KONIN

THESE ARE UNCORRECTED BOUND PROOFS. Please check any quotations or attributions against the bound copy of the book. We urge this for the sake of editorial accuracy as well as for your legal protection and ours.

KONIN

A QUEST

THEO RICHMOND

JONATHAN CAPE
LONDON

First published 1995

1 3 5 7 9 10 8 6 4 2

First published in the United Kingdom in 1995 by
Jonathan Cape
Random House, 20 Vauxhall Bridge Road, London SW1V 2SA

Random House Australia (Pty) Limited
20 Alfred Street, Milsons Point, Sydney,
New South Wales 2061, Australia

Random House New Zealand Limited
18 Poland Road, Glenfield,
Auckland 10, New Zealand

Random House South Africa (Pty) Limited
PO Box 337, Bergvlei, South Africa

Random House UK Limited Reg. No. 954009

A CIP catalogue record for this book
is available from the British Library

Paper used by Random House UK Limited are natural,
recyclable products made from wood grown in sustainable forests.
The manufacturing processes conform to the environmental
regulations of the country of origin.

ISBN 0–224–03890–7

Printed in Great Britain by
Athenæum Press Ltd., Gateshead, Tyne & Wear.

In memory of my parents
and for
Jonathan, Sarah and Simon

‘It is not your duty to complete the task, but neither are you free to desist from it.’

Pirkei Avot, *Ethics of the Fathers*

ACKNOWLEDGMENTS

I wish to thank the following former Jewish citizens of Konin and its environs for giving me the benefit of their memories and, in many instances, for welcoming me into their homes in Britain, the USA, Canada and Israel. A more remarkable and courageous group of people it would be hard to find: Natan Ahykam, Leibush Aron, Julius and Niusia Ancer, Zalman Bayrach, Gedalia Ber, David Berendt, Lola Birnbaum, Shimon Bram, Rivka Brum, Tola Cymbler, Ginny Damashek, Rywka Diament, Shlomo Ehrlich, Joe Fox, Teresa Franco, Miriam Grossman, Sam and Eva Gruen, Gloria Gutwill, Izzy Hahn, Regina Rachel Haruvi, David Irwin, Mike Jacobs, Alexander Kaliski, Henry Kaplan, Henry Kaye, Simon Kempinski, Sam Klapstein, Leib Kleczewski, Herman Krol, Jozef Lasman, Mendel Leben, Louis Lefkowitz, Maria Leszczynska, Yitzhak Lipinski, Mikhail Moskowicz, Fella Nitzky, Alexander Piekarczyk, Sidney Prost, Abraham Rundbaken, Mira Ryb, Lola Sherer, Yitzhak and Hanna Sukari, Helen Trencher, Sarah Trybuch and Yehuda Wallis. Three of the above, Natan Ahykam, Shimon Bram and Mira Ryb, committee members of the association that published the Konin Memorial Book, kindly gave me permission to quote from it.

Sadly, the following have died since I had the privilege of interviewing them: Bertha Atzmon, Shimon Beatus, Natan Biezunski, Sarah Bram, Jacob Bulka, Miriam Cherniak, Rose Dolan, Yetta Ehrlich, Annie Glassman, Guta Katzenstein, Hanna Kowalska, Morton Mysch, Hirsh Majer Natel, Jacob Perelman, Avrom Soika, Avram Sukari, Lola Szafran and Frances Taylor. They bore my relentless questioning with noble patience.

I am indebted to the following relatives of Koniners for the insights and information they provided: Miriam Trybuch Bondorowsky, Lily Beyrack Cohen, Irene Fresko, Bill Gladstone, Claude Hampel, Ginger Jacobs, Philip Lewin, Professor Ralph Lewin, Rose Morris, Bella Natel, Hyman Offenbach, Merke Ronch, Eli Trybuch, and the late Ignac Grossman, remembered with special affection.

Thanks and acknowledgments are due to: Adam Bielecki, Librarian of the Jewish Historical Institute in Warsaw; Eva Feldenkreis, Director of Archives of the Ghetto Fighters' House, Israel; Dr Benjamin Nadel, former Director of the Bund Archives of the Jewish Labor Movement, New York; Suzie Sato of the Arizona Historical Foundation; the administrators of the Yad Vashem archives, Jerusalem; and members of the library staff at YIVO, New York. Professor David Chandler responded with kindness to my research enquiries. I am indebted to Professor Jozef Lewandowski, born in Konin, who not only contributed to my store of knowledge and gave me permission to quote from one of his books, but became a friend in the course of our long correspondence.

Several individuals in present-day Konin went out of their way to supply me with information that was hard, if not impossible, to obtain elsewhere. I therefore wish to express my appreciation to: Lech Hejman, Director of the Konin Public Library; Alicja Sadowska, Manager of the Konin branch of the Polish National Archive, and her historian colleague, Piotr Rybczynski. The warm welcome I received from Teresa and Jozef Blaszczynski during my visit to Konin will not be forgotten. My most memorable encounter in that town was with someone who, for reasons of his own, does not want his name mentioned. His testimony plays a significant part in this book, and I shall always be thankful for having had the opportunity of meeting him.

A lack of funds prevented me from using professional translators as much as I would have wished, so it was my good fortune to have two friends, Martha Price and Alexandra Gore, who gave freely of their time to translate long and difficult passages of Polish and German. I must thank Danuta Lyon and Maria Nicoll, too, for their help with Polish translations. When I had almost completed the book, the Society of Authors was good enough to award me a grant that paid for some of my translation expenses. I could not have written this book without having acquired the ability to read and translate Yiddish, in which so much of my source material was written. For this I must thank two gifted teachers: Yitzhak Niborski of the Sorbonne, who taught me during a crash course at Oxford, and Barry Davis, whose weekly Yiddish class at the Spiro Institute, London, brought delight as well as illumination.

I gathered facts and hospitality from a number of my relations, among them: Eva and Lewis Graham, Doris Leverson, Miriam Popoff, Chanoch Richka, Benny Ryczke, Abraham Sarna, Hettie Sarna and Gertrude Sarner. I should single out certain members of my family who went far beyond the line of familial duty in dealing with my tiring and, no doubt, tiresome stream of requests for information as well as assistance with Yiddish and Hebrew: Leibish Glassman, David and Varda Richke, Freda Ryczke, Rachel Araten Sarna, Asher Sarna, Professor Nahum M. Sarna and his son, Professor Jonathan D. Sarna. It was to my advantage that the last two read the manuscript, as did my children Sarah and Simon, whose comments were of special help. I thank them, my son Jonathan, and the many friends who gave me much-needed encouragement.

There are others I must thank for not backing away when I foisted the bulky manuscript on them: Professor Antony Polonsky, Gerry Lewis and Harvey Mitchell. The last named was particularly generous with his attentiveness to nuance and detail. Any opinions expressed in the book and the responsibility for the facts given are entirely my own. Long before any publisher showed interest in this book, two strangers, David and Iris Freeman, heard of my quest for Konin, and spontaneously expressed their belief in what I was trying to do. I am grateful to them for being so generously supportive at a crucial time.

My literary agent, Toby Eady, took on an unknown and unproven author because of his faith in the subject of my book. I thank him for this and for encouraging others to have faith in it, especially my British publisher, Dan Franklin of Jonathan Cape, and my American publisher with the remarkably similar name, Dan Frank, of Pantheon Books. Both suggested cuts and changes with discernment and sensitivity, and I was lucky to have their advice as well as enthusiasm. I was also blessed with two superb copy editors: Steve Cox in London, and Ed Cohen in New York.

I have left to last the one person without whom etc. During the seven years I spent researching and writing this book, my wife, Lee Langley, supported me not only with her love but with the earnings from her creative writing as a novelist and scriptwriter. She was a tower of strength at times when I was a tower of weakness, in danger of toppling over whenever self-confidence grew shaky. Living with an obsessive was not easy, and she endured it with tender and selfless devotion. I inflicted every chapter on her as it was written, and there can scarcely be a page of this book that has not benefited from her constructive criticism.

A NOTE ON TRANSLITERATION AND PRONUNCIATION

To transliterate Yiddish into English is to risk upsetting someone, either the Jewish layman who clings to the traditional Germanized spellings, or the academic Yiddishist who favours the codified rules of orthography laid down by the scholarly YIVO Institute for Jewish Research. Many authors have acknowledged the problems, grappled with them, and apologized for whatever sins they may have committed. I must now join them.

One oft-recurring difficulty is the guttural *ch* sound as in the German *ach* or the word for a Scottish lake, *loch*. YIVO uses the sound equivalent *kh*. So should it be *Chasid* or *khasid* or, to be strictly correct, *khosed*? (Or Chassid, Hasid or Hassid?). I myself resist spelling the name of the creator of Tevye the Milkman as Shoem Aleykhem simply because I was brought up on Aleichem. My Yiddish teachers in London and Oxford would no doubt disagree. Another choice lies between the 'old-fashioned' *ei* or its YIVO equivalent, *ay*, both pronounced like *i* in *fine*. So is it to be *mein* or *mayn*?

In the end, I have allowed personal preference to prevail, which has meant forsaking consistency, sometimes in the cause of conveying pronunciation more clearly than would the YIVO forms. *Shabes*, printed without accent marks, would strike the uninitiated as a one-syllable word. I have therefore spelt the Yiddish word for Sabbath as *shabbes* to reduce that possibility. Where words of Hebrew derivation occur, I have sometimes transliterated from the Yiddish, sometimes the Hebrew.

As for the complexities of Polish pronunciation, which few English tongues, including my own, can get round, I offer the reader the following meagre guide: *sz* is pronounced like the English *sh* as in *sham*, *cz* like *ch* as in *chase*. This should help with certain Polish names.

Where foreign terms are used in the text, I usually follow them with a translation in brackets. Where they occur more than once, they are listed in the glossary at the back of the book.

Contents

Introduction

THIS book is about my return journey to a place I had never been to, a place of which I knew nothing except that it was a part of my past and in a curiously powerful way a part of my present. Its name reverberated throughout my childhood and adult years, sometimes withdrawing into the far distance so that I scarcely heard its echoing whisper, sometimes clamorous in the bleak and desperate early hours, always there, somewhere in the caverns of the unconscious, refusing to let go. The name of that place is Konin.

Both my parents grew up in this *shtetl*, a small Polish country town on what was then the western edge of the Tsarist empire. When they emigrated to England just before the First World War, they brought Konin with them. Not its way of life but its memory. In many respects my parents stood out as untypical among the East European immigrants who settled here at that time. Scornful of the materialistic preoccupations of Anglo-Jewry, they were oddball individualists who defied easy categorization. And yet their roots clutched; the past was neither forgotten nor concealed. My father had many close relatives still living in Konin. My mother's large, closely bonded family from Konin had come over to London. They kept up friendships with people from Konin. They founded a Konin Aid Society to help the poor they had left behind. Playing on the floor with my toys on visits to uncles and aunts, disengaged from the adult voices talking among themselves, I heard a name recur again and again: Konin, Konin, Konin.

The greater part of my life has been lived in London, where I was born. I studied, married and brought up my children here. I have lived here for more than a quarter of a century, in a house close to the Thames. And yet, that other town, also set on a river, has always coexisted alongside it – its unofficial twin. I felt that I was in some way an ex-citizen of that town, an exile. What I did not know was that one day it would in a sense reclaim me and that its pull would be irresistible.

It asserted its presence with sombre force in the aftermath of the

Shoah (I prefer to call the Holocaust by its Hebrew name) when, as a schoolboy, I learned of the fate of my Konin relatives. I had never met these people who died in unspeakable ways in the camps and ghettos. I knew little or nothing about them. And yet their erasure from the face of the earth haunted me. Konin was gone. It was time for me to let go. But I held on.

In the early Sixties a group of Konin Jews in Israel, some of them survivors of the Shoah, some veteran pioneers from the Mandate era, formed a committee to publish a Konin Memorial Book that would honour the memory of their lost families and townsfolk. At the request of my father, I subscribed to the project and thereafter scarcely gave the matter a thought.

The book committee, short on funds and expertise, set about gathering information from various parts of the world. It took years before their labours bore fruit. Indeed, I had forgotten all about it when one day, in 1968, the postman delivered a heavy parcel: the Konin Memorial Book. I opened the thick, blue-bound volume. Tucked into the inside front cover was a folded map of the town with unpronounceable Polish street names. Two wavy parallel lines showed the River Warta. Near the river I picked out a rectangle named Plac Wolnosci, which I took to be Konin's main square. There were numbers on the map marking places of Jewish interest but I could not read the key. It was a meaningless pattern of black lines. I had no bearings, no reference points. The map was for those who had been born and brought up in these streets, for those who would look at these lines and see their homes, the courtyards where they played, the synagogue where they worshipped, markets where they bought and sold. Shedding the years, they would see themselves, their lost family and friends as they were before the darkness fell.

The book was nearly eight hundred pages of history, geography, memoir, biographical sketches and much else. But I could not read it. Save for a few pages of English text, it was as inaccessible to me as a Dead Sea scroll. Paginated from back to front, written from right to left, it appeared to be printed almost entirely in Hebrew. I learned later that most of the book was in fact written not in Hebrew but in Yiddish, which uses the Hebrew alphabet. Only one section of this book spoke for itself: lists of names occupying page after page, each with the mark of mourning – a surrounding border of black.

For years the book rested on a shelf near my desk. Every now and then I would yield to its pull, take it off the shelf and look at the photographs: a synagogue exterior, a cobbled street, an onion-domed church by a wooden bridge, all as they were in Tsarist times. Long-dead rabbis and Chasidim stared out from the pages, young soldiers in the army of independent Poland, a Jewish fireman, the amateur dramatic society, a mandolin trio, moustachioed dignitaries, Zionist athletes, youngsters on a summer outing, the mobile gassing van, Jews digging their own graves.

One day in January 1987, idly turning over the pages of the book, I arrived again at the black-bordered roll-call, twenty-five pages with over two thousand names, pages with a chilling, morbid power. I was able – just about – to decipher the victims' names. That I could do so was due to a paradox in my upbringing. (Jews and paradox are never far apart.) My free-thinking parents – my mother who quoted Voltaire's refutation of the existence of God at me when I was a child, my socialist father who subscribed to the Left Book Club and viewed Judaism (at that time) as an obstacle to man's salvation – sent me every Sunday morning to religious classes – to *cheder* – where I acquired a primitive ability to read Hebrew without understanding a word of what I was reading.

Thus I was able to grope my way alphabetically through the death list until I reached the Hebrew letter *reysh* and found the surname Ryczke (pronounced rich-ke), which was my father's name before he anglicized it to Richmond. I saw the name repeated again and again: RYCZKE, Dovid (my grandfather), RYCZKE, Gitl (his wife), RYCZKE, Avrom (my father's brother), RYCZKE, Chana (a stepsister), RYCZKE, Itsik Hirsh (brother), RYCZKE, Shimen (brother), RYCZKE, Leib (brother) . . . and yet more members of the Ryczke clan in Konin. I looked closely at the Hebrew transliteration of RYCZKE: Did these ancient, oriental marks in some way stand for me? How did they connect with my world, with my present life?

I turned over the pages and knew that the decision had been made for me: I must write a book of my own about the Jewish men and women of Konin, a book that would interweave past and present, that would be a confluence of two rivers, the Thames and the Warta.

I would learn Yiddish to unlock the contents of the Memorial Book. I would embark on a search for a lost community.

Friends said I was 'searching for roots', a suggestion I rejected, not only because this root-searching activity – now almost an industry – had acquired clichéd, sentimental overtones from which I recoiled, but because I did not see my quest as springing from a need to discover my racial identity. I was not assimilated to the point where I was totally ignorant of, or uneasy about, my racial provenance. Whatever my insecurities – what Jew is without them? – they were not the result of puzzlement about the *shtetl* world my parents had left behind. I knew about that ghetto life revealed in histories and fiction, in plays, musicals and films, portrayed all too often with a thick impasto of *shmaltz*. What fuelled my curiosity was the wish to know more about one small corner of that world. I was interested not so much in the broad canvas of *The Jews of Poland* but rather in the Jews of one particular community, in the daily life once lived by my family and by my family's neighbours in a town that held a personal meaning for me – a town on the River Warta. I wanted to explore its banks and meadows, its orchards and woods. I wanted to know my way around the town, every street, every corner, every building of the Konin I might have been born in, the Konin I might have glimpsed for the last time through a gap in the timbers of a railway cattle truck.

I wanted to focus on Konin as it once was, its people and the rules and values by which they lived, their institutions and, above all, the texture and colour of their everyday lives. Parochial curiosity was my drive. I wanted to get to know the people as individuals I would recognize if I met them in the street. How were their marriages celebrated and their deaths mourned? What sort of childhood did they have? How did they earn a living and spend their leisure hours? And a hundred other questions. I wanted to know how the community met its end, and whether anything remained to mark the five hundred years of Jewish presence in the town. Of course, I felt a familial curiosity too, and wondered if I might unearth new facts about my parents' families and their lives in Konin – the Ryczke family on my father's side, the Sarna family on my mother's.

Was curiosity the sole driving force? Maybe not. Perhaps I hoped that in satisfying my curiosity about the dead I might succeed at the same time in creating a memorial to them, however imperfect. It was a way of keeping them alive. I wanted, also, to tell my children about their ancestry, for I share the feeling of the writer who recorded the lives of his Russian forebears: 'There is no way of knowing what my children will make of ancestors from the age of dusty roads and long afternoons on the shaded veranda deep in the Russian countryside. But I want to leave the road marked and lighted, so that they can travel into the darkness ahead, as I do, sure of the road behind.'[1]

I have a meagre knowledge of the holy Scriptures, but am aware of the all-important injunction to remember, of the recurring phrase in the Hebrew liturgy: *le-dor va-dor* – from generation to generation. For Jews, handing on has always meant remembering. On it has depended the survival of ethnic identity as well as religious practice. I remember, therefore I am. The Ba'al Shem-Tov, founder of Chasidism,[2] once said: 'Forgetting is exile, remembering is the path to salvation.' In the light of twentieth-century history, I would amend that axiom: Forgetting is not exile; forgetting is the Final Solution.

When I set out on the path back to Konin, I was looking for ways of retrieving the past, not only by searching through archives but by making contact with survivors, if I could find any. When I eventually met them, I discovered how inextricably linked I was to these people and their town, sometimes in the most extraordinary, unexpected ways. Questioning them about what once had been, I gradually became aware that in talking about their lives there could be no sudden cut-off point, that I would be swept along with them from Konin to the present day, that I would learn how they had salvaged shattered lives, established new roots, new hopes in lands far from their birthplace: in Omaha, Nebraska, a corner of Brooklyn, a kibbutz in Israel, a London suburb . . . I found that I was listening to a story of renewal as well as annihilation.

Part One

SETTING OUT

I

Awareness of Konin's existence was one thing; knowledge of it another. What I knew added up to little more than a disjointed smattering of facts garnered mostly from those overheard family conversations:

> Konin (pronounced with a short 'o', as in 'cot'): a clean, handsome little town near the German frontier. On a river, with a wooden bridge. Nearby meadows, orchards and forests. In winter, people skated on the river. In summer they strolled in the municipal park, where a military band played on Sunday afternoons. Soldiers of the Tsar were garrisoned in the town, dashing cavalry officers brought custom to Jewish shops. The Jewish community was composed of pious but unfanatical Jews. Religious observance coexisted with a lively interest in secular culture. Nearby shtetls (my parents would have said *shtetlekh*) looked up to the Konin community, admired its educated Jews, and envied them their outstanding library. There was a synagogue, a House of Study, and several small congregations. The Jewish quarter had a square, which was the heart of Jewish life in Konin.

No one ever told me a story that would have appealed to a child – the legend of the Founding of Konin:

> Prince Leszek, hunting in the forest, became separated from his men and lost his way. He was resting under a tree when a band of lawless woodsmen, attracted by his rich apparel, sprang on him, threatening his life. The sound of galloping horses was heard approaching, and the robbers, thinking it was the prince's soldiers, fled. When the horses appeared, they turned out to be a wild herd that had been grazing nearby, disturbed most likely by some predatory beast. Grateful to the horses for saving his life,

> the Prince decided to found a town nearby and call it Konin, *kon* being Polish for horse. To this day the town's emblem is a white horse rampant.[1]

Reference works yielded the prosaic facts: Konin lies 200 kilometres west of Warsaw, in the valley of Poland's third longest river, the Warta, a lush valley of forests and meadows. The flat terrain of the valley bed, combined with huge skies and a winding stretch of water, offer a view not unlike a seventeenth-century Dutch landscape. From earliest times Konin occupied a strategic point on the crossroads of highways running east–west from Warsaw to Poznan and north–south on what was once the Amber Route, linking the Roman empire and the Baltic. Some of the early settlers were probably boatmen ferrying amber merchants across a ford in the river. Ptolemy of Alexandria, in one of his maps of the second century, marked a place named Setidava close to the present site of Konin. A nearby town to the south, Calissia, on the same map, almost certainly refers to what is now Kalisz.

There have been human settlements in the Konin area since prehistoric times. In the early Middle Ages a city called Kaszuba stood a few kilometres to the west of Konin's present site. Changes in the course of the river led to that city's decline, and the need for a new ford brought the foundation of a trading centre that was to become Konin. Today's town – where one of the first Jewish settlements in Poland took root, flourished and, in our century, died – has its beginnings in the late thirteenth century, when Konin was granted town status.

Konin's past mirrors the turbulent history of Poland itself. Crusaders destroyed the town in the fourteenth century; fire erased most of it again in the fifteenth. Cholera decimated the population in the seventeenth century, and the assault of the invading Swedes resulted in most of the town being razed yet again. The partition of Poland in the eighteenth century brought Konin under Prussian rule. In the following century the Russians took over as foreign oppressors. The Kaiser's men occupied the town in the First World War, Hitler's in the Second. When Nazi troops entered Konin in 1939, its population numbered about 12,100, of whom some 2,700 were Jews.

Konin produced no great and famous sons. No Copernicus, Mickiewicz, Paderewski, no world-celebrated rabbis, *rebbes* (heads of Chasidic sects), Nobel Prize winners or future leaders of Israel. Before the Second World War, few people in the rest of Poland would have heard of Konin, and even today when the town has grown into an industrial and mining centre of some magnitude, its name provokes little reaction from Poles, let alone Jews.

But perhaps I do the town an injustice and risk injuring the pride of its present-day citizens, over eighty thousand of them. Foraging for some connection with the eminent, however tenuous, I came up with a nineteenth-century Jewish innkeeper of Konin, Michael Goldwasser, whose grandson, Barry, once ran for the presidency of the United States (from humble publican to top Republican in three generations). Somewhat earlier, in the fourteenth century, Kazimierz the Great, hallowed in Polish history (and a friend of the Jews), almost certainly stayed in a palace in Konin when he visited the town in 1360. King Wladyslaw Jagiello visited Konin in 1403, 1425 and 1433. In the nineteenth century, Sir Moses Montefiore is said to have stopped off in Konin en route to St Petersburg for an audience with the Tsar. An artist by the name of Eligiusz Niewiadomski, who painted some of the murals in Konin's Catholic church, achieved instant fame (now faded) on 16 December 1922, when he assassinated the first President of Poland, Gabriel Narutowicz, whose enemies claimed he was in partnership with the Jews.[2] A more famous Polish soldier and statesman, Marshal Pilsudski, honoured the town with a visit in the 1920s. A Konin writer and poet, Zofia Urbanowska, enjoyed some literary success (also faded) between the wars.[3] Konin does have one unique claim to fame – the oldest milestone in Poland, which bears a Latin inscription: 'This is halfway between Kalisz and Kruszwica. Crossing this point, weary traveller, you should pray to almighty God. Anno Domini 1151.'[4]

Refusing to abandon the search for a figure whose fame might lend lustre to Konin's image, my thoughts turned to Napoleon. Might the Emperor of the French have slept here? From his itineraries I discovered that in 1806, before he crowned himself Emperor, Napoleon took a route eastward between two towns that must have taken him through Konin. His coach, according to my calculations, rumbled over the wooden bridge during the afternoon of 16 December.[5] As he had risen before dawn that day, it is more than likely that the victor of Austerlitz was having a nap at the time.

2

I HAD WAITED too long to plunder my parents' memories. My father reached the age of ninety, my mother eighty-nine, opportunity enough to recover some of their Konin years. It was not my indifference that was to blame but procrastination, based on the delusion that my parents would never die. But they did, and my failure to record something of their youth in Poland became a source of sadness and self-reproach, which intensified when I began writing this book. I had so many questions only they could have answered.

My maternal grandfather, Simcha Sarna, died in the East End of London in 1933 when I was a very young child. I have only the vaguest memory of him, standing in a doorway of his home at No. 70 Sidney Street, a short man with a trim goatee beard, quietly distinguished-looking. He emigrated from Konin with his wife and large brood just before the First World War. Konin was dear to him and, but for his declining fortunes as a wholesale merchant dealing in a modest way in hardware and crockery, he would probably never have left the town where he was a well-known figure, respected for his Talmudic learning and modesty.

His widow, Esther-Reisl, outlived him by many years, and shared a home with us for a while in St Albans, Hertfordshire, where we had moved to escape the German bombing raids on London. My grandmother was a spry, kindly, obstinate old lady, racked with arthritis but undeterred by pain. Today I would cherish her company and show her off to my friends, but as a schoolboy, trying to blend into the gentile world of my grammar school in an English country town, the last thing I wanted was to acknowledge my kinship with her in public. Going home from school with my classmates, I would flinch as I saw the little, bent, foreign-looking old lady clothed in black approaching on the other side of the street, clutching a shopping bag that almost scraped the ground. I had my strategies for avoiding her, sometimes turning to stare into a shop window with feigned interest until I saw her reflection pass by.

My *buba* (granny) used to feed me prodigious quantities of nutritious soups to make up for wartime shortages, standing at the table after she had served me, keenly watching each spoonful disappear down my throat, exhorting me to eat, eat. How could I refuse? If I declined a third helping of her barley soup or chicken broth, she would resort in Yiddish to the ultimate emotional blackmail: '*Ikh zol azoy lebn*,' which means essentially, 'Eat it for my life's sake.' In other words, my refusing to eat would be tantamount to wishing her dead. It never crossed my mind either then or later, when I was grown up with a wife and young children of my own, to ask her about her life in Konin, where her family, the Festenbergs, had lived for many generations. Born in Konin in 1870, my *buba* grew up, married and had children in a town where the physical conditions of everyday life and many of the mental attitudes of its inhabitants had scarcely changed since the Middle Ages.

My mother, Bertha, was born in Konin in 1893, my father, Simcha, in nearby Golina a year earlier. His family, the Ryczkes, moved the couple of miles up the road to Konin when he was a young child, and it was Konin that he always regarded as his home town. They never spoke to me much about their life there – but not, I think, out of any wish to avoid my being infected with a ghetto past they had left behind. Rather, they must have felt that I, born in Britain, not speaking Yiddish, not having experienced East End life let alone the world of the *shtetl*, belonged to a different planet, and that with all of life stretching ahead of me, their reminiscing about the old country would strike me as an irrelevance, a bore. They were right. And yet not entirely right. The past is a foreign country in which I have always felt at home.

As a small boy, I spent hours browsing in junk shops. At the age of twelve I spent saved-up pocket money on my first purchase of bric-à-brac, a battered sovereign case and a Victorian carving of Disraeli, which still hangs on my walls. After school, I would wander into the local history museum, invariably deserted at that hour. My footsteps on the polished parquet broke the solemn silence as I moved among the mahogany glass cabinets of curiosities, studying the jumble of coins, pottery and artefacts dug up from Verulamium (where St Albans now stands) with their handwritten captions on curling slips of paper. But whether the Jewish world of Konin would have gripped me as much as ancient Rome is questionable. None of us knew then what was happening to that world. While I, an English schoolboy in short trousers and school cap, was gazing enthralled at the remains of a vanished civilization, my Konin relatives, some of them children of my own age, were being exterminated. The Jewish communities that had blossomed for so many centuries in Eastern Europe were soon to become part of a vanished world, like that of the ancient Romans.

In 1987, when I began my exploratory 'dig' into the ruins of Konin, the thought did cross my mind: Was I too late? A fragile urn can survive for millennia but the unrecorded thoughts of its maker are lost for ever. There could not be many Koniners left and the ranks of the few were thinning. When the last link went, it *would* be too late.

My maternal grandparents, my parents and all my aunts and uncles old enough to remember their youth in Poland were buried in various London cemeteries. My Uncle Jacob, the eldest of the Sarna siblings, would have yielded the richest store of information. He remembered Jewish life in Konin with an affectionate fervour, and with an informed knowledge that went beyond a mere sentimental attachment to *der heym* (home – the Old Country). His pride in Konin showed all too clearly when it came to the task of composing the inscription for his father's gravestone. I went to visit it recently in the London suburb of Edmonton. Carved in marble after my grandfather's name is the proud proclamation in Hebrew: CITIZEN OF THE TOWN OF KONIN.

Jacob's brother, my Uncle Eliezer, who loved paintings, luxury and fine food, could also have illuminated Konin life for me, in a more dispassionate, less reverential way. But he had died some years before, and again I was too late. Or so I thought, until one day I received a telephone call from someone related to me by marriage, a bright, entrepreneurial figure, who had heard of my project. He wanted me to know that he had taped an interview with Eliezer shortly before his death. My uncle, he said, had talked at length about his varied life. Two sides of one cassette were taken up with his memories of Konin – family detail, impressions of *shtetl* life, personal profiles . . . in short, a picture of what it was like to grow up in that small country town in the early years of this century. Recalling my uncle's urbane intelligence and humorous eye for detail, I knew I had stumbled upon treasure, a unique family record available from no other source. 'Please don't mail me the cassette,' I begged my relation, not wishing to take the smallest risk of its being lost, 'I'll come over to you.' A few days later he called again. He is a nice man and, wanting to save me a drive across London, he had taken the trouble to copy the cassette so that he could post me a duplicate. Something had gone wrong, however. Instead of copying the original cassette, he had by mistake wiped it – every word. He was most dreadfully sorry . . .

3

ONCE THERE WAS a large clutch of Sarna aunts and uncles, my mother being one of nine children. By 1987 they were reduced to three: Annie, Abie and Asher. Because they spoke without a foreign accent, I had always assumed they were born in London, but Asher assures me that only he, the youngest, can claim to be a native Briton. The other two were born in Konin and left when they were toddlers. Abie retains no memories of Konin; Annie has one: 'I was about three years old. It was evening and my mother was carrying me in her arms, and I was holding a pair of new shoes, and I was very, very happy about it, dangling them backwards and forwards with delight. We were crossing a wooden bridge over some water.'

Her names are Chana-Brocha – in English, Hannah-Blessing. Hannah became Annie. Her husband, Leibish, has taken devoted care of her during the many years she has been ill and housebound. When I visit them on a bright spring day, she is curled up on the sofa like a sick child. But soon, drawing on some mysterious reserve of energy, she is sitting up, bright-eyed and spirited. Leibish is wearing a dark suit and black skullcap. I have never known him dress any differently. His short beard, black when I was a boy, has turned a streaky grey. Born in 1910, he retired some years ago after a lifetime's career as a *shoychet* (ritual slaughterer). His weekday routine never varies: he rises at five, makes a cup of tea for himself and Annie, studies the Talmud, walks to Edgware Synagogue for morning prayers, comes home, has breakfast and studies for several more hours; after lunch he visits the sick or looks in on the lonely and returns to *shul* for evening prayers. Tolerant and humble, he is the best advertisement for Judaism I know.

Leibish acts as the family transmitter of morbid tidings, being always the first to get news of the death of a relation or family friend, and always the first to pass it on. He is guardian of the family graves, knowing the row and number of every burial plot of every relation who has died in the last sixty years. During the month of Elul – the traditional season for visiting the graves of near ones – he sets out on his annual cemetery trek. He never fails to attend a funeral, never forgets the anniversary of a death – a *yortsayt*. And with it all, he is cheerful and optimistic, his attitude to death one of fatalistic acceptance. When catastrophe strikes, it is '*min ha-shamayim*' – the will of heaven. Who is he to question the divine plan?

I address my Konin enquiries to Annie, not realizing, until he quietly reveals it, that it was Leibish's birthplace too. When his family arrived in London and had nowhere to stay, the Sarnas made room for them, which is how he met his first and only girlfriend. He moved away from Konin when he was three and remembers nothing of the town. He wonders what has set me on this trail: 'Who wants to know about Konin?'

I have a favour to ask of him: when, in the course of my Konin researches, I come across matters of religious law and custom that leave me flummoxed, may I turn to him for help? He raises two palms in an expressive Yiddish gesture, as though physically pushing away a silly question. Over the next few years I gratefully exploit him as my religious consultant, while he, in the tradition of Jewish charity, is grateful to me for allowing him the opportunity to perform a *mitzve* (virtuous deed).

I have an even greater favour to ask of my mother's brother, Uncle Asher – religion-mocking, iconoclastic, former fiery socialist, who came close to expulsion from the Jews' Free School for refusing to salute the flag on Empire Day; conscientious objector, a regular of the Prince of Teck pub, one of the best-read men I know, endowed with a brilliant mind that never brought him money or success, for many years regarded as the black sheep of the family – will he, out of the kindness of his heart, perform a task I can ask of no one else: the job of translating into English the Yiddish sections of the Konin Memorial Book, several hundred pages of closely printed Hebrew type? Asher has not looked at a word of Yiddish for over fifty years, but a kind heart prevails. An incurable insomniac, he spends the next few months dictating a rough translation of the book into a tape-recorder at two or three o'clock in the morning, swearing when a passage defeats him, skipping bits that bore him, making irreverent interjections, pausing occasionally for violent coughing bouts (he has only part of one lung), switching off when the recorder picks up the sound of birds announcing dawn outside his Earls Court balcony. In the next few months he hands me the cassettes in regular instalments, and I spend months transcribing them. Thanks to Asher's heroic efforts, I can explore the contents of the Memorial Book, abounding in discrepancies, vague about dates, repetitive . . . but nevertheless an achievement that does credit to the Konin memorializers who laboured to create it.

Reading about Konin triggers Asher's memories of life in Sidney Street. 'In a way, it was a continuation of life in Konin. When my mother heard I was involved in leftwing activities she was terrified, convinced she would see me dragged off in chains to Siberia, a scene she remembered from Poland. My father was always writing letters to Konin. He prayed in a tiny synagogue round the corner run by a Koniner. As boys we learned Hebrew from a teacher who came from Konin. There wasn't a day that we weren't visited by *landslayt*' (fellow countrymen). Number 70 Sidney Street became the Konin headquarters of London, where former townsfolk could pick up the latest news from home, get something to eat, a glass of lemon tea, perhaps a loan, even when my grandfather was himself struggling to make ends meet. With help from his sons, he ran a little translating bureau and 'forwarding agency' as it was grandly described on his letterhead. Illiterate immigrants used his services as a scribe to compose letters in Yiddish, Hebrew and English. Official letters were tapped out on a second-hand typewriter with a broken spring that had been replaced by a hammer hanging from the carriage by a piece of string like a pendulum weight.

My grandfather advised his clients on the tone and content of their letters, encouraging them to make peace if they were embroiled in family quarrels, helping them phrase a proposal of marriage, deal with the question of a dowry . . . The 'forwarding agency' dispatched parcels of warm clothing to Poland and Russia. More often than not, my grandfather was incapable of taking money from his impecunious clients. 'He suffered from a disease called compassion,' says his son Abie. Four dress-making daughters bent over sewing-machines in the upstairs workshop helped to pay the bills.

'Compared with some others, we were well off,' says Asher. 'We never went hungry, but I do remember the time when I had to wear my mother's shoes to go to school. One Saturday morning my father took me to synagogue and as we were walking along I spotted a five-pound note lying on the pavement. In those days it would have bought the equivalent of far more than a hundred pounds today. It was a fortune. I bent down to grab the note, but my father stopped me – it was the holy Sabbath. You mustn't touch money on *shabbes* [Sabbath]. We carried on to *shul*, leaving the five-pound note lying on the pavement.'

While Asher showed little interest in Jewish observance or the family's past, his older brother, Jacob, took pride in our Sarna lineage. Family history has it that I can count Rabbi Shlomo Ephraim Solomon ben Aaron among my forebears.[1] Born in Poland in the mid-sixteenth century, he was a great preacher, became Rabbi of Prague, and wrote one of the best-known commentaries on the Torah. Among other rabbis in the family were five brothers, three of whom settled in Jerusalem in 1844 where each became, in turn, head of the Rabbinical Court.[2] Jacob never forgot the family tree he was shown as a boy in Konin, which traced us back to Don Isaac Abrabanel,[3] statesman, commentator, philosopher, treasurer to King Alfonso V of Portugal, later in the service of Isabella of Spain, and said to be descended from King David. Alas, the family tree was lost and my connection with Don Isaac, not to mention King David, remains only a legend.

I once enlisted my father's help in tracing the Ryczke line. He could take it back a mere three generations. No rabbis. No grand viziers. The Ryczkes were egg and butter merchants. However, my grandfather was known for his Talmudic erudition, and the Ryczkes stood tall in the ranks of the *balbatishe* families of Konin. 'What nicer adjective is there?' asks Leo Rosten. 'To call someone *balbatish* is to endow him or her with quiet, admirable, traditional virtues.'[4]

Postscript *Annie died in May* 1988.

4

I KNEW ONLY one other Koniner in Britain, Joe Fox, an old friend of my parents. He and my father had been founding members of the Konin Aid Society in London after the First World War. As a boy I used to play with his son, Jeffrey, but we had drifted apart as we grew up, and I rarely saw him or his father. Joe Fox had made his money as a cap and clothing manufacturer. When I last saw him he was living in a detached house in one of the best roads in Hendon, where every house has a *mezuzah* (a scroll inscribed with holy words and encased in a narrow container attached to the doorpost) and every front garden looks as though it receives a daily brush and polish. Joe was in many ways an archetypal member of North London Jewry, a generous contributor to Zionist causes who spent every Passover in Israel and every Rosh Hashanah (Jewish New Year) in a kosher hotel in Bournemouth. And Joe was very, very old. How did I know he was still alive? Simply by virtue of not having heard of his death from Uncle Leibish. Not hearing from Leibish that someone belonging to or connected with the family was dead constituted sure proof that he or she was still alive. I called my old childhood friend to check on his father's health and learned that he was in good shape, long retired, living alone in the same house, but in daily contact with his children.

The man who opens the door to me is stockily built, has watery, pale blue eyes, and seems in fine form. He still drives a car and is immediately recognisable as the man I remember from my boyhood. How are you, Mr Fox? 'Mustn't grumble.' He was eighty-nine when I went to talk to him about Konin, where he was born in 1898. Seven years later, after I had traced Koniners all over the world, he still held the record as the oldest of them all. (I called him on his ninety-sixth birthday when he was still living on his own, and asked after his health: 'Mustn't grumble.') We talk not in the spacious 'lounge' with its fitted floral carpet, Thirties radiogram, cocktail cabinet and walnut-veneered furniture, but in the room next to the kitchen, now his living quarters, with an armchair permanently positioned a yard from the television set.

He starts off discouragingly. There is not that much he can tell me about Konin, he says: he was twelve and a half years old when he left the town. Does he ever think about Konin? 'I cannot forget it. I see it like I stand there today. When I went back there with your mother in 1937, I remembered every building, every corner. Nothing had changed.' We settle down to talk at the small table where he eats all his meals. He answers my questions in the slow, low-key voice I remembered, mispronouncing certain words as he always did, his foreign accent unchanged, his memory crystal clear. He remembers the windmills outside the town, the first horseless carriage in Konin, the first electric light bulb (magically illuminated by a Jewish factory owner who had his own generator), the first silent movie shown in the town, projected in a tent that was set up for a few days in the market square like a visiting circus. 'I can tell you the date – 1907 – because it was the year my father died. We went to the synagogue to say Kaddish [mourner's prayer] for him, and on the way back we passed the tent where they were showing the moving pictures. People warned me: "Don't go to see it. It's witchcraft." I couldn't go anyway – I couldn't afford it.'

His memory even stretches back to the public demonstrations against the Russian regime in 1905. 'It was like a celebration. There were lamps hanging up outside the synagogue, and the Bund [the outlawed Jewish socialist labour party] was busy organizing strikes and marches. Did *I* know what the Bund was? Of course not, but I ran around distributing leaflets. We all did it as kids. It was a bit of excitement.'

School was not compulsory in Russian times and Joe's education, like that of most Jewish males in the town, was restricted to *cheder*, where only religious subjects were taught. Joe was ten when his father, a tailor, died. 'My mother was his second wife.' Joe was one of five children. 'Life was hard. I remember my mother always had to go out and work, cooking for someone, or standing in a market selling ribbons and pins to earn a few shillings.' They occupied a small basement flat in the Jewish quarter. Basements were dark and damp, liable to flooding when the Warta overflowed. Living below ground level was a sure sign of poverty. For the residents of a basement, there could be no greater dream of social climbing than the stairs that led to an upstairs apartment. The Fox family never made it. After his father died, Joe's uncle, a cap-maker, took him in as an apprentice. Joe recalls his young hand, thimble on finger, pushing a needle through a thick leather peak.

When he was fourteen, Joe left Poland. Koniners who had emigrated to Paris were writing home about the better opportunities the city offered. Joe joined them, doing piece-work making caps. He borrowed money to buy his first sewing-machine, ate one meal a day, and when he had repaid the loan, came to London. He carried the head of the machine under his arm and had fifteen francs in his pocket, six of which – without the benefit of a *bureau de change* – went on the horse cab that took him from Victoria station to the East End, where his mother was now living with the other children. At fifteen Joe became the family's sole breadwinner. Working for various cap-makers, he set up on his own in a room in Aldgate, working all hours, often bedding down for the night on the workshop table. He narrowly escaped bankruptcy when an important customer defaulted on a bill. By the end of the 1930s he and his brother Michael, with whom he went into partnership, were manufacturing over ten thousand caps a week. By the 1950s Fox Brothers, which now included Joe's two sons, had three factories, were manufacturing clothing as well as caps, and employing about 400 people.

During my visits to Joe, I began to take my first faltering steps round the town of Konin. He went to *cheder* with my Uncle Eliezer. He remembers Jacob going off on a trip to Palestine, my mother as a little girl, my Aunt Nettie ill with smallpox when there was an epidemic: 'They tied her hands up to stop her scratching her face. That's what they did in those days.' (Maybe they did it too late. I remember visiting her with my mother when I was a little boy. Though I did not know it at the time, she was dying of TB. She lay silently in bed, still as a corpse, staring at the window. Even then, I was aware of the tiny indentations all over her pale face.)

'Your grandfather, Simcha, was the first to introduce enamel household ware to Konin. He brought it in from Germany – dishes, bowls, pails, saucepans . . . white enamel with a blue border round the edge. It was the latest thing. Before that we had clay pots and wooden buckets and things made out of iron which were hard to keep clean.' (A chipped, enamelware colander, blue with no border – once part of my grandfather's stock in Konin – hangs in our kitchen in Richmond-upon-Thames.)

Joe explains the whereabouts of my father's home – on the southern outskirts of the town, 'near the German Evangelical church'. There was a sizeable minority of Lutheran Protestants in Konin, who originated from Germany. He is not sure if streets had official names in Russian times. If they did, he is unaware of them. Nor do any of the street names on the post-Polish independence street map tucked into the Memorial Book mean anything to him. He, like the other Yiddish-speaking inhabitants of the Jewish quarter, knew only Jewish Street, Synagogue Street, Gentile Street, Cobblers Street, Tailors Street, Little Shops Street, Warta Street . . .

One of the young Bundists who fled the town in 1905 was Shima Gluba, who came to London, where he inexplicably changed his name to Bloom and became the landlord of the Lord Rodney's Head, a pub in Whitechapel Road. It is still there. The Konin Aid Society used to hold its committee meetings in a private upstairs room. There was a triumvirate of Konin immigrants mainly responsible for the founding of the Society: Joe Fox, my father, and Jack Offenbach. They distributed various titles among themselves. Offenbach was the first President, my father the Chairman. Joe was an officer too. My mother was the Secretary; later, when she gave birth to my brother, her youngest brother Asher took over her duties.

The Konin Aid Society – known to its members as the *Konin Hilfsverein* – was one of many such *landsmanshaftn* (associations of compatriots) formed in London, New York and other cities where Jews from Eastern Europe settled. The purpose of the Society was not just social but to raise money for the needy folk back home. Konin was still *der heym*. The social activities – block bookings for Yiddish plays at the Pavilion Theatre, dances and parties – were designed to raise money. One of my earliest memories is of seeing the little coloured books of Konin Aid Society raffle tickets piled up on a table.

Each year, until the outbreak of the Second World War, two or three hundred pounds – 'a lot of money in those days' as Joe points out – found their way to Konin, where they subsidized good causes: schools, vocational training, and particularly the Jewish bank in Konin, whose *raison d'être* was to provide interest-free loans for those unable to pay their rent, as well as for artisans and traders who needed money to buy tools or merchandise. During the years between the two world wars, most of the London Koniners moved up in the world, leaving behind the grime of the East End for neat houses with white net curtains in Stamford Hill, Willesden, Forest Gate, Golders Green and other salubrious London suburbs. But they did not forget their home town on the River Warts.

Where are they today? 'Passed away,' says Joe. Hope fades that he will be able to point me in the direction of other Koniners, other memories to be ransacked. He ponders for a moment and comes up with two names, one the son of a Konin butcher who was living near London last time he heard of him, the other an older man who might be in Hove 'if he is still alive'. Joe does not know their addresses or telephone numbers.

It was a tenuous lead, but I finally tracked down the butcher's son, Henry, a survivor of Mauthausen concentration camp. He in turn led me to his Konin contemporary, Izzy, in Ilford, who had survived Auschwitz, and to a Konin tailor of nearly eighty, who was still making bespoke suits in Whitechapel. I found the old man in Hove, who had been a cobbler in Konin and attended the circumcision of the butcher's son. He told me about a librarian in Pinner he remembered as a little girl in Konin, and she led me to the squire's son in Harrow, born on the family estate beside the River Warta; and the squire's son led me to an old lady in Edgware who came from one of Konin's intellectual families, who led me to her niece in south London who was a Konin sculptor's daughter and whose Bundist revolutionary uncle fled Konin in 1905 with the Tsarist secret police hot on his heels. It was a start.

5

HIRSH MAJER NATEL cultivates hydrangeas in his back garden near the seafront at Hove. He learned how to grow things in Konin during the First World War. 'Food was short, and people who normally bought produce in shops had to go out in the fields and try to grow it, otherwise they could starve.' In 1914, when Germans and Russians were fighting a battle for Konin a stone's throw from his home, Hirsh Majer sheltered in a cellar with his mother, listening to the cannon fire and the clatter of Russian cavalry charging down the cobbled street.

One Friday afternoon soon after the war began, refugees from Kalisz arrived in Konin bringing reports that a German bombardment had left much of the Jewish quarter in ruins. Thus began a rescue operation that was to become a legend in the annals of Konin Jewry. It followed the electric moment when Rabbi Lipschitz rose to his feet in the synagogue and exhorted his people to disobey one of the Ten Commandments, to join forces in desecrating the holy Sabbath. It was not, of course, a desecration, as the Rabbi explained to his startled congregation: Jewish law is clear on one thing, that the saving of human life – *pikuach nefesh* – takes precedence even over the Sabbath. The Jews of Konin, Hirsh Majer's father among them, saddled their horses, hitched their wagons and headed for Kalisz, about fifty kilometres away. 'The following day they came back loaded up with people, including our neighbours' relatives, and this is something I will never forget – it was such a moving scene.'

The Germans captured Konin and became its wartime masters. The Tsar's forces fled, and when the Russians returned thirty-one years later, it was the Red Army, inaugurating another period of Russian domination. Hirsh Majer – known now to all save his fellow Koniners as Mark – was born in Konin in 1904. His family lived next to a yard where the Russian cavalry stabled their horses. His olfactory memory can still summon up the smell. Sometimes the cavalry men threw the little boy a piece of *razuvka*, Russian black bread with raisins, as they trotted out of the yard. 'I loved watching them ride. They would gallop at full speed and lie under the belly of the horse – they were devils.'

Mark remembers, as did my mother, the Russian military band playing in the park on Sunday afternoons. 'I always went there to listen to the music and watch the dancing.' Yet even as a boy, he was aware of the darker side of life under St Petersburg's rule: 'My elder brother read books and had them hidden all over the place. My father was always worried that he would be arrested.' Mark's earliest memories take in the town crier, who attracted the crowd with a wooden rattle, a *gregger*. On Sabbath eve a beadle known only by his nickname Dokonch *Grepser* – Dokonch the Burper – went his rounds of the Jewish quarter, banging on doors and shutters with a wooden mallet, bidding the inhabitants to prayer. '*In sheeeel arayn! In sheeeel arayn!*' – Into synagogue! Into synagogue!

Mark's father, Menachem, was a trouser-maker.

We were very poor. My mother had family in America and every *yontef* [religious festival] we received some dollars from them and this helped a lot. My father became a wagoner, working for Mendel Bulka, and drove a big covered wagon, very heavy with four horses. He would leave Konin on Saturday evenings after *shabbes*. It took him two-and-a-half days to get to Lodz, load up, and then start back, with cloth and merchandise. He usually reached Konin on Friday afternoon in time for *shabbes*. If the sun set before he reached the town, he would leave the wagon with someone else and walk into Konin rather than break the *shabbes*. I went with him once to Lodz. I was only a small boy and we had to pass through big forests. Because of the danger of bandits, there were always two wagons, one following the other.

If my father didn't come home on time on Fridays, my mother wouldn't have money for the *shabbes* shopping. Go without food for *shabbes*! God forbid that anyone should know you haven't got enough in the house to make *shabbes*! When I was about six I came home one day from *cheder* and my mother, Sarah-Gitl, said to me: 'Go to your *buba* Mindl and whisper in her ear that she should lend us a little money.' I went to the marketplace where my grandmother had a fruit stall. I said: 'Good day, *buba*,' and kissed her hand – kissing the hand was a sign of respect. When my father left home, I kissed his hand. If an uncle came to visit us, I kissed his hand. I told *buba* why I had come. She stuck her little worn hand in the pocket of her white apron and counted out fifteen bright kopeks. She hung a pair of cherries over my ear, and I went home feeling very happy.

When I got back, my mother said she had borrowed money from a neighbour, and I was to take the fifteen kopeks back. I began to count them and there were only fourteen. The sweat poured off me. My heart was pounding. I didn't dare tell my mother. I went back to *buba*, looking everywhere on the way, praying a miracle would happen. And it did. Near the market I found a kopek, battered and filthy, but still a kopek. I gave the money to *buba*, kissed her hand and ran home. On the way back, I spotted something glittering on the ground and there, to my astonishment, was a clean, golden kopek.

Buba Mindl was born in 1813, when Napoleon was still emperor of the French, nearly a hundred years before the incident with the kopek. 'It was a tradition then if a child was very ill or dying, to take it to a respectable person who had lived to a good old age and "sell" the child to them. They even used to give the child an extra name.' The hope was that the child would inherit the longevity of his or her surrogate parent, and in this way thwart the Angel of Death. 'The old person handed over a small coin in exchange for the child, and this was considered a *mitzve*. My *buba* lived till one hundred and seven and was famous because she bought so many sick children.'

> I had two brothers and four sisters. We lived in two rooms, one of them the kitchen. My father couldn't afford to give me private education, so I just went to *cheder*. When we moved closer to the marketplace, there was a saddler downstairs at the back of the house and I used to watch him sitting on a wooden horse, working with thread. One day he said: 'Do you want to try?' So I began making the thread, twisting it from flax, and then I put wax and tar on it to make it strong and waterproof. He gave me a few kopeks and I was happy. My father thought I was in *cheder* and when he caught me he gave me a good few wallops. But I wanted to carry on, so he went with us to the Rabbi to draw up an apprenticeship agreement. The first year I was to get so many roubles, and for Pesach [Passover] I was to get a suit, a cap and a pair of shoes. I was not even eight years old when I went to work. Sometimes I worked from five in the morning till twelve at night.
>
> Unfortunately, my master didn't keep his word. Two days before Pesach he went with me to a shoemaker and bought me a pair of shoes. 'Tomorrow,' he said, 'I'll buy you a cap and that is that.' I said: 'What about my suit?' He said: 'I never promised you a suit.' I went home crying: 'I haven't got my suit.' My mother said: 'What! After Pesach you are not going back.'

Mark found work with another saddler. The first saddler found out about it and claimed back his apprentice. The parties went to the Rabbi, who heard the evidence and delivered his judgement, which Mark cannot remember. Rabbi Lipschitz was used to settling disputes of this kind. It was unknown for one Jew to sue another Jew in the civil courts, where the atmosphere was alien, the lawyers expensive, and the justice mistrusted. Best to keep away from officialdom.

When Mark's new employer was called up into the army, he became a shoemaker's assistant. In the *shtetl* hierarchy of occupations, few were considered lower than that of shoemaker. 'I had no choice. I would have liked to be an engineer. Once I went to a factory that made agricultural machinery to fix a leather belt. I looked round and asked: "Can I have a job here?" But what education did I have? I had no education. So I became a shoemaker. There was no alternative.'

Mark's father fell victim to the typhus epidemic that swept through Konin during the First World War. He died three days after being taken to hospital. 'We were all in quarantine for a fortnight. There were only two persons at my father's funeral, one was my younger brother, who had escaped through a window to go to the cemetery, the other was the gravedigger. Our clothes were burned. The Germans gave us something to wear and pairs of odd shoes. My mother and the children came home to an empty house, a bare table, no money, no food, no even a crumb. If there *was* a crumb, it was eaten up by a mouse. What were we to do?' Mark's mother took *buba* Mindl's place in the market where she, in time, became a fixture too, known as *di shvayge* – the silent one, 'because she accepted, because she never complained'.[1]

> There was not much work for me as a shoemaker – everyone was in hospital. There was no money around, so I helped my mother in the market. There was a rich Jewish landowner in Konin called Moishe Kaplan. In Poland he was like a squire. He had a big estate at Glinka with fields and orchards and we bought from him. He treated everyone the same, whether you were rich or poor, and he gave us credit. I used to walk to Glinka, about five kilometres away, and walk back carrying the potatoes and fruit. I had a belt over my shoulder with a basket hanging in front and another basket hanging at the back. And with my hands I carried two more loaded baskets. In those days I was strong like a horse.

(Today Mark Natel is small, slight and on the threshold of frailty.)

After two years' service in the new army of independent Poland, Mark set up on his own as a shoemaker, and remained in Konin until 1931. He joined the ranks of the autodidacts who, together with the more prosperous graduates of the Jewish high school – the gymnasium – constituted the community's intelligentsia. During the

1914–18 war, German Jewish officers had taught their uneducated Polish co-religionists German. Whether their motivation was idealistic or a patronizing attempt to elevate the *Ostjude*, one does not know. Later, some of the teachers from the Jewish gymnasium, undoubtedly of the left, set up free evening classes for Jews like Mark, who could not afford an education. Leopold Infeld, headmaster of the gymnasium, lent a hand in educating the Jewish poor. The young shoemaker borrowed scores of books from the Jewish library, studied the Marxist-Leninist doctrine, and felt a growing antagonism towards a society that offered him and so many like him no future.

His mother died in 1930. One brother was in Lodz. Two of his sisters had married and also left Konin. 'My home was no more home. I went to live in Danzig.' This raises a delicate point. A boyhood friend of Mark's, writing in the Memorial Book, records that following a Communist demonstration on May Day 1931, several arrests were made and the writer's brother and H.M. Natel 'escaped to Danzig'.[2] Although the new Republic of Poland legalized the Bund, it banned the Communist Party. Offenders risked being sent to the most feared prison in Poland, Bereza Kartuska, more a concentration camp than a prison.

The subject is delicate because, in the course of our conversation, Mark has never admitted to being a Communist in his youth. His brother Avrom served a sentence in Bereza Kartuska. Mark's sister, Adela, was arrested in Konin. Mark himself served a prison sentence for taking part in demonstrations against unemployment and racist nationalism. But he will admit only to being an 'anti-Fascist'. My guess is that when Mark arrived illegally in Britain in 1939 and was caught, he replied in the negative when asked if he belonged to an extremist party. He has had no dealings with the Communist Party since coming here, and I find it touching that a pensioner who has led a law-abiding life in Britain for fifty years should not have shaken off the fear instilled in him in Tsarist times, and later in independent Poland, of a knock on the door at midnight.

In 1938, planning to leave Poland, he returned to Konin to say goodbye to relatives and friends and to collect a birth certificate from the Town Hall. They handed him the certificate and advised him to leave town immediately. 'I said: "I have come to see my sisters and to visit my mother's grave." The official said: "I would not advise you to do this. Go straight to the station." The choice was to leave the town or be arrested. I had been in Konin only a day and a half. I went to my sisters and told them. They didn't come with me to the station and I never saw them again. I had to wait for a train for one-and-a-half hours and I am sure there was someone there to watch me. It was the fascist way of doing things.'

By 1938 Konin was no longer quite the town Joe Fox and Mark Natel remembered as boys. In some ways little had changed: the pumps that provided the neighbourhood with drinking water; the primitive sanitation, the market days, the flourishing Jewish social life insulated from the gentile world, the schismatic diversity of religious and political organizations . . . But now the town had two cinemas, moving pictures no longer inspiring a fear of sorcery. Certain irreligious Jewish bachelors were to be seen in the company of hostesses in the Olympia 'nightclub' – in reality, more of a late-night café with a dance-band. The Bundist dramatic society performed Ibsen. Secular education was compulsory until the age of fourteen. Those who could afford it – and most could not – had electricity in their homes. Some of the more prosperous merchants communicated with Lodz by telephone. The coming of the railroad in 1923, putting Konin on the main Berlin–Warsaw line, reduced its isolation from the outside world. The horse still ruled the road, and not even the richest Jew in town possessed a private motor car, but motor trucks were beginning to carry goods between Konin and Lodz.

Mark rejoined his wife in Danzig – in 1936 he had married Bella, a well-educated woman from Warsaw. In January 1939 she got permission to enter Berlin as a domestic, and worked for a family in Scotland. She tried and failed to get him permission to come as a butler. Mark found himself stranded in Danzig, running out of money. Nazi gangs roamed the streets, making it dangerous for him or anyone else with a Jewish face to go out. One night in June 1939 he and two friends rowed out to a Lithuanian cargo vessel moored in the harbour, where a sailor was waiting to smuggle them aboard. Mark hid in a coal bunker next to the boiler. The space was too small to stand upright, so he moved to a locker, where the steady drip of engine oil soaked his hair. During the storm that raged for four out of the seven days it took to reach Britain, Mark roped himself to a pipe. Conditions became so bad that he came close to surrendering himself to the captain. The three stowaways landed in a northern port at midnight. Mark borrowed money from his friends to pay the sailor, and the trio made their way to London. When his cousin opened her front door to him, she thought it was the coalman.

The police soon caught him, and it was touch and go whether he would be deported. He spent several days in jail. Bella tells me: 'After dealing with the Polish police and Nazi officials, we thought the policemen were wonderful. They gave him cups of tea. He had a temperature after the journey and they gave him aspirins. They were fantastic.'

Granted permission to stay in Britain, they worked first for others, earning very little, speaking on English, trying to build a home and bring up two sons. One day Bella had the idea of making bonnets and supplying them to stores. It worked, and they ended up with a little business manufacturing children's clothes, which they ran until they retired in 1967.

I become a welcome visitor in the home of the former shoemaker of Konin. There is always tea and cakes. When it is time to leave, he puts on his black beret and accompanies me to the car with the farewell admonition: 'Come again. Bring your wife. Do up your coat, it's cold. Next time you phone, call after six, it's cheaper.'

I discover links between us I had no idea existed. In 1945 he joined forces with my father and others to send parcels of warm clothing to the few survivors who had straggled back to Konin after the war. Mark's family was not among them. Only his brother Avrom, who had escaped to the Soviet Union and joined the Red Army, remained alive. The Nazis hanged his younger brother and murdered his two married sisters and their children in a massacre in the forest of Kazimierz, near Konin. One sister died of typhus in the Lodz ghetto. His youngest sister disappeared. His last communication from the family was a postcard dated 6 February 1940 that reached him via Switzerland. He reads it to me: 'My Dear Brother, we are all well . . .' His voice falters and he cannot go on.

Mark and Bella have a *mezuzah* on their front doorpost. They belong to a synagogue and feel 'intensely Jewish', but some time after 1945, when the truth of the Shoah unfolded, God left their lives, or perhaps I should say they left God. They ask the question so many others have asked: 'Where was He?'

Postscript Mark Natel's health deteriorated, and in 1993 it turned out that he had Parkinson's disease. I telephoned him one day in February of that year. He had walked to the seafront with the aid of a stick, and been out in the garden cutting back his hydrangeas. It was the last time he was able to do so. From then on Bella, in poor health herself, became his full-time carer. He died on 15 February 1994, a few weeks short of his ninetieth birthday.

6

THE MARKET SQUARE where *buba* Mindl sold her wares was known to every Jew in the town as the Tepper Marik (vowels pronounced as in 'turret') – Yiddish for Pot Market.[1] Of the Konin vocabulary I picked up as a child, these words imprinted themselves on my mind almost as strongly as the name of the town itself. In fact, Konin and the Tepper Marik seemed inseparable, unfailingly linked whenever my relatives set off on a trail of reminiscence. The Tepper Marik was at the centre of their memories because it was the centre of Jewish life, the quintessence of *shtetl* existence. Idealized with the passage of time, the Tepper Marik stood for all that was best about the way of life they had left behind.

The Tepper Marik was half the size of the town's main square, the *Groyser Marik*, the big market.[2] Although there were some Jewish shops and homes in the big square, its character was predominantly *goyish* (gentile). The Tepper Marik was unmistakably Jewish. As one Koniner recalled: 'We truly regarded the *Tepper Marik* as a *yidishe vinkl* [a Jewish corner] – a place where Jews felt more secure than anywhere else.'[3] The shops all belonged to Jews. The grocery stores, some no bigger than a front parlour, devoted most of their floor space to dark wooden barrels of home-made pickled cucumbers, pickled cabbage, pickled herrings, all giving off a piquant aroma of *yidishkayt* (traditional Jewishness). The *beth hamidrash* (combined place of study and worship, also used as a meeting place), more commonly known in Yiddish as *bes-medresh* – occupied one corner of the square, and next to it, in the street leading up to the park, the synagogue and the *mikve* (ritual bath house). The Rabbi lived just round the corner. The Jewish bank – a rather grand name for a couple of rooms – overlooked the square. You could choose to pray in any one of the many small congregations close by.

The Tepper Marik lay at the center of the grid of streets forming the Jewish quarter of Konin. In medieval times there were wooden houses here, overlooked by a castle. The Tepper Marik of modern times was mostly nineteenth-century, an odd assortment of buildings: poor-looking, hut-like cottages, five-storey houses with stone facings, the neo-gothic *bes-medresh* and, most conspicuous of all in its ornate bulk, the house belonging to Gluba, father of the future landlord of the Lord Rodney's Head pub in Whitechapel Road.

Each of these buildings, usually with extensions at the rear forming a courtyard, was divided into a warren of apartments that were workplaces as well as living quarters. Extended families – numerous children, son-in-law, widowed grandmother – squeezed into two or three rooms, eating, sleeping, giving birth, dying, tailoring, cobbling, making caps, clothes, leather uppers . . . The more assimilated Jews, by which I mean those who spoke Polish rather than Yiddish, who were religiously less observant and on the whole better off, preferred to live outside the Jewish quarter.

Just as light and season transform the character of a landscape, so the day of the week affected the character of the Tepper Marik. Tuesdays and Fridays were market days, when peasant farmers and villagers poured in from miles around, bringing grain, firewood, chickens, geese, ducks, eggs, butter, cheese. They sold their produce mostly the big market, but they also came to town to buy, and the Jews of the Tepper Marik supplied them with smocks, aprons, caps, hats, coats, jackets, trousers, shirts, haberdashery and other goods.

Once a month, on a Thursday, Konin had a fair, which also occupied the big square. Traders came from as far away as Lodz. On these days the Tepper Marik was busier than ever, overflowing into adjoining streets and stretching past the synagogue, almost to the end of the road, where horses were bought and sold.

When Joe Fox and Mark Natel were young, the Tepper Marik

was still known for its hand-made pots, the *tep* that originally gave the market its name, but as the century progressed, mass-produced enamelware and metal pots and pans took their place, though clay pots could still be bought until the Second World War. On market days you could hardly move for the crowd. Country customers with breeches tucked into high leather boots mingled with bearded Chasidic Jews in kaftans and 'modern' Jews in short jackets. Women in peasant aprons and headscarves picked at the merchandise alongside Jewish housewives wearing *sheytls* (the wigs worn by religiously observant married women). The noise never abated – the rattle of barrows and carts trundling over the cobblestones, droshkys trotting by, poultry squawking as they were carried off to the kosher slaughter, grain merchants trading, people haggling in Yiddish and Polish. 'There was no buying without bargaining,' says Mark Natel.

Water-carriers wove in and out of the crowd with buckets strung from wooden yokes, while those too poor to patronize them filled their pails at the two pumps in the middle of the square. In winter an icy mound formed round the pumps – iron columns as tall as a man – where children slid and the unwary broke their bones. In cold weather Blond Mordechai, who ran one of the two refreshment booths, did a brisk trade in tea, soup and hot salami snacks. The customers gripped their mugs with frozen fingers, stamped their feet, and looked longingly at the stall selling new fur hats held aloft on a cluster of wooden poles. Some time between the wars, Wolf Gruen opened his café bar where people could keep warm and listen to Radio Warsaw on his valve wireless, one of the few in Konin.

Friday was the busiest day of all, when Catholics and Jews shopped for fish. Three fish-sellers occupied the corner of the street that led down to the Warta. During the week the fish were kept alive in slatted wooden crates anchored just below the surface of the water. On Fridays they were hauled out and taken to the Tepper Marik, where they flipped around in flat wooden tubs. One of the fish-sellers was known only by his nickname, Bim-Bom.[4] After a customer had selected a fish – carp was the favourite for *shabbes* – Bim-Bom would scoop it out of the water, offer it up for approval, and give its head a loud thwack against the side of the tub.

On Friday afternoon, as sundown approached, the crowd melted away and a Sabbath calm descended. On Saturday morning, worshippers criss-crossed the square on their way to pray. After the bustle of the previous day, the Tepper Marik looked deserted and lifeless, the shops shut, no one working. Even the heavy iron handles on the pumps were idle. Everything changed in the afternoon, when families took a stroll after the parental post-prandial *shlof* – nap. This was a favourite time for groups to gather. The Tepper Marik became a debating forum. Bundists argued with leftwing Zionists, who argued with Communists, who argued with rightwing Revisionists, who argued with religious Zionists. Those who shared an ideology argued among themselves. Still others discussed books they had borrowed from the library, and topical events reported in the Warsaw newspapers. Strollers stopped for a chat.

By law, Sunday was supposed to be a quiet day in the Tepper Marik, although food shops were allowed to open in the morning. Behind closed doors, tailors and artisans – unable to afford *two* days of rest – carried on working, while merchants caught up with their book-keeping, ignoring the Christian day of rest. It was a world within a world.

7

HENIEK KAWALEK lived not many yards from the Tepper Marik as a boy, in the same house as the Natel family. When Henry was circumcised in 1927, on the eighth day after he was born – as Jewish law ordains – Hirsh Majer Natel was one of the witnesses.

I visit Heniek in Luton, Bedfordshire, where he has lived for many years as Henry Kaye, a British citizen. He is the son of a butcher, and the first Koniner I have met who was living in Konin when Nazi troops entered the town in September 1939. A young schoolboy at the time, he went through the agonies of the Shoah – deportation, starvation, concentration camps – and survived. His parents died in Treblinka. He lost his only brother. Why was he spared? 'I cannot answer that question. It was fate.' A reply I shall hear many times from other survivors.

Mark Natel traced him in Poland after the war and helped bring him over to England, where he had an uncle. Joe Fox gave him a job in his factory. Hard work and determination raised him from penury to prosperity. Now approaching retirement, he is a partner in a company that owns a small chain of hotels. He and his wife, Sala, live in a plushly furnished semi-detached house overlooking the Chiltern Hills, own an apartment by the sea at Bournemouth, and – the dream of Jewish parents – have one son a doctor, the other a lawyer. The visitor can hardly miss their bar mitzvah and graduation photographs. The war brought Henry's own formal education to an abrupt end when he was almost thirteen. Auschwitz and Mauthausen were his universities.

I have come to talk about life in Konin, but neither he nor Sala, who lined up for Dr Mengele in Auschwitz, can leave out their Shoah experiences. 'It's a shadow hanging over our lives,' she says. 'Everything comes back to me.' He says: 'After talking about this today, I shall have nightmares for weeks. We have been marked for life. You know what I mean?'

Konin, our common denominator, is more common than I had realized. My Sarna grandmother and his grandmother were close friends, he tells me. There are other personal links. But it is everyday life in Konin as he remembers it that we talk about most, he responding patiently to my stream of questions, slowly stroking his goatee beard, while Sala plies me with coffee and home-made cakes.

I come away knowing more about Konin in the 1930s, and with the telephone number of Henry's school friend in Konin, Izzy Hahn. He has a phenomenal memory, says Henry. I am about to leave when he expresses a thought I would rather he had kept to himself: 'You know something? The people who could have told you what Konin was really like in the old days are dead.'

8

HENRY WAS right about Izzy Hahn's memory. It *is* phenomenal. His powers of observation, even as a child, were remarkable, drawing every detail of life around him into his retentive brain. He had the freedom as well as the memory to absorb these details, for he gives me the impression that his parents did not keep him on a tight rein. A devil-may-care urchin with fair hair, blue eyes and a Slav cast of features, Izzy did not look any more Jewish as a child than he does today, his hair now a silvery grey.

He was born in 1928, the son of a tailor living in a basement on a corner of the Tepper Marik opposite the *bes-medresh*. 'When I looked up through the window on Friday nights, I could recognize the Rabbi's legs as he walked past on his way to *shul*.' The young boy roamed the streets in his free time, exploring every nook and cranny of the town, peering curiously through doorways and windows, eavesdropping on conversations, playing with Christian children while other Jewish boys mixed only with their own kind. An anti-Semitic taunt aimed in his direction would meet with instant physical retaliation. Izzy was short but tough. 'As young kids we was always fighting the Poles. I was never afraid of 'em. No one could ever touch me, no one.'

He grew up street-wise, able to talk himself out of any situation, a gift that came in useful later when he faced arrest and interrogation by the Gestapo. His quick wits, sharp eye and brazen nerve enabled him to spot escape routes when his life was in danger. He and his younger brother, Karol, once escaped through the electrified wires of Auschwitz, were captured and avoided death.[1] Izzy had all the qualities of a survivor, as intent on staying alive as the Germans were on exterminating him. He worked as a slave labourer, starved in Auschwitz, ate snow on a death march, endured cruelties that caused others to go under. As a boy, he saw his parents, ten-year-old brother and seven-year-old sister depart for Treblinka: 'I see them get on the train with the Germans shouting and the dogs barking. My family didn't see me. I saw the doors shut and that was it. I didn't see them no more.' He saw his aunt and uncle shot, and narrowly escaped execution himself. He witnessed hangings, tortures, massacres . . . He lived.

He came to London in 1946, speaking only Yiddish and Polish. Today he talks like a Polish-Jewish Cockney. At first he worked for a butcher. Now he is manager of the biggest kosher slaughterhouse in Europe. He met his English-Jewish wife in the East End soon after he came to Britain. He thinks of himself as a Londoner, but those formative first twelve years of his life in Konin are still very much with him. He recalls them without a pause for recollection. He describes the pattern on a wall, the number of steps leading up to a front door, the display arrangements of a shop window, the exact position of a wart on someone's nose, people's names, where they lived and what they did, distances on road signs, and the events that marked the last days of the Jewish community.

I ruthlessly exploit his memory over the next seven years, telephoning him at frequent intervals: 'Izzy, what colour was such-and-such? Who lived below so-and-so? Do you remember where they kept this or that?' Invariably he does.

9

CHILDHOOD WAS a short-lived Eden for a *shtetl* boy. It ended on his first day at *cheder*. Parents and relatives rejoiced at the start of his formal education as a Jew, showered sweets and coins on his head and dabbed honey on his lips to symbolize the sweetness of holy study.[1] Maternally cosseted one day, he found himself cast out the next into a strange and frightening world. When the boy first passed through its doors, wrapped in a prayer shawl and carried in his father's arms, he might be as young as three years old.

Today, Henry Kaye can laugh about his *cheder* days in the Thirties, but then it was a time of terror. 'The teacher had a leather whip, and we were treated like galley slaves on a boat. He also had an ivory pointer, and would shout "Speak up! Speak up!" If you didn't read loudly enough, he'd put the pointer between his teeth, grab you by the throat and nearly throttle you.' Mark Natel, who started *cheder* at three and a half, once made the mistake of challenging his teacher with a question: ' "You say that God created this and God created that, can you please tell me who created God?" I really wanted to know. He called me to the front, lifted me by the ear, tore my ear, dropped me on the table and gave me a good wallop with his whip. Later I went out, untied his goat, took it to the edge of the town and left it tied to a tree. He was a sadist. I don't want to talk about it.'

If circumcision was a boy's first painful introduction to Judaism, *cheder* was undoubtedly the second. But there was this difference: the first left its mark on the flesh but not the memory. The second did both. The undisputed ruler of the *cheder* was the teacher, the *melamed* or, as he was also known, the *rebbe*.[2] He might look like an ordinary, bearded religious Jew, wear a worn and grubby kaftan, be of lowly social standing, but the power he wielded over his pale, diminutive subjects seated on hard benches round his table was absolute. His task was to save them from being an *amorets* – an ignorant boor, no better than a peasant. He started them on the holy path of learning, teaching them the Hebrew alphabet and giving them a grounding in the basic religious texts. He was there to open their eyes to the truth and joy of the Torah. What were a few thrashings in exchange for such riches? An illustration in the fourteenth-century Coburg Pentateuch shows a teacher pointing down at his pupil's book with one hand and flourishing a whip in the air with the other.[3] Over five hundred years later, much the same scene could be observed in Konin.

Yeshia Zandberg was a *cheder* boy towards the end of the nineteenth century (my uncle Jacob was his class mate). When he became a Yiddish writer, this is how he remembered his first *melamed* in Konin:

> *Rebbe* Meyer was a Jew who seemed to get along with people. He was slender in build with a silver-black beard, a pale face and thoughtful eyes. He attracted sympathy and trust from everyone. But we *cheder* boys certainly had a different view of him. To us he was the flogger, the upholder of the full severity of the law. To us he rarely addressed a word of conversation. All we heard from him was a loud humming, interrupted every now and then by a heavy sigh. He never shouted at you, but inwardly boiled and blazed.

His chin was covered with a peculiar sort of beard. He had one long beard and a little pointed beard which seemed to grow out of the bigger beard. The little beard was named 'Junior Beard', and the other 'Senior Beard'. At times when he could no longer keep his temper under control, he would stick the little beard into his mouth and chew it. After a while he would release it, then grab it again between his teeth. And all would be well until the fatal moment arrived. He would suddenly let go of the little pointed beard and sit absolutely motionless. This was a sure sign that his patience had burst and the small boy who happened to be reading aloud at that point became speechless with fear. He would stop reading and wait for the whack . . . But on such occasions a miracle could occur. Sometimes his temper would suddenly ebb, leaving us feeling like someone who had just escaped the gallows.

He enjoyed pouncing, and therefore when the 'guilty party' was least expecting it, he would suddenly deliver a 'cut' on the elbow with the blunt edge of his open hand, or give the boy's sidelocks a fierce tug. Oh yes, he certainly had a lot of ideas, did *rebbe* Meyer! For example, he would get up from his seat with a cold stare and walk across the room. Then, when it was opportune, he would stand behind one of the boys and would remain there for a while with his hand in his belt. The young boy who was granted this honour would begin to fidget in his seat because he did not know what was going to happen. The *rebbe* would stand perfectly still and as soon as the young boy got tired and stopped wriggling and fidgeting he would let fall a slap on the pupil's face, leaving a visible sign on the swollen cheek that would linger for some time.

Moishe, the widow's child, had come to Konin with his mother from Lodz . . . He found it very difficult at first to adapt himself to these classes but he soon managed to orientate himself and in due course caught up with the others. However, this little lad was not very good at reading and always got into trouble. He used to get lost. The *rebbe* would not chew his beard for long . . . Poor little Moishe went through the entire gamut of the *rebbe*'s specialities but he still read the passage badly and would begin crying . . .

We all sat there as though turned to stone. The injustice being done to our comrade! (He later became one of the most talented actors of the Yiddish theatre.)[4] It was an injustice that

> cried out for vengeance. Still, things carried on in this way and no concessions were made, and it stuck in our throats. But what could we do other than to comfort the lad? . . . We couldn't do a thing while we were within sight of the *rebbe*.
>
> One day, all of a sudden, it happened: an event took place before our very eyes that was surely impossible. It was so extraordinary that we could hardly believe it. The boy suddenly stood up, brought his fist down heavily on the open *gemoreh* [a part of the Talmud] and shouted: 'I will not study!!!'
>
> This scene of Shakespearean drama, which the actor-to-be performed in the *cheder* – with real life in charge of the directing – cost him dear. The *rebbe*'s hand – poor man – hurt from the beating he delivered (he was after all a weakling). Eventually, after repeated blows, the boy fell off the bench, on which half the boys of the *cheder* were seated in a state of jubilant confusion. And so, with the boy lying under the table, the *rebbe* continued to kick out at him with his boot as far as he could reach.
>
> From that day on, Moishe's stature grew in our eyes. We certainly remembered that, despite his battering, he had stood up for himself and for his principles. This had never happened before. To us he seemed invincible. And in later years, in the course of life's hard struggles, we often reminded ourselves of the example he set us in those far-off days.[5]

The *cheder* teacher had a limited but effective armoury of physical weaponry. It included his hands, his feet, the reading pointer, a willow stick, a sewing-machine belt and, best remembered by those at its receiving end, the *kanchik*, a kind of leather cat-o'-nine-tails designed expressly for whacking the culprit's hand, shoulders or bottom.

The *cheder* inflicted another, even more relentless and inescapable form of pain: boredom. Learning was by rote: repetition, repetition and still more repetition. The sound issuing from the *cheder* window was of young voices reading in unison or chanting in accordance with the prescribed liturgical *nigunim* or melodies. And this torture by monotony went on hour after hour, day after day.

In winter, the incarceration was bearable. Outside, the temperature dropped below zero and gales rattled the window-panes. Inside, there was a sense of being protected from the elements. The stove gave off a comforting warmth. The *rebbe*'s voice droned on. Young eyelids began to droop, until the sudden lash of the *kanchik* snapped them awake. At the end of the day, some of the younger boys had to be carried home by their brothers, the shadows cast by their lanterns as they walked home through the narrow streets accentuating the darkness around them.

In the spring, youthful bodies became restive, impatient to feel the sun again on their pallid skin. In summer the room was stifling. In one Konin cheder 'We looked at the clock more than the *gemoreh*, but the clock went on doing what it had to do, and it almost seemed as if it had stopped.'[6] The goat outside the *melamed*'s window became an object of envy – it too was a tethered creature, but at least it was outdoors and spared having to learn biblical Hebrew.

The pupils were encouraged directly or implicitly to feel superior to the peasant youths, untutored and untamed. But on a warm day, when the *cheder* boy, struggling with the ancient language of his forefathers, found his thoughts wandering to games in the courtyard or stealing apples in the orchards or swimming in the Warta, the notion of being superior or privileged must have seemed dubious.

Friday brought relief in the form of a half-day, which was followed by the respite of the Sabbath or, rather, a partial respite, as the morning was for synagogue and the afternoon was a favourite time for the *melamed* to pay a call and test the boy in front of his father. It kept the pupil on his toes and enabled the father to judge whether the paltry fee he paid the *rebbe* was justified.

The birth of a male child was welcome news for *cheder* boys. At the home of the newborn child they would gather round the bed and recite prayers. The baby would thus hear, soon after coming into the world, the Shema: 'Hear, O Israel, the Lord our God, the Lord is One.' While reciting this precious, most fundamental of all Jewish affirmations, the minds of the young chorus would be firmly concentrated on the sweets and biscuits to follow. It was customary for the mother to hand round small goodies. In poor homes, the boys would have to settle for a nut and a raisin or a chick pea and the knowledge that they had performed a *mitzve*, a virtuous deed.

A much-anticipated annual treat was the spring festival of Lag Ba'Omer when, by tradition, the *melamdim* took their pupils on a picnic outing. For one day, the teachers became human beings, put away their *kanchiks*, abandoned their natural indoors habitat and ventured out into the spring sunlight, each at the head of a crocodile of boys making their way along the river to the Kaplan estate at Glinka, or to the top of the hill where the Russian cavalry exercised their horses, or to the tamer pastures of the municipal park.

The pupils marched with home-made archers' bows slung over their shoulders, part of the Lag Ba'Omer tradition. Once at their chosen destination, 'the *rebbe* told us the wonderful tales of Bar Kokhba and of Rabbi Akiva with his four-and-twenty thousand pupils . . . And how they fought heroically against the Romans, who wanted to destroy the Jewish people and their faith.'[7]

The boys ate their packed lunch and traditional boiled egg under the blossoming trees, fooled about when the *rebbe* was looking the other way, shot an arrow or two in mock battle with the Romans and then, when it was time to go, shouldered their bows, lined up behind the *melamed* and marched back through the town in high spirits. Next day, it was back to the stuffy room and the reading of texts, punctuated by a twist of the ear, a rap on the knuckles, a tug of the sidelocks, and the whack of leather on bare flesh.

Now spare a thought for the poor pedagogue. Even Zandberg, looking back in maturity at the flogger, detects in the old monster something the little boy never noticed: pathos. 'Did the *rebbe* perhaps see in us that joy of life of which he had been robbed, who knows how, in his own youth?'[8] The *melamed* was a sad figure in society. The writer, poet and Zionist, Shmarya Levin, goes so far as to describe him as 'one of the most melancholy phenomena in our Jewish life of the last century'. He quotes the old proverb: 'Two things it's never too late to do: to die and to become a teacher in a *cheder*.' It was, he says, 'the last resort of every failure'.[9]

To become a *melamed* you needed almost nothing by way of material resources, which is why the occupation attracted the poor, the pious and the unambitious. A few books, a table, a bench, and you were ready to set up shop. *Cheder* is the Hebrew for 'room', and room is what it usually was, more often than not the *melamed*'s combined living-room and kitchen. His wife would go about her cooking and housework a few feet away from where her husband taught his flock. It sounds homely, but in reality the dismal surroundings, often heavy with stale odours, had all the wretchedness of poverty.

The daughter of one of these teachers, a very old lady living in Brooklyn, wrote to me about her father, Tsvi Hirsh Szmerlowski, who was born in 1858 and started a *cheder* in Konin before the First World War: 'He was orphaned at the age of five and his married sisters took care of him . . . After he finished his service in the Tsar's army, his sisters arranged a marriage for him with my mother, who brought him a dowry of four hundred roubles. He used it to become a merchant. As he had no experience in business, he soon lost the money. Meanwhile, children were born.'[10] He became a *melamed*.

As a pious Jew, Tsvi Hirsh had 'suffered terribly' in the Russian army, but later, in Konin, his military service saved his life. During the early violent days of the First World War a Cossack grabbed Szmerlowski in the street and demanded money. 'Cossacks, if they happened to be in a throat-slitting mood, had a way of killing Jews even after they had taken the money.' The bearded *melamed* asked the Cossack to wait while he went indoors to fetch the money. He reappeared moments later not with money but with the medals Tsar Alexander III had awarded him for his part in fighting the Turks. 'The Cossack looked at the medals, looked at Szmerlowski, saluted, and walked away.'[11]

Within the ranks of the *melamdim*, there were gradations of status. The lowest was that of the *dardeki melamed*, who taught beginners the Hebrew alphabet and basic prayers. He was usually the most punitive of the *melamed*: beginners had to be broken in. Next in the hierarchy came the teacher of the *chumesh* (Five Books of Moses) and the rest of the Bible. At the top came the *melamed* who taught Talmud, especially the commentaries, the *gemoreh*. When a boy left the *gemoreh cheder*, at around the age of fourteen, he was ready, if need be, to be handed on to the rabbi or to a *yeshiva*.

Whatever his grade, the *rebbe* struggled to make a living. He offered his services in a competitive market. More than twenty *melamdim* who taught during the last fifty years of the community's existence are named in the Memorial Book.[12] It was against Jewish law to take money for the holy task of teaching, therefore parents and teacher maintained the pretence that the fees were for overseeing the boy's general education and moral welfare. Most teachers tried to supplement their earnings in various ways, such as giving tuition in private homes. One Konin *melamed* sold snacks to hungry boys – a slice of bread and *shmaltz* (rendered chicken fat) or a piece of herring.

One was a scribe who repaired Torah scrolls. Another gave haircuts for a small charge. Yet another carved wooden candlesticks.

To portray the *melamed* as invariably cruel and sadistic would be to perpetuate an unfair stereotype. There were humane and dedicated teachers in Konin who won the lasting affection of their pupils. Mostly they were teachers of older boys. The man who remembered Meyer the flogger so pitilessly went on to be taught by a teacher known by his nickname as Leibke *Soyfer* – Leibke the Scribe. His real name was Aryeh-Leib Mrozowicz, and he taught boys between ten and twelve years old. Although he was a strictly observant Jew, he abhorred fanaticism. 'He would laugh at the Chasidim with their wild prayer meetings and their running after *rebbes* all over the place. He found satisfaction in his work, was a fairly happy man, and stood out among the other *melamdim* of the town . . . He always took the opportunity to teach his pupils in original ways, and this is something none of his other colleagues could do. Not looking his considerable age, he was always close to his pupils, however young they were, and showed them a lot of understanding.'[13]

Leavening his instruction with jokes and puns, Leibke *Soyfer* had a gift for bringing Bible stories to life. 'His wife used to listen along with us to the stories and lessons given by the *rebbe*, bent over his book as he read aloud from the Bible in Hebrew.'[14] Leibke *Soyfer* showed mercy when others would administer a thrashing. One hot, somnolent day, when it was impossible to hold the boys' attention, he put the holy books aside and read the class a short story by the popular Yiddish writer, Sholem Aleichem. The drowsy pupils sat up, hanging on every word of the moral tale about a little boy. Leibke *Soyfer*'s methods would have shockd many of his colleagues. A *rebbe* reading secular fiction to his pupils!

There is a photograph of Leibke *Soyfer* in the Memorial Book: a little, frail old man with a double-pointed white beard and bright button eyes, posed stiffly in the photographer's studio beside a wilting potted palm. His arm rests on a small table on which a book lies open. His expression has a hint of gentle amusement. He looks like a benign gnome, his smallness emphasized by his voluminous double-breasted black coat with sleeves that are too long for him. I like to think of Leibke the Scribe as more typical of the Konin *cheder* teachers than Meyer the flogger. He was pious without being rigid. He was prepared to bend the rules in the cause of kindness. He brought a ray of light into the tenebrous world of the *cheder*.

Until I began my search for Konin I was unaware that one of the town's best-known *cheder* teachers was my kinsman, Benyumin Ryczke. He was the man I had known until then only by his nickname, *Der Geyler Ryczke*, the Blond Ryczke. The colour of his hair was one of only two facts I knew about him, the other being that he was the brother of my paternal grandfather, who was known as *Der Shvartser Ryczke*, the Dark-Haired Ryczke or, literally, the Black Ryczke. I have talked to survivors who studied under him. It seemed odd to me that none of them knew him by his nickname, but then I realized that by the time he taught them, in the 1920s and Thirties, his hair had turned grey and he had acquired a different nickname. They knew him as 'the lame *melamed*'. How or when he acquired his limp I do not know, but it gave him a lurching, unsteady gait. Strangers seeing him in the street would sometimes be taken aback: it was not often you saw a respectably dressed, religious Jew drunk.

Benyumin Ryczke taught boys at the highest *cheder* level, up to the age of fourteen. In his case it was not failure that led him to become a *melamed*. For many years he had been in partnership with his brother and a few others, exporting eggs and butter to Germany, until an event occurred that made him abandon his business for good. As told by my father's brother, Haskel, it happened like this:

> One day he was sent to Posen [then in Germany, today the Polish city of Poznan] on business in order to meet some German merchants. For this purpose he had to dress up in a short jacket and wear a gentile-style hat. He also had to trim his beard somewhat. As he related it afterwards, he was walking along the main street of Posen and happened to see his reflection in a window. He did not recognize himself, and in a state of anxious dread he asked himself: 'Am I really Benyumin Ryczke? I look like a *goy*.' When he came home he declared to his partners that he was leaving the business. He was truly learned in the Torah and when this happened, in 1910, he decided to become a *melamed*.[15]

At the age of forty-one he put away his *goyish* attire never to wear it again. He let his beard grow long, and devoted the rest of his life to teaching and studying the Talmud. In the one surviving photograph of him, he looks intimidatingly grim. He must have inherited the Ryczke gene that gave my father and his father and some of my paternal relatives the ability to wither people with their glare. Yet, as in the case of my father, the glare concealed a sensitive soul.

Once, when a boy asked the Blond Ryczke why he always shouted at him and not at other pupils who did less well in class, the *rebbe* explained that the pupils he did not shout at were blockheads. It was a waste of time to scream at them: '. . . but you, I love you, and I want you to grow up learned in the Law.' My kinsman, I am glad to sy, reserved the *kanchik* for truly serious offenders, such as the juvenile gamblers once caught playing cards under the table. In conditions of poverty, Benyumin and his wife Mindl brought up seven children. His funeral took place a year before Hitler's army entered Konin. His widow and daughter were deported and subsequently murdered in 1942. Several of his sons and most of his pupils suffered the same fate.

The Konin *cheder* boy, in general, fared better than his counterpart in communities further to the east, where there was greater resistance to change. The Konin *cheder* teachers included a higher than average number of *maskilim*, followers of the *Haskalah*, the Jewish Enlightenment, which had spread its influence from Germany in the course of the nineteenth century. They dressed in secular fashion, wore short beards, and did not beat boys. My grandfather, Simcha Sarna, an early Zionist, helped to found the first 'reformed *cheder*' in Konin, where Modern Hebrew rather than Yiddish was used to translate the Bible.[16]

The *melamed*, Israel Izbitsky, saw no incongruity in combining Talmudic learning with secular knowledge. Yehuda Leib Lichtenstein, another enlightened teacher, was an essayist, a writer of superb Hebrew poetry, and, according to an uncle who studied under him, 'a man with an encyclopedic mind. If you mentioned some obscure French poet born in 1718, he would know the name.'[17] According to my cousin, the eminent biblical scholar Professor Nahum Sarna (Jacob's son), 'He was a true genius. In a Western society he would have made a name for himself as a great academician. He was totally wasted. In Konin he starved three times a day.'

Oyzer Tzorondorf broke many of the long established *cheder* rules. Unusually for a *melamed*, especially one born in the last century, he dressed in secular fashion. His beard was short. He did not beat boys. He taught Hebrew as a language for its own sake and not exclusively as a key to religious knowledge.[18]

In the traditional *cheder* usually only one secular subject was allowed – arithmetic, an astutely practical choice for a people engaged so much in trade. In Konin, other subjects such as Russian, German and Polish crept into the curriculum, although they still played a minor role. With the introduction of compulsory secular education after the First World War, the *cheder* provided only *part* of the Jewish boy's formal education. While this spared him many unrelieved hours of religious study each day, it created a different kind of strain. When children finished school in the afternoon, gentile children and Jewish girls were freed from academic learning for the rest of the day. Jewish boys, on the other hand, had to go to *cheder* and bend over their Hebrew books. For many parents, the secular influence of the Polish school underlined the need for a Jewish education. Without it, their son would grow up a *sheygets*, an uncouth gentile. Until the Second World War Konin had two Jewish religious schools, approved by the Polish authorities, which combined *cheder* teaching with a secular curriculum.[19]

Between the world wars a startling change occurred in the *cheder* world of Konin: girls came to be admitted into what had hitherto been a male stronghold. *Melamdim* had long made a little extra money by going to better-off religious homes and giving girls private tuition. But now the doors of a *cheder* were opened to them for the first time. Chaim Kreitzer, a tiny man – hence his nickname, *Der Kleyner Rebbeleh*, the Little *Rebbe* – taught as a *melamed* in Konin for over thirty years. I have met a number of his old pupils, now in their seventies and eighties, living in America and Israel. The Little *rebbe* wore a long coat, and shoes with wooden soles. Although he was of the old school, it was he who took the innovative step of introducing a second table into his *cheder* – for girls. While he taught the boys at one table, his wife taught the girls at the other. In 1941 the Nazis lined up the Little *Rebbe* and his equally diminutive wife and shot them. I have this from one of his ex-pupils, who saw his old teacher go to his death.

In one respect the most extraordinary of all the Konin melamdim was not a *melamed* but a *melamedke*, the female of the species. The ultra-Orthodox would deny that such a thing was possible. That Rivka was able to follow her occupation before the First World War shows that Konin was not like other towns. She was knowledgeable in matters of Jewish laws and rituals, but this was not her chief speciality:

> Rivke lost her husband quite early . . . and was left a widow with five young children. In order to alleviate her hardship, she repaired household linen until late into the night, and often she went sewing in other people's houses. However, as this did not cover her outgoings, she also started to teach children and in her tiny room she founded a *cheder*. She became a *melamedke* for beginners. Her room, though stark with poverty, was always clean and cosy.
>
> Grown-up teenage girls used to come to her too, mostly servant girls, who were uneducated and could not read or write. She devoted herself to teaching them, to opening their eyes and placing in their hands the first key to education – the Hebrew alphabet.
>
> This elementary teaching work did not come her way easily. The girls would come to her weary from toil at the end of a hard working day in order to learn, and they found the initiation into reading and writing bitterly hard. But with her great love and patience, she slowly helped them out of their difficulties. Often she would guide the tired, calloused hand of one of her pupils across the page, showing her how to draw a letter of the alphabet. She felt enormous joy and spiritual satisfaction when, after long efforts, she finally taught girls how to write words of their own composition. And how much gratitude and love did each success elicit from her pupils, especially when they succeeded in reaching the point where they could write someone a letter in Yiddish all by themselves. They used to come to her overjoyed, and embrace and kiss her, bring her gifts and declare that they would never for the rest of their lives forget their teacher.[20]

During the interwar years a seamstress in Krakow,[21] dismayed at the widespread lack of elementary religious learning among Jewish women, founded the *Bes Yaakov* movement to promote religious education for girls. A *Bes Yaakov cheder* opened in Konin, which girls – mostly from Chasidic and religious families – attended in the afternoons.[22] I have discovered among my family papers a yellowing letter from Konin addressed to my mother in London and through her to Koniners in England. Dated 2 December 1937, it is a plea from the governors of the *cheder*, reinforced by a few lines from Jacob Lipschitz, the Rabbi of Konin. The *cheder* for girls, they report, is a success, growing in numbers and raising its standards, but the financial situation is grim: without outside support, they will be forced to close it. I do not have a copy of the reply. Somehow the *cheder* for girls struggled on until war broke out.

For all its failings, the traditional *cheder* did educate. At a time when the surrounding Christian population was largely illiterate, Jewish boys could read by the age of five or six. The *cheder* expressed the Jewish attachment to education and preoccupation with the written word. It produced Jews who could read the Hebrew liturgy and who knew their Bible. As secularization encroached on *shtetl* life in the years leading up to the Second World War, the *melamed*'s authority inevitably declined. But even when it failed in one direction, it often succeeded in another. It helped instil a sense of historic continuity, of Jewish national pride, which came to be manifested less in religious observance than in Zionism. Bible stories learned in the *cheder* planted in young minds an awareness of Eretz Yisrael, the Land of Israel, and the dream of returning there to build a new life for the Jewish people. One former pupil of a Konin cheder wrote as an adult living in Israel: 'Studying the Five Books of Moses, I learned and felt something new: that I am a part of a people with a long and great history.'[23]

10

AMONG THE wealthy Jews who lived in Konin between the wars few could claim a longer ancestral connection with the town than Moishe Kaplan. As that élite shrank in the course of the century, his own position grew stronger. While other rich families emigrated or packed their bags and moved to bigger cities, he stayed on, not least because his capital assets could not be packed and carried away. Moishe Kaplan owned land, a great deal of land, which he and his forebears had cultivated for several generations. Rare among Jews in this part of the world – where for centuries they had been forbidden to own land – he loved farming and the country life. He was an entrepreneur too, and the family estate at Glinka, a few kilometres from Konin, comprised not only extensive farmland, orchards and forests, but clay-pits, brickworks, and an open-cast coal-mine with its own private link to the nearby railroad.

Kaplan's hillside villa overlooked the meadows by the Warta, which offered perfect grazing for his dairy herd. His town house in Konin, also on the river, had its own private mooring. Kaplan owned pasture land bordering on the town and was the landlord of various properties including Konin's first cinema.[2] To his less well-off Jewish brethren, the tailors stitching in fusty workshops and the market traders stamping their feet on frosty mornings, Kaplan was an enviable figure, a true *nogid*, a *gvir*, a *porets*, a man of substance by any Yiddish appellation, who gave to the poor, donated the bricks for the building of the Jewish high school – the gymnasium – and supported other philanthropic causes. He was an elected member of the governing body of the community, the *kehillah*,[2] as well as a town councillor. The fruit that Jews bought at *buba* Mindl's stall in the Tepper Marik came from Glinka. They drank milk from Kaplan's cows. On the festival of Lag Ba'Omer, parties of schoolchildren and *cheder* boys hiked to Glinka where they enjoyed Kaplan's largesse.

To Jews and gentiles he was known as the *dziedzic*, Polish for squire. His servants and workers addressed him with feudal, forelock-tugging respect: '*Dzien dobry, panie dziedzicu*' – Good morning, squire. When I mentioned the name Kaplan to any of my Koniners, their response was invariably: 'Ah, you mean the *dziedzic*.' To them Glinka with its vast acres was a source of vicarious pride.

A photograph in the Konin Memorial Book, taken I would guess in the early 1920s, shows Mojzesz Kaplan – as he was known to his Polish friends – in a formal line-up with the mayor and councillors. What he lacks in height he makes up for in military bearing, bold moustache and resolute chin. His eminence in both Jewish and Polish circles earns him several mentions in the Memorial Book. His name is also listed, together with those of his wife and members of his family, in the black-bordered memorial pages. Stripped of land, wealth and social distinction, the squire died in Belsen alongside the poor tailors and market traders who once envied him.

I first heard the name Henry Kaplan mentioned *en passant* by a Koniner. 'Who was Henry Kaplan?' I asked. 'He was Heniek Kaplan in Konin – a son of the *dziedzic*.' What became of him? I enquired, fearing the worst – a recital of the familiar journey to ghetto and gas chamber. I learned that he was alive and living in London. I came away with an address that would lead me to the squire's son.

The home is a pebble-dash semi in an unremarkable road in suburban Harrow. A noisy turning of locks and the clatter of chains precedes the opening of the front door. The squire's son – words ineluctably freighted with Englishness. My mental image of him that I have brought to his door owes more to Gainsborough and Fielding than to the *shtetl*.

I feel a twinge of surprise when a small, elderly man greets me in a thick Polish accent. He is seventy-three, spry and healthy-looking. A receding hairline throws a high-domed forehead into prominence. The eyes are cautious and watchful. This is not a man who will readily open up to strangers. He wears casual clothes too impeccably neat ever to look truly casual.

The house is oppressively still as he ushers me into his sitting-room. Larger and more opulent than one might have expected from the exterior, it exemplifies the North London Jewish 'lounge', with freshly plumped velvet cushions, crystal chandelier, gleaming silver in the glass cabinet – an environment where no speck of dust would be wise to settle.

The interview gets off to a calamitous start. Kaplan is coiled up, almost truculent. 'What are your intentions?' he snaps. I had already explained my intentions in a letter, and now I explain them again. 'What have *I* got to tell you?' he says. 'Konin was like a lot of other towns in Poland. Nothing special. I don't think that what I have to say is of particular interest.' He leans forward in the big armchair and stares at me as if to say the subject is closed. I feel a sickening disappointment. Kaplan is only the fourth Koniner I have approached. He is probably the only survivor I am likely to find from Konin's small, rich Jewish upper class.

I lob a couple of questions at him, phrased more to show that I have done my homework than to elicit information. As is often the case with people who insist they have nothing interesting to say, he starts to say interesting things. I switch on the tape-recorder resting on my lap. A bad move. With a peremptory gesture he insists that he does not want anything recorded. I hastily switch off and start scribbling notes, which he appears not to mind. But he has a disconcerting habit of never taking his eyes off my pen while I write. I feel he can read my words upside-down.

He loosens up when he answers general questions, speaking slowly with occasional grammatical lapses and mispronunciations. Just as I am lulled into thinking the worst is over, he brusquely halts the conversation: 'This is no way to go about it,' he insists. 'We jump from this point to that point. We are talking about education, then life in Konin or culture. It is chaotic. You must decide what the points are and we must discuss them in some kind of order, otherwise we get nowhere.' I hold on to my temper. Desperate to win Kaplan's cooperation, I placate him with soothing words, conscious of my ingratiating tone.

Gradually he relaxes, becomes more outgoing. What turns the tide I do not know. Possibly my insatiable curiosity about Konin, his rediscovery of a past he has not talked about for a long time, or my genuine fascination at hearing about a privileged Polish-Jewish lifestyle that I know little about. Personal connections help. He remembers one of my kinsmen in Konin, not surprisingly my only rich relative there, a rather distant one, Aron Ryczke, who was a friend of Kaplan's father and a fellow town councillor. He stands near Moishe Kaplan in the Konin town council photograph, which we now look at together. The caption is in Yiddish, which Henry Kaplan does not read or speak. Polish is the language he still uses at home. This, he tells me, was a problem when he acquired the Memorial Book, but a close friend, now dead, translated the passages concerning his family. The close friend, it emerges, was an uncle of mine. We discover other personal ties. All roads lead to Konin.

I am wrong in thinking we are alone in the house. The door opens and Zofia Kaplan enters. Small and chic, she has considerable charm and her good looks have lasted. She carries a tea-tray with exquisite bone china, home-made cake and biscuits on a silver dish with silver tongs, and napkins folded into perfect triangles. The Kaplans bring a touch of continental stylishness to their suburban setting.

He used to be a technical and chemical consultant in the leather trade. Since retiring he has turned his garage into a studio and become a keen amateur sculptor. Before I leave, he takes me into his study to show me a bronze bust he has done of his father. The squire of Glinka gazes benignly down on us from the top of a bookcase.

In the course of the next few years I visit Henry Kaplan several times. He becomes more forthcoming with each visit, is generous with his time, brings out old photographs for me, and shows interest in the progress of my book. But he never completely drops his reserve, a Polish formality that I encounter from no other Koniner. To the end we remain Mr Kaplan and Mr Richmond. At no stage do I dare switch on my recorder again: his voice alone is missing from my sound archive of Konin reminiscences.

The following is the fruit of my several talks with the squire's son.

> My father, grandfather and great-grandfather were all born in Konin. At the time of the First World War, before taxation forced my father to sell some land, we owned about three thousand acres. I was born on the farm and my grandfather taught me to ride when I was about four years old. We had about a hundred horses – for riding, for working on the land and in the brickworks and coal-mine.
>
> My mother, Hannah, was also born in Konin. We had a

very beautiful house, a mansion, with a housekeeper, cook and servants. There were twelve of us children, six girls and six boys. During the school holidays the girls had a governess and we had a tutor. We had eight bedrooms for the family. We always had people staying – family and friends – and for them we had guest quarters, about twenty rooms. Sometimes we had thirty-five to forty people sitting round the table. A maid always served at table, wearing a white apron and a little hat. We supplied the food from the farm, our own eggs, milk, butter, cheese. We had our own system of refrigeration: we gathered blocks of ice in the winter, put them into a very deep cellar, put sawdust on top and they kept everything cool for weeks and weeks in the summer.

Our relationship with the Polish people who worked for us was very friendly. They respected us and we respected them. We felt no anti-Semitism from them. We did not feel we were Jews and that we should be frightened of them. We felt as good as any Catholic man or woman. We were not afraid of them, and they were not afraid of us. As children we play with their children. When we grow a little older, we swim with them, we ride horses with them. It was a completely different life from the Jews living in Konin. It was the life of a squire. We participated in country life. We had shooting parties to which big Polish landowners like our neighbour *hrabia* [Polish title, equivalent to Earl] Kwilecki used to come, and we used to go to them. We would go from one shooting party to another. We had forests of our own with wild boar and deer.

We were not very religious but every one of us boys have bar mitzvah. We have a Jewish cook and our food was kosher, though later on the younger generation starts to get less kosher. At home we have kosher meat from the town, and if we want to kill an animal on the farm, then a *shoychet* used to come. We participated in Jewish festivals and lit candles on Friday but we did not go to the synagogue every Friday and Saturday, and my father did not lay *tefillin* [put on phylacteries]. He had seats in the synagogue and Rabbi Lipschitz was a friend of our family. At the same time, my father had seats in the village church near Glinka, for our workers, and his name was on the seats.

My father was a very lovable man, very charitable. He was helping with a lot of Jewish causes. There were a lot of poor Jews in Konin and during Jewish festivals he was giving them fruit from the farm, potatoes, vegetables, corn, flour. My father also gave lots of donations to Catholics, and offered bricks for churches, so they could not say that the Jews help only the Jews.

My father was very knowledgeable in agriculture and veterinary matters, and trained some of the first *chalutzim* [Zionist pioneers] who went to Palestine. They came to Glinka from Warsaw, Krakow and elsewhere in Poland. Quite a lot of these *chalutzim* were Communists. The Polish authorities found out and did not allow my father to train them any more.

My first school in Konin was the Jewish gymnasium, where all the subjects were taught in Polish. When the Jewish school closed down, the children of those who had the money went to the Catholic gymnasium in the town and finished matriculation. The Catholic school was very different. I was one of only two Jews in my class. As there were very few Jewish pupils, we assimilated with the other boys and we did not feel great anti-Semitism. Because I went to the Polish school, most of my friends were non-Jewish. I went to their homes and they came to us.

A servant took us to school every day in a beautiful carriage and then came and collected us. Every one of us was used to this way of life. When school term started in the winter, we moved to our house in Konin. It was not always possible to travel from Glinka to Konin because of the weather – snow, mud and floods. Our stables in Konin backed onto the river, and we had a boat there too. In the summer my brothers and I went canoeing between Glinka and Konin. Our family belonged to the Konin Rowing Club. Only one other Jewish family in Konin [the Joels] belonged to this club.

There was no Jewish education at the Polish gymnasium, no Rabbi coming to the school. When there were religion lessons, the priest said: 'You sit down. There is no need to go out.' So I know as much about Catholic religion as Jewish, maybe more. To get a Jewish background I went to a *cheder* in Konin once or twice a week, only in the afternoon. The *rebbe* spoke Yiddish. Yiddish was not spoken in our home, and we always asked him what the words mean in Polish, but he could never tell us, only in Yiddish – mumble, mumble, mumble. We learned the Hebrew and all the prayers like parrots. Once he hit me and my brother Jacob with a *kanchik*. We hit him back and we did not go again. We got a good hiding for it from my father and he punished us by making us have a religion teacher at Glinka during the summer.

The teacher was living for the summer on a little cottage on the estate, and we went there for our lessons. We hated it because it stopped us riding and fishing and shooting. One day we made arrangements with our friends to go fishing, but we had religion lessons. Jacob went first. The teacher was a young *yeshiva* student who was learning to be a Rabbi. He was very thin and pale, had earlocks and wore a long black coat. He was sitting on a chair when my brother walked in carrying a shotgun over his shoulder. The teacher said: 'Why have you got that?' My brother took the gun, loaded it and hung it over the back of the chair where the young man was sitting. He was afraid to move and sat there so stunned that my brother walked out and we went fishing.

That evening the teacher was supposed to come to the house. They called him and nobody answered. They said he must be in his room and went to get him. He was still sitting with the gun hanging over the chair. He had been there all day, frightened to get off the chair. That was our religious lesson.

We had a music teacher, not Jewish, a friend of my mother's and also a teacher at the Polish gymnasium. She always spent a few weeks with us at Glinka and gave us piano lessons. She sneaked on us and related to my mother everything that happened at school. We were very annoyed with her and Jacob decided to teach her a lesson. He put pins between the keys of the piano and then during the lesson he deliberately made a false note. She hit the right note with her hand and pricked it on the pin. We never had another piano lesson. We had disposed of another teacher. [Kaplan laughs heartily, his face turning beetroot red. Zofia comments: 'Those six boys were such devils.'] We hated teachers in the summer. In summer we wanted to be free. I loved the outdoors. I loved the Polish countryside, which is more wild than here in England.

When we lived in Konin in the winter we did not hunt, but there was a factory on the other side of the river belonging to a [Swiss gentile] family called Reymond. It was almost opposite our house and it had little windows. My brother Jacob and I would

> shoot across the river with a Winchester rifle to see who could hit the highest window.

Kaplan brings out a snapshot showing him, aged about sixteen, with his brothers Jacob and Mietek. He and Jacob carry a pole on their shoulders from which hangs a deer, strung upside-down by its legs. Nothing could illustrate more vividly how the Kaplans' lifestyle differed from that of their fellow Jews in Konin. Hunting and shooting were for the *goyim*.

Kaplan produces a gun case and two ammunition boxes made of brown leather as hard and smooth as polished wood. They once belonged to Mietek, who took them with him when he settled in France before the Second World War. When he died a few years ago, he bequeathed them to his brother, who shows them to me together with an antique pair of binoculars, also from Glinka. I draw aside the white net curtains over the patio doors and train the binoculars on a neighbouring house. The Zeiss lenses that once followed wild game in the forests of Poland pick out a television aerial and suburban rooftops in Middlesex.

The Duke of Bedford, Kaplan tells me, once invited him to join a hunting and shooting club, but it was too expensive. Today he belongs to the Harrow Angling Society, whose monthly magazine rests on a coffee table: *Pike Special*. Kaplan takes his grandson angling at weekends, and in the summer he goes deep-sea fishing off the Brittany coast: 'You see, I am still with nature. I never part with it.'

After leaving school, Kaplan did his stint of military service and became an officer cadet. 'I myself did not meet with much anti-Semitism in the army. I was a very good sportsman, a good horse rider and physically strong. I could cope with anyone. In every riding and sports competition I did as good if not better than they. Therefore they cannot say: "Oh he is a Jew, he cannot do it." '

> We had family in France, and in 1935 I went to study at Lyon University, where I graduated in industrial chemistry; after that I stayed on to do research work on enzymes for my doctorate. During the vacations I went back to Konin. The saddest thing was that I saw how the atmosphere there was changing. I start to lose my connection with my Catholic friends from school because of their growing anti-Semitic attitude. Every year when I visit Konin

in the vacation I find things changing for the worse. I hear from my parents that the *Endecja*,[3] the party of fascists, is active in the area. They beat up Jews selling in the markets and smash their stalls, taking away their livelihood. The police were standing and looking.

I am proud of the culture I obtained in Poland. I was very assimilated, but as time went on and fascism and anti-Semitism started to grow, and young Polish fanatics started behaving the same way as the Hitler Youth, then I gradually start not to sympathize with this kind of behaviour by my compatriots.

My father wanted to sell everything and go to Palestine and farm there, but he was very occupied with running the estate and business, so he sent his younger brother, Joseph, to look. He came back and said to my father: 'How can you grow anything on the stones and desert sand?' Which at that time was logical because there was only bare land and desert.

My father did not want to go to France. He was a patriotic man who loved the land where his family had lived and farmed for generations. It was heart-breaking for a man of his age to move to another country, but he started to send his children abroad. Two of my brothers stayed and worked with him. And most of my sisters stayed in Poland.

Kaplan finished his research work at Lyon in July 1939 and soon returned to Konin. Crossing Germany by train, he observed the troop movements, the military concentrations close to the border with Poland, and sensed that war was imminent. A few weeks later, the Gestapo arrived at the gates of Glinka.

Fortunate in not having suffered anti-Semitic humiliations in his early youth, Kaplan is able to view his Polish compatriots more dispassionately than those who did. He does not ascribe every vice to the Poles, or every virtue to the Jews: 'You need to look at it both ways. The Jews never mixed with their neighbours. The community tried to separate itself. It was forming a Jewish high school, and Talmudic schools and little *cheders*. The very religious Jews did not dress like their neighbours. The Jews say to the *shabbes goy* [gentile who is hired to perform tasks on the Sabbath forbidden to Jews]: "Light me a fire. I must not do this, I must not do that." The Poles think: "What sort of people are they?"'

The poorer Poles were used for various kinds of dirty work

> and they resented it. They saw the enterprise of the Jews, poor Jews working at home, making clothing, selling in the markets. They themselves had no enterprise. The Polish maids saw that the Jews have *challa* [plaited white bread eaten on the Sabbath] and silver candlesticks, that the children are nicely clothed to go to synagogue – this all created jealousy. They didn't see that the Jews work hard, they thought it just came from heaven. I recognize the bad qualities of the Poles and also their good qualities. They were good companions, very jolly socially. They were not just slaving for money but enjoying life. They take pleasure from life. Jews found life sad. The Poles played and drank. It was two different mentalities, two different worlds. I was brought up in these two worlds. I was assimilated but I always felt I was a Jew and belonged to the Jewish people. I think the Jews could have mixed more with their neighbours and still kept their identity.

Like most Polish Jews, he believes that the Catholic Church was a prime cause of anti-Semitism, and helped to pave the way for rightwing violence. Hatred fostered by religion, he says, has made him fearful of all religious extremism, whether Christian, Islamic or Jewish. His own religious affiliation in England is to the Liberal Synagogue, which is as low-church as you can get. Does he feel more consciously Jewish today than he did during his early youth in Poland? 'Definitely. My experiences have converted me to being a Jew.' He laughs.

Of Moishe Kaplan's twelve children, three daughters died in the Warsaw ghetto. One survived. Four sons, including Heniek (Henry), served in the Polish army; two of them lost their lives in the underground movement. His other two sons, living in France at the outbreak of war, served in the French army and later joined the Resistance; one was awarded the Croix de Guerre.

Heniek, aged twenty-five, and his nineteen-year-old bride, Zofia from Kalisz, spent their honeymoon fleeing to Russia. From then until the end of the war their life together was one continuous fight for survival, with enough danger, narrow escapes, romance and suspense for a dozen action movies. They came through it all with unfailing resourcefulness, courage and above all, verve. 'Perhaps because we were young, we did not have the fear that older people felt. We always said: "We will fight our way through."

There were Jews who were frightened if you so much as shout at them, because they were always kept down. I was brought up on the farm with nature, with hunting, swimming, boating . . . We were built for this kind of adventure. For us this was adventure.'

The young man peddling second-hand shoes on the streets of Lvov was scarcely recognizable as the squire's son. The prisoner fighting cold and hunger in a Siberian labour camp, where so many foreign refugees ended up, had to blank out memory of the mansion by the Warta. The camp cobbler repairing boots could survive only by living in the present. The presence of Zofia, who was in the same camp, gave him strength. She was ready to take any risk so long as they stayed together.

When Hitler invaded the Soviet Union, the Russians released thousands of Polish prisoners, Heniek and Zofia among them. The couple trekked five days to the Volga, embarked on a makeshift raft and finally, after further hardships and adventures, joined the Polish army newly formed under General Anders. They remained in uniform until the end of the war. Their army travels took them to Tashkent, Kazakhstan, Iran, Iraq, Egypt, South Africa, Palestine and finally Britain, where they transferred to the British army. Back in civilian life, they looked for work and began to think about starting a home and family.

For Henry Kaplan, there was no prospect of ever becoming the squire of Glinka. The postwar Communist regime in Poland confiscated the Kaplan lands, demolished the mansion to make way for industrial development, and expanded the open-cast coal-mine, where they discovered deposits of a rare and valuable mineral no one knew was there in Moishe Kaplan's day: titanium – now used for making things like the nose-cones of spacecraft. In 1952 Henry Kaplan tried to sue the Polish government for compensation to the tune of one million pounds and failed. (Following the end of Communist rule in Poland, he has taken further legal action against the government but knows it will be a long-drawn-out struggle. 'I want them to accept liability. Perhaps one day my grandchildren will benefit.')

> I would not go back to Poland because of the sadness of my parents and so many of my relatives who perished. I love Poland but it is too sad to return to the grave. Where *is* the grave? Was

it where my father went to the gas chamber? Or the forest where my brother was killed fighting for Poland, for freedom? There is no point.

My two daughters do not know much about Konin. Maybe it is my fault. Maybe not. I wanted them to regard England as their country and so I did not teach them much Polish. They have been born here after the war and we wanted to bring them up as normal, with the culture of this country. They went to English schools, to university, and got married to Jewish boys born in England. We did not want to be martyrs, show what we suffered, be sorry for ourselves. They know about the Holocaust, they have read the books, but we brought them up as people for the future, and therefore we talk as little as possible about the past. They know about Glinka but their heart is not there. We who knew it have never forgotten.

II

HENIEK KAPLAN was twenty-five when he returned to Konin in July 1939 after completing his studies in France. 'I cross Germany by train and mention to my parents that I don't like seeing to many German troops on the border, that I expect any time they will cross. Everyone say to me: "Don't make panic. The Germans have an agreement with Poland, there will be no war." I have the same reaction from my friends. A few weeks later the Germans cross the border and the same day they are approaching Kalisz, not far from Konin. I was staying in Kalisz with my sisters, who lived there, and I know a number of Jewish friends there, one of whom became my wife. I left Kalisz and went to Konin, to my parents.'

Henry Kaplan falls silent and sits for what seems a long time saying nothing, looking down at his chest, lost in thought, absently rubbing his hands along the wide arms of the chair. Finally, in a voice drained of energy, he asks: 'Who is interested in my story?' Another silence. Then he continues.

The Germans were not yet in Konin. I had my mobilization

card and I registered there with the local infantry unit. After registration I was told to wait and report later. The German army advanced very quickly. The first bomb fell on Glinka, on a small building not in use, and various bombs fell on Konin. There was panic in the town. I was on the farm and one of my nephews had been running for cover and broke his leg. I with my sister Rozhka went straightaway with her son to the hospital. There I saw already casualties from the air raid, and a lot of Polish army retreating in the direction towards Warsaw. Many of the population, Polish and Jewish, started to run towards Warsaw. My parents decided to leave with my brothers Leon and Jacob. Another brother, Joseph, and I stayed behind looking after the farm, making sure the animals were tended, and we were supposed to leave later, in a few days' time.

The workers and servants had vanished, and I and my brother were left to do all the work ourselves. The horses, the cows had all been tied for the night in the stables or the cowsheds and they were hungry, not fed. We untied the animals and let them go into the fields. That was the only way we managed to save them, but the bombardment became more severe and some of the animals were killed. My brother and I decide to leave immediately, also in the direction of Warsaw.

This was about four days after the war started. We took the best four horses and saddles and the carriage, and we looked for my parents but we never found them. The Germans advanced so quickly, there was big congestion on the roads. Refugees were filing it, stuck, tangled in the road, refugees and army. The Germans bombed the road and there were dead all over.

We heard that my parents were somewhere in a little town not too distant. Therefore my brother decided that I stay in one place and he would go on horseback to find my parents. When I stayed, I noticed the army unit to which I belong passing by. I join them. Near Sochaczew, before Warsaw, there was the biggest battle between the Polish and German armies, one of the bloodiest fights that took place. We lost. Twice the little town was taken by the Polish army but we were defeated by the heavy mobile arms of the German army. I lost one of my cousins and another cousin buried him and marked his grave. My brother Leon was in that same battle but we never met. Later he was wounded very badly in

> the battle for Warsaw, where he was commander of a machine-gun unit.
>
> The army that survived Sochaczew started to run towards Warsaw to defend the city and organize the last battle for the capital of Poland. The army was completely disorganized. Part of the forces managed to cross the River Vistula and went to defend Warsaw, but we were trapped in a forest near Warsaw, where we were surrounded by the Germans. They shout with a megaphone: 'If you don't surrender we'll burn you alive.' We were forced to surrender.
>
> We were taken prisoner and put in a field used as a temporary camp. I removed my cadet officer epaulettes so that I can stay with some friends who were ordinary soldiers. That night I and my friends decided to escape. It was a cabbage field and easy to hide. We crawl until the searchlight comes round and then we wait. When the searchlight moves away we crawl again, and this way we escape. We had no maps, we did not know what direction to go, so the simple way was to find the railway line. There the telegraph poles had plaques nailed to them in a certain way which tells you where is the north. We also used the trees, because the moss grows on the north side of the trunks. So the direction we decided to go in was home, to Konin.

Concealing his uniform under old clothing given him by a farmer, dodging German units wherever he went, living on a diet of raw potatoes taken from fields, Kaplan made his way first to Lodz, where one of his sisters lived. Finding no sign of her there, he made for Konin via Kalisz, where he planned to see another sister and his girlfriend, Zofia Zylberberg, then nineteen.

He was crossing the bridge at Kalisz on a peasant's haycart when a German guard arrested him for not having a pass. He was thrown into an overcrowded cell. While he waited to be interrogated, prisoners from his cell were regularly taken out and shot. The Gestapo gave him a relentless grilling, but did not spot him as a Jew: 'My manner was Polish and I spoke in a distinctly educated language. I did not talk with a Yiddish accent or with the hands.' But the Gestapo held on to him. At the next interrogation two days later he gave his captors the name of a local *Volksdeutscher* (Pole of German descent who has declared his loyalty to the Fatherland) who was a friend of his father's and a prominent industrialist. The friend vouched for Kaplan, and the Germans released him with a temporary pass.

With a few minutes to go before curfew, he raced through the town and spent that night with Zofia's family. There was no news of his parents. Next morning he went to his sister Fella's home and found it deserted.

> In the cellar I found my nephew's bicycle and I started to cycle to Konin, about sixty kilometres away. The chain kept slipping but somehow, after spending a night in a village, I reached Konin. As I went through the town, I passed people who know me from childhood but they seemed not to know me. They did not look at me. I was very surprised but still I did not approach them. I was too proud.
>
> I passed the wooden bridge over the Warta and the chain slipped again. There was a column there with posters on it, and I rested the cycle on the side of the column and tried to put the chain back. I look up and I can see my name, my father's name and my brothers' names, on a poster saying: WANTED DEAD OR ALIVE.
>
> I was trembling. My legs shake and I can see why the people do not want to know me. I started to cycle as fast as I can to Glinka. I arrived and found my mother and my sister, Sasha. They had returned there and were happy to see me. 'Where is father?' I asked. 'In prison in Konin.' My mother said: 'You must leave the house at once. The Gestapo is coming day after day, checking if any of you come back. You have no chance to survive here.'
>
> As we sit and eat there is a terrific banging at the gate. It is smashed down by a car and I can see Gestapo jump out and start covering the front of the house. But I know how to escape from the back. I jump through a window and make my way to the River Warta. I swim across and hide in bushes, wet and cold, and do not know what to do next. It is in the afternoon. I lie and watch from the bushes, and on the other side of the river I can see a lot of movement near the house.
>
> Night comes. I still sat there and do not know what to do. Suddenly I hear a whistle, a whistle I know very well. My father had an old servant, a very loyal man, who was now retired. He taught us shooting and hunting when we were boys, and when we

have been hunting during the night, he makes a special whistle with the fingers. I hear that whistle and know it is old Swendrowski. I answer him with the same whistle. I know I will have some message. Slowly I can see a little boat arrive in the dark. He brings me some food and clothing. He say to me: 'Look, I cannot take you to my home but I can take you to a safe place, rely on me, rely on me. You are in safe hands.' Swendrowski was an old poacher, he knew every movement. He was like an animal who could not be caught.

We go to our nearest village, Morzyslaw, and there, next to the church, is a cemetery with old graves. He moves an old stone to one side and says: 'Get in there.' The tomb is very deep and I can almost stand in it with my head bent a little. He moves the stone back and I stay there sitting in the dark, watching the light change as dawn comes. Next night I hear the whistle. He came: 'The village is full of Germans. They know you are in the district. It is impossible to move you at the moment. Be patient until things quieten down.' He brought me some food. 'Stay here. I'll see you again. We're working on something.'

After the third day sitting in this tomb, Swendrowski came very early in the morning and said: 'Here is some clean clothing and some food. I take you on the main road to Kalisz. Your Uncle Joseph is waiting for you with a horse truck. He will have a German pass for two – for driver and helper. You will be the helper.'

Uncle was waiting there. He got the pass from the Germans with help from our friend Reymond, an industrialist in Konin [his was the factory whose windows provided targets for the Kaplan boys]. And so we left the village and went to Kalisz.

Kaplan never saw Glinka again.

Stanislaw Swendrowski proved his loyalty to the Kaplan family in other ways. When the squire and his wife, Hannah, were in the Warsaw ghetto, Swendrowski, though quite an old man by then, travelled to the capital, walking and hitching lifts, to bring parcels of food to his former employers. He remembered the squire's many kindnesses, the retirement gift of a plot of land and the bricks to build a house. Swendrowski's son, Stefan, was in Warsaw when the Kaplans were in the ghetto. On one occasion he took them some bread and, according to one of Henry Kaplan's sisters, 'the two men wept like children.'

Posing as a *Volksdeutscher*, dressed in a green jacket, high boots and a Tyrolean hat with a feather, Kaplan worked for a short while in Kalisz as a cashier in a shop, raising his arm and barking '*Heil Hitler*' whenever a German officer entered. Soon the Gestapo got wind of his whereabouts and he had to get out fast. He did so in a truck with swastika markings, provided by his father's industrialist friend.

Increasingly draconian restrictions on the Jews convinced Kaplan of the need to escape from Poland. But Zofia was still in Kalisz. 'As I was in love with her I decided to go back. I will not leave her to perish with the others.' He returned to Kalisz, where he faced an unexpected problem: Zofia's father would not countenance the impropriety of a young couple going off together while still unmarried. A rabbi was summoned, and while friends kept a lookout for the Gestapo, Heniek and Zofia and two other couples were married under the same *chupeh* (wedding canopy). It was 14 November 1939. Next day, all six fled from Kalisz and eventually succeeded in escaping from Poland. When Zofia signed her married name for the first time, it was in the register of a Russian jail.

12

I CAN HAVE BEEN no more than four or five years old when I was introduced to Puccini, Verdi and Adolf Hitler. I would sit on the stairs in my pyjamas, unobserved, listening spellbound to an Italian diva in full flood, her voice floating up from the room below with a beauty that scarcely seemed human. The music aroused my emotions in a new and powerful way. My parents thought I was fast asleep. There were many nights when I crept halfway down the stairs and waited with nerve-tingling anticipation during the overture of whistling and crackling which always preceded the musical delights. My father, holding this week's *World Radio* in one hand, twiddling the Bakelite knob on our wood-veneered radio with the other, trawled the wavelengths until he found the programme he wanted, usually opera, often from La Scala, Milan. This was how my musical education began. It was also how I first heard another, less musical voice which also did not seem quite human: an angry, declamatory voice ranting in a language I did not understand. The speaker seemed to be working himself into a rage until the crescendo of fury reached screaming pitch. This voice too was drawing an emotional response from an audience, for every now and then, as the speaker reached a hysterical climax, a vast crowd roared in unison: '*Sieg Heil! Sieg Heil! Sieg Heil! . . .*'

The Führer had recently come to power in Germany. Some years later, in 1939, I was allowed to join my parents in the 'drawing-room' while they tuned in to Berlin, the adored city of my mother's youth, and listened with anxiety on their faces to the roar of the Nazi mob. I learned the meaning of one oft-repeated German word: *Juden*. Some of these *Juden* were relatives with whom my mother had lived in Berlin as a girl. One by one they fled the country.

As war drew near, I realized that we in London were also under some kind of threat. At school they gave me a square cardboard box holding a gas-mask that smelled strongly of rubber. There was talk of evacuation. My parents began to display a new interest in our cellar. They listened more frequently to the radio bulletins and to that rabble-rousing voice from Germany.

I know now that their thoughts at that time must have focused less on our own ill-defined danger than on the vulnerability of their family in Konin. Our position was secure by comparison, in every possible way. My father had changed his name from Ryczke – which no Englishman seemed capable of pronouncing, let alone spelling – to Richmond.[1] He ran a small business importing jute matting from India. We had a house in a leafy suburb, and a tiny Austin car. My parents were citizens of the largest empire on earth, protected by the world's greatest navy. Stretches of land and a circle of sea separated us from the potential enemy. In Konin, the enemy was just down the road, ready to devour a military feeble nation whose population included the largest number of Jews in Europe.

The day before Germany invaded Poland, Leo Monczka, an educated timber merchant and town councillor, sat in his comfortable home on Konin's main thoroughfare, Third of May Street, following the news on the radio. Many years later, living in Israel, he recalled the last hours of peace ticking away:

> 31 August 1939: The whole day in great tension, listening to the radio. We hear Hitler's speeches, threats . . . Jewish families are gathered round the radio with neighbours who don't possess one, listening to bad luck approaching us . . . Konin Jewry knows how close this bad luck is to our doors. We are so very near the German frontier.[2]

Among the young Jewish army reservists mobilized towards the end of August 1939 was a young tailor, Herman Krol, born in 1912. In 1987 I found him living in London, still tailoring:

> I joined my regiment in Poznan and from there, not many hours before the war began, we were sent eastwards. The train went through Konin and we stopped there for a few moments. I wrote a note to my parents, wrapped it round a stone and threw it out into the station courtyard, where I hoped Prochovnik [a Konin Jew who transported goods to and from the station] would pick it up. He was always there and I thought maybe he will find it and take it to my parents. I don't know if they ever got my message. They died in Treblinka with my brother and sister. The train left and that was the last time I saw Konin.[3]

Monczka and his family stayed up all night on the last day of August: 'Near the radio we hear tensely [on 1 September] that German troops have crossed the frontiers of Poland.' That afternoon, a Friday, the Konin Boy Scouts posted on the fire brigade tower not many yards from Monczka's home spotted German planes approaching. Soon the first bombs fell on Konin. Jacob Krafchik, a tailor living on the big square, led his family and four workers into the cellar.

> Nerves were overwrought and tense and the one thought in all our minds was that the air raid would be followed by a gas attack, and everyone sat around . . . with handkerchiefs over their faces.[4]

Thanks to Konin's large duck population, the bombers caused little damage. Disturbed by the noise of the planes, a flock of ducks rose into the sky, sparks of sunlight flashing off their wet bodies and wings. The German pilots, thinking they were coming under heavy anti-aircraft fire, dropped most of their bombs on the boggy marshes near the town.[5] Nevertheless, this first air raid scared an already nervous citizenry. News came through that Poznan and other towns had been bombed.

> Early on Saturday morning we heard that the Germans were advancing on Poznan, and already thousands of refugees were passing through Konin travelling eastwards towards Warsaw, on foot, by car or wagons – by any transport available they came . . . day and night the refugees passed through Konin.[6]

Conditions on the roads worsened. Army units, mostly on the retreat, were caught up in the congestion. Reservists struggled in vain to reach their units. German dive-bombers swooped on the crowded highways, machine-guns blazing, leaving the roads littered with the dead and dying. Bombers devastated nearby towns crowded with refugees. An attack on the railway station at Kolo, 28 kilometres away, hit a train packed with evacuees. Some of the victims were brought to Konin.[7]

Morale soared on Sunday 3 September, when it was announced that Britain and France had declared war on Germany,[8] but the elation was short-lived. The Panzer divisions swept forward, encountering more resistance than they had expected from the hopelessly outnumbered and outmanoeuvred Polish army. The Luftwaffe, five times larger than Poland's air force, soon had the skies to itself. On the afternoon of 3 September, German planes bombed Konin's railway station. This time the ducks did not help. A second attack swiftly followed, inflicting heavy damage on the station, cutting the railway lines and causing heavy casualties. The town itself was untouched. Another raid followed that night, but again no damage was done. The Konin population learned to recognize the sound of German planes flying overhead on their way to other targets – the retreating columns of the Polish army, and Warsaw.

By 5 September there was panic in the town. Civil government collapsed as the mayor and local functionaries fled with their families, joining the mass of refugees heading east. Hoarding had emptied the shops. Everywhere large numbers of people – Christians and Jews alike – were hurrying to get out, loading their belongings onto prams, handcarts and bicycles, the better-off travelling by horse and cart. Leo Monczka, Moishe Kaplan the squire, and Jacob Krafchik the tailor, were among those who joined the exodus. Krafchik went on foot. Packed into Monczka's horse-drawn wagon were so many adults and children that in the end the men walked alongside it.[9]

The highways to Lodz and Warsaw were now in a state of total chaos. At night, the flames of blazing bridges, windmills and villages lit up the sky. People tried to make their way across fields, only to be caught in the cross-fire of army skirmishes. Monczka and his group encountered anti-Semitism on the way:

> Among the immense mass of refugees from the Poznan district are those who, though they themselves have death before their eyes, cannot be silent in their hatred of the Jews, and they point with their fingers – 'Look how the Jews are running away.'

Some Konin Jews pressed on, reaching Lodz and Warsaw, only to be overtaken by the Germans. A few eventually managed to cross the border into Russia. Many abandoned their plans to escape within a few days of fleeing from Konin. Krafchik narrowly escaped death when thirty-seven German bombers devastated the town of Leczyca, near Lodz. Learning that the Germans were not far away, and uncertain where to head next, a footsore and hungry Krafchik decided there and then to go back to Konin whatever the consequences.[10] Monczka, Kaplan and others also returned. They knew they were opting for Nazi oppression, but at least they would be in their own homes, on their own familiar territory, sharing whatever ordeals lay ahead with friends, family and fellow citizens. Perhaps they would be able to retrieve the possessions they had hurriedly abandoned. The refugees returned to Konin to face their first unpleasant surprise: the retreating Polish army had blown up the wooden bridge over the Warta.[11] The makeshift repairs made crossing the river hazardous.

On Wednesday 13 September, the eve of the Jewish New Year, families gathered in their homes to eat the traditional apple and honey, symbol of the sweet year to come. Next morning the first German troops entered Konin and raised the swastika over the Town Hall.

13

PEOPLE WILL CLUTCH at any straw to push grim reality away, and so it was with the Jews of Konin. Hitler's persecution of the most assimilated Jews in Europe, his vow to eradicate the cancer in the fair body of Germany, his demonizing of international Jewry . . . all this was known to the Jews of Konin. In October 1938 Hitler revoked the citizenship of eighteen thousand Jews of Polish origin and pushed them across the frontier into Poland. Konin's Jews saw some of these destitute refugees pass through the town. Following Germany's defeat in the First World War, its frontier with Poland had been pushed back towards the west, so that Konin was now 180 rather than 30 miles from the nearest checkpoint. But this was no great distance for a superbly equiped and motorised army. Yet, nearly a year later, when Hitler marshalled his forces near the border ready to pounce, there were those who believed he would not do so, while others clung to the belief that if he did, life under the Germans might not be as bad as some feared. Didn't Polish Jews already suffer racial discrimination, if not persecution, under an increasingly fascist government? Weren't Polish hoodlums cutting off Jewish beards, boycotting Jewish shops, stirring up racial hatred? Anti-Semitism was hardly a new phenomenon in Poland.

The First World War had brought hardship and danger, food shortages and disease. Yet Rabbi Lipschitz recalled the civilized relations he had established in those days with German officers, some of whom were Jews. Yitzhak Mysch, the bespoke tailor, rememberd the seven friendly soldiers who had camped in his back yard in 1916. Another Koniner, Lola Birnbaum, whose husband and two children died in the death camps, recalled: 'Those earlier Germans were good to the Jewish people. They brought coffee and all kinds of things to our house.' The German military presence in the town invigorated trade. Jewish shopkeepers and craftsmen, with their Germanized Yiddish, had the edge over their Polish competitors when it came to dealing with the occupiers.

After Russia's long and repressive rule, the Germans even appeared to some as liberators. The Germans of the First World War had provided Konin with public facilities unknown under Russian rule. They built the first electric power station, combined with public baths. In 1939 the same power station still provided the town with electric lighting. Only once in its history did Konin have a Jewish mayor, Herman Danziger, and that was during the German occupation in the First World War. 'When the Germans came in 1939,' recalled Yitzhak Mysch's son Morton, 'the old generation thought these were the same Germans who had come in the First World War. My father said: "Don't worry." '

Avrom Kempinski, one of the younger generation at that time, writes: 'We had known . . . what Hitlerism meant but that its arrival could from the very start reach such a horrific scale, no one had imagined.'[1] Within hours of Nazi troops entering the town, armed soldiers stormed the synagogue and brutally drove out the Rosh Hashanah worshippers.

Izzy Hahn, aged twelve at the time, remembers the scene: 'The Jews were running out into the street in their prayer shawls while a German army photographer took pictures – I suppose to use for propaganda.' His friend, Henry Kaye, was in the synagogue with his father and grandfather when the Germans broke in. He told me: 'I can hear today as clearly as then the voices of the Germans shouting: "*Schmutzige Juden Hunde, 'raus!*" Dirty Jew dogs, out![2] It was the last time Jews were to pray together as a congregation in Konin.

The Germans embarked on a campaign of terror directed at Poles and Jews alike, executing a policy designed to assert the unquestioned authority of the New Order. In this part of Poland the occupiers found ready partners among one section of the population: local ethnic Germans, the descendants of Lutheran settlers. Even before the invasion, their potential as a fifth column had attracted suspicion in the Konin area. 'People became psychotic about seeing spies everywhere,' comments one local historian.[3] The Konin Boy Scouts reported secret meetings held at night in a gazebo in the garden of a local German, who subsequently became an enthusiastic Nazi collaborator.[4]

There were several hundred ethnic Germans in the town, the second largest minority after the Jews, with a Protestant Evangelical church of their own; but far greater numbers resided and farmed in the surrounding country areas. In one village, where 70 per cent of the inhabitants were of German origin, they welcomed the invading forces with shouts of '*Heil Hitler!* At last we have our *Heimat*. We are free. Down with the horrible cursed Polacks.'[5] Local Germans who identified themselves as *Volksdeutschen*, proclaiming their allegiance to the German race, provided a corps of informers and denouncers. Among the local ethnic Germans were individuals who behaved honourably and who even became victims themselves of Nazi brutality, among them a boy of seventeen who was sent to a concentration camp for refusing to join his three brothers in swearing loyalty to Hitler.[6] Nevertheless, those who harboured a grudge against certain Poles or Jews were now perfectly placed to take revenge.

Konin's prison could not cope with the numbers arrested in the early days of the occupation. The basement of the Town Hall in Third of May Street – soon to be renamed Hermann Göring Strasse – became a detention centre where the screams of tortured and beaten Poles and Jews rang out day and night. The Germans confiscated all radios and firearms, and imposed a strict curfew. Jews were forbidden to travel without permits. Jewish males between the ages of fifteen and sixty were taken for forced labour, the women subjected to various indignities. Jews were forbidden to walk on the pavements. Beatings in the street became a commonplace. German soldiers burst into Jewish shops, robbed the owners of their goods and demanded false receipts. They extorted money from the Jewish community, giving its frantic leaders only hours in which to raise huge sums.

They ripped apart Jewish dwellings, searching for money even in the poorest homes. 'Several Gestapo men entered our house and demanded the gold that was hidden there. "We know," said their leader, "that we shall soon see the gold. If not, you soon won't be able to see anything." My stepmother stood as though turned to jelly and did not know what to answer. After giving her several blows, they began to demolish the place.'[7]

It was the home of a young tailor, Avrom Kempinski. He had been among those who had returned to the town after a futile attempt to escape. One day soon after he got back, a German patrol stopped him in the street and ordered him to get into a truck:

> I saw sitting there a group of forty-eight Jews . . . We were driven to the station . . . The fields [beside the station] were wet from a few days' rain. There the Germans drove us with knouts and ordered us with wild shouts to run into the fields, run and fall, run and fall, and to do this for one and a half hours. We could hardly stand up . . . The leader of the group of Germans asked me if I had ever swindled an Aryan . . . I told him that I never had swindled and never would. He gave me a strong blow on the head. I collapsed unconscious. The German, not satisfied, gave me more blows. I lay in the mud and could not stand up on my own . . . As I was so weak, my comrades carried me on their shoulders. We went home . . . and I lay in bed in great pain for weeks.[8]

On Thursday, 21 September, two days before Yom Kippur, the Day of Atonement, the Rabbi and elders of the community convened a special meeting. Mindful of what had happened on Rosh Hashanah, they discussed what to do about Yom Kippur services. They arrived at the view – such was their inability to come to terms with the Nazi reality – that the German masters would, if approached in the correct manner, show respect for the most sacred day in the Jewish calendar. The president of the community was an intelligent, widely admired Chasid by the name of Baruch Dzialoszynski. However, on hearing that Leo Monczka had just returned to Konin, the meeting decided that he – a worldly, unbearded Jew who had received part of his education in Germany – would make an ideal community spokesman.

Monczka, who had left Konin with his family and neighbours shortly after the outbreak of war, had returned home that very afternoon, shocked and exhausted. The poor man had just collapsed onto his bed when my kinsman, Shmuel Leizer Festenberg,[9] arrived as an emissary from the meeting, bringing the news that he, Monczka, had been given the task of going to the German commandant next morning to request that the synagogue be opened that evening for Kol Nidre (the solemn prayer that ushers in Yom Kippur). One cannot but sympathize with Monczka for responding: 'Let's see first what tomorrow morning brings.' My kinsman departed, and Monczka went back to bed and fell into an exhausted sleep.[10]

A few hours later, 'somebody banged at the windows and shouted

"Open Up." Five soldiers armed as though for the battlefield read out my name from a list and ordered me to get dressed. They would not allow me to put on a tie, saying firmly that I would no longer need it. The words rang out clearly: "In the name of Adolf Hitler you are arrested. Hands behind your neck." '[11]

They escorted Monczka to the town prison in Wodna Street. 'The doors of the cells were opened and there stood Rabbi Lipschitz and, next to him, *chazan* [cantor] Rosenberg, deathly pale.' The Germans had taken fifteen Christians and fourteen Jews as hostages. Now Monczka equalized the numbers. 'They said someone had cut some telephone wires and for this reason we were to be shot.[12] The whole night we listened to the town clock strike. It is four o'clock and nobody comes. Six, still quiet. The morning has arrived. Between seven and eight we hear wild shouting: "Get ready for the execution." '[13]

Peasants from the surrounding area were in town early for the Friday morning market. Posters were already up announcing that enemies of the Third Reich were to be executed in the big square at ten o'clock: the citizenry was ordered to attend. The German authorities, who liked everything to be neat and tidy, gave instructions for the square to be swept for the occasion.[14] According to two accounts, a rolling of drums heralded the 'barbaric spectacle'.[15] Everyone knew that the cutting of the telephone wires was merely a pretext. The execution was meant to instil fear and deter resistance.

The Germans picked two hostages for execution, a Christian and a Jew.[16] The former was Aleksander Kurowski, a man in his forties who ran a restaurant in Third of May Street. The Jew was Mordechai Slodki, a little Chasid of seventy, who traded in cloth, haberdashery and cheap underwear in Kramowa Street. On learning Slodki's fate, the Rabbi went over to him and said: 'Reb [Mr] Slodki, you are the scapegoat.' Slodki responded: 'Rabbi, we have no right to oppose God's will.'[17]

Monczka saw the two men led away: 'At nine in the morning the dors of the cells in the prison were opened. The candidates for execution were led up to the main administrative office on the ground floor where personal identity documents were registered. A military squad in full uniform marched in. Rabbi Lipschitz [aged seventy] was asked to accompany them in order to say the last prayer for his co-religionist. He collapsed and they went without him.'[18] The deathbed prayer, Vidui, is both a confession of sins and an expression of hope for eternal joy in the presence of the Lord. It ends with the Shema: 'Hear, O Israel, the Lord our God, the Lord is One.'

The firing squad marched into the cobblestoned square, and stood in a line facing the wall of the former Polish gymnasium.[19] A crowd of some three hundred had gathered. The Jews stayed away. They 'closed their doors and windows out of fear and opened their Jewish hearts to the full because they knew that the bullets that would kill Mordechai Slodki were aimed at all Konin Jewry.'[20]

But among the crowd there was a young Jewish spectator, a boy with nerve and audacity who could pass for Polish. 'When you're a boy you want to see everything. I was nosy.' Every detail of the event has remained in Izzy Hahn's memory. He remembers the exact spot behind the firing squad where he climbed onto the spout of a pump to get a view over the heads of the adults. He heard the sound of the prisoners and escort coming up the little side-street alongside Baruch Migdal's icecream shop. The crowd waited to see who was to be shot. 'The stickers announcing the execution did not give names. Kurowski's young son was standing near me. He did not know his father was going to be executed until he saw the men marched into the square. He gave a terrible cry when he saw his father.'

They stood the two men against the school wall. 'People looking on this dreadful scene were struck with silence as they saw the first of the many murders that were to take place,' another witness wrote.[21] Before being blindfolded, Kurowski received the last rites from a priest. The old Jew in his long black coat waited, perhaps muttering again the valedictory prayer, deaf to the Latin blessing which Father Zwierz is reported to have given to the Jew too.[22] Next day, Slodki was to have performed the duty of prayer leader in the Yom Kippur service, intoning the prayers that commemorate the killing of the sacrificial scapegoat in the days of the Temple.

There is a photograph of the execution in the Memorial Book, presumably the work of an official German photographer. The firing squad, rifles raised, take aim, awaiting the order to fire. Two lonely figures stand close together, isolated against a white expanse of wall. The photograph is blurred and one cannot distinguish their faces: Jew and Pole merge into one dark, pathetic shape.

A number of Jewish families lived on the big square at that time. They may have shut themselves in their homes but they could not shut out the sound of the killing. The shots that rang out must have been audible to my grandfather, Dovid Ryczke, and his family, who had moved to the square, as well as to the tailor Jacob Krafchik, who had returned to the town twelve days earlier and whose windows overlooked the execution site, to old Szyjka in his little sweet shop on a corner near the school, and to Baruch Migdal, whose house is clearly visible in the photograph of the execution. The shop is shuttered. There is no sign of life behind the little dormer windows. If one were able to swing open the façade like a doll's house, there surely would be Migdal and his family, white-faced, frozen with dread, awaiting the sound that signified the sacrificial death of a fellow Chasid. In the foreground of the picture, a German soldier stares into the photographer's lens. The shutter clicks. The guns fire. The victims of the first Nazi execution in Konin slump to the ground.

14

THE WIVES OF Slodki and Kurowski went to the prison to ask for their husbands' bodies. The request was granted 'on condition that no more than five persons attend each funeral'.[1]

The fourteen Jewish hostages remained locked in their cells as Yom Kippur approached, worrying about their families, brooding over their own fate. Monczka makes no mention of any attempt to mark the onset of the Day of Atonement. No does he convey the state of mind of his fellow prisoner, the Rabbi, who must surely have felt a sense of unreality, of dislocation, at finding himself in the town prison rather than in the synagogue conducting the Kol Nidre service as he had done every year since 1906. 'Again it is a sleepless night,' writes Monczka.

> We hear distinctly the striking of the Town Hall clock. Now it strikes four. The doors of the cells are opened. We fourteen Jewish hostages are led into the courtyard of the prison, and made to stand

in a row. Next to me is Meyer Winter.[2] He whispers: 'They won't put on a show with us; they'll finish us off here.' We hold hands and grip fingers.

A corporal appears . . . accompanied by a military functionary, who addresses us with words that ring out sharp and clear: 'You Jews have your biggest festival today – Yom Kippur. On this day it is forbidden to work. You, however, will work.' And he shows us some tin buckets and implements placed ready for us in front of the latrines. He commands: 'In the trench under the latrines is the mess left by departed prisoners . . . by 2 pm it is to be totally cleaned up. Any delay in cleaning up completely will mean punishment by death.'[3]

To save the old Rabbi from further humiliation and physical hardship, the others – younger men – hid him in a bundle of straw. 'Punctually at 2 o'clock the work was finished. We cleaned up with water from the pumps and then we were released with our fourteen Christian comrades in suffering.'[4] Other men were promptly arrested to take the place of those freed, and every twenty-four hours they in turn were replaced with other hostages.

On Kol Nidre and Yom Kippur the synagogue stood empty. Before long there was no synagogue in which to pray. The Nazis wrecked the interior, shattering the magnificent Holy Ark, the pride of Konin Jewry. Jews were forced to carry the Torah scrolls into the Tepper Marik, where a great bonfire was prepared. The historic collection of religious books from the *bes-medresh* were thrown onto the heap.[5] According to one witness, the Germans ordered Jews to set fire to the heap but 'not one obeyed this order.'[6]

Rabbi Lipschitz and his fellow Jews were made to watch while the scrolls were set on fire. The dignified bearing of the white-bearded Rabbi must have irked his tormentors, for they rammed a woman's hat on his head, and taunted him while the parchment rolls went up in flames. The Rabbi was 'made to stand against the wind so that the smoke blew into his face. The Germans pushed him closer and closer to the fire so that at times his beard got singed.'[7] The bonfire blazed for three days.[8] One boy observed the scene with his usual eye for detail: 'The colours of the flames from the parchment were unbelievable' recalls Izzy Hahn, ' – every colour of the rainbow. I stood and watched.'

Monczka returned home one day from forced labour to find that the Gestapo had called and removed documents, cash, valuable books, a new piano and various items from the wardrobe. From his business ledgers they had listed the names of customers who owed him money, then gone to their homes and collected the cash.

That evening the Gestapo called again. This time their search lasted until midnight. Having helped themselves to more plunder, they arrested Monczka 'with the warning that within fourteen days a sum of 10,000 zlotys had to be paid to set me free.[9] If the money was not produced, every day a part of my body would be cut off and sent home, at first a finger and then more. Standing by the open door, a Gestapo man – judging by his age a family man for some years – reacted to the tears of my wife and niece with the words: "Take one more look at your husband. You may be looking at him for the last time." '[10]

They took Monczka away, beat him up, made him stand in water for over twenty-four hours while forbidding him to attend to his 'physiological needs'.[11] He heard prisoners being crippled in a room set aside for torture, saw corpses lying in the yard, and contemplated suicide. He shared a cell with two Jews and a wealthy Pole, the owner of a large estate, accused of stealing part of his grain harvest.

They were in the cell one night when 'suddenly some fingers appeared at the little window . . . It was my devoted workman of many years, Wladek Staszak, who had dared to creep here. He gave me a flask of milk and a thickly spread roll and sliced of bread. Thirsty and starved, we four fellow sufferers stood close to one another as we swallowed down the milk and handed back the empty flask. Then in brotherly fashion we divided the treasure of the food in four.'[12] The Konin Memorial Book includes this tribute to a brave Pole.

The hostages' chief torturer was a *Volksdeutscher* who, in return for pledging loyalty to the Führer, had been rewarded with the privilege of breaking prisoners' spirits and bodies. He was a butcher by trade and came from a small town near Konin. Monczka refers to him as the '*Schlager*', the batterer. When, on one occasion, a German officer visited the hostages' cell, Monczka made the mistake of looking him straight in the eye:

> He says: 'Why do you stare at me so stupidly?' The officer gave a signal to the butcher. He hit my face and I fell against the wall with the back of my head. Unconscious and lying on the floor I felt my feet trembling and pushing. The result of this was a hernia. After several hours I woke up lying in the straw in the cell, my face, head and stomach bleeding.
>
> Another visit, the next day. The door . . . opens and, according to regulation, we stand up in a row. One of the functionaries goes over to Meyer Winter and his eighteen-year-old son, Itshe. He orders the son to shout at his father: 'You piece of shit!' and then strike him in the face. Behind the boy stands the *Schlager* with a dagger in his hand. The young lad . . . looks desperate. The father begs him: 'Obey, carry out the order.' Father and son stand face to face. The Gestapo man shouts: 'Hit harder.' Now the dagger . . . is close to the boy. The father, his voice shaking, begs: 'Be obedient, hit harder, really hard.' The *Schlager* lowers the dagger. The five armed Gestapo heroes have been victorious. They know that resistance is not possible, yet they have performed this scene with revolvers in hand, ready to shoot . . . We stood until the door was closed again. Our deathly pale faces expressed our feelings. Without saying a word we lay down again on the cement floor thinly covered with straw.[13]

At the last hour Monczka's family managed to raise the ransom money and he was freed. How things worked out for the Polish landowner I do not know. Meyer Winter and his son vanished in the camps. Monczka escaped from Konin in a lorry, hidden among sacks of flour.

15

THE EXECUTION OF the Pole and the Chasid had symbolized, for all to see, the shared suffering of Jew and gentile. One would like to say that it brought the two peoples closer together, but it did not. Each side concentrated on its own survival. The Jews felt more imperilled, with little hope of protection from their Christian neighbours. There were, it is true, acts of bravery and humanity towards Jews, perhaps not as many as some Poles today would like to claim, nor as few as some Jewish survivors are prepared to acknowledge.

Though the Germans were indiscriminately brutal to all, they reserved special treatment for 'the oldest enemies of the German people and of all healthy, rising nations – the Jews'.[1] The oldest enemies posed no threat to the Nazi occupiers of Konin. Their Semitic features, yellow patch, and concentration in certain streets stamped them as a conspicuous minority whose movements could be easily restricted and controlled. It must also be said that the Germans could count on an anti-Semitic element among the Polish population as well as the *Volksdeutschen* for help in keeping an eye on the Jews and identifying them in cases of doubt.

The educated Polish élite, with their patriotism, entrenched position in local society, and influence on the Polish community at large, offered a more serious potential challenge to the occupiers. This grouping, loosely defined by some as the intelligentsia, comprised those who were most likely to become resistance leaders. In Konin, as elsewhere in Poland, the Nazis identified the threat and wasted no time in dealing with it.[2] In a carefully planned *Aktion* launched on 10 November 1939, they rounded up Polish teachers, lawyers, municipal civil servants, political activists, influential local figures such as Count Stanislaw Kwilecki, and others. The fifty-six captives were driven to the Jewish cemetery and there they were shot, in batches.[3] One can only guess as to why the Jewish cemetery was chosen as the killing field. Perhaps burial among the Jewish 'vermin' was meant to lend death a final, nicely calculated touch of degradation.

A Pole who lived close to the cemetery witnessed the events of that day: 'Every one of the accused was standing over the pit and was killed by a short weapon with one shot in the back of his head . . .'[4] A Jewish account of the atrocity reports that the prisoners were beaten before they were shot. Jews who had been grabbed off the streets buried the victims – 'many of them still alive'.[5]

How often, on reading about similar massacres of the Jews, has one pondered on the passivity of the victims. The fifty-six Christians went to their deaths as quietly, as unresistingly as the Jews. It is no slur on their bravery, rather a comment on the shock, the sense of helplessness, that must numb all but the most extraordinary of humans in this situation.

The killing of Poles and Jews in the Konin district continued unabated during the first few months of the occupation. An elderly Pole was executed for owning a sword dating to before the First World War.[6] Some victims were shot without provocation in the street, others secretly massacred. Hangmen were kept busy. Bodies floated down the Warta.

On 21 September 1939, two days before Yom Kippur, a secret high-level meeting was convened in Berlin, chaired by Reinhard Heydrich, Chief of the Reich Central Security Office, to discuss the fate of Poland's Jews. One of the policies decided on at that meeting was to rid large areas of western Poland of the Jews, to move them eastwards and concentrate them in ghettos. Konin fell within the borders of the newly constituted province of Wartheland, one of the four regions in western Poland annexed to the Third Reich, and therefore to be made 'racially pure'.[7] Arthur Greiser, the *Gauleiter* of Wartheland, signed a decree on 4 November, giving the final orders for the entire Jewish population to be cleared from the region.

In Konin the announcement of the first deportation came, without warning, on Thursday, 30 November.[8] In the Hahn dwelling on the Tepper Marik, renamed Horst Wessel Platz, Gestapo men clattered down the stairs to the basement, burst open the door and ordered the occupants out. 'We had no valuables to take,' says Izzy, 'and no suitcase – in those days you didn't go away on holidays like you do now. My mother put one frock on top of another frock, and my father put one coat on top of another, and I and my brother and sister put on as much clothes as we could. It had to be done very quickly. We were scared – those Gestapo men were six feet tall, and we had low ceilings so can you imagine what they looked like to young children? Like giants. My little sister began to cry, and my mother also started crying. We had no idea what was going to happen to us, where we were going.'

The 1,080 Jews selected for deportation were taken to assembly points, held there until after midnight, and then driven in trucks to the station. 'On our way through the streets we caught a last glimpse of where we had lived.'[9] It was hard for the deportees to grasp what was happening. One day they were in their own homes, sleeping in their own beds, eating at the family table. The next, they were crammed with forty, fifty or more fellow prisoners inside a freight wagon or cattle truck, crouching or lying on rough boards, huddled together against the December cold, hungry, tormented by thirst as water ran out, inhaling the stench from the overflowing bucket used as a latrine, babies crying, old people groaning, others fainting, no one knowing where they were heading or what their fate was to be.

The train frequently pulled into sidings to make way for military transports. Sometimes it remained stationary for hours, making the agony seem more interminable than when the wheels were turning. The train followed a circuitous route, sometimes doubling back over the same ground, but its general direction was eastward. On the second morning, the guards opened the doors and gave the passengers five minutes to relieve themselves by the side of the tracks. Felig Bulka, the Konin doctor who was one of the deportees, ran from wagon to wagon giving whatever help he could. On 3 December the train pulled into the station of Ostrowiec Swietokrzyski, an industrial town in the province of Kielce. It had taken more than two days to travel the 200 kilometres from Konin. A committee greeted the strangers from Konin as they staggered off the train, fed them bread and tea, and found them accommodation in Jewish homes.

The first deportation removed about half the Jews who had stayed on in Konin following the German invasion. By July 1940 the Germans had evicted the other half, sending them initially to Zagarow, Grodziec and other villages in the countryside to the south of Konin. Here the Jews found whatever shelter they could, in barns, outhouses and rooms rented from peasant farmers.

Although the Polish population too suffered grievously during this period, 1941 was, as one Polish commentator puts it, '*rokiem zydowskim*' – the year of the Jews.[11] More trains rolled eastward, transporting deportees to ghettos such as Ostrowiec and Jozefow-Bilgorajski in the territory of the General Government in central Poland.[12] Others were transported straight to Treblinka and other death camps. Thousands of Jewish families from the Konin region were spared these nightmarish journeys. They were massacred in the forest of Kazimierz Biskupi, about ten kilometres from Konin's town square.

By mid-1942 German bureaucrats were able to produce a statistical report with a satisfying zero: not one Jew was left in Konin.[13]

Part Two

SYMBOL OF LOST HOPES

16

KONIN WAS AMONG the first twelve Jewish settlements to be established in Poland.[1] Little is known about its early days, and the few scraps of information that have come down to us do not tell us what we long to know. Who were the first arrivals? How many of them were there? How did they live? Where exactly did they come from? And why did they choose to make their home in this corner of Poland?

The flames of a Nazi bonfire consumed the community's archives, but were we to have access to these records today it is doubtful that they would add to our knowledge of early Jewish life in the town. Historians who consulted medieval sources before the Second World War, and who must have scoured Jewish archives in Konin, had to admit in the end that the pickings were lean.

From the early Middle Ages Jews came to Poland from western Europe, fleeing the Crusades, pogroms and religious persecution. Many from Germany settled in the provinces nearest to the German border, in towns such as Posen (Poznan) and Kalisz. Anti-Semitic massacres in Germany in the fourteenth century drove more refugees into Poland, where Kazimierz the Great welcomed the trading and financial skills the newcomers brought with them. (The King also welcomed with even warmer arms the beautiful Jewess Esterke, a tailor's daughter who became his mistress and bore him two sons and two daughters, the former brought up as Jews, the latter as Christians.) A great Polish Rabbi of the sixteenth century acknowledged the sanctuary Poland had given to the Jews. He even coined a pun on the Hebrew form of the name Poland – *Polin.* It derived, he said, from two Hebrew words, *poh lin* – 'here shall we rest.'[2]

The expansion of Jewish life in those early centuries followed a discernible pattern. Having put down roots in one place, Jews would start venturing further afield, scouting the region for new economic opportunities, and in time forming satellite communities, dependent at first on the mother community, then, as their sense of permanence grew, establishing their own separate status. This is probably the story of Konin as an offspring of Kalisz, the oldest Jewish community in Polish history.[3] In 1264 Prince Boleslaw the Pious signed the Statute of Kalisz, establishing the legal status of Jewish communities within his territory of Great Poland and granting important religious and economic freedoms under royal protection.[4]

By the end of the thirteenth century, the Kalisz Jews had their own burial ground, and by the middle of the fourteenth century a fine synagogue, all of which is documented, while the archival search for Jews in Konin during this period draws a blank. Therefore, it is reasonable to deduce that it was Jews from Kalisz who pioneered the first Jewish settlement in Konin, along with other Jews moving eastwards from Poznan. What the newcomers brought with them, apart from their Yiddish culture and religious practices, was financial know-how and initiative, which they put to use in their new places of settlement.

Konin was one of those towns where Jews were not allowed to settle in medieval times. But just as there were a small number of Jews in Shakespeare's England when, by law, they were not supposed to be there, so must a few individuals have been allowed to set up home in Konin, especially if they provided financial services that Christians did not or could not offer. The earliest records of Jews in Konin are to be found in local court books, written in Latin, almost all of them relating to litigation between Jewish money lenders and Christian borrowers. As the Church forbade Christians to practise usury, this unpopular service was left to the Jews. In 1397 'Sabbetai of Conin' appeared before a court in the town of Lentschitz – the first reference to a Jew in Konin.[5] The following year we meet him in the town proper, again suing for settlement of a debt. These two court records are the first and sole documentation linking a Jew to Konin in the fourteenth century. It is unlikely that Sabbetai would have lived alone without at least a few brethren nearby for fellowship and security, so there may well have been a Jewish presence in the town, albeit a tiny one, before 1397, though there is no proof of this. One scholarly paper suggests 1418 as the date when a Jewish settlement in Konin began.[6]

We learn no more about Konin Jews until about 1432, once again in the context of moneylending and litigation. For about twenty years, starting in 1434, the court books enable us to follow the activities of Kanaan,[7] evidently a successful usurer, who lent for interest as well as on pledge. The amounts involved suggest that his clients belonged mainly to the lower and middle ranks of the Polish gentry. In 1448, when one of his debtors failed to settle, Kanaan took control of two fields with all the rights of the owner.[8] As Jews were reluctant to accept the task of administering and tending land (which, in any case, they were legally banned from owning), they would usually come to an agreement with a neighbouring landowner to take this on for them. Thus a court record that Kanaan, '*perfidus judaeus de Conin*', acknowledged a certain nobleman as his 'true and good guardian and administrator of his goods'.[9] It is not unlikely that these aristocratic borrowers, like many others in Poland and Russia in subsequent centuries, were negligent landowners, high-spending *bons vivants*, needing regular replenishments of cash in order to maintain a lifestyle beyond their means.

Like other moneylenders of the time, Kanaan almost certainly engaged in trade, perhaps dealing in grain, but as these transactions were usually in cash, they seldom gave rise to legal disputes and therefore no record of them appears in the early court books. This resulted in an unbalanced picture of how Jews earned their livelihood. King Wladyslaw Jagiello visited Konin in 1425 and granted the town important concessions including the right to hold a second annual fair.[10] This also benefited small Jewish traders who then, as throughout the centuries until the Second World War, drew much of their trade from peasants and farmers coming into town on market days. Kanaan makes his farewell appearance in the court books in 1453.[11] After his death, his daughter Martha, who had sometimes represented him in court, carried on as a moneylender in her own right, and proved no less assiduous than her father in bringing recalcitrant debtors to court.[12]

After 1462 there is no further mention of a Konin Jew in the court books of the fifteenth century. The extent of the Jewish presence in the town at the close of the century is imprecise. One source states that 'approximately 150 Jews lived in the town, inhabiting 12 wooden houses.'[13] Fire destroyed a large part of the town at the end of the fifteenth century, and there was a decline in the number of Jews.[14] The powerful craft guilds, fuelled by religious bigotry and fearful of competition, maintained their exclusion of Jews, thus giving them little choice but to specialize in moneylending, finance and trade. Royalty made use of this expertise, and in 1404 a Jew, Fishl from Krakow, acquired the concession to collect taxes from fellow Jews in several towns, including Konin.[15]

A poll-tax was imposed on Jews in 1549, and the tax books for 1579 and 1580 reveal that there were Konin Jews whose poverty made it impossible for them to pay the tax.[16] The system eventually changed back to a form of collective taxation. The Council of the Four Lands – the autonomous Jewish governing body in Eastern Europe established in 1580 – undertook, through arrangements with individual communities, to pay the royal treasury a lump sum for the Jewish population, and therefore the poll-tax books ceased as a source of recorded information on Jewish activity.[17]

Father Jan Wolski, a former Konin priest, has provided me with an item about the Jews that he found while researching the subject of Konin churches: 'I came across a report from the 1595–1609 visits of the Gniezno Bishop, Albert Baranowski . . . While consecrating the foundations of a new chapel . . . Bishop Baranowski had asked if there were any Jews living in the Konin parish. The answer was yes. He then said that he would like them to be gone by the time the chapel was ready for consecration. In 1609 he asked the same question but he was then told that the Jews had always been very loyal to the town and its rules and regulations . . .'[18]

A cholera epidemic broke out in Konin in 1628, killing many of the inhabitants and starting a decline in the fortunes of the town.[19] There were 127 private houses in Konin at this time, four inns, and a few dozen artisans such as shoemakers, millers and bakers. Jewish artisans, though not specifically mentioned, must have worked in the town too, if only to cater to Jewish needs. The Jews by now had their own little quarter – 'Jewish Street' – close to the castle walls, and it was in this part of the town, the site of the future Tepper Marik, that most of Konin's Jews lived until the Second World War. In fact, a street of this name survived until 1930, and I have heard older Jewish survivors of the community still refer to it as ulica Zydowska.[20]

When the Swedes captured Konin in 1656 and put the whole place to the torch, Stefan Czarniecki, the Polish general who liberated the town, accused the Jews of inadequately resisting the foreign enemy and proceeded to carry out a pogrom in Konin and a great many other communities.[21] Royal revenue records of 1659 reflect the damage done to the town during the war. The four inns had vanished; only twenty-five houses remained standing.[22]

The plague returned in 1662, reducing the already depleted population of Konin to 200.[23] In 1707 the Swedes attacked again, this time destroying Konin's finest edifice, the castle.[24] It took almost the whole of the eighteenth century to rebuild the town.[25]

A census carried out in 1765 shows that 133 Jews in Konin were registered to pay a tax. Children under the age of one were exempt; some Jews did not register, hoping to evade the tax, and also out of fear that further taxes of a different kind would follow. Taking these factors into account, it has been estimated that the total Jewish population in that year was 168,[26] out of a total population of about 700.[27]

The same census details the occupations of the thirty Jewish heads of households, twenty-five of them of 'undefined profession', one beadle, two barber-surgeons and two furriers.[28] They lived in a collection of wooden houses set close together, forming a small marketplace. A local Polish historian has written of this period: 'It can be assumed that the inhabitants of Konin were not too well disposed to Jews, just as in other towns. They did not want Jews to buy houses and parcels of land, to ruin guilds, to take over trade in their hands.'[29] The Jews of Poland had long accustomed themselves to this situation. Certainly it did not deter the Jews of Konin from taking a decision that expressed their desire for a permanent presence in the town. The community was expanding, and local prospects seemed promising enough to encourage a bold act of faith in the future. During the years 1763–6 they erected their first synagogue, a building of some grandeur compared with the room that previously must have served as their prayer house. At last, after being affiliated to Kalisz since the sixteenth century, the Jews of Konin established a *kahal* – or *kehillah* as it was more colloquially known – an autonomous, organized community of their own.

17

THE SECOND PARTITION of Poland, in 1793, placed Konin under Prussian rule, where it remained until the victorious Bonaparte brought the country a measure of autonomy in 1807. With his defeat eight years later, the town changed hands yet again. From 1815 until 1914 Konin occupied an insignificant place on the vastly enlarged map of the Tsarist empire. Throughout this period Jews were becoming increasingly urbanized all over Poland. In 1807 there were 369 Jews in Konin – 18 per cent of the total population. By 1883, when the Jewish presence in the town was at its peak, their number had risen to 3,400 – 52 per cent of the total population.[1]

Jewish commercial flair contributed hugely to Konin's economic development as the nineteenth century progressed. The River Warta flourished as a commercial waterway, and Konin became a 'harbour' town. Sailing barges took grain, timber and other produce on board for export to Germany, and returned with goods from the rapidly industrializing West. Never had there been so much activity around the old wooden bridge or in the narrow streets leading up from the river to the big square and the Tepper Marik. Jewish carters met the increasing demand for road transport, carrying goods by horse and wagon between Konin and the bigger cities. With no railway station in Konin (it was not to acquire one until 1923), they transported produce and people to the frontier town of Slupca less than thirty kilometres away, and the German railhead just beyond it. Among the goods they carried were the eggs and butter that my grandfather, the Dark-Haired Ryczke, exported to Germany.

Jewish wholesalers traded in salt, sugar, alcohol, spices, tobacco and other goods. Manufacturing on a modest scale began around the middle of the nineteenth century, when the first factories opened, the biggest owned by a gentile.[2] Jews had no entrepreneurial monopoly, but their involvement in almost every branch of business activity was indisputable.

Until the mid-eighteenth century the town retained its medieval appearance. In 1765 the old stone church of St Bartholomew towered above the 165 dwellings, all but one of which were built of wood.[3] When a fire in 1796 destroyed most of Konin, including the medieval town hall, the burghers set about rebuilding in brick and stone. Even before the middle of the eighteenth century, terraces of tall houses with wrought-iron balconies had gone up in the big square, creating a townscape worthy of a city. A new Town Hall conveyed the municipal *gravitas* that comes with four classical columns and a grand pediment. New houses spread down Third of May Street. New streets reached out towards the meadows on both sides of the wooden bridge.

The Joel and Weiss families and a few other prosperous German Jews settled in the town, bringing with them banking experience and an elegant lifestyle that owed more to the gentile West than to the world of the Tepper Marik. Yet they retained their Jewish identity, and became involved in community affairs. Like the other secularized, well-off Jews of Konin, they were acculturated rather than assimilated.

The Tepper Marik was changing too. Houses several stories high were going up alongside the old humble cottages. In 1870 a new building graced a corner of the square, the *bes-medresh*. The house of prayer and study was the gift of a local businessman, Zalman Zander.[4] But for every Zander, Weiss, Joel, Kaplan, Leszczynski (owner of the town's largest flour mill) and Spielfogel (founder of a distillery), there were scores of others who represented the broad mass of the Yiddish-speaking, working population – the tailors, hatters, glaziers, wagoners, blacksmiths, tinsmiths, tanners, bakers, porters, cobblers, carpenters, cabinetmakers, painters, barbers, barrelmakers, stonemasons and other artisans, craftsmen and petty traders, for whom life was never easy.

Jews had no more cause than gentiles to love their ruler in St Petersburg, the Emperor of All the Russias. As conscripts – my Sarna grandfather was one of them – they wasted some of the best years of their youth serving in his armies. As civilians they suffered under a corrupt, capricious and dilatory bureaucracy. However limited their Russian vocabulary, they all knew the meaning of the word *pogrom* – 'destruction'.

In the last two decades of the century, a number of Jewish families took the path of emigration, driven not only by a growing sense of insecurity but by a desire for a life of greater liberty and opportunity. Most went to America. Many went to France, particularly Paris. Some put down roots in Germany, others in Britain. Statistical information does not exist. All one can say is that by 1897 the Jewish proportion of Konin's population had dropped to 32 per cent, not all of it due to emigration. The bigger cities in Poland, such as Lodz, were also drawing Jews away from Konin.

The majority, however, stayed where they were, through choice, inertia, or because they could not afford to take their families across the ocean. Those who remained had one reason to be grateful to the Tsar: the presence of army barracks in the town, home to his cavalry regiment, the Thirteenth Dragoons. In the latter years of the century, as traffic declined on the Warta and Konin lost some of its commercial momentum, the military population – about one thousand soldiers plus officers and wives – formed a corps of customers whose spending, by a trickle-down effect, helped to prop up the town's economy. They provided work for a host of people – a tinsmith to repair the colonel's roof, a dressmaker to sew his wife a gown, a tailor to make him a new uniform . . . The soldiery drank in Jewish inns. The quartermasters placed substantial orders for provisions and gods. My Sarna grandfather supplied the barracks with enamelware mugs, plates, and pots and pans imported from Germany.

Celebration was compulsory for everyone on one day of the year: 18 May, the birthday of Nicholas II. The cavalry paraded in the big square. The band played, the choir sang and the crowd prayed for the health of the Imperial family. There was a celebratory service in the Russian church, whose onion-domed tower can be glimpsed rising up above the trees in an old postcard view of Konin. Eager to demonstrate their loyalty, the Jewish community held a service in the *shul*. A children's choir joined the Rabbi and congregation in beseeching God to protect the despot who, in the course of his reign, consented to the massacre of thousands of Jews. They went on praying for his health until 1914. I have met a few of those children, now old men and women, who can still sing, with shaky voices, the royal hymn in Russian: '*Bozhe trarya khrani* . . .' – God bless the Tsar . . .

I have an old Jewish encyclopedia that conveys with eloquent brevity the Tsarist regime's success at suppressing a nation's identity. The entry for Poland reads: 'See under RUSSIA'. In Konin, as throughout the Empire, police spies kept subversive elements under surveillance, though this did not prevent periodic insurrections from erupting. When the Konin population participated in the January Uprising of 1863, a Jew boy by the name of Shlomo was among those arrested and found guilty. One source has it that he was exiled to Siberia,[5] another that he was hanged.[6] Jews had supported the patriotic cause in the belief that national freedom would bring Jewish emancipation in its wake.

Among the proscribed political organizations, none was more active than the Bund, founded at a secret convention in Russia in 1897. Within a few years Konin had its own cell, composed of secularists who opposed Zionism and capitalism, yet favoured the preservation of Yiddish – the language of the Jewish masses. Maurice Lewin, elder brother of the aspiring sculptor, was a student in Warsaw in December 1904, when the Tsar closed all the universities as part of an attempt to curb the widespread unrest that was threatening his regime. A committed Bundist, Maurice returned to Konin and joined in clandestine activities against the Tsar.[7] Strikes in the big cities, peasant uprisings and mounting political pressure finally forced Nicholas II to make concessions. More than sixty years later, Maurice Lewin, by then a British citizen, Fabian, Esperantist and retired aircraft engineer, set down in his adopted language an account of the heady days when he was a twenty-one-year-old revolutionary in Konin:

> In the summer of 1905 the Tsar electrified the country by granting the [elective] Duma. The press was exuberant – 'Hurrah' – freedom has been won at last! Down with tyranny! Long live the constitution!
>
> In Konin the usual vacation crowd of intellectuals gathered, and meetings, discussions, readings were the order of the day. The [Jewish] community woke up suddenly to the hope of liberation and prepared to take part in common with the gentile inhabitants in a procession through the streets to express their loyal thanks to the government. Of course, we in the Labour movement were not satisfied with these promises and were prepared to accept nothing less than street barricades in the style of the French revolution of 1789. To demonstrate our feelings we decided to march in a separate procession under our own flag.
>
> We had to find a flag. So we procured three yards of red cloth, a

quantity of gold-covered paper, needles and cotton, a pot of paste, and all this material was smuggled secretly into the cellar of the home of Saluz Zander. At 10.30 in the night, after the old people had retired, the conspirators, Felix Weiss, Abram Sachs, Saus, my sister Yetta and a friend of hers and myself went to work cutting out Hebrew and Latin letters about three inches high and sticking them onto the red cloth. The slogans were 'Down with the Tsar' – 'Long live the Social Revolution'. One side of the flag was Yiddish and the other Polish. By 2 am the job was finished and we sneaked home.

The next morning the town was humming with excitement in anticipation of the common action of Jew and gentile, the first time in remembered history. At 8 pm the two processions joined up, Poles with their banners of saints, Jews with their Sefer Torah marched to the Duzy Rynek [the big square] where they were met by the Naczelny Powiatowy [head of the local district council], who made a speech in Russian about 'Free Poland', and they dispersed with joyful hearts.

We of the proletariat would not dream of common action with the bourgeoisie so we held a separate meeting on the Garnczarski Rynek [the Polish name for the Tepper Marik], and I was asked to address the working population. I did so in Polish from the elevation of a wooden chair in order to be visible to the crowd. I used all the newly acquired slogans about the oppression of the working classes – about the fight to the death against a mock parliament [i.e. the Duma], the impending dictatorship of the proletariat, and so on. We then formed ourselves into a procession and on the way were joined by the Polish PPS group [the banned Polish Socialist Party] group . . .

When we arrived before the government offices on the Duzy Rynek, we were received by the police superintendent who came out in the company of two officials and started to deliver a speech in Russian about the newly gained liberty. This was met by shouts of 'Down with the Tsar', 'Long live Poland', after which the attendants whispered something to him, they apparently noticed in the semi-darkness the red flag and the slogans, and they diplomatically withdrew. After delivering a few more salvoes of slogans we returned to our starting point and dispersed. The day of freedom was over . . . and so apparently was the freedom.

> Konin returned to its slumber, the workers to the distribution of proclamations and the police to the task of making secret enquiries. Most of the students returned to their respective school, but one or two arrests were actually made. Felix Weiss escaped in the very early hours hidden in a baker's van [he means cart], disguised as a sack of flour, and two days later I was informed by Tomasi that the police were on my track. I, therefore, took myself to the Town Hall, obtained a day pass for crossing the Slupca frontier and actually left Poland the same afternoon with a carved walking stick as my only worldly possession.[8]

Lewin was later sentenced *in absentia* to twelve years' banishment to Siberia.[9]

The Russo-Japanese war of 1904–5 ended in military and naval humiliation for the Tsar. Five years later, the inhabitants of Konin heard with rather more concern of a Russian military decision that would have a profound effect on their future: the cavalry regiment was to move to another town:

> It was an unforgettable sight for all the inhabitants observing the event . . . The thousand cavalrymen, the band at the head of them on their white horses, rode with slow steps. Behind and on both side of them people accompanied them for a stretch, as though it were a funeral procession. Among the young people were members of the fair sex who now exchanged flirtatious farewells.[10]

My grandfather and his friends watched their best customers recede into the distance. A few years later, Isaac Leszczynski installed steam power in his flour mill on the edge of the town, which worried some of the gentile owners of windmills that dotted the Konin countryside. Leszczynski was in the habit of taking his wife for a drive at the end of a working day. One evening, as his carriage trotted past the fields of ripening corn, 'a man stopped him, and asked for a lift. He got into the carriage behind Leszczynski and put a bullet through his head.' Leszczynski collapsed into his wife's arms. Supporting his corpse with one hand, holding the reins with the other, she brought her husband back to Konin. I have met a man in London – Joe Fox – who saw Leszczynski's murderer: 'One of his competitors had hired him to do the job. When they took him to the magistrate's court, I and all the other kids ran to the big square to watch. He was chained round the waist, down and round both legs.' In 1994 Joe (aged ninety-six) told me: 'I can still hear the noise the chains made as they led him across the square.' The killer was taken to Kalisz and hanged.[11]

In 1910 refugees from pogroms in Russia trailed westward through the town, carrying their salvaged belongings. It had a profound effect on the Jews of Konin. The following year, newspapers throughout the Western world reported the trial of Mendel Beilis, who had been falsely accused of ritual murder in Kiev. In Konin, a new taunt was hurled at Jewish children: 'Beilis! Beilis!'[12] Nationalist forces were emerging in Poland, hostile to all non-Polish, non-Catholic minorities, most especially the Jews. In 1912 the rabid anti-Semite Roman Dmowski inspired his National Democracy Party (the *Endecja*) to launch an economic boycott of the Jews. Their slogan, 'Don't buy from the Jews, only from your own', was heard in the streets of Konin. My grandfather, with young children of his own and a business that was fading before his eyes, decided it was time to leave Poland. In 1913 he said goodbye to his relatives and friends in Konin and brought his family to London.[13]

18

WORLD HISTORY aside, 1918 marked a great event in the parochial world of Konin Jewry. In that year the town acquired its first Jewish high school, or gymnasium. According to one of its founders, Leo Monczka,[1] anti-Semitism lay behind the school's creation. Konin's long-established Polish gymnasium in the big square did not bar Jewish children, but most of its teachers, wrote Monczka, came from Proznan, known at that time for its virulent anti-Semitism. In any case, it was not an establishment designed to make Jewish children feel comfortable. Catholicism influenced its ethos and instruction. There was teaching on Saturday mornings. Jewish festivals, of which there were plenty, posed another problem. In time, the need for a secular high school for the Jews of Konin became 'a serious problem'.[2]

A problem, that is, for those who could afford it. Most parents had to put their children to work at the earliest opportunity. The wealthier families, which usually meant the less orthodox families, had ambitions for their sons to become graduates and join the few liberal professions open to Jews, such as medicine, dentistry and law. If university was out of the question, then at least the *matura* (Polish matriculation) certificate constituted a desirable status symbol, useful too in the marriage market. Moreover, a gymnasium provided its pupils with a sound Polish education, which could only make life easier in the gentile world and even open a few doors normally closed to Jews.

Konin parents who could afford a Jewish gymnasium education for their offspring had no choice but to send them to a bigger city, which meant being separated from them for most of the year. This encouraged the families to consider moving to major urban communities like Lodz, which also offered greater economic opportunities and a more diverse cultural life. The war years, with their acute food shortages, changed all that. Farm produce was more readily available in country areas, and this led a number of Jewish families to leave Lodz and move to Konin, thus swelling the size of the community. I would guess that when the war ended, the community elders saw the existence of a gymnasium as a way to encourage these families to stay and dissuade others from leaving.

Another factor might have influenced the school's founding fathers: Konin Jews basked in their regional reputation as an intelligent, well-educated community. They already had a secular Jewish library bigger than that of Kalisz, the capital of the province. If Kalisz had a Jewish gymnasium, why not Konin? As well as boosting still further the community's reputation, a gymnasium would help keep brainy youngsters in the town, providing them with a superior secular education without loss of Jewish identity. The foundation of the school was not, as Leo Monczka seems to suggest, solely the result of anti-Semitism.

In 1917 a meeting of interested parties met at his house and formed a committee (there could never be too many committees) that set about the formidable task of raising money, finding premises, teachers, headmaster – or rather, Director – drafting the constitution and, not least of all, satisfying strict government regulations. A delegation travelled to Warsaw, where they met Jewish members of parliament and obtained the Ministry of Education's approval to open a Jewish coeducational school 'teaching in the Polish language with Hebrew as one of the subjects'.

The first pupils of the *Koedukacyjnego Gimnazjum Zydowskiego* (Jewish Coeducational Gymnasium) – or KGZ for short – found themselves in a modest one-storey building at one end of Wodna Street, behind the big square, near the river. At the start, it was a lower school only, comprising five classes. Permission to qualify as a fully-fledged, eight-class gymnasium for boys and girls was conditional on the governors finding larger quarters.

The original building stood next to an empty plot of land belonging to the Town Council, who sold it to the school for a nominal ten zlotys, a magnanimous gesture that possibly owed something to the influence of the Jewish councillors – such as Monczka – who also happened to be school governors. The Lodz city architect drew up plans for the new building, and the governors began raising the money for its construction. Parents made donations. Sympathizers gave loans. 'Squire' Kaplan, one of the governors, donated the bricks. My prosperous kinsman, Aron Ryczke, owner of a sawmill, provided timber and other materials.

Letters pleading for contributions went out to Koniners in Europe and America. I have one of them, a cherished item in my slender family archives.[3] Handwritten in a halting English (why not Yiddish?) on the school's official stationery, it arrived at my maternal grandfather's house in Sidney Street, London E1, in March 1920. It tells of the government threat to close the existing school premises, and the consequent need to start work on a new building. The school hopes 'that our brethren in England will come to help to this weight [*sic*] aim . . . With the building of this house we must begin in the month April because the youths must know if they have the school or not.'

Construction work began. Members of the staff and the older pupils became voluntary labourers during school holidays. One of these pupils, an aspiring poet by the name of Meyer Weinstein, wrote a school song extolling their back-breaking toil.[4] Sung in Polish at every fund-raising event, it softened hearts and opened wallets:

We are the pupils of the famous KGZ
We have been brought up in a free atmosphere
By the River Warta, by the meadow
Where the KGZ has its home.
There in the quiet retreat, life bubbles.
There winds rage, there we wallow in mud,
There we swallow clouds of dust.
It is stifling and dirty there,
And breathing comes hard,
Oh there in our building of today,
The KGZ.

The finished building was a three-storey structure of a ponderous classical design. If it was meant to impress, it succeeded. It was one of the most imposing buildings in Konin, with an entrance flanked by double pilasters two storeys tall. The Jewish citizens looked on and *kvelled* (swelled with pride). But soon a scandal arose that became the talking point of the town. There are a few old pupils of the school alive today – the squire's son for one – who still remember the hullabaloo and will readily tell you about it. Here is how one of the school governors remembers it:

> There was among the non-Jewish population an element who watched with envy and hatred as the beautiful building grew, hoping that after it was finished – or at the start of the school year – it would collapse, because (as it later transpired) the foundation under the front wall was laid in a position forward of the wall . . . thus giving it no support. This was the result of the Christian in charge of building the foundations having been influenced by his co-religionists to carry out this devilish sabotage.
>
> The roof and tiles were already finished when a worker on the foundations, in a drunken moment, told his friend – one of M. Kaplan's workers – that this beautiful building would collapse after it was finished.
>
> It was a Saturday in November when suddenly big cracks appeared in the high front wall. The next day two members of the administration committee [the school governors] carried out an investigation to find out the reality behind the information the drunk worker had given. But it was not necessary, for by now it was clear that the high front wall had not been built on the

> foundations. The town architect, under whose supervision the work had been carried out, was so taken aback and frightened by the occurrence, that he took poison, but quick medical help saved him.
>
> Salvage operations were immediately put in motion. Craftsmen blocked up all the openings of doors and windows. Heavy timber and boards were brought in to support the building from ground to roof, and in this way the danger was avoided. Early next day, members of the committee presented themselves at the city architect's office in Lodz. He sent experts to Konin to carry out underpinning work. They laid new foundations under the wall and anchored it with iron bands, thus averting further danger.
>
> Before long, the man in charge of the foundation work, Tarczewski, was arrested. The contractor responsible for the foundations and walls reimbursed the cost of the new foundations. After consultation with parliamentary deputies Priluczki and Hartglass in Warsaw and also the lawyer Piotr Ken from Lodz, it was decided to abandon the idea of instituting legal proceedings.[5]

Did the conspiracy exist, or was it the product of Jewish paranoia? Former pupils of the school, who have related the story to me, remain convinced of its truth. But on what grounds? Is it likely that the man in charge of the foundations would have connived at a blunder that was bound to be exposed? Might it have been nothing more than the kind of mistake that happens all the time in the building trade? One can imagine the predicament of the Polish worker who was aware of what was happening but reluctant to step beyond his station and point it out. The charge against Tarczewski was dropped. Because he was innocent? Not necessarily. An official cover-up is not beyond the realms of possibility. Conspirators, if they existed, would have had little difficulty in persuading the police not to side with the Jews. Maybe the school governors decided not to press charges because they doubted that a Polish court would give an impartial verdict. Or, another theory: the 'why-make-trouble? They'll-only-hate-us-more-if-we-sue' line of thought.

Whatever the truth of the matter, this we know: in the synagogue and in the Chasidic *shtibl* (literally, small room; in this context, house of prayer), in shops and marketplace, wherever Jews gathered in Konin, they repeated the story of the envious and evil anti-Semites who plotted to destroy the new school, hoping it would collapse on the heads of innocent Jewish children.

In no time at all the school established an academic reputation. Pupils from nearby towns enrolled because of the quality of the tuition. The teachers were, in the main, over-qualified graduates, some with doctorates, who could not find university posts. The continental love of titles and formality ensured that they were addressed as 'Professor', but this was small compensation for an abysmal salary. None of the headmasters stayed long. Konin was a stepping-stone to better things. Some made a name for themselves in academia. One headmaster, Leopold Infeld, went on to achieve fame in the sciences. The teachers were dedicated men and women, some of whom in their leftwing idealism organized free evening classes for working-class Jews in the town. Occasionally they gave public talks and lectures. In this way the gymnasium enriched the cultural life of the community at large.

The children were exemplary teaching material, bright and highly motivated. Their peaked caps and, in the case of the older boys, heir swagger-sticks were visible emblems of privilege. Collections and fund-raising activities provided scholarships and bursaries for talented children from poorer homes. The pupils organized concerts to raise money, and sold copies of the school newspaper, one tattered copy of which has miraculously survived and is in my possession. Pupils went on to university and became doctors, dentists, pharmacists, lawyers, engineers, architects, teachers. This was a new generation of Konin Jews, steeped in Polish literature and history, French and Latin, yet at the same time at ease with their Jewish heritage. They studied Hebrew and were active in Jewish youth organizations. Many became ardent Zionists and some made *aliyah* (settled in Eretz Yisrael) between the wars.

A leading Chasid of the town, Baruch Dzialoszynski, sat on the board of governors, presumably to keep an eye on the mixing of the sexes, a cause of some worry in religious circles. Chasidim and some very religious non-Chasidim would not send their sons to the school, even though all the teachers were Jewish. For boys, a totally secular education was unthinkable; for daughters, not impossible. 'My father was reluctant to send me to the school,' a Chasid's daughter, Miriam Grossman, told me, 'because it was coeducational, but in the end he agreed.' Romance flourished, and not only among the pupils. Five of the male staff found brides among their students.

The school's financial position, precarious at the best of times, deteriorated within a few years of its opening. Jewish families continued to drift to the bigger cities and to emigrate. The opening of the railway station in 1923, though a boon to Konin in some ways, was not entirely to the advantage of all its Jewish merchants and traders. Important customers in the surrounding region could obtain manufactured goods more cheaply by buying directly from Lodz or Poznan rather than from middlemen in the town. And the inflation that raged in the early Twenties destroyed business overnight and caused widespread misery. School salaries could not keep up with rocketing prices. As economic conditions worsened, fewer parents could afford fees and donations. Physical amenities needed upgrading and the government put increased pressure on the school. Governors, staff, parents and pupils frantically stepped up their fund-raising activities, but to no avail. Staff morale dipped further. By 1922 the number of pupils had dropped from 200 to 120. During the academic year 1923–4 the number fell to eighty. In 1919 the Jewish inhabitants of Konin had formed nearly 45 per cent of the total population. By 1928 the figure had dropped to 24 per cent. Various attempts to save the school failed, and in 1929 it finally closed its doors.[6]

Pupils who are alive today, about three women and half a dozen men spread around the world, remember their *alma mater* with affection and gratitude. More than seventy years after it opened with such high hopes, an old lady in North London[7] sang some lines from the school song for me in Polish, her voice clinging precariously to the melody of a popular *czardas* of her youth:

> Let him live who gives of himself,
> Who desires to look to the future.
> Let him who does not think of himself alone, live.
> *Vivat*, let him live!
> Let him soar higher and higher.
> May the future of the KGZ live!

19

LEOPOLD INFELD was the fourth headmaster of the Jewish gymnasium.[1] He stayed in the town for two years and hated every minute of it. Contemptuous of the Jewish community and everything it stood for, he fled at the first opportunity, and drew a sad and unflattering picture of Konin in his autobiography, *Quest: The Evolution of a Scientist.*[2] Nonetheless, eight pages of the Konin Memorial Book are devoted to him, accompanied by a photograph proudly captioned 'Prof. L. Infeld'.

No matter that Infeld broke away from Judaism and became totally assimilated, that from an early age he longed to escape from a Jewish world for which he had neither regard nor affection, that his impressions of Konin were completely at variance with the Memorial Book Committee's own nostalgic memories. They knew – and we are speaking now of the mid-Sixties when the book was being prepared – that Infeld had achieved international eminence as a physicist, and if some of that eminence could brush off onto Konin, all the better. They venerated Jewish intellectual achievement, and Leopold Infeld was one of its most outstanding examples. His photograph, probably taken in his late fifties, shows a forceful face, strong-jawed, almost pugilistic. Pictures of him as a younger man – much as he must have looked in his Konin days – reveal a tall, slender figure, sensual mouth, attractive cleft chin and humour in the eyes.

Born in Krakow in 1898, Infeld was brought up within the strict conformity of the ghetto. His father, Salomon, a leather merchant, prayed in the synagogue each morning before breakfast. He sent his son to *cheder* where, at an early age, he was 'plunged in a hopeless ocean of boredom'. He was warned he would go blind if he gazed at Christian holy images. His home background was claustrophobic though not impoverished. Until he was eighteen he slept on a sofa, sharing the room with two sisters and a hostile Orthodox grandfather. He heard Yiddish spoken all around him, a language he grew to dislike. Almost everything about the world he was born into disgusted him: the dirt and smell of the ghetto streets, the religious narrowness, the cultural isolation. As a young boy he felt 'hate, hate, hate' towards his Jewish environment.[3]

Hate worked as a dynamic force and from it he 'drew the strength which carried me toward the outside world . . . To escape I was forced to fight against my environment.'[4] He succeeded brilliantly and went on to win academic distinction. For many years he was Albert Einstein's closest associate. When he received his Ph.D. in Krakow in 1921, it was the first doctorate in theoretical physics to be awarded in independent Poland. He had gained it in the face of every obstacle, including the opposition of his own father, who rejected out of hand his son's plea to be sent to a gymnasium, which would have set him on the path to university. He wanted Leopold to follow him into business. Undeterred, the boy got hold of textbooks, mastered new subjects on his own, including Latin, and against all odds passed the formidable oral and written *Matura* examinations with first-class honours.

Five years later, when he received his doctorate in a solemn and pompous ceremony at the ancient Jagiellonian University in Krakow, Infeld had every right to feel that the gods (he rejected the one and only God) had rewarded him for his struggles and perseverance. That he was a man of outstanding brilliance and promise there could be no doubt. In Poland at that time there was a scarcity of lecturers in theoretical physics. An academic post should have landed in his lap. A year later, the young but by now disillusioned Dr Infeld accepted the only work available to him: teaching children in a Jewish school in the backwoods of Poland, in Konin. 'The bleak reality deformed the once glorious dream,' he writes. All academic doors in Poland's five universities were closed to him: 'It was at the universities that anti-Semitic and reactionary slogans sank in most deeply.'[5] That was the bleak reality.

Prejudice of a different kind stood in the way of his finding a teaching job in a Jewish school: 'To the Polish world I was a Jew. To the Polish Jews I was not sufficiently Jewish.'[6] I suppose it is to Konin's credit that he was sufficiently Jewish for them. At the age of twenty-four he was appointed headmaster of the coeducational Jewish gymnasium beside the River Warta.

Infeld moved into rooms on the opposite side of the river not far from the wooden bridge, settled into his new job and began two of the most frustrating and despairing years of his life. Recalling them nearly twenty years later, at a time when success had come his way, when a book on physics that he had co-authored with Einstein was a bestseller in the United States, when he had just obtained his first professorship, when he was in love and newly married, he still retained bitter memories of a place where he had wasted two of the most valuable years of his life. His unhappiness springs off the pages of his memoirs: 'There is still a name in my memory which has always remained a symbol of lost hopes: it is Konin.'[7]

Infeld felt himself to be an exile, cut off from everything he held dear. 'While I was there my world was divided into two parts: isolated Konin in which, I thought, I should probably die, and the rest of the world which I should never see.'[8] He found the people boring, the provincialism oppressive. All around him he saw the sadness of a town that had seen better days, where the rich were moving away, where runaway inflation was demoralizing the middle class and the poor were getting poorer. Having fought to free himself from the shackles of the ghetto, eager to rid himself of all traces of his Jewish upbringing, he now found himself confined once more within a Jewish community, the headmaster of a Jewish school, controlled by a board of Jewish dignitaries who represented everything he abhorred. The school itself was crowded into a tiny red-brick building.

> It comprised a little more than a hundred students. My colleagues were young and even less experienced than I. Wherever we went we encountered each other. We got on each other's nerves, and wild quarrels, accusations and counter-accusations broke out between us for the most trivial reasons. Our salaries were nearly worthless a week after we received them. They were measured in thousands of Polish marks at the beginning of the school year and millions at the end. The school was in constant financial difficulty and each month, we thought, would be its last. I lectured to the parents on the importance of learning and concluded each speech with an appeal for money, lest the teachers die of starvation. When I returned home I could not bear to look at my scientific books, collected during years of study. I did not believe that I would ever open one of them again in my life.[9]

Glancingly, in just one sentence, Infeld reveals a facet of Konin life of which I was totally ignorant: 'Each evening I saw the same two prostitutes walking for hours round and round the square . . .'[10] Prostitutes! Parading openly in the street! In Konin? Nobody, least of all any member of my family, had ever so much as hinted at this. Maybe they felt that such matters were too distasteful to discuss, even to acknowledge. One of my relatives once assured me in solemn tones that marriage was so sacrosanct in small Jewish communities like Konin that infidelity simply never happened. Never. Now this shocking revelation of carnal vice in the town square! Infeld provides no further details. Indelicate curiosities obtrude: did the prostitutes have Jewish clients? I knew that questioning Koniners on such matters would be an awkward task.

How objective is Infeld's portrait of Konin? Is it too jaundiced, too warped by his own disappointment and sense of failure? Life in any small Polish town would have compared woefully with the cultural riches, friendships and café society he had left behind in Krakow. He was unable – probably unwilling – to see anything of worth in his place of exile. This leads him at one point into blatant inaccuracy: 'There were no pavements, no library, no movie, not one house with a bathroom.'[11]

On two of those counts – the absence of a cinema and modern plumbing – he was right. But no library? To prove him wrong, here before me is the revised printed catalogue of the Jewish lending library in Konin dated March 1922, the very year that Infeld arrived in the town. It lists every book on the shelves: Milton, Rostand, Ruskin, Shakespeare, Tolstoy, Cervantes, Wilde, all the great Polish writers and poets . . . Yet the library failed to impinge on Infeld. No doubt he was pining for the great academic libraries where he had studied in Krakow.

I am not sure that he is right about the pavements either: they can be seen in some of the postcard views of the town dating back to Tsarist times. He was probably thinking of the muddy streets near his home, on the other side of the river, away from the town proper. If, as he admits, he walked through Konin 'hating the streets, buildings and faces around me',[12] perhaps his unhappiness distorted his vision.

Infeld was glad to get away from Konin even though his next job brought him no closer to achieving his life's ambition. Was there much point in holding on to this ambition? He saw a path of failure, of opportunity denied, stretching endlessly ahead of him. His new post – teaching physics in a Jewish gymnasium for girls – offered one consolation. It was in Warsaw. He packed his scientific books and belongings, turned his back on the Konin Jews and headed for the capital. In all, Infeld spent eight years as a schoolteacher: 'The best years in the life of any scientist, the years in which imagination reaches its peak. Those years were gone.' The whole of quantum physics was developed during what he calls his 'provincial sleep'.[13] It makes his subsequent achievements all the more remarkable. What far greater heights might he have reached without the loss of those years? Infeld was thirty-one before he got his first foothold on he academic ladder.

In 1928 he had met a Jewish girl, Halina, at a meeting of the Polish Physics Society. They fell in love and happiness transformed Infeld's life. Their marriage ended tragically four years later with Halina's death from a harrowing and protracted wasting disease. Crushed by grief, unable to work and desperate to get away from Lvov, Infeld applied in 1933 for a Rockefeller Foundation Grant in Cambridge, and was successful. He writes about his year in England with unreserved affection. He felt secure there, as he never had in his native Poland: 'I was brought up in a country where a Jew going through the streets outside his ghetto had the feeling, consciously or subconsciously, "These are my enemies." '[14]

The convivial collegiate atmosphere of Cambridge and the challenge of his work made him dread the return to Lvov, but the academic year ended and he had no choice but to go back. The political situation in Poland had deteriorated during his absence. A weak government was yielding to fascist forces. Gangs of nationalistic students disrupted lectures and resorted to increasing violence, sometimes resulting in deaths: a gang 'would arrive suddenly each carrying a stick. In some of the sticks a narrow groove had been cut and a razor blade inserted so that its sharp edge was barely visible. Having pushed the attendant away they would rush to the lecture room and beat the Jewish students with the sticks and razor blades until the blood flowed . . . In the lecture room there was always someone who would silently indicate the Jews to the gang leader.'[15]

Infeld could see no future for himself in Poland: 'I want to leave Poland,' he said to a colleague. 'I cannot bear the feeling of being unwanted.'[16] He wrote to Einstein, whom he had once met, and with his support was awarded a modestly funded fellowship at the Institute for Advanced Study at Princeton. Before departing for the United States, he went back to Krakow to bid farewell to his family:

> I wandered through the ghetto of my town. On a summer morning the voices of Jewish boys singing in chorus the words of the Torah reached me through the open window of the school. There may be among them someone who hates this place as I hated it and who dreams of going to a gymnasium. I went nearer. The school windows were open, the first-floor windows of a dreary house. I smelt the foul air of the room. It was the same air, the same smell of onions and potatoes, which I had smelled over thirty years before. I saw the tired, thin, badly nourished faces with burning dark eyes, and for the first time in my life I was conscious of a touch of poetry in this sad ghetto scene.[17]

In 1936 he left for America. 'Away – away from the air saturated by hate which darkened the sun and shadowed all my days! Away from the endless talks of the Jewish problem, from whispers of the still darker future and of lost hope.'[18] At Princeton he began an exhilarating period of fulfilment as a scientist. He worked with Einstein on motion and general relativity, a problem 'rooted in the foundation of physics' and one that was to be Infeld's principal research interest for the rest of his life.

Infeld's fellowship came to an end the following year. He was fast running out of money. A letter arrived from the professional academic body to which he belonged in Poland informing him that, as a Jew, he could no longer consider himself a member. The influx of highly qualified refugee scientists in America made it impossible to find an academic post. Diffidently, he suggested to Einstein that they collaborate on writing a popular exposition of modern scientific ideas. Einstein accepted the proposal and threw himself into the project with enthusiasm. *The Evolution of Physics* became a critical and commercial success, bringing Infeld the money he needed to stay on in America. In a typically self-aware passage in *Quest* he writes: 'Mine was a perfect example of reflected glory. To the end of my life I am stamped as the "collaborator of Einstein".'[19]

Quest, sadly long out of print, is an imaginative and poignant book, filled with historic as well as personal insights. Looking back at his past, particularly at the Jewish background from which he had sprung, he recognizes that his lifelong attempt to break himself free from it would never entirely succeed: '. . . all my attempts to tear off the bonds only prove that these bonds exist, and they will exist to the last day of my life. Hate and scorn carry subtle overtones of love and attraction.'[20]

The memoir covers Infeld's life up to a day in September 1939 when, on vacation in Maine with his new wife, he picks up a newspaper and reads: 'German planes raided the centre of Warsaw this afternoon.' World War Two had begun. Infeld feared for his family in Krakow. The flow of letters from a small provincial town called Konin, where he had once taught, dried up: 'letters from my old pupils, begging me to help them emigrate to this country . . . invariably sent by registered mail, full of pathos, sent by men and women who, for the price of a postage stamp, bought hope for a few weeks, waiting for an answer which in most cases buried this hope.'[21]

Infeld spent the following years as professor of mathematics at the University of Toronto. He did war work on ballistics, and continued his scientific collaboration with Einstein by correspondence. One of his former students in Toronto, the late Alfred Schild, has written of him: 'There was nothing of the hermit in his makeup. He had an appetite for life and a curiosity about everything. He liked to gossip, to eat and drink, to discuss the world in all its aspects . . . There was something magnetic, even exotic, about the big, talkative, brilliant man . . .'[22]

One day soon after the war ended, Infeld was writing an article about Einstein for an American journal. His thoughts turned back to a winter's evening in 'a small Polish town', unnamed but surely Konin: 'I was a schoolmaster in a small Polish town and I did what hundreds of others did all over the world. I gave a public lecture on the Relativity Theory, and the crowd that queued up on a cold winter's night was so great that it could not be accommodated in the largest hall in the town.'[23]

The crowd that turned out that night to hear the head of the Jewish gymnasium lecture on Einstein would almost certainly have been a Jewish crowd. They would have walked there in the dark and the cold of a Polish winter, many of them workers who spent their days bent over a tailor's bench or a cobbler's last, toiling and shlepping, buying and selling in wind-swept markets. Why were they there? Was it the same poignant thirst for knowledge and education that brought them to the Jewish library? Was it the respect for learning that had begun long ago with the holy books and was now finding secular expression?

Jozef Lewandowski, a Koniner with whom I have discussed these questions, believes that: 'It was not perhaps that they were so interested in the mathematics and physics. It was rather that Einstein was a symbol for all of us, for Jews who wanted to go out of the ghetto and live a modern life. He, a Jew, had achieved a dream, and this was a great help for us. If he could do it, we could do it, perhaps not at the same level but at least at some level.'[24]

Infeld makes no mention of that evening in *Quest*, but in a different context he does offer an explanation for the phenomenal worldwide popular interest in Einstein's theory in the early 1920s. He, too, suggests that at the heart of it lay a dream born out of the experience of the First World War: 'Everyone looked for a new era of peace and wanted to forget the war. Here was something which captured the imagination: human eyes looking from an earth covered with graves and blood to the heavens covered with stars. Abstract thought carrying the human mind far away from the sad and disappointing reality . . . Romantic scenery, a strange glimpse of the eclipsed sun, an imaginary picture of bending light rays, all removed the oppressive reality of life.'[25]

And so, for one reason or another, there were many dreams in Konin that night, floating in the air like, one is tempted to say, the *shtetl* visions of Chagall: a temptation to be resisted, for to evoke the colours of Chagall's palette – that of a rich bouquet of flowers – would be to romanticize the scene in that dismal provincial hall. The sooty images of a silent movie might convey it better. Open with a wide shot of the packed hall: the locals, some of them shabbily dressed, squeezed up on rows of wooden benches. Cut to medium shot of the youthful lecturer as he turns to the blackboard propped on an easel and reaches for a piece of chalk. Big close-up of his hand filling the screen as he writes $E=mc^2$. A flickering caption: THE FORMULA THAT CHANGED MAN'S THOUGHT ON TIME AND SPACE. Cut back to the lecturer, then to a montage of faces in big close-up: weary faces, faces that know suffering, faces of the ghetto.

But how to reveal the dreams behind those sad eyes? The dream of a better life in Poland for themselves and their children. The dream of returning to Zion. The dream of the brilliant young physicist, aching for the chance to develop his own theories in a great centre of learning. Between audience and lecturer there is a vast gap in education, a chasm bridged by dreams. On both sides there is a fear, perhaps a dreadful inner certainty, that the dreams will never be fulfilled.

In 1949 Leopold Infeld revisited his native land after a thirteen-year absence. In *Quest*, written when he had reason to think he might never see Poland again, he expressed his longing for 'the Polish fields and meadows, for the air smelling of flowers and hay, for vistas and sounds which can never be found elsewhere . . . I will never forget my country.'[26] Now back once more in Poland, he received an invitation from Warsaw University to take up a temporary position the following year when he was due for sabbatical leave from the University of Toronto; Infeld gladly accepted. It was a decision – and this is a comment on those Cold War years – that created a national furore in Canada, where suddenly he found himself at the centre of a political scandal and the target of a McCarthyite campaign of vilification. Rightwing circles accused him of being a Communist and a potential traitor to Canada. He was suspected of passing atomic secrets to the East – secrets he was never in a position to possess.

While denying all these charges, he made no attempt to hide the fact that his sympathies were on the side of the postwar regime in Poland. In prewar Poland, he had held 'progressive' views, leaning to the left like most of those who opposed nationalist extremism and the increasingly anti-Semitic attitude of the government in the latter years of the Thirties. Just how far to the left his views were at that time it is hard to say. An essay on the history of revolutionary activity in Konin, published in Poland shortly before the Communist regime collapsed, says of Infeld that: 'It was under his direction that the young people of that particular gymnasium began being interested in Communist ideals.'[27] After the Second World War, Infeld was a leading campaigner for nuclear disarmament. In common with many other prominent intellectuals of that time who combined humanitarian sincerity with monumental gullibility, he supported the Moscow-orchestrated peace movement.[28] Yet Infeld, always an independent spirit, was also the first to scoff at the propagandist sloganizing of Communist apparatchiks, and in later years he bravely opposed government censorship in Poland.

Here is not the place to deal in detail with this period of Infeld's life. He himself has given an anguished account of it in *Why I Left Canada*. Suffice it to say that when he went to Poland in 1950 for what was intended to be a temporary stay, the Canadian embassy in Warsaw asked him to surrender his Canadian passport. Later, his two young children – born in Canada – were stripped of their Canadian nationality. Infeld and his American wife, Helen, a mathematician, shipped their belongings to Poland and started a new life in Warsaw. Much fêted in the land where he had once been rejected, Infeld became a member of the Praesidium of the Polish Academy of Sciences and the recipient of scientific honours in several Eastern Bloc countries. In Warsaw he set about creating an important international centre of theoretical physics.

At the age of sixty-five, working on a collection of autobiographical essays, *Sketches from the Past*,[29] Infeld's thoughts turned again to a small town on the Warta. In one short essay he set down his memories of the place where he had lived and taught as a young man. This 'sketch' subsequently appeared in the Konin Memorial Book, translated into Yiddish.[30] Infeld has not forgotten the 'empty years', the years of stagnation, but time seems to have softened the hard edges of his memory. He does not mention the prostitutes. He does not refer to the lack of a library. He omits that despairing summation of Konin as a symbol of lost hopes. In a rare and significant lapse into repetitiveness, he informs the reader twice, using almost precisely the same words, that the town is 'situated picturesquely on the bank of the River Warta'.[31] Of the incessant in-fighting among his fellow teachers, not a word. They were badly paid, yes, and were driven on one occasion to strike, but they were also 'full of enthusiasm and willingness to work'. The pupils, on their part, responded with 'their full confidence, I would even say their love'.[32]

The school governors, dismissed in *Quest* as a bunch of pompous tightwads, now appear in a more human light. He recalls the day when, faced with yet another financial crisis at the school and deciding that enough was enough, he called a meeting of the school board with the intention of handing in his resignation. Unusually, the governors turned up that night armed with bottles of vodka. Had they guessed what Infeld had in mind? Or had he already told them? He has forgotten. What he cannot forget is the way the meeting ended, with everyone paralytically drunk, including Infeld, who seldom touched alcohol. One member of the board began dancing with a bottle on his head. Infeld joined in, threw up, and staggered home supported on the arms of two of the governors. He was still the headmaster.

Ten years later, in 1934, by a coincidence that would seem far-fetched in a work of fiction, Infeld bumped into one of the school governors in London. At that time Infeld was engaged in advanced research work in Cambridge in collaboration with the eminent physicist Max Born.[33]

> Every half year the Royal Society had an evening affair to which they invited those who had published in the *Proceedings* during the last period. The guests were given champagne and an opportunity to talk with members of the Royal Society about their scientific results. For those occasions a white tie and tails were obligatory. I was much honoured by this invitation, and, since I did not have tails, I set about having them made by one of the best London tailors.
>
> Thus, dressed in my beautiful tails, I went to the top of a London bus, delighted with my marvellous appearance and my wonderful invitation. In the almost empty bus I heard someone speaking Polish, a rather unusual event at that time. I turned around and there I saw Mr Maczka, member of the school board in Konin. [Either Infeld's memory has slipped or he has deliberately changed the name, for it was Leo Monczka.] It was fairly dark and Mr Maczka did not recognize me. I turned to him:
>
> 'Excuse me, sir, but am I in London or Konin?'
>
> We began a pleasant conversation during which Mr Maczka said:
>
> 'I was terribly bored in Konin. I thought I'd go crazy. I saved up and came on an excursion to London.'
>
> 'And how about the school?'
>
> 'It went out of existence long ago. When you left, Mr Headmaster (for in Polish everyone is called by a title and I remained headmaster to him), the number of students dropped again. We were only able to keep up the school for another year.'[34]
>
> 'Piccadilly Circus!' called the conductor. I had to get out, quickly taking leave of my former board-member.[35]

Monczka, the educated and much-travelled timber merchant, had been the youngest of the school governors, and the only one with whom Infeld felt any rapport. He survived the war and settled in Israel. It was probably in the early Sixties, perhaps at the very time that Infeld was writing about his surprising encounter with the ex-school governor, that my father telephoned me one day to say: 'Monczka has arrived in London and is coming over to see us.' The name was vaguely familiar to me as one of those Konin names I had heard many times over the years. I could tell from the tone of my father's voice that he was excited about the visit. Monczka was President of the Konin *landsmanshaft* in Israel. Maybe – this is mere conjecture – they were going to discuss the idea of publishing a Konin Memorial Book. All I could foresee at the time was a long evening during which he and my parents would reminisce about old times and people I had never met. My mother would undoubtedly seize the opportunity of showing the visitor that she had not forgotten her gymnasium Polish.

My father invited me to join them for dinner. I know now that it was not so much that he wanted me to meet Monczka as that he wanted Monczka to meet me, his son, the university-educated Englishman. Boasting was alien to my father's character, but perhaps my presence that evening would have been a sign of how far he had come since leaving Konin, he penniless, teenage son of a small-time egg merchant. This visit, which happened long before my obsession with Konin began, meant little to me at the time. I declined the invitation, perhaps for a genuine reason, more likely after inventing an excuse. My father did not press me and I thought no more about it until I began this book. It has bothered me ever since. I never met Leo Monczka. He died in 1976.

But to return to Infeld and his essay on Konin: more than twenty years had passed since he wrote *Quest*, time enough for the bad old days to seem not quite so bad. He had become an honoured physicist, a familiar figure at international conferences, a man with access to top government circles in Poland. Perhaps the memory of those wasted years in Konin had lost its sting. But now he was burdened with a knowledge he did not possess when he wrote *Quest*. Then, he was writing about a community he wanted to forget. Now he was remembering a community that had been exterminated. The Polish ghetto Jews for whom he once felt such distaste had been systematically annihilated, over three million, his own family among them.

In the autumn of 1922 the twenty-five-year-old teacher from Krakow trotted into Konin by droshky along a country lane. In June 1963 the eminent scientist from Warsaw entered the town by car along a tarmac road. Konin was becoming an industrial centre, rapidly expanding in size and population. Modern high-rise blocks for the workers were going up in the new town. But the change that must have struck Infeld most powerfully of all when he walked round the old streets he once knew was the absence of Jews. They had vanished. Of all the teachers at the school, only he had survived. The children he once taught were a lost generation. 'I have tried to find out what happened to my best pupils. What happened to Bulka, extremely intelligent; what happened to Lewin, the best in mathematics; what happened to Weinstein, the most promising poet? Always the same answer: murdered, murdered, murdered.'[36]

Infeld ends his essay on Konin thus: 'Of the people I once knew no one remains except one pupil. She told me about her husband, whom the Nazis murdered, and of her graduation certificate which was lost. Then she asked me for a statement that she had passed. I signed it as the former headmaster of the school in Konin.'[37]

Nearly a year elapsed between my reading of *Quest* and my discovery of Infeld's *Sketches from the Past*. During this time I traced a handful of ex-pupils of the Konin Jewish gymnasium, now men and women in their late seventies, living in Britain and Israel. Few had actually been taught in the classroom by Infeld. Most of them had joined the school after his departure. Nevertheless, they remembered him, perhaps from seeing him in the street and observing him as their future headmaster. One of them, the squire's son, recalled Infeld visiting his home in Glinka on a number of occasions. Infeld was a fine man, said the squire's son, and his wife a charming woman. Wife? Surely Infeld was a single man when he lived in Konin? His marriage to Halina, which ended so tragically, did not take place until well after he left Konin, and there is no reference in *Quest* – a self-portrait of exceptional frankness – to any previous marriage. I reminded Henry Kaplan that Infeld had shared his home in Konin with a younger sister, Bronia, who taught at the Jewish elementary school in Konin. Infeld must have visited Glinka in the company of his sister; a young boy might well have mistaken a Miss Infeld for a Mrs Infeld. Kaplan, a stubborn man, stuck to his facts and I decided not to argue further, aware that we were talking about events of long ago.

The mystery was solved when I read Infeld's essay on Bronia. He writes: 'I fell in love when I was sixteen and married when I was twenty: before I was thirty the meaning had gone out of my marriage.'[38] Beyond that he tells us only that the marriage ended in divorce, *after* which he married Halina. Why did he omit any mention of his first marriage in *Quest*? One could speculate, but I see no purpose in doing so here. I raise the matter only because it does have a bearing on Konin, or rather, on Infeld's reminiscences of Konin. Small wonder that the place remained for him such a potent and unforgettable symbol of lost hopes: the hope of escaping the ghetto, the hope of becoming a scientist, the hope of a happy married life.

Leopold Infeld died of a heart ailment in January 1968, shortly before the vicious anti-Semitic campaign of that year reached its hysterical peak with a wave of arrests and a ruthless purse of the universities. Had he lived just a few months longer, Infeld might once again have found himself branded as an unwanted Jew in Poland.

After his death, obituaries appeared in *Time* magazine, the *New York Times*, the London *Times* and other leading journals in the West. They described his career as a physicist, his collaboration with Einstein, his writings, scientific honours and achievements. Only someone in the grip of a parochial obsession might have hoped for a mention of Konin.

Postscript For years my search for a photograph of Leopold Infeld during his time in Konin had proved fruitless. Then, one day, Henry Kaplan called me to say that he was sending me a snapshot his brother in France had found among some old papers. I looked at the small, blurred photograph of a group of students on an outing in the woods at Glinka. With them was a tall young man – it was Infeld.

20

MAREK LEWIN set his sights at an early age on becoming a sculptor. It was an unusual ambition for any Konin youth, particularly a Jew. The prohibition of the Second Commandment, the Prophets' battles with idolatry, the teachings of the rabbis, the cultural and economic traditions of the Ashkenazi Jews, all militated against a fostering of the visual arts. The only reference to painting in the Old Testament is in the context of lewdness and whoredom.[1] The Jews are not a people of the image. In the synagogue they press their lips against the word, not an icon or a holy statue.

How did Marek, born Meyer in 1889, become interested in sculpture? Maybe it began with his mother, who was a milliner. I see an affinity between her skills – the moulding and modelling of three-dimensional forms, the arranging of materials into plastic shapes – and those of a sculptor. Rivka Lewin's hat shop in the main street, advantageously sited opposite the Town Hall, contained an item in the window which at a stroke lent her establishment a touch of big-city style. It was a mannequin head on a stand, the only one in Konin! On it she displayed her latest concoction of felt, velvet, ribbon and net veiling, giving passers-by – Russian officers' wives, Jewish matrons, Polish peasant girls – a glimpse of what was currently à la mode in St Petersburg or Warsaw or, more probably, what *had* been fashionable there a couple of seasons back.

Rivka Lewin, born in 1847, was a conventional middle-class matriarch from a religious family, a small, determined woman who dashed about, rarely without a bonnet on her bewigged head, attending to a multitude of commercial and domestic affairs. It was not uncommon in that society for the wife to bear more than a fair share of family responsibilities. While she ran the workshop, served customers, gave birth to seven children and looked after the household, her husband, Isaac, busied himself – if that is the right verb – with less strenuous duties such as book-keeping. His granddaughter, whom I found living in London, remembers him usually 'warming his hands, combing his beard or sitting with his grandchildren on his knees, teaching them how to tell the time by the town hall clock'.[2]

From time to time Rivka travelled to Warsaw to buy new stock and acquaint herself with the latest fashions. Since Konin was not yet on the railway line, this involved a journey of twelve hours by stagecoach plus another three hours by train – the same for the return trip. 'I still marvel,' her son Maurice wrote many years later in London, 'how my mother, who was never in robust health, could have stood it.'[3]

The Lewins had three sons and four daughters.[4] Marek, the youngest son, became apprenticed at the age of fifteen to David Zucker, a Jewish wood-carver in Konin. That local churches commissioned work from Zucker must be taken as a comment on his reputation. He was noted for his hand-made furniture decorated with intricate carvings of flora and wildlife. Marek Lewin spent two years with Zucker, learning how to chisel patterns on the rock-heavy wardrobes and sideboards that were *de rigueur* in bourgeois homes at that time.

When Marek's elder brother Maurice had fled Konin in 1905 after taking part in anti-Tsarist demonstrations, he became a student in Darmstadt in Germany. There a contest was organized in 1906 for artists and craftsmen, who were to compete in decorating thirty façades in the city's 'artists' quarter'. Hearing that wood-carvers were in demand, Maurice wrote immediately to his younger brother and invited him to join him.

It is not difficult to imagine the impact Darmstadt made on a youth who had never travelled beyond the villages around Konin, never stepped inside an art gallery or museum. Darmstadt, with its long cultural past, was proud of its university, institute of music, and several museums. It had the additional prestige of being an imperial residence. But perhaps what excited the newcomer most was Darmstadt's colony of artists and craftsmen who shared his interests and passions. Astonished and exhilarated, Marek stepped into a new world, a new life.

Darmstadt must have strengthened his resolve to become an artist, but all too soon, at the end of a year, his work there came to an end – perhaps his money too. Reluctantly, he returned to the parental home. If Darmstadt came as a revelation after Konin, how must Konin have seemed after Darmstadt? Marek was eighteen or nineteen years old. By all accounts he had a naturally cheerful disposition, but it is reasonable to suppose that he returned to Poland with lowered spirits and fears for the future. He had glimpsed a larger, more vibrant world.

A return to routine commercial wood-carving was hardly what he wanted, but this is almost certainly what he did for the next couple of years, probably working for his old employer Zucker. Onto the Konin scene at this point stepped a man who was to become for a while an important influence in Marek's life: Chanoch Glicenstein, 'under whose supervision', writes Maurice, 'Marek managed to develop his talent.'[5]

Glicenstein, eighteen years older than Marek, came from the *shtetl* of Turek, a few miles from Konin. The son of a tombstone carver, he had worked as a sign-painter and wood-carver. He had known hardship and debt. But in 1907, when Marek returned to Konin, he found Chanoch working as a professional sculptor. The previous year, Rodin, at the peak of his career, had been so impressed with Glicenstein's *Messiah* that he asked that it be exhibited beside his own work in the cental rotunda of the Grand Palais in Paris. Later the same year Glicenstein was elected, on Rodin's recommendation, an honorary member of the Société des Beaux-Arts. To Marek Lewin, Glicenstein was living proof that his own hopes need not remain a dream.

Glicenstein had relatives and friends from his youth living in Konin. He may have had an affection for the town, so much more spirited and intellectual than his own smaller community of Turek. Perhaps he never forgot that the Jewish lending library had exhibited his work when he was still unknown, that friends in Konin had lent him money when he was broke. It must have been during later visits to Konin, when he was a successful artist, that he and Marek spent time together. In isolated Konin, Glicenstein was Marek's sole link with the outside world of art. From him Marek would have heard about the work of contemporary artists in Paris, about a young Spanish avant-garde painter and a new movement called Cubism.

In 1910 Marek left Konin to rejoin Maurice in Germany, this time in Chemnitz. There Marek enrolled in the art academy for one year, supporting himself by craft work. At the end of the year he returned to Konin. Four years later came another breakaway: he went to Dresden to study sculpture. A pattern emerges from these years: stints of humdrum work in Konin interspersed with study periods abroad.

Marek arrived in Dresden three weeks before the outbreak of the First World War. Exactly how long he remained there we do not know but, almost certainly as a result of the war, he returned to Konin, now under German occupation. According to his brother's account, this was the start of an artistically productive period of his life. One of his sculptures, *A Dying Jew*, was exhibited in a Warsaw art gallery: his first recognition as an artist. The *kehillah* invited him to paint frescoes for the synagogue walls. The municipality commissioned a wooden plaque of the city emblem – a white horse – for the façade of the Town Hall, just yards away from his parents' hat shop.

Frances Taylor, who was born in Konin, tells me she remembers her young uncle best in the years just before 1922, the year she left for England. 'He certainly liked having a good time. He was well-dressed, wore a beautiful hat, was good-looking and had all the girls round him. He played the mandolin, took part in amateur dramatics and played football. He liked singing and dancing. He was a wonderful fellow to have at a wedding.'

Like the majority of the youth of Konin, Marek was a Zionist, and when the war was over he began to think of making *aliyah*. Like many others, he was finding it hard to scrape a living in inflation-torn, postwar Poland. Helping to rebuild the Jewish Homeland might be the one worthwhile alternative to being an artist. He had passed his thirtieth birthday. Glicenstein at this age had already won the Prix de Rome (twice) and was launched on a distinguished career. If one can rely on his sister Yetta's memory at the age of ninety-one, Marek's decision to emigrate was not entirely idealistic: 'He was six months too old to enter the Paris Art School, so he decided to go to Palestine.'[6]

He contacted a group of *chalutzim* who were on their way to Eretz Yisrael and arranged to join up with them in Vienna. On arriving there he learned that their plans had come disastrously unstuck: the necessary permissions had been suspended or withdrawn. There was no chance of entering Palestine. Yetta, then living in London, wired him funds to go to Paris for the time being. Her laconic summary of this period of his life is as follows: 'In Paris he again tried to enter the Art School. He was very artistic and unhappy. He met Sarah, who was married.'[7]

Marek arrived in Paris some time between 1922 and 1924. By

then he had Westernized his name to Mark. Paris was the start of 'a period of hard years' to quote his brother Maurice.[8] He was alone, cut off from family and friends. Learning German had been no problem for a Yiddish-speaking Jew. In Paris he was lost. His penury makes his one final attempt to become an art student all the more puzzling. Was it a final burst of irrational optimism before the door slammed shut?

Mark Lewin had a daughter, who was born in Paris in 1930. Like so many French Jews, she might have ended up in Auschwitz. The reality, as I discovered, was that she had survived the war in France and was now a Londoner, living a few miles from my home.

Charming and youthful-looking, Irene is unmistakably French: in accent, urbanity, and style. She knows Konin as the name of her father's birthplace, but it has not impinged greatly on her life. She visited the town for a holiday with her mother and sister when she was five years old. They stayed with her grandmother, Rifka the milliner, and met all their Konin relatives. Irene remembers the fuss everyone made over Mark's two little French daughters who could not speak a word of Yiddish.

From Irene I learn more about Mark Lewin's life in Paris: 'My aunt Yetta had a friend with a beautiful sister whose name was Sarah, whom my father met and fell in love with.' Sarah was a divorcée with a young son when they met.[9] She had come to France from Poland as a child, and spoke both French and Yiddish. In or about 1924 Mark and Sarah were married. Irene's knowledge of her father's early years in Paris is short on detail but of one thing she is certain: it was a bad time. Either before or soon after getting married, he went back to the work he had done as an apprentice in Konin: 'My father couldn't make a living out of fine art, and so he was carving these huge pieces of furniture and using very strong-smelling glue, which can make you ill. It was very hard on him. I was told he had to stop working after a while because it affected his health and made him cough.'

Mark's first child, Dora, was born in 1927, followed three years later by Irene. Sarah's small son by her first marriage lived with them. 'He adored my father,' says Irene. Around this time,

Mark was searching for some new means of supporting a family.

> He decided to start in the fur trade. All of a sudden a complete change! My mother was working with her parents making fur coats for ladies, and he joined them to learn about the trade. But making coats was not enough for him. To make use of his skills as a sculptor he decided to venture into something that had not been done before: he made pyjama cases out of fur. They were in the shape of a dog lying with his paws in front. I haven't got one now but I remember them so vividly. The dog had a zip on the belly and inside was a red velvet lining. The heads were amazingly natural. He made moulds out of plaster of Paris. I remember the moulds – the inside of them was painted red – and he made *papier mâché* shapes of the head inside them. When they came out of the moulds he stretched fur over them, and he clipped the hair of the fur exactly the way it would be on a dog.
>
> He made different breeds of dog, a pekinese, a greyhound, a papillon . . . and he used different kinds of fur for each breed. He decided to introduce the idea to the big stores in Paris, and eventually he got orders for them. My parents worked late into the night, just the two of them, making these dogs. They used to buy glass eyes for the dogs, and he placed them in an artistic way within the fur to look exactly like real eyes. The fur dogs were a perfect copy of each breed, with the right expression. He used to prick little dots with a soldering iron – I can still remember the smell – and insert the whiskers. My mother used to make deliveries by day and then work during the night. They were always in the workshop, which was in the apartment where we lived, in Rue du Cardinal Lemoine in the 5th *arrondissement*, behind the Panthéon.

Had she sensed that her father was unhappy? 'No, not at all. Life was not easy, I knew that. A man with his training would have preferred to be doing art, but there was no way he could afford it. He must have been frustrated but as a child I didn't realize it.' Life began looking up for the Lewins. The pyjama-case dogs were selling, and Sarah was now running a tiny furrier's shop not far from their apartment. Their elegant stationery was headed: 'M. Lewin – *Fourrures*'. Yet Mark and Sarah were still tied to a relentless daily grind of work amid the dust of furs, the smell of tan, and the clatter of an industrial sewing-machine. Their apartment, recalls a

British-born nephew who spent a holiday with them once, was 'up two flights of narrow, smelly stairs' with a 'small odoriferous WC on the landing, and no bathroom.'[10] Mark wore a black beret, liked wine with his meals, drank *café filtre* for breakfast, and smoked Gauloises.

Mark never lost his love for sculpture, but art was now a hobby. 'I remember my father working at his sculpture in the apartment, the wooden stand that he used, like a tall stool with a square top for modelling which he could turn round. We had a fireplace in our apartment with a beautiful ornate mantelpiece that he carved with two columns, and he put some of his pieces of sculpture on this.' Mark's brother-in-law, a furrier, was a patron of the arts who socialized with painters in Montmartre, but Mark never became part of his circle. Perhaps he – a now bourgeois furrier selling kitsch – felt he no longer fitted into an artist's milieu. Or perhaps he did not wish to be reminded of the life that had eluded him.

Irene tells me that a number of his works survived the war. She, as their curator, has moved them protectively from place to place. They are now displayed in her London home. One or two are cast in bronze but mostly they are small figures and busts in white plaster of Paris. Some are *shtetl*-inspired: refugees fleeing a pogrom, a Chasid holding a candle, and *A Dying Jew*, the work exhibited in a Warsaw gallery that seemed at the time like the turning-point in his career.

Irene shows me several busts he did of her mother, a self-portrait dated 1935, busts of Irene, and an unfinished head of her sister in brown plasticine, still tacky after half a century. On her wall hangs a bronze medallion plaque of Mark's parents, Rifka and Isaac. There are no wood carvings among the collection. Perhaps the years spent slaving over Konin sideboards and Paris *armoires* spoiled that medium for him. To an unqualified critic's eye, his work has worthy qualities: humanity, compassion and technical assurance. If it has a weakness, it lies perhaps in its academic conformity. Whether this means he had no original talent, or never had the chance to develop it, or lacked the single-minded dedication of a committed artist, who can say?[11]

Irene brings out a family album and shows me a snapshot of two little girls – herself and her sister during their visit to Konin in the Thirties. There are photographs of her father, one of them as a young man posing beside a sculptor's modelling stand. He wears an artist's smock and a flamboyant cravat, both of which look newly bought like clothes for a wedding picture. It was probably taken while he was studying in Dresden. This is how he saw himself and how he wanted the world to see him: The Artist in His Studio. He must have sent copies of the photograph, which is printed on the back like a postcard, to his parents, relatives and friends in Konin, and one to his guide and mentor, Chanoch Glicenstein, with fraternal greetings from one artist to another.

Postscript Mark Lewin died of lung cancer in Paris in 1938, his death hastened by glue fumes, fur dust, and forty Gauloises a day. His wife and daughters hid from the Germans during the Second World War. Dora died in 1942 aged fifteen, her mother in 1963. Mark's father, Isaac, died in Konin in the 1930s. Three of Mark's sisters, together with their husbands and children, died in the Shoah, along with his mother, Rivka. According to Irene: 'She was ninety-three when she was taken away and forced to walk a long distance. She pretended that she was much younger than she was and she tried to walk well, but in fact she was almost carried by those on either side of her. She hoped that she would be selected for work when they reached their destination, but she was not too successful, and the Germans shot her.'[12]

Chanoch Glicenstein, twice winner of the coveted Prix de Rome, achieved international success as Enrico Glicenstein. Among his sitters were Pope Pius XI, Hindenburg, Mussolini, Einstein, Franklin D. Roosevelt, Lord Balfour and Israel Zangwill. He made his home in Italy, but the rise of fascism in the Thirties led him to emigrate to America, from where he returned all his Italian medals and honours. He died in New York in 1942 at the age of seventy-two after being struck down by a cab. The Israel Bible Museum (formerly the Glicenstein Museum) in Safed, Galilee, is devoted to his Bible illustrations, and there is a street in Tel Aviv named after him.

21

AT THE END OF six months, Konin's presence was invading my home. Maps, books, files, papers, letters and research material encroached on every spare space. The River Thames flowed near the house; the River Warta flowed through it. I had tracked down the handful of survivors living in Britain and explored their pasts, learning something from each of them. Frances Taylor, formerly Franya Bulka, having said she left Konin in 1923 and could remember nothing worth telling me, then talked fascinatingly about her Uncle Maurice, the Bundist. Teresa Franco, formerly Blumcha Zylberberg, now a librarian, gave me a vivid image of a little girl coming away from the Jewish library in Konin hugging books under both arms – Balzac, Dumas, Brontë – and devouring them at home, where mother sewed shirts and the children earned a little money wrapping sweets on the kitchen table. Herman Krol, a Konin tailor and ex-fighter in the Polish army, now nearly eighty and still making suits, said when he set eyes on me: 'You look like a Ryczke.' He was a friend of my father's brothers in Konin. Jack Offenbach, a founder member of the Konin Aid Society, was long dead, but I tracked down one of his sons, Hyman, hoping to glean a few more facts. And I did. In 1930 his father took him to Konin for his bar mitzvah, and I was able to view the Tepper Marik through the eyes of an English schoolboy. Only one Koniner refused to see me, prevented from doing so by her ultra-Orthodox son, who viewed my secular project with deep suspicion.

I was getting to know my way about the faraway town and the Jews who once lived there, their foibles, reputations, nick-names: Hirsh Turn-head who banged the big drum in the fire brigade band, Moishe Pot-of-Semolina, Stein the Cossack, Simcha Shnorrer, Crooked Nose, Water Head, Goat Beard, Moishe Bottom, Mad Malke, Mordechai the Peasant, the Little Rebbe, the Red Rebbe, the Lame Rebbe, the Rebbe with a Hump, and the poorest market porter in the town, known to all as – 'Rothschild'.

I became familiar with family relationships: Mendel and Lola Gruen were the children of Chaim Gruen who was married to

Zipporah, who was the daughter of Gusta Offenbach, who was the mother-in-law of Wolf Gruen, who made soda-water, and who had another son, Shmulek, who was related to . . . I learned to distinguish between Rabbi Lipschitz, Moishe Lipschitz, Esther Lipschitz, Lipschitz who lived on the big square, Lipschitz the stone mason, Lipschitz the tailor, Lipschitz the teacher, Lipschitz the shoe-shop owner, Lipschitz the clogmaker, Lipschitz the driver, Lipschitz the upholsterer, Lipschitz the paint merchant, and the Lipschitz who was not quite right in the head.

A broad picture of the community's class structure was emerging: in the middle, the solid core of respectable burghers, the shopkeepers and businessmen who controlled most of the trade in the town; below them, the more successful tailors and artisans, and below them, at the bottom of the pile, the struggling piece-workers sewing at home, the porters, manual workers, the generally unsuccessful, the poor. At the top, a small stratum of the wealthier merchants and businessmen, the owners of land and property. And each of these divisions was subdivided into more subtle gradations. The poor, for example, could be divided between 'the poor and the hopelessly poor', to borrow a phrase from Irving Howe.[1] Economics alone did not define class; education, Torah knowledge and family pedigree also counted.

The more I knew, the more I became aware of what I did not know. There were gaps that neither the handful of British Koniners nor the Memorial Book could fill. At the outset I had thought that six months would be all I needed to research this book. Now I realized I had to look to more distant shores. Most of the survivors had settled in America and Israel. I had a cousin, David Richke (named after Dovid the Dark-Haired Ryczke), living near Tel Aviv, whose father had been a leading light on the Memorial Book committee. I set him the task of tracing every Koniner he could find in Israel.

Meanwhile I began a hunt for Koniners in the United States. I had already written to former Senator Barry Goldwater, who had subscribed to the Memorial Book and had an interest in his Konin ancestors, the Goldwassers. I received a friendly, constructive reply, expressing interest in what I was doing, but turning down the idea that we might meet.

Someone had given me an old letterhead of the Konin *landsmanshaft* in New York that had an obviously obsolete address printed at the top, and a telephone number with an exchange that no longer existed. The association of compatriots might well be defunct by now, like its opposite number in London. Eventually I tracked down one of the names on the letterhead, Morton Mysch. Pictures in the Memorial Book showed him as a young man in the early 1930s. Was he still alive? I wrote to him and got a reply from his son, Leon, a school-teacher living in Brooklyn. His father was fine, he told me, but no longer able to cope with correspondence. I learned that the Konin Society in America *was* to all intents and purposes moribund. The membership – much reduced in number – met only once a year, for a Yizkor gathering – remembrance service – for the Konin victims of the Shoah. He enclosed the names and addresses of the members, and said his father promised to give me all the help he could.

I sent off a letter and a questionnaire to every Koniner on the list, about thirty-five in all, including a few who lived in Canada. Not too many replied. Some, as I discovered later, did not want to awaken painful memories. Others could not face the strain of writing in English. Some were too old. Still others succumbed to inertia. But a few replies began trickling in and they were encouraging. Mendel Leben, a Konin Chasid's son and an American college graduate, wrote to say he had lived in the same house as the Ryczke family and grew up knowing my grandparents, uncles, cousins . . . Sarah Trybuch (née Ozerowicz), writing from Florida, had a past I wanted to hear more about: she and her husband had been partisans in the forests during the war. I heard from a Konin horse-dealer's son, Julius Ancer, twice wounded in the Polish army before ending up in a concentration camp . . . He and his wife, also from Konin, invited me to stay with them in Minneapolis if I decided to visit the States. Another heartening message from a Mrs Miriam Grossman in Omaha, Nebraska: 'We want to assure you that you will be our honoured guest with comfortable lodging and food at our table.'

I telephoned Morton Mysch and heard his voice for the first time, so soft as to be almost inaudible, its accent formed by Konin and Brooklyn. He sounded old. The annual Yizkor meeting, he said, was to be held in Manhattan in a few weeks' time. The date was not firmly fixed but it would probably be in October or, at the latest, 'da foist November'. It would be my only chance to attend a gathering of Koniners – the few who were left. Would I come?

Part Three

AMERICAN JOURNEY

22

MORTON MYSCH, wearing a flat cloth cap and dark overcoat, greeted me warmly at Kennedy Airport, shook my hand, and in the unemphatic voice I was to get to know so well, announced: 'You are twenty-five years too late.'

His son, Leon, drove us to Morton's home in nearby Canarsie, Brooklyn, and though we chatted all the way, I could not take my mind off those opening words. They stayed with me throughout the classic Sunday brunch of bagels and lox, followed by fruit – Morton's wife was particularly insistent that I eat fruit. She called him Motek, which suited him far better. I discovered our many Konin connections. Motek grew up in a house that belonged to my aunt Frieda's grandparents. He lived near my Ryczke grandfather and knew all my uncles and cousins. He remembered my father's visit to Konin in the Thirties.

At last I voiced the question preying on my mind: why was I twenty-five years too late? Twenty-five years ago, he explained, some of the most intelligent, best-informed Koniners in New York were still alive, the Konin Society was flourishing, and memories were fresh. I should have come then. Nevertheless, he wished me good luck because the Konin past was close to his heart and he wanted the younger generation born in America, his own son and daughter included, to know more about the community from which their parents had come. He began talking about that past, his memory undimmed, and I knew I had found a precious key to Konin's past. I had come in time for him. But the others, the Koniners I had missed? Was he right? Was I too late?

It was time to head for Manhattan. Brooding thoughts receded as the famous skyline came into view. No uniformed lackey awaited me at my hotel, one of New York's oldest, described as 'in the European tradition'. The deserted lobby retained an echo of old-time style but its days of glory were long past. I had asked for their cheapest room and, when I saw it, I knew this was what I had got: scuffed walls, grimy paintwork, a velvety layer of dust along the picture rails.

Particles of plaster from the flaking ceiling sprinkled the carpet like dandruff. The European tradition with a vengeance. What could one expect for sixty-five dollars a night?

That evening I began telephoning Koniners. My heart sank at the thought of talking to so many strangers, instantly needing to win the good will on which everything depended. I tapped out a number. A voice answered. There was little time to establish rapport. I had to persuade them to allow me, a stranger from London, into their homes to ask them about their past, a past some of them wanted to forget. I came to hate the sound of my voice repeating certain lines like a well-rehearsed sales pitch.

I knew something about most of these people. Some had completed my questionnaire, and Motek Mysch had given me thumbnail sketches of the Koniners in America. Going through the list with him, I had marked an F or NF against each name to indicate *Frum* (religious) or Non-*Frum*. This was to avoid the *faux pas* of calling a *frummer* on the sabbath or during the approaching festivals of Sukkot (Feast of Tabernacles) and Simchat Torah (Rejoicing in the Torah). There were not many Fs.

The voices at the other end of the line belonged unmistakably to Polish Jews who had spent a good part of their lives in Brooklyn or the Bronx. At times Hyman Kaplan, Damon Runyon and Jackie Mason jostled for supremacy. I had to concentrate intently until my ear became attuned. No problem with 'toity-toid'. Nor with 'plis haf a void vid mine dotter'. But I was totally flummoxed when a man inexplicably began telling me about his employer – 'you want the boss' – until I realized he was advising me on public transport. My English accent must have struck them as equally outlandish – even to my ears it began to sound prissy.

Two priority names on my contact list were Gloria Gutwill and Louis Lefkowitz, mainstays of the Konin Society. They, together with Motek Mysch, were largely responsible for keeping it going in recent years: both offered unstinting help. Gloria, a forceful personality who had taken on the vocal manner of a Polish countess without losing her Konin-bred hospitality, wanted to pin me down straightaway for lunch or dinner in Forest Hills. 'Might you be free tomorrow, Mr Richmond? The day after? What would you like me to cook for you?'

And so began my daily journeys to Brooklyn, Queens, and more remote parts of New York. I soon became a familiar face to the garrulous Italian driver of the M25 express bus to Brooklyn who picked me up each morning at the same time. Cramming as much Konin activity into each day as I could, taking no time off, I soon realized that my stay in New York was going to be longer than I had planned. The hotel room was becoming increasingly oppressive, but a tight budget ruled out anything more luxurious. I had heard of another hotel, better situated for my purposes, in Midtown Manhattan. Its name was off-puttingly quaint and it was cheaper than my place, therefore likely to be a bug-infested flophouse; but it was worth a look. I liked the Pickwick Arms the moment I set foot in it, not least because it made no attempt at Dickensian décor.

The room was cabin-sized but cheerful, and the European tradition refreshingly absent. With shower, phone and colour TV, it cost $56 a night: a *metsieh*, a snip. Right opposite the hotel was the Sutton Place Synagogue – 'The most innovative and dynamic synagogue in New York,' one of its leaflets claimed. Its social activities included a Singles Hotline and a Singles Party – 'Socialize and network with over 2000 young professionals'. Strangers were invited to dine 'al fresco' in the rooftop *sukkah* (booth erected for Sukkot) and join in a Bar-B-Q party with hamburgers and hot dogs.

I moved into the Pickwick Arms next day.

A daily routine established itself. In the morning I would set off by bus, subway or overground train for Brooklyn or Forest Hills or distant suburbs like Monsey and Mount Vernon. My hospitable hosts invariably wanted to feed me. There is an old Yiddish song of the *shtetl* that goes: 'Sunday potatoes, Monday potatoes, Tuesday and Wednesday potatoes . . .' For me it was 'Sunday bagels, Monday bagels . . .' usually accompanied by mashed tuna fish and a glass of orange squash. I was grateful for this and the occasional more varied meal.

Sometimes I managed to cram two visits into a day (Monday *twice* bagels . . .) or filled a gap between meetings in the library at YIVO (Institute for Jewish Research). Evenings were for sorting through notes, diary-keeping, fixing more appointments . . . It cost less to telephone from the lobby, so I spent part of each evening standing under a plastic hood alongside other cheapskates trying to save a few cents.

There were rewarding moments during these first few weeks when the search for clues led to unexpected treasure; when a Koniner might casually say something seemingly trivial that opened up a new field of enquiry. It was elating to see a missing piece of the jigsaw click into place, revealing a part of the picture previously obscure. My knowledge of Konin was growing from day to day. Sometimes, when Koniners struggled to recall some fact from the distant past, I was able to supply it, reminding them of the name of their next-door neighbour, of their *cheder* teacher, of the street that crossed with theirs. To my delight, some of them spoke to me as if I myself had been born in Konin.

It was when I was on my own that Jewish *Angst* descended. I worried about petty failures and missed opportunities. Rich and unexpected sources of information were coming to light each day, and yet I fretted about gaping holes in my knowledge that might never be filled, about contradictory facts and confusing discrepancies I might never sort out. Each night I would crash into bed, fall asleep the moment my head hit the pillow, and wake up an hour later, mind whirling, unable to get away from that town on the Warta. Too restless to read, too agitated to watch old movies, I would lie and listen to the sounds of Manhttan: a taxi door slamming below, the grunting horn of a fire-engine racing along Lexington, the distant hum of traffic. And through it all I heard a voice whisper: 'You are twenty-five years too late.'

23

IT WAS NATURAL for fellow townsfolk newly arrived in a strange land to turn to one another for comfort, companionship and support. The first instance of Koniners clubbing together in an institutionalized way dates back to 1879, when the B'nai Tsvi Amsterdam was established in New York. The Konin connection is revealed in the name – that of Konin's first Rabbi, Tsvi Hirsh Amsterdam. Firm facts about the society's early days are hard to come by, but it is more than likely that Koniners played a key role in founding the Society. By the late 1960s, when it was beginning to peter out, few of its members came from Konin. Today the Society no longer exists.[1]

Another organization more specifically tied to Konin is recorded in a Yiddish publication dated 1896: *Constitution of the Konin Young Men's Benevolent Association*. Founded in New York four years previously, it was, as its name suggests, a mutual aid society designed to meet practical rather than social needs, the most important being burial rights and relief at times of financial crisis. The membership, which stood at nearly a hundred in 1896, declined in the course of the present century as the young men became old men, and finally, some years after the Second World War, it too came to an end.

On 20 October 1923, a charter adorned with the blue seal of the State of New York was granted to the Ladies' and Men's Society of Konin, Inc.[2] 'The enthusiasm was great,' according to a report in the Memorial Book, 'but that did not last long and the organization fell apart and was revived from time to time.' No reason is given for the collapse: a diplomatic omission perhaps. Status-seeking and petty in-fighting, not unknown in Jewish organizations past and present, may well have divided the Society during the Twenties.

The Thirties brought a revival in the Society's philanthropic activities, prompted, it is safe to guess, by the communal cry for help coming from Konin, the reports of growing anti-Semitism and economic hardship. In 1935 the then president of the Society, Philip Charof,[3] visited his home town as an emissary, taking with him 'a big sum of money, with the aim to provide constructive help'. He spent two months in the town, helping to put 'the religious school for poor children, *Yavne*' on a more secure financial footing and alleviating the poverty of its pupils. Thanks to the cash injection from America, 'the school was heated and the pupils were provided with hot meals, warm clothing for winter and a pair of shoes.'[4]

Like the Konin Aid Society in London, the *landsmanshaft* in New York went into limbo during the Second World War. All contact with Poland ceased. Koniners in America were by now socially and economically established, no longer dependent for comradeship on their fellow Koniners. The Society's charter still had legal standing, but to all intents and purposes the Society was moribund.

The new influx of immigrants after the war once again provided the incentive for creating a fraternity. Koniners emerged from Russian labour camps and Nazi concentration camps broken in health, penniless and in many cases alone in the world. Insecurity bred interdependence. Having lost so many of their own kith and kin, those who came to America in the late 1940s and early Fifties turned to one another for friendship and the consolation of shared memories. More altruistically, they remembered fellow survivors still stranded in Europe or struggling to make ends meet in the harsh economic climate of the new State of Israel.

With encouragement from veterans of the prewar Konin Society, the newcomers decided to take over the 1923 charter and revive the Society. Morton Mysch and Gloria Gutwill were among the newcomers who served on the first provisional committee. Thus the Ladies' and Men's Society of Konin, Inc. rose like a phoenix from the ashes of the camps.[5] Its two to three hundred members (including spouses who in only a few cases came from Konin) felt an intense pride in the community from which they had sprung and inconsolable grief at its annihilation.

For some years the members met in each other's homes. The first gathering in a public meeting place was held in a rented room in the Bronx in October 1953: 'A big crowd of *landslayt* met for the first time in our own place. The enthusiasm was beyond description.[6] Thereafter the members met eight times a year. There were Chanukah parties, Purim parties, strawberry parties, dances . . . They attended each other's *simchas* (celebrations), fund-raised for Israel, sent money every year to the Konin Society in Tel Aviv, gave financial aid to their own members, bought burial plots for Koniners in a New York cemetery, and contributed two thousand dollars towards the cost of publishing the Konin Memorial Book.

The most solemn, best-attended event in the Society's calendar occurred each fall, when Koniners came together for the annual Yizkor service, to say Kaddish for their murdered families and friends.

Inexorably, the average age of the members rose and their number declined. Their children, born in America, knowing little or nothing about their parents' native town, found nothing to tempt them into the Society's mostly Yiddish-speaking fold. One by one the last of the old-timers from the prewar Society faded away. Of the remaining members, some became frail and home-bound, or retired permanently to Florida or warmed their old bones there in the winter. The younger of the postwar immigrants, reaping their reward for years of unremitting toil, moved to new and plusher homes, and immersed themselves in the lives of their children and grandchildren. The intimacy that had once bonded the Koniners was weakening. Mutual contact came to depend on the once-a-year Rosh Hashanah greetings card. The Koniners had become Americans.

No one observed the Society's decline with greater sadness than Morton Mysch. Universally respected, devoted to the memory of his lost community, he became the natural figurehead of the Konin Society in America. He served for six years as its president, and long after that continued to hold the dwindling band together.

Social gatherings ceased altogether in 1981. Members no longer paid annual dues but continued to pledge donations at the Yizkor meeting. With funds no longer needed to alleviate hardship among American members or survivors in Europe, these donations were passed on to Zionist causes and helped meet the maintenance costs of the Konin memorial in Tel Aviv.

A handful of Koniners in New York chose not to belong to the Society, or belonged but rarely participated in its activities. These were mostly the ultra-Orthodox and the Bundists, who were not attracted to the idea of indulging in small-talk and nostalgia. They had a secure anchorage in ideological worlds of their own, and the companionship of fellow believers.[7]

In an attempt to prolong the Society's active life, some members mooted that it should be amalgamated with another society. The most obvious match was the larger and still active Kalisz Society.[8] The two communities were linked by geographical proximity and history. But the Koniners were sharply divided on the issue and the result was deadlock. Motek Mysch was one of those who opposed amalgamation. For him, it would be merely the demise of the Konin Society in another form.

The list his son sent me in 1987 totalled fifty-five members (including non-Konin spouses), of whom thirty-one lived in the environs of New York. The Society's social activities had by then shrunk to one – the annual Yizkor gathering. The Society continued to have a president[9] and officers, but there was little for them to do save for arranging the memorial meeting. Motek, supported by a few others, doggedly kept the event alive. For them, this act of remembrance alone justified perpetuating the Society. Otherwise, the only reason for Motek and the few remaining stalwarts to come together from time to time was to bury another Koniner.

24

THE CHEAPLY printed handbill might well have been a piece of ephemera from the Lower East Side of long ago. The Yiddish heading is printed in bold Hebrew characters, the English text in a typographical jumble of chipped typefaces and smudged Gothic capitals. Someone has enlisted an old typewriter to insert details of date and venue. This is the invitation to the annual Yizkor gathering.

YIZKOR MEMORIAL MEETING
LADIES' & MEN'S SOCIETY OF KONIN, INC.
MEMORIAL FOR KONINER & VIC. MARTYRS.
SUNDAY AFTERNOON, OCTOBER 18, 2:00 P.M.

Dear Members and Friends:

Forty-four years have passed since our dearest and beloved ones have perished by the bloody hands of the Nazi murderers. Their last will was DO NOT FORGET US. The memory of our martyrs will never be forgotten, but will forever live in our hearts.

We ask you to attend a
Yizkor Meeting
on SUNDAY, October 18, 2:00 P.M.
at FREE SONS OF ISRAEL, 180 Varick Street
14th floor room 5
New York, N.Y.

An appropriate program has been arranged – and it is the duty of all KONINER and VIC. to attend and together pay tribute to our martyrs who are no longer with us!

Mournfully yours,
THE KONINER MEMORIAL COMMITTEE

There is a final line in Yiddish: 'Come and honour the KONIN MARTYRS'. The 'VIC. MARTYRS', I deduce, are those who lived in the vicinity of Konin.

On 18 October 1987 I wait outside a building in downtown

Manhattan, eerily deserted at the weekend. Motek Mysch arrives, dressed in his *shabbes* best: well-cut, dark blue suit and waistcoat, white shirt and gleaming black shoes. Perhaps to hold this formality in check, he wears a sporty corduroy hat.

Once inside, he puts on a black yarmulke, and I don mine, brought from London for the occasion. The meeting place is a rented room, square, windowless, with harsh neon strip lighting and black and white checkerboard vinyl flooring. Rows of chairs face a trestle table where Gloria Gutwill, the resplendent, Junoesque Chairlady for the afternoon, is setting out a cluster of *yortsayt* candles. Gloria passed successfully as an 'Aryan' when the war began, risking her life to smuggle food into the Ostrowiec ghetto, where her family and many other Koniners had been deported. When the Germans rounded up her sister, she chose to go with her to Auschwitz. Her sister lived. Gloria saw her mother shot. She lost her father and brother in Treblinka. When the Russians liberated her in Czechoslovakia in 1945, she was too weak to chew or swallow bread.

Louis Lefkowitz, the Society's Chairman and Treasurer, arrives carrying a heavy six-branched candelabra fashioned from plumber's copper piping. A man of quiet authority, Lefkowitz is in the tailoring repair business and lives in one of New York's outer suburbs. He was born and grew up in the VIC. of Konin. He is a survivor of twenty-one Nazi camps and is here to remember those who did not survive, among them his parents, four sisters and two brothers.

A few more people arrive, Koniners and their spouses, short, dapper-looking couples who have not met since the last Yizkor meeting. Hugs, kisses and shrill greetings create a hubbub that belies their small numbers. All seem to be talking at once, catching up with a year's news in English, Yiddish and, just occasionally, Polish. '*Nu*, how are you Captain?' someone greets a man who served as an officer in the Polish army nearly half a century ago.

Nearby is the 'baby' of the American Koniners, Sam Klapstein, sixty-three, over six feet tall, glowering above the others like a skyscraper among a huddle of cottages. Sam is a genial kosher butcher from New Jersey. In Konin his mother eked out a living in the family kitchen, baking cakes for wedding parties. Sam (Simcha then) spent his teens in twenty-eight camps, one of them Dachau. His mother, father, two brothers and two sisters were deported from

Konin and executed. In his wallet he carries a small photograph of a family group taken when he was about six years old: his parents, brothers and sisters. Faded, creased and crumbling at the edges, it stayed with him throughout his years in the camps. 'When there was a search, I put it in my mouth.' He cups the precious fragment in the palm of his hand and holds it out for me to see. The only one of his six siblings to survive is a sister who lives on a kibbutz in Israel. He was twenty-one when his emaciated fingers shook the hand of his liberator, General Eisenhower, in May 1945.

The Society's current President, David Irwin, stands next to Sam. His father, Jakob Iwanowicz, was a prosperous cloth merchant in Konin. Irwin manufactures ladies' underwear in the Bronx. He was separated from his family, including his twin brother, in 1942 and never saw them again. When he was liberated from Buchenwald on 14 April 1945 he weighed sixty-five pounds and was close to death.

About ten people have arrived. Gloria keeps glancing anxiously towards the door. 'I wish more people had come,' she whispers, 'I'm so discouraged.' 'Every year it's fewer,' says Lefkowitz. 'People are dying, moving away, they're getting older, they're getting sick. We used to have over a hundred people.'

The women get busy with the catering. They unpack brown paper bags bulging with provisions, and with professional speed set about making ryebread sandwiches. They slice cake, fish pickled cucumbers out of huge jars, and stack paper plates. The janitor walks in hugging a steel catering urn.

Matrons start badgering me like persistent saleswomen, pressing me to taste their wares. When I hesitate, they adopt expressions of disappointment, pain, even shock: 'This is the best Jewish bread you've ever eaten. Take!' I take. Another woman spears a slice of pastrami on the end of a fork and dangles it close to my lips: 'Here, eat this.' I eat. 'Try the cake.' I try. 'Have some more coffee!' I have some more coffee . . .

Proud *bubas* extract family snapshots from capacious handbags and coo over pictures of bar mitzvahs, weddings and their grandchildren. A photograph of three impassive infants is held up for my admiration: 'Look, my *eyniklekh* [grandchildren] in California.' A woman invites me to stay with her when I visit Florida: 'You mustn't stay in a hotel. We've got a nice room.' I thank her for the kind offer but explain I shall be staying with a cousin. 'No! You will stay with us.'

The name Ryczke is familiar to everyone in the room, and I am aware of being an object of interest. Threads tie me to most of these people. A man called David Berendt, sweet-faced and gentle, comes up and tells me that as a boy he went to Benyumin Ryczke's *cheder*. Another man has a surname I heard as a young child and could never forget: Rundbaken – Roundcheeks. My Sarna grandfather had a friend in the East End who came from Konin and was called Rundbaken. I am talking to his nephew. Fella Nitzky tells me she grew up in the house where my Ryczke grandfather and his family lived: 'I remember the time he went to visit his son in London.' That son was my father. I was a toddler at the time and I have no memory of the bearded visitor from Konin who must have held me in his arms.

Berendt remembers my grandfather coming back and telling everyone about the princely lifestyle of the Jews in England. 'He told us that his son's house had a garden at the back and a garden in the front.' The everyday domestic comforts that I, as a boy, took for granted were outside my grandfather's experience: flush lavatory, running water, gas geyser in the bathroom. Bathroom!

It is 2.45 and there is no sign of the meeting getting started. Maybe the socializing is a normal part of the proceedings. People study photographs of a Konin Society dance taken twenty years ago and point out Koniners who have 'passed away'. The women gaze at glossy black-and-white photographs that showed them as they then were, their brows smoother, waistlines slimmer, and sigh as only Jewish women of a certain age can sigh.

A little man with a magnificent nose and an inquisitive eye walks into the room, strides up to Gloria and demands: 'Who are you?' 'Konin,' she replies, much as a character in Shakespeare might declare 'Gloucester' or 'Somerset.' 'Konin!' he exclaims. 'I know Konin. Many your members don know where Konin is.' Visibly irritated, Gloria assures him that the members do know where Konin is. 'I tell you dey don know. Many of your members don know where Konin is. Anyway, I'm from Israel buns.' Who is this confident intruder, a salesman for a kosher bakery? I am told he flits from meeting to meeting fund-raising for a good cause: selling Israel Bonds. He looks around appraisingly, clearly decides we are not in the mood for buying buns and, still insisting that most of us have no idea where Konin is, strides out.

By 3.20 the number has crept up to sixteen including me. Gloria confides despairingly: 'Never yet so few people. Unbelievable!' The supply of sandwiches is beginning to run low but an addition to the refreshments catches my eye: a bottle of Scotch. I am handed a thimble-sized plastic container, half-filled. '*L'chaim!*' No one presses me to have another.

It is nearly 4 pm and the *chazan* who has been hired to lead the prayers has still not arrived. 'Gloria, when can we start?' asks someone plaintively. Morton Mysch deputes one of the men to lead the afternoon prayers. The congregational drone starts up, recalling the hours of numbing boredom I endured in synagogue as a boy. Anyone who has shared my background will be familiar with the sound: a tuneless mumbling, muttering, chanting and humming, a slur of words gabbled at breakneck speed as though a competition is afoot to see who can get to the finishing post first. Every now and then the drone is punctuated by a loud *Oomeyn!* (Amen), the nearest to unison they ever come. People start chatting during the prayers. A reproachful 'shshsh' silences the culprits, but only momentarily. The unstylishness, the indecorousness, the Ashkenazi ghetto Jewishness of it all, makes me cringe. But would I prefer High Mass in St Peter's?

As the prayers comes to an end, two latecomers appear. Gloria's attempt to start the official proceedings is thwarted by general concern for the welfare of the new arrivals, now heading anxiously towards what is left of the food. 'Let them eat!' someone shouts. 'Let them eat!'

This urgent priority attended to, Gloria opens the meeting with an eloquent reminder of the tragedy of the murdered six million. She calls forward five women, one at a time, to light a symbolic candle in the menorah. She herself lights the sixth, then invites us to step forward and light one of the small memorial candles in the name of our dear ones.

'I would like to light this candle for Franya Beatus as there is nobody alive from her family.'

'This is for the Slodkis and for the Weisses.'

'I want to light a candle for Benyumin Ryczke, who was my *rebbe*.'

'This is for Dzialoszynski.'

A candle is lit for the martyred children: 'Over one million children. Can you grasp it?' Gloria asks the audience. 'This next candle is for our past beloved Rabbi Lipschitz of Konin. In his honour one of our members will light this candle, and I think Motek Mysch should do it. This is a very big honour, Motek.' Those who have already lit candles start chatting among themselves. 'Please!' pleads Gloria, calling the meeting to order. 'This is a solemn occasion.'

Candles are lit in memory of late President Murray Blum, and other past luminaries of the Konin Society. Someone demands: 'How about for Schwartz?' A candle is lit for Schwartz.

Louis Lefkowitz lights a candle 'For all my friends who were together with me in concentration camp, including my brother who perished.' Finally, Gloria calls on me: 'Theo Ryczke, would you please light a candle.' I light a candle for my lost family.

Motek Mysch stands up and urges everyone to help me in the task of gathering material for my book: 'This is not for us but for our children.'

About now I become aware of a disturbance in the room, of people trying to pacify a man sitting near the front. Suddenly he erupts. In a high-pitched voice he vehemently attacks Gloria for failing to introduce me properly. He is so incoherent with rage that it is difficult to make out what his grounds for criticism are. A heated altercation ensues. A few minutes later, a contretemps blows up with another member over some trivial matter. Struggling to restore a touch of grace to the occasion, Gloria casts her eyes heavenwards.

Louis Lefkowitz delivers a quiet, thoughtful address. He speaks of the memories revived on this day of remembrance, memories of experiences which he, 'a graduate of many places of extinction', now looks back on with disbelief. 'Did I really survive all these incredible days? Was it real or was it a nightmare? My young years were shattered by the arrival of the Nazis. I was stolen away from my family and thrust into a world of despair, one I did not understand. I guess God and nature gives us the mechanism that allows us to function under the most intense stress and suffering. It also gives us the time which is supposed to heal and help us forget. But how does one forget years of degradation and humiliation? How does one forget the hunger, the sickness, the stench of burning flesh, and the corpses of young and old staring at you then and even now?'

A little later, in the middle of another speech, the man who exploded earlier stands up and declares out of the blue: 'I want to make a proposal. I propose that all our meetings from now on we conduct in Yiddish.' His wife shrieks: 'Why nut?' An opponent retorts: 'We forgot already Yiddish.' The disrupter screams at the top of his voice: 'Our fathers, our grandfathers talked Yiddish so I want to talk Yiddish.' Lefkowitz tries to silence him but the Yiddishist, now beside himself, continues protesting while his wife interjects again: 'Why nut?'

A peacemaker in the audience proposes that the meeting be conducted in both languages. The disrupter, even more put out, cries: 'Official should be Yiddish!' Pandemonium reigns. What am I doing here? I ask myself. People shout, wave their arms about, make shushing noises. It is an unseemly sight, the Jews as I do not like to see them: undisciplined, petty, disputatious, disunited. Here, on a small scale, are the divisive forces that have afflicted the Diaspora and are the curse of the State of Israel.

Motek Mysch, discomforted, stares down as if wanting to detach himself from the proceedings. Others have no qualms about joining in the fray. Gloria, who wants to carry on in English is, curiously, the first to speak Yiddish, or rather, exquisite Yinglish. She blazes at the man: '*Zay nisht azoy* a fascist all of a sudden.' (Don't be such a fascist all of a sudden.) 'You've been a member for a very long time,' she tells him in Yiddish, 'and you have never raised this question before. Suddenly it is so imp –' He interrupts, screeching hysterically: '*Ikh hob* a proposition. *Ikh hob a rekht tsu makhn* a proposition.' (I have a proposition. I have the right to make a proposition.)

The *chazan*, a weary-looking man in a trilby hat, who has silently appeared from nowhere and seems utterly unfazed by the goings-on, stands up and says quietly in Yiddish: 'Let us sing a verse of *Tillim* [Psalms], and then say Kaddish.' His words work like magic. The assembly falls silent. He seizes the moment and launches into a Psalm of David.

Before Kaddish is recited, the lights are switched off. The tall candles in the menorah and the squat candles around it flicker in the dark, lighting the surrounding faces like a Caravaggio. For the first time, a sense of awe and holiness attends the occasion. The *chazan* leads us in the familiar words of the Kaddish: '*Yisgadal veyiskadash shemeh rabah* . . .' The driving rhythm of the Hebrew is lost in translation: 'May His great name be magnified and sanctified in the world that is to be created anew, where He will revive the dead, and raise them up unto life eternal . . .'

The *chazan* sings the poignant prayer, '*El moleh rakhamim*', O Lord full of compassion. No matter that the voice is past its best. The outpouring of supplication fills the room and invades the heart. It is a sound of the Middle East, unashamedly emotional, a sobbing, imploring cry of suffering, a humbling before the ancient God of Israel. The darkness in the room erases the here-and-now. The *chazan* is invisible. His voice soars in a soulful vibrato and the sound floats across the desert air where the tents are pitched that night. The Jews in the room need only reach out to touch the fingertips of their ancestors.

Are they crying for their murdered faith as well as their murdered families? Motek Mysch, whose first child, a baby daughter, was speared on the end of a Nazi bayonet, is not the only one in this room who has rejected the God who looked away when his People cried for help. There is one woman here who wears a *sheytl*, who abides by Judaism's strictest rules and does not know the meaning of doubt. But the others? How many believe in this God of mercy and compassion? And yet they pray – Motek too, because this is what you do at a Yizkor service, and because this is what they know the dead would have wished.

The neon lighting comes on. The names of more martyrs are recited, and then Gloria calls on me to say a few words. Before I can do so, the disrupter starts up again but is hushed into silence by the others. I talk briefly about my links with Konin and my reasons for writing the book, its function of recording, of remembrance, its purpose in handing on what might so easily be lost for ever. I ask of my audience only that they give me their time and the benefit of their memories. They listen attentively.

The formal part of the meeting ended, the men chat while the women clear away the food. Gloria and the disrupter kiss and make up. He is calm now but his features are drawn, his eyes red-rimmed. Has he lain awake these last few nights haunted by the nightmare years, by images of his parents led away from the selection lines, stripped naked, choking in the gas chambers? Why did he live and they die? Does he, like Primo Levi, believe that 'the worst of us survived'? During these sleepless hours has he tried again to make sense of the inexplicable, to come to terms with the unacceptable, repressing a rage that has found its release today? Maybe he is over-emotional at the best of times, or maybe I have seen a man literally mad with grief.

Before we part, Motek Mysch asks me how I liked the meeting. I give him a non-committal reply and he tactfully refrains from pursuing the subject. I come away despondent, feeling trapped in my Englishness, an outsider, an alien, denied yet again the elusive joy of belonging.

25

IN AMERICA he is Morton. To his fellow workers in the rag trade he was Mort. To his friends from Konin he is still Motek. In his youth he was a gymnast, something of a rarity in a community whose cultural tradition valued brain over brawn. Today, at seventy-seven, after two heart-attacks and a bypass operation, he confines his gymnastics to daily work-outs on an exercise bike and rowing machine. Motek Mysch has angina and circulation problems but deflects talk about ailments: he comes of a stoical breed. Outwardly, he looks fit and has kept his trim, upright figure. In character he retains the attributes that made him one of the best-liked young men in Konin. Someone described him to me as 'Mister Konin – the finest of the Koniners'. 'To us as young children,' recalls Koniner Henry Kaye, 'he was a hero.'

His American passport states his age as seventy-eight, perpetuating a bureaucratic error made in Tsarist times. The registrar in Konin entered his date of birth as the impossible 31 February 1910.[1] Years later, when Motek tried to get the date amended to 3 March, he was told that for administrative reasons this would not be possible. Instead they changed it to 3 March 1909. To argue with Polish bureaucrats, says Motek, was to waste one's breath. Long ago he grew resigned to being a year older than he really is.

He was fourteen when he left school in 1924 to join his father and brothers in the family business. A sign outside the small shop in Third of May Street depicted a dandyish figure in black coat and top-hat. Motek's father, Isaac, was a bespoke tailor whose craftsmanship and figure-flattering skills attracted the custom of Polish officers as well as Jews. The workshop, filled with the warmth of charcoal-heated flatirons and the smell of freshly pressed cloth, adjoined the family apartment.

Motek spent what little free time he had on developing his prowess as a gymnast. His was the first generation in Konin to benefit from a new and radical Jewish attitude to physical exercise. Zionism, with the most practical of motives, had made muscular development a desirable thing for young Jews who dreamed of starting life afresh as pioneers. They dreamed of going to Eretz Yisrael not to sit cross-legged at a tailor's bench but to make the desert bloom: to sow rather than sew. Working the land required a sturdy body. Physicality thus acquired a value it had been denied before, nationalistic rather than religious, Jewish if not kosher. When young athletes from different countries staged a gymnastics display at the Fourth Zionist Congress in Basle in 1903, there was no mistaking the message they were sending to ghetto youth.

The message filtered through to Konin, where Motek began his physical education at the age of seven under Mr Goldberg, an insurance agent who worked part-time as an instructor in the town's recently formed Maccabi Club. In 1917, not long after Motek joined, the first parallel bars arrived from Germany, creating a buzz of excitement. He was keen on soccer too. His first football was home-made, created from *shmattes* (rags) off the workshop floor. At seventeen he was the only Jew in Konin to possess a pair of genuine soccer boots with studs.

By the time he left Konin for military service at the end of the 1920s, he had become an accomplished all-round sportsman and athlete. With his fair hair, light skin, pale eyes and perfectly coordinated body, he disconcerted his army NCOs by not conforming to the stereotyped image of the Jew, a general image not altogether undeserved – as Motek concedes – where sporting activity was concerned.

'When I was a recruit the corporal took us over to the parallel bars and explained what they were for. He pushed himself up, down, up, down, and asked the first young man to do the same thing. Then it came to my turn. I walk over and I start to do somersaults and scissors – you swing, you cross your legs, you fall down on the bars, turn over, swing again, scissors again, turn over – then I jumped down on the ground. The corporal was furious. He came over to me and said: "I didn't ask you to do this!" I suppose it was a humiliation for him.'

Motek became a high-scoring player in his army unit's soccer and basketball teams. 'One day, when we were playing a match and my face was burned from the sun, the major asked: "Who's that guy with the red face?" "He's Jewish," they said. He called me over and gave me a cigarette. You know what this means in Poland? A cigarette! From a major! It was like I would get a medal.' One of his sergeants was a devout believe in punishment by press-ups. Motek crouches down on the carpet, kicks his legs out behind him and proves that his muscles have not deserted him.

Home on leave, he became a voluntary, unpaid instructor in the youth section of Po'alei Zion, the Zionist socialist workers' organization to which he now belonged. Throughout the Thirties he taught young Jews to excel at activities that would once have branded them as *shkotsim* (coarse, uneducated gentiles). 'We had boys of twelve or thirteen who walked with bent shoulders, and in one year they were straightened.' A few days after this conversation I met one of his former pupils in Manhattan, now an old man, but with a back, like Motek's, as straight as a rod.

Politics and politicking, argument and debate Motek left to others. 'I was interested in gymnastics and sport. This was my life.' His enthusiasm bubbles up when he recalls those times: playing in the soccer team, encouraging weedy young tailors to toughen their sinews, gain physical self-confidence, perform acrobatic feats on the bars, leap onto one another's shoulders to form a three-tiered pyramid.

Twice a year Po'alei Zion hired Staszinski's theatre near the river and put on a fund-raising display of gymnastics and dancing. Gymnastics were for males; the girls joined in the dancing. The show included Swedish gymnastics – 'all done with the arms,' explains Motek, 'sometimes holding wooden clubs.' He demonstrates, raising his arms above his head, swinging them slowly first to one side, then up again. His movements still have the graceful flow of a ballet dancer.

He recalls the show-stopping moment when the lights in the theatre were switched off and the gymnasts, each holding an electric torch, wove patterns in the dark. The audience oohed and aahed as if watching fireworks bursting in the sky. Then the grand finale: the performers zigzagged about the darkened stage, finally coming to rest in the shape of an illuminated Star of David. The show was a sensation. The young Zionists took it to Kalisz, Kolo and other nearby towns. The proceeds went to help hard-up young Koniners go to Palestine. After each performance the seats were cleared away, a live orchestra started up, and dancing went on until six or seven in the morning. 'It was a good life,' says Motek.

Has he perhaps forgotten the bad times? 'I'll tell you something. Bad things I remember very well, but even with the bad times it was a happy life. Happy because we got together and enjoyed ourselves. There was a lot of activity. I cannot remember that I should be bored, have nothing to do. In some ways I think I had a better youth than my son in Brooklyn.'

Konin, he claims, had some special quality. 'We were more emancipated than many others in Poland because we were near Germany.' He and his friends had a freer rein than many of their contemporaries in *shtetlekh* where religion and tradition kept a tight grip on daily life. In Konin there was an intellectual liveliness in the air, a reaching out for new ideas, a thirst for secular knowledge. While the older generation studied in the *bes-medresh*, the youth performed Ibsen. 'We had a reputation as a community for our intelligent youth. We produced a nice few doctors and lawyers, teachers and students. We had a much better Jewish library than Kalisz and yet Kalisz was a much bigger town.'

> Poverty was a problem. People managed but it was a big problem. My father was a good tailor. He was working on a suit maybe three or four days. The busiest time was before Passover when people wanted new coats and suits, but he didn't get the money from the customers straightaway, and after the holidays they came and said that this doesn't fit right and this doesn't fit right, and he had to wait for the money. So he had to go out and get a loan from the Jewish bank. I remember a neighbour once saying to my father after Passover: 'Itshe, did you have plenty of work for Passover?' and he replied (ironically): 'I had so much work I didn't have time to go and get a loan.' We had credit with the food stores, so we took home the food until my father was paid. Some customers paid him

with a *veksl* [promissory note drawn on a bank] and when, in say four weeks' time, the customer didn't have the money to pay the bank, the man had to extend the loan and pay more interest.

In 1904 my father had to run away from Konin because of a strike by the tailoring workers. They wanted to cut the working hours which I think were twelve to fifteen hours a day. My father was a boss at that time and chairman of the Konin Handworkers' Union [*Handwerkerverein*], which was a union of the bosses. He was against the strike. The workers belonged to the Needle Union [*Nodlverein*].

One Saturday my father went out with my mother for a walk along the Slupca street to Czarkow. People used to go for a walk out of town on a Saturday afternoon. While they were walking, a few guys – *undzere menshen* [our people, namely, Jews] – came over to him with sticks and grabbed hold of him. They said to him: 'If you don't agree with the strike we're going to kill you.' My father was prepared. He knew there might be trouble and he had a *kanchik* which the *cheder* teachers used. He took it out and they began to fight. Later he got some information – that if he did not leave Konin they were going to kill him. That same Saturday night he left Konin and went to America, leaving a wife and four children. I think the strikers won but I'm not sure – it was before I was born. My father came back in 1907. He would have stayed in America but he did not want to work on Saturdays.

I met here once a man who used to work for my father in Konin around 1910. He said the workers were sometimes there until ten at night. I remember when I was a young boy, mothers and wives used to come with a piece of herring and two slices of bread at about four in the afternoon and hand them in, and the workers ate while they were working.

There were good times when my father had six, eight people working for him. They were usually paid on Friday. On Thursday, the wife of one of the workers used to come and stay under the window because she needed money. The bosses and the workers – *both* sides – had a bad deal: this is how I see it now. I can't talk for the wife of that worker. I can only talk for myself, and for me it was a hard life but a happy life. We were close together. Compared with how we live in America we were poor, but I enjoyed my poor life in Konin very much.

A year or so before the war, Motek married a girl from Kolo and had a daughter. Mother and child were early victims of the Nazis. Motek fled to the Soviet Union and endured the rigours of a Siberian labour camp. With no family left alive in Poland after the war, he joined two brothers who had long settled in America. He earned his first wages in a garment factory, sitting at an electric sewing-machine, underpaid and overworked. In the world of mass production, his skills as a craft tailor counted for nothing. To escape from the assembly line, he switched to tailoring repairs, took part-time courses in cutting and design, gained two certificates, and ended up as a designer-cutter in a garment factory where the money was good but the pressure relentless. He and his wife Sonia, whom he met in the Soviet Union, were able to give their son and daughter a good start in life. In 1974 he had two heart attacks and had to give up his job.

Home is a modern terraced house on a main road in a residential area of Brooklyn. Seaview Avenue has lost its view, hidden by buildings across the road. Beyond them lies Jamaica Bay and the Atlantic. The neighbourhood has a characterless suburban propriety and is predominantly Jewish. Dr Fred Zatz has his dental surgery a few doors away.

Motek's home is modest compared with some I have visited. It is clean and comfortable, but has no swag curtains or crystal chandelier. A faded washable plastic cloth covers the small kitchen table where we eat. It is the home of people who were never keen on conspicuous display and now are too old to care about replacing and renewing.

Sonia suffers from Parkinson's disease and only superhuman effort enables her to cling to a near-normal daily existence. No bigger than a slightly enlarged elf, she is so frail that one fears a breeze could blow her away. Their ancient miniature French poodle, Ernie, is almost weightless himself, and constantly at risk of being crushed to death. Ernie, says Motek with just the faintest hint of a smile, is their 'votchdog'.

While Motek and I sit and talk, Sonia pads around silently, often entering the room without my hearing her. Occasionally she says something to me in a whisper so soft that I fail to catch her words. It takes a while to discern the bright mind still functioning within this alarmingly fragile frame. One day, when she is out of earshot, Motek tells me she is a highly educated woman and was once a teacher. In her younger days she was athletic, a wonderful swimmer, a good dancer, and a keen cyclist who used to hurl herself downhill at great speed. Now many of the domestic chores fall on Motek. Both insist on feeding me the minute I appear, whatever the time of day, pressing food on me as though I have just emerged from a refugee camp. Motek brushes aside my 'Please don't go to any trouble' with 'I am from Konin. It's no trouble.'

One day Motek and I are talking at the kitchen table while Sonia, a few feet away, prepares the Friday evening dinner, which they have insisted I stay for. She goes over to the fridge, loses her balance and crashes to the floor. She lies spreadeagled like a rag doll, staring up at us with wide, frightened eyes. As we help her to her feet she whispers again and again: 'I'm all right, I'm all right.' Once she is steady again, we carry on as if nothing has happened. Motek's face is expressionless, but behind the eyes . . .

A few minutes later there is another mishap. A colander filled with freshly cooked *lokshen* has just dropped from Sonia's hand, strewing the contents onto a shag rug and across the floor. Again we rush over, and while Motek picks her up I gather the wet noodles, slippery as eels, and drop them into the pedal bin. None of us says anything. Motek and I resume our chat, but for the next few minutes his mind is elsewhere.

There are no *shabbes* candles. Though he still belongs to a synagogue, the Shoah destroyed any religious faith he might have had. But the meal remains traditional: gefilte fish with horseradish sauce accompanied by Manishewfitz's 'specially sweetened' blackberry wine, which a *sommelier* might question as the ideal accompaniment for gefilte fish. The next course is *lokshen* soup without the *lokshen*. In Konin, says Motek, his mother used to start making the *shabbes lokshen* at noon on Thursday. 'My mother's soup had a layer of fat and she always made sure my father got the first helping with the most fat.' Sonia serves us roast chicken and broccoli and, like any good Jewish mother, coaxes me to have seconds. When I decline, she quotes a Yiddish saying: '*Koyekh ligt in der shisl*' – Strength comes from the cooking pot.

26

MOTEK AGREES, when pressed, that the situation of the Jews in Konin changed for the worse in the course of the 1930s.

We in the Zionist youth weren't afraid of the anti-Semites. Once a group of students from Poznan came on a Friday. Four or five of them were standing in the corner of the Tepper Marik where all the Jews have to go to the *shul* and *bes-medresh*. They tried to grab every Jew that passed and were trying to cut off his beard.

We lived quite a long way from there. A boy called Kawalek came to the house and he says: 'Motek, some hoodlums have come from Poznan to beat up Jews.' I went there and the students had already got a beating. We had some good boys there, one of them a baker, a very strong guy, and he beat them up, all of them, so much they were almost crippled. When I got there I helped also a bit but it was already over. The police sent us tickets that we broke the quiet of the city, that we caused a disturbance. Can you imagine? A few of us were in prison in Konin, three or four days. On the floor were a few sacks of straw for sleeping. It was no shame for my family – I didn't steal.

In the last years it was very, very bad. Once I had to run away from the town. One day, all of a sudden my father comes in where we are working and says: 'They're standing outside and won't let in even one customer.' There was an anti-Semitic organization – boys of sixteen or seventeen – and they were standing outside the shop and they wouldn't let anyone in: 'Don't buy from Jews.' My father said: 'It's already three o'clock and I have to pay for merchandise and I've not taken a penny.'

So I walked out and I see one of the boys. His grandfather rented a garden at the back of our house, so I know him. I say: 'What you doing here? Why are you doing this?' He said: 'We don't let our people go into the Jews.' So I hit him, and he start to scream and to yell. They all yelled – 'A Jew has killed a *goy*.' They start to come in, maybe fifty people, so I went to the back, and after this a policeman came, who had a good relationship with my father. He said: 'Tell your son he should leave Konin.' That's what I did. Through the back yard I ran to the fields, to the train, went to Kolo, and I was staying there maybe over a week until things quietened down.

Once I went home late at night with my friend Kott. I said goodbye to him and walked on my own to our house a few yards further on. All of a sudden a young cripple with a stick came from behind me – he was with somebody else – and hit me a blow with a stick. He took me by surprise. I walked into the house and later on I thought: 'I will catch you.' Next morning I am going through the town to buy some trimmings and I meet him. I say: 'Hey Stefan, why did you hit me yesterday?' He said: 'Because you are a Jew.' He had a bad leg but he could run fast. Eventually, I caught him and gave it to him.

Another time, also around 1935, Kott and I were going home, and the same Polack came from behind and stuck a knife in the back of Kott's leg. We took him to the doctor who sewed him up. He was in hospital for a few days. I didn't go after him this time. If I had started with him, all the Polacks in the town would go mad. Kott wanted to sue him but people said, No, don't. The judge is a Polack, you won't win. This was life in Poland at that time.

27

The anti-Semitic boycott of the Thirties duplicated that of two decades earlier. The same extremist forces, now grown in power, and inspired by the victory of fascism in Nazi Germany, brought their anti-Semitic slogans to Konin. *Endecja* thugs gathered outside Jewish shops and businesses, blocking their doorways and handing out anti-Semitic leaflets. The message they preached to the peasants, the unemployed and other disgruntled citizens of an agriculturally and industrially backward country was clear: the Jew was the cause of all their ills. The government in Warsaw showed no inclination to clamp down on the agitators. On the contrary, it embraced the anti-Semitism that was boosting its right wing extremist opponents' popularity.

After the First World War, the constitution of independent Poland granted Jews the equal rights they had been denied under the Tsars. In fact, though, discriminatory practices and restrictions continued and were to characterize the whole interwar period. By the time Jozef Pilsudski, the leader of Polish independence, died in 1935 (in Konin the Jewish population went through the motions of officially mourning a man who, in the end, had done nothing to curb their enemies), any Jewish hopes once vested in him had long faded.

Changes in local government boundaries in 1938 came as a special blow to Konin Jewry, transferring them from the administrative jurisdiction of the province of Lodz to that of Poznan, where the *Endecja* held greater sway. One of the first effects was to make the local slaughtering of kosher meat illegal. Sometimes the meat brought in from outside the province during the summer months was putrid by the time it reached Konin.

Despite all this, communal life during these years continued with an outward semblance of normality. The whirl of social activity, if anything, intensified: political meetings, lectures, fund-raising, Zionist youth gatherings, athletics, balls, amateur drama productions . . . Feeling increasingly alienated from the gentile world, the Jews huddled closer together for comradeship and safety. Zionists brought renewed ardour to their hopes for a Jewish Homeland. Members of the rightwing Zionist youth movement, Betar, put on their brown military-style uniforms and did marching exercises, seeking self-esteem through discipline and self-defence. The religious prayed. Only Jewish Communists, who constituted a small minority of the community, joined forces with Christians to form clandestine cells, distribute counter-propaganda, and plan May Day demonstrations, during which they were invariably arrested. It became established custom for the police to put the ringleaders in jail a few days *before* May Day.

Of some comfort to the Jews of Konin was the knowledge that most of the boycott organizers were outsiders, students from Poznan, who did not have the full support of the local population. Some Polish customers slipped into Jewish shops through the back door. Others shrugged off the troublemakers as a passing phase. There were liberal and radical Poles, mostly from the ranks of the intelligentsia, who sympathized with the Jewish plight. They were the one section of Polish society that was philo-Semitic. They knew it was not just the Jews who were in danger but democracy itself and, ultimately, their own liberty.

Though the Jewish population of Konin had little cause to fear for their lives at this time, they heard of violent anti-Semitic outbreaks elsewhere in Poland. They saw Jewish stalls overturned in small towns near Konin. The possibility of a pogrom – that ugly word branded on the Jewish psyche – could no longer be dismissed out of hand, unlikely though it seemed in a town like Konin, where Polish-Jewish relations had for long been as good as anywhere in Poland. Christians and Jews had served together harmoniously on the town council. The wealthier, more Polonized Jews enjoyed genial business relationships with their gentile counterparts. There had been no slaughter of Jews in Konin since the mid-seventeenth century, though they came close to it two centuries later, as I discovered from a report in the *Jewish Chronicle*, published in London on 27 November 1842:

MALICIOUS CHARGE AGAINST THE JEWS OF SACRIFICING HUMAN BLOOD

FRONTIERS OF POLAND, *November* 10.

. . . A Christian girl of the town of Konin having disappeared, the report was industriously spread, that the child had been stolen and sacrificed by the Jews. A witness even came forward to state that he had seen a Jew on the previous evening carrying a sack on his back, from which he had perceived the legs of a human being suspended. The mob, hearing this, became fearfully excited and enraged. The Burgomaster, who unfortunately is not one of the most liberal-minded, sent for the Chief Rabbi [the Rabbi of Konin], and ordered him to have all the Jews of the town . . . (it was midnight) . . . assembled in the Synagogue, where he was solemnly to command them to give up the hapless sacrifice, or to detect and surrender the thief. The Chief Rabbi refused obedience, declaring that his co-religionists were incapable of such a horrid deed. Meanwhile, the streets became crowded with the furious mob, who were armed with sticks, pitch-forks and various instruments of destruction, swearing to be revenged on the Jews. Indeed, bloodshed would have been the immediate consequence, had not an officer, with thirty veterans armed with

> well-loaded muskets, hastened to the spot, and threatened to fire upon the mob if they perpetrated any act of violence. The effect of this threat, however, was but momentary. A very few minutes after, the lawless and numerous crowd, in defiance of the much smaller number of soldiery, prepared to fall upon the Jews and attack the military, when suddenly a peasant appeared in the scene of confusion, carrying a child in his arms, which he said he had found asleep on the common, and kept meanwhile under his roof till he found out the parents of the child. The resurrection of the (alleged) dead child put an end to the uproar. The Jews immediately sent estafettes [mounted couriers] to the authorities of Kalish and Warsaw, requesting investigation and satisfaction. Six of the ringleaders have been since arrested. It is hoped that the Burgomaster will be called upon to account for his, to say the least, strange conduct in this affair.

Every Koniner I meet invariably turns at some point to the subject of Polish anti-Semitism. 'The Poles take in anti-Semitism with their mother's milk' is one refrain I hear. 'It's in their blood' is another. The anti-Semitism they experienced from childhood onwards permanently soured their attitude to Poland. My mother, who left Konin as a teenager to live with her uncle and Konin-born aunt in Berlin, never forgot how differently the German Jews viewed their own country. Her cousin Siegfried, who was about her age, would sit at the piano every day and play the national anthem, '*Deutschland über alles*'. 'You see,' he would say to my mother, usually reducing her to tears, '*I* am entitled to play this because *I* am a German. You are not because you are an *Ostjudin*' – a Jewess from the East. Some years later, Siegfried received a beating from the Gestapo and fled penniless from Germany.

Few of the Koniners I speak to were not deeply scarred as children by constant, if not daily, experience of anti-Semitism and the familiar cry, 'Dirty Jew!' Polish has a thesaurus of abusive nicknames for Jews – *Zydek*, *Zydy*, *Zydowa*, *Zydziak*, *Zydlak* . . . 'How could we feel Polish if they never regarded us as Poles?' asked Koniner Herman Krol, who fought in the Polish army. ' "Jews, go to Palestine!" they shouted at us, and when the Jews wanted to go to Palestine, they didn't like that either. We weren't allowed to be civil servants or have a government job. We couldn't work on the railways, in banks or the post office. We were second-class citizens, and they expected us to love them?'

Cheder boys took it as a given that they would be ambushed and pelted with stones on their way home in the dark. Rivka Brum remembers her first day in the State secondary school during the Thirties: 'In my class were five Jewish girls and perhaps thirty-five Christians. Some of them refused to sit with us and called us "Yid, Yid." But the headmaster was a fine man. He sat me down next to the mayor's daughter.'

Ah, so it is not true that *all* Poles were anti-Semitic? Grudgingly, they agree, but add: 'There were few who weren't.' They relate the story of another teacher, a Catholic, who happened to be headmaster of the Jewish State primary school. Known for his habit of making anti-Semitic gibes in front of the children, one day he went too far and the pupils, aged between seven and eleven, marched out in protest and went on strike. A delegation of parents met the headmaster. He promised to exercise more restraint in the future, and the children called off the strike.

Jewish boys whose parents allowed them to play in the streets and toughen their muscles learned how to cope with enmity from the *goyim*. 'I gave as good as I got,' said Izzy Hahn, 'and they had respect for me.' Leib Kleczewski, the son of a tinsmith, told me: 'Whoever was scared got beaten. I wasn't scared, and I had Polish boys who were my friends. I remember the time when Shmulek Glowinski came back to Konin after training at an agricultural college. He was tough from working in the fields. A hooligan gave him some trouble so he picked him up and threw him through a barber's window.'

One Koniner gave me what she regarded as a typical example of Polish contempt for the Jews: 'If a Chasid went into a bank and tried to speak Polish, the Poles used to laugh in his face.' Without excusing such ridicule, one can understand why many Poles found it extraordinary that a people who had lived in Poland since the Middle Ages showed so little desire to learn its language. Until the First World War most Jewish boys received only a *cheder* education, speaking Yiddish in and out of class, mixing in a world where only Yiddish was spoken. As adults they acquired enough Polish for everyday transactions in the marketplace. This shut them off not only from Poles but from those fellow Jews who had received a secular education.

Girls, less cloistered in their education, could communicate more easily with the gentile world. My mother spoke an educated Polish and developed an enduring love for Polish literature, while my father spoke the language awkwardly and felt no affection for Poland. In many Konin homes the daughters spoke Polish while their brothers spoke Yiddish. The Koniners I meet are mostly men and women who attended Polish State schools in the Thirties. They spoke Polish among themselves, Yiddish with their parents.

Jewish parents discouraged their children from forming friendships with Polish children. 'My father would not let me bring *shikses* into the house,' one woman remembers, 'and he would not let me go to their homes in case I ate *treyf* [non-kosher food].' Socializing between unmarried Jews and Christians of the opposite sex was taboo. 'If a boy went out with a *shikse*, everyone in the town knew about it,' Mike Jacobs recalled. That way lay intermarriage, social ostracism and lasting parental shame. Thus Jewish apartheid, which began with compulsory segregation in the medieval ghetto, persisted not solely as a result of Christian prejudice but through choice. Ethnic exclusivity was a means of preserving the species.

Religion was the supreme divider. Catholics inherited the age-old stereotype of the Jew as Christ-killer. This instilled in Jews a visceral fear of the Church that continued long after Jews stopped being tortured on the rack. Natan Biezunski told me: 'I remember like today the Catholics went in processions to holy places and through the villages with banners and holy statues, and when we saw them we ran away as though from a fire. When I walked past a church and smelt incense I felt frightened.' That was a recollection from Konin in the 1920s. Jozef Lewandowski, recalling his Konin boyhood between the wars, writes: 'The readiness to beat Jews was directly proportional to piety. Perhaps beating passed for a religious duty . . . when Corpus Christi day was celebrated, no Jew dared to appear in the street. It was the same on Good Friday and even on Sunday during High Mass.'[1]

There is a terrible sadness about the words of the Polish-Jewish writer, Adolf Rudnicki, when he asks: 'How was it possible to live together for a thousand years and know nothing about one another? Nothing.' To which the sociologist, Zygmunt Bauman, has recently added: 'Poles and Jews did not live *together* but beside each other . . . While histories intertwined, life-worlds stayed hermetically sealed.'[2]

When Christian and Jew did try to break down the barriers that separated them, the outcome was not always a happy one, as Jozef Lewandowski, relates. Around 1934 his father, an upholsterer in Konin, went into partnership with a Polish upholsterer, his friend Mr Boguslawski:

> . . . the worthy gentlemen failed to take account of social considerations. Father became unacceptable to the Orthodox Jews, Boguslawski non-kosher to some of his Catholic customers. Both went beyond the limits imposed by unwritten but harshly binding statues. Rich folk such as landowners and industrialists could join forces, but not the poor masses. After a few years they split up.'[3]

Responding to the argument that Jews who chose to dress in alien garb, follow peculiar customs and speak a foreign language could hardly blame the Poles for regarding them as aliens, my Koniners point to the fate of German Jews and the discrimination directed at totally assimilated Polish Jews like Leopold Infeld. I asked one university-educated Koniner who served as an officer in the Polish army if he thought the Jews could ever have been accepted as equals, however hard they tried. His reply was a despondent 'No!'

What ultimately reinforced the anti-Polish feelings of the majority of the survivors was the Shoah. To quote historian Antony Polonsky: 'Far from healing the divisions between Poles and Jews, the Nazi Holocaust, carried out as it was largely on Polish soil, considerably strengthened those barriers of suspicion, fear and even hatred between the two communities which had already begun to grow alarmingly in the last years before the outbreak of the war.'[4]

More Jews could have been saved, insist many of the survivors I meet, if the Poles had not been so incorrigibly anti-Semitic. They rarely mention that Poland was the sole country in occupied Europe where the penalty for helping or even trading with a Jew was summary execution together with your family. They do not speak of *Zegota*, the organization set up by the Polish underground to aid Jews.[5] They do acknowledge that there were brave Poles, over four thousand of whom are honoured in Yad Vashem in Jerusalem for risking or giving their lives to save Jews. But they cannot overcome the trauma of the anti-Semitism that was part of their everyday life before the war.

The compilers of the Memorial Book did not omit to acknowledge the courage of several Poles who helped the Jews during the war, including the priest who comforted Jewish deportees expelled to villages outside Konin in the summer of 1940. Driven out of their homes at short notice, they arrived exhausted and frightened.

> One ought to emphasize the help we received from the priest of Grodziec, who occupied himself with handing out coffee and tea to us, and distributing milk to the children and the sick. Until late into the night there were warm kettles in the square. Bread was also given out. Besides that, the priest went around appealing to the peasants to give accommodation to the deportees, and help to the homeless. He had recently lost a brother in a concentration camp, and he knew that he himself was also in danger. The Germans sought an opportunity to arrest him and this happened after he helped he Jews in Grodziec. Soon afterwards came news of his death.[6]

I have talked to Koniners who feel it is time to end mutual recrimination, who desist from wholesale condemnation of the nation that allowed Jews to create a great and unique culture of their own. Some of them, though far from affluent themselves, sent food and clothing parcels to Polish friends in Konin during the time of severe shortages after the Second World War. Sometimes, when I hear them recalling scenes from their childhood – skating on the frozen Warta, swimming in the summer, gathering mushrooms and wild berries, picnicking by the meadow and stream or in the stillness of the forests – it occurs to me that they retain more affection for Poland than they would care to admit.

For most, the knowledge of how that life in Poland came to an end is too tragic for nostalgia. Those who served in the Polish army during the war cannot forget the anti-Semitism they encountered even when Jew and Pole were fighting a common foe. One woman who served with the Polish army in Britain told me she could still hear the words of the priest giving a lecture to the troops: 'When the war is won and we return home, we shall finish off the Jews.'

28

MOTEK MYSCH keeps the Konin Society's membership records, a set of file cards covered with faded handwriting, in an old cigar-box. Other records – minutes of meetings, accounts, correspondence and so forth – must surely have accumulated in the course of so many years, but whenever I raise this with him, he looks vague. Today he has something to show me. I follow him down a flight of narrow stairs to the low-ceilinged basement, divided into two rooms. The rear room is crammed with lumber and the detritus of an abandoned lifestyle: an outmoded record-player rests on what was once a bar. He and Sonia held parties down here when they were younger. I notice a brass plaque presented to Motek from the Konin Society in recognition of his services as President.

The front room, windowless and starkly lit, has two ancient sewing-machines, racks of coloured bobbins, a tailor's dummy and work-bench. Cardboard cutting patterns hang from a spike. Tissue-paper patterns fill an old cabinet. This is where Motek worked as a freelance after ill health made him give up his full-time job nearly fifteen years ago. At the far end of the room stands a boiler, a washing-machine and an old chest of drawers. One of the drawers is half open, revealing a cat curled up fast asleep on a blanket.

Motek shows me one of his fashion drawings, one of the most successful 'lines' he ever designed, a leather coat edged with fur. 'They called it the bar mitzvah coat.' Because women bought it to wear at bar mitzvahs? 'No, because it was running for thirteen years.' We laugh.

He opens a black briefcase busting with Konin Society files and papers he has not touched for years: letters from the Memorial Book committee in Israel, receipts, invitations to the annual memorial service in New York, drafts of some of his speeches, lists of Koniners long dead . . . Absorbed in this, I am unaware of Sonia's presence in the room until I hear her behind me struggling with a can-opener. I help her open two cans of pet food, one for Ernie the votchdog, one for the cat, who suddenly leaps out of the drawer.

Motek produces a Polish letter he received from Konin in 1968, from the last Jew left in Konin after the war, Magdalena Leszczynska, known by her Polish diminutive, Madzia. She came from the family who owned the largest flour mill in the town. The man who had introduced steam power into the mill, and been murdered as a consequence, was one of her relations. Madzia was one of Leopold Infeld's pupils at the Jewish gymnasium, the only one he found alive and living in the town when he made that brief return visit in 1963. She was the woman, unnamed in his essay, who asked him – as her former headmaster – to certify that she had passed her *Matura* examination. Madzia's husband died in the Warsaw ghetto. She and her young daughter, passing as gentiles, survived, returned to Konin in 1945 and stayed on.

The following is a translation of Madzia's letter to Motek Mysch:

12 December 1968

Dear Sir

I must ask a great favour of you. I have heard that you are a leader of the Konin townsfolk. I am in a very bad financial situation and absolutely cannot manage. I cannot help myself any longer. I am very ill with a heart condition and I am getting old. I know that your organization sends quite a lot of money to people, but we too need help. I am asking for help on a regular basis if it is possible, and if you will listen to my cry for help. If you are prepared to take this on, the money could be sent to me through PKO [a Polish bank]. Mr Jakubowicz [a Koniner living in America, who had recently visited Konin and made contact with her] could give you more information about me. He is in constant touch with me. If you ever knew me, you will understand that I am the sort of person who is used to giving, and that writing this letter causes me a lot of pain. But what can I do? I am forced to ask for help from my friends be they near or far. I would be very grateful if you would be kind enough to reply. With regards to everyone from Konin.

M. Leszczynska

Did the Society help her? No, replies Motek. A leading member opposed the idea, arguing that Leszczynska had married a Christian and converted to Christianity. So far as Motek knows, this is true. Other members felt that asking for what amounted to a regular pension verged on the *chutzpedik* (impudent). Koniners in New

York who had been destitute after the war remembered that Madzia Leszczynska took over her uncle's ironmongery business when she went back to Konin in 1945; now she was taking it for granted that the survivors in America were awash with money. Her alleged conversion to Christianity was almost certainly what hardened their hearts against her. I suspect that class enmity may have been a factor too. Before the war, Madzia had belonged to the upper stratum of Konin society, educated, privileged, mixing in social circles where Yiddish was not spoken. For the members of the Konin Society, coming from more humble backgrounds, this may have been an unconscious cause of resentment.

Motek sent Madzia a few dollars in his own name. One or two others did the same, including the Koniner most opposed to Madzia's petition. There was no further contact with Madzia, who died some years later. Motek feels contrite about it now. He is sorry they rejected her plea.

He forages around to find the Charter of the Konin Ladies' and Men's Society, Inc., dusty and stained inside a battered frame. Before I leave, he places a sheet of paper on the work table, a diagram showing the layout of the burial plots reserved by the Konin Society in a cemetery in Flushing, New York. Some of the old-timers he wishes I had met are buried there. There are six graves still awaiting occupancy. He has bought two, for himself and Sonia.

29

THE AMERICAN writer and satirist George Axelrod once said he would rather know what Caesar used for toilet paper than how he won the Gallic wars. Koniners are taken aback when I ask about their lavatories. Motek Mysch provides the following description:

> At the back of the house there was a wooden shed with seven toilets. You went up three steps at the end of the shed and past a row of seven doors. Six of them had locks and each family had their own key. We shared our toilet with two other families. One door did not have a lock and was open – sometimes you had an

emergency! The shed was away from the house so you had to walk about fifty yards every time you needed to go.

When it came to cleaning, every family had to do it – wipe the wooden seat and so on. The seat was on top of a kind of wooden box. Underneath was a deep hole in the ground. Everything from the seven toilets went into the same hole. Late on Friday night a Polish peasant with a horse and cart came along. There was an opening in the ground outside the shed. They used a long pole with a bucket on the end to get everything out – there was a big smell. They poured it into a tank on the back of the cart and took it to the farmers who used it as manure, so they took it away for nothing.

Everybody had to bring their own paper. We used newspaper which we cut into pieces. If I wanted some, I used to go to my father – he was in charge. He always kept two or three pieces in his back pocket. We'd say in Yiddish: '*Gib mir a shtik papir*' – Give me a piece of paper. Maybe rich families had special paper but I don't remember ever seeing it. Even newspaper was a problem.

These were the sanitary arrangements in Motek Mysch's home in Third of May Street before the Second World War. They were typical of those that prevailed throughout the town in the Twenties and Thirties. My mother would recall, always with a shudder, the revulsion she felt as a small girl when, lying in bed, she heard the nightsoil man in the yard going about his evil-smelling work. Here is one of her memories as used by a novelist in a book set partly in a Polish *shtetl*:

There was the man who came, mysteriously, in the night, every month or so, to empty their earth closet, the little shed screened by bushes, which stood in the corner of the tiny yard by the side of the house.

No one ever talked about him, the nightsoil man with his horse and creaking cart. He came when they were all supposed to be asleep and it was proper to behave as though he did not exist. But sometimes, waking, Leah heard weird noises – scrapings, and thuds and once a muffled curse – and she longed, sick with fright, to know more. To see him. Hirshl told her once that the man also skinned dead animals: horses and dogs, and she wondered horrified, whether he came to their yard with his hands dripping the blood

> of dead dogs; were his clothes made of many skins sewn together with the guts of disembowelled cats?[1]

Mike Jacobs, who lived on the Tepper Marik, gives me a boyhood memory of the Thirties:

> I remember the stink when they came ten o'clock at night to empty the outhouses, a man and a horse. You could smell it a mile off. The outhouses at the back of our house had plenty of rats. I remember my brother used to take a brick and throw it and kill them. You could see two or three at one time, that's why we had so many cats. The rats – grey rats – were inside the pit; you could lift up the boards and see them crawling around. They walked along the roof of the outhouse during the day. We used to stuff bottles in the rat holes. My uncle lived close by and I used to go and use his place because it was cleaner and there were no rats.

Lavatorial visits stayed in Leopold Infeld's memory too: 'Our outhouse was about 220 yards from the house. I still remember my visits there at night with a candle in my hand and despair in my heart.'[2]

The reek of human excreta rose to a peak in the heat of summer. In winter you had to trek across the yard in rain or snow, in biting winds and arctic temperatures – not ideal conditions for lowering one's exposed flesh onto an icy seat. One man had a special seat of his own, upholstered and jealously guarded. He took it with him each time he went, looped over his arm like a giant bagel. My aunt, Freda Ryczke, told me: 'As he walked through the kitchen on his way out to the yard, people would laugh and say: "Ah, there goes Hirsh with his crapping machine."'

Most people were made of sterner stuff and, knowing no different, became hardened to conditions we would find insufferable. For all that, even the young and healthy could not have relished leaving the comfort of a warm stove or a quilt-covered bed when nature called. For those living in upstairs apartments, it meant going down unlit flights of wooden steps before stepping out into the cold: too much for young children, the sick and elderly. For them the *nakht*-top, the night pot, and the commode came into their own. When morning came, the able-bodied – or the maid if there was one – carried out the capacious chamber pots brimming with their saffron broth. In genteel homes a piece of cardboard served as a lid.

My mother, a woman of great fastidiousness, gave me an early potty training with questionable effect on my psychological development. The sight of crumbs on a tablecloth would offend her as they do me. Other women's children were allowed to have messy faces when they ate jam buns; the merest speck would be instantly wiped from my lips. Her attitude to bodily functions was inhibited and 'refined'. Unlike her siblings, she had been accustomed to modern sanitation since her adolescent years in Berlin. She had long taken the flush loo in our well-appointed London home for granted. When she visited Konin in the Thirties, the malodorous and not so private privies, which she had not experienced since her early teens, must have revived her childish horror of the nightsoil man. How did she refrain from retching? I can only guess. Her handbag was never without a bottle of Yardley's English lavender water. She also carried with her a neatly folded, daintily embroidered handkerchief. These two items were surely her survival kit. I see her approaching the outhouse, handkerchief pressed to her nose like a medieval prelate with a pomander proceeding through the smelly populace.

Joe Fox, who had left Konin before the First World War, accompanied my mother on her visit there in 1937. 'I wasn't used to it any more. I was there two days, and I didn't eat because I didn't want to use the lavatory. I waited until I got to Germany.'

Motek Mysch could not remember ever seeing a roll or packet of toilet paper in Konin. Nor could any of the other Koniners I have spoken to. Even the squire's son recalled squares of newspaper hanging in their superior privy. Or as another Koniner remarked: We always had the news on our *tukhes*' (bottom). Given all this, it seems likely that my mother's handbag survival kit included a third item: several sheets of interleaved Bronco lavatory paper brought from England.

Jack Offenbach went back to see his family several times between the wars. The white suit he wore is still remembered today. He stayed with his mother and relatives but refused to use their thunderbox. His way of dealing with the problem was rather more expensive and time-consuming than my mother's. Every morning he hired Izzy Hahn's uncle, Szwiatowicz, the droshky driver, to take him over the bridge and across the meadows to the one place in Konin that could boast a flush toilet: Konin's railway station at Czarkow.

Shtetl Jews, remembering that the Kaiser often attended State ceremonies mounted on a white horse, used to quote a Yiddish saying when they headed for the lavatory: 'I am going where even the Kaiser has to go on foot.' Not Jack Offenbach. He went by horse. His fellow Jews, seeing the droshky roll by at the same time each morning with its white-suited passenger, must have thought back to the penniless lad who left Konin with a one-way ticket to London in his pocket. Now he could afford to take a carriage to the station every day just to have a shit. What greater sign of affluence could there be?

30

A FAMILIAR bearded figure makes his daily rounds of Konin, shoulders bowed by the heavy churns he carries from house to house: Aryeh-Leib Witkowski the milkman – just Aryeh-Leib to his fellow Jews, who liked to conjoin Hebrew and Yiddish names. *Aryeh* (Hebrew) and *leib* (Yiddish) both mean lion. Yet Lion-Lion was no lion, except, possibly, in his moral strength, He is remembered as a quiet, honest man, who 'trusted everyone and as a result was often exploited'.[1] He was the part-time beadle of one of Konin's many small congregations, a God-fearing man, unaggressive, underprivileged, the archetypal *posheter Yid* – a simple, decent Jew – who went unregarded on this earth and achieved immortality in the works of Yiddish writers such as Peretz and Sholem Aleichem. Aryeh-Leib and the more famous milkman, Tevye, are close cousins.

Aryeh-Leib was born around the end of the 1850s. As a young man he worked as a labourer in Burzinsky's store in the Tepper Marik, unloading back-breaking crates of glassware. Tall and active, he served his apprenticeship in what was to be a lifelong career: shlepping. Not his sole career however. In 1880 he married a local girl, Hendl, and soon realized, as did many others, that one job was not enough to support a wife and family. Survival demanded versatility.

Aryeh-Leib's main sideline depended on well-off families finding suitable husbands for their daughters. A betrothal announcement was good news for Aryeh-Leib. It meant a wedding, which meant a celebration, which meant guests, which meant Aryeh-Leib had a job. In those days guests were not expected to make their own way to a wedding party. The bride's father provided them with transport in the form of a carriage, a coachman, and Aryeh-Leib.

On these occasions, seated next to the coachman, Aryeh-Leib underwent a transformation almost as splendid as Cinderella's. No longer the drably dressed market-square shlepper, he cut a stylish figure in black jacket, top-hat and white gloves. Joe Fox remembers Aryeh-Leib's 'black, glassy shoes which he rubbed with oil so they had a gloss like a mirror'. I suspect that the custom of collecting wedding guests in this fashion began with the rich German Jews who lived in Konin before the First World War and who knew – and perhaps liked to show they knew – the meaning of style.

When Aryeh-Leib participated in these *simchas*, his manner underwent a change too. He was not putting on an act – he was too straight a man for that. It was more the nature of his duties that wrought the change. As the host's representative, he was there to greet the guests at their front door, be their escort and attend to their comforts: spread out a travelling rug when it was cold, hold aloft a protective umbrella when it rained, and extend a white-gloved hand to the ladies when they stepped in and out of the carriage. He performed these duties with a natural grace.

When the guests were assembled and it was time to get down to the serious business of the evening, namely eating, Aryeh-Leib, still wearing his white gloves, assumed another role: that of waiter, helping to serve the wedding feast. Returning home in the early hours of the morning, richer by a few groshen, stomach comfortably full, he would put away his black jacket, top-hat and white gloves, fall into bed, and a few hours later be back at Burzinsky's, shlepping.

Some time after the First World War, Aryeh-Leib decided to shlep for himself. He became a milkman, rising every morning before dawn to walk into the countryside with his little cart and bring back milk. These journeys often took him to the

Kaplan farm. The squire's young sons sometimes stayed in Konin while their parents lived at Glinka, and at such times they would collect their weekly pocket-money from Aryeh-Leib, who would simply deduct it from what was owing to the squire for milk. From time to time he odd-jobbed as a glazier, and made wooden packing crates for people who were emigrating. Throughout these years, as he grew from youth into middle age, he carried on as Konin's one and only wedding guest escort.

Aryeh-Leib and his wife and five children shared two rooms in a street near the Tepper Marik. The three Witkowski sons and two daughters were noted for their exceptional intelligence. His eldest daughter graduated from the Jewish gymnasium and went on to Warsaw University. The other children educated themselves – brilliantly. One of these sons, Mendel, became the leader of the Bund in Konin, a town councillor and a member of the governing council of the *kehillah*. He enlisted his siblings as fellow ideologues and turned the Witkowski home into a Bundist cell. Arey-Leib's home became a party headquarters, political debating chamber and distribution centre for leftist books, manifestos and newspapers. The Bund, though legalized when Poland became independent, continued to come under the suspicious eye of the police. While the old milkman went uncomplainingly about his daily chores, his children campaigned for the rights of the working man.

Aryeh-Leib was in his early seventies when he died in 1932, followed shortly after by Hendl. Mikhail Moskowicz remembers him. He told me: 'He lent all his savings to someone he trusted and they never returned it. He was so upset he stopped eating, became ill and died.'

As a wedding guest escort, Aryeh-Leib had a predecessor[2] but no successor, and weddings were never the same without him. He kept going almost to the end, though with a certain falling off in style – the fault of the times rather than the man. Most of the old moneyed families had left the town. The grim economic scene after the First World War probably deterred those Jews who still had money from flaunting it in public. In any case, the spirit of the age was against him. Twentieth-century fashion was turning away from formality. At some point, impossible to date precisely, Aryeh-Leib discarded his black jacket and top-hat. But he still turned out with a coachman and carriage to collect the wedding guests. The grand days were over but he clung to one last vestige of finery: Koniners today who were children when Aryeh-Leib's wedding run was coming to an end have not forgotten the white gloves.

I am chatting with Motek Mysch over a lunchtime bagel when he mentions a Koniner by the name of Lola Szafran – a name I have not come across. He tells me she is a widow who lives in New York and for reasons of her own has nothing to do with the Konin Society. He thinks its pro-Israel activities probably put her off – all her family had been ardent Bundists. What's her maiden name? I ask. 'Witkowska.' The bagel stops midway to my open mouth. She is the only one of the Witkowski family left, he says, adding: 'A very intelligent family. I remember her father, Aryeh-Leib.' Motek has had no contact with Lola Szafran for years and it could be that she has died. If she is alive, she would be a very old lady. Motek is puzzled by the intensity of my interest in Mrs Szafran, but after lunch, dear man that he is, he gets out his old file cards and finds a telephone number I could try.

I long to call the number there and then. Aryeh-Leib is one of those *shtetl* characters who were vanishing even before Hitler came along. His daughter would be able to expand my knowledge of the Bund in Konin. The Memorial Book has little to offer on the subject, and most of the Konin survivors were Zionists who played no part in its activities. The fact that Mrs Szafran has distanced herself from her townsfolk hints strongly at the ideological divide.

In the course of the next few days I call her number repeatedly. It rings but there is no reply. Perhaps she has moved, or is away. Or dead. I go on trying. On the day of the Konin memorial service I decide to make one last attempt. A woman's voice answers, gentle, with a pronounced Polish accent. It is Lola Szafran. She has been in hospital after a fall and has just come home. I explain why I would like to meet her. She sounds friendly but points out that she lived in Lodz from 1934 and has no knowledge of Konin after that date.

I sense polite resistance. She asks if I know that her old schoolteacher from Konin, Mrs Friedlander, who taught generations of Jewish children and is ninety-three, lives in Manhattan quite near her. I do not. More tantalizing tid-bits follow, but when

I try to set up a meeting, she backs off. She would be delighted to meet me and help me if she could, but her leg is still in plaster and she would prefer to wait a little while before we meet. We agree to talk in a few days' time.

I wait two days and can no longer restrain my impatience. I call her again. She is feeling 'slightly better' and is as friendly as before, but may we leave it that she will call me as soon as she feels ready? Four days pass without a call. I worry. How clearly did I convey what I am trying to do?

I have a copy of the introductory letter I sent from London to Koniners in America. It is more detailed and effective than my words on the phone. I attach a note saying how much I look forward to hearing from her, and I deliver it to her Manhattan apartment on Eighth Avenue and Twenty-Fifth Street. No call that day. Nor the next, until late in the evening when, just as I am losing hope, she calls to thank me for my letter and to invite me to tea in two days' time. She asks me to call her half an hour ahead of our meeting, just to make sure she is feeling well. She sounds much brighter and says she has found a number of things connected with Konin that she wants to show me.

Precisely thirty minutes before our arranged meeting, standing at the phone booth in the lobby of the Pickwick Arms with my coat on, flowers at the ready, I call Mrs Szafran. No reply. I try again and again for over an hour. Should I go and knock on her door? I decide not. Paranoia sets in. She is sitting there with the telephone ringing, knowing who it is, not answering. Or is she stretched out on the floor after a stroke, her hand vainly reaching for the ringing phone? Should I dash right over and save her life? Or is she back in hospital? Or has she simply forgotten the appointment and gone out? On calm reflection I decide to call her later. But pessimism creeps in. I shall be leaving New York soon in search of other American Koniners. When I get back, there will be just a short interval before I return to London. Shall I ever meet Aryeh-Leib's daughter?

Two days later I happen to mention my problem to a woman from Konin. She says she will call the Bund offices – they will know what has happened to Mrs Szafran. Am I hearing right? Has she just said 'the Bund offices'? The Bund is history – romantic, revolutionary history. I would be no less startled to hear her say she intends telephoning the Chartists or the Decembrists. She puts the phone down and says, yes, someone at the Bund has just told her that Mrs Szafran is back in hospital.

The Bund lives. On Twenty-First Street, Manhattan. Celebrating its ninetieth birthday. Their archives look like a set-designer's idea of archives. Cabinets and bookcases are crowded together leaving scarcely any room for human beings. Stacks of shelves reach to the ceiling, bending under the weight of bulging brown paper packets, tied with string. Tens of thousands of items: newspapers, periodicals, pamphlets, documents, books, in more than ten languages: a unique record of the Jewish labour movement.[3]

I am the only visitor. Occasionally the ringing of a telephone breaks the silence and I hear Yiddish spoken. The Bund propagated socialism through Yiddish, and today still promotes the language and culture. Leo Greenbaum, a young Polish Jew wearing jeans who works in the archives, tells me the Bund has about three to four hundred members in New York and more in other parts of the country. He knows Mrs Szafran, who worked in the organization's offices until just a few years ago.

There is disappointingly little on Konin, but Leo finds two original photographs: one a group of workers' children at a Bund summer camp near Konin in 1931. Among the grown-ups is Lola Witkowska. Leo says he can recognize her. Her brother Mendel is in the other photograph.

He pulls out a file on Lola Szafran containing material that she has presented to the archives. From the letters, papers and documents, it is possible to flesh out more of her past. In the 1930s she became a nurse in Lodz, later escaping during the war to Russia, where she worked as a slave labourer in a Soviet copper mine in the Urals in conditions worse than anything Zola described in *Germinal*. She gave condemnatory evidence about these conditions to the UN in 1949. There are pages photocopied from Menachem Begin's *White Nights, The Story of a Prisoner in Russia*, published while he was Prime Minister of Israel: 'In a wretched mud-hut in a little Uzbeki town, at Dzhizak, between Tashkent and Samarkand, I settled down together with my sister's family and a friend of theirs from the time of the deportation. Her name was Leah Vitkovska [*sic*]. Vitkovska, a kind-hearted woman, was an active worker in the Bund.'

The file contains a photocopy of her last Polish passport and other papers. Estera Laja (Leah) Witkowska was born in Konin in 1907. Passport photographs are rarely flattering and this one shows a somewhat masculine face, hair parted down the middle, and bold, heavy-lidded eyes. She wears an army shirt and tie. In the latter years of the Second World War she served in Scotland as a nursing sister in the Polish Army in Exile, ending up with the rank of captain. A bundle of wartime correspondence contains letters in Yiddish from Bundist friends who address her as Comrade Lola. She came to America after the Second World War and married a fellow Bundist. I find a New York newspaper clipping of a Death Announcements column from May 1962 that includes the name of Natan N. Szafran.

Leo shows me an authoritative three-volume work on the Bund, published in Yiddish,[4] which contains several informative pages on the Witkowski brothers. It was edited twenty years ago by a historian of the Bund, J.S. Hertz. A frail old man with twinkly eyes shuffles into the room, wearing a formal brown suit which no doubt fitted him better when there was more flesh on his bones. He engages me in conversation, automatically speaking Yiddish, not every word of which I grasp. He chats fervently about the Bund, tells me his name is Jacob Sholem Hertz and shuffles out again.

An archivist arrives who happens to be a friend of Mrs Szafran. She reports that Lola is on heavy doses of cortisone, but she has just spoken to her and this seems one of her better days. She is lucid and not in pain. She thinks Lola would be pleased to see me. I get the address of the hospital and decide to go there. Now.

31

A HOSPITAL in Lower Manhattan. Outside, a chill December night. Inside, hot as the Sahara. My small bunch of flowers is wilting by the time I find my way through a maze of corridors to her ward. I open the door of a room shared by three elderly women. One of them is curled up fast asleep. Another sits in a chair and fixes me with an unblinking gaze. The third, propped up on pillows, looks at me, gently curious. Her eyes have a glossy darkness set off by the dreadful pallor of her face. Her skin, stained with liver spots, has that strange transparent look that comes to the gravely ill. Thinning silvery hair is brushed straight back in a bun, Victorian governess style. Her nose is prominent in a face that has lost too much weight. Somewhere in those features – maybe in the eyes, which have best withstood the years – I can make out the younger woman in the passport picture, and the still younger woman at the Bund summer camp of 1931. I introduce myself to Lion-Lion's daughter.

As she begins to talk, life returns to her face. Personality triumphs over weary flesh. When she makes a gesture it is graceful. Like her father, she has a natural dignity and finess. She knows immediately who I am, and says how upset she was that our arrangement did not work out. On the day we were to have met, alone in her apartment, she had collapsed with an internal haemorrhage and had nearly bled to death. She apologized for breaking our appointment, as if guilty of bad behaviour. 'For the last few years I have had to fight several illnesses. I fought cancer twice and each time I have come back, but now it is something rare, and they will soon decide if I can go home or whether I must have surgery.'

Her manner is calm, her tone uncomplaining, but there is no disguising the note of anxiety. Perhaps the fighter has lost the taste for battle. I observe a mannerism my Sarna grandmother and my mother acquired in old age: an uncontrollable fidgeting of the right hand. First she plays with a rolled-up bandage, tapping it up and down on the narrow table cross her bed. Then she makes smoothing gestures across the surface of the table as though brushing away crumbs. Then she plucks at the sheets. The rest of her body is still and composed, but the hand seems to have a life of its own.

She is slightly deaf and sometimes I have to repeat my words loudly, which makes the woman in a dressing-gown sitting nearby stare at me even more intently. My throat is parched. The flowers droop. Lola Szafran is sitting up in bed, one arm propped behind her in an uncomfortable position. I fear this will be our first and last meeting. There is so much I want to ask, and so little time. It is like being at a railway station, seeing off someone who is about to depart on a long journey, and finding in those last few precious minutes that there is nothing to say.

I begin by chatting inconsequentially about my family background, and at the mention of the name Sarna she flattens her palm against her cheek in a gesture of surprise. 'Among the old Konin generations you will always find the name Sarna.' She asks if I am related to Jacob Sarna. Yes, he was my mother's brother. Lola Szafran says she met him when she was on leave in London during the war. She once spent a Sabbath eve in his home and remembers his hospitality. I say how nice it is to discover this link between us. 'You know the Yiddish saying,' she says. '*Mir zenen geknipt un gebindn*' – we are knotted and bound to one another.

She recounts how she was in London's East End one evening, searching for an address in the dark. A little old lady who showed her the way asked her in Yiddish: 'Who are you?' She replied: '*Ikh bin Aryeh-Leib's tochter*' – I am Aryeh-Leib's daughter. No surname was necessary. The woman knew immediately who she was. Her own father came from Konin: '*Un ikh bin Kopl-Dovid's tokhter*' – And I am Kopl-Dovid's daughter. Kopl-Dovid – a name from my earliest childhood – was one of my Sarna grandfather's closest friends in London, a distant relative, and religious teacher to three of my uncles. Lola Szafran does not know just how many knots and bindings she is revealing.

The conversation flits here and there, never wandering far from Konin: 'If you would come to my house, I have so many pictures of horses. I like horses because the name Konin is from *kon*, the Polish word for horse. Konin' – she draws out the sentence, stressing each syllable with her attractive Polish accent – 'Konin was the most beau-ti-ful town I have known in my life.' She enthuses about the river and bridges, the rich social and cultural life, how wonderful it was growing up there: 'You know what it is like when one has memories of a time when one was young and full of life.' As she says 'full of life' she spreads both arms out in a wide, unfolding gesture. 'We were proud of our town. There was something in the air. The intellectual atmosphere was much higher than in other small towns in our region. It was different. It was a place that accepted Western culture. We had a wonderful library. We used to bring lecturers from Warsaw, actors, we had our own dramatic groups.' Talking about Konin recharges her. Some of the pallor goes.

'I have some pictures to show you at home. I am really sorry I could not be there that day.' I remind her that I shall be going back to London before too long. 'I have your address. I will follow you,' she says with a laugh. My thoughts at this moment become inward-turned, unseemly. I want to see those pictures. They are in an apartment nearby and yet I cannot get to them. She adds: 'I have a family photograph of my parents with all the children, and I have pictures of other people from Konin. I have prepared books for you, especially about the Bund. My goodness, how much I would show you if I was home. Maybe I will be able to, let us hope so.'

She talks about her father. 'He was not an educated man,' she says, not disparagingly but as though pointing out a blessing life had denied him. 'He used to sell butter and cheese as well as milk. Rabbi Lipschitz used to buy from him – "If Aryeh-Leib says it's kosher, it's kosher."'

She tells me more about his everyday life: where he lived (No. 8 Slowackiego Street in a house that belonged to Moishe Kaplan), where he prayed (in Mendel Bulka's house). She mentions the pair of white gloves he wore for weddings. 'He tried everything to make a living. He used to repair windows, and I learned how to do this from him. When I wanted to help my father, we went together to the villages and put glass in the windows. I am a Jack-of-all-trades.' She laughs again. The woman in the chair never takes her gaze off me. The one curled up in bed remains as still as a corpse. The heat is suffocating.

'If my father was not well, I used to go for the milk and collect the newspapers. To support a family and send them to school was not an easy thing. But we made a living. We went to school nicely dressed. You know the story of the immigrants on the East Side – they worked hard but their sons are professors. There is in Jewish life something that makes you want to learn, to know. One of my brothers, Moishe, worked so hard to know everything. You know what they called him?' I let her tell me: 'They called him "the walking encyclopaedia".' I hear about her elder sister who attended the Jewish gymnasium and university, and she tells me that she herself studied for the gymnasium entrance exams and passed, but there was no money to send her. 'At home we spoke Yiddish, but we were the best students in Polish in school. We had the ambition, you see, to be better than the others.'

Sometimes, while we talk, she emphasizes a point by touching me lightly on the arm, a gesture of human warmth. She connects. She creates her own knots and bindings.

We talk about the Bund. 'I used to help my brother Mendel, who for many years was on the City Hall Council and helped the poor. You know what a *shik-yingl* is? It is someone who runs here, runs there, takes care of this and that. I was his *shik-yingl*, his helper. All my family was involved, including my father.' His daily trek into the countryside took him past Konin's railway station at Czarkow, where the night train from Warsaw used to drop off the newspapers in the early hours, among them the Bund's Yiddish daily, *Di Folkstsaytung*. The paper was legal but the Warsaw authorities were in the habit of confiscating issues that contained anti-government material they considered subversive. It happened sometimes that by the time they got round to stopping the presses, early copies were already on their way by rail to towns like Konin. Tipped off by Warsaw, the Konin police would go to the station in the morning to grab the papers, only to find they were not there. Aryeh-Leib had already picked them up from the deserted station, hidden them in his milk churns and smuggled them into town. 'My father was not interested in politics but he liked to read our newspaper and to help us. He was a nice man who cared for justice, who tried to help everybody. In all groups of life there are people who know what is right and what is wrong, and they will do what is right whether they belong to an organization or not. That was my father.

'We had an open house. Our address was "The Bund, Konin"' – she laughs. 'I was born and raised with the Bund.' Has she remained a committed member of the Bund? 'Of course!' she replies, amazed that I should ask such a question. 'We were never Communists, always Bundists. We believed in democratic socialism. The Bund was an organization that took the poor and made them dreamers for justic. Oh yes, we are still the same today, though of course in other conditions.'

She left Konin for Lodz at the end of 1933 and she and the rest of her family never went back. She is glad they were able to bury their parents in Konin when they did. 'It was the best way to die – in peace.' Her three brothers and their families perished in the Shoah. She has no children or close relatives.

We skitter around a few more topics, both of us aware there is no time to dig deep. I have been with her an hour and she is beginning to flag. It is time to go. Suddenly her energy drains away as quickly as it came, and the shadowy crescents under her eyes darken. She leans back against the plumped-up pillows. A nurse peers round the door. Time for another injection.

She waves aside my apology for having tired her: 'I am so glad you came. It is a mission you have taken upon your shoulders.' I attempt a disclaimer, but she merely looks at me closely with her dark, intelligent eyes and says: 'I understand.' I wish her a speedy recovery, the words ringing hollow as I say them. She replies: 'I am trying very much to be alive.' I remind her that she is a fighter: 'Oh yes,' she says, 'and how!'

Postscript I learned what I had already suspected: that Lola Szafran was suffering from leukaemia. When I telephoned her a few days later, her voice sounded anxious, slightly breathless, and we did not speak long. She remembered the Konin photographs and said she would write to me about them. She was still hoping to go home. I said I would try to come and see her again before I left. She said she was not feeling up to receiving visitors, but would I please call her again before I left New York. I did so just before boarding my plane to London, and she asked me to give her regards to the Koniners in England, and wished me a safe journey.

I heard no more from Lola Szafran. I wrote to her but received no reply. When I telephoned the Bund I learned she was still seriously ill. She died at the age of eighty-one on 29 December 1988, one year after we met. I wrote to her executor, explaining my interest in the Konin material she had so much wanted to show me. He did not answer. A few months later, I heard from a kind soul at the Bund archives whose help I had enlisted. He had gone to her apartment to look for the Konin material but it was too late. It had been thrown away, probably by a maintenance man who had helped clear the place. There was just one item he had managed to save: a studio photograph taken in Konin of Mrs Szafran's parents with their three sons and two daughters, one of them Lola. He sent me a photocopy and so I had my first view of Lion-Lion, a bearded, patriarchal figure, powerful hands resting on his knees. But no white gloves.

Some time later, I wrote to the Bund to ask if I could have a better-quality copy of the photograph. Helpful as ever, they looked for it in their archives but, mysteriously, it had disappeared and could not be found. That dark and not very distinct copy is the only picture I have of Aryeh-Leib.

32

MY MOTHER disparaged doctors throughout her long life and always discarded the pills and medicines they prescribed for her, which probably accounts for her longevity. I wonder if it had something to do with her Konin childhood at the turn of the century, when doctors could do little if anything to combat major diseases and were scarcely more effective at curing the minor ones. Most people, in any case, could not afford a doctor, and relied instead on well-tried folk remedies, which were cheaper and just as efficacious.

My mother's sceptical view of the medical profession was equalled only by her confidence in the curative properties of the cabbage leaf. The remedy had worked in Konin and she saw no reason why it should not work in London. The cabbage leaf – it had to be raw and green – was especially effective, she believed, in dealing with cuts, boils, blisters, bruises, swellings, inflammations, sprains and septic wounds. She ignored my derision. If I came home from school with a cut knee, she wrapped a cabbage leaf round it. A sprained wrist? On with the cabbage leaf. Once, when I had a seriously infected ankle that resisted hospital treatment, it was only her devoted application of cabbage leaves that finally did the trick. After that, I scoffed less. I know she got the cabbage leaf therapy from Konin because *her* mother believed in it too. My *buba*'s way with an inflamed or swollen throat was to apply a poultice made of hot breadcrumbs well wrapped in a large, warmed cabbage leaf. I remember my mother telling me that the peasants in Konin treated cuts by laying a spider's web on the open wound. I was spared having to go to school with a spider's web on my knee.

Both my mother and her mother, who lived with us when I was a boy, had extraordinary powers of endurance, a heroic capacity for putting up with illness and pain, which must have had something to do with being brought up in an era that offered little choice but to put up with it. In Konin, unless you were well off, you summoned the doctor only in cases of mysterious and alarming symptoms, serious illness or emergency. Why waste good money on doctors if the body could heal itself, helped along by a warm bed, herbal remedies, chicken broth, lemon tea with honey, invocations against the evil eye and, not least of all, prayer?

In 1900 there was only one elderly Jewish doctor in Konin. Their number grew after the First World War and included two former pupils of the Jewish gymnasium, Isador Kawa and Felig Bulka.[1] Kawa is the Polish word for coffee, while Bulka means bread roll, hence the tired joke inflicted on someone who felt unwell: 'What you need is a coffee and roll.' A little before their time, another much-respected Jewish doctor, Julian Joel, practised in the town. He came from a German banking family and was the only Jew – other than the Kaplans – who belonged to the exclusive Konin rowing club. 'When he began practising as a doctor in Konin and came into contact with the Jewish masses and with their situation, he attached himself more closely to Jewish life . . . As for taking payment for medical treatment in poor homes, it did not enter his thoughts.'[2]

The very rich could afford consultations with eminent doctors in Lodz, Warsaw and Vienna, and to go to fashionable spas for a 'cure'. Most ordinary folk in need of medical help for the less serious illnesses and minor surgery summoned not the doctor but the *feldsher*, descendant of the medieval barber-surgeon, whose presence in Konin long preceded that of the doctor. He was a sort of paramedic, or what the Chinese would call a bare-foot doctor. People trusted the *feldsher*'s practical experience.

The census of 1765 lists two Jews as having the occupation of *feldsher*. The first to be mentioned by name lived in much more recent times. Chaim Warmbadt specialized in treating children. His expertise included 'tearing teeth' – to use the almost too graphic Yiddish phrase – a service he performed in his barber's shop opposite the Catholic church. Later, between the wars, there was a qualified Jewish dentist in the town, Shlomo Neuman, but he cost more, and why mess about with fancy treatments when it was much simpler to have the thing pulled out and be done with? Even cheaper than the *feldsher* was the tooth-puller who did his work in front of the public on market days, though this figure seems to have disappeared from Konin life around the time of the First World War. A dental mechanic was kept busy between the wars making false teeth for those who could afford them.

There was a woman *feldsher* too,[3] reputed to be good at resetting children's dislocated bones, but the *feldsher* most surviving Koniners remember was Warmbadt's son-in-law and heir to the business, Jacob Strykowski. He began to practise before the First World War and remained active until the 1930s, running his barber shop as well as working as a paramedic. With a diploma that entitled him to write prescriptions, Strykowski was no ordinary *feldsher*. His bone-setting skills were said to be better than any doctor's. (He also happened to be my paternal grandfather's landlord.)

Strykowski's range of treatments included cupping, much favoured for maladies such as fever, asthma, bronchitis and rheumatism. The cupping-glass, shaped like a round eye-bath, was called a *banke* in Yiddish. The *feldsher* would put a drop of methylated spirits in the glass, ignite it to induce a vacuum, and swiftly clap it onto the required part of the body, most frequently the back. The patient could end up with *bankes* all over his or her back, sucking away for ten minutes or more to draw blood to the surface of the skin. This was said to relieve deep-seated congestion. Some thought it helped to draw impurities from the body. As each *banke* was removed, the release of the vacuum produced a hiss and a pop. The reddish circles left on the patient's skin could take days to fade. '*Bankes* were good,' said Avrom Soika. 'They worked – no question about it – especially for heavy colds.' Another, rather more cynical Koniner, Mike Jacobs, said: 'So long as people believed in it, it helped.' *Bankes* have given rise to an expressive Yiddish saying, used to describe an action that has proved totally futile: '*S'hot geholfen vi a toytn bankes*' – 'It helped like using *bankes* on a corpse.'

The *Oxford Companion to Medicine*[4] confirms that cupping 'is now obsolete', which was my impression too, until one day in 1992 when I went to a young physiotherapist in London for treatment for a bad back. To my amazement he suggested cupping, which he said he used to great effect on some of Britain's top rugby players. How could I refuse a treatment known to so many of my Konin forebears? As I lay on my stomach, I felt the *bankes* sucking gently at my skin

– not an unpleasant sensation – and heard the pop when each glass was removed. It didn't do much for my back.

Cupping took two forms, dry and wet. I experienced the dry. Rivka Klapstein experienced the wet, and remembers it more than fifty years later. Wet cupping – called in Yiddish *geshniteneh* (cut) *bankes* – was less pleasant than the dry: 'I was about nine years old and had a very high fever; mother's treatment – making me take some kind of oil – didn't work, so she called in Strykowski and he put *bankes* on me. Before each *banke* was applied, he nipped the skin so the bad blood should come out. I screamed and screamed. Years later when I gave birth to my first child, the pain of those *geshniteneh bankes* came back to me.'

The *feldsher*'s other favourite form of treatment, also long recorded in the history of medicine, was blood-letting by *piavkes* (Polish for leeches). The leech is a sluglike creature with a sucker at one end and three sharp teeth to pierce and grip the skin while it gorges on blood. One famous French physician[5] of the early nineteenth century who believed that many diseases are due to inflammation prescribed leeching for almost everything. In 1833 over 41 million leeches were imported into France.[6] I have no statistics for Konin, but there was certainly a steady sale in leeches, which the apothecary kept in a jar of water. Izzy Hahn remembers his grandfather applying leeches to a rheumatic leg. 'They sucked for perhaps twenty minutes and when they had drunk enough blood, they dropped off.'

There was another treatment that the *feldsher* administered in people's homes, always with the chamber pot or commode at the ready: the enema. Strykowski probably used a rubber appliance for this purpose, a technological advance on equipment used in the previous century, which my mother could recall from her childhood. Here, too, her memory found its way into a novel:

> Life was full of sinister, unmentionable figures who lurked, thrust out of sight, in the back of Leah's mind: like the enema woman her grandmother talked of sometimes, from her village. The gross, red-handed enema woman with her goose-quill and her sheep's bladder, who came to deal with those whose over-charged systems needed clearing.[7]

Strykowski's hour of glory came during the First World War, when a typhus epidemic struck Konin, as it did other parts of

Poland. With no Jewish doctor in the town, the *feldsher* was much in demand. The typhus symptoms were unmistakeable: high fever ushered in with the shakes, a tongue that turned from white to yellow to brown, disagreeably coated teeth and, finally, the eruption of rose-coloured blotches. As the patient declined, he or she stared blankly at the world in a state of wakeful stupor. Anyone found suffering from typhus was taken to hospital, and the rest of the family put in quarantine. their home was disinfected and sealed. If healthy members of a poor family were thus prevented from working, it could result in destitution. In such cases, Strykowski – humanely but perhaps irresponsibly – often would not report a typhus case to the authorities, despite the risk of a heavy fine.

Conditions in the town during the war were ideal for typhus: overcrowded housing made worse by the influx of refugees, under-nourishment, a shortage of soap, bad sanitation. The epidemic, by no means the first in Konin's history, broke out in poor homes and spread through the whole town. The death toll rose steeply until the German authorities promulgated quarantine regulations, appointed a 'sanitary commission' to go from house to house checking for cleanliness, and brought in a cumbersome contraption like a huge steam kettle to fumigate homes and kill the lice that were spreading the disease. Only a few years had elapsed since medical science discovered, in 1909, that the disease was louse-borne.

It was the Germans in the First World War who established Konin's first hospital, in the Kalisz suburb of the town, a long walk from the Jewish quarter. Designed originally to deal with the typhus epidemic, it came to be used as a general hospital after the occupiers had departed. Jews, especially if they were religious, did not like entering it. The problem was not anti-Semitism but rather the whole ethos of the place which, to an observant Jew, was disagreeable if not horrendous. Imagine yourself to be a Chasid, lying in bed in the Hospital of the Holy Spirit, as it was called. A nurse – which means a nun – comes over you and the crucifix hanging from her neck swings to and fro, almost brushing your lips. You close your eyes and frantically mutter, Hear, O Israel, the Lord our God, the Lord is One. You open your eyes and the black-robed figure has gone. But facing you on the opposite wall is a candle-lit icon of the Virgin Mary, and above the doorway hangs the one-whose-name-must-not-be-mentioned, nailed to the cross. The Catholic priest seated by a patient in the next bed utters a prayer and crosses himself. On some days the smell of pig flesh fills the air. Not the ideal environment for Orthodox Jews, who would enter the local hospital only *in extremis*. The nearest Jewish hospital was in Kalisz.

One of the greatest misfortunes that could afflict a couple, especially if they were religious and therefore had a holy duty to be fruitful and multiply, was infertility, for which there was no remedy other than prayer and various superstitious rituals. When my Uncle Jacob travelled to Palestine as a young man, an aunt who had been married several years without having a child made him promise to perform a duty at Rachel's Tomb that would fulfil her dearest wish. He was to measure the circumference of the tomb with a piece of string and bring the string back for her. This was an infallible remedy for barrenness. Unfortunately, illness and various emotional crises drove the matter from my uncle's mind, 'and here he was back in Konin, his mission forgotten and his aunt's imploringly hopeful eyes upon him.'[8] In desperation he left the room, found a length of string, cut off a piece and presented it to her. Almost a year later she gave birth to a child.

A small-town community in which there was considerable inbreeding was likely to produce a fair number of the mentally handicapped. The dangerously mad were packed off to an asylum in a larger town. The rest became part of the everyday scene in a society where parents could no more put away their mentally sick children than children their geriatric parents. One of my own relatives, killed in the Shoah, was mentally retarded in a moderate way. A shopkeeper in the Tepper Marik had a crazy daughter who went three times a day to pray at the statue of the Madonna. Another deranged Jewish woman used to hang around the station and accept overtures from men without taking money from them. Nor was there any shortage of gentiles who were mentally unhinged. Children enjoyed running after crazy people in the street, taunting them with their nicknames.

I was talking to a group of Koniners one day when I heard the story of a woman who used to walk around wearing outlandish hats and crazy clothes. Asked why she dressed this way, she replied: 'Because I have no one in the world. This way, when I die, people will remember me.' Some sixty years later, when other and saner members of the community had been forgotten, she was still being talked about.

Illness was dreaded not merely for the pain and suffering it inflicted, but because in a society where health insurance and State welfare were unknown, it could mean the difference between a decent life and abject poverty. A few years before the Second World War, the Konin municipality opened a small clinic that provided free medical advice, inoculations and hospital referrals, but the Koniners I met had little to tell me about it; perhaps because most Jews preferred to call in their own doctor if they had the money, or like generations before them, the *feldsher*. For those who were thought incurable – the ashen-faced, bed-ridden consumptives, the victims of a stroke, the cancer sufferers and others – there was not much to be done: their 'sanatorium' was a cot in the corner of a shared bedroom, where they lingered on till breath and hope ran out.

33

MOTEK MYSCH remembers:

There were some special old women in the town who, if someone was sick, used to come to the house, take hot charcoal and put the burning coals in a pottery jar; smoke would come out and they would make as if to spit three times through the smoke onto the sick person – *tfou*, *tfou*, *tfou* – and so take off the evil eye. Or if a person was dying, she would spit three times and beg God: 'Take away the Angel of Death!' My aunt, Chana-Rivka Bayrach, was one of these women.

She used to go to the cemetery and yell to the dead that they should do something for such-and-such a person so that he should be healthy, earn a living and so on. Whenever there was someone in trouble, she was running to the cemetery. Let's say there was a sick girl who had a *zeyde* [grandfather] buried in the cemetery. My aunt went to his grave and she would start to plead with him in Yiddish: 'Go to *Reboyne-sheloylem* [literally Master of the World, that is, God], ask him to help her, she's a young girl, she must live to be a bride and be married . . .' all kinds of things, and she was screaming and crying. People who heard her believed that she was talking to the dead.

When we had my mother's *yortsayt*, my aunt used to go with us to the cemetery at seven o'clock in the morning and we came home seven o'clock at night. My mother was her sister and died very young. On that day we always went without breakfast and lunch. For us it was a *Yom Kippur* day, a fast.

At the cemetery my aunt knelt, she lay down flat on the ground and was talking to the grave: 'Sheva, I am here with your children. Plead for them, that they should be healthy, that they should earn a living, and that no evil eye should harm them.' And she was crying and we were crying. After that came the *shammes* [beadle] from the cemetery and he made *El moleh rakhamim* [the prayer: Lord who art full of compassion].

People asked her: 'Go tell the dead they should run to the Almighty to beg a small favour of him and that they should say to God: "Chana-Rivka was here and has pleaded that you see that so-and-so gets well." ' The dead were to act like a messenger to God. My aunt did not take a penny for this work. She was a fat woman, and when people saw her running across the Tepper Marik they knew Chana-Rivka was off to the cemetery. She was a saint.

In our town of Konin, you were not meant to go past the synagogue after midnight: *Sheydim!* Ghosts! They said a man once went past the *shul* after twelve o'clock and a ghost said to him: 'Come and make a blessing.' He went inside and had to make a blessing over the Torah in total darkness. There were people who believed it and were afraid. We of my generation walked past the *shul* at midnight and we always used to say to each other as a joke: 'Be careful or they'll call you in.'

They used to tell a story about someone who said: 'I'm not afraid to go in the cemetery after midnight.' So they bet money with him. 'How are we going to know you went there?' they asked. 'You should knock in a stake as proof.' So next day they went to the cemetery to check, and found him lying dead. Why? When he knocked in the stake in the dark, it went through the bottom of his coat, and when he moved away he thought dead people were clutching him, and he died of shock.

34

THE FIRST JEWS to settle in Konin were too few and too insecure to think about establishing a local burial ground of their own. Many of the early settlers came from Kalisz, and it would have been natural for them to wish to be buried near their families. And so it was to Kalisz that the body of a Konin Jew was taken for ritual burial. The journey could be hazardous. A royal decree had granted the Jews the right to transport their dead from one town to another, but this did not remove the threat of attack by bandits and highwaymen. The forests between Konin and Kalisz were ideal for ambushing a slow-moving cortège. Robbers looking for hidden valuables might disturb the dead, a desecration of the corpse, which had been ritually cleansed according to Jewish custom.

The journey itself was arduous in bad weather, both in the cold of winter and in the early spring when wagon wheels stuck in the quagmire of Poland's appalling roads (which Napoleon was to curse when he crossed the country some three hundred years later). The journey to Kalisz took the best part of a day. Several precious working days would have been lost by the time the mourners got back to Konin. Thus there was no lack of incentive for the Jews of Konin to create their own burial ground, their own House-of-Graves or House-of-Eternity, to give the literal translations of some of the Hebrew expressions for cemetery.

A contributor to the Memorial Book speculates that Konin had its first Jewish burial ground 'most likely at the beginning of the sixteenth century'.[1] There must surely have been some kind of consecrated ground to receive the victims of two cholera epidemics, one in 1628 and another thirty-four years later. At the start of the seventeenth century the Jews were paying an impost to the local clergy in the form of 'butter and two fishes' for each funeral, which seems proof enough that there was a local burial ground in or near Konin at that time.[2]

I have spoken to Koniners who have childhood memories of the old Jewish cemetery near the hamlet of Czarkow, where the new industrial town of Konin stands today. Whether or not this was the site of the first burial ground is not known.[3] It was sited on the slopes of a hillside to protect it from the floods that washed over the valley floor in the spring. The old headstones were plain slabs of local sandstone, no more than twelve to sixteen inches in height with pointed tops. They bore Hebrew inscriptions primitively carved in shallow lettering, which 'gave the impression of amateurism'.[4] Evidently, there was not enough work in the locality to support a Jewish stonemason. The inscriptions, written in 'Rashi script',[5] were as simple as the stones themselves, stating merely the forename of the deceased, the forename of his or her father, and the date of burial.

Konin's Jews not only grew in number but persisted in the habit of dying. Their brethren from smaller settlements close by, such as Golin, began using the cemetery, and in time the rows of stubby little headstones spread across the hillside until there was no way of extending the burial ground in a flood-free direction. By the end of the eighteenth century it was obvious that a problem was looming.

Other factors encouraged Koniners to search for a new site. Czarkow was hardly ideal. It was a few kilometres out of town and on the wrong side of the river. In the thawing season it was not unknown for the fast-flowing Warta to hurl a boulder of ice at the timber framework of the bridge, rendering it impassable. Then a boatman would row the black-clad mourners and their shrouded corpse across the river like Charon ferrying his charges across the Styx.

The community acquired a new burial ground on the town side of the river, only fifteen minutes' walk from the Jewish quarter, on land just beyond a wooded area that would one day become Konin's municipal park. The *kehillah* most probably paid a symbolic sum for the land because, according to custom, Jews must not gain title to the ground for a cemetery without paying for it. The 'new cemetery', as it came to be called, was established in the years 1806–8.

The first Jew to be interred in the new cemetery was a woman whose family name was Zilmonowicz. It is said that on the night after her funeral, she entered the dreams of all her family in a state of great distress, weeping and wailing. She explained, between sobs, that she could not bear the loneliness of being the only person in the cemetery. Night after night she returned to her relatives with the same heart-rending lamentations until, in desperation, they sought advice from the Rabbi.[6] He decreed that a guard should be posted near the grave throughout the following night. The man's company was clearly to the lady's satisfaction, for she did not disturb her relatives' sleep that night. The watchman was kept on until a second body had been interred. Mrs Zilmonowicz never complained again.

The new cemetery was enlarged more than once, and in time ceased to be new. 'Here, for over a hundred years, they buried the Jews of the town. Here people came to visit the graves of their close ones when there was a *yortsayt* and on Tisha Ba'av,' a day of mourning for the destruction of the Temple. At other times people would visit the cemetery 'to invite the deceased members of the family to a wedding'.[7]

Motek Mysch's old aunt, Chana-Rivka, and others like her had a special, almost holy, gift for enlisting help from departed relatives residing in heaven, but there were those who relied on their own powers of supplication. Imploring the dead to intercede with the Almighty on their behalf, they would 'tear their hearts out', light candles, or place notes of prayer and petition between the stones of the tombs of Konin's rabbis.[8] When all such entreaties failed, the last resort was to measure the grave of a close relative and donate an equivalent length of white linen to the poor for future use as a shroud.

The first three rabbis of Konin were buried near one another in a pat of the cemetery that came to be specially honoured. Some of this honour was bound to rub off onto nearby burial plots and, just as someone's social status in the synagogue could be judged by the proximity of his seat to the eastern wall, so a hierarchy established itself among the dead. Near the rabbinic tombs were buried the most eminent members of the community, the exceptionally pious and the wealthy, who paid extra for the privilege. The Memorial Book contributor offers a wry comment: 'It seems that even after death it is good to be a rich man.'[9]

The tombstones faced east, in the direction of Jerusalem. As the community grew, so the stonemason's art began to flower. The inscriptions became more ambitious. Non-sacred languages – Russian, Polish, German – were added to the Hebrew. Certain symbols became visual clichés: palms covering the eyes for the tombstone of a Cohen;[10] an open book for a Talmudic scholar; a flower with a severed stem or a hand with a sickle cutting off a young twig to mark the grave of a child; a pair of snuffed-out candles or a snake wound round a tree flicking out its poisoned tongue, for a woman. The monuments were indicators of worldly success. The more imposing of them were grandly enclosed by posts and chains. Between the two world wars, granite and polished marble came to replace local stone.

In the cemetery, as in the synagogue, the sexes were separated. For men and women to lie together in a public place was considered unseemly. However, it was permissible for a woman to be buried at her husband's feet. In 1921, following the death of a wealthy member of the community, his widow made a formal request to the honorary officers of the Chevre Kadishe (burial society) that she be allowed to buy the plot next to her late husband's grave as her own final resting-place. The burial society, bound by precedent, refused the request, whereupon the widow threatened to kill herself. The officers took the threat seriously enough to reconsider their decision. Finally, on the grounds that even the most sacred of laws may be put aside in the cause of saving a human life, they reversed their decision. (That the widow's worldly fortune and the sum she was prepared to pay for the plot might have contributed to the volte-face is a suspicion that will cross the minds of only the cynical.)

A few days after this break with tradition, three Konin Jews suddenly dropped dead. There could scarcely be a clearer sign of heavenly displeasure. Public agitation and protest ensued. The burial society, under heavy pressure, revoked its consent, whereupon the good widow repeated her firm intention to do away with herself. Rabbi Lipschitz convened a special *beth din* (rabbinic court) to consider the matter. After much deliberation, the court announced what is known in legal circles as a Judgement Reserved. It was a brilliant delaying tactic, and it worked. The fuss died down. The widow did not commit suicide. More than forty years later the old lady was still very much alive in Israel.

The less desirable parts of the cemetery, those close to the perimeter wall, were reserved for the poor, for persons who had 'earned a bad name', and for those who had committed suicide. The latter occupied a separate area of special ignominy and were always buried in the evening. But there is a long and humane tradition among rabbis – maintained to this day – of doing everything possible to deliver a verdict of not proven when considering suicides. I like to think that my relative (by marriage) who hanged himself in Konin was a beneficiary of this tradition and received a decent burial before sunset.

Until around the middle of the nineteenth century, Jews who had parents or grandparents buried in the old cemetery at Czarkow continued to visit the peaceful hillside. As time distanced each new generation from their ancestors, these visits dwindled. By the time of the First World War, the disused burial ground looked forlorn and forgotten. The depredations of rain and frost had eroded the soft stone, erasing the names of the dead. The rows of headstones leaned over at crazy angles, some snapped off, others lying in fragments on the ground. Streams of heavy rainwater had washed away the soil in places, revealing human bodies. Cattle grazed among the graves.

One could rebuke the Konin Jews for allowing this dereliction. They, I suppose, would point to more urgent priorities: the needs of the living as well as the financial burden of maintaining the 'new' cemetery. In the early 1920s, the burial society wrote to my Sarna grandfather in London and to other well-known Koniners abroad, pleading for contributions toward the cost of rebuilding the cemetery wall, which had been damaged by floods. The wall was built.

Joe Fox, born in Konin in 1898, has a memory of going through Czarkow one day as a child. The adult accompanying him pointed at the hillside as though at a curiosity and said: 'Look, that's the old Jewish cemetery.' Other boys found it an intriguing adventure playground. Few Jews gave much thought to the disused cemetery until 1927, when an unexpected event occurred that suddenly made every Jew in Konin not only aware of its existence but frantic to preserve it.

In that year the local government gave notice that the hillside was needed for development purposes: the old cemetery would have to go.[11] The news set the entire community in an uproar. Jews who scarcely ever visited the cemetery could now talk of nothing else. It is forbidden under Jewish law to disturb or move the remains of the dead, and there was communal fury over the 'evil decree'. Petitions and urgent pleas for help went out to Jewish organizations in Warsaw, to Jewish deputies in parliament, to rabbis in the capital. To no avail. The government was able to invoke a law that gave local authorities the right to take over any disused cemetery where no burial had taken place for over a hundred years. The Jews of Konin had to yield.

The Rabbi begged the community to calm down. He offered reassurance to those who feared they might be punished in the next world for agreeing to the plan to move the dead. They were to say, at the appropriate time, that he, Rabbi Lipschitz, the Rabbi of the town, had taken upon himself the full moral responsibility for moving the bones of their ancestors. The community elected a committee of leading citizens to organize the winding up of the old burial ground. As matters of holy ritual were involved, the elders of the Chevre Kadishe were to supervise the transfer of remains to their new resting-place.

The local government offered compensation in the form of extra land for extending the new cemetery, plus considerable quantities of topsoil brought from outside the town. The task of transferring the bones began in 1928.[12] On a series of Mondays, designated as fast days, a team of volunteers composed of men, *yeshiva* students and boys headed out of town in the direction of Czarkow. Their wagon rumbled over the wooden bridge, crossed the wide expanse of flat meadow, turned right at the crossroads and arrived at the hillside. The volunteers dug up the graves and carefully placed the bones from each grave in a white linen sack. When the wagon was fully loaded, the slow procession made its way back to the town and the cemetery behind the park, where a mass grave had been prepared to receive the bones. Jewish and gentile shops closed as the cortège went by. Each Monday the Rabbi officiated over a funeral service and recited Kaddish. This went on week after week until all the bones had been reinterred. The old gravestones were dug up too, and those that were still intact were re-erected in a row not far from the mass grave.

Everyone felt a sense of relief when the succession of Monday fasts and funerals came to an end. They had done their duty according to the precepts of their faith. They felt secure in the belief that the earthly remains of those who had lived and died in Konin and its surrounding villages for centuries, having been disturbed, could now rest at peace for all eternity.

35

'EVERYONE was buried with dignity,' said one Koniner emphatically. Listening to accounts of funerals in Konin, I get the impression that the dignity sprang in no small measure from the vehicle in which the deceased made their last earthly journey. Rich man, poor man, wealthy widow or penniless spinster, all could die secure in the knowledge that they would travel to their graves in style. Konin's communal hearse, the *agoleh*, introduced a note of outward show that would have been alien to the primitive simplicity of most Jewish small-town funerals. One Koniner, struggling to do justice to its magnificence, compared it favourably with the Queen of England's coronation coach. The hearse was black rather than gold. But what a black! Coat upon coat of burnished lacquer produced a mirror-like gloss that glittered even on the dullest day. The hearse was open-sided, with swagged curtains drawn back to afford a discreet view of the body draped with a black cloth.

This elaborate conveyance, reminiscent of funereal pomp in its Victorian heyday, was used until the Second World War to bear Konin's Jewish dead to their final resting place. I go along with one Koniner's theory that the funeral carriage was the product of Western assimilationist influence from across the nearby frontier. It certainly owed nothing to *halakha*, the Jewish law.

The coachman, perched high in front, wore a black coat with a half-cape and a black top-hat as shiny as the lacquer work. 'He was a porter who usually walked around in rags,' Joe Fox remembers, 'but when there was a funeral he looked like a lord.' The pair of horses, which had been hauling bricks or sacks of flour the day before, were similarly dressed up for the occasion, superbly caparisoned with black coats edge with a white border, their eyes trimmed with white decorations. They came from Leszczynski's mill, from Kaplan's stables, or from Ancer the horse-dealer, all of whom would lend the horses gratis, as a *mitzve*. The horses themselves were not black, nor did they sport black plumes, but such details apart, the hearse would not have shamed a State funeral.

The dead person was usually placed on a bed of straw at home, with the feet pointing to the door or towards the east – Jerusalem. 'I remember I was three years old when my mother died,' recalls Motek Mysch. 'I remember her body lying on the floor. My grandmother died and I saw her on the floor. Even when I was grown up, it was not so pleasant to stay in the house with the dead. Some of them, if they died on a Friday, would lie all day Saturday until Sunday morning.' Hirsh Meyer Natel, the Konin cobbler, was a small boy when his one-year-old brother died. 'I looked at him and was thinking, why doesn't he breathe? He was lying on the floor so I lay down as well.'

The Chevre Kadishe took charge of all the ritual associated with death and burial. The members of this highly respected society were volunteers, impeccable men of religion, who observed special feast and fast days. They delegated a guard, a *shomer*, to stay with the body all night and recite the Psalms, because a dead person must not be left alone. 'This was necessary not only for religious reasons,' a Konin woman told me, 'but because it had been known for cats to get into a house and start chewing the corpse.' Volunteers from the burial society performed the duty of ritually closing the eyes, purifying the body and wrapping it in a white linen shroud. This duty, like that of circumcising, was considered an honour and therefore went unremunerated. A candle was lit and placed at the dead person's head. A poor family with a lot of children occupying one or two rooms would find everyday life difficult with a corpse lying in the middle of the floor, and in such cases the cleansing rituals were performed in a room at the cemetery set aside for this purpose, the *ta'ara shtibl* or purification room.

When the horse-drawn hearse arrived at the home of the deceased, officials of the burial society carried the body out in a shallow, plain wooden coffin without a lid and placed it on the hearse. In the case of a man, his prayer shawl was spread out over the black cloth covering the body. Close family and other mourners followed the hearse to the cemetery on foot. Some Jewish communities in Poland, such as Krakow's, followed the example of the Holy City and forbade women to attend funerals. Women were allowed to attend in Konin but had to walk at the rear of the procession, separated from the men. It was necessary to keep the sexes apart because, as a Chasid's son in Brooklyn told me, 'Satan dances at funerals, according to the holy books.' Someone from the burial society walked alongside the cortège, rattling a *pushke* – an alms box – at bystanders while chanting repeatedly the traditional refrain: 'Charity rescues from untimely death.'

Shops closed as the cortège approached, and opened again as soon as it had passed. Christians paused and removed their hats as a mark of respect. The synagogue was in the road that led to the cemetery and it was the custom for the procession to pause for a minute outside the building. The sobs, shrieks, moans, wails and lamentations, particularly of the women, filled the air. The Jewish upper lip was never stiff.

The service at the graveside – the prayers, the Kaddish, the Rabbi's oration – would be familiar today to anyone who has attended a Jewish funeral. Departure from present Diaspora custom came at the point of burial. In Konin, as in most of Eastern Europe, a dead Jew was not interred in a coffin. There is no Jewish law that a person must be buried in a coffin. The Book of Genesis tells us that Jacob, who died at the age of one hundred and forty-seven, was put in a coffin to be taken to Hebron for burial, and that Joseph travelled in the wilderness for forty years in a coffin. In both cases, a long journey made a coffin a practical necessity. Burial in a coffin is a custom of relatively recent times, the result of copying or conforming to local non-Jewish practice. In present-day Israel, Jews are buried simply in shrouds, as they were in Konin. Izzy Hahn remembers that the shrouds in Konin had pointed hoods like those worn by the Ku Klux Klan.

An official of the burial society pulled back the hood and placed four shards of broken pottery over the dead person's eyes, nose and mouth. This is not a Jewish law but a tradition (not generally practised today) dating back to ancient times, probably founded in superstition: a way of confirming that the body was truly dead, that the cadaver would not open its eyes and start breathing again. This ritual completed, the body, wrapped in its white shroud, was lowered into the grave. In the case of an adult male, his prayer shawl was buried with him.

Pieces of timber lined the sides of the grave from the bottom to a point about halfway up. Once the body was in place, often with a little bag of soil from the Holy Land tucked under the head, planks were laid across the grave over the body, their ends resting on the tops of the upright timbers. Thus, when the earth was shovelled into the grave, there was no risk of hitting and disfiguring the dead. One Koniner remembers a mourning relative placing a locked padlock in the grave and throwing the key away, almost certainly a superstitious custom to guarantee that the dead would stay where they were and not return to earth to haunt the living.

After the funeral, the mourners walked home, ate a snack of herring and hard-boiled eggs (which had been slowly cooking in the ashes of the stove), and drank a glass of home-made plum wine. The hearse returned to its shed behind the *bes-medresh*, and the horses went back to hauling bricks and sacks.

One of the most memorable Jewish funerals to take place in Konin was that of Dr Joel, who died in the early Thirties, having won the hearts of Jewish and non-Jewish patients alike. Civic dignitaries turned out for his funeral and all the shops closed. A long procession of Jews and Christians trailed through the streets of Konin in honour of a dedicated and compassionate doctor. He had contracted appendicitis and, either because he distrusted his fellow physicians or because he wanted to widen his experience as a surgeon, he decided to operate on himself. The experiment was not a success.

36

KONINERS CAST moderation aside when they extol their former *shul*. Some say it was one of the most beautiful synagogues in all Poland. An old picture postcard view shows a single-storey building set back from the road behind wrought-iron railings. The oriental-style windows, decorative details and onion-dome finial lend it a distinct charm. In a large city it might not count as grand; in the context of a small country town it must have seemed imposing, especially to the Jews living in the dark, overcrowded houses all around.

The synagogue was built not many yards from the Tepper Marik in or around 1829.[1] In 1818 the old wooden synagogue was in such a decrepit state that there was a serious risk of its collapsing, and the Konin Jews applied for an indefinite lease of the ground it stood in, with the aim of building a new *shul*.[2] Koniners reserve most of their praise for its interior, of which there is little photographic record. One of the two photographs that have come to light shows the Holy Ark, the *aron kodesh*, with balustraded steps leading up to an elaborate, tiered structure of carvings, Hebrew inscriptions, classical pilasters and an embroidered velvet curtain covering the Holy of Holies. This Ark, the work of Zanvel Barash, was probably transferred from the earlier wooden synagogue.

Asked to be specific about the splendour of their *shul*, Koniners invariably mention the Ark first, especially its gold-leafed carvings, then the glitter of the chandeliers hanging from the painted ceiling, the four magnificent pillars at the corners of the *bimah* (the raised central podium from which the Torah is read), the stained-glass windows, the elaborate ironwork of the two women's galleries, the walls colourfully decorated with murals and Hebrew inscriptions . . .

The *shul* was Konin's principal Jewish place of worship. Here the Rabbi officiated and sermonized, the cantor sang, the wardens wore top hats, and the choirboys clustered on the steps of the *bimah*. Here the grandees and the leading non-Chasidic figures of the community prayed. Chasidim apart, the congregation represented a good cross-section of the community, including those who were too poor to afford a seat of their own. But it was the middle classes, the merchants, traders and shopkeepers, who formed the solid core of the worshippers. Where they sat reflected, in a sense, where they stood. The closer to the eastern wall, the greater the honour. Upstairs, in the women's main gallery, status rippled outwards with diminishing honour from the *rebbetsn*'s (Rabbi's wife's) seat in the front row.

The members were, in the main, conventional Jews who kept kosher homes, observed the Sabbath and sent their sons to *cheder*. While the Chasidim were, without exception, strictly observant, the same could not be claimed for all who prayed in the *shul*. Among them were some who were – by Chasidic standards – tainted by assimilation. They read secular newspapers and books, sent their children to secular schools, had wives who did not wear a *sheytl*, daughters who did not attend the *mikve*, sons who were socialist Zionists. In the years preceding the Second World War, the few grandees still left in the town were rarely seen at the regular Friday night or *shabbes* services. The High Holy Days and main festivals aside, the *shul* did not draw a packed congregation.

Most of the oral evidence I have gathered comes from those who lived in Konin during the interwar years, and I must be wary of applying their experiences to other periods of history. Unfortunately, there are no sources to draw on for a precise survey of religious observance in earlier times. One can only assume that regular synagogue attendance in Konin remained on a high level until it declined somewhat in the latter half of the nineteenth century under the liberalizing influence of the *Haskalah*, and dipped sharply after the First World War as Zionism, secularism and leftwing ideologies tempted yet more congregants away from the religious path.

Influences from the West, especially from the country on the other side of the nearby frontier, affected the way the services in the *shul* were conducted. Some aspects of the old, free-for-all style of worship gave way to the more orderly practices of the German Jews. To the Chasidim, the *shul* services seemed tepid and half-hearted. There was outer splendour and dignity perhaps, but where was the fervour? For them, the decorum of the *shul* smacked of the ways of the gentile Church. Today a choir, tomorrow an organ.

That said, I must not give the impression that Konin's synagogue Jews resembled in any way the mute and passive worshippers to be found in the majority of 'progressive' synagogues today. Every Hebrew word, every prayer and blessing – drummed into them from early childhood – came readily, even noisily to their lips. Yet for the Chasidim praying in their *shtibl*, there was insufficient show of exuberance and joy in the Torah. One could say – exaggerating in order to make the point – that the *shul* was to the *shtibl* what an Anglican cathedral is to a black Baptist chapel in the Deep South.

Still, the Jews at prayer in the synagogue suffered a physical deprivation not demanded of their Chasidic brethren: the place was unheated, even on the coldest winter day. According to one religious Koniner, custom forbade the burning of wood or coal inside a synagogue. He would not endorse my own theory that the prohibition had a secular origin, dating from the time when synagogues were made of wood and therefore vulnerable to fire. Equally, he rejected my other thought – that heating the synagogue's large interior for a service of just a few hours' duration would have been an extravagant expense. Whatever the reason, on Sabbath days in the depths of the Polish winter, 'when icicles hang by the wall', the older members of the congregation huddled in their coats as they prayed. 'I was young and didn't mind,' recalls Izzy Hahn. 'We was used to the cold. We didn't even know what central heating looked like. In any case, once you got some people inside, the place heated up a bit. Compared with outside, I tell you it was warm!'

On weekdays, a stove created a snug warmth in the small anteroom where morning services were held. The *shtibl*, being a place designated for study as well as prayer, was heated throughout the winter, protecting those who spent their days there from the threat of frostbite.

Next to the synagogue stood the *bes-medresh*, its Gothic-oriental architecture echoing that of its older neighbour. The two buildings blended harmoniously to form the religious nexus of the community. The interior, with its four-pillared *bimah*, also borrowed stylistically from the *shul*, though the Ark, furnishings and décor were of a more modest order. A row of three clock-faces on the wall showed the time of that day's morning, afternoon and evening services. No cantor sang in the *bes-medresh*: a lay member of the congregation would lead the prayers. Long tables and benches, where men could sit and study, lent the place an informal, slightly disorderly atmosphere.

The *bes-medresh* was proud of its rare and valuable collection of leather-bound religious books, some centuries old, stored in large heavy cupboards that looked like wardrobes. Favoured by the seriously religious, the *bes-medresh* was a scene of constant coming and going, of Talmudic exegesis and argument, of wagging beards and waving hands. *Yeshiva bokherim* (students) and boys preparing for *yeshiva* spent their days here, though they dwindled in number after the First World War. Older men pored over the commentaries. When a study group reached the last sentence of a holy book, it was traditional to celebrate with a glass of wine. At one table might sit a learned man helping a group of the less educated to study that week's portion of the Law.

Chasidim came here, too, to use the library. Visiting preachers and orators delivered 'moralizing sermons'. A tailor or a shopkeeper might pop in at some point during the day to attend a service and catch up with local news before going back to work. At times of international crisis or when there was rumour of a pogrom, everyone would crowd round a copy of the latest newspaper from Warsaw. Eating, which was forbidden in the synagogue, added another informal touch, and at midday spiritual nourishment gave way to the munching of bread, herring and a piece of onion. The *bes-medresh* was, in fact, a typically Jewish blend of the spiritual and temporal. It lived up to the Hebrew words for synagogue, *beth knesset*, a meeting house. In wintertime, the stove blazed on into the evening, while the Rabbi conducted study sessions. In the latter years of the last century, the *bes-medresh* became a meeting place for religious Zionists, among them my grandfather, Simcha Sarna, one of the first members of the early Hovevei Zion, Lovers of Zion, movement.

There is an old joke about the Jew shipwrecked on a desert island who built himself two synagogues, the second being the one he would not be seen dead in. When it comes to places of prayer, Jews like choice, and there was no lack of it in Konin. If the *shul*, *bes-medresh* or *shtibl* failed to cater to a man's religious or social tastes, he could shop around for a suitable *chevre*. The *chevre* – a small society of kindred spirits – flourished in Konin as it did throughout Eastern Europe.

Like the cafés in Franz Josef's Vienna, each *chevre* attracted its own circle of habitués. And just as a Viennese leisure-seeker would patronize a particular café not merely for the quality of the coffee or *Sachertorte*, but for its camaraderie, gossip, business chat, or artistic and literary discourse, so the Jew in Konin chose a *chevre* not just for its distinctive religious flavour but for its congenial company and fellowship. The Yiddish word *chevre* derives from the Hebrew word for comradeship. In this sense, the *chevre* was more than a society or house of prayer. It was like a club. An all-male club.

The *chevre*'s appeal lay in its lack of pomp and stiff decorum, its intimate, personal atmosphere. In the confined society of the *shtetl* where any mark of social distinction was valued, the *chevras* were able to spread the bestowal of rank. The more *chevres*, the greater the number of men who could acquire the title of warden. The more Sabbath services, the greater the number of recipients for the honour of being 'called up' to the reading of the Torah. A man of lowly means and modest learning could become the beaadle of a *chevre* and feel that he was a somebody. *Chevras* – at least those favoured by the poorer strata of the community – also acted as benevolent societies, holding funds from which small interest-free loans could be made to those who were ill and sinking into debt.

A *chevre* was not necessarily a person's one and only place of worship. It was quite common for a man to attend his *chevre* on weekdays and take his family to the *shul* or *bes-medresh* on *shabbes*; or he might pray in the *chevre* on weekdays and *shabbes*, and join the larger congregation in the *shul* for the major festivals.

If a *chevre* may be described as a kind of club, the most exclusive of them all was indubitably the Chevre Shas, the *chevre* of the Talmud. At this point, I cannot resist the temptation to brag. Both my grandfathers, not to mention other members of my family, belonged to the Chevre Shas. These two words were part of the Konin vocabulary I absorbed as a child without knowing what they meant. When Uncle Jacob recalled the rich Jewish life he had left behind in Konin, he never failed to invoke the Chevre Shas. Is it surprising that when he came to list the Konin *chevras* for the Memorial Book, he should give it pride of place?

Writing about this exclusive bethel as he remembered it before the First World War, he describes it as 'the gathering place in all Konin of the learned, the *maskilim*, and Zionists'. Theirs was a Judaism free of fanaticism; they did not isolate themselves from the culture of the outside world. As early Zionists, they opposed the view that the use of Hebrew for other than religious purposes was blasphemous. The members of the Chevre Shas were the élite of the enlightened religious Jews of Konin. Although Talmudic knowledge rather than wealth was expected of its members, there were a few who were fortunate enough to possess both. Until the First World War they attended Sabbath services 'aristocratically dressed in black frock coats, top hats and gaitered boots with high "Louis XIV heels" '.[3]

It is not known exactly when the Chevre Shas was founded, but it had already been in existence some years when, in 1872, it received a never-to-be-forgotten honour. The great Sir Moses Montefiore, so my uncle reports, was on his way to St Petersburg for an audience with the Tsar when he broke his journey at Konin. Where did this famous Jew who had the ear of the Empress of India, the Tsar of all the Russias and the Sultan of the Ottoman Empire choose to worship? The Chevre Shas.

At that time it was housed in the home of my kinswoman, Rivka-Rokhl Karp, and her husband, Abraham Karp, who must have been among the welcoming party to greet the distinguished English Jew – all six feet six inches of him – as he stepped out of his carriage and entered the *chevre*'s homely quarters.

Many years later, in the Twenties, letters from the Chevre Shas arrived at my grandfather's house in Sidney Street, asking for donations to its interest-free loan fund. Times were getting harder in Konin. No more top-hats or Louis XIV heels. Belonging to the Chevre Shas still counted for something, but the membership was getting smaller, poorer and older. After moving premises several times, it spent its last few years in a room above the *mikve*. The glorious days of the Chevre Shas were over.

In addition to the *chevre* of the Talmud and the Chevre Kadishe, Konin had a *chevre* of the Psalms, a *chevre* of the Bible, a *chevre* of the Guardians, a *chevre* of the Keepers of the Sabbath, a *chevre* of Zion and a *chevre* of the Tailors.[4]

The *goyim* had two churches.

37

THE CHASIDIM formed a minority within a minority, and therefore were bound to be a minority among the survivors too. There were few enough of them in 1945, and by the time I began my search in 1987, Konin's Chasidim were an endangered species on the point of extinction. Finding the few who were left would be difficult enough. Getting them to talk would, I feared, be harder still. I was right on both counts. Britain, so far as I could tell, could not boast a single Chasid from Konin. I tracked one down in Brooklyn and called him twice, only to be fobbed off each time by a stonewalling intermediary. There was no point in persisting. I was a secular Jew, an untouchable, not welcome in that tight-knit world.

I pinned my hopes on one other Koniner, the son of a Chasid, brought up in the pietist tradition and, though not a Chasid himself, committed to an Orthodox life. Although Mendel Leben was on the Konin Society's membership list, he had distanced himself from its activities. However, unlike the majority of Koniners who failed to return my questionnaire, Leben responded with a friendly and cogent letter. One of the youngest of the Konin survivors – still at school when the Nazis entered Konin – his wartime story was the familiar list of horrors: deportation, the camps, the murder of his parents, close encounters with death, liberation in 1945 . . . But what came after that was exceptional: arriving in America straight from a DP camp, the former inmate of Auschwitz and Buchenwald went on to attend Columbia University – paying his own way and graduating in electronics.

His letter revealed something more, a connection not merely with the town, but with my own family, leading me for the first time to their very doorstep. 'Not only was I born and bred in Konin,' he wrote, 'but in fact we lived in the same house with your Ryczke grandfather and his wife and their two sons. In addition, your father's eldest brother and his sister also lived in the same house.' I had no idea where that house stood, nor much else about the Ryczke family in the years before the war.

I called him soon after I arrived in New York. There were heavy demands on his time, he said apologetically. As well as doing his own professional work, he taught Talmud to religious adults every evening (unpaid, I learned later), and devoted part of each day to preparing for these classes. Just as I was fearing the worst, he said he would see me.

I sit warily at one end of the graffiti-smothered subway carriage, avoiding eye contact with the only other passengers, a pair of down-and-outs who take regular swigs from bottles wrapped in brown paper bags. It is a scene I know well from American movies, usually the prelude to an act of blood-spattered violence. Fortunately they ignore my presence. I descend from the iron-girdered elevated railway and find myself among the black-clad Orthodox, their coats flapping as they make their way – some with that strange, duck-like waddle – towards 'glatt kosher' stores (the term denotes extra-vigilant religious supervision). This is Borough Park, Brooklyn.

Mendel Leben has a genial smile that belies the sorrowful Jewish eyes. He wears black trousers, a crisp white short-sleeved shirt, and a black yarmulke. The previous day a Koniner's observant husband had asked me to cover my head when I visited their home, so today I have come prepared. Mendel sees me draw the skullcap from my pocket and says with a waving gesture of the hand: 'You don't have to worry about that. I don't believe in foisting my ideas on other people. Everyone must be free to have their own feelings on these matters and do as they wish.' Religion with a tolerant face. In the best Konin tradition.

Volumes of the Talmud in handsome leather bindings fill bookshelves lining one wall of his living room. Talmudic study is part of his daily life, as natural to him as eating or sleeping. Twice a day he prays in a nearby Orthodox *shul*. What exactly he does for a living I never quite elicit. His answers are brilliantly imprecise. I gather that he is engaged in some way with computer retrieval systems. Among all the religious tomes, a physics book lies open on the table. The house is silent. His wife is at work: she runs a jewellery business with the help of their son. A thought occurs: but for the Nazis and the war, might Mendel Leben today be leading the life of a Chasid in Konin, his days given to prayer and study while his wife takes care of the business?

We talk about our families: the Lebens and the Ryczkes. They were good neighbours, he tells me, living in a large detached house divided into several apartments. His parents sold kitchen utensils from a small store on one corner of the building; my father's sister, Bayla Prost, ran a grocery store on the other. On Sukkot the Ryczkes and the Lebens ate meals together in the *sukkah* they built in the shared courtyard behind the house.

I have brought along some photographs of the Ryczkes. Mendel stares at the faces of his former neighbours, faces he has not seen since he was a boy, and gasps with recognition: 'Yes, that's your uncle, Itsik Hirsh!' He sighs. 'So many years ago.' He picks up another picture. 'That's your grandfather, Dovid Ryczke! You know, he was a religious man and a very learned Talmudist.' The photographs trigger other memories of the Ryczke family. He shows me where they lived – on the edge of the town near the German Lutheran church. I add another dot to my street map of Konin.

Mendel Leben visited Konin in 1985 to garner family information from the register of births, marriages and deaths. On arrival he went straight to the new town, where the municipal offices were located. He was in two minds about crossing the river to have a look at the old Konin where he was born. 'I said to my wife: "Something attracts me there like a magnet." But why should I want to go? There was nobody to meet. And still there was this irrational attraction.' He went, and found only two Jewish landmarks still standing: the synagogue, busy with workers restoring the wrecked building, and the *bes-medresh*, now a public library. Its interior had been gutted after the war and was completely changed.

Much of the old Jewish quarter had been demolished, but the house where the Lebens and Ryczkes lived still stood on the outskirts of the town. His colour snapshot gives me my first glimpse of their home. He points out my Uncle Itsik Hirsh's balcony, right above the Leben shop.

He tries to describe his emotions as he walked round Konin for the first time since he and his family were deported in November 1939: 'It is hard to express. It was like bleeding inside. Wherever I went there were memories. Here I saw this man, and there I saw another. We went into one store because my wife needed some slippers and suddenly I remembered that the *mohel* who circumcised me used to have this very store.'

Mendel vaguely remembers my father visiting Konin shortly before the war: 'I think he wore a beret.' Until recently I would have said his memory had served him wrong: I cannot recall my father ever wearing a beret. But rummaging through some family papers shortly before leaving for New York, I came across a snapshot of him walking along a street with one of his stepbrothers. It was taken during his visit to Konin in 1936, and he is wearing a beret. That his headgear should have made such a lasting impression on a small boy says something about Konin, how cut off it was from the outside world, how unused its inhabitants were to anything that departed from local convention. When my father left Konin as a teenager, he must have looked like any other local Jewish lad. England changed him and clearly it showed. 'Your father looked a foreigner,' says Mendel.

Archives and records kept by the Chasidim in Konin have disappeared, probably destroyed in 1939. We do not know exactly when the Chasidic movement first manifested itself there. Its founder, the Ba'al Shem Tov, won over the masses in the eighteenth century, offering those who had little or no learning a way to God through fervent prayer and religious ecstasy. But the movement took some time to reach Konin, where most of the Chasidim belonged to a sect that was not established until the late nineteenth century.

Situated close to Germany, relatively enlightened and prosperous, Konin lacked the soil in which Chasidim could flourish. The great majority of Konin Jews stayed faithful to traditional rabbinic orthodoxy. In nearly eight hundred pages, the Memorial Book has vitually nothing to say about Chasidic life in Konin. The men who produced the book were secular Zionists, while the contributors who wrote about the religious life of the town were *misnagdim* (religious opponents of Chasidim), like my Uncle Jacob, who devotes all of one sentence to the *shtibl*, the Chasidic house of prayer.

According to Mendel Leben, there were seventy Chasidic families in Konin between the wars, representing a little over 10 per cent of the total Jewish population. They were, with few exceptions, Gerer Chasidim, followers of the *rebbe* of Gur.[1] The exceptions were four adherents of the Alexander *rebbe*, two or three followers of the Sochaczew *rebbe*, and one who was a 'dead Chasid'. He, I should point out, was alive; it was his *rebbe* who was dead. He had died in 1812, leaving no dynastic successor. Left without a living *rebbe*, his followers became known in Yiddish as the '*toyte Chasidim*', the 'dead Chasidim'. Konin's 'dead Chasid', Chanoch Rus by name, was an unworldly character, known for his absent-mindedness and phenomenal Talmudic learning. About thirty years old when the Second World War began, the 'dead Chasid' met his death in the Ostrowiec ghetto, where he was murdered.

In most respects the Konin Chasidim dressed according to tradition. They wore a black cloth kaftan with a belt – a *gartl* – tied loosely round the waist as a symbolic divider between the spiritual upper and profane lower halves of the body. Their headgear was generally a cap known as a *yidishe hitl*, made of black cloth with a high crown and narrow peak, which some of the non-Chasidic religious Jews also wore. On *shabbes* and festivals they would don a silk kaftan with a fringed belt made of interwoven silk threads, and a velvet *hitl*. In the later years, few wore what I consider to be the one attractive feature of Chasidic garb, the round, fur-edged hat, the *shtrayml*.

One aspect of their appearance differentiated them from Chasidim in other parts of Poland, and from their present-day brethren in Stamford Hill or Crown Heights: the Konin chasidim kept their *tsitses* (the fringes of an undergarment worn by Orthodox Jews) inside their trousers and did not have them hanging out on view. *Peyes* (earlocks) were kept short and tucked behind the ears. The married Chasidim wore beards, the young bachelors – the *bokherim* – in the main did not, another significant sign that the liberal Jewish ethos of Konin influenced the ways of the Chasidim too. A contributor to the London Yiddish newspaper, *Di Tsayt*, writing about Konin in 1915, comments on its Chasidim who 'have already become modern, wearing little collars, and whose daughters can speak not a word of Yiddish'.[2]

The Chasidim of Konin worshipped in a room in the same building as the *bes-medresh*, known simply as 'the *shtibl*'. It had a *bimah* and a velvet-draped ark, but its general character was plain. The services differed from those in the *shul* and *bes-medresh* in that they were conducted according to the Sephardic rite, as are all Chasidic services today.[3] Females were not just segregated, but excluded altogether. The Chasidic womenfolk used the gallery in the adjoining *bes-medresh*.

Forming a *minyan* (a quorum of ten males over the age of thirteen) was never a problem in the *shtibl*. On ordinary weekdays, when only a few worshippers gathered in a small ante-room of the big *shul* for morning prayers, there were well-attended morning, afternoon and evening services in the *shtibl*. On Friday nights the place was packed. 'Everyone went on that night unless they were sick,' says Mendel. On Saturday mornings the crowd was less numerous only because the bachelors, perhaps wanting to run their own show, worshipped separately in a room down the road. At some stage the young Chasidim split into two factions, each praying separately. The non-Gerer Chasidim would no doubt also have liked to set up their own house of prayer, but being too few to command a *minyan*, they had no choice but to worship alongside the Gerer majority. In this respect, Konin did not fulfil one of the criteria a Yiddish writer once light-heartedly listed as defining a *shtetl*: 'Two prayer rooms for Chasidim, one for the Gerer and one for the Alexander Chasidim.'[4]

The *shtibl* was the hub of Chasidic life in the town. There were no concessions here to the changing world outside: no whiff of acculturation, no adoption of *goyish* styles of worship, no choir or cantor. Wrapped in large linen prayer shawls, the congregation swayed and rocked, beat their breasts with unrestrained vigour when breast-beating was called for, prayed noisily and fervently, their lips moving like speeded-up film. But it was on celebratory occasions like Simchat Torah that the Chasidim came into their own, embracing a Torah scroll in their arms as dancing partner, singing until lost in holy ecstasy, the one form of inebriation the Jews allowed themselves.

Given their divergent attitudes to Judaism, it is not surprising that clashes occurred between the Chasidim and their opponents. A controversy over *shechita*, the slaughter of animals according to Jewish ritual, tore the community apart in the late Twenties. Kosher butchers in the town sold meat only. A housewife wanting a chicken for *shabbes* went to the market, bought a live bird and carried it squawking to the slaughterhouse near the synagogue. There she handed over a coupon which she had previously bought from the *kehillah*. The slaughterer, the *shoychet*, tore the coupon in two, retained one half, then proceeded to wield the knife. At the time of which we are speaking, there were three *shochtim* in the town, all in the employ of the community.

Mendel tells the story as it was told to him:

> There was a man by the name of Lassman, who dealt in fowl. I think business was not going so well for him and the community wanted to help him out. As they needed a *shoychet* – I think one had just retired – they told him to become a *shoychet*. However, there was a problem. The Chasidim were strongly opposed to Lassman. They said that, firstly, his wife did not wear a *sheytl*, and secondly, his beard was a bit short. The opposing side supported Lassman. He was appointed but the Chasidim refused to accept him.
>
> In the *shtibl* was a man who was not officially a *shoychet* but who had probably practised as one. He was a very learned man, and so the Chasidim went to him to have their fowl slaughtered at his house. Rabbi Lipschitz, who was on the side opposed to

> the Chasidim on this matter, declared that anything slaughtered privately by that man would be forbidden as *treyf*. There was a big fight. In fact, my father who in general was a liberal Chasid – not extreme – felt this was an issue where you had to toe the line. This caused a problem with our neighbours when Sukkot came round. My father was best friends with your uncle, Itsik Hirsh, but since the Rabbi said you are not allowed to mix with the Chasidim because they are eating *treyf*, my father built a separate *sukkah*. How was the dispute resolved? In the end I think they came to some kind of compromise: the man's wife put on a *sheytl* and his beard grew longer. But – so I have been told – there were two Chasidim who didn't want to use him for a couple of years until a new *shoychet* came to Konin.

Politically the Chasidim were to the right, as one would expect, supporters of the Agudah Yisrael religious party, which stood opposed to Herzl's Zionism. They represented the most rigid wing of the community in religious matters, and it would be all too easy for me to portray them as reactionary fundamentalists. Yet it was their strict, uncompromising attitudes that helped to sustain Judaism in Poland and preserve a culture whose loss many in the West today lament, including those who never go near a synagogue.

Despite their differences, the Chasidim and their opponents maintained a peaceful coexistence most of the time. The Chasidim tended to keep themselves to themselves, and were known for the way they came to each other's aid in time of trouble. They had their own administrative committee (Mendel's father, Moishe, was a leading member), which met weekly to discuss *shtibl* affairs and the running of their religious educational institutions. These included a full-time school for boys, the Yesoydes Hatorah, which Mendel attended, and the Bes Yaakov *cheder* for girls. For all that, it was not possible to maintain rigid separatism. Lacking the numerical clout needed to lead a totally insulated existence of their own, the Chasidic elders participated fully in community affairs. The most prominent Chasid in Konin between the wars, Baruch Dzialoszynski, was chairman of the *kehillah* as well as a town councillor and a governor of the Jewish gymnasium. He was known for his generosity in helping the needy whether they were Chasidim or not.

Mendel Leben has not broken all his links with Chasidim. Occasionally he prays in the Gerer *shtibl* in Brooklyn, worshipping according to the rite he learned as a boy in Konin. His credentials as a learned devotee of the Talmud, as an obsevant Jew married to a *sheytl*-wearing wife, are impeccable; but not quite good enough for his local Chasidim. They frown on his secular mode of dress, his lack of sidelocks and, most difficult of all to accept, the absence of a beard. In short, he is, as he points out with an amused expression but with no wish to ridicule – 'too modern'.

38

BETWEEN 1810, when the Konin community appointed its first Rabbi, and 1942, when the last Rabbi died, only four men held this post, and three of them had as their first names Tsvi Hirsh. *Tsvi* is the Hebrew, *Hirsh* the Yiddish, for deer: they are not uncommon names among Ashkenazi Jews, but the fact that so many Konin men have borne them owes something to their rabbis and the vicarious honour their names bestowed on newborn males. My own Jewish name is – Tsvi Hirsh.[1]

The panegyrical accounts of Konin's rabbis in the Memorial Book permit no failings. As youngsters they were prodigies; as adults, learned, pious and saintly. Faithful upholders of the Torah, they were everything a Rabbi should be, venerable teachers whose conduct set an example of how a Jew should live. If their eulogists err on the side of uncritical veneration, why not?

Until the early years of the nineteenth century, Konin's community was not large enough to support a Rabbi, though it had built a fine synagogue. There were learned laymen in the congregation who would have no difficulty in leading the prayers or reading the Torah. They also had a beadle, a cantor (who doubled as *shoychet*), and a scribe to look after the records, correspondence and administration. When serious matters arose, such as the need for a decision on Jewish law or to settle a dispute, the community would turn to the Rabbi in a larger town, usually Kalisz.

With Konin's population showing healthy signs of growth at the beginning of the nineteenth century, the community decided it was time to have its own religious leader, and they appointed a Rabbi from Germany, Tsvi Hirsh Amsterdam. He was a member of an 'aristocratic rabbinical family', the son of a distinguished Rabbi, and he had studied with a teacher whose illustrious reputation enabled him to pick and choose his pupils.[2] Tsvi Hirsh, we are told, was among the best.

About his term of office in Konin little is known, which probably means that it was not marked by great divisions and upheavals. He founded Konin's *yeshiva* – never destined to become one of Poland's eminent seats of learning – and produced writings on the Torah. There is only one story told about him: after he married off his children he summoned the elders of the community and declared that as his outgoings were now reduced, the eighteen guilders he received each week was too much: twelve would be enough, and the rest could go to the community. A gesture worthy of a man who 'with charity and good deeds loved the poor and always spiritually uplifted the rich'.[3]

After his death in 1849, Konin 'laid the crown of Torah and honour'[4] upon the head of Tsvi Hirsh Orbach, the son-in-law of a Rabbi and, needless to say, a man of learning, wisdom, nobility and saintliness.[5] The sight of him crossing the street on his way to the synagogue, wearing his prayer shawl, filled even Christians with awe. They recognized him as a man of God. His alleged superhuman powers became the stuff of legends. Once, when the parties to a dispute refused to execute his judgement, he banged his hand on the table and the imprint of his fingers was burnt into the wood. On another occasion, when one of the disputants refused to attend his court, the good Rabbi said: 'He will soon want to come but it will be too late.' That same day, the offender fell off a balcony, broke his foot, and limped for the rest of his life.

Tsvi Hirsh Orbach was Rabbi of Konin for thirty-four years. Christians and Jews attended his funeral in 1883. Joe Fox remembers a story told to him when he was a boy in Konin, not that many years after the Rabbi's death. Shortly before he died, he gave the order – probably as an act of modesty – that people should not name their sons after him. 'That year, so my aunt told me, four boys were born who were named Tsvi Hirsh, and every one of them had something wrong with him.'

Nothing was more likely to provoke quarrelling and squabbling within the community than the appointment of a new Rabbi. Each function had its favourite candidate. Rabbis eager for the post came from all over Poland, delivered sermons in the *shul*, were judged, criticized, argued about and sent away. The friction following the death of Tsvi Hirsh Orbach was particularly intense. Some favoured his son, Rabbi Yitzhak, as the successor. The more orthodox felt he was not sufficiently qualified to rule on all questions of *halakha*. Finally the matter went to arbitration and it was decided that Rabbi Yitzhak should become the next Rabbi but only on condition that someone else should be appointed to deal with complex matters of Jewish law. The whole affair came to an end when the Russian regime, in an act of reprisal against Germany, issued a decree that all German nationals in the country had to relinquish their jobs and leave. This disqualified Rabbi Orbach Jr, who was German-born. He subsequently became a Rabbi in Berlin.

More candidates arrived to deliver Sabbath sermons, and were found wanting by one faction or another, until the third of the Tsvi Hirsh triumvirate, Tsvi Hirsh Biezunski was given the post in 1884. Surprisingly, he was a Chasid, and who can say what complex political manoeuvring led to his appointment? Biezunski was a Kotzker Chasid, whereas the Konin Chasidim were mostly Gerer, and this may have allayed fears that the Rabbi would become a puppet of the *shtibl*. On the other hand, Biezunski had been close to the first Gerer *rebbe*, who in turn had been a pupil and brother-in-law of the Kotzker *rebbe*,[6] all of which would surely have counted against him with the opponents of the *shtibl*. Perhaps he owed his post to being a compromise candidate. Or he may have so outshone his competitors that there was no choice but to give him the job. As well as being (need one say it?) 'a scholar of genius', Tsvi Hirsh Biezunski was also 'a man of culture' who spoke Russian and had passed an examination in that subject, thus satisfying a government law that the Rabbi of a town should know the official language of the country.[7] A tall, imposing figure, he wore a long beard, a frock-coat and a *shtrayml*, but these were not enough to allay misgivings in certain Chasidic quarters, as I was to learn when I met his great-grandson, Natan Biezunski, in Israel:

My great-grandfather died before I was born, but your uncle, Jacob Sarna, remembered him and told me stories about him. For instance, when he applied for the post of Rabbi of Konin, some of the Chasidim were against him being given the job even though he himself was a Chasid. Why? Because they were worried that his trousers had a crease and that he wore silver cufflinks. He dressed too much like a gentleman – a Chasid, according to them, should be a *bisl farshlumpert* [a bit scruffy]. Also, they were not so happy about him having studied Russian. Russian? Why Russian? What's wrong with Yiddish?

Your uncle also told me that there was a big flood when the Rabbi died, and it was impossible to get to the cemetery. They had to put down planks of wood to make a kind of bridge so they could get his body across and bury him. Some of the Chasidic zealots said this was a punishment from God. Even here in Israel, many years later, a Koniner once told me: 'You know, your great-grandfather was a Rabbi but he was not kosher.' I said: 'What do you mean he was not kosher?' 'Well,' he said, 'he went about with pressed trousers and with stiff cuffs showing.'

When Rabbi Biezunski died in 1905, it was decided that as an act of love and remembrance all boys born during the thirty days of mourning would be named Tsvi Hirsh.

In 1906 Jacob Lipschitz became the fourth Rabbi of Konin. He was a *Litvak*, a Lithuanian Jew, and it took some time for his flock to get used to his accent. The son of a Rabbi and one of three brothers who were all rabbis, he was – need it be said – a young genius as a pupil and studied under the greatest teachers. He was also educated in secular studies, spoke Russian, German and Polish, and was, perhaps, the most progressive and tolerant of all Konin's rabbis, the right man to lead the community into the twentieth century. The fact that he allowed himself to be photographed – only one picture of him exists – and to have his portrait painted by the local Jewish artist, Chanoch Glicenstein, was a sign of his enlightened attitude. He was a handsome figure, impeccably turned out, with a silver, patriarchal beard. Koniners remember him as a humane and kindly man, who sometimes turned a bind eye to the letter of the law in order to observe its spirit.

One of the Rabbi's customary tasks was to give his verdict on meat or fowl suspected of not being kosher. (The person bringing it to him for inspection, usually a woman, would leave a few coins on the Rabbi's table.) Some flaw or deformity in the innards of a hen could easily render it *treyf*. Rabbi Lipschitz knew that a negative verdict on the fowl in question would cause hardship for some families, who were depending on it for their Sabbath meal. Therefore, when a poor woman came to him with a suspect bird, 'he did not hurry to forbid it and declare it *treyf* but . . . sought every means to make it kosher. He knew that not every family could afford to buy another.'[8]

During his early years in Konin he used to bake matzos, rolling them with a mechanical device rather than by hand. This outraged the Chasidim, who banned their brethren from eating the Rabbi's matzos. They were none too happy either about his willingness to join the dignitaries of the town in greeting a visiting cardinal, or his uncondemnatory attitude towards the young who desecrated the Sabbath. His son, who was ordained as a Rabbi but did not serve as one, once shocked the Orthodox by attending a *socialist* Zionist meeting in a *short* coat![9] But in general, his was a harmonious reign, and even those who disregarded or opposed religious practice never dared show him disrespect.

During the First World War, as I have mentioned, he did not hesitate to invoke the Jewish law that accords the saving of human life precedence over observance of the Sabbath. When the Nazis invaded Konin in 1939, Rabbi Lipschitz was one of the first to be thrown into jail as a hostage. After his release, he did his best to alleviate the situation of the Jews, even presenting himself at Gestapo headquarters to protest at the way they were treating his flock. He was among the second batch of Konin Jews selected for deportation, first to the nearby countryside and then, in March 1941, after a long journey by train without food or water, to Jozefow, near Lublin. There the last Rabbi of Konin met his death.

39

LOLA BIRNBAUM, born in Konin in 1903, is hard of hearing, almost blind, and lives on her own in an apartment block in Queens, New York. Her war experiences in a score of Nazi camps, the loss of her husband and two children have done nothing to shake her belief in a benevolent God. Thoughts of mortality do not bother her. She has bought a burial plot in Israel, where she wants her bones to rest. Death will come when it will come. But until the Angel of Death beckons her, life is there to be lived.

Once tall and shapely, she has become a redoubtable old lady, unyielding and uncompromising, refusing to surrender to her age. She wears glasses with bottle-end lenses and goggle-style side-pieces. These and an unsmiling countenance give her a forbidding exterior. She talks in a penetrating, sometimes screechy singsong, the vocal equivalent of Yiddish shrugs and gestures. Her sentences combine Konin Yiddish and Brooklyn English. She substitutes the Yiddish 'mayn' for the English 'my', says 'in' when she means 'and', and 'mit' when she means 'with'. Thus: 'I vent mit mayn fudder in mayn mudder.' She forms the English past participle as though it were Yiddish: I swallow, I have geswallowed – or, to render the way it sounds, gesvollerd. There is also gepunished and gehired.

'Tank Gott I remember a lut from Konin,' she says. She remembers her mother calling her to the door when she was twelve to watch the Tsar's cavalry fleeing the town. She was in the big square when the Kaiser's soldiers attached messages in cylinders to the legs of pigeons and released them into the air. I become her memory's beneficiary in a more personal, unexpected way. She remembers my maternal grandfather when he was living in Konin. This means before the year 1913, when Simcha Sarna emigrated to London. Lola is also probably the only person alive who can tell me the name of the street where he lived shortly before he left the town, a discovery that thrills me in a way I do not expect anyone else to understand. I am not sure I fully understand it myself. Is it the satisfaction of fitting another piece of the jigsaw into place? Would it matter if mankind had remained eternally ignorant of where Simcha Sarna traded in kitchenware?

Lola remembers going into my grandfather's store when she was about nine years old to buy some dishes. It was in the Krum Gesl, as the Jews called it; ulica Kramowa in Polish; Shop Street in English. It was one of Konin's shortest and narrowest streets – hence *gesl*, the diminutive of *gas*. It provided a useful short cut between the Tepper Marik and Third of May Street, which Lola calls by its old name from Tsarist times, Long Street. Little shops belonging to Jewish merchants lined both sides of the *gesl*. Lola herself had a shop there once, long after the Sarnas had departed.

Lola's family name is Bulka. There were many Bulka families in Konin, all interrelated in some way. Rivka the milliner was a Bulka. One of Leopold Infeld's most brilliant pupils was a Bulka. ('What happened to Bulka, extremely intelligent? Murdered, murdered, murdered'). Konin's Jewish lending library was housed for most of its life in the home of a Bulka. One of the old Koniners now living in London is a Bulka. The Bulkas indubitably belonged to the social category of *bekovede menshen*, honest, decent, respectable folk, the backbone of the community.

Lola was born in Ogrodowa Street, where her parents, Mendel and Taube, owned a house next to the *bes-medresh*. There was a baker in the basement, a cobbler in the attic and several other tenants in between. Her father let one room rent-free to the Chevre Tanach. The chanting of Jews at prayer was a part of everyday life for the little girl as she grew up, just across the hallway from the chevre of the Bible, of which her father was a warden. When a new velvet cover was needed for a *Sefer Torah*, the honour of sewing it naturally fell to Mendel's young daughter.

Mendel served five years as a trumpeter in the Russian army, showing sufficient talent to take him to the Imperial theatre in Moscow. After his return to Konin, he and his brother Leibish became partners in a transport business, carrying goods by horse and wagon mostly between Konin and Lodz, 100 kilometres away. When the brothers began their partnership in 1904, they would take it in turn to make the slow two-way journey each week, sometimes in a convoy of up to six wagons.

In the First World War the brothers smuggled contraband goods between Konin and Lodz. Because it was so near the German frontier, quite a lot of contraband goods passed through Konin. No one suspected that the little girl asleep on the top of the loaded wagon had bags of sugar tied with shoelaces to the inside of her clothes. Her father concealed flour and other produce in the mattresses of second-hand beds. 'Everyting hot men geshmuggled' – one smuggled everything. But one day the brothers were caught. Mendel's affluent son in America had sent him a hundred dollars, a fortune in those days, as a donation towards Lola's dowry. It was invested in contraband. The Bulkas were caught and the whole lot confiscated. Lola breaks into a cackle as she tells the story. The next time she engaged in smuggling was in Auschwitz, when she found a small piece of gold that might once have filled a tooth: 'Ikh hob gesvollerd it.'

After leaving school at the age of fourteen, Lola began helping her father, and would accompany him on the journey to Lodz. Sometimes the coachman handed her the reins and the young girl felt what it was like to be in charge of four powerful horses. Before long the boss's daughter went in his stead, sometimes riding on top, more often walking alongside 'votching everyting be in order'.

From Konin the wagons carried letters, commercial documents, parcels, barrels of alcohol from Spielfogel's distillery, and other merchandise. Lola helped with the packing and unloading – 'I had baggage on mayn shoulders, two hundred pounds, three hundred pounds.' Konin merchants entrusted her with the money to pay for cloth and other products to be collected in Lodz. The wagons trundled back to Konin laden with textiles and other manufactured goods. Lola looked after the paperwork on these trips, and got her first experience of book-keeping. At sixteen, physically attractive, lively but responsible, of good family but not too rich, she was a desirable match.

One day Lola was travelling back from Lodz in heavy rain when she recognized an old man from Konin standing by the roadside. She stopped and offered him a lift. 'So he came home and said to mayn fudder: "Mendel, I like your dotter. Ve have a son. *Lomir makhn a shidekh.*" [Let's arrange a match.] So we make engagement and der vas dancing. I always say: "If you dance at der engagement, you don't dance at der vedding."' On this occasion she was proved right.

Lola and the young man became affianced at a *tnoyim* (engagement ceremony), when the dowry settlement and other matters were formally agreed. In the presence of their parents and close family, the couple gave their word to one another,[1] signed a solemn and binding document, and smashed a plate, for even at moments of joy Jews must remember the destruction of the Temple. From this point on the two youngsters officially became a new entity: *chosn-kalleh* – groom-and-bride. The assembled company celebrated with the customary cake and wine.

Five months later, Lola announced that she wished to call off the engagement. She does not describe the moment when she broke the news to her family, but I see the shocked pressing of palms against cheeks and I hear voices crying in unison 'Oy vey!' foretelling calamity like some ancient Greek chorus. Breaking an engagement in those days, says Lola, was 'vorse than a divorce' – a scandalous thing to do unless one party had a justifiable and serious grievance against the other. For the rejected it meant public humiliation and unavoidable devaluation in the marriage market, perhaps disastrously so in the case of a spurned female. Breaking an engagement was more serious than a *get* (deed of divorce) because, for one thing, a *get* could be granted without the parties forgiving each other, whereas nullifying the engagement contract required mutual absolution. Few of those who were rejected found it easy to forgive their rejector. Lola must have been aware of the family pressure that would be brought on her to change her mind, but she held her ground, displaying the determined spirit that years later helped her endure the camps. Why did she not want to marry the young man? 'Because I didn't like him' – a view not generally regarded at that time as a sound reason for rejecting a prospective husband from a decent family.

Unsurprisingly, the rejected bridegroom and his near ones retaliated. Accusations flew back and forth: that she was simply after a suitor with more money; that he was unbearably jealous. The acrimony fuelled the town's *yentes*, *yakhns* and *pliotke-makhers*. (That Yiddish offers a goodly choice of words for trouble-making gossips says a lot about *shtetl* life.)

There was only one tribunal to turn to at a time like this

– the Rabbi. Lola's father, uneasy at breaking a contract with a fellow townsman, was reluctant to pursue the matter personally before Rabbi Lipschitz. Instead, his wife attended the rabbinic court to argue her daughter's case against that of the fiancé's incensed father. Rabbi Lipschitz found in favour of the young man and awarded him suitable compensation. The parties forgave each other and peace returned to the two households. When, later on, Lola accepted Jonah Birnbaum's offer of marriage, it was not for mercenary reasons. She liked him. 'I no have a *shadchen*' (matchmaker).

Lola was eighteen when she married Jonah, a business associate of her father's who came from Lodz. A few years older than she, he had observed her development from schoolgirl to nubile teenager, a tall and sparky figure striding beside her father's loaded wagons on the road to Lodz. They married in 1921. She remembers the date straight off – 27 November, 'two weeks before Chanukah' (religious festivals were the calendar landmarks by which all important events were remembered) – and the day of the week – a Tuesday.

Tuesday was no arbitrary choice. The Book of Genesis records that on the third day, Tuesday, God surveyed his creation and – not once but twice – 'saw that it was good'. On Monday he appraised his day's handiwork without noting even once that it was good. Therefore Tuesday was a much-favoured nuptial day, while Monday was best avoided. On Monday, the day before her wedding, Lola went to the *mikve* for her premarital ritual purification.

The wedding took place in the early evening. For hours beforehand, the Bulka living-room became a strictly female domain, where Lola's mother, assisted by a flock of aunts and cousins, fussed over the bridal toilette. A dressmaker had moved in two weeks earlier to complete the trousseau and sew the calf-length wedding gown, which was made of pale lilac silk, a gift from Lola's brother in America. Most other presents from friends and relatives would arrive after the wedding, always in the form of things for the home, never cash. It was the role of the bride's father to be the cash dispenser at this stage of the game, a fate he bemoaned as the tradesmen's bills poured in. As though the wedding was not costing enough, his daughter needed a new kitchen set, a new bedroom suite 'mit der mirrors' and goodness knows what else. 'My fudder said to me: "Ven I married I had a table mit three legs."'

Lola shows me her sepia wedding photograph – 'Dis is my husband.' Looking uncannily like Gustav Mahler, he is formally dressed in an old-fashioned wing collar and bow tie, and a superior piece of tailoring with a white handkerchief tucked into the top pocket. The bride, poised and beautiful, could well be a high-society heiress from Berlin or Vienna. Across her smooth forehead, edging the hairline, lies a braid of pearls ending in drooping circlets just below the ears like delicate ear-rings: the creation of her relative Rivka the milliner.

The photograph carries a special ache. I know how the marriage ended, how the children of this union forged on a propitious Tuesday met their fate. The old lady shows no emotion as she watches me looking at the photograph with the knowledge of what came after.

Back to the wedding day: when word reached the sitting-room that the menfolk were ready, Lola's attendants lowered her veil and gave the folds of her gown a final pat before she set off to join the groom under the *chupeh*. The door of the sitting-room was opened and the bridal party set forth, the bride escorted on one side by her mother, on the other by her future mother-in-law. The procession did not have far to process. Facing them on the other side of the hallway was the entrance to the *chevre* of the Bible. The small hallway, normally dim at this hour on a November evening, was illuminated by a double line of flickering candles, held aloft by women forming a path of honour between the two doorways. ('Valking to de *chupeh*, both sides stand de pipl, mosten de vimen mit candles.')

The bridal entourage entered the packed, dark-suited, all-male province of the *chevre* where, under the wedding canopy, her father, the groom in his *kitl* (white linen robe), the groom's father and Rabbi Lipschitz stood waiting. Aryeh-Leib the milkman was in attendance in his official capacity as beadle of the Chevre Tanach.

The proceedings went smoothly, according to the Law of Moses and the people of Israel. The bride circled the groom seven times. The groom placed the ring on the bride's finger. The bride accepted his consecration. The women sniffled. The Rabbi pronounced the Seven Blessings. The groom stamped his foot on the wineglass. The entire assembly – the men filling the room and the women crowding the hallway and the children trying to look in – all cried with one voice: '*Mazeltov!*'

The guests dispersed back to their homes while the final touches were put to the wedding feast. The fragrant bouquet of *heymishe* cooking was already filling the air, tantalizing the palates of the groom-and-bride, who had been obliged to fast all day. Now they went into a separate room where they were left on their own to break their fast with the customary bowl of *goldene yoykh*, the special broth reserved for this occasion, its unskimmed surface cholesterol-rich with golden globules of fat.

Meanwhile, Aryeh-Leib was busy setting up tables in the *chevre* for the men, and in the sitting-room for the women. In the kitchen, Miriam Klapstein, Konin's ace professional cook, was keeping an anxious eye on the food: steaming pans of broth, platters of gefilte fish and plain fish, huge baking dishes crammed with roast chicken and meat, pots of *tsimmes*, a sweet, succulent mix of vegetables, and, of course, large quantities of the cakes for which Mrs Klapstein was renowned.

When the signal was given, Aryeh-Leib put on his white gloves and top-hat and set off with the coachman to collect the guests. A gathering of about seventy crowded into the Bulka home. There were no speeches. A *marshelik* (professional master of ceremonies-cum-jester) set the party spirit going with couplets and jokes made at the expense of the leading personages present. A *klezmer* trio played. The guests punished their digestive systems. Aryeh-Leib, now in his role of waiter, helped to serve the food. The men drank wine and schnapps – in moderation says Lola. They chanted the grace said after a wedding feast and blessed God 'in whose abode is joy, and of whose bounty we have partaken, and through whose goodness we live'. The mothers silently prayed that their own daughters should also find such a match. The children larked about. There was singing and dancing until the early hours. Then, when the last guest had gone, Jonah and Lola retired to their bedroom newly furnished mit der suite and der mirrors.

Honeymoon? 'How knew from honeymoons?'

Lola and Jonah were still living with her parents in 1925 when she opened her little shop in the Krum Gesl where she sold haberdashery and fancy goods, known by the Polish word *galanteria*. Jonah traded in stockings on his own account, and became increasingly involved in the transport business as his father-in-law's health declined. In 1927 Mendel Bulka died.

Lola gave birth to her first child, a son, Yitzhak, in 1925, in the house where she herself was born. Two years later she had a daughter, Shana. After that the Birnbaums moved into an apartment above her shop. Lola's mother came round each day to help look after the children. When they were unwell, *buba* Bulka placed a picture of Rabbi Meyer the Miracle-Worker[2] beside their bed, lit two candles in front of it, said a prayer, and left the revered second-century sage to perform another miracle. He never failed. The children always recovered.

As the Thirties progressed, the worsening anti-Semitic climate affected the Birnbaums like everyone else. Pickets blocked the entrance to her shop. By dint of hard work the family got by, hoping for a better future. Thoughts of departure from Konin centred only on their son, a bright boy at school, who wanted to become an engineer. Lola and Jonah cherished the dream of sending him, when he was older, to the Technion in Haifa.[3]

Lola brings out two battered wallets crammed with family photographs. Today she would not possess a single picture of her parents, husband, son or daughter – now her most treasured possessions – were it not for these photographs dutifully sent from Konin before the war to relatives in Israel and America. Lola picks up one of a cluster of magnifying glasses lying on the table and scrutinizes each photograph before handing it to me. The most striking is a portrait of Lola herself, in profile, looking like a *femme fatale* of the silent screen, in a high fur collar and magnificently 1920s hat with a long lampshade fringe: Rivka the milliner at her most bravura.

There are photos of the Bulka family, Shana aged five with classic shadowy Semitic eyes, and Yitzhak at thirteen, self-conscious in his bar mitzvah suit. The ceremony took place in 1938 in the big *shul*. That morning, *buba* Bulka tied a red ribbon inside her grandson's pocket '*az me zol nisht gebn keyn eyn-oreh*' (so that no one should cast an evil eye on him). Others helped thwart the demon forces by dropping a clove of garlic in his pocket. It was a happy day.

One year later Lola and her son looked on helplessly as the Holy Scrolls from the synagogue, including the one he had read from on his bar mitzvah, were flung into the middle of the Tepper Marik and set alight. The Birnbaums were deported to Ostrowiec. Finally, separated from each other, they ended up in the camps. There the

Nazis took the lives of Lola's mother, her husband, daughter, and almost certainly her son.

She tells me of the last time she saw Yitzhak, then seventeen. It was in Auschwitz. Neither new the other was there or even alive. They had not seen one another for two years. One day in 1943 he suddenly caught sigh of her in the camp. 'It vos Yom Kippur. He recognize me. I no recognize him.' He called out to her and she knew who he was, by his voice. Later, she managed to smuggle a piece of bread to him in another part of the camp but he sent it back. 'He said: "You need it more than me."' He was moved to another camp and they did not meet again.

Lola wears a plain chain necklace from which hangs a heart-shaped frame containing three minuscule photographs of her son, her daughter, and of Lola and Jonah on their wedding day. 'I wear dem over mayn heart. I know mayn dotter pass away and dat dey buried her. I know she is dead. Mine husband vas killed in a camp. I know mayn mudder vas killed, I know. My son I don't know if he is dead or alive. Dis is de voist ting for me. I live in hope . . . because nobody told me he vas dead, nobody give me proof . . . Somebody told me three days before de liberation he was living, and I'm looking all over de vorld for him.'

Her fellow Koniners, her friends and others, have tried to convince her that he is dead, but she hearkens to her own inner voice. She has searched all over America and Israel, tracking down those who were with him in the camps. She has firmly established that he was alive in Bergen-Belsen a few days before the camp was liberated. But what does that mean? When British troops entered Belsen on 15 April 1945, they found '10,000 unburied bodies, most were victims of starvation. Even after liberation three hundred inmates died each day during the ensuing week . . .'[4]

Sick and emaciated at the time of her own liberation, she trudged back to Konin in the hope that Isaac would turn up. Her conviction that he lives is unshakeable. She tells me that an American priest once said to her: 'Lola if you don't find your son on dis oith you'll find him in heaven.' She answered: 'I don't want find him in heaven. I want to find him on de oith!' I ask the obvious question: were her son alive, would he not have traced her by now? She has a theory: perhaps the nineteen-year-old lad took shelter with a Christian German couple after he was freed, lived with them, fell in love with their daughter, married her and chose to reject the past. 'Maybe he don't want to be found. *Un dis ligt oyf dem harts*' (And this thought burdens my heart).

She speaks of these things with no outward sign of grief, as though there are no tears left to shed. The one and only time her voice breaks, momentarily, is when she speaks of God: 'I still believe in God. *Muzn* in someting *glaybn.* [One must believe in something.] I believe in God from childhood. He is vid me. He give me courage. He direct me to do everyting. You know, vhatever comes I take it – all the sickness; it hoit me here, it hoit me here, it hoit me de feet. I have de eyes bad, in *dis* is bad in *dis* is bad. I never complained. I say: "I survived Hitler, I vill survive dis." I soffer. I accept it. Everyting. I accept the years in de camps. But I don't vont to be alone, you know, because vorse ting is *bay nakht az me shloft nisht* [at night when I can't sleep]. Everyting comes in mind. Every day, all de time, I tink about my son.'

At eighty-four she makes a valiant effort to live in the present: 'I don't like a qviet life. If I'm mit people I'm out of de past.' Voluntary work takes up most of her week, as it has done for the last fifteen years. On Tuesdays she goes to a home for the blind, where she helps the residents make toys and dresses. She points at the stuffed animals perched along the top of her sofa and a tiger occupying an armchair: 'I put de bows on, I put de eyes in, I finish it.' On Thursdays she goes to a club run by the National Council of Jewish Women, where she crochets sweaters and makes blankets. On Friday she works in the blind home's pharmacy: 'Mayn blind people count de pills. I check.' She gives much of her time to working with retarded children. She belongs to Hadassah and other Jewish organizations, is a member of the Forest Hills Synagogue, goes on senior citizen coach outings, and is about to set off on her own for a holiday in Israel. She has been there many times, and always tries to go to Tiberias to say a prayer at the tomb of the man who used to cure her children when they were ill – Meyer the Miracle-Worker. She regularly donates part of her German reparation money, her main means of support, to Zionist causes, and to the Technion in Haifa.

She arrived in America after the war with a few clothes, a pillow, a spoon, a press iron and two dollars. She lived for a while with her brother in New Jersey. Keen to be independent, she looked around for work, bluffed her way into her first job with spurious claims of catering experience, and was hired as a cook in a Jewish hotel. She carried on in catering, working the wedding and bar mitzvah circuit, until she retired.

Now she has no close relatives left. A slight note of bitterness, but no self-pity, creeps in when I raise the subject of her fellow Koniners in New York. She used to see them: 'I know all de Koniner and now no Koniner know me. *Ikh bin tsu alt.* [I am too old.] So I keep avay. Tank Gott I don't need nobody.' She no longer attends the annual memorial service: it is too far for her to go by public transport, and she says no one offers to take her.

She did not buy the Konin Memorial Book. 'I don't need de book. I know de past, so vot I need it?' I point out that the Koniners who have bought the book also know the past. '*Zey hobn kinder.* [They have children.] If my son had lived, I vould have subscribed a book for him, and it might have been interesting for de grandchildren, but now, for whom? But ven you have finished your book, please send me a copy and I pay you.'

Before I leave, she opens a glass cabinet, its shelves jammed full with china animals and knick-knacks. She asks me if I would like to take something as a souvenir. 'Perhaps for your children?' She is disappointed to hear they are too old for such things. Perhaps a bead necklace for my wife? We pass near a bookcase, which reminds me to ask her about a Yiddish writer from New York named Ronch, whose name was unknown to me until last week. I know little about him other than that he was born in Konin and died a few years ago. Lola is unaware of his Konin connection but thinks she has one of his books translated into English. She peers along the bookshelves, her nose almost touching the spines, and pulls out a novel with a torn jacket, *The Awakening of Motek* by Isaac Ronch. She thrusts it at me as a farewell gift. 'Of vot use is it to me? Have it! Have it!' I accept it gratefully.

It is dark when I leave her. She asks me to take care. 'Call me ven you get home,' she shouts as I walk towards the elevator. The *shtetl* legacy is evident all around as I make my way along Queens Boulevard to the subway, passing a score of doctors' and dentists' plaques – Ekstein, Lieberman, Tregerman . . . And kosher butchers with the Star of David. The bunch of old folk who had been sitting outdoors earlier, chatting in the October sunlight, have hobbled home with the aid of their rubber-tipped sticks to fall asleep in front of the television. The gift shop selling Israeli souvenir shlock is shut. The Knish Nosh snack bar is busy selling Cocktail Knishes; elsewhere matzo ball soup, gefilte fish and latkes are on offer. *Shtetl* culture flourishes – in the alimentary canal.

I hang around on the gloomy platform at Sixty-Seventh Avenue, deserted but for two other passengers waiting for the R train to Manhattan. I sit alone on a bench near the tunnel, a figure in an Edward Hopper painting. Remembering warnings not to travel on the subway at night, I hide my shoulder-bag behind my feet. Distant rumblings produce no train. I open up *Motek* and read the blurb: '. . . the story of a childhood in a turbulent era preceding World War I.' Set mainly in Lodz, the story begins with references to the small, unnamed country town where Motek's family used to live. I flip over the pages and my eye catches sight of a familiar name, Dluga Street; and another, Zhelona Street; and another, the River Warta. The author mentions the lending library where the young used to gather. I know this place, this 'provincial backwoods town' he is describing. And I certainly recognize the boy's family: 'The Sarnes had carried on a trade in crockery since time out of mind . . . the Sarne womenfolk of that time had been vastly more enterprising than the men, who had been mostly of the scholarly type and haunters of the synagogue.'[5]

In Poland my family spelled their name Sarne. I am reading a description of my grandparents.

Postscript In 1990 Lola settled in Israel. No longer able to look after herself, she moved into an old people's home in Rehovoth. I hear from her occasionally, a few wavering words in her own hand, accompanied by a message written on her behalf: 'Everybody in Israel is very busy. They never have time to visit. I am very lonesome here in my room. I'm sorry I'm complaining.'

40

I FIND MYSELF discussing the subject of revenge with Louis Lefkowitz a few days after his eloquent address to the memorial gathering. In his apartment in Mount Vernon, outside New York, the former tailor of Kleczew and Konin calmly recounts some of his experiences as a 'graduate of many places of extinction', including Buchenwald and Theresienstadt. His wife, Miriam, endured Auschwitz. They try to block out – but with little success at this time of the year – memories of what they went through, what they witnessed, what was done to their loved ones. I raise the question of revenge, wondering if he had ever felt the desire for it. I remind him of a troubling poem in the Konin Memorial Book: an impassioned plea to God to remember those who remembered Him in their final hour. The poet, mindful of his own mother's constancy of faith as she went to her death, begs God for more than remembrance: he wants *nekomeh!* Revenge![1]

'I saw *nekomeh* in Theresienstadt,' says Lefkowitz. 'For two days after the liberation, the Russians let us do whatever we want. I was too weak to join in, but I saw our boys bring in Germans who were running away on horse and wagons. They brought them in – whole families on the wagons. They put gasoline over the people and burned them up. Wagons with whole families were burning day and night for two days.' The Germans in charge of the camp and all the guards had made good their escape. Those put to the torch were civilians fleeing from the Russians.

'When I saw the Germans burning, did I have feelings? No, I had more compassion for the horses. I said: "I hope they don't do nothing to the horses. It's not the horses' fault." ' Was it, I ask, the fault of the German children they burned alive? 'What did the Germans do to *our* children?' But the German children had done no wrong. 'And *our* children did something wrong? You must understand, we were so outraged, so bitter. Now I wouldn't do it. Now I would think differently. I would have to separate the guilty from the innocent.' But when the camp gates were thrown open, did he want revenge? 'Of course, who didn't? Once I went out to the latrines where we had German soldiers cleaning up; it must have been about three, four days after the liberation, and the latrines were overflowing. A couple of our boys were standing there and one said to a German guy: "Why don't you clean it up?" He said: "I'm not going to clean it." The Jewish feller knocked him down, and I said to him: "Now drown him!" I said: "Drown him!" I said: "Drown him!" He drowned him right there. They drowned *our* boys. In Buchenwald there was a swimming-pool but there was no water in that pool, just human shit. The Germans hanged Jewish boys and threw them in. I saw it.

'There was a young lad with us, Shloymeleh, younger than me, who lost a finger in the camp. Why did he lose a finger? The Germans saw a ring on his finger. Shloymeleh wanted to keep that ring so bad he cut his finger off to get the ring so *they* wouldn't get it. You know what he did? He came back to the camp one day – the second day after the liberation – carrying a sack. I thought he had potatoes in it. There were fifty men in the room. I was lying in bed sick, and I saw him empty the sack – three dozen or more fingers fell out with rings. I felt nothing. I was numb. I didn't have no feelings for nobody, especially for the Germans.'

In Lodz, one night not long after the war, Lefkowitz was walking along the street with a couple of Jewish friends, one of them a former lieutenant in the Soviet army. 'A Polack walking behind us stared cursing the Jews. This Russian lieutenant said: "We have to do something about it." We were near a house with a courtyard. He took the Polack into the courtyard and finished him off. He said: "One anti-Semite less," put his knife in his coat, and we walked away. We lost six million. Six million is enough.'

It was from Louis Lefkowitz that I learned how a Koniner by the name of Leon Danziger met his death. The stories I had heard about him were vague and contradictory. Leon Danziger ('May his name be blotted out,' cursed one Koniner in Yiddish at the mention of his name) was not someone his townsfolk were keen to talk about. Danziger became a Kapo, eager to prove to his masters that he was as good as any German at beating Jews. He thought it was his route to survival. In the end, his fellow Jews drowned him in a latrine, or so I was told. Another report has it that Danziger ended up like his victims in the gas chamber.[2] None of this is correct, says Lefkowitz, the first Koniner able to give me a first-hand account of the Kapo's fate:

> I was with him when I was deported in March 1941. From the first day he became rightaway a *makher*, a big shot. I'll tell you how. He was a Communist before the war, and he was put in jail because of his politics. We were standing on this open space where they gathered us together to be deported, and the German commandant said: '*Ist da jemand der in Gefängnis war vor dem Krieg?*' [Is there anyone here who was in prison before the war?] Everyone was scared, but Danziger put up his hand. The Commandant said: '*Warum?*' Danziger explained; and you know what the Commandant said? '*Komm 'raus. Solche Leute darfen wir.*' [Step forward. We need people like you.] And right away Chasid put on his band and became a *makher*. 'He didn't go to work like the rest of us. He walked around the huts in the morning to see that everybody is out, shouting '*Raus! Raus!*' He hit Jews many times. I saw him do it, with a whip.[3] He always had a girlfriend. Nobody was allowed to look at a woman, but he had a woman.
>
> He travelled with us from camp to camp until we came to Riga in June 1944. The Germans said to him: 'No more *makhers* here. You're going to work.' First, some Jewish guys beat him up in the camp, and he could hardly go to work the next day. These were guys who hated him because he mistreated them badly. I didn't have no pity on him because I saw what he did. He was pushed in a latrine, sure, but he came out again.
>
> Our work in Riga was loading timber onto boats, and you had to walk across a plank to board the ship. As he was going along that plank with a bunch of boards on his shoulder, somebody pushed him – just touched him – and he fell into the water. This was the port of Riga and it was deep, maybe fifty, seventy feet deep, and he never came out. The Germans who were on guard did nothing, they didn't care. You think I would jump in and save him? No way. He wasn't worth it. So that was the finish of Leon Danziger.

Which of us does not deplore the spirit of revenge, we who have never had our high-mindedness put to the test, who have not suffered at the hands of others as Lefkowitz has done? Today, nearly half a century after his release, content with his life in America, his son put through college on the proceeds from dry-cleaning and alterations, Lefkowitz says that the desire for revenge has left him. Justice, yes; punishment according to the law for those found guilty, yes; blind revenge, no. He cannot blame today's generation of Germans for the sins of their fathers. But in earlier times, when he was starving and could hardly stand on his swollen knees, when he saw his comrades beaten to death and hanged, when he himself nearly died in the typhus epidemic that swept through Theresienstadt after the liberation, when he grieved for his brother and his father and other relatives and friends, what then? Yes, then it was different.

41

At 2 pm on the afternoon of 20 January 1945, the first troops of the Soviet Eighth Mechanized Corps under General Ivan Dremov entered the outskirts of Konin. That evening, following a skirmish with retreating German forces, the Soviets occupied the town and began mopping-up operations. On 23 January a Red Army communiqué announced that Konin was free.

Before the end of February the first handful of Jews began trickling back. Others, still in captivity and clinging to life, had to wait until May and the end of the war for their freedom. When it came, some were too ill, too physically and mentally wrecked to make the journey home. They became Displaced Persons. By the end of the year a total of forty-six Jews had returned: twenty-four men, fifteen women and seven children.[1] Not all were originally from Konin. Survivors came and went in the course of the year, and it is unlikely that there were ever more than twenty-five Jews in the town at any one time during most of that period. I estimate that of the 2,700 or so Jews living in Konin in 1939, perhaps 200 lived to see the defeat of their enemy, including those who for one reason or another did not or could not return home.

The journey back to Konin called for superhuman will-power from men and women confused and demoralized after their ordeal. Psychiatrists have observed that many survivors became even more acutely traumatized when the daily preoccupation with survival ceased. 'For many it was only then [after liberation] that the realization of the loss of most or all of their nearest relatives, friends and extended family and the world they had known, began to penetrate their consciousness.'[2]

Returning home sometimes entailed trekking hundreds of miles and crossing several frontiers. Everywhere cities were in ruins, roads and bridges destroyed, means of transport broken down, shops empty, money valueless. Izzy Hahn was seventeen, his brother Karol fifteen, when they were liberated in Czechoslovakia. It took them weeks to reach Konin, walking, hitching lifts, and taking circuitous journeys by train, living off beetroots dug up in fields, free meals from the Red Cross, and sometimes food extracted by threat. In his London home, Izzy recalled those times:

> We had no possessions, no money, no papers, nothing and we were wearing our striped camp uniforms. In German villages we demanded food. I went into one house and a smartly dressed German comes out, wearing a watch and chain. I took it away from him. I says: 'Have you got something to eat?' He brought a box, put in a dozen potatoes and wanted to give it to me. I slung it in the corner and went in and helped myself to a good meal. They saw our striped suits, they knew the Russians were coming, and they were scared. We picked up weapons lying in the road, slept in empty houses, and picked up jackets and trousers on the way.

Izzy caught a last glimpse of his parents in Ostrowiec when he escaped from he *Aktion* that sent them and thousands of others to Treblinka. Did he hope to find them alive after the war? 'Not really, not after what I'd seen in Auschwitz and other camps. One of my uncles got shot in front of me. I saw my mother's sister shot, and many other people I know murdered. I knew what was going on. But I thought: "Perhaps, perhaps . . . maybe a miracle will happen and somebody will come back." ' After eight months in Konin, he knew the miracle was not going to happen, and he left.

Tola Zeidlitz and her mother were liberated from Auschwitz in January 1945. Turning down the offer of medical treatment in Sweden, they made it back to Konin hoping other members of the family would do the same. In New York, where Tola now lives, she told me: 'We walked to Krakow. We were like *toyte menshen* [dead people]. We had nothing to eat and had to beg for food. When we showed people the numbers on our arms, some of them said: "Maybe the Jews did it themselves." After we got back to Konin, my mother used to go every day to the station to see if Father was coming home or my brother, but they never came.'

Julius Ancer, whom I met in Minneapolis, was one of the first to return to Konin, in February 1945, after escaping from a camp: 'I arrived by train . . . and walked from the station. My one possession was a worn-out blanket . . . which served as a jacket . . . My only clothes were what I was wearing – a set of warm underwear, torn slacks and shoes, and a British army short woollen jacket – a gift from a British prisoner of war . . . The only feelings I remember at arrival was being cold, hungry and practically starving and worn out.'[3] Ancer's fiancée arrived a few weeks later. His parents, like hers, had been killed by the Germans. 'My biggest hope,' he said, 'was that my older brother, Mathes, with his wife and sons, aged six and four years old, who were concealed as a gentile family, had survived. Later on I learned that a Polish peasant woman reported their hide-out to the Gestapo, who shot the four of them in the summer of 1944, just weeks before the Russian army marched in.'[4]

The first Jew he encountered in Konin was his former neighbour, Leo Monczka, who, the reader will recall, had left Konin in 1939 hidden among sacks of flour on the back of a lorry. After spending the war years in the Soviet Union, he went back to Konin in February 1945:

> Like several survivors I travel to Konin to find out if any of my relatives might still be alive. The train stops. I hear the call 'Konin.' It is night and as I step out I realize that my miserable luggage has disappeared. My belongings were a symbol of poverty but at that time this poverty represented my fortune. [A policeman at the station, who recognizes him, tells him that local boys have become adept at boarding moving trains, stealing luggage and jumping off before the next station] . . . In the meantime all the horse cabs to town have left. I intend to walk. The policeman is very helpful and tells me that the iron bridge was blown up by the Germans when they left,[5] and it is very dangerous to walk that way in the dark.
>
> [The station master allows him to sleep on the station.] I wait for morning. The moment daylight seems near, I begin the slow

walk to the town . . . Here is my house, my apartment. Without thinking I knock on the first window. It was from here that I always used to be given the key of the door when I returned from a journey. A young man with a revolver in his hand opens the window and says roughly: 'What cheek at this early hour.' He is an officer of the UB [Urzad Bezpieczenstwa, the secret police]. I tell him: 'Not so rough, young man. I am the owner of this house and of this apartment.' He puts the revolver away and, somewhat embarrassed, he replies that he doesn't know me from earlier days, and that the other half of the place is occupied by my caretaker. He calls the caretaker who, surprised to see me, receives me warmly. I get a bed with a whole lot of bed linen that comes from my own household and other unfortunate neighbours' . . .

Several former Christian friends came to visit me . . . The conversation makes me feel as if I had come back from hell and now find myself in a different world. I visit the municipal offices and am warmly greeted by the secretary to the council, Stanislaw Jarecki, who has been an official there for over fifty years. I am received in the office of the Mayor . . . We go into the splendid town council chamber. The beautiful pictures hang on the wall like before, nothing damaged. I seat myself in the same place where, as a councillor, I participated in council meetings for so many years.

Next morning at eight o'clock I receive an invitation from the Starosta [district prefect] to come to his office at midday. I fill the time in between visiting the Tepper Marik. It was there and in the sidestreets that the Jewish inhabitants mostly lived. The houses have been burned. I walk towards the street where the *bes-medresh* used to be and, next to it, the magnificent synagogue, now a dreadful sight, especially the inside, all ruined, proof of vandalism by the criminal hands of the Nazis. The building is used as the town's store for old junk.

After this, I follow the road to the park and try to visit the cemetery. The surrounding wall has disappeared, the bricks plundered. All the gravestones, the plain ones as well as the most precious ones made of marble and granite, are gone. Everything has been taken, from the smallest to the largest. The Nazis have not honoured the dead either. They have vandalized the resting-places that existed here for generations. No sign of a grave is visible. Grass grows on the site . . . There are cattle and goats grazing.

It is a bright day but my eyes darken over. The soil is moist, wet in places, and I have the impression that it is soaked with blood. With slow paces I make my way to the big square and I am now at the entrance where the sign says: *Starostwo*. The Town Hall clock strikes twelve.

As I enter, functionaries recognize me from the old days. The door of the Starosta's office opens and he asks me in. He introduces himself. He is from Poznan but nevertheless knows who I am. He has heard about me and is authorized by the town council to propose to me that I re-establish my former building materials yard. What I built up over thirty years is still there, and he and the town council will put materials and everything else at my disposal.

I sit with half-closed eyes, my mind filled with the impressions of the last three hours. I am asked if I have heard the proposition, and I answer that it would mean my staying in Konin . . . I ask what would happen when I died. The Jewish cemetery no longer exists. There would surely be no room in the Catholic cemetery for a non-believer. I also ask what they would do in my place, coming back to their former home and seeing what has happened, as I have just done. He understands me and asks my pardon.

It is a short stay. I stand near the railway tracks at the station. The incoming train stops and they call out 'Konin.' I board the train. It is evening. In the compartment I stand by the window. The high street lamps of the town are visible, lighting the place as in the old days. The train moves, the lamps become ever less visible and disappear. As in a dream I see figures moving, the figures of those on whom this light once fell, and who are no longer among the living.[6]

A few survivors were able to return to their former homes. Lola Birnbaum, bereft of her husband and two children, lived for a short while in her parents' house, where she had married Jonah. 'Der caretaker take me in. I vas veighing eighty-five pounds. I live four weeks on flour un milk.' Most of the returning survivors found that their apartments had either been demolished or taken over by Poles. They were reluctant to claim them back for fear of trouble. Another Lola – Lola Sherer, née Moskowicz – who now lives in Haifa, was one of those who found their former home occupied:

'Upstairs was a woman I knew and I spoke to her. She said: "You're still alive? What are you doing here?" But she was friendly and gave me a meal and said I shouldn't leave Konin: "Stay here, become a Christian and get married to a Christian. Why go away? Stay here. Don't go. I knew your parents, your mother." But I could not stay. I felt dreadful.' After a few weeks Lola left with my cousin, Felunia Prost, another survivor who had gone back.

On his first day in Konin, Motek Mysch knocked at the door of his apartment. 'I wanted to find some photographs and look around, but the occupier wouldn't let me in. He thought I was dead. "How come you're still alive?" he asked.' Motek left the next day and never returned.

When Alex Kaliski, who had served in the Russian army, visited a Polish family he had known well before the war, they fed him and showed him kindness: 'The father said: "Alexeyu, stay in Konin. Have my daughter, marry her, stay here." I told him that Poles always used to say to us: "Jews, go to Palestine." So I'm going.'

Fella Nitzky, whom I met in Brooklyn, arrived in Konin after leaving Auschwitz, knowing that her parents and other members of her family had perished. She walked to the house on the edge of the town where she lived before the war as Fella Leben, sister of Mendel, the Chasid's son. My Ryczke grandfather and his family had been close neighbours in the same building. Fella described her trepidation as she walked through the main entrance and approached the door of the apartment she had last seen as a schoolgirl in 1939. The door was slightly ajar. There was no sound from within, no sign of any occupants, nothing to stop her entering her old home. 'But I just stood there frozen, unable to touch the door.' She fled and never went back.

Izzy Hahn and his brother walked to the corner of the Tepper Marik to find that their house was no longer there: 'They told me the Germans had pulled Jewish houses apart looking for the gold that was supposed to be hidden in the walls. Then they used forced labour to demolish the houses. One whole side of the Tepper Marik was knocked down. I found somewhere to sleep – there were empty places you could occupy where *Volksdeutschen* had been living. They saw the Russians coming, left everything and ran. You just went into a place and said: "This is going to be mine." '

Julius Ancer went to the council offices to claim back his

parents' house in Third of May Street. The top bureaucrat, 'a fanatical Communist, at first turned down my claim, stating to my face that the Jews wanted this war and deserved to be punished. Finally, after threats and arguments, he gave me a small one-room-with-kitchen apartment in our house, because I was a returning army veteran. Where my parents lived was given to three Russian officers.'[7]

It took Henry Kawalek (now Henry Kaye) several months to get home, travelling from Mauthausen, where he was liberated, to Poland via Yugoslavia, Hungary and Romania. 'I went to see the house where we used to live but I was frightened to go in. Poles were living there.' His mother, father, brother, aunt, grandfather and other relatives had died in Treblinka. 'I thought if *I'm* alive, there might be others.'

> I travelled back with an uncle, my mother's brother, Marcus Yutkewicz, who was looking for his wife, Lotka. We went first to Lodz where he found a sister-in-law who told him that his wife was alive and in Konin. I remember coming into the town and seeing my aunt and uncle reunited. It was like a miracle. She was living with your cousin Felunia, in Lola Birnbaum's house.
>
> My aunt, Lotka Blum, was a girl from Konin and they married before the war and had a baby daughter, Renia. When war broke out, they gave her to a Polish family. After they were reunited, they looked for Renia but couldn't find her and didn't know if she was alive or dead. They went back to the Polish family who had no idea what had happened to her. They said she had been taken here and there. The girl simply vanished.
>
> After a while, my uncle and aunt went to live in Lodz, and I stayed on in Konin for a couple of months. I went to see the house where we used to live but I was frightened to go in. Some Jews in Poland were killed trying to claim back their homes. It wasn't a very safe time. I stayed with Chaim Czerwonka,[8] who was living in his old flat in the Tepper Marik. One day I went to Warsaw with Izzy Hahn to buy a drum. In those days you could travel free. In Warsaw we went to Joint,[9] who had a big canteen – the only place where you could get rice pudding with milk.
>
> While I was sitting there eating, I became aware that a woman sitting opposite me was looking at me all the time. You know

how it is when someone is watching you, you can't eat. In the end I got a bit annoyed and said to her: 'If you're so hungry, why don't you eat?' She said: 'No, it's not that I'm hungry. It's just that you look like somebody I know, a young girl.' I thought of my uncle's daughter and said: 'Where is she?' 'Oh, a long way from here.' I said: 'Give me the address and I'll go there.' She gave me the address of a convent in Poronin, a small place about six hundred kilometres away, not far from Krakow.

I left Izzy in Warsaw to get the drum, and I set off. I came to Krakow and was very hungry and went to the Jewish Committee and they fed me, and told me where Poronin was. It was in the Polish mountains and the convent was up a very steep slope. I got there about seven o'clock in the morning and opened the door to see if someone was about, and my cousin was standing there. I recognized her at once and she realized who I was and we started to cry, both of us. She was seven years old and knew nothing about what had happened to her parents. I stayed in the convent one night and took her the next day, and they let her go. I took her back to Lodz. The journey took ten days. Her parents had no idea I was bringing her back. I opened the front door and left her downstairs. I didn't want to give them a shock, so I went upstairs and it was early in the morning. My uncle opened the door and said: 'What are you doing here so early?' I said: 'Don't be alarmed. I've brought Renia home.' The girl came upstairs and saw her parents. This is a true story, and it all happened because someone was staring at me while I was eating rice pudding.'

It was a relief to hear a story with a happy ending – there were so few; but Henry's story was not quite over: 'A few years later, while they were living in a Displaced Persons camp in Germany, Renia contracted TB and died.'

In 1945 the gentile citizens of Konin were also emerging into the daylight after a long occupation. They had lost husbands and sons in the war, had seen family carried off to Germany for forced labour, had lived in fear and tasted Nazi brutality. But the Jews who came back were consumed with their own troubles. If there was to be any competition in suffering, they felt they had the edge. The Germans had not embarked on a systematic plan to exterminate the entire Polish race. No Christian mothers in Konin had seen their babies torn from their arms and killed before their eyes. Nor had their families been transported to death camps to be gassed. The few Jews who came back saw Polish families inhabiting the homes they occupied before the war, sleeping in the same beds, eating round the same tables. Their church and their cemetery were intact, their community still in place. The Russians were their new masters, but Poland was, and would continue to be, their home. The Jews were lost, without family, without anchorage and seemingly without a future. Even before the war, when there were nearly 3,000 of them, they had felt vulnerable. Now they numbered no more than a couple of dozen. Polish neighbours greeting them on their return made remarks that rankled, like: 'So many Jews have come back.' The Jewish community had been exterminated and yet, so it seemed to the survivors, the Poles regarded them still as too numerous. Questions like 'How is it the Germans didn't burn you too?', asked out of bald curiosity with no ill will intended, struck Jews as hurtful and insensitive.

Meanwhile, searching for family and wondering where to go next, the revenants faced the immediate problem of getting by from day to day. The Red Cross set up a kitchen to feed homeless Jews and refugees passing through the town. The local authorities handed out bedding and basic furniture.

Towards the end of 1945 the Jews in the town formed a committee to make contact with *landslayt* in England, America and Palestine, but it took time before they managed to establish lines of communication with the outside world. I have in my possession the original letter dated 10 December 1945, written in Yiddish, which the committee sent to the London Konin Society, asking for help: '. . . We have no money. The bones of the dead are littering the ground [of the former Jewish cemetery]. We hope that you will send help as soon as possible with money and clothing. We greet you in the name of the Jews of Konin.' Mark Natel, Joe Fox and my father got together to help their *landslayt* in Poland. Among old records kept in a cardboard box, I have found registered parcel receipts attached to handwritten lists of pullovers, trousers, underwear and other items of clothing dispatched to Konin at that time.

Avrom Soika, whom I was to meet in Montreal, was one of the founders of the Jewish Committee formed in Konin in 1945.[10] He had returned in March after escaping from the Germans in Ostrowiec with the help of two Poles, whose bravery he has recorded in the Memorial Book.[11] Back in his native town, Soika found himself penniless and alone. Of his extended family of eighty, only he and one nephew – living in a DP camp – remained. He rented a room, acquired a needle and cotton, and began working at his trade. Konin once again had a Jewish tailor – one where there used to be dozens. 'Poles came in to have something repaired or to have a coat made. I wouldn't take money because it was worth nothing. They paid me with food.'

Tola Zeidlitz, who had been educated at the Polish gymnasium in Konin, found a good job as a book-keeper in a government office and in 1948 was one of the last Jews to leave Konin. Madzia Leszczynska successfully reclaimed the family ironmonger's, the only Jewish business to reopen after the war. Janina Ryczke, wife of my kinsman Aron, came back with her son and resumed her job as a schoolteacher. Simon Kempinski, formerly a tailor, and his wife Rose began to manufacture small quantities of boiled sweets on their kitchen stove. Jews without resources or a trade – many were schoolchildren when war broke out – found themselves in a hopeless position. A few turned in desperation to illegal currency dealings.

No organized Jewish religious life re-established itself in the town. It was not just that all the places of worship had been devastated or that there was no Rabbi. There was simply no will to thank the God who 'sustainest the living with loving kindness, revivest the dead with great mercy, supportest the falling, healest the sick, loosest the bound, and keepest faith to them that sleep in the dust.' Two Jewish couples got married in postwar Konin. Julius Ancer and his Konin girlfriend, Niusia Brzostowska, had a civil ceremony in April 1945. No wedding canopy, no benedictions. 'Eight persons attended my wedding, one of them was Jacob Kotowski, who wore a nice suit and himself had hopes of marrying Niusia. He arrived in Konin on my wedding day not knowing about the wedding and stayed in my place. I asked him if I could borrow his suit. As I told him afterwards, he ended up sitting in his underwear while I, wearing his suit, was marrying the girl he came to propose to.'[12]

Another couple, who had already had a civil marriage ceremony, asked their friend Lefkowitz to 'marry' them as best he could according to the Jewish tradition.[13] Lefkowitz found a prayer book which a Pole had rescued and given him, covered his head and recited the Seven Blessings over his friends. The bridegroom stamped his foot on a glass, and the word *mazeltov* was heard again in Konin.

The survivors found no pleasure in being back in their old town. Wherever they turned they were reminded of the dead. The Jewish population in Poland, once numbering almost three and a half million persons, was reduced to about 250,000 in 1945.[14] Life in Poland was, in the words of Julius Ancer, 'like being engulfed in a cemetery atmosphere, with tragic memories reappearing and anti-Semites threatening us. Three Jewish survivors returned to their small home town of Tuliszkow, near Konin, and were murdered the next day by Polish anti-Semites.'[15] It strengthened the survivors' conviction that anti-Semitism was and always would be an ineradicable element of Polish life. Louis Lefkowitz heard one Konin Pole say to another 'You know the dirty Jews are back.' He returned in September 1945, wearing a German jacket and two left shoes. A local official he had known before the war wept when he saw him, gave him a small grant and helped him find somewhere to live: 'I couldn't get back our apartment.' One night he and three friends were crossing the Tepper Marik in the dark when some locals with guns yelled 'Dirty Jews' and fired at them. The bullets missed, shattering the windows behind them.

'The secret police started to bother us,' Simon Kempinski told me when we met in Forest Hills. 'I was making candies – it was my whole *parnoseh* [livelihood]. The police arrived one day and asked: "Where is your factory?" The "factory" was my apartment, which consisted of one room and a kitchen. We cooked the candies in a little pot. That was my factory. So they started to look for money. Money? You know how rich I was? My left shoe was a completely different style from the right one. Anyway, I saw what is going on and realize it was no more a place to stay. I took my wife and put our things in a shopping bag and we went out on the road to Kolo in the hope that a horse and wagon would come along and give us a lift. We were afraid to go to the station in Konin.'

One of Julius Ancer's neighbours, Wieslaw Kurowski (son of Aleksander Kurowski, who was executed in the big square alongside Mordechai Slodki), showed up one day and presented him with a hand-gun so he could protect himself. 'He told me not to be a sitting duck. Otherwise, I should leave the town.'[16] 'I had no desire to stay there,' said Izzy Hahn. 'No, there was nothing there, no future.' The pogrom in Kielce in July 1946, when an anti-Semitic mob murdered forty-two Jewish survivors and injured many more, served as a warning that could not be ignored.

One by one the Jews left Konin and, finally, the Polish People's Republic. Before leaving, a small group visited the Kazimierz forest near Konin to nail a wooden plaque to a tree in honour of the thousands of Jews from the region who were massacred and buried there. I have a small, out-of-focus snapshot of the grim-faced group standing amid the shadows of the forest.

Only three Jews chose to remain in their native town.

42

JOZEF LEWANDOWSKI was sixteen in 1949 when he escaped from Konin and made his way across war-torn Poland into the Soviet Union. Today he is a retired professor of history in Uppsala, Sweden. In 1947, while serving as an officer in the Polish army, he went back to Konin, not with any intention of staying, but to satisfy a need to revisit the ground of his childhood, to see what had become of his old town. He visited the Jewish cemetery. It was still in a state of total dereliction, littered with pieces of broken tombstones and fragments of human bones.

By then most of Konin's Jews had made their postwar exodus, and he spent much of his stay meeting up with Polish neighbours and acquaintances. As an acculturated Jew who spoke an educated Polish, he was able to relax in the company of gentiles more easily than most Jewish Koniners. While retaining his sense of Jewish identity, he felt a love for many things Polish, and did not see an anti-Semite in every Pole.

One of the Jews living in Konin at that time was a man known before the war as Beniek Danziger (no relation of the Kapo). Lewandowski had no knowledge of him – or at least, thought he had none. Danziger was away during his four-day visit, and the two men never met. Nevertheless, the locals made quite sure he was aware of Danziger's existence. The following is from Lewandowski's absorbing account of his brief visit to Konin:

> [During my stay] I heard many sentimental stories, but the one I am going to tell you sounds as though taken from trashy literature. I had to listen to it about ten times, this story about the adventures of Danziger. The excuse that I had already heard it ten times was not accepted. It was obvious that these adventures were very important to the people who were telling them, and that they wanted the world to understand and value them.
>
> In 1939 Danziger was hidden by a hostess from the Polonia 'nightclub'.[1] During the war it was '*nur für Deutschen*' – for Germans only. The girl hid Danziger through the whole long war. He did not put his nose outside the little flat, and during visits by officers and gendarmes Danziger was hidden in a box under her bed. He came out of hiding after the war and married the girl. He changed his name to Gdanski, which was the Polish equivalent of Danziger, and he became a conductor of a dance orchestra in Konin.
>
> I could not remember this Danziger and yet I knew everyone in the town. I did recall a man of that name, Beniek Danziger, a bit of a rascal, who so far as I knew had no talent that would quality him to be the conductor of an orchestra, not even of a dance band, not even in a dive. I remember that when I said this it made people bitter and even suspicious that I, for some unknown reasons, did not want to know about this story. My [Polish] friends wanted me to go and see the flat in which the girl had hidden her Jewish lover. I did not go. I knew the house. I knew the apartment – before the war, No. 26 Wodna Street, first floor – because I spent my early childhood in No. 28. But I truly did not know this Danziger. Perhaps I might have recalled him if my friends could have told me where he lived before the war.
>
> But still for years afterwards greetings were passed on to me from Gdanski, who certainly knew and remembered me, and was delighted to hear about me and always asked after me. In 1961 I asked about him and learned that he was dead. He had died of diabetes and cirrhosis of the liver caused by alcohol consumption. So the question of identifying the man ceased to be important. But not quite. One sleepless night in Sweden there suddenly

stood before my eyes a young Chasid who, just like myself, had taken violin lessons from Mr Gabrylewicz, the conductor of the fire brigade band . . . He was a tall Chasid who stopped being a Chasid, trimmed off his sidelocks and shortened his long coat so that it looked more like a jacket. Nevertheless, on Saturdays he continued to attend the Chasidic synagogue [the *shtibl*].

He was about ten years older than me, not among my circle of friends, and at Gabrylewicz's I met him only once or twice. His father had a little shop with iron pots and crockery . . . But of course I knew him; I simply had not remembered him. Now I recalled that we had sold my violin to him when I was ten years old and it was obvious that I had no talent. Yes, he stood there trying the violin. He liked it. But even remembering him with his frock-coat shortened, I could not reconcile him with the Danziger and the dance band in Konin. It is obvious that within Gdanski was a personality that differed from his exterior. There was also in him an artistic sensibility that eventually found an outlet . . . What a lot we two would have had to say to each other, we pupils of Mr Gabrylewicz, we fiddlers in the wind, each trying in his own way to escape from the Chasidic synagogue. But how could we have this dialogue? Damn!

I mentioned that the story sounds like cheap literature, but are my words not a gift to conventional thinking? A dance hostess, a person from more or less the depths of society, displays the highest humanity. She does it in unusual circumstances where others, respected and of a higher class, let you down and fail the test. She earns her living pretending, yet she proves capable of great and dangerous love. In military actions, heroism and sacrifice are mostly single acts, often done on the spur of the moment. She stood the test not for a moment or for a day but for almost six years. Time has proved pitiless even in the case of good marriages that have never been subjected to this kind of test. And what love anyway can withstand the pressure of time? But the dance hostess made it and Gdanski made it. Not only did he survive the war years but also a number of years afterwards. It remains only for one to bow one's head. The people of that town have every right to feel proud of them, and it is to their credit that everyone, without being asked, bored me with their story.[2]

It was a gripping, not to say inspiring, story, but I read it with growing puzzlement. Was Danziger hidden in Konin throughout the war? It did not tally with what I had heard from Izzy Hahn and Henry Kaye. They both knew Beniek Danziger and remembered that before the war he played the accordion in what they described as Konin's 'nightclub'. 'He was a brilliant musician,' said Izzy. 'As a boy I used to stare through the window of the club and listen to him.' He played at weddings and parties too, also in his spare time. What his everyday job was I have not been able to establish with any certainty. One Koniner seemed to remember that he worked as a clerk during the day. Another insisted he was a tailor. Everyone agreed that he walked with a slight limp.

Izzy and Henry confirmed independently that Danziger did indeed marry a dance hostess after the war, and that he formed a band of his own. They said (as have others) that he was one of the few Konin Jews who decided to rebuild their lives in Poland. In the immediate postwar period he remained close to the group of survivors who came back to the town. He played the accordion at Julius Ancer's wedding. The letter that I have from the Jewish Committee in Konin, asking their London brethren for help, bears two signatures; one of them is that of the 'Secretary: B. Gdanski'. He kept in touch by correspondence with at least one Koniner in Israel.[3] After Henry Kaye came to England, he received a number of friendly letters from Danziger. 'He always used to ask me to send him pens, which were not easy to get in Poland at that time.'

So far so good. But, insist Izzy and Henry, Danziger was deported with them to Ostrowiec in 1939. 'While we were there,' recalled Izzy, whose memory has been proved accurate again and again, 'Beniek became a German policeman – a good one. They just put a uniform on him. He was really too gentle to be a policeman.' Izzy and Henry were with him in the same forced-labour camp. 'He used to march us three miles there and back to the steel works every day,' recalled Izzy. 'After that, he was in Auschwitz with me. We separated there and met again in Konin after the war. I heard him playing in Konin in 1945 in a new place on the big square. One day he needed a drum, probably for the new band, and Henry and I went to Warsaw to get one for him. After I came to London, he sent me a photograph of himself and the band.' I have seen the small, curling snapshot inscribed in Polish on the back: 'To my dear friend as a souvenir. B. Gdanski and orchestra Melodia-Jazz, Konin 1947.' How does Izzy explain the story about the dance hostess hiding her Jewish lover through the war? 'Believe me, it isn't true.' Henry Kaye concurs, as does the New Yorker Simon Kempinski: 'Danziger was deported to Ostrowiec and later went to Auschwitz. I later met him in Konin in 1945. He was living with a Polish girl.'[4]

So I am left with questions. Was the Chasid who bought Lewandowski's violin the same Danziger who married the dance hostess? The fact that he was taking violin lessons lends credence to his becoming a musician, albeit playing another instrument. Lewandowski says that the young Chasid was pulling away from religious orthodoxy, as did many others. From what I have been able to work out, the band leader was indeed about ten years older than Lewandowski. I myself believe that Danziger *was* deported to Ostrowiec, as my three informants have assured me. Had he remained hidden in Konin throughout the war years, would not the returning survivors have been the first to know about it? And would not the extraordinary circumstances of his rescue have stayed in their minds for ever? On the other hand, I do not believe that the Konin citizenry would conspire to invent the story, however useful it would be in demonstrating how one of them risked her life to save a Jew.

I have juggled with several theories. Could it be that the woman protected her lover for a few weeks between the beginning of the German occupation of the town and the first deportations in November 1939? Or might he have been moved to another camp from Auschwitz, escaped and returned to Konin just before the Germans left? As a Jew, he would not have been able to declare his presence. Instead, he would have crept during darkness to his girlfriend's flat, where he remained – at considerable risk to her – until the Russians arrived a few weeks later. Once the Germans had gone, neighbours would become aware of his presence and, setting eyes on him for the first time in nearly five years, they might have assumed he had been hidden there all that time. Izzy, Henry and Simon Kempinski have good reason to dismiss these theories.

So how did the myth, if myth it is, begin? Like all enduring myths, it has an aspect of unreality but also something about it that makes it endure. Myths are created to fulfil a need, and perhaps one should not examine them too closely.

43

FORTY YEARS after serving as headmaster of the Jewish gymnasium in Konin, Leopold Infeld returned to the town where he had spent two of the most miserable years of his life – the 'empty years' as he has called them. I have described his visit in 1963, when he found only one former pupil living in the town, a woman who mourned not only for her murdered husband but her lost high school graduation certificate. He did not reveal her name but I knew who she was because so many Koniners had mentioned Madzia Leszczynska to me, always in the context of her decision to remain in Konin after the war. The Leszczynski family, of which there were many branches, had been one of the most affluent in the town. 'They had a telephone and a typewriter, the acme of Jewish wealth.'[1]

In the early 1930s Madzia married a fellow graduate of the Jewish gymnasium, Meyer Yehuda Ejzen, known as Idek Ejzen. After graduating in law at Warsaw University (where Madzia studied music at the Warsaw Conservatoire), he returned to Konin and set up in practice. His family, living opposite the synagogue, was *frum* and poor, at the opposite end of the social spectrum from hers, but their shared secular education and his professional status placed the young couple in the ranks of the more assimilated Jews of Konin, open about their Jewishness yet having little else in common with the Yiddish-speaking inhabitants of the Tepper Marik. Idek, I was told, had died fighting in the Warsaw ghetto. His wife and young child, having eluded the concentration camps, returned to Konin in 1945, where Madzia took over the ironmonger's that had belonged to her uncle before the war.

After her fellow survivors left the town for other lands, there was no contact between them and the Jewess who had stayed on. Her decision to throw in her lot with the Poles, to remain in a town whose every corner was haunted by the Jewish dead, won her no sympathy from her *landslayt*, as we have seen from their rejection of her request for financial help in 1968. Rumours that she had married a Pole and converted to Catholicism were construed as the ultimate betrayal.

A London Koniner[2] who visited the town in 1964 found Madzia a sad figure, living alone with an aged maid. Another Koniner, Mike Jacobs, looking round his old State school in 1975, heard from one of the teachers about a Jewish woman who lived close by – the only Jew left in the town, he was told. It turned out to be Madzia Leszczynska, then aged about seventy. He knocked at her door. 'Her daughter and granddaughter had come to visit her from Warsaw. I was impressed that she had the same lady as domestic help as before the war. Her apartment seemed well furnished and the only indication she gave regarding her situation was a comment that we should ask Joint to send more food packages. She was proud to serve us American coffee. I believe she had Lipton tea as well – she kept these in a locked compartment of a cupboard.'

None of the Koniners could tell me more, and it was from a non-Jewish source that I learned in 1988 that Madzia had died in Konin some time in the late 1970s. In October 1990, I received a card from a woman in Warsaw, saying that she would like to establish contact with me. She had heard that I was writing a book about the Jews of Konin and had obtained my address: 'I am a lawyer, living alone, and I have a grown-up daughter and one granddaughter. Until 1978 my mother lived in Konin and I am very interested in that town. If it is possible, please drop me a few lines.' The card was signed Maria Leszczynska. I wrote back immediately and thus began, with the help of translators in both countries, a correspondence that grew in warmth and frankness with each letter.

My fears about how she might respond to prying questions about her life proved unfounded. She was pleased that someone who had links with Konin wanted to know about her past. In her very first letter she wrote: 'I am very attached to my past, a bad way to live. In spite of that, I always go back to my childhood and youth.' She was born in 1933 and one of her earliest memories was visiting her Leszczynska grandmother every *shabbes*, a routine she loved, not least of all because of her granny's musical potty. The little girl would hardly be through the front door before announcing an urgent need. Granny would produce the potty and the little girl would sit on it while it played a Polonaise.[3]

'On 1 September 1939 my childhood, my family happiness, ended.' Her father enlisted, was seriously wounded in battle and came close to losing a leg. She and her mother and a number of relatives joined the refugee trail to Warsaw, where they were finally trapped in the ghetto. Her father joined them there. It was in the Warsaw ghetto that her father learned that his mother and sister had committed suicide by taking poison: 'It was the only time I remember my father crying.'

He was caught up in the Ghetto Uprising of April 1943, escaped through the sewers and, thanks to help from the Polish underground, he and his wife and daughter found refuge in an apartment on the Aryan side of the ghetto, where they joined seven other Jews in hiding. They remained cooped up there for a year, hoping to sit it out until the Russians liberated the city. Maria became ill during this period – she had already nearly died from typhoid – and it was arranged that a nun would collect her and take her into the countryside. The nun came a day earlier than arranged, on 16 May 1944: 'Fate desired it.'

Next day 'the doorbell rang . . . and my mother, wearing only her dressing-gown, looked through the peephole and recognized the Gestapo. She had been washing her hair. She ran to my father, who told her to escape through the back door in the kitchen. She did this, went to the floor below and asked the people there to hide her. She told them she was a maid in the flat above, which was being raided by the Germans.' Meanwhile, upstairs, the Germans had burst into the flat where they found Idek Ejzen standing near an open fourth-floor window. Idek grabbed one of the Germans, pushed him out of the window, and then threw himself to his death. Barefooted and still wearing only her dressing-gown, Madzia left the house and saw the bodies lying in the street. With no time to think, she placed herself at the mercy of a Polish policeman. He took her to his home, where he fed her and gave her money to enable her to rejoin Maria in the country. Later, Madzia learned how the Gestapo had traced their whereabouts. One of the Jews in the same apartment had a beautiful wife who was concealed in another house. The landlord's son became besotted with her, grew jealous of her husband, and finally betrayed his hiding-place to the Gestapo.

Madzia and daughter, passing as gentiles, roamed the countryside penniless, close to starvation and occasionally reduced to begging. They returned to Warsaw at the time of the Uprising of 1944 and once again were caught by the Germans, who deported them, as gentiles, to a forced-labour camp for agricultural workers. Here they remained until they were liberated at the beginning of 1945.

'By foot, train, horse and cart, any transport there happened to be, we returned to Konin, my mother wearing a German soldier's jacket with a hole in the back, given to us by a Russian soldier . . . It was February. Mother wore a sweater and I had a rabbit skin on my back and wooden clogs. All we possessed was an old sheet holding a few bits and pieces.' When they arrived in Konin they went straight to the man who had been manager of the Leszczynski mill before the war, and he gave them a bed for the night. 'He received us very well. I remember that night because we ate such a lot and after going a long time without food it made me ill. I vomited all night and this continued for several days.' The former manager of the mill returned items of family silver that he had been safeguarding for Madzia during the war, and granny's musical chamber-pot, still in perfect working order. 'Many people returned a lot of things to us, but many robbed us too.' Madzia never retrieved her jewellery.

Germans who had been living in their former home had stripped the place of many of its contents when they left, and local people were now living there. The Town Hall allocated to Madzia the home and ironmongery store that had belonged to her mother's brother before the war. Maria's old nanny, Manya, who had worked for the Leszczynski family from the age of twelve, rejoined her former employer. Madzia changed her surname from the German-sounding Ejzen back to her maiden name, Leszczynska, which then became Maria's surname too.

One day a woman arrived at Madzia's home, tearful and frightened. Her husband, who had been a policeman in Warsaw during the war, was under threat of being sentenced to death for collaborating with the Germans. She wanted Madzia to sign a statement confirming that he had saved her life. Madzia went to Warsaw to attend the trial, and kissed the man's brow. He was acquitted, but died soon after.[4]

Maria was twelve when she saw Konin again after an absence of four and a half years. 'We went back full of hope that our near and dear ones would return. How long we hoped against hope, discussing the subject each day.' None of her mother's or father's large families in Poland had survived. 'I did not go near either of my grandparents' homes – it was too painful. And yet at the beginning life was good. A big and pleasant home, animals, two dogs, cats, rabbits, a garden cared for by Manya. Every day people called, remembering the family. It was cosy and warm. Everyone sympathized with us for a while, and then I started school and things changed.' Maria found herself excluded from the scouting movement because, as a Jew, she was not able to swear on the cross. Anti-Semitism made daily life at school a torment, alleviated only by the presence of one brave defender. 'One day I accidentally tripped over a boy who said to me: "Don't touch me, filthy Jewess." My defender hit him and the other boy hit back, breaking my defender's nose. He had to go to hospital in Poznan and there he declared himself to be Jewish. He said he wanted to know what it felt like to be persecuted because of your race rather than the sort of person you are. He returned to Konin a confirmed philo-Semite and we have stayed in contact for more than forty years.' Life at school failed to improve. 'Girls did not want to play with me. That was in 1946, the year of the pogrom [in the Polish city of Kielce]. I ran away to Lodz, where I said I was a Jewish orphan who wanted to go to Palestine via Cyprus . . . My mother found me and took me back to Konin.'

Madzia had no business experience, times were hard for everyone, and her store foundered. The State had taken over the flour mill. I asked Maria why her mother had stayed in Konin when other Jews had seen no future there. She wrote back: 'I'm not sure what she would have said if asked. I suppose her answer would be: What can a lonely forty-year-old woman with a child and no profession, no money and no family in the world do?' In Konin at least she had property, friends, and the ever-faithful Manya who cooked, cleaned and knew the family history. That gave us a small portion of family happiness. I suspect, though, that she simply lacked the strength to start again. In 1957 she tried to find out from a cousin in Israel if it might be possible for us to emigrate there. The cousin dissuaded her by telling her about all the hardships to be encountered. Another thing – my mother was sufficiently well assimilated into the Polish community and felt at home among Poles, unlike the other Jews who came back.'

Maria said her mother never remarried after the war, which compelled me to raise the question of Madzia's alleged apostasy.

It drew a heated response. 'I was very upset by your information about my mother's conversion. It is an absolute myth, gossip that weighed heavily on her in the last years of her life, so much so that she sometimes cried on account of it. I think that the Jews who happened to come to Konin or who lived there for a short while after the war came to that conclusion. The first indication she had of it was through a letter from friends of her family living in the United States, which was really insulting. After that came years when nobody would help us materially, which was all associated with the gossip. I know Mother contacted various individuals for help but all in vain. She sold her prewar piano and sewing-machine to keep us . . . I think Mother always retained a resentment towards these Jews until the end of her life.'

Manya, the servant, stayed with her mistress to the very end, though in the last few years it was the mistress who had to look after the older woman. Madzia was seventy-three when she died of heart failure in July 1978. Manya died the following year at the age of eighty-seven. Unhappy at the thought of her mother being buried where no one would visit her grave, Maria went to Konin and brought Madzia's body to Warsaw. 'She is buried in the civic cemetery, and I shall end up there too.'

Bit by bit I learned more about Maria's adult life. Following in her father's footsteps, she studied law in Warsaw and became a government lawyer, 'married badly', gave birth to a daughter, and divorced, after which she changed her name back to Leszczynska. By then, she told me, it was too late for her to leave Poland. All else apart, she did not want to leave the country while her mother was still living in Konin: 'I loved her very much till the end . . . She was so full of life, proud and witty . . . She tried to give me everything . . . To this day I cannot come to terms with her death.'

Maria underwent a change in the course of our correspondence. Her early letters emitted a dreadful sadness: 'In spite of surviving we have not escaped the poison and have become psychological invalids for ever.' About to retire as a lawyer, she was pessimistic about the present, uncertain about the future, living alone in a tiny flat, finding little pleasure in life apart from her granddaughter. Her unsuccessful marriage had been to a gentile, and she had no contact with Jewish life, no ethnic 'heritage' to fall back on as one of memory's comforts. There had been a visit to Israel some years earlier to stay with a relative but there was no follow-up. Then, in June 1991 she and a group of other survivors went to New York as guests of the Lauder Foundation to participate in a conference on the wartime 'hidden children'. Three 'Righteous Gentiles' who had helped to save Jewish lives were invited too. The programme of activities exposed her to new experiences: 'We were soaking up Jewishness, the Sabbath; we went to a Chasidic club . . . The Polish consulate entertained us with a kosher reception . . . After twelve days we all came back different people.'

Soon after her return she spent a holiday at a Jewish summer camp, where she received her first tuition in Hebrew, listened to American rabbis discourse on the Torah, describe the holy festivals, enact a Jewish wedding under a *chupeh* – and tell Jewish jokes. She became increasingly active in the Association of Holocaust Children in Poland. Her letter of August 1991 began: 'From the time in 1990 when I sent you a shy letter begging for an answer, so much has changed in my life, and I am no longer the same frustrated, bitter woman who wrote to you then. You played a part in this because our correspondence, in spite of its difficulties, means a lot to me.' The 'difficulties' refer to my questions, which had reawakened bad memories and caused her 'sleepless nights and loss of appetite'.

Some weeks later, in a letter, headed 'Sukkot', she wrote excitedly: 'Theo! For the first time I have observed Rosh Hashanah and Yom Kippur, and today I am dining out on the occasion of Sukkot.' In December she announced she was about to attend her first Chanukah party, adding: 'I am glad I have returned to my people.' The following year she joined a group from Warsaw that attended an international Holocaust gathering in Israel. She wrote to me on her return, describing her visit to the Dead Sea, Jericho, Jerusalem and Yad Vashem. This time she signed herself Miriam.

44

OMAHA AIRPORT. A small, grey-haired woman. Pale eyes behind plainish spectacles. Anonymous grey coat. Someone who would rather merge than stand out. She is hesitant to make the first move. 'Mrs Grossman?' We shake hands, and I sense her charm, gentle and unmannered. Her voice, smile, movements – all have a delicacy untouched by worldliness and modernity. She guides me towards the exit: 'My husband is waiting for us outside with the car.'

We emerge into the crisp autumn sunlight and Miriam gives a gentle wave in the direction of a car parked nearby, a beaten-up Ford with rusty dents and dusty windows, its former white paintwork matt and parched. The car pulls up and from it steps a short man wearing a red and blue check lumberjack shirt. His loose-fitting trousers are supported by belt and braces. Thick round glasses lend an owlish look to his weathered, not too closely shaven face. Like Miriam, he must be in his mid-seventies, but when we shake hands I can feel the strength still there in his arm. He is or has been a worker. This is Ignac (pronounced Ignatz). He smiles, picks up my hefty suitcase as though it were a briefcase and stows it away.

Miriam and I chat easily while we drive along. Her thoughtful attempts to draw Ignac into the conversation fail: I sense a hint of shyness, which is explained when he finally speaks. The English language commands him rather than he the language. His accent is so thick, his sentences so liberated from any constraints of grammar, that for a moment I think he is addressing me in a Slavonic tongue. I have the greatest difficulty understanding a word he says. Miriam and Ignac are an odd couple: he gruff, unpolished and inarticulate, she neat and refined, expressing herself in a perfect, slightly formal English spoken with a soft and beguiling Polish-American accent.

We drive past a sleepy lake in a deserted park, through a residential suburb, and draw up at a detached clapboard house with a porch, a patch of well-kept lawn and a white picket fence: more than a touch of Norman Rockwell. In sharp contrast, the area at the back of the house looks like the corner of an industrial estate. A clutter of aged machinery too long exposed to the weather has turned the same colour as the autumn leaves. Chunks of rusting iron and cogwheels litter the approach to a long, shed-like structure built out of cement blocks. An immobilized bus, its entire surface – even the windows – sprayed with silver paint, adds a faintly surreal touch. The bus is backed up so that one end almost touches the house. The other, facing a busy road, displays a home-made sign:

WELDING
All kinds

Waving his hand to and fro like a windscreen wiper, Ignac refuses to allow me to unload my case and insists on carrying it into the house. We enter through the side door and I am struck by how different the interior is from most of the other homes I have visited. This is the home of people who have had to do their own decorating, make their own curtains, watch their pennies. It is by no means shabby, but it is not smart either. It has the well-worn feel of a home where little has changed for a long time, an uncoordinated look that has never been influenced by fashion. It has a distinct flavour of Central Europe.

I had asked Miriam to book me into a hotel, but she would not hear of it. I follow her up a steep staircase squeezed into a space between two walls little wider than my shoulders. Upstairs the smooth wooden flooring and solid timber doors are all darkly varnished. 'This is your apartment,' says Miriam quietly. She ushers me into a small room and points to a writing-table and chair: 'This will be your office.' Then into a big double room with a dividing archway and curtain: 'Here is your sitting-room, and over there is your bedroom.' The tour continues across the landing, and I feel like a tenant about to settle in for a long stay rather than just two days. 'Here is your bathroom, and this is your kitchen.' She leaves me to unpack my things. Soon I hear the clink of pans and dishes in the kitchen below. Appetizing smells waft up.

I rejoin her below, where she seats me beside her on a bulky sofa. Ignac has gone off somewhere. It is a long, high-ceilinged room, originally two rooms which have been turned into one. There are knick-knacks everywhere. At one end, a dining-table and chairs. At the other, an enormous double bed where Miriam and Ignac sleep.

Miriam has a quality that distinguishes her from most of the other Koniners I have met: she *listens*. She wants to know about me, how my work is going, how I am feeling, whether I am homesick . . . It makes a refreshing change to be asked rather than to ask questions. There is a maternal kindliness about her. Her eyes can look unutterably sad one moment, then light up with amusement the next. She has a youthful laugh and a Garboesque way of pronouncing certain vowels.

Miriam was born in Konin and educated at the Jewish gymnasium. As though reading my mind, she mentions Ignac's problems with the English language and how much it bothers him. He had more limited educational opportunities than she, Miriam explains without a hint of superiority. 'He was an engineering machinist in Czechoslovakia before the war and he has always been confined to a workshop.' Mostly he speaks Czech to her, while she speaks a mixture of Czech and Polish to him. Americans usually call him I.G. or Iggy but Miriam prefers Ignac. She is worried about his health: five months ago he fell and badly damaged his shoulder. He is in pain much of the time but refuses to make a fuss about it. There are other, more long-standing problems.

Ignac reappears and Miriam suggests that he show me over his workshop while she finishes preparing lunch. As we cross the yard, he points at the number on his left arm: 'Auschwitz! Auschwitz!' On the other arm is a tattoo of his own choice, a heart.

The workshop is huge, with aisles separating rows of workbenches and machinery: great power-driven hammers, shearers, grinders, turners, machines for drilling holes in solid steel, chains hanging from the ceiling for hoisting heavy weights. There is space enough here for twenty men to work, but where are they? My ear is slowly becoming attuned to Ignac's speech. It emerges that he is the sole worker here, though I can't quite fathom what he does. One thing is obvious: his affection for the machines. You can tell it from the way he looks at them, pats them, strokes his thick fingers along dark iron handles worn smooth as polished gems. 'I lof my vife, I lof my kids and I lof my machins.'

With great chuckles he puts on his working headgear for my benefit: first a sinister welding mask, then a high skullcap that Miriam made for him out of brown corduroy, and finally, for hot summer days, a straw hat in the shape of a jungle topi sprayed with the same silver paint as the bus. Lying on one of the benches is his current project, an old metal hat-rack that belongs to the cantor of their synagogue. The *chazan* is so fond of his hat-rack that he wants Ignac to make him two exact copies. For reasons I cannot understand, it has turned out to be a tricky job, and Ignac wishes the *chazan* had never thought of the idea.

We go in for lunch. Miriam cooks at an old-fashioned stove near an antiquated white sink with no cupboard unit below it. She looks fastidiously tidy, a fresh cotton apron over her neatly pleated skirt. Below the kitchen window, in the narrowest part of the room, a small Formica table is squeezed between two banquettes, diner-style. The window is like a frame round a pop-art painting: a cut-out of a glittery silver bus pasted on a sheet of blue.

Miriam serves *lokshen* soup, roast chicken with cauliflower, followed by home-made zucchini cake, all delicious. She coaxes me to eat more. A little more soup? A little more chicken? Another piece of cauliflower? A second helping of cake? Miriam eats slowly with ladylike table manners. Ignac slurps his soup. She appears not to notice. They have lived in this house for thirty-five years. It was a wreck when they bought it. They restored it themselves, doing the plumbing, electrical wiring, woodwork, everything with their own hands. 'Day un night I vorrk,' says Ignac. 'She help me. She help me ven I need dis holden, dis tool.' After lunch he disappears into the workshop, leaving us to talk at the kitchen table.

Miriam was a teenager when she and her family left Konin for Lodz in the late 1920s. At first my Konin street map means nothing to her, but soon a landmark here, a landmark there, triggers the chain reaction of memory and suddenly the map becomes a route back to her childhood. She reads out long-forgotten street names once as familiar to her as the name of the street she lives in now. The distant past comes surging into the present, and now it is Omaha's turn to recede into the background: Ogrodowa Street? Yes, the *bes-medresh* on the corner near the big synagogue . . . the Tepper Marik . . . Trzeciego Maja (Third of May Street), where her grandmother and parents shared a store, leading up to the big square. Plac Wolnowsci, Freedom Square, where she used to live. The Memorial Book contains three photographs of the square. To my surprise, she has only the vaguest knowledge of the book's existence.

She leafs through it eagerly, her eyes sweeping across the Yiddish text, absorbing the chapter headings, the group photographs, the bearded *cheder* teachers, turning more pages, wanting to take it all in at one go like a thirsty person gulping water. 'Oh I would love to have this book! I would love to have it.' We come to a photograph showing one side of the big square and she recognizes it immediately. Another photograph taken from a side angle shows the line of façades receding in perspective: buildings of varying height, one with a classical pediment and pilasters, some with small shops and little doorways. The shadow cast almost directly under a bushy tree suggests it is nearly noon on a sunny day. A few tiny figures, blurred by the poor printing, walk along the pavement, perhaps on their way home to lunch. A cart – or is it a van? – is parked in the roadway.

Miriam scrutinizes the photograph for a moment, presses her palms together in excitement and exclaims: 'I see our house!' It is a three-storey building towards the far end of the square. 'This is where we lived, on the middle storey.' The effect of the camera angle is to narrow the windows into a row of five dark slits, occupying an area smaller than the nail of Miriam's little finger. She picks out two of the slits. 'These are our windows!' The human imagination gets to work. Two black marks on a sheet of paper become panes of glass through which Miriam, like a ghost gliding through a wall, enters her girlhood home of sixty to seventy years ago. Memories start flooding back. 'Here at the top of these little steps is the bakery where we used to buy *bulki* [bread rolls], and in the back was a man who sold herrings, and underneath us was a Mr Lipschitz who sold cloth . . . And these windows next to ours is where our gentile neighbour, Mr Wodzinski, the attorney, lived . . .'

I show her a third, older-looking postcard view of the square. Here, two ornate wrought-iron balconies, missing in the other picture, adorn the façade of Miriam's house. They must have been removed at a later date.

'I remember Mr Wodzinski's balcony, here, next to our window. As a girl I loved to see the sky, which I did by sitting on the window-sill and leaning my head backwards to watch the stars. I loved to watch the stars this way in the evening. And then we as children have been a little bit mischievous, so from this window one evening as it was getting dark I and my sister climbed onto our neighbour's balcony. It was very dangerous: we could have fallen, and when my parents found out they were very angry, and that's why I remember it, but we were so proud that we were able to achieve it.' I leave the room for a moment while she leafs through the book. When I return I see that she has been crying.

I have good memories of home. My father's name was Avrom Dovid Golomb and we lived on the Duzy Rynek. In Yiddish everyone called it *der Groyser Marik*, which also means a big square. Later on it was called Freedom Square [to mark Poland's independence]. We were a Chasidic family and there were nine children, five boys and four girls. My mother was a very gentle and peaceful woman.

We had a store on Third of May Street which my mother ran with my grandmother. My mother worked there more than my father because he had stomach ulcers and he had a lot of pain, so my mother tried to release him so he could rest more at home, and this is how he contributed to bringing us up properly. My father was strict but I did not clash with him. It was a beautiful Chasidic home.

We were a middle-class family and it was a custom that middle-class families had maids. I remember another non-Jewish woman, who was my beloved nanny for maybe ten or thirteen years, and she had her bed in the kitchen, and I slept many times with her because I loved her, and she loved me too. We also had a Jewish cook who used to come in to help. There was one incident when we had a maid who wanted to desecrate something Jewish, and one Friday night we found a piece of pig's leg in the chicken soup. I remember my father was very upset about it. We had to discard many dishes.

Although we had a maid, the children also had their responsibilities, like one had to help with keeping order in the house, and another helped in the store, and one watched over the younger ones and so on.

Our parents spoke Yiddish to each other. I spoke mostly Yiddish to them, and to my brothers also. To my sisters I spoke Polish. My brothers went to *cheder* all day. We girls went to the Jewish gymnasium and spoke Polish. And we had the maid in the house and neighbours and friends to whom we spoke Polish. My father and mother could both speak Polish, maybe not perfectly. My sisters, cousins, friends called me by my Polish name Marysia. My parents and brothers called me Marjem, which is Miriam. I was called a *shikse* because I was reading books on *shabbes*, not Jewish books but Polish books I borrowed from the Jewish library. I combed my hair on *shabbes* and that also made me a *shikse*.

Our apartment had five rooms: a kitchen, a dining-room, a *salonja*, a room for the children, and my parents' bedroom. On Saturday afternoons Jewish families used to walk round and round the square, and young people used to stroll here, especially on our side of the square because at one end of the square was the main street. At the opposite end was a street leading to the wooden bridge over the Warta, and from there it was a nice walk to Czarkow and the countryside. So people coming from the Tepper Marik area would walk across our side of the square on their way to the bridge.

We had neighbours of high standing. Our neighbour with the balcony was the lawyer, Wodzinski. He came from a prominent family. He even had a title, like a lord or something. Another neighbour was the dentist Selig Neuman. He was Jewish but an agnostic. My father engaged in a lot of conversations with Neuman, and also with Mr Wodzinski, with whom he discussed politics, Torah, law, everything under the sun. It was very interesting because they had respect for one another and they learned from one another. If I recall correctly, there were many times when the lawyer would ask my father questions about Jewish law. My father had a whole wall with Talmudic books. They exchanged views on Jewish law and civil law. I was always interested in what the older people were talking about. I was not allowed to question or have my say, but I was listening.

My father was a respected man, very wise. People used to come to him with their problems. He had short *peyas* and always wore a Chasidic coat. He had a woollen attire for the week, and a silken attire for the Sabbath and holy days. In the morning whenever I woke up I saw him studying. But he was a constructive man. He was engaged in the Jewish community, in dealing with people, in the conflicts people had. He helped out in the store whenever he could. He did not divorce himself from it. Some Chasidim did but not all.

My father was a *Gerer* Chasid and prayed in the *shtibl*. There was no place for women in the *shtibl* but I remember it with special pleasantness when it was *Simchat Torah*. The Chasidim had a way of showing joy with the Torah. By comparison, the people who prayed elsewhere were more orderly. In the *shtibl* they just went wild with rejoicing, and we liked this emphasis on the happiness, how the Chasidim could find such joy and make merry. They danced with the Torah and they danced with each other and they sang and threw candies and the mood was so elated. They were dressed in their long frocks and most of them wore the caps with small peaks which the Chasidim used to wear. Some of the rabbinical students wore *shtraymls*. I was a young girl and I used to stand with the women who gathered at the entrance of the *shtibl* to look inside and see the joy.

I was envious of my brothers because they had the right to study the Torah with my father. They were regarded as future heads of families and in this way they were more highly valued. To us, the girls, he said: 'You have the obligation to carry a home.'

He was a talented man. He made himself a violin and taught himself to play. He had a beautiful voice, and he and all the five boys made a choir and they sang at home. Every *shabbes* it was a requirement to sing songs of praise – *zmirot*. It was lovely and there was a nice mood. Mr Wodzinski could hear it from his apartment. He told us how much he enjoyed it. He loved our family. I have good memories of home.

Every *shabbes* my father brought home a Sabbath guest. There were Jewish soldiers stationed in the barracks in Konin who used to come. And *yeshiva* students sometimes ate with us. *Shnorrers* were not taken into the house. They just went from door to door begging money, but they did not expect to be invited in. A *shnorrer* was never refused, not in our house.

All the festivals were beautifully observed in our home. There was Passover when we all gathered round for the Seder. On Rosh Hashana we had honey and apples and the new fruit on the table, and the blessing over these things was done with such appreciation. I watched a television programme yesterday about American Indian culture. They had reverence for nature and for everything that lives – trees and grass and flowers and running water. To them it is a living spirit. It reminds me of that; when my father said the blessing over the wine, and the blessing over the fruit, it was also with a reverence. It is a reverence for the things which God gave us and it's different from when you sit down and just gobble up the food. That is why when I eat a meal I always say a little blessing. For bread, *hamotzi lekhem min ha-aretz* [who bringest forth bread from the earth]. Or *shehakol niyeh bidvoro* [by whose word all things exist]. Or *borei peri ha-adomah* [who bringest forth food from the earth]. It just shows appreciation for the bounty we have. When I am with my family, especially with my husband, we both say it aloud. But when I am with other people and perhaps they will not understand it and may be critical of it, I say it to myself.

Thinking back, I realise that she had not said a blessing aloud during lunch; I asked her not to regard me as a stranger. 'May I put a question to you?' she asks tentatively, waiting for my consent. 'What do you think about God?' It is a question I have put to most of the Koniners I have met. Now on the receiving end, I flounder, groping for the right words to convey my inner confusions and conflicts, the lifelong tug-of-war that pulls me towards and away from belief. I share her urge to give thanks, but to whom or to what? I pull back at the brink, unable to ritualize my gratitude as I would wish, unable to utter the poetic Hebrew words that heighten an awareness of life's bounty: the grace before and after meals, the ancient blessing over bread and wine, on smelling herbs, on seeing beautiful trees, on observing a rainbow, on smelling sweet-scented wood . . . I regret the absence of holiness in my own daily life, the spiritual vacuum, yet I cannot fill it with the divine, cannot pray. The result is a vague inner reaching for the transcendental that is perpetually frustrated.

Miriam listens attentively and explains the nature of her own belief:

I feel with all my being that there is someone above me, beside me, beyond me, a ruler who created the world, who gave us what we have. That spirit, that Being, that Almighty – we must call it something – is unimaginable because our minds are not big enough to do that. We are just the work of Him so how can we conceive of Him? I feel that since I have received so much, I have to give something in return, and give Him verbal thanks. [I compare the eloquence of her simple declaration of faith with my own tangle of uncertainties.]

I am not as religious as my parents were. Ignac and I make it a habit to go to the synagogue every *shabbes* morning. It is called an Orthodox synagogue but men sit with women, and we do drive there because it is quite a long way away. I think that if it were not for me, Ignac would be much less observant than he is, but he has developed a love for Judaism now. As a young man he always used to be with non-Jewish boys and girls, but when he was in concentration camp he saw a *siddur* [prayer book] and he endangered his life because of it. He saved it and brought it out with him when he was rescued. There is that spark in us which is very hard to extinguish.

My father, I feel sure, would rather I had married a Chasid, but I know that if he would be here under these circumstances he would understand that I am trying to keep up the Jewish heritage the best possible way. We did give our son a Hebrew education. I am keeping a kosher home. I bless the candles on Friday night. I have three sets of dishes, ***milkhik, fleyshik*** and ***pesachdik*** [separate crockery for meat, for dairy dishes, and for Passover], and I am trying to have my father and mother always before my mind. Today we have different opportunities and different ways of doing things, but I feel, as a Jewish daughter, that I do try to fulfil my Jewish duties, and I treasure my upbringing. I treasure my faith.

It is time for a coffee break and Ignac reappears. Battling with the recalcitrant hat-rack has put him in a tetchy mood. Work not going well? I ask. 'No good arbeit. Ach, too much troubles. Vere is bread?' 'He always gets upset,' says Miriam, 'when work doesn't go the way he wants. It causes him annoyance and when he is annoyed he sometimes lets it out on me.' He smiles and sighs simultaneously: 'Ai-yai-yai-yai-yai-yai, ai-yai-yai-yai-yai, ach shveetheart!' He makes a playful stabbing gesture at her with his fist: '*Bandita*!'

She hands him a mug of coffee: 'Give me bigger! In old contry I got big von, a haf-litre of coffee.' She gives him a bigger mug. 'Too hot! Bisl cold vater here.' 'I'm going to bring some more milk, honey.' He turns to me: 'If you need in the night milk, is in Frigidaire opstairs.' Miriam says: 'I will show him.' She offers me some cake. Ignac raps impatiently: 'Bread! Bread! adding softly: 'Mamushka.' He has the Slav's masculine ability to be rough one moment, tender the next. 'This is the sweetest name in the world,' says Miriam, 'Mamushka – Mama.' Ignac sighs: 'I loved my mudder, ach she vere a gut mudder. Die German banditen, di sonovamongoose. Ja, mein farder, seventy-five years old, dey take avay ulso. Ai-yai!' He pushes his glasses onto his forehead and wipes his eyes.

He spots the Memorial Book on the table. Miriam opens it at random and reads a passage aloud in perfect, unhesitating Yiddish, which she has not read or spoken for several decades. The passage describes the deportations from Konin, the day when the Germans rounded up Jewish families and herded them into freight trucks. Miriam reads and Ignac listens, both totally absorbed, motionless: she seated at the kitchen table, one hand resting lightly on the open book, he in his workshop apron and corduroy skullcap, standing behind her, leaning over her shoulder to peer at the book. The window casts soft daylight onto the plain wall behind them.

While Ignac is in the workshop struggling with the cantor's hat-racks, Miriam feels compelled to talk to me about Auschwitz:

> I went there after they cleared out the Lodz ghetto, probably at the end of 1944 or the beginning of 1945 – I am not sure of the date: it is like a film with three exposures on it, so many impressions imposed on other impressions.
>
> We were gathered in the open at Auschwitz for the selection, exposed naked. There was a table and there were soldiers sitting around it. Mengele appeared, in breeches, holding a whip. We stood in a line, moving forward slowly and they were looking at us. Mengele made a motion to the left or to the right. At that time I was with the remnant of my family, Yetka my youngest sister, my cousin and one of my sisters-in-law. Only I was to survive. They were all taken to one side and I was taken to the other. Of course we didn't know what for. Finally, I found myself in a group taken to work, and the others – my sister and the others – were taken away in a covered motor truck. They were naked – standing, bodies pressed together as they were taken away. The picture will never fade from my mind.
>
> Our group was taken to a shower to clean up and given a garment and we were all marched to a railroad station. On the way, the Kapo – it happened to be a very sensitive girl – waited for a moment when no one would see her, and she told us in a quiet way: 'You are going to live, and you are going to be taken to work, but remember you must not mention that you are from a small city because they need intelligent people to work in this

> particular factory and they do not have a high esteem for people from a small city, so you have to say a city which is a large one, and you must not be over this-and-this age because if you are older than that they will not take you, so you have to remember in your mind for ever the date when you were born and the name of the city.' I told them I was born in Lodz, not Konin, and I made myself several years younger than I was. It all happened in a kind of trance.
>
> I was assigned to a factory that made parts for airplanes. Towards the end I got very ill and had a terrible gall-bladder infection. I was so ill that one day we were standing for a roll-call and I just dropped to the ground, and they picked me up like a piece of rag and they threw me in a corner, just to die because there was no medical attention there. And I was lying there and didn't know what is going on and I don't know how long I was there, but suddenly I heard a cry and some laughter and I didn't know what happened. I couldn't lift myself up. I was lying on the floor on straw and my consciousness came back and forth, back and forth. I came to and heard the words 'The war is over,' and I rolled myself over to see what is happening and I saw Russian soldiers embracing girls and there was crying and laughing, and the soldiers brought food for the girls and I passed out. Then I found myself on a horse buggy because they took the very sick people into the hospital, and there I got my first medical attention.

In time she learned that her three sisters, three of her brothers and nearly all of her aunts, uncles, cousins and other relatives had died in the Shoah. Like others who have kept their faith, she blames humans not God for what happened. 'It made me aware of the cruelty which is in people. I feel justice should be done to those criminals who have been caught, and I am upset when it is not done. But I do not have revenge in me. Revenge would change me to being one of them.'

> Every time we go to the synagogue and they say the kaddish, I see in front of my eyes a heap of bones and I say the kaddish for the heap of bones, because I know that so many have no one to say kaddish for them, and many of my close relatives were among the bones. It doesn't go out of my mind. I am living a normal life and yet I am not. And as for my husband, not one day goes by that he will not speak about the losses, the horrors

and the cruelties, and he is outwardly such a cheerful man with a smiling face and his passion in his work. Every day he speaks about it. We live a double life, because we cannot stop living and we should not stop remembering.

My son has never asked us any questions about our experiences. It could be that he doesn't want to wake up our pain. I don't know what it feels like to be the child of a survivor. If someone else would ask him, I am sure he would give some answers. We told him about our experiences only in a broad sense. We told him we were in the ghetto, in the concentration camps, that we were deprived of our identity, that we were threatened and mistreated and things like that, but not as I am speaking to you, with the details. I don't know how he would take it, and I didn't want to take the chance of injuring him. That was our fear. But we want him to know, and he may know from the records which we leave behind, but it's a big load on the child of a survivor to hear the details – it is such a terrible pain and as a parent I don't want to inflict that on him.

Her son, a graduate of Omaha University, lives not far away and does research work on electronic aids for handicapped children. 'Alex came home one day and he said: "Ma, I'm going to get married." And I said: "Wonderful. *Mazeltov*! Who is the girl?" He said: "She's not Jewish," and lightning struck me. I didn't say a word, and he said: "Don't cry. When I marry, she will be Jewish." So she went through the whole thing and became Jewish.

'They do not go to *shul* every Saturday like us. They are working all day long, all week long. They are too much under strain, under pressure, so what gives is God. Well, he will wait, he will wait.'

Miriam makes me *matzo bray* for supper, a Passover dish I loved as a boy, an unashamedly fattening mixture of broken *matzo* soaked in milk and fried in beaten egg. Like my mother, she learned to make it in Konin, and the taste is exactly as I remember it: the first mouthful, soft as pasta, carries me back to my childhood days on a wave of gustatory nostalgia: one man's *madeleine* is another man's *matzo bray*. We recite aloud a blessing of thanksgiving.

When Miriam and Ignac arrived in the United States in 1949, their first stop was New York, where the refugee organization HIAS [Hebrew Immigrant Aid Society][1] suggested there might be a suitable job for Ignac in Omaha. 'We did not know where Omaha was, what Omaha is. We didn't even know the map of America. But we said we will go to the end of the earth so long as we can build a new life. So they put us on the train with a ticket and we came to Omaha. The Jewish Community Center here was notified that there is coming a family of parents and a child, and they are looking for a job. So the Center found Ignac a job as a body works mechanic in a car repair shop.'

Thick snow was falling on the day they arrived in Omaha. At first they stayed in an unheated hotel room with no means of warming the baby's bottle; later they moved in with a kind woman from the Jewish Center who took them into her own home until they found an apartment.

> We didn't even have a bed to sleep on. We were sleeping only on the floor, on a ruined mattress because the apartment wasn't furnished. Finally, they got a bed for us and a couch that was all holes and some old dishes, but Ignac injured his back and he couldn't even lift the mattress to the bed and I had to carry it. I was sick too, and he couldn't move. It was just horrible. But little by little we got on our feet until I was very sick and had to undergo an operation. We had to give the baby to an institution while I was in hospital. Ignac was earning only seventy-five cents an hour. It was the bottom, impossible to live on, but we didn't have anything else. We were paying rent but I cooked for the landlady because she was old and didn't see very well, and fixed things for her. We were trying to be useful. We wanted to feel that we have a family. We wanted to attach ourselves to someone and she and her sons were very kind to us. They showed us feeling and this is what counted. They showed us compassion.
>
> So this is how we lived three years. But Ignac wanted to have a place where he could fix an old car and do things for himself, and we found a man who loans mortgages who came from Bohemia like Ignac, and they developed a friendship. He gave us a mortgage although we didn't have any collateral: it was a trust of friendship. We had another friend, also a survivor,

> who lent us the $500–$600 down-payment for this house and we moved over here. We didn't have furniture of course, but a family gave us things, like the dining-room furniture inside, and we did everything by ourselves. But then we couldn't meet the mortgage payments and so we decided we're going to convert this house upstairs and we put in the kitchen and bathroom ourselves and we rented it for fifteen years until the mortgage was paid. Ignac could not increase his earnings much although he was a skilled man because he did not know the language, one thing, and second thing, I went through several major operations and he couldn't take a risk over the job.
>
> Ignac adds: She sick. I tink so she voll die. Sixty-five per tsent out stomach. Qvarter lung out. She got pneumonia, ja. I think so she die. Var harrd.

A stroke of bad luck that they find too distressing to talk about, even so many years later, resulted in their receiving no reparations money from Germany. 'But we always had our Jewish comfort: we say: "Whatever happens, it could be worse." '

They had no money to pay for her first major operation. The surgeon waived his fees but Miriam felt it was wrong to accept his services for nothing. Their only possession of any value was a Leica camera they had bought with their combined savings before leaving the DP camp. It was meant to be a gift for their baby son when he was older. They sold the camera and paid for the operation. Four other major operations followed. She cannot recall ever receiving a communication about the Konin Memorial Book, but it could be that it arrived when she was desperately ill: 'I was on the verge of dying a long time, and the only concern I had was about my family because there would be no one to look after them if I was gone.'

After supper Miriam takes out her sewing things and sits in the kitchen mending Ignac's velvet prayer-shawl bag while he potters around, occasionally contributing a few words in his own inimitable language. The conversation switches back and forth, from the nightmare past to the mundane present and then back again into the darkness. Mirim wants to know about my wife and children and life in London. Ignac shows me a sepia photograph of himself standing beside an army truck, taken in 1928, when he was a lieutenant in the Czech army. And another photograph of him as a small boy with fair curly hair. He does not know when or where his parents died. He saw them last when they were taken away. All he has is a photograph of them which he kisses every night before going to sleep. Miriam has no photographs of her parents.

They worry about their geriatric dog, Smokey, whom they have had since he was a puppy. 'He is nice dog. German shepper. He can no more valk. I hate give him kill it. Dey fish der air from der lung and he die.' 'No, we cannot do it,' says Miriam, 'because he still enjoys food, he enjoys our presence. He just can't walk, so we have to take care of him, feed him and clean up after him.'

Half-teasingly, half-admiringly, Miriam turns the conversation to Ignac's obsession with the workshop. 'He says he loves me more than his machines but I would not like to put him to the test.' Ignac grins benignly. 'He built the shed himself. He welded the beams. He did everything.' Ignac goes over to her and kisses the back of her neck. A little later he appears in an old-fashioned check dressing-gown. Time for bed.

Miriam reminds me that there is fruit in the upstairs kitchen and that I am to eat it. 'Do it for my pleasure,' she pleads. 'Maybe before you go to sleep you might like to have a banana. And remember, there is milk in the fridge.' We say goodnight. Ignac wanders off. Miriam opens the Memorial Book and settles down to read.

Next morning, when I wake at dawn, one of the sash windows in my bedroom is a rectangle of glowing pink. Soon the sun rises above the distant low horizon, at first a blood-red semicircle then an undefined epicentre of fiery orange and yellow. The house is silent. Below, two old people lie in their double bed. Are they awake, thinking of their bunks at Auschwitz? Or worrying what to give me for lunch?

At breakfast I notice how frequently Miriam coughs, always turning her head away and politely covering her mouth. She apologizes for being such a slow eater. Ignac dunks his toast in the coffee and declares: 'I am fast eater. I vher all der time. I vas when I vas yong boy at home I vas fast, fast, fast, fast.

I vork fast, but now I slow down.' He gets up from the table. 'I moss go vork. You tok. Goodbye, Mamushka darling, my shveetheart.'

Miriam has spent half the night reading the Konin book and it has dredged up more memories. A cluster of fresh pencil dots peppers my street map. Miriam had many shopkeeper relatives in Konin: the Szyjka family (chocolate and sweets), Rachwalski (*galanteria*), her Neufeld grandmother ('dry goods' in one half, glass and china in the other), the widowed Mrs Neufeld (newspapers, stationery and school supplies).

> The book reminded me of our lovely park. Every Sunday they had an orchestra playing in the gazebo, and people were enjoying themselves, and walking around, and having picnics. It was very pleasant especially for young people. There, when I was about twelve, I experienced the first shock of sexual behaviour. It was daytime, and I saw a man lying on a woman and she was screaming and I didn't understand as a young girl this act and know what kind of scream it was, a scream of joy or a scream of horror, but she was screaming and I was so horrified by seeing the man overpowering the woman that I ran and I called 'Help! Help! Help!' So people came round and it was in the bushes. They saw the scene and they turned away and started laughing. I remember this because it was my first encounter of a horrible thing, not knowing what it meant. It might have been an encounter of love but to me it was a horrible scene, this man overpowering a woman.
>
> My parents never discussed sex with me. We spoke about marriages but in a very mature, sacred way, about the responsibility of being married, of being together and being faithful, and creating families and caring for them. Of course every young person had a phase when they were romantic. We read about Romeo and Juliet and so we dreamt about, oh, being kissed, or hugged, it didn't go further than that. There were questions that intrigued the curiosity, but they didn't have a form. I had a sister who was married and it was a natural thing to have a family and children, but sex as such, no, it was not discussed.

When she was a young girl in Konin, Miriam had a dream about the end of the world.

> A skeleton covered with a white sheet, seated on a horse and with a whip in his hand, was riding through the town: the Angel of Death. Wherever he went there were people, but whatever he left behind him turned into water and lilies. When he came to our house everything turned into water and we turned into water-lilies, and I turned into a lily and I was growing in the water like a lily, not as a person but as a flower. And this happened until he went through the whole town and it was just water and lilies. And I, as a lily, was aware that I am living but I am not living as a person but as a flower, and the quiet all around was so astonishing. The world was completely water and lilies, left in his wake as the skeleton with the white sheet and the whip rode through Konin. Here there were people, but as he went by there was only water and lilies left behind.
>
> When I woke up and told my father that I had a dream like that, he said: 'This is a very significant dream but it is something I cannot understand.' I can't forget it. Looking back now I see it was like a prophetical dream. In some way it prophesied the end of the community.

Might there be a more prosaic explanation? I have in mind the great flood of 1924.

'Yes, I remember that flood – vaguely.'

For the Warta to flood its banks in the spring was a normal cyclical event, a sign of winter's departure. As the ice melted along the course of the river, the current quickened, the water surged and roared, spilling into neighbouring marsh and meadow, creating shallow lakes and a second sky. The people of Konin would, in the normal course of events, find it a heartening sight, knowing that soon the fruit trees would be in blossom and that summer lay ahead.

Nineteen twenty-four was different. The level of the water rose and kept rising until the Warta overflowed into the streets of the lower part of the town. Cellars filled up like sinks. Muddy water cascaded into the basement homes of the poor and swamped the shops of their better-off neighbours. It was the worst flood in living memory. Third of May Street, about half a mile long, became impassable, vanishing under the inundation and cutting off one end of the town from the other. Some means must be devised of keeping this main route open. The answer was to fetch every wagon that could be found and line them up end-to-end along the whole length of the street, creating a wooden causeway along which people could walk, stepping from one wagon to the next.

A photograph in the Memorial Book records part of this scene in the main street; a closer shot shows a farm wagon, wheels half-submerged, placed in front of one of the houses. Some men and boys standing on the wagon pose stiffly for the camera. Across the bottom of the picture are scrawled a few words in Polish and the date. Miriam translates them for me: 'Konin, the house of the Wiener family in Third of May Street during the flood, 28 March 1924.'

I feel the prickle of gooseflesh, as I always do when some fact leaps unexpectedly out of the past to bind me to the life of this town. My father's brother, Haskel Ryczke, who settled in Palestine in the 1930s, married a girl from Konin, Fella Wiener, now a widow living in Israel. I know her well, as Freda. I had looked at this picture before, without connecting it with her. Little of the house is visible, but enough to show the floodwater lapping just below a window-sill. This was once her home in Konin. The Mysch family lived in the same house.

'I remember the horror of the flood,' recalls Miriam. 'I saw it from the distance because they didn't let us come close. There was much concern because a desperate rescue squad of young people were almost drowned trying to rescue other people. There was great danger.'

The flood made a lasting impression on Leopold Infeld, the young headmaster from Warsaw:

> Moving cakes of ice crashed against the bridge. Someone wearing an armband shouted insults at the Konin Jews who tried to cross over to the other side of the river. At that time I felt anti-Semitism everywhere, perhaps even where it did not exist. It turned out that the unknown person was an engineer who had been made responsible for the bridge. We began to exchange sharp words. The result: a court case against me for abuse of a civil servant while on duty.

> This was my only contact with Polish courts. I defended myself and prepared a moving speech. The judge was human and gave me the smallest possible sentence – only a fine. Independently of this affair, the bridge did collapse, the water overflowed its banks, and my house was inundated. Fortunately I lived on the first floor up, where the water did not reach. But Bronia [his sister] and I were cut off from the school and our fellow teachers. For many days following this, I remember that the school janitor took me by boat straight from my door to the school.[2]

The big square where Miriam lived was situated on higher ground than the main street and so escaped the flooding. Leaning out of her window and looking sharply to the left she would have been able to see the bridge: the commotions as people fought to get across before it collapsed – peasants on this side trying to get back to their villages before nightfall, Koniners on the far bank wanting to come home, policemen trying to keep order, small boys jostling for a view of the icy torrent, maybe a well-dressed young man locked in fierce argument with a civil servant. She must have overheard her parents discussing the plight of families whose homes had been ruined, whispering about the threat of further destruction: all designed to arouse anxiety in the mind of a young, impressionable girl. Surely it was this event, the great flood of 1924, that her sleeping mind later transmogrified into the apocalyptic skeleton galloping through the town, leaving a desolate expanse of water and lilies in his wake. Miriam sticks to her theory that it was a prophetic dream, one which at the time neither she nor her father could understand but which, in the light of subsequent events, makes sense. Not entirely. For the Jews of Konin, the reality was far worse than the dream.

Ignac retired from his job about ten years ago. Since then he has earned modest amounts from welding and repair jobs, enabling him to buy more tools and second-hand machines. Nowadays he often charges nothing for his labour. The proceeds from work he does for the synagogue go to charity. 'This workshop of his is a blessing. He's got an interest. He does not do it for money but because it is his passion. I derive happiness from his happiness. I do sewing alterations for some people. I look after the back yard, and I look after Ignac.'

They never take a holiday. 'He fears that people will come and steal his machines and tools. I think this is a psychological block because he has lost so much in the past, things he worked for, like the loss of his workshop in Czechoslovakia before the war. He and his brother had forty mechanics working for them. Whatever he has now has been acquired with such great effort, with such great sacrifice.'

Life has settled into a quiet routine; there is the synagogue and, for Miriam, a monthly meeting of the Jewish reading circle. She misses the years when Alex was at school and she was involved in PTA activities. Occasionally she still addresses audiences of young people on the subject of the Shoah – 'This is my obligation.' Drawing and painting were once her hobby, and art classes a weekly joy, but these days she does not want to leave Ignac on his own.

They first met in a DP camp in the American zone of Austria. Here her nursing experience in the Lodz ghetto hospital helped her find work in the camp's ambulance station. Another nurse from the Lodz ghetto, who had a fiancé, tried to fix up a companion for her shy, retiring friend. She had Ignac in mind, but her first attempt to get them together was unsuccessful. On her second attempt she bought four tickets for a camp show, two for Miriam and Ignac.

> When we were sitting together he was watching me and I was watching him, and through our minds went: Is this going to be my husband? Is this going to be a good wife? We didn't know what was happening on the stage because we were so absorbed with the questions we had to decide. Do we want to get to know each other or what?
>
> So anyway he told my friend that he likes me and wants to get to know me a little better. I was scared, but we lived across from where he did and I could see him in his room from our second floor, and from that time on I tried to watch him through the window because he had no curtains. He restored a burnt-out room in order to live in it.
>
> It was winter, and he was a man who tried to help people. He brought wood for them. One time he came upstairs to our place where we four girls lived together and he saw that we are freezing, that we have nothing in the stove. He didn't say a word. He went down, he brought up wood and he made the fire and he

> warmed up our room, and this showed his character. He shared things with others. In Auschwitz he shared his food with a young boy, took him under his wings and saved his life.
>
> One of my friends had an acquaintance, a lawyer, an educated man, and he came over to visit her and he wore his coat and was complaining about the cold, but he didn't do anything. They were both freezing and he didn't do anything. So in my mind I worked this out, that a man even with education, even with the care he has for this lady, did nothing, while here is a hard-working man with dirty hands, and he brought in the coal and the wood and warmed up a room for four people. So this quality in him came through to me. He invited me into his little compartment to see how he lives, and when I came in I saw that a woman's hand is very needed.
>
> So I applied myself, I cleaned up and so on. And somebody asked him to drive a truck some place and he said: 'Well, I'm sorry I have to go, but please wait for me.' While I was waiting I prepared something to eat, and this was for him something precious because nobody prepared anything for him, and he was touched by my attention, that I tried so much to make him comfortable. A few months after we met he asked me to marry him. I said: 'I am hesitant but I trust you that you'll be a good man to me.' And he said: 'I love you.' I didn't say: 'I love you' because I didn't feel that I love him. I just trusted him. So until this day he always says: 'I can't forgive you. I love you right away and you didn't tell me that you love me,' and I say: 'Haven't I shown it for forty years?'

Does she mean she grew to love him? 'Yes, I grew to love him. It was something that developed. It doesn't have to spring up like lightning.' A Rabbi married them in the camp in 1947. A friend lent her a dress and a pair of stockings. Other friends made sandwiches, borrowed instruments and formed a band.

> We nurses didn't get paid but we received a CARE package from the United States, and two or three nurses shared one package – some canned goods, a packet of cigarettes, a bar of chocolates. My dowry was part of a CARE package. But I also saved parts from two or three packages so I was able to fill a box and it fitted under the bed. I moved into his room. One wall was gone so he and a friend put up a wall. Our table was a wooden crate covered with a

sheet. As a wedding gift the head nurse and the doctor, who were English, gave me a wedding gift – a hospital bed; and I also got a gift of some bandages and some cotton cloth diapers from which I made curtains. We lived in this one room, and here Alex was born.

I consider myself a lucky woman because there is not a day going by without my husband saying: 'I love you,' not a day in forty and more years. I know this is sincere. This helps me to bear his moods, his frustrations, his sometimes improper words because he is a very emotional man. When I point out that he hurts me with a word, he apologizes. He is disappointed that he cannot do more. He would like to do everything and know everything but he is limited now with his age and his state of health. He has blood pressure and other problems. But he still expects too much of himself and that is hard on him and hard on me but that is my challenge and I try to face it. He always has some longing which he cannot satisfy. And I know there are limitations which we have to accept.

We sleep badly because of worried minds, and because of physical discomfort. As I told you, not a day goes by that Ignac does not speak about the past. I have to listen and comfort him and understand. Yes, we do live with it, but since we are still blessed with life and were given enough strength to have conquered all this and we were privileged to have a child, we must appreciate that, and the feeling of appreciation makes our pain a little more bearable. Many times I myself cannot understand how I can smile, how I can laugh, can enjoy things, but I suppose that we are endowed with this quality to be able to survive.

I feel gratitude to this country for giving us another chance to live, for accepting us into this society. People have been good to us, Jews and non-Jews. In Poland I was always an inferior person because I was a Jew. It was my home country but I was unwanted.

We admire the nature when the leaves are coming up, the liveliness when they flutter or the serenity when they are still, the time when the trees are naked, and then when they are covered with snow, how beautiful they look. We always talk about it. Ignac loves the nature but he doesn't have the time to dwell on it, but I am much more in touch with it because I take care of a few flowers. Every year I take the seeds of the marigolds, dry them and

> start them anew. I get my own seeds from the old plants. I already have three jars of seeds and I share these seeds with a friend of mine, and I put them in the ground in our synagogue and they were so beautiful this year even the president of the synagogue sent me a thank-you note.
>
> I'm also a barber, trimming my husband's hair, trimming my son's hair and my son's beard. They never go to a barber shop, isn't this a funny thing? [She presses both palms to her cheeks in a gesture of mock bashfulness and laughs.] So there is plenty to do. I can't complain.

At the end of the afternoon, when it is dark, I hear voices outside and Miriam says: 'Oh, the children are here.' She goes out to greet them. Alex, her son, is a big fellow, over six feet tall with a full black beard. There are Chasidic faces exactly like his in the Memorial Book. His smile is diffident and at first he seems ill at ease, not quite sure what to do with his hands or his eyes. His wife, Mary, is relaxed and outward-going. Both show interest in my quest and ask penetrating questions. While we talk, Miriam amuses her two grandchildren at the other end of the room. Ignac appears and Alex says: 'Hi, Dad!' Ignac waves back and stands in the doorway beaming happily at his family before vanishing again.

Alex says he has never heard the name Konin before. I ask if he is curious to know more about his parents' past. His body language tells me I am treading on sensitive ground. 'I never asked my parents questions. I guess I didn't want to know too much. I'm not very comfortable with stories about the Holocaust. Maybe I feel a little guilty.' Why guilty? 'I don't really know. Maybe it's because I think: Why didn't it happen to me instead of to them?' His affection for them is apparent: 'The older I get the more I appreciate them.'

When they have gone, Miriam praises her son's qualities: he is helpful, sincere, honest, to which Ignac adds: 'Oh ja, oh ja. Gut boy, gut boy.' He wants to say more but gets stuck: 'I am butcher in English. I ken Jewish, Czechish, Hungarian, Polish. I ken no English. You know vhy? I talk to her too much Bohemian.' He lifts a dish of apple compote to his mouth and drinks the juice. Miriam puts some noodle kugel on the table. He says: 'She is gut girl. Look those eyes, look those eyes, gut girl,' and he admires her eyes, which are indeed beautiful, a pale greenish blue.

It is another flawless autumn day, erasing my night of bad dreams. I shall be leaving after breakfast. Miriam refers to it laughingly as The Last Breakfast: 'Now I am getting a little bit sad. When you leave I am going to feel the vacuum. We have got used to you. You have permitted me to get back into my childhood, and it is my personal gain.' She asks me to stay longer. The apartment is mine for as long as I want it. But she understands when I say I have to move on.

The phone rings in the other room. Miriam takes the call and comes back into the kitchen: 'It is your wife calling you from London.' Is it Jewish *Angst* that makes me fear the worst at once, expect to be told that one of my children has died? The news does concern death: my cousin Felunia, one of the many Ryczkes who lived in Konin until 1939, a survivor of the camps, my sole source of information about the family between the wars, has died unexpectedly in Israel at the age of sixty-four. She had been impatient for me to visit her so that we could talk. There was so much she wanted to tell me.

Time to leave for the airport. Miriam wants to give me something to eat on the journey: 'So you can remember me with a piece of cake.' Ignac appears. He has a gift for me: his Czech army cap-bedge, a rare souvenir of his youth. Touched, I reach out to shake his hand. He ignores my formal English gesture, grips my shoulder, hugs me tightly and presses his stubbly cheek against mine. When he has released me, I look more closely at the badge and, as I do so, I can see at the edge of my vision that Ignac is lifting his glasses and dabbing his eyes. I feel uneasy about accepting the gift and tell them that I cannot take it, that it must stay in the family. 'No, you must have it,' says Miriam. 'We know you will treasure it.'

Postscript Two years later, in the summer of 1989, Ignac became increasingly unwell. In January 1990 he was only just able to summon up the strength to lift the Torah scroll in the synagogue and hold it aloft before the congregation. The following month he was diagnosed as having cancer of the liver. By this time he had become too weak to work, though he continued to attend synagogue. One

Saturday morning the cantor asked how he was feeling. He replied in Yiddish: '*Ikh gey aheim*' – I'm going home. A few days later, on 29 March, he died.

Miriam's health has declined. Increasingly frail, she has moved to a small apartment in Omaha, drawing pleasure from her family, still trying to come to terms with Ignac's death, still trusting in God.

45

'A FINE LIBRARY,' my Uncle Jacob used to say – no small praise from a serious bibliophile and book-dealer. 'A wonderful library,' said Lola Witkowska in her hospital bed in Manhattan. Miriam Grossman praised it in Omaha. Every Koniner I have met has waxed lyrical about it, citing it as evidence that theirs was a community of enlightened Jews, of 'intelligent people'. Invariably, they compared their home town's splendid collection with those of larger Jewish communities that had fewer books. In fact, Koniners find it hard to talk about their library without sounding downright boastful. Some assured me it was one of the biggest and best secular Jewish libraries in all of Poland. A case of community pride blurring reality, I felt sure.

The Bund archives proved me wrong. They yielded little on Konin but one item alone made the search worthwhile. Inside an old brown paper packet was a copy of a Yiddish-language journal published in Warsaw in 1922[1] that contained a survey of Jewish secular lending libraries in Poland, 138 in all. Konin was among them. What I learned was astonishing. At the time of the survey, the neighbouring town of Kalisz, the capital of the region, its name known to thousands of Polish Jews who had never heard of Konin, had a collection of 855 books, all Yiddish. Konin had a total of 5,225 books in Yiddish, Hebrew, Polish, Russian and 'other languages' (including, I happen to know, German and Esperanto). In 1921 Kalisz had a Jewish population of 15,566, compared with Konin's 2,902.[2]

Far more extraordinary is the comparison with Lodz, a major city with a population of over 150,000 Jews. Its three libraries had between them 2,300 books in Polish as compared with Konin's 2,600, and 900 books in Yiddish compared with Konin's 1,275. The survey reveals that Konin had more Polish books than any other Jewish lending library in the country. Nationwide, the average of number of books per reader was six; in Konin it was fifteen. Who could blame them for boasting?[3]

A community composed in the main of tailors, cobblers, artisans, wagoners, small-time merchants and shopkeepers built up a collection of works that went far beyond the popular Yiddish authors of the day: Goethe, Byron, Heine, Shelley, Diderot, Kipling, Rabelais, Mark Twain, Copernicus, Tolstoy, Rochefoucauld, Nietzsche, Schopenhauer, Mickiewicz, Sienkiewicz, Dostoevsky, Kraft-Ebing, Flaubert, Marx, Cervantes, Ruskin, Ibsen and, of course, Szekspir (William), to name but a few.

I can tell you the title of every book on the shelves of that library in 1922, for sitting on my desk is a small volume published in that year, from which I have picked the above names. It belonged to Uncle Jacob and is a rare copy of the catalogue of the Jewish library in Konin, its brittle, flaking pages so frail I hardly dare touch them.[4] My uncle's passion for books, which led him to create a distinguished library of his own in London, may well have owed something to that library in Konin whose catalogue he preserved until he was an old man.

The story of the library begins with the progressive youth of Konin at the turn of the century, mostly the sons and daughters of better-off families that had not necessarily abandoned their Judaism or community fealty but had allowed their sons and daughters a degree of freedom denied to the children of the strictly observant. Whether they knew how far their offspring were taking this freedom I doubt. The young were excited by the prospect of a library, 'of having unlimited reading material in a town where most people had to rely on the miserable stock of the travelling book pedlar . . . who appeared on market day every few weeks with a tattered selection of sacred Hebrew works for the men and a few Yiddish tales aimed at the inferior minds of women.'[5]

Some youngsters risked arrest and banishment to Siberia for belonging to the Bund and engaging in anti-Tsarist subversion. I have written about one of them, Maurice Lewin. When he was nearly eighty, he described the early days of the library. His account opens in the year 1901.[6]

> We started out by a door-to-door collection of any books that we could obtain and within a few days amassed a heterogeneous number of volumes. This we augmented by a number of second-hand books that we managed to buy in Warsaw.
>
> The nucleus of our library we carefully catalogued and numbered and established it in a tiny room in the flat of my parents. We then enrolled a number of about sixty readers who paid twenty kopeks monthly, and we issued books to them on Tuesdays and Fridays during afternoon hours. Hels Fernbach, Flondrovna, and my sister Zenia were acting as librarians.
>
> As we obtained no official permission for running this library, indeed it would never have been granted to us anyhow, we took every precaution that there should not be too many readers crowding in on us at the same time, as this would have attracted the unwelcome attention of the police. Gradually, however, we became bolder, and it became no uncommon sight to see members gyrating round the big square with a batch of books under their arms. This became a sort of status symbol.
>
> We used the money collected as subscriptions to buy more and more books from Warsaw, and in a short time we became so affluent that we were able to acquire the stock of the Yiddish library, the property of a young bookbinder, Skowronski. In this way our collection soon assumed so great a size, and the number of subscribers grew so fast, that we had to find larger premises and we therefore transferred the library to a cellar in Danziger's house. For such valuable (!) stock we thought it expedient to guard it, and Abram Zachs and I took over entirely and made it our living quarters. Once we had a scare. We were given a hint from outside that the police were planning to raid us. The news spread quickly, and a dozen students arrived secretly with sacks and baskets to pack and disperse our valuable collection and hide it in neighbouring houses. By evening the shelves were empty – no police appeared in the end. Was it a hoax and by whom? And why? Anyhow, after a few days our fears subsided; the books were all brought back and we continued as before.

Any mention of Konin in a newspaper article was enough to

make Jacob Sarna reach for his scissors. Among the cuttings he began gathering after he came to London is an article about the town published in 1915 in the London Yiddish daily, *Di Tsayt*. It refers to the Konin library, which was founded 'first in secret and then legalized. This institution suffered a great deal of troubles. Today it continues to exist. It has about 5,000 Polish, Russian and Hebrew books, and a very nice reading room with 35 newspapers and journals in five languages. This institution was the pride of Konin.'[7]

What were the 'troubles'? Possibly troubles with the police, even after delegates from Konin had gone to St Petersburg to swear allegiance to the Tsar and to obtain, in return, permission to open the library. Possibly troubles with community elders anxious not to antagonize the authorities; troubles with raising money to buy books; troubles from certain religious quarters opposed to setting up an institution that would entice youth away from the only work worth studying: the Torah. Were a man to spend every minute of every day of his entire life studying the Torah, say the rabbis, he would extract only a small part of its riches. If the holy tongue provided the key to wisdom, what was the point of wasting time on Esperanto and other *narishkeytn* [foolish things]? It mattered not one jot if a town had no secular library, so long as it possessed the holy works in its *bes-medresh* or *yeshiva*. Konin had no *yeshiva* proper but it did have a *bes-medresh* endowed with an outstanding library. Here, so its habitués would argue, was the proper place for a young Jew to exercise his mind and find spiritual nourishment.

Both libraries, the religious and the secular, were places for exploring ideas, for analysing and interpreting the written word. Judaism provided the focus in the former, more recent isms in the latter. The one valued books, the other *the* Book. The library that had the ancient tradition, though it opposed the values of the newcomer, yet unwittingly helped ensure the upstart's success. Those who drank at the well of the Enlightenment grew up in a religious community that encouraged reading from an early age, respected learning and thrived on abstracts. In his history of the Jews, Paul Johnson observes: 'Pious Jews saw heaven as a vast library, with [an archangel] as the librarian.'[8] (Hell had its library too. Two days after the Jews of Vilna were driven into the ghetto, they opened a library.)

Some Jews managed to straddle both worlds, holding on to their faith while engaging with modernity. But inexorably the numbers of the deserters from religion grew, and youngsters who might once have teased the meaning out of a commentary by Rashi turned to grappling with the complexities of dialectical materialism. Some found themselves caught uncomfortably between the two worlds. Avrom Soika, a young man in Konin in the 1920s, had a 'fanatically religious' mother, who insisted that he attend *cheder*, 'lay *tefillin*' and go to synagogue twice a day. Without her knowledge, he borrowed books from the library and read them in a secluded part of the park. 'I led a double life,' he told me. His *melamed* once caught him reading Modern Hebrew poetry. 'He was shocked. He shouted: "*Haskoleh! Haskoleh!*" [*Yiddish for Haskalah*]. Hebrew was the *loshn koydesh*, the holy tongue. He went to my mother and told her: "He's growing up a *goy*, a devil." ' Natan Biezunski, a descendant of one of Konin's rabbis, was another furtive library user: 'Who would read a book other than the Torah? Secular books were *shmadkeytn*' – things associated with converting to Christianity. Was he ever found out? 'God forbid!'

There was among the Jews a huge and unsatisfied hunger for knowledge, which the new library did its best to satisfy. Such was its success in the Twenties that one Koniner recalls 'long queues waiting to change books'.[9] They were not all earnest autodidacts bent on intellectual self-improvement or politically-minded idealists shopping for ideologies. The readers of Yiddish sought diversion from the cares of everyday life. They warmed to the human stories of the founding fathers of Yiddish literature, Mendele Mokher Seforim, Sholem Aleichem and Isaac Leib Peretz, who found their raw material within the ghetto and created characters their readers immediately recognized – Tevye the Milkman, Bontshe Shvayg and other *shtetl* heroes. Sholem Asch, Abraham Reisen and other authors produced works of fiction that were in constant demand, their merit spread by word of mouth on street corners and in the Tepper Marik. Zionists preparing for *aliyah* could turn to the works of Herzl and Max Nordau, or find inspiration in the Modern Hebrew poetry of Hayyim Nahman Bialik that so shocked Avrom Soika's teacher. Some came to the library to read the newspapers, which hung in rows, clipped to bamboo holders.

The library also welcomed a section of the community that was excluded from the *bes-medresh* and the *shtetl*: the female sex. More girls than boys attended Polish schools, where, like my own mother, they acquired a taste for the poetry and literature of Poland. The sight of brothers and fathers bent over books must have had its influence, and the establishment of the library meant that girls too could steep themselves in books, albeit of a different kind. Long winter nights and a dearth of entertainment provided the ideal conditions for nurturing a love of reading, as in the case of the young Blumcha Zylberberg, who was to become a librarian: 'Jack London – I used to read all his books, Israel Zangwill, Balzac, Dumas, Maeterlinck, Thomas Mann, a lot of Polish books . . .'

When illness and old age forced Avrom Soika to retire as a tailor in Montreal, his favourite refuge was the local public library. 'When I am there, I fly. I am free.' He first got a taste of that freedom in the Jewish library in Konin. All those who felt trapped in a world from which they longed to escape had the opportunity to open a book and take off like a bird. No sooner had they finished a book and returned to earth than they opened another and soared again into the sky to glimpse a bigger world below.

The library moved premises several times. Its first proper home was in Moishe Klotz's house in the big square. Later, probably around the time of the First World War, it moved to the upper storey of Lipman Bulka's house near the Town Hall. Once it lost its clandestine character, the library became an official community institution, with a constitution and officers and committees, all giving their services on a voluntary basis. The library's popularity spread to Jews living in the villages around Konin who borrowed books when they came to town. Gentiles came to use it too, perhaps not entirely satisfied with their own Polish library, which was run by a charitable organization.[10]

Once it was firmly established, the Jewish library opened from 5 to 10 pm every weekday except Fridays. The volunteers who ran it not only helped with the administration but would advise readers, especially children who did not know what to read next or were too hooked on Karl May's popular stories of cowboys and Indians. Borrowers were not allowed access to the shelves. They had to choose a book from the catalogue and the duty librarian went and got it for them. As few homes afforded the luxury of a 'salon', reading was generally done at the kitchen table, with predictable effects on the condition of the books. I have found a photograph – the original has sadly vanished – of a bookmark containing a message in Yiddish addressed to THE READER: 'I beg you not to fling me down carelessly on the table . . . Do not read me while eating at the table because you will stain me . . . Do not use me to snuff candles . . .' It is signed, THE BOOK.

Increasingly, the library came to be a centre for cultural and educational activities. Speakers from bigger towns came to give talks and lectures on a variety of topics. Audiences, mostly composed of the young, gathered in the library on Saturday afternoons for readings and discussions. Yiddish culture flourished, and on the anniversary of the death of Isaac Leib Peretz, beloved champion of the Jewish working masses, his bust was put in a place of honour.

The library was always strapped for cash. Benefactors among the wealthier, more enlightened members of the community would donate books from time to time. Subscription fees, paid either monthly or annually, brought in revenue, but free membership was given to those who could not afford it, with particular lenience shown to children from poor homes. The library housed fund-raising events, such as an exhibition of early works by the painter and sculptor Chanoch Glicenstein, who befriended the aspiring artist, Mark Lewin. As a souvenir of his visit, he painted a portrait of Rabbi Lipschitz and his son.

In 1936 the library moved to its final address, the building of the former Jewish gymnasium, where it settled down under the same roof as the Jewish social club. By now its collection must have outstripped the figures given in the statistical survey of 1922. One Koniner has put on record that by 1939 there were 20,000 books, but I am inclined to accept the figure of 12,000 which appears in a Bund publication.[11] The move to the new address marked the end of the library's golden years. Though still valued, it opened fewer days a week as the number of users began to fall off. 'The cinema, youth clubs, Zionist organizations, political movements, athletics, games and other social activities were drawing away the young,' I learned from Natan Ahykam, a former of the library committee.

The books from the library of the *bes-medresh* went up in flames in 1939, and we know exactly where the bonfire was lit. The fate of the secular books remains a mystery. Perhaps they were burned after the Jews were deported from Konin. If so, did the Germans in their zeal unwittingly cast their own Nietzsche and Kant and Schiller into the flames? Whatever the truth of the matter, the fact is that when a handful of survivors returned to Konin in 1945, their library was gone. There is a particular poignancy about the destruction of a library, and though the Jewish Communal Library and Reading Room of Konin hardly ranks with that of Alexandria, its loss is mourned by all who tasted its pleasures. And by one who did not.

46

'MENDEL BUYS NASA space ships and sells them for scrap. He's a millionaire, they say.' I first heard about Mendel Jakubowicz from a Koniner in London who teased my curiosity but failed to satisfy it. I learned that he came from a fairly poor family in Konin, had been in Auschwitz, and was now breaking up obsolete spacecraft. I heard one other intriguing fact: he had refereed top soccer events in the USA, including a match between the Moscow Dynamo team and the Texas Tornados.

Alas, my Koniner had lost Mendel's address and could remember only that he lived 'somewhere in Texas'. I tried to trace him through other sources without success. When Motek Mysch's list of American Koniners arrived some months later, I ran through it quickly but could find no Jakubowicz. Studying it more carefully, my eye paused at the name Michael Jacobs of Dallas, Texas. Michael Jacobs? Mendel Jakubowicz?

On 6 November 1987, a warm, almost summery day in Dallas, Texas, I drive down a dirt road into the scrap yard of JACOBS IRON & METAL COMPANY, INC, to meet its founder from Konin, Poland. At sixty-two Mike Jacobs exudes physical fitness. He has a healthy crop of hair, keen grey-blue eyes and a restless energy. The scar below one eye adds to the macho personality. There is an engaging, likeable quality to the man that counterpoints the tough aura. He talks in a foreign-accented flow of lively English. He wears an open-necked, short-sleeved shirt that reveals the number on his left arm: B4990.

He takes me on a guided tour across a wide expanse of dusty

wasteland from which rise jagged mounds of metallic detritus: automobiles flattened into layered slabs as though they had been through a mangle, steel offcuts, iron pipes and brass, mouldy-looking copper, silvery soft-drink cans . . . Mike points at a pyramid of rusting metal hoops – 'worth half a million dollars'. Cranes shift massive chunks of iron, trucks roll up with new loads of scrap. Wagons on a railroad track bear his name and the slogan SCRAP IS BEAUTIFUL. He tells me it was his idea. To him scrap is indeed beautiful, if for no other reason than that it has brought him a good living. But where are the discarded NASA spacecraft? Sadly, that part of the story turns out to be myth.

The soccer refereeing, on the other hand, is fact, although it was always a part-time activity, from which he has now retired. His office walls are covered with photographs of soccer events, team pennants and trophies. A past President of the Texas Referees Association, he has refereed local amateur players as well as matches between world-class professional teams in some of the biggest stadiums in the United States. And yes, he did referee a match in Dallas between Moscow Dynamo and the Texas Tornados.

Mike arrived in Dallas from Austria in 1951, at the age of twenty-six, having come by sea from Bremerhaven in Germany to New Orleans and from there by rail to Dallas. When he stepped off the train, his worldly wealth was twenty dollars. He carried no suitcase because he couldn't afford one. Instead, he had a wooden crate containing his personal possessions, the most precious among them a pair of soccer boots, soccer clothes, a sweatshirt, tennis shoes and racket, and several sports trophies he had won after the war. He spoke no English.

Two years later, after he had 'worked his tail off' at various forms of employment and married a local Jewish girl, he started up on his own in the scrap business. His young wife, a teacher with two degrees, helped get a loan from the Teachers' Credit Union to buy a used Chevrolet truck. He learned how to drive, and she joined him in scouring the countryside in search of scrap. He began the business on the present site in 1955, after raising a bank loan to buy a small parcel of land. The sign went up: JACOBS IRON AND METAL. His wife took care of the book-keeping. When he was out on the road, she bought scrap and worked the scales.

Mike accepted a single payment from the postwar West German

government as compensation for the loss of his parents' valuables. He never applied for regular, lifelong reparations money for his own sufferings: 'I didn't want it, even when I had no money.' For some years Mike has run the business in partnership with two of his three sons. He has expanded the site, now owns thirty-five acres in all, has installed a railroad siding, and employs over twenty men. His wife no longer needs to lend a hand with the book-keeping or scrap-buying. The plant we are looking at would 'cost five million dollars and more. Everything you see – the bailers, the hydraulic shearers, cranes, magnets – everything is paid for. I'm an old European. I pay for everything cash. I like to be secure and sleep at night.' He sings America's praises. I have heard the paean from other Konin immigrants, and the words are becoming familiar: 'It's a beautiful country. You're free, and if you work hard there's opportunity.'

Mike has worked hard. He owns several properties around Dallas, including a 152-acre farm. He is part-owner of a marina and has his finger in various other investment pies. But for all that, his wealth is probably less prodigious than rumour among Koniners suggests. He is no top 'Dallas' tycoon. He has no chauffeur, no live-in servants, but his home is certainly on a grander scale than that of any other Koniner I have met.

The Jacobs residence is a long, low, ranch-style building with a drive leading to a front portico that can accommodate two large automobiles. Glass doors and double wooden doors open onto a black-tiled lobby from which the visitor steps down into a vast, thickly carpeted living-room. The high ceiling slopes down to a wall of smooth-hewn boulders. In a space like this the grand piano shrinks into insignificance. Through a glass wall I can see the 'free form' swimming pool outside, forty-two feet long, with Hockney patterns undulating in the sun and reclining chairs scattered about. Lawns slope down to a natural stream.

The leather-padded bar is equipped with ice-making machine, stainless-steel sink and, unusual for a Jewish home, a wide rang of alcohol. There are long sofas and fat chairs, and *objets* everywhere – over one hundred at a quick count, not including pictures and prints. Crystal ornaments glitter on glass shelves lit from below. Mike collects naturalistic bronze figures, which are everywhere. The top of the grand piano has clusters of framed family photographs. Despite the affluent trappings, the place is homey, not the work of an interior decorator.

Mike and his wife, Ginger, do not themselves project ostentation. She is an energetic woman who was born in Dallas, speaks Hebrew and feels intensely Jewish. She has an MA in sociology, and does research work on local Jewish history. Mike admires her intellectual attainments and leans on her for help on any matter for which he has neither inclination nor patience. All the letters I have received from them were written and typed by her.

They have His and Hers studies. Hers is book-lined and paper-strewn. His looks untouched, the walls covered with gold-framed certificates testifying to Mike Jacobs's generous support of Israel – 'The Zionist Organisation of America gratefully acknowledges . . .' Beside that is a 'Citation of Honour' in recognition of Mike Jacobs, President of Jewish National Fund of Dallas 1982–1983 . . .', a 'Certificate of the Prime Minister's Club' for 'exemplary service to Israel . . .', 'In grateful appreciation to Mike Jacobs from B'nai B'rith . . .' Still more certificates acclaim Mike Jacobs's achievements in the world of sport. The occupant of the study has a large 'canvas-effect' colour portrait of himself on display, as well as snapshots taken when he was a Displaced Person in postwar Austria: winning a trophy, winning a 400-metres race . . .

A presentation pen-holder incorporating a Hershey chocolate bar wrapper has a bizarre link with the Mauthausen death camp where Mike was freed on 5 May 1945. He describes that moment:

> I looked out from the barracks and I see tanks coming with white stars. At first I think they are German tanks. I say to my friends: 'Hey look, the Germans have changed from a swastika to a white star.' Two hours later I see some more tanks coming. I walk out and I start waving. The guy comes out of the turret. He waves back and throws me something. It was a bar of chocolate. I grabbed it and run into the barracks and say: 'Hey guys, look, I got a bar of chocolate. And can you imagine! – the name of the chocolate is Hershel[3] [a common Yiddish name]. I didn't read the wrapper properly, so the first American food I eat is a Hershel bar.
>
> I remember I took the piece of chocolate and cut it into very small pieces. Everyone was standing around. I gave everyone a piece. I could see the look on their faces – they didn't want to swallow it, they wanted to keep it. I looked out again from the

> barracks and I see a guy, a civilian with a red cross who is with a soldier with a machine-gun, and the man with the red cross waves. None of the others wanted to go up to him. Who goes? Mike. I went over there and he said: 'You speak German?' and I say 'Yes.' He says: 'You are free people now. The Americans are here.' I walk to the barracks and say *'Mir zenen fray. Di Amerikaner zenen do. Mir darfn nisht moyre hobn'* – Guys, we're free. The Americans are here. We've got nothing to fear. I was nineteen and a half years old and I weighed seventy pounds.

Today, Mike is an honorary member of the American army division that liberated him. The inscription on his pen-holder reads: 'Presented to Mike Jacobs, a Mauthausen Survivor, 41st anniversary, May 5 1945–May 5 1986, given by his friends and liberators of the 11th Armoured Division.' It was their idea to add the chocolate wrapper to the souvenir.[1]

Mike shows me a video that was shot in the Dallas Memorial Center for Holocaust Studies in 1985. Made originally for schools and special audiences, it has since been shown many times on local television. Speaking directly to camera, he describes the end of his normal life in Konin at the age of thirteen, and the six years he spent after that as 'a dead teenager'. He recalls the day he and his family were rounded up, their deportation, the death of his parents and brothers and sisters at Treblinka, and the harrowing atrocities he witnessed. He shows some of the exhibits at the Holocaust Center, including his own striped cap from Mauthausen – 'soaked with blood and sweat where I used to be beaten . . .' He talks of the non-Jewish prisoners, the Gypsies and Jehovah's Witnesses who also perished, and he pays tribute to the 'Righteous Gentiles' who died helping Jews. His concluding message is that we must cherish our freedom and ensure that such a catastrophe never happens again: 'We must not forget. We must remember.' It is an eloquent statement, all the more effective for not being delivered from a script.

It is over forty years since he was liberated from Mauthausen. Since then he has rehabilitated his life, built up a flourishing business, has a supportive family, lives in a society where he feels happy and secure. Yet the Shoah still defines him. He has an unswerving, one might call it obsessional, determination to bear witness. The Dallas Memorial Center for Holocaust Studies was his brainchild. He was its first President and he is still caught up in its affairs.

He gives up much of his free time to lecturing on the Shoah. 'Officially, I've been talking since 1956. Unofficially, I've been talking since I left Mauthausen.' He visits schools all over Texas, and has a thick file of appreciative letters from schoolchildren. He addresses adult audiences, the overwhelming majority of whom are gentiles. 'I speak a lot about freedom but I don't speak with hate. Hate breeds hate. My closing line is: "You are privileged to listen to a Holocaust survivor. We're getting fewer and fewer. You can tell your children you listened to me. And you will be the spokesmen who will hand the message on. Take nothing for granted. Germany was one of the most cultured nations in the world and look what happened there. We must not forget because it is so beautiful to be free. That's my life, that's my dedication." That's how I end.'

Now he wants to show me another video, which he is sure I will be thrilled to see. It is a film of Konin that he shot when he visited the town a few months ago with his wife, and son Andy. I plead tiredness. I remind him that I left Nebraska early this morning, that it's been a long day and my head is spinning and maybe it would be better if I looked at the video tomorrow. Mike, who does not know the meaning of tired, is dismayed. Don't I want to see what the town looks like today?

The truth of the matter is that I do, but not this way. How can I explain to him that however much I long to see Konin, I want to experience it through my own eyes not his, that I want Konin to be my final destination, not a video stop-over in Dallas? I cannot think of a way of telling him this without being hurtful. In any case, I *am* tired and aching to have a wash. Reluctantly he gives way. I go and unpack my things. He and Ginger, generous people, have invited me to be their guest for the next few days.

My arrival in Dallas is on a Friday, and this evening I join Mike and Ginger and members of their family in welcoming in the Sabbath. We do not eat in the chandeliered dining-room reserved for formal social entertaining but, more to my liking, in the kitchen which nevertheless, like the rest of the house, is on a Texan scale. I meet the Jacobs's eldest son, Mark: Ginger introduces him with conscious humour as 'my son the lawyer'. He is twenty-eight, a bachelor, and has his own place in Dallas.

I meet their daughter, Debbie, their son-in-law, Wayne, and their three young granddaughters.

The *shabbes* candles flicker on the table. The *challa*, baked by Debbie and still warm from the oven, is placed on the table in front of the master of the house. The men wear yarmulkes. Mike intones the blessings over the bread and wine, and conducts the whole ceremony with effortless command. As one would expect, his pronunciation of the Hebrew is Ashkenazi, but more than that, it is Konin. In the delivery of each word, the melodic rise and fall of each phrase, I hear an uncanny echo of my father's voice.

Up to this point the proceedings have followed in the ways of our Konin forebears. The meal that follows is not quite so traditional: Texan barbecued chicken with baked beans and broccoli, followed by pecan pie. Mike's father, Moishe Jakubowicz, might have found his son's brand of Judaism somewhat perplexing: Mike is honorary treasurer of the Dallas Conservative synagogue yet does not attend Saturday services. At home he ushers in the Sabbath with due ritual yet does not treat the Sabbath as a holy day. His religious observance, like that of many Diaspora Jews, extends not much further than Yom Kippur, the Pesach Seder, and a *latke* (potato pancake) party at Chanukah, yet he and Ginger assure me that they would, with not a minute's hesitation, sever relations with their sons and banish them from the family home were they to marry gentiles.

Dinner over, Mike talks about his family in Konin. They lived on the Tepper Marik, just across the square from the *bes-medresh*. His parents, Moishe and Dora, had four sons and two daughters. Mendel was the youngest. They lived in two rooms and a kitchen. The daughters helped with the housework. During the day, one of the two rooms served as a tailor's workshop. 'I shared a bed with my mother, and my older brother slept with my father in the same room in two separate beds. In the workshop my two sisters shared one bed, my other two brothers slept in the other bed. The workshop had a large table and two or three sewing-machines. Sometimes if someone wanted to sew, they sat on the bed. We managed. The home was very comfortable.'

Moishe Jakubowicz was an able violinist, who had served as a musician in the Tsar's army. A tanner by trade, he cared little for the work and tried other ways of earning a living. For a while he was a book-keeper, then started a small grocery store in the

Tepper Marik that failed. Finally, deciding to be a drayman, he bought a horse and wagon and carted freight between Konin and Kolo. His luck was shaky: one horse after another went lame on him. He struggled on, occasionally supplementing his income by buying and selling rabbit skins.

His eldest son, Avrom, worked at home tailoring, making bespoke suits and coats. The next, Reuben, worked for Hershel Ancer, making leather uppers. Mrs Jakubowicz contributed to the family coffers by baking Passover matzos.

> There were only a few people in Konin – maybe two or three – who made matzos for selling at Pesach and one of them was my mother. She must have done it for many years, I cannot say how long, but I remember as a small boy she always made matzos for Pesach, and she went on making them until the war. When she started, it was with a partner, and when he passed away my mother carried on by herself.
>
> Zadik, who made candy, also baked matzos for Pesach but she didn't want him as a partner. She could handle it herself, so finally he opened up across the street and was in competition with my mother. There was always a big fight between them because everyone want to buy from my mother. The bakers who made bread all the year, they didn't bake matzos.
>
> My mother used to take over an old bakery that was no longer being used and she rented it for a few weeks. When she moved into the bakery we used to clean it out, kosher it by burning lots of wood in the oven for one or two nights, making everything red-hot. Usually she began baking after Purim. People came in from Slupca, Golina and other *shtetlekh* and used to order matzos from us.
>
> She had Polish women helping her. There were a lot of matzos to make. It was hard work, but the same women came every year. They knew how to do it and my mother treated them right. When they come in to make the matzos they had to wash their hands. It was not only to be clean but to make sure there was no *chomets* [leavened matter]. When the *goy* brought water, it was poured into the barrel through a cheesecloth because maybe there was some *chomets* in the bucket.
>
> They mixed the flour and the water and kneaded the dough.

Then it went over to a person who cut it into small pieces, and other women used to make them into balls and roll them flat. The matzos were round.

They had to be very careful when they rolled the dough flat to make sure no part of the matzo folded over at the edge. If it did, it was *chomets*. After the matzos were rolled out, they were put on another table for the *reydl* [small wooden implement with a spiked wheel]. I used to help with the *reydl*, running it up and down to make the holes. I know how to bake too. When I was in Austria after the war I used to bake the matzos for Pesach.

My mother had a man who put the matzos in the oven with a long shovel. I think he was a Ryczke. [Quite likely, as two of my Ryczke relatives were bakers.] You had to know how white the matzo should be after it was baked. You didn't want it to be too brown. If it was too brown people didn't want to buy it. From the broken matzos my mother made matzo meal.

We used to rent an empty store at Pesach and all the matzos were taken there, and people came to buy, two kilo, five kilo or ten kilo. They were bought loose. The women put them in baskets or wrapped them in a sheet or a pillow case. I remember lots of people want to buy the matzos from us. It was a nice matzo, a thin matzo. All the customers knew my mother: '*Mir geyn tsu Doyra koyfn matses*' [We're going to Dora's to buy matzos].

My mother worked from early morning until late at night. Sometimes she make money, sometimes she didn't. It depends on whether she sells all the matzos. Sometimes people were going to the competition, to Zadik. And there were the people who worked for her who had to be paid. The mills – Leszczynski or Kowalski – didn't give everyone credit but when she bought flour they gave her credit. She did not have to pay a penny until after Pesach. They knew it makes no difference whether she makes money or not, she will pay them. She was never behind with payments.

The Chasidim would not eat my mother's matzos. On the last day of baking they came to my mother when all the matzos were finished and they say they would like to have the bakery. They paid my mother so much money and took over the bakery to make '*shmureh* matzos' [made under the strictest religious supervision]. No female was allowed to touch the *shmureh* matzos. Only men. All the Chasidim went over there. They used to knead the dough, and a guy used the *reydl*, and they baked the matzos.

The Chasidim used to watch how the corn for the *shmureh* matzos was harvested to make sure there was no *chomets*, and watch it until it goes into the mill, and watch it when it was in the mill. That's why it is a *shmureh* matzo. But I couldn't eat their matzos – they were dark and thick.

Houdini, son of an unsuccessful Rabbi, once eulogized with classic *shtetl* understatement: 'If God ever permitted an angel to walk on earth in human form, it was my mother.' Mike feels much the same about his own mother. She was 'a golden lady', whose selfless love bound the family together.

My mother wore a *sheytl*. She had two *sheytls*, a weekday wig and a Saturday wig. The *shabbesdikeh sheytl* would rest all week on a wooden head. Every Friday I used to take it in a cardboard box to the woman who looked after *sheytls*. There were lots of other *sheytls* in the room on wooden heads. I can see it now. She used to put waves in the *sheytl* and comb it out. She had hot irons – curlers. Very poor people combed out their *sheytls* for themselves, and I guess they wouldn't be able to afford two.

Our family was a very loving family, very close. It always gave me lots of strength. I remember it as a happy childhood. I never was ashamed of what my family did. We weren't rich, and I wouldn't say we were poor. Poor meant people who didn't have for *shabbes*, who didn't have nice clothes, who lived in basements and had to come to the community and ask for help. We always had fish for *shabbes*, we always had chicken or geese and *tsimmes* on the table, and on festivals the same thing. There were seven families living in the same house as us. Some of them were people who didn't have money to heat their homes. What did they do? They came to us because we had a stove. They used to sit, put potatoes in the ashes, eat them with herring and then go back to their cold rooms.

One time when Jack Offenbach came to visit Konin he brought from London a tricycle for his sister's boy. The biggest thing in my life was being able to ride on it. I can see it now. It had a big wheel in front and two little wheels at the back. Sure it was a sensation. Who could afford a bicycle? Who could afford toys? Who heard about toys? We made our own. We had a long stick. Someone else threw another stick and you hit it. If someone caught it, you were out. You had to run to base – like baseball.

My father was not a Chasid but he always wore a hat, and he went every morning to *shul* and in the evening to Ma'ariv [evening prayers]. He prayed in the *shul* but sometimes it was difficult to get a *minyan* and he went into the *bes-medresh* or a *chevre*. My father sometimes used to stop at night on the way from Kolo and say evening prayers in the forest. I'd say: 'How can you pray without a *minyan*?' He'd say: 'The trees are a *minyan*.'

My father had his own seat in the *shul*. Well-off people with top hats sat near the eastern wall. My father's seat was in the middle, near the **bimah**. I was standing up, next to him. He couldn't afford a seat for me. I sometimes used to sit on the floor and fall asleep on Yom Kippur. I was in the choir when I was five and a half years old until war broke out. Not all my brothers went *shabbes* to *shul*. It didn't bother my father. He was modern. Life in Konin was changing.

My brothers belonged to the Jewish library – it was a tremendous library. Reuben was reading all the Jewish books in Yiddish. I remember he belonged to one particular group of boys. They would read a book and stand on the corner of the Tepper Marik discussing it, debating. When Reuben sat at the machine and sewed uppers, he used to have a book in front of him all the time and read. His boss used to say my brother was doing such a good job it didn't bother him.

Talking to Mike about his family, I realize that he and I are related by marriage. One of his first cousins married Zalman Ryczke, son of the *cheder* teacher, Benyumin. Zalman, I learn, was 'a bit of a joker'. He used to sew by an open window overlooking the Tepper Marik. His needle always had an excessively long thread, and the wide sweeping movements he made with his arm as he sewed were like a conductor's. He worked to the sound of music. Next to him stood a gramophone with a large horn whose sound wafted down to the cobbled square below.

No hope of Mike forgetting about the Konin video. He is not a survivor for nothing. He never gives up. When I try a delaying tactic he goes into a sulk, and a cloud of gloom pervades the house. He is used to having his own way. I surrender, and his good humour returns as quickly as it vanished. I, on the other hand, feel unreasonably resentful: Why should he pre-empt a precious moment, my first sight of Konin? While Mike feeds the cassette into the player, I resign myself to his tour of Konin. In the event, the video is a succession of home-movie shots, shaky pans and pointless zooms. The images are blurred because there was a problem with the camera.

In the course of the next few days we talk endlessly about Konin, in a variety of settings: in the kitchen, beside the pool, at Fudruckers ('The World's Greatest Hamburgers'), at a Dallas engagement party ('I can't believe my luck,' the fiancé's father whispers in my ear. 'She's white, she's Jewish, and you know something – they want to keep a kosher home!'), at a lavish fund-raising 'tribute' dinner in honour of one of Dallas's wealthiest Jews and his wife. On all these occasions Mike mixes easily, is a genial, high-spirited presence, obviously much liked. But it is never difficult to extract him from the immediate scene and take him back to Konin. He steps readily into a past that in some way feels more real to him than the present. Others want to avoid the pain of remembering and the remembering of pain, and have no wish ever to return to the place of their birth. For them, the past torments and embitters. For Mike, it invigorates and restores. 'Every time I visit Konin,' he says, 'it gives me inner strength.'

He has returned three times and is planning a fourth visit with his youngest son, Reuben. Mike did not go back to Konin after he was liberated. There was no point. He learned that his brother Reuben (after whom his son is named) had joined the partisans and been killed, and that the rest of his family, distant as well as close relatives, had been gassed. Mike remained in Germany and Austria until he emigrated to the United States. When he went back to Konin in 1975, it was as a fifty-year-old American citizen. He was fourteen when he left Konin. The Polish school he had attended was still there, although the staff had changed and there were no Jewish pupils. He found one Jew left in the town, Madzia Leszczynska.

His former home had been demolished, along with many other houses in the Tepper Marik. The cemetery was gone, the synagogue dilapidated and locked. 'I felt the buildings are closing in on me. I say: "Ginger, let's go." ' Mike waited thirteen years before his next visit. This time they took their son Mark, and the visit was rewarding for both father and son. Mike found the house where he had gone to *cheder*, the tree whose trunk he used to try to encircle with his arms when he was a small boy, the river where he fished and swam, and other landmarks from his early youth. The synagogue was now in the early stages of restoration. Mike showed Mark the spot where he and his father used to pray, where he once sang as a chorister. Afterwards, as they walked round the town, Mike felt the place reaching out to him once more. 'People cannot understand that when I walk in the streets of Konin I don't walk, I float. It's important for me to take the kids back to Konin where I laughed, cried and was happy, where my father and my grandfather lived, where I played with Yankeleh and Chaveleh and Moisheleh.'

Mike decided to pay another visit to Konin the following summer, with his son Andy. This was a few months before my arrival in Dallas. On the eve of their departure from Poland, Andy wrote his father a letter, and Ginger wants to read it to me now. It is a tender letter in which Andy asks his father to re-examine his attitude to the past and begs him 'to go forward with life . . . accept the things that have happened and move on in a positive way . . . As you can see, we no longer have a life in Poland. All we have is memories, memories that should be cherished but not memories that should be dwelt upon . . . Please move on as we all must do.' Later, when Mike is out of the room, Ginger says: 'I don't think the full meaning of that letter has got through to Mike.'

Andy, twenty-three, tells me: 'Since we got back he doesn't seem to harp on the past so much. I guess he's finally leaving it for good. He's handling what he has much better instead of experiencing his guilt. He is more giving. He deals better with problems. Every time he goes back, it's better. Okay, this *did* happen. Okay, his brothers *did* die. These things occurred. So what next? Now he's finally saying: "So what next?" I've always been Konin-conscious and it was wonderful to go there and see where he came from, but it's time to move on. Remember, yes, but there comes a point where it becomes destructive and you can't enjoy what you have if you always remember what you've lost.'

Mark says: 'When Dad came back from Poland we noticed an immediate difference. He was more relaxed, would start helping around the house, was more in tune with himself and with us. There's more niceness when he goes to Poland. It is a reminder of the fact that he survived and is free, not only in the physical sense but emotionally. Probably it is only since he went back that he has been free emotionally. More of the demons are exorcised.

'It seems trite to say this, but he could never remember the names of friends in Texas. It's to do with not being here, a sign of not living in the here-and-now. I think the Holocaust greatly influences the way he lives his day-to-day life – whether consciously on his part or not I don't know. But it's there. It's like a low-level hum.'

On a Sunday afternoon, with rain sheeting down, Mike decides to take me to the Memorial Center for Holocaust Studies, part of the huge Dallas Jewish Community Center. Before we left, Mike had been pacing restlessly at the front door and didn't want to be bothered with lunch: 'Come on, come on, let's go, let's go.' When Mike wants to do something, nothing must stand in the way.

It is impossible not to feel the intensity of his commitment to the Holocaust Center. He shows me round with a proprietorial air: the well laid-out exhibition room, the railway freight car brought from Europe, the room dedicated to the six million, with human bones from Birkenau sealed in an urn, the well-stocked library and study area where a woman is addressing a group of teenagers on the rise of anti-Semitism in prewar Germany. Seventy-five per cent of the visitors to the Center are gentiles, Mike points out.

A numbing horror takes hold of me again as I look at the children's shoes from Maidanek, charred bones from Treblinka, a striped shirt from Buchenwald, bricks from Crematorium No. 1 at Auschwitz-Birkenau, soap made from human fat, the photographs I have seen so many times. There is one, taken in Mauthausen, that I have not seen before: a band of musicians, bony figures in pyjama stripes, tramp lifelessly across a compound, providing the musical accompaniment for the execution of a fellow prisoner. Head bowed, limp and resigned, he stands on a primitive wooden trolley being hauled along by other prisoners, taking him to the gallows.

How did anyone survive this phantasmagoria? How did Mike survive? In answer he points at one of the exhibits, an object that appears at first sight to be a normal wrist-watch on a strap. A closer look reveals that it has no inner works, no face, no hands or numbers. It is not a wrist-watch at all, merely a piece of solid aluminium fashioned into the shape of a watch. Mike explains: 'This is what kept me going. When I saw the SS people, the civilians, wearing watches I said to myself, Why can't I have a watch? They say I am dehumanized, that I have no brains, but I knew I had brains. I made me a watch from parts we were making for Messerschmitts, and I put my camp number on it, 188860. If they caught me wearing the watch I wouldn't be here today to tell the story. My arm was very thin and I could wear it high up, under the sleeve. When I looked at the watch I could tell the time. I knew I couldn't really tell the time, that it was make-believe. It was more than the watch. I made it. It's mine. I have something to hold on to.' Today, he can no longer wear it high up on the arm: the strap scarcely reaches round his wrist.

Mike tells me he feels no hate for his former oppressors, none at all. I ask him bluntly whether that is because he, as an official Jewish spokesman, feels obliged to adopt a diplomatic line, but he rejects the suggestion. He says he feels no bitterness towards those Poles who betrayed the Jews. Anti-Semites in the Polish resistance killed his brother Reuben, he says, along with eleven other Jewish partisans. But he cannot point a finger and say that the entire nation was guilty. Nor has he ever had a wish for revenge against the Germans, not even while he was a prisoner. He at no time hated his enemy, he insists, not even the SS or the Gestapo or the people who murdered his parents. 'The hate would help nothing, so the only thing it would do is weaken my purpose of survival.' 'But now?' 'I am sometimes asking myself: "Do you hate or do you not?" I don't hate.'

I am unsure how to respond to this. I sense he is being honest with me, and yet the words are in some undefinable way out of tune with his personality. I press the point. I ask him how he feels about Sergeant Holzer. Mike has talked a lot about Sergeant Holzer, an SS man for whom he worked in the ghetto at Ostrowiec. Mike's duties included helping Holzer clear out possessions from the homes of Jews who had been executed or deported. Mike's stories about Holzer had made my blood run cold, stories of events he had witnessed: 'I don't tell nothing what I didn't live with.' Here is one of the events he lived with:

> There is a small child left outside in the street, a baby. The mothers, before they were taken away, they left the children. The child was outside crying. I said to Sergeant Holzer: 'You're not going to do it are you, you're not going to do it?' He said that if I say one more word I will get the same thing. He took out his gun and emptied six shots into the baby. I cannot believe it, that he could do this to a little child not a year old. The baby still looks at him with bright eyes. He was so mad he run to it, grabbed it by the little feet and hit its head against the wall. It's hard to believe. Sometimes I say: 'Mike, you are dreaming aren't you?' I am not.

So now, in the Holocaust Center, I question Mike about his feelings towards Sergeant Holzer. 'I feel no hatred. Just dislike.' Dislike! Is that the word for someone who smashes a baby's brains against a wall? Mike holds his ground: 'I cannot help it. I sometimes say to myself, Mike, why don't you hate? I cannot hate. One woman visitor, a gentile, embraced me and said: "Thank you for not hating" and that made me feel good. I didn't hate in the camp. I was worrying about food, about not being beaten, not being selected for the gas chambers. I didn't go around hating. I had to preserve my strength for something else.'

I ask myself: does Mike's attitude to his former enemies spring from a rational, ethical conviction? Possibly. But might not another explanation lie in a remark made by his son Mark? 'One of the ways survivors survived is that they suspended a certain part of their being, and for a lot of these people that suspension continues.' If Mendel Jakubowicz had to anaesthetize his feelings in order to endure, could it be that more than forty years later the anaesthetic has not worn off?

A small group of visitors is in the exhibition area and Mike's antennae detect the makings of an audience. He launches into a talk. 'I am a Holocaust survivor. I was born in a small city called Konin, not too far from the German frontier . . .' The words are familiar. I have heard them on the video and in the course of our discussions.

From his opening words he has the audience in his grip, but for me the one-time spontaneity has degenerated into a pat repetition, each phrase honed and over-rehearsed. He has even perfected the sure-fire joke: 'I'm sorry if you don't understand all the words I am saying to you. That's because I speak with a strong Texas accent.' Mike gets his laugh.

I tiptoe out and look at a display of photographs showing scenes from Jewish life in prewar Eastern Europe. There are no other visitors. The Center is silent save for the sound of Mike's voice in the background. I can tell it will be a while before his talk ends. I go into the library and wander aimlessly past the bookshelves. A large white book catches my eye: *Memorial to the Jews Deported from France 1942–1944* by Serge Klarsfeld. The sub-title reads: *Documentation of the Deportation of the Victims of the Final Solution in France.* Thoughts turn to my father's brother, Shimen, who left Konin as a young man, went to Paris, married and had two children. About his end I know nothing other than that he died at the hands of the Nazis. The pages are crammed with list after list of thousands of deportees, grouped chronologically according to the departure date of each convoy. The information is logged in four columns: surname of deportee, followed by first name, date of birth, and place of birth. The details must derive from German sources: their orderly, bureaucratic efficiency strikes a chill.

Mike's voice has stopped; through the walls I can hear the muffled soundtrack of an audio-visual presentation about the death camps: a grimly apt commentary as I start working my way through the lists in search of my uncle. It is soon apparent that the task could take hours. There are over six hundred pages and the book has no general index. I remember my father once mentioning that his brother had died towards the end of the war. I turn to the back of the book and start working my way through to the front, page after page, with no success. On page 515 my finger runs down the list . . . ROSENBAUM, ROZENBERG, ROZENCWAJC, RUDOLF, RYBACK, RYCZKE. I read across the other columns: SIMON. 14.01.01. KONIN.

Shimen of Konin – subsequently Simon of Paris – departed from France in Convoy 68 on 10 February 1944. On board the train were nearly 1,500 prisoners, men, women and children: I find a Lucien (age ten), an Yvette (age six), a Jean-Claude (age three), 'five Waks children without parent', and many more. The train's destination: Auschwitz. On arrival, 200 men were selected and received numbers . . . 61 women were given numbers . . . The other 1,229 people were immediately gassed.' Was Simon Ryczke among the 200 or the 1,229? I do not suppose I shall ever know. And does it matter? He died in Auschwitz.

Mike's talk ends and the audience leaves. The survivor of Auschwitz and Mauthausen goes round locking up the doors. We get into his grey convertible and drive back to the house and the swimming-pool. I am not in a talkative mood. He, having just surfaced from the depths of evil, seems recharged, buoyant, almost elated. Is it the exhilaration that comes from being centre-stage, with an audience in your grip? I put the question to him as bluntly as that. 'I'm buoyed up because I'm doing my duty. I'm the mouthpiece for the millions who died. If I don't do this they will have died in vain. So long as people want to listen to me I will speak, speak the whole truth. When I speak I get lots of inner strength knowing they will remember. I don't want their children or my grandchildren to go through what I did.' Of his sincerity and sense of mission I have no doubt; equally I cannot reject the possibility that he enjoys being in the public arena. As George Steiner has said: 'Even the Holocaust survivors have been impresarios of their own pathos.'[2]

There is only one occasion during my stay when he draws back sharply from discussing a wartime experience. He has been so frank about the past, so unsparing in giving painful detail, that I am emboldened to pose a question I would normally regard as tasteless and intrusive: I ask him how he came by the scar on his cheek. 'With a whip!' he replies with curt intensity. The topic is closed.

When I am alone with Ginger in the kitchen, we discuss Mike. She talks about him admiringly, lists his qualities – courage, integrity, generosity, decency – but she sees his weaknesses too, with clear-eyed affection. 'As you have probably gathered,' she says with a laugh. 'Mike has a healthy ego.' I ask her how she interprets his renunciation of hatred. 'Look, you haven't seen him when he's having one of his rages. His eyes bulge and his whole face goes red. It's always over minor things. It's a displacement of his emotions. All this pent-up hatred comes through in different ways – it's still there. You know, the only time he has cried was when we visited

Treblinka for the first time, and I thought to myself it's sad, doubly sad, that he is not able to express himself, that he still brings to bear all those survival techniques.'

Next morning, on my way to the airport, I visit JACOBS IRON AND METAL for a final chat with Mike. While he is on the phone, I look at the Moscow Dynamo pennant pinned to his office wall, the framed certificates awarded him by the United Nations Relief and Rehabilitation Administration for outstanding performances in athletics, a collection of medals received from various Texas soccer clubs . . . He comes off the phone and tells me about a Konin memory that has just come to him that morning. 'I never told you about my bar mitzvah did I? My bar mitzvah was in the *shul*. I remember I started singing with a high octave and everyone thought I wasn't going to make it, but I did. Afterwards there was vodka and herring in the little room off the *shul*. That's all there was. There was no party at the house. We couldn't afford it. You know what my bar mitzvah present was? An old book in Yiddish. And it was a book we already had. But I wasn't disappointed. I was proud of it. What should they have given me? A pen?'

A truck with scrap metal pulls up outside and drives onto a weighing platform. The Boss goes over to the window overlooking the waiting truck and works the scales, an old-fashioned, almost antique contraption. He slides the weights smoothly along the horizontal bar until a balance is reached. Andy, his son and partner, wants to instal computerized equipment but his father opposes the idea: 'Who needs it? It gives me something to do.' Mike is in an exuberant mood this morning. He likes being back at work after the weekend. Also, he spoke on the radio earlier this morning about his experiences in the camps, and has already received a congratulatory telephone call. For a survivor who never tries to, or wants to, forget his Holocaust past, Mike Jacobs is a remarkably happy man.

One thing in his past does remain a cause for regret and self-reproach, something he did soon after arriving in America, over thirty-six years ago. He is reminded of it every time he has to state his name. 'When I came to Dallas they said: "Why don't you change your name from Jakubowicz to Jacobs?" – because a lot of people couldn't pronounce Jakubowicz. So I changed it, and I shouldn't have changed it. It would have carried on my family name. My kids say to me: "Daddy, why don't we change the name back?" They would like to be Jakubowicz and carry on the family name. I say no. Maybe when they were small it would be okay, but now I say no, it's too late. I shouldn't have changed my name. I regret it. When I lecture at the Center I always take visitors over to the wall with the names of survivors' families who perished and I say: "There's my name. My name is not Jacobs. My name is Jakubowicz." '

47

THE HISTORY OF persecution, the chronicle of repeated massacres and pogroms, of daily insults and humiliations, all arouse compassion for the victims and, at the same time, an irrational impatience with them, a maddening frustration at their apparent readiness to be victims: so much submission, so much passive acceptance of suffering. If suffering was indeed our tribal badge, why did we not wear it with defiance rather than resignation?

The Memorial Book inspires these thoughts: pages filled with descriptions of the torments inflicted on a community of innocents, who submitted and went on submitting to the very end. In their place, I would no doubt have submitted too. It is not for me to reproach them. Yet when I finally came to a chapter called 'Jewish Partisans'[1] I realized how badly I needed to read about Jews who fought back.

The author of the chapter, written in Yiddish, is Sarah Trybuch, née Ozerowicz, whose wartime experiences distinguish her from her fellow Koniners. One of those quirkish combinations of decision and chance rescued her from the path to extinction that most of her townsfolk followed. She was twenty-eight, married, and had given birth to her first child two months before the Germans entered Konin in September 1939. Two months later, she and her husband and baby daughter, Miriam, left Konin, heading eastwards, intending to cross the Soviet frontier and reach two of her brothers who were living in Baranowicze in Belorussia. After several hair-raising ordeals, she and her child ended up not in Baranowicze but in Lesnaya, a tiny country town not far away. Here she joined a few dozen other Jews. In the upheaval, she had become separated from her husband. It was the last time she saw him, and she was to learn that he had been killed in 1942.

In 1941 the German invasion of Russia caught up with Sarah. The Jews in Lesnaya were confined to a ghetto. Only men on forced labour were allowed out, and only under guard. She writes:

> One day in February 1943, when there was a dreadful frost outdoors, the men came back from work and told us that in the forest, about two kilometres from the ghetto, two long graves had been dug. We knew for whom these were being got ready. Now we resigned ourselves to awaiting the moment, which alas did arrive, on 13 March 1943. At dawn, when the men were out at work, we were encircled by the Germans who, together with the White Russian police, set about liquidating the ghetto. With yells and abuse, and amid the terrible weeping of the victims, they drove the people with whips in the direction where the graves were prepared.

Sarah avoided the round-up. Wearing only her nightgown and carrying Miriam in her arms, she crossed a railway line and entered the forest as day broke. She met no other Jews. Soon she was lost in the forest, without clothing, food or money. 'It is difficult to convey the next five days and nights,' she writes, but convey it she does.

> On the first evening I knocked at a cottage on the edge of a forest . . . My desire was to see someone and not to be alone and lost in the vast forest. Fate wished it that I met up with good people who had sympathy for me. I received an old torn coat and some rubber galoshes for me and the child. I put them on our bare feet. The ragged bits and pieces saved us from freezing. I also received a little flask of milk for the child, a piece of bread in a small bag, and let myself head out again on my destined path.
>
> This happened at the time when the snow was thawing. The mud, mixed with snow, created large puddles, obliterating the tracks and footpaths in the forest. At night, under a tree, frozen to the ground, clasping the child close to me, I warmed her with

my body. At night I feared the wolves, and by day a German – or a peasant who might hand me over to the Germans. I couldn't imagine what might happen to us next. The forests in Belorussia stretch for long distances.

Having nothing to lose, I went further. I walked in the snow, not feeling the frost and hunger. I understood that one could go under in the forest, not meeting a living soul. How long could we go on like this, seeing death waiting for us everywhere? What hurt me especially was the sight of my small child, who was so heroic, as if she understood the situation. She didn't cry and didn't even yearn for home. Just when I thought that my end had indeed come, I suddenly noticed straw on a footpath. The thought occurred to me that I must be near people. And the sign led me to a little bridge made of freshly cut timber. I crossed the little bridge and met up with a partisan guard. When I encountered someone who was on our side, I felt as though a heavy weight had fallen from my heart, as though I would no longer be entirely on my own.

With beating heart I waited for the commander of the partisans to accept me into the camp. But to get such permission was hopeless. A woman in a partisan group was regarded, with scarcely any exceptions, as a nuisance, and on top of that a woman with a small child, and without so much as a weapon! A child in a partisan camp certainly posed something of a danger. It disturbed the routine of the camp and, above all, the sound of a crying child could be heard loud and clear from far away and so disclose the whereabouts of the camp.

It was a Jewish partisan group going through a bad time, having just been raided and driven out of their old camp. They were on the run, without food, seeking a new site.

But I had no inkling of this. I was happy with the first drop of soup made from mouldy potatoes and beans that came my way. It tasted better than anything I had ever eaten in my life. Later on I learned that for taking me and the child into the camp I had to thank my present husband, the then partisan. He had warmly received me when I encountered the partisan guard. He was very popular in the group. Just for him they made an exception, thus allowing me into the camp.

Suddenly the reader is plunged into the partisan fighter world of Primo Levi's *If Not Now, When?* Sarah became part of that world, caught up in a life as dramatic as Levi's novel. Her Jewish partisan group was equipped with pitifully few weapons: their armoury consisted of two guns. One day a well-armed anti-Semitic partisan group attacked the Jewish camp as the men were returning from a sortie, and took away their guns.

> After this we dragged ourselves through mud so deep that we almost drowned in the forest, where no human foot had ever trod – without weapons, without food, all of us feeling like death. I and my friend [the partisan whose intervention got her into the camp] took turns to carry the child on our shoulders. At one point I and the child sank into the mud, which came over our heads, and we would certainly have drowned but for the men who threw us a rope, which they hastily made from scarves, and in this way hauled us out. We at last dragged ourselves to a small clearing and there established a new camp.

The Soviets parachuted men into the area to amalgamate the bands of partisans into one fighting force. Sarah, her child and her friend became part of a larger camp of about five hundred men, almost entirely gentile. The encircling forest and swamps made the camp virtually inaccessible. The partisans lived in log huts half-buried in the ground, camouflaged with turf and branches to make them invisible from the air.

Russian planes dropped weapons and supplies to the partisans, who kept in continuous radio contact with Moscow, receiving news and instructions. Sarah was one of only three women in the camp, the others being Russian peasant women. Hers was the only child. Shortly before her arrival, there had been an incident in the camp involving a family with three young children. The Germans were close to tracking down the partisans. The children began to cry, threatening to give away the partisans' position. The commander, a Russian colonel, urged the parents to keep the children quiet. When their frantic attempts to do so failed, he silenced them with three quick bullets. After that, no one wanted children in the camp, and yet Sarah and Miriam were allowed to stay. Her Jewish friend and protector must have been a persuasive man and valued fighter.

The child grew accustomed to the spartan conditions, living

off frugal meals cooked over open fires, never seeing or playing with other children, having no idea of the outside world. When German bombs fell on the camp, the toddler cowered under trees. When the camp had to be evacuated, Sarah scooped her up as the partisans fled, cold and hungry, through the forests.

They continued to harass the enemy, inflicting damage on railway lines, industrial targets and German garrisons. The radio brought news of a turn in the course of the war. The Germans were retreating from Stalingrad. One day orders came to blow up a railway line used for transporting German ammunition, wounded soldiers and supplies. The target was some distance from the partisan camp, which meant having to move across open terrain in daylight. Nearly three hundred partisans set out, with Sarah's friend leading one of the main groups. They succeeded in blowing up the line, but he was carried back with a German bullet through his foot. Three men did not return.

Sarah's story ends with the events of a July day in 1944:

> Representatives of the Red Army appeared, who had freed the territory of German occupation. They led us out of the forest. We all danced and kissed each other for joy. Dancing in a circle, we departed from the forest. On a small wagon ahead of us was my daughter Miriam, dressed in a Russian uniform, which my husband-to-be had sewn for her. My daughter could not work out how aeroplanes could travel on the ground: the 'aeroplanes' were freight lorries – something she had never set eyes on in her life. Aeroplanes that dropped bombs she knew only too well. Having seen only log cabins, she was filled with wonder at the sight of a simple village cottage, thinking it was the palace in which Stalin himself lived.

DISNEY . . . DISNEY . . . DISNEY . . . The signs flash by on the highway taking me north from Orlando Airport, where the nearby Magic Kingdom processes the tourist hordes. The air-conditioning in my rented car dries my clammy shirt and keeps out the Florida smell of wet jungle. Palm trees become travelogue silhouettes as the sun sets gaudily in the west. Soon it is dark. It is years since I have driven in America. I am not sure of the route. All too easy to go wrong at intersections. My nerves are frayed by the time I reach the small town where Sarah lives. I pull into the first motel, collapse onto the bed, and call her to let her know I have arrived. We fix a time to meet next morning.

Sarah had returned my original questionnaire with a charming note: 'If you ever plan to visit America, please include us in your itinerary.' Her home in central Florida is a trim apartment house in a quiet backwater off the main highway. I walk upstairs, ring the bell, and there she is, a well-fleshed figure with wavy white hair, dark eyes and pale, plump arms. She wears a plain top with check cotton trousers, very Florida Senior Citizen. At seventy-six she moves with the vigour of a younger woman. She greets me warmly.

Behind her in the hallway lurks a man wearing a black beret. He is smaller than Sarah, thin and frail, with a birdlike, fine-boned face. We shake hands. His lugubrious, ungiving expression does not change. It is Eli, the former partisan fighter.

The sitting-cum-dining-room, casual and lived-in, has the mandatory glass-fronted cabinet, framed colour snapshots of grandchildren, wedding and bar mitzvahs, and needlework pictures on the walls. A brass fan hangs from the ceiling. Brilliant sunlight bleaches the small balcony from which concrete steps lead down to the street at the back of the house.

Sarah's English, though heavily accented, is fluent and expressive. Eli remains silent, a brooding, slightly unnerving presence. I am asking Sarah some opening questions about herself when he begins a series of interjections: '*Excoose* me!' he says each time with a challenging edge to his voice. '*Excoose* me! Why are you doing dis?' '*Excoose* me! There are so many books about the Holocaust and nobody reads them.' '*Excoose* me, but you know what I was doing with the partisans?' He fixes his penetrating blue eyes on me. I explain that I very much want to talk to him about the partisans, that it is one of my reasons for coming to Florida – but first I would like to ask Sarah a few questions. This fails to placate him, and more interruptions follow. Then suddenly he stands up and retires to another room. Sarah is unperturbed. Having established beyond all reasonable doubt that I am not in desperate need of nourishment, she is ready to talk.

She was born and grew up in a house near Konin's Protestant

church, on the road leading to Kalisz. Thanks to Mendel Leben, I know exactly where she lived. The Ryczke family, she confirms, lived a few doors away. Her father and my grandfather prayed daily at the same small congregation that gathered in Leszczynski's mill across the way. Both families got their water from the same supply – cold water from a pump, hot water fetched from Spielfogel's distillery, where the water ran to waste after industrial use. One of her brothers, Tsvi, emigrated to Palestine about the same time as my uncle, Haskel Ryczke, and they had stayed friends in Tel Aviv. Both had been active in publishing the Memorial Book. She remembers my grandfather in Konin as a 'very religious man in a long black coat. The Ryczkes were very respectable, upright people.' I produce a few of my family photographs. She looks at her former neighbours, scrutinizes my features and says yes, she can tell I am a Ryczke.

Her father, the son of a *cheder* teacher, owned a successful store, selling cloth – 'yard goods' – in one part of the store, and 'colonial goods' – spices, tea, sugar etc – in the other. He also dealt in grain. Sarah was one of six daughters and four brothers. She graduated from the Jewish gymnasium, which she attended for eight years. 'Even now, after all these years I have not forgotten the school song.' She sings it for me in Polish. 'Early in the morning, when my husband is sleeping, I walk two to three miles, wintertime too, and sometimes, as I walk along, I sing the school song.'

I mention the Tepper Marik, the focal point of Konin's Jewish quarter. 'I was there but I have no connection with these people.' She says 'these people' in a matter-of-fact way, not meaning to sound superior. I ask about class divisions in Konin, and she says, yes, they did exist. 'I belonged to the better class and I had no connections with those other people. After the war I meet a few of them in Israel and this time we were all one family because of what we had been through.'

What differentiated her from the Tepper Marik people? 'We were educated, this was the first thing. My whole education was in Polish. My parents spoke Polish to us but Yiddish between themselves. My Yiddish comes from my husband. We had a tutor living with us in the house who taught my brothers Yiddish and Hebrew and religious studies. I had a private teacher who came to the house and he prepared me for the gymnasium. We have a maid, a *shikse*, who did the cleaning and dirty work. And we had a Jewish girl from a poor family who did the shopping and cooking. She was like family. My mother was working with my father in the store.' By the end of the 1930s the family's fortunes had declined.

We are chatting about Konin when a woman appears in the doorway of the balcony, smiling at us. She is in her forties, has a healthy, burnished complexion, good bone-structure and auburn hair. Wearing gold ear-rings and a softly gathered skirt, she looks slim and glamorous beside Sarah. Mother and daughter Miriam hug. Sarah gets busy laying the table. Eli appears, and we all sit down to eat. Miriam calls Eli *Abba*, Hebrew for father. She has an Israeli-American accent.

Can she recall any of the experiences her mother describes in the Memorial Book? No, she says, she was too young. Eli picks up my copy of the book. Without waiting for a pause in the conversation, he begins reading Sarah's article aloud in Yiddish, at the point where she is wandering barefoot through the freezing forest, clutching her small child – the woman sitting beside me on a hot day in Florida. He reads in a steady monotone, showing no sign of stopping, indifferent to whether we want to listen or not. While he carries on reading, Miriam says of her mother: 'It was her will to survive.' Does she marvel at how she and her mother did survive? 'No, I don't really think about it. It's as though it happened to someone else. That's why it doesn't cause any emotion. I have to think hard to remember that this is me she is talking about, okay?' She laughs.

Miriam was a baby when she left Konin. 'Konin doesn't mean anything to me. To all intents and purposes, I am not a Koniner. I heard something about it from my uncle in Israel.' Her seventeen-year-old son Sandy, she says, probably does not even know the name of the town. But he has shown curiosity about his family's wartime experiences. By now Eli has stopped reading aloud. Miriam looks at her watch, apologizes, kisses her mother, and dashes off down the balcony steps on her way back to work.

After lunch, Eli falls asleep on the sofa. Not many months ago he had a heart attack and developed pneumonia. In a week or two he will be eighty. While he dozes, we chat about Konin, about people she remembers from her youth. Most of the names are familiar to me, as though they were part of my youth too. She shows me photographs of Miriam's teenage son, and of her own son, a dentist, who is married and lives in Washington. He was born after the war.

I ask her, does she still think about her escape from the massacre in Lesnaya, or does she push it to the back of her mind? 'I no push. I cannot push. You cannot forget the cries of the people, the beating, the dogs. You can never forget that.' Her account in the Memorial Book does not explain how she eluded the Germans on the day of the massacre. She tells me now:

> It was in the morning, five or six o'clock. There was noise – loud, loud, loud. I look outside and I see everybody runs. Then I took Miriam. We have no time to put on something. The door from my room was smashed in and fallen down. I stay with Miriam under the door and they no see me. After everybody go, I leave. There was a deep gully and I sit there with Miriam and nobody was looking on me because they was busy searching in the houses. The Germans took everybody, maybe twenty, twenty-five people. There was one girl more who escaped – not with me. I walk across the railway and into the forest.

When she was wandering in the forest, did she think that she and Miriam might die? 'I was not afraid, not so long I have her in my arms, because I know I have to be strong for her. And I never was afraid. We were sitting night-time under a tree and it was so cold, my body was frozen, but her I keep warm and I was not afraid. Even when I heard from afar the wolves, I was absolutely not afraid. If I be afraid, I be finished, and her. The whole of my journey I was no afraid. And if I think about this today, you know, I get gooseflesh.' Looking back, is she amazed that she was able to do what she did? 'No, I think everything was by accident. It was only accidentally that I go the right way. *Mazel* – luck. I was with a baby in the forest, miles and miles with no human being. And how I come out from this, I cannot understand. I ask the baby: "Miriam, in what direction we go? Here? Or here?" And she showed me with the finger – here. And I go here.'

What made Eli help the bedraggled stranger who stumbled across the partisan camp clutching a baby?' 'It was *beshert*' (fated), says Sarah. And her first impression of him? 'To tell you the truth, at the time I was not thinking. Everything comes after. Every good thing is in this man, his heart, his mind, everything. He is good.

He is brave. And the most important thing is that he was such a good father. He regarded Miriam as his daughter.' She remembers the times she watched him leave on a sortie: 'So many young men not come back but I never was thinking of it. You cannot think about everything bad. You have to live.' I try to imagine Eli as a young man, a partisan with muscles, a thick mop of hair, and a gun. I glance across at the old man dozing on the sofa.

Sarah learned how to handle a rifle and stand guard when the men were away, but she never joined them on fighting expeditions: no one was prepared to take responsibility for the child if Sarah was killed. 'The men in the camp, they bring her soup. They bring her shoes from the village. They love her. Today I am thinking: how I kept her clean? I remember I have to bathe her. Was frost. Was cold. We put blankets around two or three trees and we make a fire, and I wash her, and she was always clean. She was so beautiful.'

Sarah and Eli married in Russia after the liberation. They were penniless. Nearly every member of her large family in Poland, including three brothers and three sisters, died in the Shoah. One brother escaped to Russia. Another survived Auschwitz and Theresienstadt. The Germans murdered her parents in the forest of Kazimierz, near Konin. In 1945 she returned to Konin 'to see if I find something or somebody, but I was a short time there, only three days. I stay with some people who had also gone back. What can I tell you about it? How can I stay there? I walked the streets and everyone look at me – they know me from when I was baby. They remembered me. I was afraid to go to the house. It was dangerous to be there. The Polacks were afraid I come and take my belongings from them. They no like us before, and they no like us when we come back, because all of our neighbours have something of ours. The first thing they do when they took the Jews out of the houses was that everybody loots something. Our house is still there. I have all the papers. But I can do nothing. No, I never want to go back there.' Her son has told her he would like to visit Konin. 'He told me this a few times. I don't want him to. No. For what? For who?'

He was born in Poland in 1949. The following year Sarah and Eli emigrated to Israel, where they remained for ten years, running a small store in a suburb of Tel Aviv. In 1960 they decided to join Eli's sister and two brothers in New York. They opened a dry-cleaning and alterations store in Brooklyn. Sarah dealt with the customers,

Eli did the alterations. Life was hard but they managed to put their son through dental college. The monthly reparations payments from Germany were, and still are, important to their finances. Miriam, who had stayed on in Israel to finish her military service, visited her parents in 1962, met her future husband and decided to stay in the States. Sarah and Eli moved to Florida in 1978, some years after they had retired.

Eli has woken up from his nap. He says he feels lost living in a smallish town in Florida. 'In New York I feel I am with my people. Here I am stranger.' There is no lack of Jews – there is a local community to which they belong – but more a lack of the kind of Jews with whom he feels at home. He resents the fact that even the old people in the Jewish Community Center do not want to speak Yiddish. 'If I speak to them in Yiddish, they say: "Why can't we speak English?" They have an American flag and an Israeli flag, but it is the American national anthem they sing.' He has other causes for complaint. He looks wan and downcast.

I try to ask him about the partisans, but he wants to leave the topic until tomorrow. He takes me into another room and shows me heaps of boxes filled with audio cassettes. These are recordings he has made of himself talking about the Shoah and the past. He often comes in here, turns on the recorder, sits on his own and talks. Always in Yiddish. He shows me reams of paper filled with his Yiddish handwriting.

For some reason he suddenly changes his mind about discussing his partisan days. He tells me about the night he escaped from a German labour camp, taking with him rifles and ammunition. He is now talking to me in Yiddish, expressing his thoughts with greater coherence. I encourage him to carry on in Yiddish, but contrariness makes him switch back to English. He says the Jews had no chance to fight when the Germans invaded: 'Sixty-five per tsent help the Germans kill the Jews. You know who help? The neighbour, the *goy*. You no can fight. You have no chance to fight when you be the same as a mouse. When you stick the nose outside, he catch you and bring you to the Germans and they kill you.'

I ask him to describe the moment when he first set eyes on the cold, starving woman and her small child. He is reluctant to talk about it. A silence falls. I sense a tension between them. Sarah says there is a problem and ask him to tell me what it is. The following facts emerge: their son, who is thirty-eight, does not know that Miriam is a half-sister. He does not read Yiddish and has never learnt the truth from the Memorial Book. He believes that he and Miriam share the same parents. Eli explains: Sarah lost her husband; he himself lost his wife and two children. He wanted to bury the past, to start afresh, and he wanted Miriam and Eli to grow up as brother and sister, as part of one family.

Sarah went along with him at the start, but now she wants to tell her son the truth. Miriam feels the same. In any case, says Sarah, she thinks it is very likely their son knows the truth. I remind Eli that Koniners who have read the Memorial Book must know the facts, just as I do. He replies: 'The Koniners are old and dying.' Sarah and I gently suggest that perhaps the time has come to be open with his son. Should there be a secret between two people who love one another? Eli shakes his head. It is too late, he says, too late to tell the truth now. 'If my son finds out, he will think I am a terrible man, that I have lied to him.' But is it not more likely that he will understand the reasons and respect him for sharing the truth with him? Eli stubbornly holds his ground. 'To him I am God. What will he think?' He withdraws into himself and the three of us sit silently for a while. He takes off his glasses. His eyes are a washed-out blue, the pupils scarcely visible.[2]

Sarah goes into the kitchen to prepare the evening meal, leaving me alone with Eli. I've been thinking about the way they met; now I put something to him: did he persuade his commander to accept the stranger and her baby because he thought God was offering him a child to replace one of his own children? 'Yes,' he replies quietly. 'The Germans killed my two children. When I saw the small baby, I remembered my child.'

Speaking Yiddish, he describes the German atrocities he witnessed, the terrible things done to old people and babies, the smell of burning flesh when the Germans threw grenades into Jewish homes. I would rather not listen but I know that nothing will stop him. He shows me the scar at the bottom of his leg: 'The foot was just hanging on by bits of skin and they wanted to amputate, and today I can walk on this leg. It is a miracle. I used to feel bullets brushing my ears. It's a miracle. There was an epidemic of typhus and nothing happened to me. It is a miracle. And so I believe in God.'

One day, when his partisan group captured a German soldier,

the commander said to Eli and two other Jews: 'Jews, here, take your revenge.' The others dug a grave and stood the German in it and then stabbed him to death, just kept stabbing him with their knives until he fell into the grave. Did Eli join in? 'No, I couldn't. I felt sick.' But later they captured three German soldiers, young lads. 'They shat themselves with fear, and I helped to hang them. Then I wore one of their uniforms when I went out on a raid.'

Speaking Yiddish again, he recalls the time the Germans entered his home town of Spolpce:

> The SS asked the *Judenrat* [Jewish Council] to send them a good tailor, and if they didn't send a good tailor they would take twenty Jews and shoot them. I was a good tailor and they called me and asked me to go to such-and-such a place, where the SS headquarters were. They needed a tailor. It was the first week that they entered the town. I went in and the head of the SS came over to me and said: 'You are a tailor?' I say Yes. He took a swipe at my head and my hat fell off. He took out a white uniform jacket and put it on. It was a little too wide on him. He said: 'Do a good job,' and handed me the jacket. He looked at his watch: 'If it is not ready by five o'clock' – it was then noon and it was a job that needed a minimum of a day's work – he pulled out his revolver: 'This will be your end.'
>
> I was shattered, ran home and worked, didn't eat, didn't drink and on the dot – on the dot, believe me, I swear it on the world, this was a miracle – I went with the jacket. He was standing on the steps and looked at his watch. I went in. He put on the jacket. There were two others with him, and they looked at him, and he said: '*Sehr gut.*' [Very good.] He wrote something on a piece of paper and sent me down to the kitchen, where the cook gave me whatever I liked. And why did he need the uniform? He took two hundred and fifty Jews and led them out of the town and shot them. This is what he wanted the uniform for.

Yiddish changes him. His tongue no longer stumbles and flounders. His sentences flow with pace and rhythm. His personality seems to expand, acquire confidence. He draws comfort from my comprehension of his words. He is less guarded. We no longer speak across a barrier.

The son of a tailor, he started tailoring himself when he was twelve. Had he lived in Konin, he and Sarah would have moved in different circles, she speaking high-school Polish, he Yiddish. She belonged to the comfortable middle classes. He was one of the underprivileged, a member of the Bund. He is grateful to his tailor's needle: 'The needle with which I sewed saved my life.' It also came in useful during his partisan days when he stitched bits of parachute silk into clothes for Miriam. Occasionally he did some tailoring for a peasant in return for a piece of bread and meat for the child. In Brooklyn it helped his son become a dentist.

The sun goes down. Sarah gives us dinner. Eli talks, and when he talks he will brook no interruption. More bitterness wells up when he turns to the subject of anti-Semitism. On the day the Germans came, one of his gentile friends lobbed a stone at him and drew a finger across his throat to indicate that Eli's days were numbered. He believes that all *goyim* are anti-Semitic. I mention the Avenue of the Righteous Gentiles at Yad Vashem, the individual Poles and Russians who helped Jews (I forget to remind him of the 'good people', to quote Sarah's own words, who gave her and the baby food and clothing when she was on the run in the forest and saved their lives), but he does not want to know. All *goyim* are anti-Semites. Sarah does not agree. She reminds him of a gentile neighbour, a man who just a few months before, when Eli was in hospital, showed extraordinary kindness to her at a time of crisis. Eli says nothing. He remembers too many betrayals.

Dinner over, Eli wants me to hear one of his Yiddish tapes. He places a battered cassette player on the table. Plastic fragments fall off as he fiddles with the controls. A continuous hiss drowns his voice. Exhaustion sweeps over me. I have been in the apartment all day and I feel stifled. Eli presses me to stay for the night. When I decline, he suggests I have breakfast with them tomorrow morning. He is extending human warmth. We walk downstairs together and he sees me to the car. The motel is just a few minutes' drive away. I park on the dismal tarmac, and walk round and round the motel, inhaling great breaths of the cool night air.

Next morning, when I enter their living-room, Eli is seated at the table, head propped wearily on his hand, ineffably sad, in the very pose of Rembrandt's *Jeremiah Lamenting the Destruction of the Temple*. The cassette player is on the table and Eli is listening, through crackling and hissing, to a cantor singing a Hebrew prayer of lament, a sound that, like no other, evokes the tearful Jewish past. One word stands out: Yizkor. Eli does not look up when I walk in. His eyes are fixed absently on the table as he listens to the prayer. It takes a while before he reacts to my presence. He plays another cassette, a speech he heard at a Holocaust gathering in Washington a couple of years ago. Sarah says: 'The Holocaust is with him day and night.' Eli listens to the recording, absorbed and abstracted. This is his past, his legacy of loss. The force that helped him survive is used up. He is left only with grief.

Eli insists on taking me to the Holocaust exhibition at the Jewish Community Center. The three of us set out in their car. Head bent low over the wheel, peering intently through the windscreen as though he is making his way through thick fog, Eli drives fast, heading at speed towards red traffic lights and braking at the last moment. At the entrance to the exhibition, a quotation from Elie Wiesel: 'Whoever forgets becomes the executioner's accomplice.' After I have looked once again at the photographs of the camps, and the six lamps burning for the six million, Sarah asks the librarian if she can borrow the Konin Memorial Book, which she donated to the Center some time ago. 'I'm going to read it again because your visit has refreshed my memory.'

Driving back to the apartment, we are held up by road-works. An excavator with a long neck and an iron grab is shifting piles of earth. While we wait alongside it, Eli recounts a wartime incident: the Germans had a machine like this, shifting sand. One of the Germans ordered a small Jewish boy to go and collect some sand. As the boy bent down, they dropped the end of the grab on him and smashed his skull. 'Did you witness this?' I ask. 'Yes, I saw it with my own eyes.'

They ask me to stay for lunch, but I have to drive to Miami. 'You want a sandwich?' says Eli. 'I make you a sandwich.' A kind offer, but I shall be stopping for a snack on the way. Eli presses two pears, two oranges and some grapes on me. I thank him and say that just a pear will do. He goes away and hurries back with more grapes. Sarah fetches a paper napkin and stuffs it in a bag with the fruit. They come down and stand waving goodbye. I look in the rear-view mirror, and when I reach the end of the road they are still waving. The Florida day is warming up. I hit the highway going south.

48

WHILE THE PARTISANS were fighting in the forests, Konin itself became the scene of a brave if short-lived gesture of defiance. The German occupiers, having rid themselves of the local Jews by massacre and deportation, had brought in slave labour from other parts of Poland to work on railway construction in Konin. Some 1,100 Jewish men arrived there by train in March 1942, and were housed in wooden barrack huts close to the station. Water was in short supply, the food scarcely adequate for sustaining life, let alone unremitting labour. Infested with lice, their feet swollen, men collapsed daily from hunger, exhaustion and beatings. Those who became unfit for work were dispatched to Chelmno, the camp where the first gassing of Jews took place, where the Final Solution was inaugurated. Cold, malnutrition and summary executions killed many of these who remained in the Konin camp. Some were transported elsewhere once their labour was no longer needed. Within fourteen months only sixty Jews remained, among them a thirty-year-old Rabbi, Yehoshua Moshe Aaronson.

He knew Konin well, having once lived in the town and studied under Rabbi Lipschitz. He married a Konin girl before becoming the spiritual leader of another community.[1] Now back in Konin as a prisoner, he began keeping a secret diary in the hope that it might survive even if he did not. His fellow Jews made a camouflaged hiding-place for his writing materials. When his activities became too dangerous, he found a new place to write – the camp mortuary, where he continued the task of recording 'for those who may come to study this age of ours'.[2] As a Rabbi he could not help recalling an earlier Jewish captivity in the time of the Pharaohs. He referred to the Germans as his 'taskmasters' and gave his diary the title, 'The Scroll of the House of Bondage in Konin'.

Sometimes he wrote his notes hurriedly. At other times he was able to revise, adding dates and details. As well as chronicling the camp's routine of life and death, the Rabbi wrote on the subject of Jewish resistance. He wanted those who might one day read his words to understand why Jews went obediently to their deaths.

Most did not realize until it was too late, he pointed out, that they *were* going to their deaths. Others were held back by the knowledge that any action against the Germans could result in the deaths of fellow Jews – men, women and children who might otherwise have survived. Not least of all, hunger and cruelty left the victims 'so weakened in spirit and body that we are simply unable to do anything'.[3]

The Rabbi asked himself: 'Why should we go on living when we have lost our families and know what is awaiting us? Why do we have intelligent people who do not commit suicide but go on serving our oppressors with the last of our strength?'[4] Judaism's express injunction against suicide, based on the principle that only God should decide when a person is to die, provided one answer but, like Hamlet addressing the same question, he too acknowledged the hidden force that makes us cling to life even when life is not worth living. He knew that some of the prisoners were considering suicide, and tried to dissuade them. Only when he saw they could not go on bearing the oppressor's wrong did he condone the idea, on condition that they die in the course of striking at the enemy. The Warsaw Ghetto Uprising, which had taken place just a few months earlier, served as an example.

A group of plotters planned a revolt, whose objective was, in the words of one prisoner, 'to behave like Samson'.[5] Towards the end of July 1943 Moshe Aaronson wrote his last entry:

> . . . Yesterday the Gestapo men came and made a list. The signs are the same as they were last year, for those taken to the valley of the shadow of death at Chelmno. We all have the impression that they will soon come to take us. Our question is whether we are finished and about to perish. But our own wills are as naught before the will of the Most High, the True Judge.[6]

After the war, a survivor, Shmulek Mottel, wrote his own account of the camp's last days:

> On 7 August 1943 the Gestapo returned and we understood straightaway that there was to be another 'selection'. We knew well enough what this meant. It meant yet more torture, suffering and death. We decided not to allow ourselves to be led like sheep to the slaughter, and that as the last choice open to us – if

it were to become clear that the end was near and that we were to be martyred as Jews – we would join together to destroy the camp by fire.

On 9 August the uprising broke out [this date is almost certainly a mistake: there is evidence to suggest that the uprising occurred on August 13].[7] Tabaczinski and Kleinot from Gostynin, and Kamlazh from Gombin, set fire to the sheds and hanged themselves in the blaze. In the main barracks, Seif from Gostynin and Philip from Gombin hanged themselves. The same fate befell Nusenowicz and Shlomo Michelski from Gostynin and Dr Knopf, a Jew from Germany.[8] The bloody nightmare of that event will stay with me all my life.

. . . After firemen put out the blaze, we miraculously remained alive, surrounded by a strong guard. The Germans ordered us to drag out all the dead, the burnt and the hanged, and asked me and an elderly Jew from Gombin to deal with the corpses . . . As it happened, the first body was that of a young friend of mine, Shlomo Mechelski. My brother cut him from the rope, and kept the rope in order to hang himself – such was the suicidal psychology that swept over us that day. When we cut Shlomo down, he was still alive, and an SS man put a bullet through his eye.

I went up to the dead man, and despite all that had happened to him, the hanging and the shooting – and with it all he had always been a weak lad – he, to my great shock and distress, opened the other eye and recognized me. I could not stand the heartache. I approached the German and begged him to shoot me. As usual, they refused a request . . . The bloody spectre of those hard days in the Konin camp whirls round and round in my head like a demon, wherever I look or turn.

The tragic occurrence made a powerful impression on the people of Konin. We, the fortunate survivors, stood with bowed heads before our heroes who would not allow the name Jew to be shamed.[9]

The Germans closed the House of Bondage two weeks later and sent the remaining prisoners to Auschwitz. Before he left Konin, Rabbi Aaronson concealed his notes and some other documents[10] in two bottles, which were entrusted to an elderly and religious Pole who worked in the camp. After the war, one of the prisoners, Abraham

Hirsch Mottel, went back to Konin, retrieved most of the papers and took them with him when he emigrated to Israel. They eventually found a home there in the collection of the Ghetto Fighters' House. For some time it was thought that the author of the diary had been killed, but in 1951 Aaronson also arrived in Israel, having survived Auschwitz, Buchenwald and Theresienstadt. It was some time later that he learned that the greater part of his chronicle had been saved.

Postscript Rabbi Yehoshua Moshe Aaronson died in Israel in November 1993.

49

I GET OFF THE bus at the usual stop in Brooklyn and walk along the empty, tree-lined streets towards Motek's home. A few weeks ago my feet scattered the crisp autumn leaves. Now the branches are bare.

It is good to see Motek again. He has taken a powerful hold on my affections. Sonia, frail as ever, whispers a greeting. I have come to report on my travels, on my meetings with Koniners he has not seen for years. 'Did they ask about me?' Coming from a man so lacking in self-concern, the enquiry is touching. I cannot tell him the truth: that Koniners have a weird, almost disturbing lack of curiosity about the lives of fellow survivors with whom they have lost touch.

Motek questions me closely about them. Each name sparks off memories. Julius Ancer: 'He lived a few doors away from us.' Sarah Trybuch in Florida: 'My sister was married to her brother.' Shmulek Gruen in Minneapolis: 'He was a good friend of mine, the best-looking young man in Konin' . . .' These names trigger other names, which carry us back to Konin and his youth and the days when he taught gymnastics. Motek is in great form.

A week or so later, when I return to say goodbye, he is not well. His face is flushed, his voice drained of energy. It is not a good day, he admits reluctantly: angina. But the pills will help. Over our last meal together, he is more himself. We go onto the balcony at the front of the house, and I place my camera in Sonia's fragile hands so she can take a picture of us as a souvenir. When I go to photograph her with Motek, she shies away.

Towards the end of my visit, after we have talked about Konin and Koniners for hours, I ask him the question that has been on my mind since I first met him: Does he still feel I am twenty-five years too late? Yes, he says; he cannot help thinking of the people I have missed. I have prepared myself for this answer. Mentally donning a yarmulke, and adopting the homiletic story-telling style of my rabbinic ancestors, I try to convince him he is wrong. One of his regrets, he once told me, is that he does not possess a single object from his parents' home in Konin. If I were to tell him now that I had found his father's prayer book, would he be happy? He looks puzzled. 'Of course!' And if the back cover of the book was missing, would he still want it? 'Yes.' And if some of the pages were missing too? 'It would make no difference.' He agrees he would treasure the *siddur* however incomplete it was. The book I am trying to write, I tell him, will also be incomplete, partly because I have waited too long, partly because of my own limitations. But my hope is that whatever fragments I save will be worth treasuring, and that he will be glad to have them.

Motek is silent for a while, and I am uncertain what thoughts are running through his mind. Finally he tells me that he has another reason for wishing I had started earlier: 'I want to be alive to see your book, and who knows?' The tone is pessimistic. I have not seen him like this before. I wish him '*Biz hundert un tsvontsik*' – the traditional Yiddish wish that he lived to be a hundred and twenty, like Moses. I adopt a cheerful tone but he has infected me with his sadness. He says he will drive me to the bus-stop but I insist that he does not, and his lack of resistance is proof of just how bad he is feeling. I say goodbye to Motek and Sonia. He stands on the little balcony and waves as I walk away.

Postscript Motek and I kept in touch. I wrote to him from time to time to report on my progress with the book; we sent each other New Year and Passover greetings. I wrote to him in late December 1988, a year after we last met. A week later, I came home one day to find a message on my answering machine from Motek's son, Leon. He said his father had not seen my letter because he had had a stroke and was seriously ill in hospital. Worse news came when I spoke to Leon: His father had just had a second stroke: 'My Dad's in a coma, but I read him your letter tonight, and his breathing changed when I mentioned the word Konin.' Motek never recovered consciousness. He died on 20 January 1989, and was buried among his fellow Koniners. Some of his old townsfolk were among the crowd of mourners at his funeral. In the fall of that year about fifteen people attended the annual Konin memorial service. They lit a candle for Motek. It was the last gathering of the Konin Society, Inc.

In 1993 I received a letter from Leon about his mother:

> She died on March 17 after being burned in a fire in her apartment. I was upstairs playing with my nephew, Michael, when I smelled smoke. I ran down to my mother's apartment and found her on the floor in flames and her clothes burned off. The floor around her was burning as well. I put out the fire on my mom with my hands but it was too late. She was, as it turned out, fatally burned. The doctors at the burn unit gave her forty-eight hours to live but through some remarkable inner strength she lasted ten days. Until the last couple of days she was quite lucid and even asked me to do some food shopping for her.
>
> She explained to me that she had been boiling some water for tea and reached over to get the pot when her bathrobe caught fire. As you know, she had Parkinson's disease and couldn't move quickly and thus couldn't take her bathrobe off fast enough or get to the water faucet which was just a couple of steps away. Instead she fell to the ground . . .

Part Four

IN THE LAND OF ISRAEL

50

HRYCZKE: the name is engraved on a small brass plate on the front door. Haskel Ryczke – my father's brother, born Konin 1910, died Tel Aviv 1975. Waded ashore as an illegal immigrant 1934. The only one of my Ryczke uncles I was able to meet.

His son David unlocks the door and we enter the silent apartment where Haskel lived until his slow death from cancer seven years ago. The place is charged with his presence. One of the books lining the cramped hallway catches my eye: the Konin Memorial Book. In this small, friendly flat in central Tel Aviv, Haskel and his wife Freda lived most of their married life. Here they brought up their two sons: Chanoch and his elder brother, David, who has just picked me up from Ben Gurion Airport.

On a side-table in the living-room stands a framed photograph of Haskel and Freda, caught at a moment of shared laughter, she resting her head lazily on his shoulder like a lover. I took the picture in the early Sixties during my first visit to Israel. In the bedroom I find more photographic links with my past: a snapshot I took of my mother with my first camera; one of my father, looking uncannily like Haskel; my cousin Felunia, who died in Tel Aviv just a few months ago, cheated of her desire to talk to me about her early life in Konin.

David has to dash back to his high-pressure research job at Israel Military Industries. We have met only rarely over the years but feel like brothers. His mother will soon be here. I step onto the balcony overlooking the rear of other low-rise blocks, typical examples of Tel Aviv Bauhaus. Housewives standing on identical concrete balconies hang up washing and shake out rugs. The tinkly sound of someone practising their Czerny mixes with Hebrew voices coming from the yard below and the hum of traffic from nearby Dizengoff Street. The view is fairly hideous, but who cares? The Mediterranean is five minutes' walk away, it is a perfect spring morning, and I can feel the warmth of the sun after an interminable London winter.

Freda arrives, loaded down with provisions for me. My aunt, who is seventy-eight, has pale blue eyes and fine, Slav features. Her teachers in Ciazen, near Konin, used to tell her that she did not look 'like other Jewish people'. Her childhood friends were gentile because hers was the only Jewish family in Ciazen – and later she attended a Polish gymnasium.

Haskel's death has dimmed but not destroyed her spirit. When she visits her younger son in Miami, this indefatigable granny, born into a rural world where horses were the only means of transport, climbs into the cockpit of his light aircraft and, once they are in the air, takes over the dual joystick. 'What's so difficult about flying?' she asks as they head for the Gulf of Mexico.

We communicate in Yiddish, I stumbling along as best I can, she soon finding her fluency, with occasional slips into the Hebrew that has been her everyday tongue for more than fifty years. I have not seen her for several years but we are instantly at home with each other, laughing over hoary family jokes, mostly aimed at the Ryczkes, whose idiosyncrasies and eccentric ways she insists I share.

Freda (Koniners know her as Fella but the family calls her Freda) starts to prepare gefilte fish for the Passover Seder in a few days' time. Making gefilte fish for the Seder is her traditional, self-appointed role. She spends most of the afternoon in the kitchen, and much of the next day – a reminder to me of what it must have been like for the Konin housewife, catering for a huge family without the benefit of a refrigerator and electrical gadgets, dependent on water that had to be carried from a pump several streets away, cooking over the fierce heat of a coal- or peat-fired range. Freda, making gefilte fish for eighteen people, hums to herself as she skins and fillets and slices and chops.

During these visits, she breaks off every now and then to have a cup of tea with me and talk about her past. Her mother died soon after giving birth to her in 1910. When her father remarried and went to live in another town, Freda was handed over to her grandparents in Ciazen, and accompanied them when they settled in Konin in 1924. The elderly Wieners lived off rents from several apartments in the house they owned near the far end of Third of May Street. One of their tenants was the Mysch family: 'A nice family,' comments Freda, adding in a lowered, confidential tone: 'But sometimes they were a little behind with the rent.' This must have been at times when, as I remember Motek telling me in Brooklyn, his father's customers took their time paying for their suits, probably because they, in turn, had to wait for *their* customers to pay up.

Freda and Haskel met as members of a Zionist youth movement in Konin, of which he was a leading figure, serving on the committee and teaching Jewish history to his juniors. He scraped a living from tailoring for his cousin, Zalman Ryczke, son of the *melamed*.

> Haskel did not want to be a tailor. His ambition was to make *aliyah*, but it was difficult to get an immigration certificate and he had no money. In the end, he decided to go illegally. When he left in 1934, he said to me: 'I'll find someone there with English papers and he will come for you, and we'll get married in Eretz Yisrael.'
>
> He applied to the Polish authorities for a passport, telling them that he was going on a walking tour of Europe. Because it might have aroused suspicion, there was no big farewell for him at the station as there usually was when people left for Yisrael, no dancing and singing. He travelled on a Saturday but he didn't want his father to know he was travelling on *shabbat* so he said goodbye to his family on Friday. Your father – who was in London – and Itsik Hirsh [in Konin] lent him money, and he had a little bit of savings of his own.
>
> He and another Koniner, Chaim Fordoynski, went by train to Greece, and from there they caught a ship going to Haifa. They and a group of other illegal immigrants had planned to land by rowing-boat, but the English were on the lookout and there was a sudden alarm at the last minute, so they had to swim for the shore. Haskel and Chaim, knowing this might happen, had practised swimming in the Warta before they left Konin. *They* got safely to the shore, but a young man and a young woman were drowned.
>
> Haskel had to leave his case on the ship. He was wearing two pairs of trousers, one on top of the other, he had with him some documents to present to the people who were waiting for him in the dark with special signals. He landed on a beach at Kfar-Vidkin, north of Tel Aviv. From there he and the others travelled by donkey to a hiding-place. Friends from Konin helped him with

clothing to make him look like a *chalutz* [Zionist pioneer], and gave him a bed. Haskel stayed an illegal immigrant until we got our independence in 1948.

Haskel had a friend in Rehovoth called Sender Kaliski, a baker from Konin, who had gone to Palestine officially in 1927 and who had a British passport. In 1936 he went back to Konin to see his parents. Haskel asked him to marry me while he was in Poland – merely as a formality so that I could acquire a British passport – and Sender agreed. The two of us went from Konin to Warsaw and we were married there in the English consulate. It was all arranged by a Jewish fixer in Warsaw, whom of course we paid. He was one of the witnesses at the wedding, the other was a consulate clerk. And so I became Mrs Kaliski. After the wedding we went to a Rabbi in Warsaw, who wrote a statement declaring that we had not been married according to the Jewish faith.

When all the formalities were completed, Sender invited me to join him for lunch. 'After all,' he said, 'we've just got married!' We had a good laugh. But not everyone laughed after such marriages. Sometimes the young men did not want to let the girls go, and sometimes the other way round, and it could all end in tragedy. In fact, Sender wanted me to be his real wife; his mother was crazy about me, but he said: 'Mama, this is my friend's girl.'

He went back to Yisrael and I returned to Konin to wait for my new passport. Unfortunately, the police in Warsaw arrested the fixer and put him in prison. They found letters from various people asking him to fix passports, and one of these letters came from me. They must have communicated with the police in Konin because one day a policeman came to my grandma's house to make enquiries about me. I was lying low at the time, staying with Marysha [Dovid Ryczke's stepdaughter], who lived across the road. The police asked Grandma to make a statement but she said she knew nothing about it. When the policeman wrote out a statement and asked her to sign it, she said she couldn't write – in fact, she was a highly educated woman. The policeman knew her and her family and so he left her alone. He knew all right where I was.

Eventually the passport arrived, and it was shortly after this that your father came to Konin to visit his parents and to meet Haskel's *meydl* [young woman]. I remember showing him my new British passport and I can see him now, standing by the window examining it. He said he was very proud that I was going to Eretz Yisrael.

Freda places a deep, square biscuit tin on the table, a souvenir tin commemorating the coronation of Queen Elizabeth II. My parents sent it from London in 1953, the coronation year. The tin has become rather battered over the years, and much of the Queen's regal splendour has rubbed away. The tin serves as a storage place for old letters, photographs and documents, including the British passport that my father held that day in Konin. Now it is my turn to hold it – Passport No. 1094, issued to Mrs F. Kaliski in Warsaw on 8 May 1936.

> When I left Konin, the policeman was at the station and said goodbye to me. After I departed, my brother-in-law gave him some money. I went by ship to Haifa, where Haskel and Sender were waiting for me on the quay with a bouquet of flowers.
>
> We went to a Rabbi, who understood the situation, and Haskel and I got married. A few friends from Konin were at the ceremony but not enough men to make a *minyan*, so the Rabbi called in some workers who happened to be standing around outside and that's how we got married. A *nadn* [dowry]? Haskel used to say to me jokingly: 'Where's the *nadn*?' And I used to reply: '*I* am the *nadn*.' Neither of us had any money. He found me a job in the factory where he worked. He ended up with a managerial position in one of the largest organizations in Israel, Hamashbir. In the early days we experienced hard times when there were food shortages and we couldn't get things like sugar, but your father used to send us little parcels every month, and he did this for years.

Freda begins to go through the contents of the biscuit tin: photographs of long-dead Konin relatives I never met, pictures of me as a boy in London, now a stranger too. She has snapshots of my three children standing in my parents' North London garden – another vanished world. How right they are who say photography is an inherently morbid medium. She has letters too, bundles of them, some from prewar Poland, written on paper that has become permanently creased and friable. A postcard from Poland dated 1941 was the last communication Freda received from her family. Somehow it managed to reach Palestine during the war, probably via the Red Cross. It is from a cousin who had just been deported to a ghetto in eastern Poland with her husband and young children, all destined to die a year or two later. The brief message ends cheerfully: 'We came here to create a new life.'

Freda hands me another picture: a group of about twenty young men and women in Konin, carefully arranged in rows for the camera. Two small holes puncture the smooth surface of the photograph where someone has stuck a pin through the eyes of one of the men: an act of hatred as primitive and disquieting as a voodoo rite. The two holes catch the light, lending the man's visage a hideous blankness. It is Leon Danziger, the Kapo, whose fate I have described in an earlier chapter. Freda defaced the photograph many years ago, while looking at it in the company of someone who described how he had maltreated his fellow Jewish prisoners.

The photograph reminds Freda of a story she heard from her uncle, Maurice Wiener, about another Danziger who was not related either to the Kapo or to the mayor of Konin with the same name.

> In 1924 five Jewish girls in Konin married Polish soldiers and converted to Christianity. It caused a big stir in the town. One of them was the daughter of Herman Danziger, who was my uncle's partner: they ran a tobacco shop in the big square. Danziger's daughter was a beautiful girl who had blonde hair and didn't look at all Jewish. She fell in love with a high-ranking officer of German origin named Erben, who was exceptionally handsome and came from an aristocratic family. She converted and they married in the Catholic church in Konin.
>
> For the Danzigers it was a tragedy. People said that the mother attended the celebration ball after the wedding but I don't know if it is true. The father sat *shivah* [the seven days of ritual mourning following the funeral of a close relative] just as if his daughter had died. He took down all the pictures of her and threw them out. The girl's name was Guta, which was quite a common name among Jewish girls, but she changed it to Griselda after she married. She moved to Warsaw, had a daughter, and lived like a queen.
>
> One day, a few years after she left Konin, Herman Danziger was in Warsaw walking along the street and suddenly who does he see but his daughter coming towards him. She went up to him

and said 'Father', and he fainted. After that incident he got it into his head that life was not worth living, and some years later he hanged himself. She and her daughter ended up in Buchenwald, where they died. After the war the Poles accused Erben of being a traitor and murdered him.

Our tea-break over, Freda puts away the biscuit tin and goes back to the gefilte fish.

51

FREDA EMERGES from the bedroom transformed, a triumph of style over age, dressed all in white, matching the whiteness of her perfectly groomed hair. Her fragile, lace-trimmed blouse awakens a memory of Edwardian photographs of my mother in the family album. Religious women in Konin, says Freda, always wore white for the Seder, just as the head of the household wore a white linen robe. She is not a believer, but keeps to the tradition of wearing white on the first night of Passover.

My own attire is less traditional: a much-travelled sports jacket, grey trousers past their best, and a black polo-neck: irreverently casual by London Seder standards, and yet, entering the living-room in Kfar-Sava where the family is gathered, I find myself conspicuously overdressed compared with my male relatives, who are wearing jeans, lightweight trousers and open-neck shirts. The women are festively dressed.

The Seder table in Kfar-Sava, though laid with care, dispenses with the formality of starched white tablecloth, best china, the ceremonial platter and other details that go to make this night different from all other nights. I miss the silver candlesticks we have at home, which were my Sarna grandparents' wedding gift to my parents, who passed them on to me. I miss the assortment of battered silver goblets, the *bekhers*, from which we drink the four ritual cups of wine. My grandparents brought them over from Konin. Not much bigger than thimbles, they are unsteady on their rounded base and therefore doomed to tip over at some point in the evening. They say no *Haggadah* (the story of the Exodus recited at the Seder) is complete without its wine-stained pages.

The Seder has a potent appeal even for an irreligious Jew like me, not least of all because its ceremonial belongs not to the synagogue but to the home. The dialogue is between father and son rather than between rabbi and congregation. Like no other Jewish festival, it combines homeliness and holiness. The table is the altar. I marvel at the obstinate survival of a festal meal whose origins reach back more than three thousand years. The Last Supper was a Seder. Were Jesus to return to earth and attend Mass in the Vatican or Holy Communion in a Protestant cathedral, he would find the ritual mystifying, the language unintelligible, whereas he could sit down and join in as one of us at the Seder table.

Fourteen members of the family – grown-ups, children and babies – have gathered around this Seder table to celebrate the festival of freedom. David, seated at its head, uncovers the three ceremonial matzos and begins to read from the *Haggadah: 'Ha lakhma anya di-okhalu avhatanu be-ar'a de-mitzrayim'* – This is the bread of affliction that our fathers ate in the land of Egypt . . . For me and many other Diaspora Jews, Hebrew remains a foreign language. For the ultra-Orthodox it is a sacred language reserved for Holy Writ. For David and the other Israelis round this table, the language of the *Haggadah* is their language, archaic in places no doubt, with passages in Aramaic (like the line above), but nevertheless their language, using words they read in newspapers, hear on television and speak in their everyday lives. When, according to tradition, the youngest male child recites the *Ma nishtana* – 'Why is this night different from all other nights?' – the small boy reads the lines aloud as he would from any other story book. Attending a Seder in Israel for the first time, I am more intensely aware than I ever could be in London of the reality of the Return, the fulfilment of a hope never abandoned. In London and New York that hope is still expressed: 'Next year in Jerusalem.' In Kfar-Siva the old city is a bus-ride away.

The younger guests are less than engrossed in the story of the departure from Egypt. The aroma of Freda's chicken soup drifting from the kitchen has a stronger hold on their attention. I sense a growing impatience with the recitation of the *Haggadah* which, it has to be admitted, indulges in repetition and ceaseless praise of the Almighty, who delivered us from Pharaoh's bondage. The people round this table have learned not to wait for the delivering hand of the Almighty.

When the Dark-Haired Ryczke's great-grandson urges David to get a move on, to skip a few passages, even draw the ritual to a close so that we can get down to the serious business of the evening, David – one generation closer to *Der Shvartser Ryczke* – visibly stiffens. I feel tension rising, the way it often does when families come together for a much-anticipated reunion. David's voice finally runs out of steam. Discouraged, he closes the book. *Der Shvartser Ryczke*'s great-great-grandson gurgles happily on his mother's lap. He is only a few months old. The past still lies ahead of him.

Each of the women has contributed to the feast. Freda's prize-winning soup and fish are appreciatively consumed. Freda does not notice. Her mission accomplished, she withdraws into silence, her face drawn with exhaustion. Perhaps she is thinking of the past, of Poland, and a different kind of Seder without Coca-Cola, without the bowl of exotic fruits, which they would not even have heard of in Konin.

After the meal there is no traditional debate or discussion of rabbinic interpretations. No one opens the door for the prophet Elijah, herald of the Messiah. The children do not search the room for the *afikomen*, the hidden piece of matzo, in order to win the finder's reward. No festive songs. The table cleared, I chat for a while with my young Israeli relatives, descended, like me, from the Ryczkes of Konin. But they do not ask me about Konin or my reasons for being in Israel. To them the *shtetl* past is a foreign country about which they know little. Nor do they want to know more.

52

I HAD MET my cousin Felunia a few times – on holiday in Israel and when she stayed with us in London – hardly long enough for us to get to know each other well, yet our relationship had a closeness that might have owed something to her status as a family survivor. The daughter of my father's sister, Bayla, she was the only close member of his family in Konin to remain alive after the war. Her existence meant everything to him. It showed in his practical concern for her welfare and in the caressive Yiddish nickname he coined for her: to him she was not Felunia but always Felunia *kroyn gduleh* – Felunia crown of glory. She, having lost her mother, brothers and other near family, cherished the few Ryczke kin she found after the war in Israel and Britain, of whom I was one.

She was a woman on whom Auschwitz had left its mark in more than a literal sense. Beneath a cheerful social presence lay an undercurrent of anxiety and emotional frailty. Yet whatever her private torments, she had an exuberant spirit that probably contributed to her survival. Laughter came to her as readily as tears.

In 1949, newly arrived in Israel, Felunia began rebuilding her life, grateful to have her mother's brother, Haskel, and his wife, Freda, close by to act as surrogate parents. She married a kindly fellow survivor, produced two sons and, after years of effort and thrift, achieved the settled domestic life she had been denied in her youth. Tragedy struck when her husband died prematurely, leaving her life once again in ruins. A veteran survivor, she battled on.

When our cousin David told her of my plan to write a book about Konin, the news excited her. We rarely telephoned each other, but on the eve of my departure for New York, she called me to wish me luck. I could tell she was impatient for us to meet. She had written about some of her wartime experiences in the Memorial Book, but not about the Ryczke family.[1] She had information about them that no one else could give me. Just how impatient she was I did not know until some time later, when David recounted a call he received from her one day. She told him she felt an irresistible urge to talk about Konin, about things she had never discussed with him. He suggested that she old back until my arrival, but she would not be put off, and called him again. The intensity of her request made it impossible to refuse. She had no knowledge then of the cancer that was shortly to kill her. Looking back, David wonders if she had a foreboding that she would not live long enough to see me.

She visited his home one evening in late May or early June 1988, and after dinner, when the children had gone to bed, she began talking about her life, her childhood in Konin, her family circle, the murder of her family . . . She talked compulsively, hardly pausing, and went on talking until three in the morning. David had little need to play the role of interviewer. The flood of memory was unstoppable, as though this was a last chance for her to put the past on record.

David taped the session, thinking it might help me to listen to it before I talked to her. I was none too happy when I read his letter explaining about the recording he had made: it seemed pointless in the light of my forthcoming visit. Moreover, I feared it would blunt her spontaneity when I went over the same ground with her. I was in Omaha when news of her death reached me and changed everything. I felt only gratitude for Felunia's persistence – or premonition – and for David's decision to record her memories. When I arrived in Israel, one of my top priorities was to go through the tapes with him.

My cousin is a brilliant graduate of the Technion. For many years he has headed a scientific research team, working with computerized, space-age instrumentation. It comes as a sad irony to learn from a somewhat crestfallen David that something went wrong with his recording. The old domestic radio-recorder he used for the purpose proved faulty. Felunia's words are unintelligible. This had not seemed catastrophic when he discovered it because he knew I would be meeting her. But now she is dead . . .

One morning in Kfar-Sava, the clear spring light of Israel brightening the room, the two of us sit down at his dining-table to sample one of the tapes. What I hear is a continuous roar and hiss through which, in the background, another sound can be faintly heard, just about identifiable as a human voice, which David assures me is Felunia, speaking in Hebrew, not a word of which is decipherable. But I have underestimated David's tenacity, his flair for rising to a challenge. All too aware of my disappointment, he decides to try to salvage something from the tapes.

He presses his ear against the speaker, plays a short snatch, rewinds, listens again, rewinds, listens again, and finally, after several more patient attempts, succeeds in rescuing two or three sentences. The retrieval system inside his own head gets to work too. A phrase here, a phrase there triggers his memory of the conversation he had with Felunia that evening, and this helps him stitch together the ripped patches of words. The exercise is excruciatingly slow and laborious. In addition, David bears the burden of having to translate her words into English.

He and his wife Varda labour for hours and days, and finally I end up with a transcript of Felunia's recording, albeit with inaudible passages here and there that no amount of effort can restore. This salvage operation enables Felunia's voice, a voice from the dead, to reach me – not loud and clear, but all the more precious for having been so nearly lost.

Her mother, Bayla, married a local man by the name of Zalman Prost. They had two sons, Moniek and Abramek, followed, in 1925, by a daughter, Felunia.[2] The Prosts rented a tiny grocery store on the corner of a house on the southern edge of the town. Upstairs lived Bayla's eldest brother – my uncle, Itsik Hirsh – and his wife. Bayla's father (my grandfather), the Dark-Haired Ryczke, had rooms at the back of the house, where he lived with his second wife, Gitl,[3] and their two young adult sons, confusingly bearing the same names as Felunia's brothers: Moniek and Abramek. At the time she was growing up, in the Thirties, my grandfather had long retired as an egg merchant.

The Prosts' financial situation was dire. Belonging to a *bekovedik* (respectable, dignified) family like the Ryczkes only served to make it worse. No poverty is more shaming than genteel poverty. With relatives and neighbours living cheek-by-jowl – just across the hall-way or up a flight of stairs – the strain of keeping up appearances must have been unbearable.

About Felunia's father I have gleaned virtually nothing. Perhaps he lacked drive or commercial flair or was plain unlucky. With Bayla running the tiny shop, I am not sure how he filled his days. A sense of personal failure must have preyed on his mind. One day in 1932, Zalman treated his wife and children to tickets for the circus, which had just come to town. He stayed home that afternoon. Bayla and her three youngsters were watching the show when someone told her to return home immediately. She and the children raced back to find Zalman dead. He had hanged himself.

To his religious father-in-law and brother-in-law, Zalman's suicide was a cause for shame. Jewish law would require that Zalman's body be buried in a separate part of the cemetery reserved for suicides. On that evening when Felunia poured out her past in Kfar-Sava, she remained silent about her father. After fifty-five years the subject was still taboo. It was from another Koniner in Israel that I learned the details of his death.

From the Felunia tapes:

> I was seven years old when my father died. At that time the economic situation was bad generally, and especially for us. This I remember: my mother was left with three children and it was tough. She kept the shop going, but it was difficult for her to make a living. I remember very clearly Uncle Itsik Hirsh who lived upstairs. He was a clever man and a very religious Jew – I liked him. He was a grain merchant and had no children. His economic situation was good while ours got worse and worse.
>
> Grandfather became very old and wasn't capable of doing anything. He had high blood-pressure, and they treated him with leeches. He always smelled of garlic – he used to walk around eating it raw. Today I know why.[4] Whenever I was close to him I wanted to run away because I couldn't bear the smell of garlic.
>
> My brother Moniek was very talented and badly wanted to study. He had the qualifications to enter the gymnasium and mother cried a lot because she could not afford it.[5] But she did not talk too much about her situation. She didn't want people to know. My other brothers, Abramek, learned to make knitwear on machines in an ORT[6] workshop in Konin. I was an excellent student and it was said that my uncle in England – Uncle Simcha [the author's father] – would take me to live with him, so that at least one of us would study. Well, this didn't work out because of the war.
>
> I remember that every month Uncle Simcha used to send grandfather money. It was about four hundred zlotys, and this enabled the grandparents to live very nicely. He also sent parcels of clothes, and even us he helped from time to time. He sent us money at holiday times and also parcels. Mother used to sit up all night making clothes for herself and for us, and in this way we had something to wear.

How well I remember, as a small boy, accompanying my mother on forays into department stores in Ilford or the West End, where deferential assistants put customers' cash into tubular metal containers which, at the pull of a lever, whizzed along overhead wires to a cashier, who took the money and sent the change whizzing back. Here my mother picked up sales bargains – cardigans and pyjamas, pillow-slips, and dress lengths at 'one-and-eleven-three' a yard[7] – destined for Konin.

> Mother had a very hard life. She could not afford to have domestic help and when we had to do the laundry, she had no strength for it, so my eldest brother – and this I shall never forget – at night, when no one was looking, prepared the water and everything, and he did the laundry for her. It was not customary that a boy like him should stand at the scrubbing board and do the laundry. And mother did not want the neighbours to see that our situation was so difficult, or even that the rest of the family living in the house should know he was doing the laundry. It wasn't very pleasant to let others know that you couldn't afford to pay someone to help with the laundry. We were a respected family. The laundry was done in an enormous vessel on the top of the stove. It took three days to do.
>
> At the time when we could afford a washerwoman, we always had some herring and a bottle of vodka ready for her.

Fetching and heating large amounts of water was both onerous, time-consuming and costly, so a lot of families would let their dirty laundry – large household items like sheets – pile up for a few weeks, and then call in a Polish washerwoman to deal with it. These women earned so little that even not-so-well-off families could afford to employ them.

> There was a market twice a week, and this is when the villagers came to town and did their shopping. These were the two days for good takings, but to have takings you needed goods on the shelves. Mother never had the money for merchandise, and she was always sending me to various people here and there to borrow money, and then she filled the shelves, sold some goods, and gave the money back.
>
> When the licence fee for the shop had to be paid, not only mother but all the other little Jewish shopkeepers were running to find the money. One would take a small loan from the Jewish bank.

One would borrow from the other. They were sewing patches on patches. Actually, I don't know what would have happened if the war had not started. I don't know how mother would have carried on. To this day I remember this heavy burden of how to keep going, how to buy clothes, how to pay the rent. Mother could sew and knit, and we were always neat and tidy. But I have the impression that we ate the store clean, because the shelves were really empty. And she was not well, not strong.

My mother had two women-friends [the context suggests they were gentiles] with whom she studied in the Russian gymnasium [when Konin was under the Tsars]. They were good friends and helped us during the war . . . [inaudible]. She had a way of making friends with people.

My mother was an educated and talented woman, and when we asked her about things we learned in school, there was nothing she didn't know. And she cared very much about our education. I nagged her because I always feared that someone in the class would do their homework better than me, so in the mornings she would stand in the store wearing a fur jacket because it was cold, while I recited by heart everything I had learned. I knew she didn't have the time for me but she listened until I knew everything as I should. It is a pity things weren't easier for her.

It was a period when anti-Semitism began to get worse in Poland, and more than once we found DON'T BUY FROM A JEW scrawled on the door. Pickets were standing in front of Jewish shops so people wouldn't buy from Jews. There were some *goyim* who were really afraid to enter our store, and they used to come in secretly. A short time before the war broke out, the anti-Semitism was really unbearable. From month to month it got worse. We could feel their hatred of the Jews.

Then the war broke out. Mother remembered the Germans from the First World War, a cultured nation. She said it was impossible what the Germans were supposed to be doing to the Jews. She could not imagine it. She remembered that her father had been a trader in eggs and dealt with Germans all the time. They used to come to our house, and we had many German buyers living in Poland, and they were real friends of ours, and she judged the Germans by this. When I was in the war and saw so many horrible things, I thought of how innocent she had been.

The German soldiers [who occupied Konin in 1939] wanted to buy butter and cheese, and Mother was selling to them. They were very nice and glad that Mother spoke fluent German. One night one of them came to visit us – probably Mother used to speak to him during the day. He was not a young soldier, and they sat round the table and talked. I understood that he told Mother that bad times were coming, and there would be murder; he told her what Hitler had done in Germany – killing old people, the sick and handicapped, and he felt he must warn her because he had seen her a few times and saw she was a widow with children. He apologized because he would not be coming again to buy, but he advised Mother to do something, to disappear, to leave, because things would be very bad.

Mother called on one of the neighbours . . . [inaudible] and he simply wouldn't believe her. They thought she was fantasizing. We talked about it among ourselves all day. After a few days, the Germans took hostages, and two of them, a *goy* and a Jew, were executed in the big square. They said we had to wear a yellow patch and walk only in the road. For me it was terrible because Polish school friends of mine walked on the pavement and were laughing at me. And I was the one who went on errands because it was dangerous for my brothers to go out. Having to walk in the road made me feel so ashamed. I didn't know where to put myself. Many times, without telling Mother, I took off the yellow patch and walked along with my heart pounding. I wasn't afraid of the Germans because they didn't know who I was. I was afraid that the *goyim* would reveal that I was a Jew.

As I mentioned before, we had many friends among the local Germans [citizens of German origin, 'ethnic Germans']. When the Nazis occupied the town, these people acquired German nationality and, willingly or unwillingly, they were enlisted in the militia and the police. Among them were many from the villages who were friends of ours and grandfather's, and they were so used to us that they left their bicycles with swastikas on them in our yard.

Once I was caught and taken with another two girls to the police and made to clean the floor. Suddenly one of the men [a local German] saw me, came over and said: 'Aren't you Prost's daughter?' I said: 'Yes,' so he said: 'Go home.' I said I was afraid I would be caught but he said: 'I'm sending you.' This happened to me and my brothers several times. Some other [local] Germans brought cheese from their village that their mother sent for us. Some of them of course were willing helpers of the Nazis. There were all sorts of people among them.

Life could not be called life. You went to sleep in the evening not knowing what would happen next morning. Jews were severely beaten. People were afraid to go out. We sat together, with neighbours, wondering what to do, where to go, how to prevent disaster. We thought they would beat us, take money, but no one could imagine the Shoah. Some Jews with money ran away, and many families escaped to Russia. They found no paradise there but at least they stayed together as whole families. We couldn't move because we had no money, and we didn't have food.

One day they said that no one was allowed to leave their home, and that the Germans would go from house to house and we would be sent way from Konin. In our house everyone packed a suitcase. Our Aunt Marysha came to us and put her two little children on the floor to sleep. We were all together, except for our grandparents who were in the town,[8] and we were sitting and waiting for the Germans to come and tell us to leave. Then, in the corridor outside, we heard one German say to the other: 'Prost lives here. She stays.' We heard this, but knew it was not a good idea to go out and look.

They took about sixty per cent of the Jewish families and sent them away.[9] At that time we didn't know where they were going, but later we learned they were sent to Ostrowiec. We remained in Konin, and for some reason grandfather and grandmother also stayed.

In July 1940 Bayla and her children were evicted from Konin along with the other Jewish inhabitants remaining in the town, among them my grandparents and their sons. Felunia was just fifteen years old. The deportees were sent initially to villages and country areas near Konin. In March 1941 the Prost family and other Konin Jews (including Rabbi Lipschitz) were deported to an open ghetto in Jozefow, a village nearly four hundred kilometres to the east.

Before their deportation, my grandfather had the good fortune to die a natural death. His sons, Moniek and Abramek, were deported to Jozefow with Bayla and her children. Whether his wife, Gitl, was deported or murdered locally is not known. What is almost certain is that Itsik Hirsh and his wife were among the thousands of Jews put to death in the Konin region – either by gassing in mobile vans or by shooting – and buried in mass graves in the forest of Kazimierz, twelve kilometres from Konin.

Life in Jozefow went from bad to worse. 'Bread and potatoes were luxury items.' Many Jews died of hunger-related illnesses while others fell victim to a typhus epidemic.[10] Felunia's brother, Abramek, decided to make his way to Ostrowiec to see if conditions there were any better. I resume Felunia's account one morning in Jozefow in 1942.

> On Sundays we didn't work, so my brother Moniek decided we would go to the woods to collect some berries for mother. We set out at about 5 am. Mother was still asleep.
>
> We were joyful because we saw such big berries. We filled our little baskets, then suddenly we heard some shooting. We were scared but didn't know what it meant. We [inaudible] the road and saw many *goyim* coming from the town. It was about 8 to 8.30 am. When they saw us and realized we were Jews they started crossing themselves. They said to us: 'Where are you going? They've killed all the Jews.' What happened? They said they had gone to pray in church but were not allowed to enter the town. Some of the inhabitants told them that in the morning an SS commander had come and given an order to the Jews to leave their homes. We had left home at five, and this happened at six. The Germans went from house to house, took all the Jews to the middle of the town, led them to a quarry and mowed them down.
>
> 'Do not go into the town, you'll be walking into trouble. They will kill you.' None of them volunteered any suggestions or offered to take us. What were we to do? There was one old *goy* who told my brother: 'Go into the forest and see what happens [inaudible].' So we did.
>
> All day long we lay there in the forest, and before evening it became cold and damp. We were hungry and wet and looked around and found the forest warden's house. We knocked and he opened the door and said, yes, he knew us. He knew that all the

Jews had been killed and said: 'I'll give you a blanket, some bread and water and show you the way, but I haven't seen you, I haven't heard you, and I don't know you.'

First we rested. I was the youngest in the family, the little one, and I cried 'Mother, Mother.' The night passed and before dawn the warden came and spoke to my brother and told him: 'Listen, I've been to town and heard that there is not one Jew there. They took everyone to the quarry, and I suggest that you stay here. Partisans sometimes turn up round here and you're a young fellow. I don't know if they will take her, but they'll certainly take you.'

When I heard this I began to cry again. First of all, I didn't want to be separated from him. Second, I wanted Mother. I had a feeling that she must have got wind that something was about to happen to the Jews. Perhaps she went to the neighbour's house [a kindly gentile neighbour in Jozefow, for whom Bayla had worked in the fields], because the neighbour had said that they would save us if something bad happened. Moniek also wanted to return [to the town]. It's possible that if I hadn't asked him to stay with me, he would have escaped and maybe stayed alive.

There was a way of entering the town via a hill. Our house was below the hill. This was where one of the worst moments happened: we were on the hill at five or six in the morning and no one was around, when suddenly someone comes running towards us, a woman with her hair sticking out all wild, like a totally mad woman. I recognized her immediately. Her daughter was at school with me. The woman had gone out of her mind. What had happened? The Germans had come to her place and she had hidden in an empty barrel and stayed there [inaudible]. From her story we gathered that when she realized her husband and two daughters had been taken away, she wandered around and met a local Pole who told her all the Jews had been killed. So she went out of her mind. She ran away, towards the hill, and suddenly she saw us and knew us. She looked at me and called me by the daughter's name and hugged me so that I couldn't escape from her grip. My brother had to take her hands to release me. I don't know what happened to her eventually. She was probably killed.

We left her and walked down the hill and entered our house. It was open, and my brother [inaudible]. When she [probably the

> gentile neighbour] saw us she was transfixed, as if someone had come back from the dead. We asked if what we had heard was true. She said Mother had indeed run to her and hidden in the cellar. But then Mother remembered that she had left a pair of trousers behind, and the best coat she had. I don't know if she would have been [inaudible; presumably the sentence ends: 'saved if she had not gone back.'] She went out for the pair of trousers, but when she wanted to return, the Germans were at the door and took her.
>
> What were we to do? I was afraid to go out into the street because I was not supposed to be alive. What the neighbour's husband then did was this: the Germans were rounding up Poles to bury the Jews. He said: 'I shall look for your mother and if I find her, I shall bring you back a piece of her dress.' So he took a pair of scissors with him, and he found her. And what she was wearing on that day was a dressing-gown that Uncle Simcha had sent from England. I kept this piece of my mother's dressing-gown with me until I got to Auschwitz. It was with me until everything was taken from us and I was naked with nowhere to hide it. Until then I always held on to it.

No detail pierces me as profoundly as this – the piece of Bayla's dressing-gown, probably one of the sales bargains my mother bought in Ilford or at Selfridge's in Oxford Street. Was I with her when she bought it? Had I perhaps once touched this scrap of cloth cut from a blood-soaked corpse in a quarry in eastern Poland?

Felunia's account becomes somewhat confused at this point in her story. It seems that she and her brother Moniek decided to join their brother Abramek in Ostrowiec.

> Now how do you travel when you have such Jewish faces? you are frightened of the Poles because they can recognize a Jew immediately. We reached Ostrowiec and saw someone who seemed a Jew. He said: 'I shall show you where to find people from your town. The ghetto is still open,' and he led us there. We entered a house where there were some Jews and we told them what had happened. They had relatives in Jozefow. We told them everything about the killing of the Jews, including our mother, and we gave names of families who were killed. They took Moniek . . . to the Rabbi, who lit two candles and made

him swear that what he said was true. This was the stupidity of the Jewish people – that they didn't believe. They were still in an open ghetto.

Even if one hears that horrible things have happened, the normal brain cannot grasp it. If everyone had believed these things there would have been many more survivors because people would have had a greater urge to escape, to survive, to try, because they would have had nothing to lose. It helped the Germans that the Jews didn't know [what was going to happen to them].

In Ostrowiec, Felunia was reunited with her other brother, Abramek, who had managed to obtain a work permit.[11]

From time to time we heard about people who were murdered, beaten, and this came to seem natural. As time went by, rumours became worse and worse. Why do I say rumours? Because everyone said they were rumours. One rumour was that they were burning Jews. What did this 'burning' mean? How is it possible to burn people? We saw people being killed but at that time we didn't see people being burned.

At the end of 1942 and beginning of 1943 the Germans enclosed the Ostrowiec ghetto. Felunia was parted from her brothers and did not see them again. After the war she learned that they were transported to Treblinka.

One day, suddenly – things like this always happened suddenly – the SS came and rounded us all up. As usual, they separated people and wanted to take the children. Not far from where I was standing was a dry well. It was round and very, very deep. Near me stood a woman who was our neighbour [in Konin]. They took her child. Her brother, who was a [Jewish] policeman, knew what would happen to her if she went with the child. He pulled her back as she tried to join the child. He fought with her, frightened that the Germans would see. He pulled her back to the line, and the child was taken away, shouting 'Mother! Mother!' She began crying. Near me, another woman stood with what later I realized was a baby hidden under her clothing. The German was very near to her and she, in a second – I don't know how – jumped into the well with the baby. We heard the thump. They were killed immediately. The German didn't even look round and we – well,

> you can imagine what a state we were in. They took the children and some old people, and we were left.

The Germans tightened the boundaries of the ghetto and Felunia's situation grew more desperate. Shootings and public executions became the norm. She describes several heart-stopping moments when her own end seemed imminent, but each time her will to survive saved her:

> I always said, No, they will never catch me, not me. I shall escape. That was a time when we heard more rumours about them burning Jews and I said to myself: I will not be burned. I don't mind them killing me but not burning me. I imagined that it would be very painful, something terrible. Today it is easy to say we should have resisted. With what? There was nothing with which to resist. It was so painful, so frustrating when you stood there facing them, without strength, with nothing, and against you are those Goliaths with dogs and everything else, so what can you do? You always think that just being passive will keep you alive.

In August or September 1944, Felunia was transported out of Ostrowiec together with the last remaining Jews there, mostly from local forced-labour camps. The four-day train journey ended at the gates of Auschwitz, where Felunia bade a silent farewell to the boy who had become her first love. They had travelled to Auschwitz in the same wagon. 'We said that after the war, if we stayed alive, we would try to find each other.'

She and a number of other young women were selected for work. She became familiar with the smell of Jewish bodies burning in the crematoria, and the sight of newcomers arriving:

> A train passes, coming from Hungary. They were nice trains, and at the window women with furs and hats and men with thick woollen scarves, girls with dolls and teddy bears, all of them looking out with curiosity, trying to figure out where they have come to; and you stand and know that this train is bringing them straight to the crematorium.

a She passed several selections, some supervised by Dr Josef Mengele.

> If I close my eyes I can see his boots and whip. I did not dare

> look up. I was scared. He used to come and go. We were naked and the girls rubbed the skin of a beetroot on their faces because they looked half-dead; and he just said 'left' or 'right', right to life, left to . . .

At the beginning of 1945 Felunia and other slave labourers, almost dead from hunger, were transported by train to a munitions factory in the former Sudetenland; and from there, as the Russians drew nearer, she trudged on a four-day march to yet another factory. On 9 May, three days after her twentieth birthday, the Russian army freed her.

While others, on being liberated, stayed where they were so as to give themselves time to recover strength, Felunia impatiently set off for Konin, but fell seriously ill on the way. After a spell in hospital she pressed on and arrived in Konin, where she hoped to find her brothers. Not finding them there, she moved to Lodz. She wrote several letters to my father (she knew our address by heart), but got no reply as we had moved away in 1940. Felunia lived in various DP camps, and in one of them she was reunited with her boyfriend, who was seriously ill. She watched him dying for three months in a German hospital. From Germany, she traced Haskel in Israel and my father in England. He sent her a ticket to London, but she decided to make her life in Israel, and arrived there by ship in 1949.

The Memorial Book contains an account by Francesca Bram of the massacre that began in Jozefow on the morning when Felunia and her brother were picking berries in the woods. In the early hours of that day, 13 July 1942, a German detachment arrived in Jozefow to kill the women, children, elderly and sick. Young males capable of work were separated from the others. Trucks ferried to and fro, taking those doomed to die from the village square to the execution ground in the nearby woods.

> In the square, among the weeping crowd, was Dr Fürt, a Jew from Vienna, aged over seventy, a former colonel in the Austrian army . . . He turned round and said to us: 'It is hard to die, I know it. But think of this – your tormentors will die a hateful death. Generations to come will have no pity on them. May a misfortune

> befall the nation of these murderers.' Because he spoke loudly and in German, they [the Germans] stood with wonder as if turned to stone . . . They saw his medals from the First World War. Dr Fürt cried out to the Jews: 'If any of you survive the war and by chance come across my son, tell him that his father was not afraid of the Hitler murderers!'
>
> The Germans tore him to pieces. His wife was a Christian from an aristocratic Austrian family. She died with him.[12]

During their search of Jewish homes, the Germans killed on the spot all those who were too ill or frail to make their way to the square. Among them was Jacob Lipschitz, the last Rabbi of Konin. They shot him in his bed.[13]

Postscript In the summer of 1993, after I had written about the massacre at Jozefow, I happened upon a chilling work, *Ordinary Men*, by an American historian, Christopher R. Browning.[14] While studying an extensive collection of documents in Stuttgart, where the Federal Republic of Germany was coordinating the investigation of Nazi war crimes, Browning had come across an indictment concerning Reserve Police Battalion 101, a unit of *Ordnungspolizei*, the German Order Police. *Ordinary Men* is based largely on pre-trial interrogations of the men of this battalion, mostly middle-aged, working-class family men from Hamburg. The atrocity in Jozefow was Battalion 101's initiation into mass killing. Browning's account of that murderous day, 13 July 1942,[15] tells us about the massacre from a different angle – that of the killers. Save for a few discrepancies, the accounts tally, though with this main difference: the picture of the bloodshed that emerges from *Ordinary Men* surpasses in horror anything to be found in the Jewish sources.

Browning reveals that while the Jews were being rounded up and assembled in the village square, the battalion doctor and a sergeant gave some of their men a quick lesson on how to dispatch their victims. The first truckload of thirty-five to forty Jews was driven to woods a few kilometres outside the village. (Nowhere does the German evidence quoted by Browning mention a stone quarry.) When they arrived, 'an equal number of policemen from the First Company came forward and, *face to face*, were paired off with their victims.' The Jews were ordered to lie down in a row. 'The policemen stepped up behind them, placed their bayonets on the backbone above the shoulder blades as earlier instructed' and on a sergeant's orders, fired in unison.[16]

'When the first salvo was heard from the woods, a terrible cry swept the marketplace as the collected Jews realized their fate. Thereafter, however, a quiet composure – indeed, in the words of German witnesses, an "unbelievable" and "astonishing" composure – settled over the Jews.'

The executions continued hour after hour. The men from the Second Company, who also participated in the massacre, had received no preliminary instructions on how best to kill their victims – by using their bayonet blades as an aiming guide. Browning quotes one of the men: 'At first we shot freehand. When one aimed too high, the entire skull exploded. As a consequence, brains and bones flew everywhere.' Placing the bayonet point on the neck brought unforeseen results. 'Through the point-blank shot that was thus required, the bullet struck the head of the victim at such a trajectory that often the entire skull or at least the entire rear skullcap was torn off, and blood, bone splinters, and brains sprayed everywhere and besmirched the shooters.' A small number of Germans had earlier asked to be excused from duty that day, and their request had been granted. A few others found excuses to slink away from the slaughter. All were in need of the copious quantities of alcohol provided when their work was done.

At the end of a long summer's day, the Germans drove away, 'literally saturated in the blood of their victims', leaving behind the bodies of 1,500 Jewish women, children and old men lying in the woods where they had been killed. Some of the dead were sprawled in doorways in the village streets, where they had been shot on the spot trying to hide or escape. My Aunt Bayla must have been among these, and one can guess how her neighbour's husband came by the scrap of cloth. He probably helped to carry the corpses left in the street to a makeshift mortuary, and, while doing so, came across Bayla. Wishing to spare the young girl the ordeal of seeing her mother's bullet-ripped body, he went to the mortuary and there cut off the piece of cloth from Bayla's dressing-gown.[17]

53

I HAVE GOT used to – almost addicted to – the noisy, frenetic atmosphere of my local supermarket in Ben Yehuda Street. But now a new and startling sound, stomach-churning in its urgency, invades the store: the high-pitched note of a siren. Everyone freezes. One moment the scene is a moving picture, the next a tableau vivant. The old man ahead of me in the check-out queue, extracting money from his wallet, freezes in that position as though paralysis has suddenly struck him. The check-out girl rests her still fingers on the keyboard like a pianist in suspended animation. No one speaks, no one moves. Only the piercing single note of the siren breaks the silence that has fallen on the shoppers. It is Yom Ha-Shoah, the day of commemoration for the six million.

Outside, beyond the plate-glass windows plastered with garish stickers, the driver of a delivery van stands motionless as a statue, cradling a cardboard carton in his arms. Cars and buses are halted in the middle of the road, engines silenced, the drivers inanimate at their wheels. Ben Yehuda Street is crowded but nothing stirs. Waxwork figures populate the pavements. The siren howls on for an interminable two minutes till at last it ends with a fading growl. The tableau unfreezes. The clatter returns. The check-out girl rings up the total, and the old boy hands over his money. Outside, motorists unleash a cacophony of impatient hooting.

The Shoah is the one bond that unites all Jews in this disunited country, and today there will be State ceremonies at Yad Vashem, shown on television along with the mandatory newsreel shots of the deportation trains, the ghettos, the camps . . .

A week later the siren sounds again, this time to mark the Day for the Fallen in Israel's wars. More memorial ceremonies, more expressions of national grief. And the following day, 20 April, another orgy of remembering as Israelis celebrate Yom Ha-atzmaut, Independence Day. It is the State's fortieth anniversary. There is official flag-waving, and boisterous crowds fill the streets of Tel Aviv, singing and dancing and banging each other on the head with plastic hammers. On television they show the military parades in Jerusalem, the fly-pasts, salutings of the flag and more old newsreels – rusty ships overloaded with refugees limping towards the coast only to be turned back to Hitler's Germany by the British and, finally, the reading of the Declaration of Independence. Jews are good at remembering, and nowhere do they indulge in it more than in Israel during the month of April, the cruellest month. 'Jews remember too much. That is their misfortune,' says a character in a story by Isaac Bashevis Singer.[1] For one young Israeli, at least, this excess of remembering has become a form of oppression: 'Every year the children sing: "Slaves we were, free we are today." Are we free, or enslaved by our memory?'[2]

No place on earth documents the Shoah more meticulously, more horrifyingly, than Yad Vashem in Jerusalem. I spend a sunlit April morning plunged in the darkest past. In the Hall of Remembrance, where the State ceremony of commemoration takes place on Yom Ha-Shoah, the names of the death camps are carved in the stone floor, beneath which are buried ashes gathered from the camps. The walls are hewn of basalt boulders, supporting a roof shaped like a tent. Smoke from the eternal flame curls up to an opening in the centre of the roof. The only sound is that of birds singing outside.

It was in a Texas library that I learned the fate of my Uncle Shimen in Paris and the date on which his train left for Auschwitz. So far I have drawn a blank on my uncle in Belgium, about whom I know less than any other of my father's brothers. One of the most important buildings at Yad Vashem, the Hall of Names, houses a register of victims of the Shoah. This vast catalogue of the dead, containing over three million names, is not designed for easy reference, but eventually I settle down at a desk with a black leather-bound volume listing deported Belgian Jews whose name begin with R, and in it I find Ryczke, Lajb, born 18.4.06, Convoy No. 1/238, departed from the assembly camp of Malines on 4.8.42 – the date of the first deportations from Brussels. Next to him is listed Ryczke, Golda, presumably his wife, who left on the same date on a different convoy. Their precise destination is not given, but twenty-eight of the thirty-one convoys listed here ended in Auschwitz, Buchenwald or Ravensbrück.

April is not quite over. On an oppressively hot day, David picks me up and we drive to Holon, a suburb of Tel Aviv known for its vast cemetery. Like most Jewish burial grounds of modern times, it is a hideous place. No lilacs out of the dead land here. No trees of any kind, not even a hedge or a bush. The flat land stretches away as far as the eye can see, covered with thousands of modern marble monuments shimmering in the heat. I suppose that I, who have always had a secret longing to be buried by a yew tree in an English country churchyard, will be buried in a place like this.

From a distance I spot the memorial that far-flung Koniners have erected in memory of their murdered townsfolk: a tall, upright slab of black marble proclaiming in bold Hebrew letters KONIN; and below it, MAY IT BE RESTORED – not the town but the Beth Hamikdash, the Holy Temple, whose rebuilding work will mark the final redemption of the Jewish people. The outlined shape of an eternal lamp contains the word 'Yizkor'. Set at right-angles to the main memorial is a low white marble wall bearing the names of the *shtetlekh* in the region of Konin, including my father's birthplace, Golina. The wall supports six wrought-iron candlesticks, fashioned by a Konin blacksmith, Jacob Atzmon, who died in Israel. An urn buried below the memorial contains some bones and hair gathered from the mass graves in the forest of Kazimierz.

A number of Israeli Koniners lie buried close by: Haskel Ryczke, Tsvi Ozerowicz (brother of Sarah, the ex-partisan in Florida); Leo Monczka (former town councillor of Konin), and others I have never met but whose names and lives are now so familiar to me. Before leaving, I place a pebble on the Konin memorial, the traditional way of showing that someone has been and remembered.

How much more remembering can one take? It consumes each day, this compulsive preoccupation with the past, this fight against forgetting that gets in the way of living. Is it a quest or an escape? A mission or an evasion? Have I too become a slave to memory?

54

UNTIL NOW, talking to Koniners in Britain and America, I have not had to worry about language. They all speak, at varying levels of fluency, the language of their adopted land. My native tongue, not theirs, has been the key to the door of their Polish-Jewish past. In Israel, I can no longer depend on this. Here, Koniners had to learn Modern Hebrew in order to build a new life. I have never spoken Hebrew. But I have another key, misshapen and rusty, which might work. I shall try it now, speaking to Rivka, on Kibbutz Shefayim. The key is our *mameloshn* – the term by which Yiddish is affectionately known – our mother tongue. Thanks to my Konin *buba*, who lived with us for a while when I was a boy, my ear quickly attunes to Rivka's rapid flow. Listening to her, I experience an eerie sense of recognition: every nuance of her Yiddish is the same as my grandmother's. She speaks with the same local accent, the same regional bias in favour of German pronunciation and vocabulary. Maybe my own speech has something of that common denominator too, enabling her to make sense of my fumbling, ungrammatical sentences.

Yiddish gives our exchange a resonance, an emotional charge. It is not just the uniquely piquant flavour of the language itself. Rather it is that I am hearing about Jewish life in Konin in the language of the Jews who lived there for centuries: the language that she and her parents and my family spoke in their everyday lives. When she quotes a line of conversation from her childhood, something her mother or father said to her, I am hearing the actual words they spoke in their two rooms in Staszica Street. Her voice sends phrases winging into the past, and back come echoes from a lost world.

Rivka's home is a plain, one-storey house in the kibbutz grounds, but the interior, with its trim furnishings, marble-chip tiled floor and appliance-packed kitchen, speaks more of urban living. We could well be in an apartment block in Tel Aviv. It was not always like this. When she first came here in 1945, an illegal immigrant, not long out of Dachau, there was no running water, no sanitation.

Two of her Konin childhood friends in London had told me about Rivka Klapstein, married to Mordechai Bram, an irrigation engineer. Others had talked to me affectionately about her mother, Miriam, Konin's champion cake-maker. In New York I had met Rivka's tall brother, Sam – she still calls him Simcha. He showed me a fragile photograph of his family in Konin that he managed to keep with him throughout his years in the camps. Sam is a kosher butcher whose farewell gift I could hardly forget: two long salamis that he slipped into my coat pocket with a magician's sleight-of-hand.

At sixty-five, Rivka is one of the youngest of the Konin survivors. Small and cosily rounded, she wears a workaday short-sleeved frock that, when she is seated, does not quite cover her stocking tops rolled to just above the knees. My suspicion that her opaque dark glasses are worn partly as a means of concealment is borne out later: typhus contracted in one of the camps left her with a permanently damaged eye. When she arrived at her first concentration camp at the age of eighteen, she had long fair braids. A pair of German scissors snipped them off. Her short hair is now dyed black.

Uncrushed by her experiences, her laughter has an unforced jollity. Grief is concealed, like her bad eye. Less well suppressed is a nervy undercurrent: she is apprehensive at the prospect of talking about Konin and her childhood years. Her Konin roots, she says, go back four hundred years on her father's side. At one time the Klapsteins owned a wood mill and counted among the haute bourgeoisie. But by the time her father, Fishl, was born, the family fortunes had floundered. Rivka grew up in a home where every penny mattered. One is tempted to describe her background as poor, but to Rivka, being poor in Konin meant not being able to pay the rent, having no money for food or clothing, being dependent on charity. By these criteria, the Klapsteins were not poor.

Fishl Klapstein changed jobs at various stages in his life. At one time he worked for the horse-dealer Ancer, helping with the horses and collecting rents from Ancer's tenants. He did a bit of horse-trading on his own account and dealt in grain, but never ranked among the businessmen of the town. At home his sole luxury was a wind-up gramophone with a big horn and a collection of ten records, all of famous cantors like Sirota and Kusevitzky.[1] Rivka remembers their sonorous voices singing through the hissing and crackling of old 78s. 'People came to Father for lessons in singing the blessings. When that happened a girl was never allowed in the room. Not even my mother could enter.'

> My father wanted us to pray, to be *frum*. He wanted us to learn the Torah. I went to the *Bes Yaakov* for girls where I got a good grounding in the Bible and Torah. My mother wore a *sheytl* and went to the *mikve* every month, and once I reached a certain age I went with her. When I didn't want to go, my father beat me.

> The money we paid for the *mikve* could have bought me a seat in the cinema but my father would regard going to the cinema as a *shandeh* [something shameful]. It meant one was assimilated, that one was not a 'Jewish daughter'. A Jewish girl must always remain on the sidelines, must always be modest. My father used to beat Simcha because he was only interested in football. I once asked my father: 'Why do you pray?' and he gave me such a wallop! There was discipline in those days. When my parents came home from the synagogue, I kissed their hands. You had to show respect. We were four girls and three boys. In the morning we stood and said *Moyde ani* ['I give thanks unto Thee' – the first words of the morning prayer, said upon rising], and we prayed when we went to bed. Yes, it was an observant home.
>
> On Yom Kippur my father wore a white cotton robe, which was kept in a white silk bag my mother made for him. After she washed the robe, we weren't allowed to touch it, so that it should remain kosher. On the morning of the day before Yom Kippur he woke up all the children and we had to take our little prayer book and say a blessing before the ritual of *shlogn kapores*.

Shlogn is from German for 'beating'; *kapores* is from the same Hebrew root as *kippur*, atonement; the two words are the Yiddish term for an ancient custom dating back to Biblical times when sacrificial offerings were made on the eve of Yom Kippur. According to one commentator on the Jewish Festivals: 'It was already a widespread custom amongst the Jews of Babylonia in the tenth century [BCE] . . . The *kapores* ceremony is to be found not only among Jews, but among many peoples, for an old belief, a primitive conception that was common to most peoples, forms the basis of the custom. The belief is that it is possible to transfer illness, pain, or sin to a living thing or to a lifeless object, as, for instance, a stone or stick. The belief still persists among primitive and semi-civilized people.'[2]

Rivka and her young siblings living in Central Europe in the twentieth century participated in a ceremony that would have been perfectly familiar to their oriental forebears of three thousand years ago. The Poles living across the yard, glimpsing the scene through the window, might have thought it some bizarre form of Jewish black magic, thus confirming their suspicions that the Jews were in league with the Devil.

> Mother and father bought hens and roosters specially for the occasion, the hens for the girls, the roosters for the boys. [The comb, being red, was meant to be particularly efficacious in chasing away devils and evil spirits.] We had to bend down by our big table and when it was Simcha's turn to be blessed, father took a rooster, a live rooster, and waved it round his head three times, saying in Yiddish each time: '*Zay kapores! Zay kapores! Zay kapores!* [May you be the sacrifice of atonement!] – I can't remember the exact words. And then he said: '*Mir tsum leven, er tsum toyt!*' [Life for us, death to it!], and he threw the rooster under the table, where there was a huge commotion from the chickens. He did this for each child, even if they were not yet old enough to stand or sit up. When he was finished with everyone, he prayed. We children were kneeling all this time and impatient to get away. Inwardly, we were having a good laugh. What was this stupid activity, we wondered. It was like some rite carried out by savages in the jungle. Today I find it hard to believe that this went on.
>
> After he had finished, we collected all the birds and put them in wicker baskets. Simcha and I then carried them to the slaughterhouse near the synagogue, not very far away. There were two *shochtim* at work on that day, and there was a huge crowd. We felt sorry for the birds when they were slaughtered. They still twitched after they were dead. Simcha couldn't bear to see the blood and once he fainted.
>
> Afterwards, we gathered the fowls together and went home and helped mother pluck them. She lit a fire and scorched off what was left of the feathers and then she opened the chickens. I couldn't bear to look as she put her hand in and took out the entrails. I used to throw up, I just couldn't hold back. By the time Yom Kippur came round, the weather was already starting to turn cold. We had a wooden shelf outside our window and this is where mother used to keep the dishes of chicken when they were cooked. That was our refrigerator.

Why 'beating' *kapores*? One explanation given me is that it was traditional for some Jews to give the sacrificial bird a symbolic tap on the ground before it was slaughtered. I am told that when my

Sarna grandfather came to London he maintained the annual Yom Kippur custom of swinging a rooster round his head.

Today, many religious Jews give money to charity as a substitute for the sacrificial bird. A welcome change. There's a disquieting irony in the idea of Jews, who have suffered as scapegoats through so much of their history, seeking scapegoats, or even scapebirds, of their own.

The Jewish mother-figure, idolized and idealized, emerges in many of my Konin conversations. 'My mother,' says Rivka, 'was the most beautiful woman in Konin. There is no beauty on earth to compare with it.' I have heard about Mrs Klapstein's good nature but not about her exceptional beauty, but then it occurs to me that her daughter may not be thinking primarily of physical beauty. The Yiddish word for beautiful, *sheyn*, has an ethical connotation too. A *sheyner Yid* is a good Jew, not a good-looking Jew. In Yiddish, beauty is goodness, goodness beauty.

Miriam Klapstein was also a dedicated homemaker with a brilliant command of every domestic skill. Yiddish has a word for such a woman: she is a *balebosteh*. Mrs Klapstein made ingenious use of every scrap of food, every piece of fabric, keeping house and children spotless, going to bed only when she was no longer able to stand. She made cakes to order: four-layered tortes, chocolate cakes, honey cakes, ginger cakes, cakes flavoured with her own home-made wine, enriched with her own home-made cherry and blackberry preserves. Her reputation was unrivalled, enabling her to augment her husband's meagre earnings.

Rivka is carried away as she describes the delicious flavours, the mouth-watering fragrance of warm pastry that pervaded the kitchen when a big wedding order was under way. The Klapstein children lent a hand, even the little ones, helping to break the eggs, beat the white, mix the dough, whip the cream, and deliver the finished product to the customers. 'There was an enormous tray about a metre long with handles at each end. I held one end, Simcha the other, and we used to walk through the street to deliver the cake, which was covered with a white cloth. The cake was sprinkled with crumbs made from butter and sugar and milk. Quite a lot of these had disappeared by the time we delivered it! My mother used to decorate the wedding cake itself with a design of roses and, in Hebrew letters, the words *Mazeltov chosn-kalleh* [Congratulations to bride and groom].'

Miriam Klapstein's talent attracted Polish as well as Jewish customers. 'At Shavuoth Mother cooked *blintzes* made with sugar and filled with cheese or blackberries: we called them *shtolnikehs*. They had a *tam vi ganedn* [a taste of paradise]. People used to swoon at the sight of them. The Poles are great noshers and they used to come and order *shtolnikehs* from Mother.'

Her reputation as a *pâtissière* spread to the Mayor himself. He was an anti-Semite, says Rivka, but when he invited the mayors of the surrounding villages to a special civic reception, he and his guests stuffed themselves with strictly kosher cakes and pastries. In addition to baking at home, Miriam Klapstein used to help out at wedding parties, for which she was sometimes paid in kind: a sack of rice from the owner of a food store or a length of dress material from a cloth merchant.

> My mother worked hard. She was so clean, you could eat off the floor. We cleaned everything. We took out the beds, we burned naphtha to deal with bedbugs. She washed our heads every Thursday to make sure, God forbid, that we didn't have something in our hair. Yes, mother was a *balebosteh*. She knew some Torah but had no other education, yet she would sacrifice her life in order that we should be able to study – buy us writing books for school. Father prayed and prayed. She wanted only that we should not have as hard a life as she had, that one shouldn't have a child in one's belly every year. As long as I remember, my mother always seemed to be pregnant. She was pregnant when she went to Treblinka.
>
> Mother had eight children altogether, one died at birth. When women were in labour the children were usually sent to relatives or to neighbours. I was the eldest child at home so it was my job to go and fetch the midwife, a Jewish woman. I remember it as clearly as if it were today. Mother's bed was hung all around with sheets like a tent, so the children shouldn't observe what was going on if they came in, and perhaps so that no evil eye should see the child. Rich people had beautiful hand-embroidered hangings but we used just ordinary white bedsheets. A small red band was tied on the bed,

also to keep the evil eye away.

A few centuries earlier she would have had the Book of Genesis and a knife under her pillow to ward off the she-devils drawn to women in labour, such as Lilith, eager to harm the newborn, or Shivta, who broke the necks of infants as they emerged from the womb.

There was a big pan on the stove and the water was boiled and everything sterilized. After the midwife arrived, mother gave me two zlotys. She said that when the time came for the midwife to put the newborn child in to be washed, I should quickly put the two coins into the water. It was a custom, some *meshugeh* [crazy] idea.

When I slipped the two zlotys into the water, the midwife pretended she didn't see them. But by the time she had washed the child, they had vanished. If it was a boy, there was a huge fuss when the circumcision took place. The boy was put on a beautiful silk cushion which was part of my mother's dowry. Mother used to hang some words from the Torah on the wall which were taken down afterwards and put away for the next time. But if it was a girl, they didn't go in for all this hullabaloo. There was no show. They said: 'Ah! Another girl, another one!' Yes, among the religious it is like that. Only a boy matters.

The minute a girl was born, a mother started thinking about the *nadn*. She saved up every groshen she could. When a girl was born they straightaway made or bought a nice chest that had a lock and a picture painted on top. And over the years things were put in it – towels, bed linen, pillows, lengths of material for dresses . . . My mother did it for me and for my sisters. If she asked me to do something for her and I refused, she would say: 'I won't put anything into your dowry chest.' Or: 'If you don't get five for your homework' – the top mark at school was five – 'I won't put anything in.'

Even the poorest girl wanted a *nadn*, and my mother worked hard so that we should have one. My parents' marriage was an arranged one. My mother came from a very nice, respectable family, not rich, but father took her because she had a large *nadn*. That is what mother told us. Sometimes, if she was angry

> with him, she would say: '*Nu*, give me back the *nadn*.' She was a clever woman. She had patience and she understood him. She had only to look at him and she knew how to play her cards. Sometimes she told a white lie. She used to say: 'It won't hurt me and it won't hurt him.'

Rivka attended the Polish State school until she was fourteen. Did Polish girls ever visit her home? 'No, I was frightened of father.' Was she allowed to visit them? 'No.' Was this because he thought she might eat *treyf*? 'I ate *treyf* without him knowing. On Yom Kippur the Polish girls, who knew it was a holy fast day, used to bring me ham on bread. I was perhaps thirteen at the time and becoming a little bit assimilated.' To the point where she ate ham on the Day of Atonement? 'I was hungry. Mother and Father locked all the cupboards, but Simcha made a key. He was two years younger than me and a little rascal. He made a key and said to me: "Reginka" – at home they called me Reginka – "would you like to eat something?" I had already eaten the ham, so I said: "No, I'm scared." Simcha didn't know that I was full.'

I have been talking to Rivka in her sitting-room. Now I join her in the large kitchen, where she has gone to make us coffee. She is crying. Her voice quavers: 'You know, this is the first time I have talked about home. Before you came, I was so worried: I thought I wouldn't be able to talk about it. And now the memories are pouring out like a spring.'

Konin was a good town, she says. The young had a great social life. She praises the 'cultured Jewish youth', and the Jewish library, where she was a frequent visitor.

> I remember Natan Strykowski [now an old man whom I am to meet in Israel], who helped run the library as a volunteer. You had to pay a subscription but he knew there were children whose parents could not afford the library, so he took no money from them. I used to take four books out at a time and three days later go back for more. I loved *di shvester Brontë* – I read all their books – and Sherlock Holmes. I read the great Polish writers, the Russian writers. When I took a book back, he always asked me what it was about, so whenever I went back with a book I thought: 'What can I

> say to him that will impress him?' He stood there and I told him. It was a wonderful time. Yes, I had a happy childhood but my youth went in the war.

Rivka won a scholarship when she was fifteen, funded by the better-off members of the Jewish community, which enabled her to attend the Polish gymnasium. She was happy to be studying but felt ashamed to be accepting charity, guilty at not earning money that would help out at home. She left after one year. Unable to find employment, she earned a pittance coaching younger children.

The night air is fragrant when I leave. Rivka says I must come again so she can show me round. Her house is on the extreme edge of the kibbutz and through the trees I can see the headlamps of the traffic hurtling along the Tel Aviv–Haifa highway. Rivka hands me a carrier-bag bulging with oranges grown on the kibbutz. She thanks me, and I say I don't know why she keeps thanking me. 'Because I am back in Konin,' she says. She hugs me and kisses me on both cheeks. '*Du bist a bruder*' – You are a brother. '*Du bist a Koniner.*'

On my second visit, a few days later, I ask Rivka to tell me more about the *mikve.* There must have been a ritual bath in Konin from the time the Jews first settled there, as Jewish law forbids them to live in a place that does not have one. Even a synagogue may be sold in order to build a *mikve.* The last Rabbi of Konin, like his predecessors, would not marry a woman until she had been to the *mikve.* Marital relations, prohibited during menstruation, cannot be resumed until the wife has immersed herself at the end of her period. Yet the true purpose of the *mikve* is to cleanse the spirit, not the body.

The word *mikve* sets Rivka laughing. Perhaps there is a slight embarrassment at talking about menstruation, a subject she was never able to discuss with her mother, for all the closeness of their relationship.

> Never once. Sex was taboo. If I knew anything, it was only from older girls. Once my sister talked to me about it. When menstruation began, I thought I had cut myself. I was too embarrassed to ask my mother. Every month at the time of menstruation I used

to go with mother to the *mikve,* which was in a separate building next to the *shul.* I was twelve when I began going. I think it was twenty groshen per person. It does not sound a lot but it was to those who didn't have it. You took your own towels and paid when you went in. Near the door was a kind of kiosk with a window, like in a cinema, where you got a ticket. The *shammes* used to take the money. He would have liked to take the girls too! [Rivka rocks with laughter.] He was thirty or perhaps a bit older. You could also pay the *rebbetsn* [the Rabbi's wife, Mrs Lipschitz], and my mother preferred to put the money straight in her hand so she could keep it if she wanted to. She was a fine woman. In the *mikve* she wore a long skirt and a kind of brown kimono.

It was a big room with a high ceiling. The walls had little dividing partitions sticking out, where we undressed and put our clothes on benches. My mother took off her *sheytl.* Even rings had to be removed. There were brown leather sandals with wooden soles which you put on to stop you slipping. You took them off when you went into the water. The pool was maybe two by two and a half metres in size, so a number of women could go in at a time. [She laughs heartily.] It was like the Ganges, all a bit primitive.

In one of the walls there was a hole – a kind of small porthole window – and the *shammes* used to look through it at all the young girls. [Hilarity engulfs her again as she folds her arms across her bosom to show how the young girls covered their breasts.] He would yell through the hole: '*Nem arop di hent! Nem arop di hent!*' [Drop your hands! Drop your hands!] We understood. He was such a *zhulik* [rogue]! We used to laugh.

When you were in the water you said the *brokhe* [blessing] and then went in as far as you could, immersing the head. In the winter they warmed the water a little. The rich women did not go to the *mikve.* They went and had a bath at the *Elektrownia* [public baths at the power station]. It was used by gentiles as well as Jews but they still said they had been in the *mikve.*

In 1938, when I became seventeen, I said: 'I am not going any more.' I belonged at that time to the Chalutz Hatsa'ir [Zionist youth organization], where Motek Mysch was one of our instructors. My parents didn't know I used to go. The youngsters there were more assimilated, and they laughed at me for going to the *mikve*:

> I felt embarrassed. They said: 'You still go to the *mikve* with your mother! What are you, a young child?' When I said to them at home that I didn't want to go, my father beat me. My mother was a tolerant woman. She said: 'All right, don't go, but don't tell your father.' So he thought I still went.

Her mother colluded with her again when she left Konin in August 1939. Her father thought she was going to spend a few weeks with relatives in another town. Her mother knew that she and three young men from Chalutz Hatsa'ir were going on *hakhshara* [kibbutz training] in the town of Brest-Litovsk. A young cousin, Esther Lipschitz, one of the leaders of the Zionist youth in Konin, helped Rivka persuade her mother to let her go, the idea being that Rivka would eventually make her way to Palestine, join a kibbutz and have a better future.

'Esther talked to my mother because she knew my father would not agree, that he would say the only thing to do is pray, study the Torah, and eat kosher. Esther said to my mother: "Do you want your daughter to spend her life like you, cleaning and cooking?" I begged my mother to let me go and finally she agreed.' Miriam Klapstein spent the revenue from a year's baking on filling a huge valise with clothing for Rivka – 'I could hardly lift it.' On 20 August she said goodbye to her father and kissed his hand. Szwiatowicz, the cabbie, who lived in the same house as the Klapsteins, drove Rivka and her mother to the station in his droshky. Rivka left for Warsaw. She never saw her parents or Konin again.

Two weeks later, the German army occupied the town and advanced across Poland. Rivka, aged eighteen, found herself caught up with thousands of other refugees fleeing from the Germans. A long and perilous journey, much of it by foot, brought her to Vilna (today Vilnius); from there on to another Lithuanian town, Siauliai, where she met her future husband, Mordechai, who was also on the run. At one point he was arrested by the Gestapo and nearly shot. Both narrowly escaped being herded into a synagogue that the Germans packed with Jews and set alight. She and Mordechai spent three years in the ghetto at Kafkass, Lithuania. They married in 1942 and worked as slave labourers in an ammunitions factory.

Rivka launches into a detailed account of these horrific years. My time with her is precious. I want to concentrate on Konin. I ask her again to give me the main landmarks of her war years – the names of the camps she was in, when she was liberated, just basic facts. The request goes unheeded. The words pour out. She cannot stop. Her voice quickens, becomes more tremulous. She must tell me, she must.

> The Germans announced an order in the ghetto that until June 1943 children may be born, and after that it was not allowed. I was pregnant, in my fifth month, which meant that my child would be born after that date, so they took me and other women and removed the children from our wombs. The Germans were the gynaecologists. As long as I live I can never forget that trauma. Women died. We lay down and they cut open our bellies and took the living children from us. Mine was a little boy, already five months in my belly.

She takes me on a train journey, the passengers packed into cattle trucks, old and young, the sick, the blind, the dying, without food or water, a journey that ends at the death camp of Stutthof, about twenty miles from Danzig, where she sees the smoke of the crematoria chimneys and smells the stench of burning flesh. I hear about children torn from their mothers' arms, wives from husbands, the selections, the gnawing hunger, and I try again, gently, to move her off the subject. She stops and looks at me: 'Have you not got the time?' I cannot see the expression in her eyes, hidden behind the dark glasses, but I can tell she feels rebuffed. 'This is the first time I have talked about this to anyone. I must get it out of my system.' I am humbled.

> From Stutthof they took us by train to Landsberg.[3] I think it was July 1944. The commandant of our camp was an SS man called Vorster, a beast, who had been in charge of rounding up Jews in the ghettos: a man of power and terror. We left the train – about three thousand women – to enter the camp. He said that when we enter the camp we must not speak. He would shoot anyone who opened her mouth.
>
> I last saw my brother Simcha in 1938 when he was about to have his bar mitzvah. I had not seen him for five years. I did not know if he was alive or dead. I didn't think about him. The Germans did something to us that made us stop thinking.

We thought only about hunger. When you are hungry it is not the stomach that hurts but here [she touches her throat]. There is no worse pain in the world. It turns a person into an animal, a beast. We thought only of hunger. We did not think in a logical way.

But I go in and see this group of children and I go up to them and say in Polish: 'Perhaps there is someone here from Konin?' To this day I do not know why I did it because they could have shot me for speaking. That's all I said before we were moved on. Later, I was lining up for soup made from cabbage with white maggots, and a friend said: 'The SS are coming. I think they are looking for you because you spoke.'

I went into an empty barrack hut where we had bunks and I stood there trembling. After a while I see that all the others were coming back, including my friend. She shouted at me: 'Why did you have to speak? Are you mad?' Then we heard them coming, the sound of their boots – a sound I shall never forget. The door of the hut was flung open, and a young SS officer stands there. He walks through and we all sit like stones.

He asked: 'Who was it that spoke?' From behind I felt people pushing me, pushing me. He said: 'If you do not tell me within one second who it was, we shall burn you all.' What was I to do? I stepped forward and said in German: 'It was I who spoke.' He did not move towards me because he was frightened of touching me and infecting himself, because I was not a human. He said: 'Come outside!'

I go out and the SS man seems to disappear. I look over to another hut and there stands a tall young fellow dressed in prison stripes and he gives a cry – 'Reginka!' I fainted. Simcha had recognized my voice when I asked the children if any of them came from Konin.

He poured some water on me and I came to. He was holding my hand and he began to weep along with me. And now the SS officer was standing a bit away from us, and he did not come over. He saw that we were sitting and whispering. Simcha said: 'You can see that I am alive, but none of the family has survived.' I don't know what else he told me. He stood up to go but the SS officer came over and said to him: '*Nein, nein, wart ein Moment! Ich gib dir eine Stunde mit deiner Schwester*' –

No, no, wait a moment. I'm giving you one hour with your sister.

He went to the hut from which I had come out, opened the door, and everyone in there thought he was about to shoot me. There was a great cry and commotion. Everyone was driven out of the hut, and he came over to us and said to Simcha: 'Go in there with your sister.' I went into the deserted hut with him. We sat down and we began to recount things to each other. The two of us together, alone at such a dreadful time.

Simcha told me that they took our parents to Treblinka. He had stayed in Lodz and been taken as a personal servant by an SS officer – the same officer who had come in and asked who had spoken. He liked Simcha, who cleaned for him, cooked, did whatever work was needed. He came from an aristocratic family and had some royal connection. Simcha had been with him all these years, in all the camps, perhaps eight camps. He went everywhere with that German. He was a murderer who had organized atrocities against the Jews, but he had trust in Simcha. He was scared of being poisoned and trusted only Simcha. When someone else did the cooking, Simcha tasted it first to make sure.

Simcha said to me: 'If one day we are freed – perhaps it will happen – you must search for me and I will search for you.' And we both wept. We sat I don't know how long. And then the door opens and a new SS man comes in with two Kapos, a man and a woman, and they have on their shoulders two sacks. They dropped them to the ground and left. Simcha said: 'Don't touch it. It could be an explosive.' But we opened the sacks and inside were pieces of ham and bread, and other things: whatever you could imagine, it was there – all of it, you could say, soaked in Jewish blood: gold watches, diamonds, necklaces, a fur coat, a pair of women's boots. I was barefoot. From the day until I came here to the kibbutz I wore those boots: beautiful brown boots. They saved my life in the camp.

The SS officer sent the sacks. Why? Perhaps there was a crumb of humanity left in him, just a tiny morsel, and this played a part. To this day I do not know. Perhaps he was moved. Perhaps. Maybe. It sounds impossible. It is impossible. Simcha says: 'He was my officer and to me he was like an angel. To others he was a murderer.' *S'iz geven beshert* [it was fated]. Perhaps God listened. Perhaps it was the *skhus* of our parents. [There is a Jewish belief that heaven rewards us for the merit and good deeds of our forebears.] Since I was liberated I ask myself questions and I have no answers.

We were hungry and ate the food. We ate fruit with sugar. There were two spoons in a box, one for Simcha and one for me. We sat and talked until someone knocked at the door, and Simcha's SS officer walked in. I have forgotten his name. He is no longer alive. That Vorster, the commandant, killed him when we went on the death march. People saw it. Simcha's officer came into the hut and said to him: *Komm heraus. Das alles ist für deine Schwester*' [Come outside. All that is for your sister]. There were ten sewing kits with buttons and threads. There was everything, a brassiere, underwear, I don't know what else. Simcha and I kissed each other and I think he cried.

I remained alone in the hut with the sack. The woman Kapo came in – a German prisoner – and she began to hit me. 'What are you doing here? Everyone is busy at work. Get out! And make it fast!' I said: 'I have just been given this. Perhaps I can take it.' She said: 'What have you got here? Let me see.' She emptied the sack with the necklaces and jewellery, and she took everything, and left me with only a piece of bread and the pair of boots.

In April 1945 the American forces were approaching Munich. The Germans decided to evacuate the camps at Landsberg. The emaciated prisoners set out on a death march to Dachau, nearly 100 kilometres away. Thousands died on the way, overcome by hunger, cold and disease. Rivka's boots helped her survive. She reached Dachau. The Americans were still getting closer. The survivors set out on another march. More fell by the way, some sitting down in the road to die. On the night of 29 April, Rivka, one of a group of several hundred exhausted, starving women in rags, scarcely recognizable as humans, was trudging through a forest, escorted by SS guards with dogs.

> On this night there was a dreadful downpour, with thunder and lightning. It was as though the heavens were opening up, and the Germans grabbed their dogs, who were barking, and ran away, leaving us on our own. They knew the Americans were near. We lay in the forest and there was thunder and lightning. And when there was lightning you could see the whole woods. The scene reminded me of the Goethe poem about a father riding with his dying child through the forest at night. I learned it at school in Konin.

Rivka cannot remember the name of the poem. I can – not simply because 'Erlkönig' is a well-known Schubert *Lied*, but because I too learned the German lines as a child – from my mother, who learned it at school in Konin. I quote the opening words to Rivka, and she joins in, the two of us reciting the lines with their galloping rhythm – '*Wer reitet so spät durch Nacht und Wind?/Es ist der Vater mit seinem Kind.*' ['Who rides so late through night and wind?/It is a father with his child.'] 'Yes! Yes! Yes!' she says excitedly. 'I learned it at school in Konin.'

> It was a fearful night. We lay in the forest and prayed, yes, we prayed. We wanted to clasp each other. I was lying on the ground. When I was a child I used to read the works of Karl May, and when his characters wanted to know if the Red Indians were approaching, they used to press their ears to the ground and listen. In the forest, in the most ghastly moment of one's life – because one was hanging on to life minute by minute – I thought of such a thing! I put my ear to the ground and I hear things moving. The earth is reverberating, I think: either the ground is shaking under us and will open up and swallow us, or the Germans are coming with tanks and machine-guns. What was one to do? There was a terrifying flash of lightning and we see tanks with men. All of us are lying on the ground. Afterwards, so someone told me, the men thought we were animals in the forest, animals of a kind they had never seen before.
>
> We are lying there and we hear speech, and what we hear is not German. A Dutch woman doctor lying next to me says: 'I think I hear English.' She lifts her head and I push it down. She says: 'No, no,' these are not Germans. And another madness seizes us, and I start to cry: '*Shema Yisrael . . .*' ['Hear Oh Israel,

> the Lord our God the Lord is One.'] We see the soldiers running towards us. They see that we are unarmed, that we have nothing. We begin to stand up and hysteria overwhelms me. Someone ran to me and I was in such a state of ecstasy that I had froth on my lips and they thought I had epilepsy. A soldier runs up to me and wipes my mouth and he says in Yiddish: '*Shush, ikh bin a Yid*. There are Jewish soldiers here and I am a Rabbi, an American.'

Rivka stops, overwrought, takes a deep breath and exhales a long sigh: '*Oyyyyyyy!* So much for a person to endure. I had to tell you about this. I have not told it to anyone before.'

The car bounces over the ridges of the freshly ploughed field, disturbing a flock of birds. The translucent edges of their wings catch the sun as they rise into the postcard-blue sky. Daisies and wild hyacinths border the edge of the field. A nearby orange grove in blossom fills the air with fragrance. 'There were wild fig trees growing everywhere when we first came here,' says Rivka.

Her husband, Mordechai, points over to the left: below us, the sea comes into view, stretching to the horizon, a heart-stopping vision of the Mediterranean. 'All this is mine,' says Rivka with an amused proprietorial gesture. Their home is a few minutes away, yet here the striped earth is the only sign of man's presence. There is a feeling of untouched natural beauty rare in this part of Israel, where so much is new and where nearly everything new is ugly. Here by the edge of the sea on this perfect spring day the Land is how it ought to be. This is the Eretz Yisrael that Rivka and her young friends dreamed about when they sang their songs of Zion on winter nights in Konin.

We leave the field and drive down a winding, poppy-strewn track that takes us through a small sandy ravine and straight onto the beach. A man fishing in the distance is the only person in sight. I try not to see the plastic detritus lining the shore. Rivka has brought me to this spot for a reason. The brim of her cotton sun-hat flaps like a sail as she leads me towards the water's edge, where the sea gently laps the smooth sand. 'This is the exact spot where we came ashore.'

We stand looking out to sea. She and Mordechai describe how

they and 170 other illegal immigrants, all survivors of the Shoah, arrived here on a small Italian ship, how they nearly sank off the coast of Greece, how they evaded British patrol boats at night on the last stretch of the voyage and dropped anchor here, where members of the *Palmach*, the striking arm of the *Haganah*,[4] were waiting in the dark and came out in rowing-boats to ferry them ashore. This is where she, a woman of twenty-four, not long out of Dachau, landed with Mordechai on 19 September 1945, here at Kibbutz Shefayim, where they were to spend the rest of their lives.

'I kissed the earth when I arrived. I wanted to remain alive if only to tell someone what happened. Now, at last, I have told you. And now I feel so much lighter.' She touches the back of her head. 'I have had a pressure here for a long time. It was so bad I went to see a doctor about it but he could not help me. It's been a terrible pain, here at the back of my head, a tight, tight pressure which I've had for years. And now the pain has gone! It has gone!'

I ask her why she has remaind silent until now. 'The Konin *landslayt* are busy, they've got their own problems and some of them don't want to talk about these things. As for the people on the kibbutz, some of them said: "You went to the slaughter like a herd of cows." They couldn't understand how it had happened; those who had not been through it – people with faces bronzed from working in the sun. They looked at us, with our white faces, and somehow they could not understand.'

She has three grown-up children: has she never told them? 'I was frightened that if I told them they would perhaps suffer on account of what I went through. I didn't want my problems to become theirs. I did not want to tell them of these terrible things.'

We agree to meet again soon for a third and final talk, but I am not allowed to depart without more gifts. My protests are ignored as she thrusts a carrier bag into my hand containing a box of matzos and a large cylindrical white cheese of her own making. She hands me a tiny plastic lapel badge, in the form of three Hebrew letters on the end of a pin. The letters spell the word *zkhor*. From the same root as *yizkor*, it is the Hebrew imperative: Remember!

A week later I am standing by the side of the Tel Aviv–Haifa highway. The bus has driven off, melting into a mirage in the wavering heat rising from the roadway. The concrete bus-shelter stands alone, the traffic roaring past. Grateful for the six inches of shadow at the back of the shelter, I wait for Rivka. Across the road I see a white cotton hat bobbing in and out among the kibbutz trees. Then she appears next to me, having crossed the road through an underpass. She hands me a perfect pink rose she had just cut.

Inside her cool house we chat about her early years on the kibbutz when she and Mordechai lived in a primitive hut. We talk about the links that join us to Konin and to each other. My cousin Felunia, who died a few months ago in Tel Aviv, was a close friend of Rivka as well as a fellow Koniner. Rivka has heard a lot about my parents and their attachment to the English ritual of 'four o'clock tea' – Felunia had given her an amusing account of it after visiting us in London.

We stroll slowly round the kibbutz, among trees and lawns. Shefayim lives off agriculture, light industry and tourists, though none of the latter are in evidence today. Sprinklers play on flower-beds surrounding the guest houses and public rooms. Unable to suppress her pride, she shows me the vast dining-hall which can seat hundreds of visitors. Here, from one of the tables, she snaffles two peaches for me. We walk around Shefayim's main tourist attraction: a complex of outdoor swimming-pools, water slides and jacuzzis worthy of southern California.

'These are my riches, all mine,' she says, her arms flung wide to take in the gleaming blue pools around us. 'And yet,' she adds, 'I cannot afford to go to Konin.' Would she like to go? 'Yes. I want with my whole heart to see the town where I was born, to tread on that earth. I know the whole of Poland is a cemetery but I want to see Konin before I die. My children want me to go. They want to buy me a ticket.' She talks about her childhood again, about her home in Staszica Street and her lost parents and family. She clasps her hands in front of her: 'I want to cry.' She lifts her dark glasses to wipe her eyes. She looks up. I catch a brief glimpse of her eyes – the colour of the sky – before the black shields come down again.

We stroll across dappled lawns in the late afternoon sunlight, pausing to admire the trees – fig, lemon, grapefruit, pecan. 'It is so beautiful. In the morning I stand and stare and consume the beauty here, see what God created.' I remind her that she does not believe in God. 'No, but there is a force that guides the world, there is a power. In the morning, I just stand here and breathe in the smell of these trees, and if I have any upsets during the day, I say I don't care. I smelled the trees, and I remember that.' On a sudden impulse she hugs me. Her affection is neither theatrical nor sentimental, simply too plentiful to be contained.

She accompanies me to the bus-stop, holding a plastic bag filled with farewell gifts. The two peaches have become six. There are chocolates and biscuits, and one of Rivka's home-made cheeses for my aunt Freda, who was once kind to her. We wait for the bus. The sun has dropped low in the sky and the heat of the day is draining away. The bus arrives in a swirl of dust and takes me back to Tel Aviv.

Postscript In May 1993 Rivka accompanied a group of children from her kibbutz on a visit to Poland. After paying homage to her parents' memory at Treblinka, she made a detour to Konin. The house where she lived was still there: 'I remember the yard being full of life with the sound of laughter and the crying of children, and now all was so still.' The grandson of her former Polish neighbour appeared: 'He was amazed on hearing my name. His grandmother, before her death, had told him about us and about that terrible night when the whole family was taken to the transports. She could hear the screaming and the weeping till the moment of her death . . . My throat felt choked; I burst into tears and all the girls and boys with me cried too. It was terrible and yet there was something comforting in all of us crying together . . . I lit a candle and prayed for the souls of my family, the Klapsteins.'

55

ISRAELI KONINERS to whom I mentioned his name branded him a *farbrenter Komunist*. The Yiddish adjective inimitably conveys fiery and irredeemable fanaticism. Zalman Bayrach, born in Konin during the First World War, makes no bones about his entrenched views when we meet in the spring of 1988, the time of Mikhail

Gorbachev's *Glasnost* and *Perestroika*, and a thaw in the Cold War. Zalman is an unreconstructed Communist of the old school, in favour of Gorbachev's loosening of the system but unwilling to condemn the totalitarian past. Like the Communist undergraduates I knew at the London School of Economics, he is a starry-eyed admirer of the Soviet Union and the People's Republics of Eastern Europe. Communism has achieved the society he longed for, classless and caring, a paradigm for all mankind.

Marxist terminology pours forth as Zalman lectures me on the class war, the exploitation of the proletariat, and the evils of imperialism, capitalism and the *bourgeoisie*. Questions are brushed aside. The gulags? Exaggerated stories. Stalin's bloody reign? He did not murder people. The plight of the Jewish refuseniks? Soviet Jews are free to learn Hebrew, Yiddish, anything they like. Shcharansky? A CIA agent. The Solidarity strikes in Poland? American-sponsored. Pointless to argue.

We converse in English, he seizing the opportunity to 'brush up' the language he learned as a soldier in the British army during the Second World War. His mother tongue in Konin was Yiddish; today his everyday language is Hebrew. He left school at an early age and has spent the rest of his life making up for it. He expresses his thoughts and theories with voluble force, supporting his arguments with references to Galileo, Darwin, Gorky and Oliver Cromwell.

Zalman is short and stocky. Elderly is not a word that suits him, despite his age. A well-rounded paunch bulges beneath his shirt but his body retains an aura of muscular strength. He worked as a welder until about six years ago. Kitty, his nimble and intelligent wife, grew up in Paris and spent the war years interned in a camp in France. She speaks a precise Parisian French and manages quite well in English. Obliged as I am to stumble now and then from English to Yiddish to French, I hear myself, at one point, asking in quick succession: 'Why? *Farvos? Pourquoi?*'

The Bayrachs occupy an unshowy apartment in a typical cream-coloured Tel Aviv apartment building. On each of my three visits they press their hospitality on me, reluctant to take a no when I cannot accept their invitation to stay for a meal, offering delectable cuisine and excellent wine (a rare treat in Israeli homes) when I say yes. Others make me feel like a *landsman*. They treat me like a comrade.

I discover that Zalman and Motek Mysch are first cousins. Their mothers were sisters. I am talking, in fact, to the son of Chana-Rivka, whom I learned about in Brooklyn – the good-hearted soul forever running to the cemetery to plead with the dead. Zalman, like Motek, describes his mother as a 'saintly woman'. She raised money for widows, attended the funerals of the poor, and dispatched saucepans of soup to the mourners' homes – transported by her young son Zalman. She regularly visited the sick, an efficacious *mitzve* according to the Jewish sages, who tell us that an individual performing this duty removes one sixtieth of the sufferer's illness. If this is so, Chana-Rivka contributed hugely to the general health of the community.

Zalman remembers his mother's visits to the cemetery, prostrating herself, imploring the dead to have a word in God's ear. 'My mother would say to Him: "May Motek have a fine bride, may his sisters have a good bridegroom, may they all make a living . . ." ' I recall Motek's affectionate imitation of his aunt's Yiddish supplications. His son tells me she was ill in health but always optimistic in spirit. Zalman dotes on her memory.

The Bayrach family lived in the Jewish quarter, in Slowackiego Street, which ran between the Tepper Marik and the river. Zalman names some of their neighbours – the affluent Chmelniks, the Piekarczyks, whose children spoke Polish and went on to university, the Horonchiks,[1] so well heeled they could afford to go to Vienna for medical treatment; and, just round the corner, on the river, Moishe Kaplan, the squire of Glinka.

Zalman's father was a cap-maker, who worked all hours trying to support the family. His mother ran a small grocery. They and their two sons and three daughters lived in two rooms and a kitchen at the back of the shop. When I suggest to Zalman that his parents were typical of Konin's Jewish *petite bourgeoisie*, it is too much for his Marxist sensibilities: 'I would not classify my family as *petit bourgeois*,' he insists, overlooking the fact that the *petit bourgeois* can be poor too.

In truth, his family was not exactly poor, as he himself admits. He says there was an infallible test for judging whether you were poor: 'We ate butter on our bread. Poor people ate dry bread. We had fish for *shabbes*. They did not. You understand the difference? When I went to *cheder* my mother packed me a roll with butter, while other boys had nothing; so sometimes they pinched mine or I had to divide with them. If you could afford butter, you were rich. I remember once we needed a *nadn* for my oldest sister when she was twenty-five. But we have no money for a *nadn*. To marry a merchant, you have to pay for it. So you must have money. My sister didn't get married. When Hitler comes in 1939 she was thirty-one and not married. She was a beautiful girl.'

He shows me a family photograph taken in 1921. No need for me to consult the stamp on the back to know it was the work of Konin's leading photographer, the Pole, Pecherski. I recognize his style and props, his visual tricks for upwardly mobilizing the social status of his sitters. He has placed a rolled-up document in the cap-maker's hand, much as an eighteenth-century English painter might depict his patron holding an architect's drawing of the stately home glimpsed in the distant parkland. A little *cheder* boy of five, whose leisure activity is kicking a pebble round the yard, stands in the centre of the group, holding a riding crop. The young master is Zalman.

The family group, whatever Zalman might say, has an appearance of comfortable *bourgeois* respectability. The photograph is meant to reassure, perhaps impress, the recipients: family in Palestine, America and other faraway places. In their best clothes and best footwear, they look more prosperous than they really are. Their faces, their figures give no hint of the reality behind the pose.

> My father's name was Yitzhak – Isaac. The kitchen was his workshop. He had his sewing-machine over here, and my mother cooked over there. It was a large room. My father specialized in caps, all kinds of caps, caps for the army, for the police, winter caps made of fur. He did not make Chasidic caps – that was a different speciality. People used to say that Isaac Bayrach was a good *hitlmakher* [cap-maker]. He was working very hard. He goes to Lodz twice a year to buy cloth for the caps. He comes back and he puts it on the kitchen table. In September he buys a lot, for the whole winter.
>
> Like many Jews in Konin, he went to sell in markets, in Konin and in the villages and *shtetlekh* near Konin. In the 1930s, when fascism grew, the market place gave anti-Semites a good opportunity for agitation, but we carried on.

The farmers came to buy caps for themselves and their children. As a young boy I used to go with him. We go from home at about two o'clock in the morning. There were usually three, four or more wagons – all small traders – travelling in convoy. The traders shared the wagons, which were loaded with all kinds of goods – shoes, suits, cloth, caps, gloves, *galanteria*. We went twenty, thirty kilometres and if I will tell you exactly how the scene looked, you will think it comes from another world – the world of Sholem Aleichem.

I remember one frosty winter night when we were travelling through thick forest. The horses were going slowly, step by step, and we were all sleepy. The wind was whistling and I had childish fantasies of bandits and robbers. Suddenly, some thieves jump on the last wagon in the convoy. Off the back of the wagon they pull a bundle of merchandise and it falls to the ground. But the bundle was a passenger wrapped up and fast asleep. The 'bundle' woke up and began yelling. The thieves ran away – they thought it was a ghost.

We used to arrive at the market at seven in the morning. You have to get there early to get a good place. When it was wintertime and there was frost and snow, we were wearing a coat and on top of that another coat and still another coat. In one of these little towns was a *bes-medresh* where they had a warm stove. All the Jewish merchants went in there. It was dark, very dark, and so you went in and found a little place to lie down and – [he makes a snoring sound] – until it was day. In the dark I step on somebody and he shouts 'Ahhhhhhh!' Then I find a place and lie down and sleep.

In the market a customer comes to try a cap, then he goes to another seller, then to the third one, then he comes back to you and he starts to bargain with you – 'I will give you this.' 'No, I will let you have it for this.' When I was fifteen I was ashamed of it. I did not feel good. I disliked this system of living. All right, you can say: 'My father's life was the same, my grandfather's also, I will do the same, and so will my children.' But I did not want to be like this.

From selling caps you can't earn a living, but my mother's grocery shop was a system of living I didn't like either. If I tell you how hard my mother worked! For example, she used to make *challah* for the Jews to eat on *shabbes*. We had a baker opposite our house. His name was Bekker [Yiddish for baker] and he *was* a baker – *der shtimer bekker* we called him – the dumb baker – because there was something wrong with him and he couldn't speak. We make an arrangement with him so he allows us to use his wood oven.

My mother starts Thursday at noon. She takes flour, eggs, sugar, yeast and she makes a big dough. Late in the evening it was ready, so she wakes up both my sisters – one was eight years older than me, one five years older. They were rolling the dough and making the strips, and my mother did the plaiting. She was the specialist at plaiting, and so quick. This room with the big table was like a little factory. At eleven, twelve o'clock at night the girls finish their job and go back to bed. Then you have to wait till the dough rises.

At about one o'clock in the morning, we take a big metal tray and carry it across the street to the baker, and we wait. When he finishes baking his bread, the oven is ready for the *challahs*, which do not need so much heat. We wait and then we push the *challahs* in the oven. After about an hour we bring home the bread. When the oven is cold, the baker is left with charcoal, which he sells to the tailors, who use it in their pressing irons.

At seven o'clock on Friday morning our grocery opens and people come to buy. My mother has had about one hour's sleep. She has swollen legs from standing. Because she works day and night, we have a Polish woman who used to come in every day to clean and look after the children when they were small. I loved this woman very much. Every *shabbes* I went to her home and brought her a pot of coffee and Jewish cake which my mother sent her. My mother brought us up to help people. I remember as a child some poor Poles from a village near Konin used to buy at our grocery. They said: 'We have no money to pay.' So my mother said: 'Okay, bread I will give you without money, and when you have, you will pay back.' She had a big book for people who paid with credit.

She could not make a living just from making bread. She sold other things, for example, pickled herrings which she made, and pickled cucumber. My father heps with the cucumbers. We buy wooden barrels and repair them so they don't leak. In summertime, in June, there are one or two weeks when all the cucumbers come out. They ripen overnight in the fields. Then you buy cheap. You make an arrangement with the farmer and he brings a wagon with cucumbers. You buy them by the *shok*. A *shok* was sixty. I think it was a measure from old Tsarist Russia.

We have a little courtyard, where we clean the barrels, wash the cucumbers and put them in the barrels. You put in salt, water, garlic and also dill. When the barrel was filled with water it was very heavy. We rolled the barrels down a plank into our cellar and it stays there for several months. The cellar had an iron key about nine inches long.

In October we buy cabbage from the farmers. We had a hand machine – a *hubl*, a kind of plane, which fits over the open barrel. The *hubl* has a little box. You put the cabbage inside, and you move it back and forth, back and forth, so the cabbage is sliced and falls into the barrel. Then you have a big wooden stick and push it down to flatten the cabbage. I did it with my father – it is strong work. Then you put in salt, some apples, but no vinegar – just a little water, because the cabbage gives water.

In winter, when there are no fresh vegetables, a customer comes to buy a cucumber or some cabbage to make sour soup. Everything is preserved for the winter. The farmers dig a big hole in the ground, put in the potatoes and cover it. The same with carrots and beetroot. In the cellar we had a lot of straw where we kept onions and apples.

By government rules you were allowed to open the shop at seven in the morning and must close at seven in the evening. A good rule, but rules are not for Jews. If a customer wants to buy at eight o'clock at night, he goes to the door at the back. If a policeman catches you, you have a fine. The police knew this was going on. Some took bribes, some didn't.

I remember one Sunday morning a policeman comes to the back door and says: 'Okay I catch you, I have you.' My father was inside the shop with a customer. My mother quietly locks the door to the shop and says: 'My husband went away and took the key with him.' The policeman says: 'But somebody is inside there.' She says: 'There is nobody there.' Then my mother tells him: 'Maybe you want something to eat? A little fish?' You know, the Poles liked Jewish fish. He sits down, my mother gives him a plate with a *kop* fish [head of the fish] and he eats it. It was a bribe.

It is unbelievable how hard people worked at that time, and it got harder. We all helped our parents with their work as much as we could, and this was how a family lived so as to have a roll with butter, a little meat, and to eat fish on *shabbes* and look good in a photograph.

Isaac Bayrach prayed every day in the *bes-medresh*; his wife wore a *sheytl*. But the teenage Zalman, like others of his generation, rejected religion: 'A new culture, a new life, was coming from outside the home.'

My older brother and my sisters had friends who were moderate Jews, and I see how the young people live. I was not allowed to skate on *shabbes* like them, or go and collect chestnuts. As a little boy I have to go to *cheder* in the morning and in the afternoon. I go till seven o'clock in the evening, even in winter, with a candlestick in my hand because it was dark. I disliked it so much as a child, therefore I did not like my father because he forced me to go.

For a short time, when I was about eight or nine years old, my *melamed* was Benyumin Ryczke. He was handicapped a little, a little bent and he had something wrong with his leg. I was a little *mamzer* [literally, a bastard, but in this context a rascal], so I used to imitate how he walked. He had also something wrong with his hand. When he took out a little cigar, his hand was not steady, and when he put the cigarette case back, his hand missed the pocket and we all laughed. He did not hit me and I do not remember him having a *kanchik*. He was the best *rebbe* really, and I do not say this because he was your family. He told us religious jokes. He knew how to interest you. He was a clever man. I knew all his sons, and not one of them was religious.

When I was a little older, I was going to the State elementary school in the morning, and in the afternoon I have to go to the *cheder*. And this was a horrible time for me and for the others in the class. So one time I revolt. I said to my father: 'I don't want to go to the *cheder* any more.' My mother said: 'Don't go.' But my father said: 'You must go.' He took me by the hand – what can I do? – and he brings me to the *cheder*. I cried, I wept like a little child, I remember it. He opened the door of the *cheder* and said: 'Go in.'

The *rebbe* – it was not Benyumin Ryczke – said: 'Come in, my child' but I would not go in, and I cried and cried. Then my father said: 'Okay, if you don't want to go.' So I win. I win! I was joyful. My fight has come to an end. So I stop going to the *cheder*. I was eleven, already a rebel. When I was bar mitzvah I did not go to the synagogue. I ran away. I don't remember what I said to my father. I just ran away. He was angry. I didn't want all this religion. Today, of course, I am an atheist.

I start to eat on Yom Kippur when I was thirteen years old. I remember one Yom Kippur when the fathers were inside the synagogue, and the youngsters gathered outside. A fellow older than me gives me money and tells me: 'Go and bring us some *chazer* [pig] food.' I took the money and I bring it behind the synagogue, and they eat.

My mother found out that I eat on Yom Kippur, and that I eat pig meat. A neighbour saw me buy it and told her. I think I was sixteen when she said to me: 'You think I don't know you eat pig meat?' My face was getting red. I was ashamed. I didn't answer. I was very upset when she told me this because I had for my mother a very high respect. When I was fifteen, sixteen I begin to understand how she works for our existence. She said to me: 'I don't want you to bring it into the home.' My father did not know about it.

Zalman's first political affiliations were to the Zionist youth movement, Chalutz Hatsa'ir. He had friends who were Bundists and Communists but he was never tempted to join them. 'They wanted socialism in Poland. I also wanted socialism, but in Israel.'

His future in Konin, never bright, became even less promising during the anti-Semitic Thirties: 'Anti-Semitism was in the interests of the rich, the bourgeoisie, to divert the minds of the people. The priests said to the poor and unemployed: "Those who killed Jesus are responsible for your troubles." Religion is part of the political system. The government, the big capitalists, used the Church in their interests.'

Like other young, idealistic Zionists, he pinned his hopes on making *aliyah*. His elder brother, Pinchas, emigrated to Palestine in the early 1930s, and it was not long before Zalman decided to follow.

He left Konin in 1935 to spend nearly four years in other parts of Poland, training to be a kibbutznik. It was a suitably tough preparation for muscular Zionism: digging, ploughing, making bricks, working in an oil mill, building, sweating in the fields . . . In January 1939 he returned to Konin to say goodbye to his family. 'My mother wept. She told me: "I will not see you any more." Then I also wept. I said: "Mother, don't worry, we're going to build a *Yidishe medina* [Jewish land] for us all." '

In February 1939 he waded ashore at night, near Haifa, a kitbag slung over one shoulder. Another illegal Jewish immigrant had eluded the British. His brother, who earned a meagre living in Haifa, dissuaded him from joining a kibbutz. 'He told me he had a job for me and we have to send money to help our mother. He said he would get me identity papers.' A few days later, Zalman was summoned urgently to a hospital in Haifa. He got there to find his brother dead. Someone had shot him down in the street. No one saw the killer but it was assumed that a member of an Arab anti-Zionist group was responsible.

His brother's death changed Zalman's life and led him to become a Communist. His brother's widow, left with a young child, bravely fought a losing battle against poverty. There was no welfare safety net. The 'Jewish establishment', as he calls it, did not give her the support he thinks they should have done. He himself became a manual labourer, heaving sacks of coal, working in Haifa's refinery, running out of money for food when no work was to be had.

These experiences intensified his sympathy for the working class, for the helpless victims, as he saw it, of a heartless political system. He began to probe the subject of Arab-Jewish relations and ask himself why it was that Arabs and Jews were killing each other. He found an answer. British imperialism, and its old policy of divide and rule. 'When I came here I changed from being a leftwing Zionist. I found out that I was wrong, that it was impossible to make a socialist State together with the *bourgeoisie* because the *bourgeoisie* want to exploit me.' In 1940 Zalman joined the Communist Party in British Palestine. Later, among the committed comrades who made up his new circle of friends, he met Kitty, the girl he was to marry.

In 1942 he joined the British army as a volunteer, hoping to fight the Germans. The army decided he was to be a welder, which gave him his career when he was demobilized. After being in the ranks of the proletariat most of his life, he finally set up a small workshop of his own, employing an assistant. Was this not a class betrayal, I ask, a defection to the *petite bourgeoisie*? He takes my teasing in good part. His loyalties were and remain with the workers.

Some years ago he underwent several major operations, one of which failed. The Party flew him as their guest to Moscow, where another operation proved successful. What he saw in the Soviet Union – or rather, what he was shown – impressed him as it did Bernard Shaw, the Webbs, and others who visited the 'New Civilization' in the Thirties. 'The care they took over me was so touching it made me weep. I ask the professors in the hospital: "Why do you help me as if I am a king, a prince?" They say: "We do it for everybody." '

He and Kitty experienced war as soldiers in the Israeli army. Their three grown-up daughters have done military service. He believes Israel is in greater danger than its generals will admit: 'I wish for peace because we are a little nation among more than 150 million Arabs. Our generals say: "We are not afraid." But if we lose one fight, we shall lose everything.'

If the threat of war hangs over Israel, the blame, in his view, lies with Zionism: 'They say Zionism is a national movement of the Jewish people. It is not. Zionism today expresses the interests of the big magnates, the big capitalists, the multinationals.' He wants Israel to leave the occupied territories and go back to the 1967 borders. He feels shame at seeing Jews practise racial discrimination: 'Why can't an Arab live in Tel Aviv? Why does a qualified Arab engineer have to work as a labourer?'

He and Kitty are the only Israelis I have met who invite Arab friends to their home. ('Are you not afraid?' asked one horrified neighbour.) They, in turn, visit homes in Arab villages. Most of their Arab friends are Party comrades. Zalman reduces the complex problems that bedevil Middle East affairs to ideological terms of black and white. For all that, I find his absence of bitterness towards the people who killed his brother, his idealistic affirmation of friendship for his Arab neighbours, more attractive than the shrill hatred emanating from nationalist and religious extremists in both the Jewish and Arab camps.

When he speaks of prewar poverty in Poland, his sympathies are not confined exclusively to his fellow Jews. He talks of the plight of peasants trapped in poverty, forced to sell their last horse and cow, surrendering their sons to rich landowners as cheap labour, their daughters as skivvies. When he speaks about conditions under the Nazis, it is refreshing to hear a Jew speak of Polish as well as Jewish suffering: 'The Germans killed them, robbed them, destroyed their intelligentsia. Of course they had collaborators, but you cannot accuse a whole nation because of this. You cannot live with hatred.'

Most of Zalman's family died in the Shoah. After the war, a survivor who was deported from Konin with his mother told him how she spent most of the journey helping others. Another survivor – my cousin, Felunia – told Zalman that Chana-Rivka died in a mass shooting of Jews in 1942, the day Felunia was collecting berries in the woods.

About the future, Zalman is irrepressibly optimistic. For others, perhaps, Communism is the God that failed. His own millenarian vision, his belief in the perfectibility of human society, shines as brightly as ever. Though he may not live to see the day, the ideology he has espoused for forty-eight years will, he is sure, triumph in the end: 'My ideology is the brotherhood of man and peace among nations. It is a dream but it can be fulfilled.'

Postscript In the ensuing years, which witnessed the tearing down of the Berlin Wall, the break-up of the Soviet Union and its empire, the end of the Cold War, and the ugly eruption of nationalism in the Balkans, I have often thought of Zalman Bayrach and wondered what effect these events would have on his loyalties and hopes. I wrote to him more than once but, sadly, he never responded.

56

'THIS IS IN YEAR one thousand eight hundred forty-seven,' he translates ponderously, pausing while he gropes for the right English word. 'At the hour of nine in the morning there came to me er, er, a Jew, Leizer Piekarczyk, a *shuster*, which is er, er –' – I help him out – 'yes, a shoemaker, here in Konin, and he is thirty-two years, and in the presence of er, of er, witnesses, Shlomo and so on and so on, living in Konin, they showed me two children – er, er, how you call them? – yes, twins – who were born in Konin in this and this date, yes, 23rd March, and they told us his wife was Golde and so on, and they knew the children had been cir- cir- cir–' – 'circumcised?' – 'Yes, circumcised and after circumcised they received these names, the first Mordechai Piekarczyk and the second Hirsh Piekarczyk, and here is the grandfather and here the two witnesses.'

Alexander Piekarczyk, tall, gaunt and stern in demeanour, hands me the document recording the birth of his Konin ancestors. I catch sight of the signature of one of the witnesses: Abraham Karp. Genealogical threads reach back to 1847 and intertwine, connecting me to this stranger in Tel Aviv. I tell him that Abraham Karp was married to my great-aunt. This scrap of paper is evidence of our shared past. Mr P. is not in a listening vein. He launches straight into his next interminably slow sentence as though I had not spoken.

I am not given the chance to tell him that Abraham Karp connects me in the same way to another man with Konin ancestors, an Arizona-born Episcopalian named Barry Goldwater. Abraham Karp signed the birth certificate of the Senator's Jewish grandfather, Michael Goldwasser, in 1821.

Mr P.'s ancestral document turns out to be a copy. He got it from Salt Lake City, where the Mormons keep an international archive of family records. This leads Mr P., whose attitude so far has been somewhat distant, to insist that I am steering my researches in the wrong direction, that my time would be better spent with the Mormons than with him. In fact, he cannot understand why I want to talk to him. Yet I had written him a long letter explaining the purpose of our meeting. I try to explain again but Mr P. persists in droning on about the Mormons. I point out that archives are always there to be consulted whereas mortals are less easily reached once they are dead. My argument falls on deaf ears. He remains determinedly unsmiling, with the slightly authoritarian manner of someone who dislikes being even mildly contradicted. His brown eyes, unwavering beneath white bushy eyebrows, fix me with an intimidating stare.

My cousin David glances anxiously in my direction. He has accompanied me to act as my Hebrew interpreter, but Mr P. insists on speaking English, slowly, painfully slowly. Polish, not

Yiddish, was his language in Konin. Mr P.'s social manner, more stiffly formal than I have been used to, must owe something to his Polish background: his years at university in Warsaw, his life there as an architect, his service as an officer in the Polish army. Formality has always been a part of Polish life. Perhaps it is just that Mr P. is a naturally private person. However hard I try, I cannot get through to him.

He leaves the room to fetch something. I look round at his airy, uncluttered living room, the attractive paintings, the books on art and architecture. Mr P., as I discover in the course of our meetings, is in the habit of disappearing into another room whenever he wants to dig out a relic from his Konin past. I build up an image of a Konin archive tucked away in this other room, a hoard of treasures I shall never be allowed to see. I am tempted to probe, but caution – or cowardice? – holds me back. There is something daunting about Mr P.

He returns and shows us a Piekarczyk family tree dating back to 1815, which he has drawn with help from the Mormons. An asterisk beside names near the bottom of the tree denotes 'perished in the Holocaust' – his mother, two sisters and other close relatives. My host, I see with surprise, was born in 1909. He looks a good deal younger. Gradually, I manage to draw him away from Salt Lake City and coax him onto the road to Konin.

His father, Meyer, sold fishing-tackle. As an observant Jew and solid member of the community, he welcomed the establishment of the Jewish gymnasium in 1918 and had all five of his children educated at the school, with the help of reduced fees. He was a well-established middle-class shopkeeper, but as in the case of other Konin families, business declined as the twentieth century advanced.

At school, Leopold Infeld taught Alexander Piekarczyk physics. I open my copy of the Konin Memorial Book and turn to the gymnasium school photographs. He picks out the young Alexander, sitting cross-legged in the front row. Mr P. leaves the room again, obviously heading for the secret cave. Shall I follow him? Club him to the ground and make off with the spoil?

Mr P. comes back with part of his Konin collection: the school song, specially printed on thin card for a concert held on 30 March 1921 to raise money for a new school building. I know the words. I even know the tune: the partisan sang it for me in Florida. I desist from revealing this to Mr P. and reap my reward: as he recites the verses to me in Polish, the stern expression gives way to a smile; he laughs for the first time, perhaps amused by the naive optimism of the lyrics, perhaps rejuvenated by the memory of himself as a schoolboy.

He fetches a photograph album and shows me pictures taken in Konin when he was young: in his gymnasium cap, a family group, a snapshot taken on Kaplan's estate at Glinka: one of the two young women with him was the squire's daughter. The photograph that holds my attention longest shows Alexander sixty-four years ago, aged fifteen, standing beside an artist's easel with a hint of youthful vanity. He meets the camera's eye, holding his brush aloft as though about to apply the next stroke to the canvas. He has the bee-stung lips of adolescence. His cheeks have not lost their boyish plumpness.

I open my map of Konin to establish where he lived. It has become a map of families rather than streets, of men and women whose names I know, whose lives I have entered. It has acquired a sprinkling of dots, each dot on the map representing a family that was wiped off the map. Mr P.'s pencil comes down to stake out his presence on a bare patch of white. He and his family lived here, in a two-storey corner house in Slowackiego Street, which leads from the Tepper Marik down to the river. Aryeh-Leib the milkman, and his Bundist offspring lived in the same street, as did Zalman Bayrach. My map, for some reason, fails to impress Mr P. He has something better, he says. He goes off to the muniments room and returns with a large architectural drawing on squared paper, executed in the confident forehand of a professional. It is headed in Hebrew: THE HOME OF THE FAMILY PIEKARCZYK, KONIN.

It is a plan drawing, to scale, of the entire ground floor of No. 8 Slowackiego Street. The building was several centuries old, with walls over two feet thick. Originally a granary, it was built in the days when the Warta was a major waterway for transporting grain and other cargo. An arrow at the top of the drawing points in the direction of the river: '250 metres to the Warta'.

A wide passageway splits the ground floor in two, leading from the street to a large courtyard at the back in the style of an English coaching inn. The neighbour's apartment, to the left of the passageway, is depicted in bare outline only. The Piekarczyk home, to the right, is busy with detail: outside steps leading up to the kitchen door, steps leading down to a cellar, cellar grilles, doors embellished with a quarter circle to indicate which way they opened.

The drawing is scattered with circled numbers and letters, accompanied by a detailed key. Any architect, I suppose, would do much the same. What makes this drawing special is that Mr P. has drawn a bird's-eye view not merely of the rooms he knew as a boy but of their contents: tables and chairs, bedside cupboards, wardrobes, sofa, desk, tiled stoves, basins and jugs, garbage bin, mother's sewing-machine, even the wall clock above his parents' bed. Here, springing to life off the page, is the home of a typical Jewish middle-class family in Konin in the early decades of this century, probably as it was throughout most of the nineteenth century and even earlier.

The retired architect, back in his professional world, begins to look at ease for the first time. The pencil between his fingers is as comforting as a cigarette to a smoker. His quick, deft sketches reassure him that he has not lost his touch. Soon the discordant atmosphere evaporates. We are now talking unselfconsciously. He enjoys explaining an architectural drawing, I appreciate the information it yields. He is still reserved, protecting his private inner space, yet at the same time throwing open the doors of his Konin home and inviting me in to explore its every nook and cranny.

We follow the pencil tip through the door on Slowackiego Street into the front room, which was his father's shop. There are two counters and a small window for displaying fishing-rods and tackle. Among Mr Piekarczyk's important customers were the owners of big lakes near Konin who used to buy nets from him, hundreds of metres long, for commercial fishing. Filial pride, oddly touching in an old man, is undisguised as Mr P. draws one of the ingenious nets his father designed. The River Warta generated a steady supply of customers – from serious anglers demanding the finest imported fishing-rods to little boys buying a single hook.

Mr P.'s guiding pencil takes me on a tour of the living quarters: two rooms and a kitchen in which nine people cooked, ate, washed, sewed, slept, kept the books, did homework, prayed, played, celebrated and mourned. Each room opens straight into the next. A door at the back of the shop takes us into his grandmother's room. In the centre stands a large table with eight chairs: the whole family ate here on weekdays to make it easy to mind the shop. Four of the children slept in this room: 'My grandmother's bed was over here. I slept in this bed with my brother, Chaim. My two sisters, Zosha and Renia, shared the other bed.'

We go down a few steps into the next room, the kitchen, which has a door opening onto the courtyard: the entrance to the apartment. Mr P. points out the main features of the kitchen, including the maid's bed in one corner, and the place where the water barrels stood. Looking at the plan, I can follow the water-carrier's daily route: he enters from the street through a wicket gate – a detail the punctilious Mr P. has not overlooked – set into one of the heavy wooden gates; he walks through the shady passageway, crosses the courtyard, enters the kitchen on the right, unhitches the pails from his yoke and empties their contents into the barrels standing on the left near the cooking-range.

On his way out, the water-carrier might glance into the last and largest of the rooms, measuring about eight metres by five, the parental bedroom-cum-family-room-cum-salon. Two beds placed together stand at the far end of the room. A large sofa across the foot of the beds helps to screen them from the living area. The youngest child, Jozef, also slept in this room. A dining-table (its two flaps visible on the drawing) and eight chairs occupy the centre of the room. The children did their homework at this table. The family ate here on *shabbes* and festive occasions.

Mr P. points his pencil at one corner of the room, at a small, confined space to one side of the parental beds. For him as a boy this was personal territory of the utmost importance. To create an illusion of private enclosure, he would swing open one of the doors of a huge wardrobe to form a fourth wall. This space is where Mr P.'s easel stood, where he used to draw and paint. This, it says on the drawing, was 'Alexander's *Atelier*'. As he says the words, he laughs quietly to himself. The wardrobe door stands open in the drawing, affirming his private space.

We return to the kitchen and out into the courtyard. A dotted rectangle indicates the position of the *sukkah*, the tabernacle erected annually on the festival of Sukkot. It was shared by the four Jewish families who lived in the house. Mr P. points out a practical arrangement: the *sukkah* butted up against a window which became a serving hatch for hanging food through to the men seated in the *sukkah*. 'Here' – his pencil touches a spot just outside the window – 'here stood my father's chair.'

There are several outhouses, mostly storerooms where customers would come to choose goods. Also a chicken house, a garbage pit and, next to it, the two earth closets, each shared by two families. With the help of Mr P.'s scale, I calculate that going to the lavatory in the winter entailed a walk – run? – of about thirty-five feet each way across the courtyard to the freezing shack. A little further away, tucked between a warehouse and the chicken-run, is an unexpected facility: a '*pissoir*' in the form of a short section of fencing. Would not the backs of the men using it have been visible from the courtyard? 'Sure,' says Mr P. 'Like in Paris.' He breaks into a laugh.

It was only recently that he decide to dip into his Konin past and do a drawing, entirely from memory, of the home he last saw fifty-one years ago. How could he remember the dimensions after so long a time? 'I am an architect,' he replies. He knew the size of the beds – that was a useful starting-point. What motivated him to make the drawing? His reply contains no nostalgic sentimentality, only the practicalities one might expect from an architect. He found it an interesting example of 'how to solve ergonomics problems. Nowadays people want rooms and more rooms and more rooms. I made this for my son and my nephew to show how in Konin nine people have been living in this space. 'Just four days previously, at the Passover Seder, he had presented copies of the drawing to younger members of his family. If his motivation was more personal than he lets on, if he felt a need to record a past that was dear to him, he is not the sort of man who would admit it. Mr P.'s wife, a slender, quietly stylish woman, puts in a brief appearance. She sees the drawing on the table and says in perfectly pronounced English: 'Alexander did that for the next generation.'

It is time to leave. I ask if I might have a copy of the drawing and he goes off to get one from his Konin archives. We go down together in the lift, he to collect his morning mail. He grants my request for another meeting, but I can sense him starting to withdraw again into his private space. In the lobby, preoccupied with his envelopes, he gives us a mechanical '*Shalom, shalom,*' and we depart.

Our second meeting again starts on a stiff note. He agrees to let me photograph him but directs an icy stare at the lens. Mr P.'s appearance and officer-class manner, his departure from Konin at the age of seventeen for university and a professional career in Warsaw, might lead one to expect a Jew who assimilated easily into Polish society, or at least sought to assimilate. One would be wrong. The gymnasium, though almost entirely secular in its curriculum, enabled its pupils to keep their sense of Jewish identity. The staff was Jewish. The children came from homes that maintained Jewish traditions even if they were not strictly religious. The young Alexander mixed exclusively with Jews in and out of school. He remembers just one Polish boy with whom he used to play in the courtyard, but it never became a friendship.

It was at university in the late 1920s and early Thirties that he first encountered violent anti-Semitism. He saw gangs of nationalist Polish students setting upon Jews, driving them out of the classrooms and lecture halls. As chairman of a Jewish students' society, he protested to the authorities and organized physical resistance. His political allegiance was to the rightwing Revisionist movement, which believed in fighting back. Once, when he was on vacation in Konin and out walking with his father, a group of youths assaulted the old man. Mr P. fought them off. Whenever he filled in official forms he would categorize himself as a 'Jew of Polish extraction' rather than the more conventional reverse: 'This has been a reaction to anti-Semitism – to say: "We are here, we will not assimilate." The gentiles did not like Jews who wanted to be Poles.'

He was commanding an artillery battery in the Polish army when he was taken prisoner soon after the outbreak of the Second World War. He escaped, returned to Warsaw, rejoined the army and was recaptured. The rest of the war he spent as a lieutenant in a Polish officers' POW camp in Germany. When a small group of officers who were architects in civilian life formed a club of their own in the camp, they excluded him from membership. He was 'always aware of anti-Semitism' among his fellow officers.

He did not return to Konin after the war. He remained in Germany, acting for a time as a liaison officer with the US forces. American immigration papers could have been his for the asking. He chose to go to Israel: 'I think it is the only place for us.' Yet he has this to say for his native land: 'Poland has had anti-Semitic parties but they gave the possibility to Jews to live and develop as Jews, to live any place they liked, to make our own schools, to have our own theatre, to be Zionists, to study Hebrew, to emigrate to Palestine. There have been Jews in Parliament. Jews were allowed to make demonstrations. They did not arrest a Jew because he was a Jew, but they arrested a Pole because he was a Communist.' Given the chance, would he visit Konin today? 'I don't know.'

Mr P. is a better listener than I give him credit for. When I telephone him to ask if I may visit him again, I mention *en passant* my regret at not having a clear idea of the physical inter-relationship of the three main Jewish religious buildings in Konin. Now, at our last meeting, Mr P. places two architectural drawings on the table in so casual a fashion that for a moment I overlook their significance, not realizing at first that he has drawn them specially for me. Both are to scale. One is a plan of the buildings – the *shul*, the *bes-medresh* and *mikve*, a simple drawing that shows their siting at a glance. The other is a more detailed scale plan showing the full layout of the synagogue interior, of which no photograph exists.

He goes over the key features, identifying the four-pillared *bimah* in the centre, the steps near the entrance leading down to the main floor of the synagogue, and the steps leading up to the ark. The *aron kodesh*, the Holy Ark, is sited, as always, on the east wall. To one side of the Ark is the Rabbi's seat. He points out the two women's galleries, the windows, stairs . . . Narrow elongated rectangles represent the rows of wooden pews, marked off into individual places. His pencil point touches one of them – his father's seat. Mr P., who appears to have no particular religious leanings, has again relied on his memory and architectural skills to reconstruct an interior that was part of his distant youth. He gives me the two drawings. I express my gratitude but he plays down what he has done, behaving as though he has not heard my thanks.

My image of Mr P.'s undisclosed treasure hoard undergoes a change. It swelled into realms of fantasy while he was ungiving. It shrank once his response became more human. I back away now from asking if there is any Konin material he has not shown me, partly because I am still not entirely at ease with him, partly because I doubt that there is much else to reveal. In any case, a touch of superstition prevents me from pushing my luck too far.

Mr P. may not have given of himself, but he has handed me gifts from his past in a form no one else could offer. I just wish I had got to know him a little better.

57

I HAD MET Natan Biezunski briefly in Israel many years ago. He and my father's brother, Haskel, had been friends since *cheder* days in Konin. They both emigrated to Palestine in the Thirties. I remembered Natan as a tall, cultivated man, whose quiet probity reminded me of my father and his brother. Until I immersed myself in the Konin Memorial Book, I was unaware that he was the great-grandson of Tsvi Hirsh Biezunski, Rabbi of Konin from 1884 to 1905. I had lost touch with Natan, but when he hears my voice he knows instantly who I am. We meet a few days later in my aunt's flat, a place full of memories for him, recalling the years when his old Konin friend was alive. The two of us sit and talk under the gaze of Haskel's photograph.

Natan, approaching eighty but as upright and fresh-faced as I remember him, has busied himself since retirement with voluntary research work for an Israeli writers' organization. Like most of the Koniners who settled in Palestine between the wars, he is a secular Zionist and supporter of the Labour movement, a committed but totally irreligious Jew. Had I been asked to guess his educational background, I would have said he attended Konin's Jewish gymnasium and perhaps went on to university in Warsaw. I would have been wrong. He tells me he did not go to school at all. He was a Chasid's son whose formal education – some private lessons in mathematics apart – was entirely and narrowly religious, most of it received at the little *cheder* run by Benyumin Ryczke. He studied for three years in a *yeshiva* in Lodz, and had he stayed on the religious path, might well have become a Rabbi like his great-grandfather.

I lived with my grandmother, who was a widow. My grandfather, Natan – the Rabbi's son – died quite young. I am named after him. After finishing at *yeshiva*, he learned to be a *shoychet* but a few days after he started to be a *shoychet*, he came to his father and said he could not carry on. He could not bear to see the flowing of blood. So he stopped being a *shoychet*. Instead, he helped his father with his rabbinic duties, and carried on living the life of a Chasid. He went every day in the morning to the *mikve* for the ritual bath. Once, during a very hard winter, the *mikve* was frozen over. He broke the ice and went in. Three days later he died of pneumonia.

My grandfather did not leave much – a rich man he was not. So the community gave his widow the monopoly in selling *shabbes* candles, and yeast for making *challahs*. But of course this was not enough to support her two sons – one of them my father – and two daughters, so the children went to live with Rabbi Biezunski so that she could carry on with her candle business – big business! This was the life in Poland.

My father, Yehuda, married and went to live in Grodziec, a small *shtetl* south of Konin. He did not have to earn a living at first because he was *oyf kest*. If a *yeshiva* student married the daughter of a man with a bit of money, he took the new son-in-law into his home and gave him free accommodation and food so that he could study Torah all day and not worry about making a living. This is what they called *oyf kest*.

Then my mother's father bought him a little knitting factory in Kalisz – just as the First World War began. Kalisz was the first town in Poland to be burned by the Germans, and my father left. When he went back, he found his factory destroyed. He had kept there things which his grandfather, the Rabbi, had left him as an inheritance – the Rabbi's silk kaftan, his *shtrayml*, his official stamp as Rabbi of Konin, and twelve boxes of his books and manuscripts. To my father it did not matter so much that he lost the factory, that all he had left was the key to the door. What he could not get over was the loss of the books.

When I was old enough to go to *cheder*, I went to live with my grandmother in Konin. Being a great-grandson of Rabbi Tsvi Hirsh Biezunski was considered *yiches* [family pedigree, something to be proud of]. In today's world this [patting his jacket] is *yiches*.

Benyumin Ryczke taught me my bar mitzvah *drosheh* [Talmudic dissertation]. Today, a bar mitzvah boy reads a few words from a piece of paper, and thanks his mother and father. A boy from a Chasidic family like mine had to give a *drosheh* for maybe ten or fifteen minutes on a subject of *gemoreh*. It was in Yiddish and

Hebrew, and you could not look down at a piece of paper. You had to learn it by heart again and again until you knew every word. You had to give the *drosheh* for the men in the *shtibl*, and afterwards they discussed and debated it among themselves. Then you gave the same *drosheh* at home in the evening, after the end of *shabbes*.

When I came to Grodziec for my bar mitzvah, my parents invited the whole *shtetl* to come to our house and listen to my *drosheh*. What happened if one forgot a word? The moment your friends saw you were in difficulty, they started singing songs and became *freylekh* [merry]. When I was in the middle of my *droseh* at home, I could not think of a certain word, so the Chasidim started to sing and dance and that was the end of my *drosheh*.

I *davened* [prayed] every day in the *shtibl*, and of course we prayed with enthusiasm. There is a saying in Aramic: *Rakhmana liba ba'ay* – The All-merciful One wants your heart. He wants you to pray with feeling, with all your heart.

We studied every day except on Christmas Eve – *nitl*. On *nitl* we played cards. Why? Because if you studied the Torah on the night the *yemakhshemoynik* [one whose name should be blotted out] was born, it might have an influence on you, and so you had to be careful and not give him this chance. Whenever a Chasid found he was walking past a church he said in Hebrew: *shakets teshaktsenu* [It is an abhorrence].

I remember at *Pesach* I helped to bake the *shmureh* matzos. I and my father and other Chasidim put on our silk kaftans with a belt and we sang *Hallel* [Psalms] as we kneaded the dough: 'From the rising of the sun until its going down may the Lord's name be praised.' We had to work in a rush because, God forbid, the dough might ferment and start to rise. Another half-minute and it could happen; so we had to work very quickly to reduce the risk of *chomets*.

When we look back on these things we can laugh or smile and say it was a naive life. But they believed in it, and they thought it was worth while to suffer, to go hungry, not to have money to buy shoes for your child so long as people could say about him: *Er vakst a Yid* – he is growing up a real Jew; this child was preserving the whole Jewish nation. And until Zionism came, this is what kept the Jews together in the Diaspora and kept *yioishkayt* alive. It was a way of keeping identity. If people did not keep themselves apart, there would be assimilation like in America today, where fifty per cent of young Jews are marrying non-Jews.

At *yeshiva* in Lodz *hot men gegesn teg* [literally – one ate days]. You know what that means? Most of the *yeshiva bokherim* came from poor parents, so the head of the *yeshiva* went to Jews in the town who were a bit richer and said: 'We have a *yeshiva bokher* – one day a week you must give him to eat.' And that is how we managed, eating a day here and a day there. My father had two relatives in Lodz, so I ate one *shabbes* with his relative and one *shabbes* with the other. On a weekday, if there was nowhere to eat – well, I fasted. I had nowhere to sleep when I came to Lodz but someone told me: 'There is a Chasid who has a business and he will let you sleep in the storeroom on a big table.' I went there to sleep the first night, and he locked me in with a huge key.

One day I got a letter from my father telling me that my mother is very, very ill, and they tell her she must go to Kalisz for an operation, and he does not know what to do. How can you go and have an operation without the advice of a *rebbe* [in this context, the head of a Chasidic sect]? There was big opposition then between the Gerer and Alexander dynasties, and we belonged to the Gerer Chasidim, but I needed a quick decision so I thought – Okay I'll go to the Alexander *rebbe* who was nearer. He was about seventeen or eighteen kilometres from Lodz and I had no money and it was winter.

Somehow I got there – it took a long time. A friend came with me and waited outside while I went in to get the *rebbe*'s advice. I told him: 'My mother is very ill and the doctors say she must be operated on, and my father asks what he should do.' The *rebbe* thought about it for a while and finally said: 'Whatever your father does, God will help him. The Lord of the universe always gives help.' And I went back to Lodz.

It was not his first taste of disillusionment. Doubt had begun to gnaw at his faith even during boyhood. He observed how boys from less religious families, such as the pupils of the Jewish gymnasium, spent their days and envied them their freedom. He longed to borrow books from the Jewish library but dared not incur the wrath of his religious mentors.

Natan's father would have liked him to become a Rabbi – 'He wanted someone in the family to continue *di goldene keyt*' [the golden chain]. In 1934, after finishing *yeshiva*, Natan found a job in a textile factory in Lodz, and a few months after that he joined the religious Zionist movement, Mizrachi. He prepared for *aliyah* and finally, in 1937, obtained an immigration certificate and left Poland for good. Zionism rather than Judaism had become his hope for the future of the Jewish people.

> The Chasidim said we must wait until the Messiah comes. There is a saying in Hebrew – 'We must not put pressure on God to send the Messiah before the time is right.' He will come, and until then we must wait. In the meantime came Treblinka. It is said that when the brother of the Gerer *rebbe* was led into the gas chambers and knew he was going to die, he called out for water. '*Wasser, Wasser, Wasser*.' Why water? So that he could wash his hands and say his last prayers, Vidki. The Shoah finally stopped me believing.

The Nazis shot Natan's brother. His three sisters died in Auschwitz shortly before the end of the war. An uncle, an aunt, several young cousins and other relatives died in a similar fashion. 'In the Cabbala there are words which mean that there are times when God is hiding away and does not see what is going on – not because he does not want to be there, but because it just happens to be a period of *hester ponim*, when he is not looking. Can you believe that God sometimes does not see, and in the meantime Hitler comes and kills all his people?'

Natan has brought along something to show me: a Hebrew manuscript in a stiff, worn binding, a Talmudic exposition written about 1878. It is the only surviving manuscript written by his great-grandfather, the Rabbi of Konin. His official stamp, in Russian, is on the first page. Natan, like his father, had assumed that all the Rabbi's books and writings had gone up in flames in 1914, but on a visit to Britain after the Second World War, Natan met a relative who showed him this manuscript. He had inherited it from his father in Cardiff, Rabbi Nathan Grunis. Now he wanted Natan to have it.

It is a much-travelled book – from Poland to Wales and from Wales to London and then across the Mediterranean to Israel. I open the book: the flowing Hebrew script has turned brown with age. My fingertips move lightly across the page and touch the Rabbi's hand.

Postscript Natan Biezunski died in Tel Aviv in March 1991.

58

WHERE ARE THE missing papers? Rotting in a cupboard, gathering dust in an attic? Destroyed? They have vanished and no one can tell me what happened to them. I lament their loss, but the Israeli Koniners are less bothered. The Memorial Book was published twenty years ago, and that was that. Why keep hunting for them as if they were the lost plays of Aeschylus?

To explain, I must go back to the early Sixties when the book committee wrote to Koniners in many parts of the world, appealing for memoirs, stories, information about their murdered kin, photographs, picture postcards, ephemera of any kind connected with the Jewish community's past. The response was slow, but finally the committee found itself with a great heap of material, some of which appeared in the book. I wanted to find that material, the handwritten bits of paper in English, Yiddish, Hebrew and Poland and, more important, the dozens of original and irreplaceable photographs. Some had been printed, but inferior block-making and printing had given them a fuzzy look on the page.

Knowing the way committees work, especially in Israel, I cannot believe that every contribution was conscientiously returned to its owner. I want to study the articles that were *not* published, some of which might be more illuminating than the editors realized. It seems logical, as a first step, to make contact with the man who edited the book, a professional – not from Konin – engaged to handle layout and production.[1] I learned that he died some years ago.

What about Tsvi Ozerowicz,[2] whose driving energy helped to produce the Memorial Book? He was no longer among the quick either, but his son might know something. His son has nothing but a vague memory of his father handing over some papers to another committee member. He is dead too; so I visit his elderly widow. Yes, she had found a heap of things to do with Konin after her husband's death – papers, letters and so forth – and she had put them all in a big sack and thrown them away.

Hopes rise again when I hear about the 'Konin cupboard'. It was at the headquarters and meeting place of the Association of Jews from Poland in Israel, where each individual *landsmanshaft* has its own cupboard. David, who has resigned himself to having no time to himself while I am in Israel and who, it must be said, is now himself bitten by the Konin bug, sets off to hunt for the key to the cupboard – and finds it. But the old Koniner in charge of the key has little idea what the cupboard contains as it has not been opened in a long time.

One evening David and I set out to investigate the contents of the cupboard. Up a shabby staircase to the first floor of a cheerless building containing a series of dreary meeting-rooms and an office marked SECRETARIAT, where an old man – the only soul in the place – sits writing at a desk, showing little interest in our presence. Without much trouble we find a row of grey metal lockers – the sort they have in gym changing-rooms. One of them is labelled KONIN in both Hebrew and Roman letters. We open the door with a tinny clang that echoes down the empty corridor.

Inside, on metal shelves, are little piles of stationery printed with the official name of the Konin society – *Irgun Yotsei Konin B'Yisrael* (Association of Konin Jews in Israel); an accounts ledger; orders for copies of the Memorial Book; some pencils, a collection of rubber stamps – Konin Jews share the East European passion for rubber stamps – and other odds and ends. There is an item of some pathos: a small, self-standing aluminium nameplate bearing the Hebrew word *HANHALAH* – MANAGEMENT. The society's officers and committee used to place this on their green baize-covered table at annual general meetings. It is not just the craving for status that is pathetic, but the fact that there no longer is a MANAGEMENT. I come away empty-handed save for a few sheets of official stationery that I cannot resist filching.

I visit the head of the Konin society, the 'Mr Konin' of Israel – Natan Ahykam, born in 1906. A retired customs official, he changed his name from Strykowski when he arrived in Israel after the Second World War.[3] He and his wife Sarah have prepared a vast array of gâteaux, biscuits, strawberries, nuts and other delicacies, which cover the entire surface of the table. They brush aside my exclamation at the delicious spread – had not my parents given *them* a wonderful reception when they visited London in the Fifties? I had no idea they knew my parents. Yes, they remember my parents well, how my mother had enthused about Polish literature, and how my father had talked proudly of his son.

I discover a more unexpected link – with my maternal grandfather, Simcha Sarna, who left Konin long before most of the Koniners I have met were born. Natan's father, Shmuel, and my grandfather had been the closest of friends. I take out my street map and mark with a dot yet another address where the Sarnas lived, ulica Zydowska (Jewish Street) near the Tepper Marik. Natan was a little boy when he last saw my grandfather, but he remembers the day, shortly before my grandfather left for London in 1913, when he visited the Strykowski family – perhaps to say goodbye. Natan showed him the new shoes his mother had just bought him. My grandfather admired them and said they were so beautiful that he would take them with him to London, at which the proud owner of the shoes burst into tears. It was some time before the little boy was persuaded that my grandfather was only joking, and wiped away his tears.

It is an anecdote of no consequence, telling me nothing new about my grandfather or his life in Konin, and yet hearing it causes a *frisson*. Could it be that it lends reality to a man I scarcely remember? I see him standing in the hallway of 70 Sidney Street when I was perhaps four years old, an image so ethereal that he appears in my mind's eye like a ghost, a transparent presence through whom I see the dark wallpaper and brown paintwork behind.

Simcha Sarna and Shmuel Strykowski were clearly of a similar mould. Both worshipped in the Chevre Shas, were pious men who knew their Talmud and Hebrew, but who despised fanaticism. Both wore European-style jackets rather than kaftans. Both embraced Zionism when the movement was in its infancy. Shmuel Strykowski's Zionist beliefs, his son tells me, once caused an uproar in the town. 'In 1919, on the fifteenth anniversary of Herzl's death, there was a talk in the *bes-medresh* about Zionism, and my father stood up and compared Herzl with Moses. Moses, he said, led the

Jews out of Egypt, and Herzl also wanted to bring out the Jews and take them to Eretz Yisrael. Can you imagine? To compare Herzl with *Moishe Rabeynu* [Moses our Teacher]! There was a big scandal and the Chasidim wouldn't let him talk further. To them, Herzl was an *apikoyres*' [a non-believing sceptic].

Natan reminisces about the Jewish library, on whose committee he served in his latter years, about the Jewish gymnasium, of which he was one of the first pupils, and about life in Konin before and after the Tsars. He left the town as a youth to study jurisprudence at Warsaw University, but there were few prospects for a Jewish lawyer at that time, and he returned to provincial Konin to help run the family business, selling iron materials and hardware. Here he remained, devoting most of his free time to the rightwing Zionist youth movement, Betar, until war broke out. In October 1939 he escaped from occupied Konin and crossed the River Bug into Russia, where he spent the war years. His elder brother, Mikhail, a veterinary surgeon, died fighting in a bunker in the Warsaw ghetto. His mother, sister and many other relatives died in the Shoah.

In 1950, two years after arriving in Israel, Natan and his fellow Koniners – those who had come to Palestine in the Thirties as well as survivors of the Shoah – formed a Konin *landsmanshaft*, to help those still lingering in Europe and the scarred survivors who came to Israel. They elected officers and a committee and Sub-committees and a council, all of which helped Israel's flourishing rubber-stamp industry. The first president was Leo Monczka. The society organized social gatherings, and collected donations from more prosperous Koniners in America, Canada and Britain. Some of the funds raised went to individual members as interest-free loans.

Another aim, of deeper emotional import, was to perpetuate the memory of the murdered Jews of Konin and the surrounding *shtetlekh*. In 1968 the members gathered for an emotional ceremony at a newly erected Konin memorial in Holon cemetery. Here, each year, between Rosh Hashanah and Yom Kippur, sixty to seventy members of the Society used to gather to say Kaddish.[4]

How stands the society today? 'There is no more a society,' replies Natan. His account of its decline parallels that of the Konin Society in New York: members becoming less interdependent, growing old and frail, and dying, until too few are left to sustain an organization. At one stage an attempt was made to recruit young members over the age of eighteen, the Israeli-born children of Konin parents, to carry on the society after the old-timers had gone. Few showed interest, and the scheme foundered.

'The last president of the society was Jacob Atzmon, and he died some years ago. Now there is no title of president. I do the work. We have a committee of three – myself, Bunim Bram and Mina Ryb – and we hold our meetings on the telephone.' Another Koniner, Leib Kleczewski, helps in various ways. The interest-free loans are down to five. Twice a year, on Pesach and Rosh Hashanah, the society continues the tradition of giving a little money to four old Koniners who are not well off. Members of the society, the few who are left, still pay an annual subscription but there is not much money left in the kitty. 'There is no future for the society, but if I live to be a hundred and twenty, I will carry on.'

The society's most ambitious undertaking was the publication of the Memorial Book. It took years to prepare and cost more than they had bargained for. Natan declines to talk about the squabbles and rivalries that marred its history, and the divided opinions about the end-result, especially the criticisms of those who resented the predominance of Yiddish, which made it a closed book to the younger generation. Now is not the time to rake over the past, he says. So where are the 'missing papers', the material that must have remained when the printers delivered their 320 copies of the book? Natan has no idea, and I can understand why this old and splendid man does not share my desire to read the unpublished papers and hold the original photographs taken in Konin in Tsarist times. He is weary and he has done his bit.

Postscript Natạn and I have kept in touch, and he wrote to tell me when his wife died after a long illness. The last Konin memorial gathering took place in 1991, by which time Natan had moved away from Tel Aviv. The committee's telephone conferences have ceased. Their final act was to give a needy Koniner the last two hundred shekels of the society's funds.

One day in March 1992 Natan received a call from the Israeli-born son of a Koniner to say he had some old papers and photographs that had been lying around his home for years. They were of no interest to him and he proposed throwing them away if Natan did not want them. Thinking of me, Natan asked him not to throw anything away: 'David Ryczke has a cousin in London who is writing a book about Konin. Hold on to the material a bit longer.'

He immediately called David, who was about to set off for the funeral of a dear friend. After the burial, David drove straight to the man's house. There he was shown a plain cardboard box, somewhat damp and slightly chewed by rodents. It had been lying for years in a backyard, under a canopy, exposed to winter cold, summer heat and field mice. The box was crammed with files and photographs. 'It's good you came for this stuff,' said the man. 'Another day and I would have thrown it out.' David took the box home and excitedly informed me of the find. Neither of us would trust the material to the mails, and in any case some of the contents of the box needed careful drying out and conservation, which David selflessly undertook.

I had to restrain my curiosity for a year until David came to London, bringing the material with him. We spent three days going through the haul. Not all the 'missing papers' were here, but enough to justify jubilation. Among the wads of Memorial Book page proofs were numerous photographs of Koniners long dead, of religious teachers and their pupils, of people I had met – Motek Mysch and his Zionist athletes – and of those whose names I would never know: Chasidim at the entrance to the *shtibl*, young Zionist hikers beside a haystack, the only original photograph I have come across of Konin's last Rabbi; pre-First World War picture postcards; a very old photograph of a football team wearing Maccabi badges, and one of the badges itself, sewn on faded silk; a sad postcard dated 1941 from the Ostrowiec ghetto; a tattered copy – surely the only one in existence – of the Jewish gymnasium's school newspaper, *Gazetka Szkolna* No. 1, dated 20 January 1921; a photograph of my father addressing a gathering of the Konin society in Israel in 1958.

There was a copy of a letter dated June 1967 from Jacob Sarna to Barry Goldwater, and an envelope from the Senator with a photocopy of his pre-publication cheque for a copy of the book; a photograph of Jews digging their own grave – beside the face of one of them someone has scrawled in ink the name of my uncle, Itsik Hirsh Ryczke; many letters, documents, faded ephemera – over three hundred items that had miraculously escaped destruction. Fragile survivors.

Part Five

RETURN TO KONIN

59

THE JEWS who left Konin for other lands before the First World War knew that the community they had left behind was still there, however changed, with its synagogue, *bes-medresh* and *shtibl*, its *cheders*, *chevres*, *mikve*, and the cemetery where their forebears were buried. Relatives and friends still crowded the Tepper Marik on market days, strolled in the park and across the river on Sabbath afternoons. In the East End of London and the Lower East Side of New York, in Jerusalem and Tel Aviv, the postman brought letters and postcards from relatives residing in the streets and houses they themselves had abandoned. Impending military service for the Tsar, economic travails, lack of opportunity, anti-Semitism, the lure of Zion – whatever the reason, they had left Konin of their own volition. With the passage of time, a rose tint began to colour their memories of the place where they had stayed only until they could afford the fare to leave it.

With a few exceptions, those earlier émigrés were not the Jews I met in the course of my quest, the ones who were living in Konin in September 1939. These were to leave the town under very different circumstances, and few would live to see it again. Not many of the survivors I met, happy with their status as citizens of Britain, the United States or Israel, expressed a desire to visit the town where they were born; most said they would not go even if they were paid. 'What for?' they asked. 'Who is left?' Even the graves of the dead could not be visited. Going back could give them nothing but heartache.

And so only a few chose to visit the town after it became *Judenrein* once again in the postwar years. Mark Natel went out from London in the early Sixties, hoping to trace a sister he thought might still be alive. For him, at least, there were Poles he wanted to meet again, old buddies from his Communist days with whom he used to share a Konin prison cell every May 1st, now honoured citizens of a town where the Red Flag flew and the word of Karl Marx was holy writ.

Teresa Franco, the London librarian, spent a few hours in the town in the Sixties, but her reason for being in Poland was to visit a sister in Warsaw rather than linger in the place where she had spent her childhood as Blumcha Zylberberg. Mendel Leben of Brooklyn went to Konin in 1986 with the sole purpose of obtaining some official papers and stayed as briefly as possible. Alone among the Koniners, Mike Jacobs – Mendel Jakubowicz – went back not just once but again and again, responding to some deep need that Texas could not satisfy, exceptional in his capacity for drawing pleasure as well as pain from walking the streets of his youth.

One day in the summer of 1988 I was talking to Izzy Hahn in London, milking his memory of prewar life in the town. I told him I had contacted and met all the Koniners I could trace – several dozen of them, in various countries – and now I was thinking of going to Konin myself, nervous at the prospect, not sure how to go about it, wondering how I would cope with the language difficulties in a provincial town unvisited by tourists. The Polish government travel office in London could provide me with an interpreter, but at an exorbitant fee. In any case, would a Pole who was himself a stranger to the town with no knowledge of its former Jewish life be the ideal guide?

'Tell yer what,' said Izzy cheerfully, 'I'll go with you.'

60

MOSCOW, Warsaw, Berlin, Frankfurt, Paris: the names on the platform signboard fired the imagination, stirring romantic images of great train journeys across Europe. Konin, one of the stops, did not rate a mention. The train was late – late enough to dissipate the romance.

Izzy last saw Konin in 1945. Liberated from camp in Czechoslovakia, he struggled home by train, horse and cart, and on foot: 'There weren't many trains and they were packed, with people lying anywhere they could.' Sometimes he climbed up the iron rungs at the end of the coach and stretched out flat on the roof amid the smoke and soot. 'We was young. We didn't know about danger.' What about luggage? 'Luggage? What you talking about! A jacket and a pair of trousers what we was wearing. No money. Nothing. Just me and my brother. The Red Cross kept us alive.' Now, forty-three years later, he was making another journey back to Konin, this time travelling First Class. Trousers knife-sharp creased, shirt immaculate, shoes polished, he looked as though fitted out in brand-new clothes.

Since our arrival in Warsaw the day before, he had wanted to prove to me and to himself that he had not forgotten the language he spoke as a boy. At every opportunity he struck up conversations with strangers, jubilant when the words came rushing back, as though he had never left Poland. Now, waiting on the platform for the Konin train, he began chatting to a cheerful young engineer who seemed equally keen to practise his English. He joined us when the train pulled in, and waved goodbye at the first stop: 'Have a good time in Poland!' We settled back in our comfortably upholstered compartment. The ticket collector came round. After he had gone, Izzy said: 'In 1945 all I needed to show them was this.' He pulled up his sleeve to reveal the bluish number on his skin.

The countryside unrolled, flat and boring, as we headed due west. No villages, churches, log cabins; instead, breezeblock barns with corrugated iron roofs, a few cows, and deserted fields. One lone combine harvester reminded Izzy of the peasants near Konin at harvest time, twenty of them, each holding a scythe, moving in line across the field. An hour away from Warsaw the afternoon sun vanished behind stormy clouds. The air grew heavy. My temples began throbbing insistently. The pressure had been there since breakfast, a tremulous apprehension, a fear knotting my stomach. And now, getting closer to Konin by the minute, I felt the knot tighten.

We had been on the train two hours. Another half-hour to go. I asked Izzy how he was feeling. I had forgotten his training in not feeling, or rather, in concealing feelings. He replied: 'Okay. I take things as they come. I would have feelings if there was someone there to meet me.' He tried to sound casual but his face, a healthy pink when we left London, had lost its colour, looked thinner.

The skies brightened again. The countryside improved. We passed an orchard laden with bright red apples. Flocks of white geese pecked at a green slope, a naive painting come to life. We raced past a tumbledown cottage with an unkempt thatched roof. Clumps of birch trees. A farmyard pond. Round, narrow haystacks with poles sticking out of the conical tops.

Izzy stared out of the window: 'Kolo next.' Kolo: another name from my childhood, a name without meaning to a small boy in London playing with his balsa-wood glider on a front room carpet while the adults reminisced about '*der heym*'. 'There it is! There's the station. Same as Konin.' The station flashed by, leaving a subliminal impression of Dutch gables painted green and white. Fifteen minutes later the train began to lose speed. Several bleak apartment blocks came into view, creeping closer to the railway line as the train continued to slow down. No sign of the old town.

Dirty grey clouds appeared, dimming the afternoon light. A storm seemed to hang once more in the air as we pulled into the station. The platform was on our left, as Izzy had predicted. 'You see, I told you!' he exclaimed. It was becoming one of his regular refrains. 'And there's the water tower over there. You see, I told you.' The train came to a halt at the far end of the platform. I looked through the window at the sign. Five letters filled my vision like a cinematic close-up: KONIN.

We hauled down our cases and looked around. 'The old station's gone,' he said, looking along the platform at a steel and glass building. As we left the station he pointed out other changes. 'There used to be large stone balls like globes on either side of wide steps. And there, over there, was a big circle with flowers where the droshkys used to wait.' His grandfather, Luzar Szwiatowicz, drove a droshky, ferrying passengers across the meadows between the old town and the station. This was the New Konin, the product of bureaucratic planning, designed without love, constructed without the resources, or possibly even the desire, for materials that would age with grace. We could see the old water tower more clearly now, the only remnant of prewar days, a neo-medieval folly, conjuring up images of châteaux and ramparts.

We joined a short queue at the taxi rank and stared at the line of freight wagons in the sidings nearby. Were we thinking the same thoughts? Was he remembering that his life in Konin ended at this station, that it was from here that he and his family were deported? He said: 'You see those small openings on the sides of the wagons. They used to put barbed wire across them.'

A kiosk with the sign *GALANTERIA* reminded me of Lola in New York, who once sold fancy goods in the old town. The kiosk was shut. Its 'gallantry', displayed behind a dusty pane, consisted of two tired blouses, two pairs of cheap sunglasses, some plastic broochs in the shape of bows, and one T-shirt stencilled PARADISE ISLES.

The hotel was only a minute away. In London, New York or any other big city the driver would have scowled at the shortness of the journey. Our genial cabbie did not seem to mind, partly due to Izzy's flair for winning over strangers. They talked away in Polish. I caught the words Szwiatowicz and droshky. Izzy was talking about his grandfather to someone who had not been born when the old boy last cracked his whip. We pulled up outside the hotel and the driver made an announcement in the manner of a tourist guide. Izzy translated: 'Here we are, Hotel Konin, Category Three Star.'

Hotel Konin had the put-up-cheap-and-fast look of a hotel on the Costa Brava. A pretty girl wearing a bright pink dress, pink Day-Glo ear-rings, pink lipstick and pink fingernails sat behind the reception counter in the deserted lobby. She welcomed us with that singularly Polish blend of charm and style.

Izzy and I squeezed into the tiny lift with our cases. My room was not much bigger than the lift, with scarcely enough space to open my case. A whiff of disinfectant drifted from the adjoining bathroom, which had a stained bath, a cistern operated by a piece of string, and army-issue toilet paper. But the room was clean, had the basic comforts and a phone. And it was very, very cheap. In any case, there was nowhere else to stay. The old town no longer had a hotel.

From my window on the seventh floor I looked out over new Konin. The international language of architectural banality divested it of any local character. A large illuminated sign, ALUMINIUM, was visible in the distance above a long industrial building. This was almost certainly the aluminium works I had read about, the largest in Poland – one of Konin's new claims to fame. Below me lay a municipal park with lawns and well-tended flower-beds. Over to the far right I could see open countryside. The meadows of the Warta? I wished I could catch a glimpse of the old town, whose proximity invaded my mind to the exclusion of all else. The anonymous streets below me, the concrete blocks, the aluminium works, had nothing to do with my Konin.

The next day's itinerary was beginning to form itself. I would rise early, maybe as the sun cast its first slanting light across the meadows, and I would walk the two miles or so to the old town, following the route my mother would have taken by droshky when she visited Konin for the last time in 1937. I would cross the Warta where the old wooden bridge used to stand, walk into the main square, make my way to the Tepper Marik and the synagogue. I wanted the town to unfold slowly, poetically.

My phone rang. It was Izzy. Would I come down and meet him in the lobby? There I found him chatting to a pleasant man of about forty with gold-rimmed glasses, and his dark and pretty wife. Izzy did not tell me who they were. Neither of them spoke English. 'Let's go,' said Izzy, without telling me where we were going. It was difficult to interrupt his flow of Polish. A Lada taxi with KONIN stencilled on the side stood outside the hotel. The man with the gold glasses was the driver.

Izzy sat in front, talking non-stop. I sat in the back with the taxi-driver's wife, who leaned forward to join in the conversation. I heard Izzy repeat a phrase that was to become a familiar refrain: '*Ja pamienta . . .*' (I remember) followed by a stream of Polish. He pointed at the road ahead of us: '*Ja pamienta . . .*' The driver had a counter-refrain which sounded like an imitation of a woodpecker: '*Tak! Tak! Tak!*' (Yes! Yes! Yes!) Driving quite fast, leaving the new town behind, we headed towards an iron bridge and with a shock I realized what was happening. I wanted to shout 'Stop!' but Izzy was still talking, too carried away to notice my attempts to interrupt him. We drove through a criss-cross of girders. I did not look down at the water, although I knew it was there. Out of the corner of my eye I was aware of a green flatness, but this was not how I wanted to view the meadows for the first time. Then we were driving through the old town, the Konin I had waited so long to see. I knew that at the next intersection we would be crossing Third of May Street. Our driver's foot stayed hard on the accelerator as we tore across. 'There's the Town Hall!' said Izzy. By the time I turned my head it was gone. We drove round a square and pulled up. 'Here we are,' said Izzy triumphantly. We were outside the synagogue.

Izzy again forgot my presence, and who could blame him? He was looking at an empty building site opposite the synagogue and I knew he was telling the driver and his wife that his home once stood here, that this is where he lived until the Germans knocked at the door one day and rounded everyone up. *Ja pamienta . . .* He pointed at something else that triggered a memory. I wished I knew what he was telling them. *Ja pamienta . . . Tak, tak, tak! Ja pamienta . . . Tak! Tak! Tak! . . .* I moved away.

The synagogue was prettier than I had imagined, glowing white in the grey light as if catching sunlight that was not there. The keyhole-shaped windows, an echo of Moorish Spain, brought a touch of exotic orientalism to the dour Mittel-European surroundings. The building had a quiet, graceful presence free of synagogual pomposity. Trees in the front courtyard soared above the roof, their dark trunks silhouetted against the fresh white stucco. The builders could not have long finished their restoration work. The freshly varnished double doors were locked. The place was silent.

The original wrought-iron railings in front of the synagogue were still there. I marvelled at their survival, particularly at a detail of their design too small to be visible in the old photographs: four Stars of David. How odd that the Germans, who despoiled the synagogue and burnt the Holy Scrolls, had allowed this symbol to remain. Between the synagogue and the railings was an area where young children used to play during the long High Holy Day services.

The locked gates, the absence of people, the weight of memory, gave the place a desolate air in spite of the fresh paintwork. The mournful, muted sound of horns and trombones – the sort of clichéd soundtrack film-makers lay over shots of out-of-season seafronts – drifted across the road from a music school on the corner of a small street opposite the synagogue. Down this street, on the right, was the Jewish slaughterhouse where housewives took their Sabbath chickens, where Rivka Klapstein and her brother Simcha brought the scapebirds on the eve of Yom Kippur. I walked across, hoping it might still be there, but it had gone. The small building next to the synagogue, which was once the *mikve*, was now a bakery.

The first light drops of rain began to fall. Izzy and his new friends had not stopped talking. I felt like a diver who had been lowered into the depths of the ocean without being given time for his lungs to adjust. I was not ready for exploring the Tepper Marik.

The *bes-medresh*, next to the synagogue, was still recognizably the building of former times, though stripped of some of its ornamentation. Metal struts protruded from the roof supporting a large sign: WOJEWODZKA BIBLIOTEKA PUBLICZNA. It was now a public library – still a place of books, at least.

I glanced down Ogrodowa Street (renamed Obroncow Westerplatte), most of whose inhabitants at one time were Jewish, the street where Lola Birnbaum was born and married, where my great-uncle, the Blond Ryczke, had his *cheder*. Across the far end of the street stood the squire's town house, and behind that, hidden from view, was the Warta.

Izzy was impatient to see more of Konin before it got dark. We drove in the direction of the river and pulled up alongside a high grassy embankment that blocked our view. We walked to the top and below us stretched the river, winding away eastwards across an unspoilt vista of flat meadowland. Dark clumps of river weeds and wild flowers softened the edges of the banks. A lone angler leaned forward, staring at his line. The tranquil, gently flowing river reminded me of stretches of the Thames above Oxford. I had expected a more assertive river, broad and daunting, like the rivers in Russian novels. But rivers change with the season, and this was not the time to see the Warta's destructive face.

To the west, the view lost its timeless quality. In place of the old wooden bridge – still here in Izzy's day – was a modern steel footbridge; and some way beyond that, a road bridge carrying the main highway between Poznan and Warsaw, and further still, looking towards Glinka, electricity pylons and signs of industrial development.

Izzy wanted to move on again. I preferred to stay here on my own. We arranged to meet up later and the trio disappeared down the embankment. I stood by the river's edge and smelled the grassy dampness and watched the drops of rain prick the shiny surface of the water as the light slowly faded. The river cast its calming spell.

Not many yards from where I stood, fishermen once kept their crates anchored just below the surface, keeping their catch fresh for market day. Young boys used the crates as diving boards. For centuries the Jews of Konin came to the river's edge on Rosh Hashanah for the annual ceremony of Tashlich. Facing east, towards Jerusalem, they would turn out their pockets and empty crumbs into the river to symbolize the casting of their sins upon the waters. I do not suppose it would have crossed their minds to stand and stare at the beauty all around them. They were too busy praising its creator.

The rain began to fall more heavily, and I made my way back to the synagogue.

61

THE NEXT MORNING, I said to Izzy – firmly – that I wanted to walk, not drive, into Konin. We set off down a wide road leading away from the station, past the public gardens and the House of Culture. The concrete apartment buildings looked marginally more cheerful in the sunlight. Few people were about. The road dipped gently as it took us nearer the valley bed of the Warta. In the old days the droshky horses had it easy along here. On the way back their flanks felt the lash of Szwiatowicz's whip.

Leaving the new town behind, we came to a major highway intersection. Traffic headed towards Poznan in one direction, Warsaw in the other. This was once sleepy Czarkow. Koniners took leisurely strolls here on weekend afternoons. Centuries ago the Jews brought their dead here for burial on a nearby hillside. The road to old Konin and beyond that to Warsaw stretched ahead, cutting straight across an expanse of flat, treeless meadowland. Patches of still water lay like mirrors cast among the lush grass. Cows grazed in the foreground. In the distance, a low horizon and an enormous sky: a landscape by Cuyp.

Lorries hurtled past as we approached a wide stretch of water crossed by the iron bridge. This was not the Warta proper but a channel cut across a meandering loop of the river. A van pulled up alongside us; the driver wanted the way to Kalisz. Izzy did not hesitate – straight ahead, through the town, along the main road to the end, turn right and just past the church take the left fork and you're on the road to Kalisz. The driver pulled away and Izzy beamed. After an absence of more than four decades he was still a local.

We stood on the Meccano structure of girders, struts and rivets while Izzy recalled a September day in 1939: 'I was playing here on the bridge with a couple of Polish boys. We saw a mass of German bombers come across the sky. We were so silly, we didn't know whose they were, and we was counting them in the sky. Suddenly we saw two bombs come down and drop into the water near the bridge. They never exploded but we ran for our lives.'

Ahead of us and slightly to the right, a narrow road petered out a few yards before it reached the highway. We stepped across a patch of earth and joined the smaller road. Looking back, I saw that it lined up with the iron bridge. We were now on the original road leading into Konin from Slupca, Golina and Czarkow. The highway we had just left curved away, bypassing the old town.

We left behind the noisy world of traffic and entered a peaceful, shady avenue, the first intimations of a small country town. This was the old Slupca road. The tarmac, worn away in places, revealed patches of the original granite cobblestones beneath. In 1905 the young Bundist revolutionary, Maurice Lewin, came along this road disguised as a Chasid, making for Slupca and the German border. Seven years or so later, my father, still in his teens, passed this way with his few belongings, heading for England. A year after that, my Sarna grandparents and their large brood followed in the same direction.

We walked past large houses set back from the road. Izzy pointed out where my wealthy kinsman Aron Ryczke lived. We came to plain, smaller houses lining both sides of the street, some with pretty iron balconies above the front doors. Two sweaters for sale drooped on a plastic hanger in the front window of a house. A butcher's shop was open but completely bare. It was 1989 and Communism's lease had one more year to run.

The road came to an end at the Warta, flowing like a moat in front of the town. Today the main highway carried traffic over the river at another point. Ahead of us, where the old wooden bridge used to stand – once the scene of so much coming and going of Jews and peasants, of carts and wagons and carriages – was a boring span of metal, a footbridge. Just before it, overlooking the river, stood a mansion of crumbling grandeur, with columns, classical statues and a broad pediment: the former home of Konin's gentle industrialist, Ludwik Reymond. It was now split into flats for less affluent occupants. The gardens were overgrown; peeling stucco contributed to the general air of neglect. Yet one could see why Jews living in two dingy rooms would have described it as a 'palace'. A television aerial graced the rooftop, its mast brushing the podgy cheeks of two stone cherubs perched above the apex of the pediment. Their feet dangled over a stone plaque on which was carved the motto of a self-made man: PRACA JEST ZRODLEM POWODZENIA, Work is the source of success.

Reymond's engineering workshops, with their tall brick chimney, stood at a decent distance from the house, looking like a disused Victorian factory. The Kaplan boys used to take potshots at its windows from the other side of the river. I gaze down at the gently flowing water. I am no stranger to a river's mystical power and presence, its way of insinuating itself into one's life. Had I been born in Konin, this Polish river would go on flowing in my mind, whatever the sadness and bitterness of other memories.

It had stayed in Izzy's mind. Memories returned, of swimming, diving, fooling about. He remembered the Polish festival of Wianki, when flowers and candles floated under the bridge on a warm summer's night. He showed me a small platform that jutted over the water where he used to watch the ice float by on winter days.

He pointed along the river at the backs of houses that belonged to Moishe Kaplan. He once saw one of the Kaplan sons rowing along here on his way from Glinka. One could picture the scene: Izzy – Srulek then – the streetwise urchin, son of a poor tailor, sitting idly on the river bank, watching the squire's son skim along the sunlit water, a creature from another world. *Ja pamienta . . . Ja pamienta . . .*

Like its wooden predecessor, the footbridge provided a perfect entry point to the town. A short road on the opposite bank led straight into the big square. It was a grander space than the photographs had led me to expect. The scale of the architecture reflected Konin's growing prosperity in the first half of the nineteenth century. The cobblestones had gone. Municipal rose-beds occupied the centre of the square where the pumps once stood. But in essence the square was unchanged. The neo-classical façades remained intact, one with 1840 carved within its pediment, another having a double flight of stone steps leading up to a graceful portico. No cold purity of architectural unity here, but rather a mixture of buildings, an accretion of styles from various periods, such as one finds in English country towns. I recognized one of the oldest buildings in the square, a cottage with a wavy roof of pantiles in a dozen shades of burnt orange: Migdal the Chasid had his icecream shop here between the wars. 'That's right!' said Izzy.

I remembered it from a photograph taken in 1939. In the foreground stood a German firing squad about to execute the first two hostages in Konin. Migdal's shop was in the background. Izzy had witnessed the execution. The two men, the Christian Kurowski and the Jew Slodki, were shot standing against the wall of the old Polish gymnasium. A commemorative plaque now marked the spot.

The square was busy with shoppers, although there was little enough in the shops to buy. A long line of women waited outside a butcher shop where a truck had just pulled up with a delivery. There was a pathos about the shopkeepers' attempts to brighten their windows with home-made paper cut-outs of flowers and trees, the sort one sees on classroom walls in infants' schools.

A leather bicycle saddle was the sole item on display in one of the windows. Izzy decided to look inside. I followed him up the two small steps, marvelling at his self-confidence. We entered a tiny shop that belonged to a bygone era. Motes of dust danced in a shaft of sunlight shining into the dark brown interior. The pungent smell of leather filled the air. Leather objects waiting to be repaired lay everywhere – saddles, handbags, old footballs, straps . . . The old shopkeeper reacted to Izzy in a way that was to become familiar among the locals encountering him for the first time: initial wariness of the Polish-speaking visitor dressed like a foreigner, which quickly evaporated once he revealed his connection with the town. Maybe the pale blue eyes helped. He always revealed that he was a Jew, but he looked more like one of them than the Jews they remembered from long ago.

We walked round the square and looked at Mrs Neuman's newspaper and stationery shop, now a motor club office, at Szyjka's chocolate shop, now the Café Europa, at other shopfronts: 'They used to sell clocks in there . . . That was a Polish butcher's . . . They sold good pastries there . . .' Izzy took me through a passage that led to the rear of the building. The contrast between front and back was startling. At the front – a smooth façade with classical detailing. At the rear, a Konin more like the Middle Ages: an enclosed courtyard surrounded on all sides by wooden galleries supported by rough-hewn timber posts. It could have been an Elizabethan theatre.

We found ourselves on a half-landing raised above the level of the courtyard and below the galleries. Water dripped from washing draped over the wooden handrails. Old rooftops with tiny dormer windows completed the tumbledown setting. In a communal courtyard like this the women of the *shtetl* would have felt at home.

Two housewives with pails of washing spotted our presence. Izzy talked to them, telling them he was a Koniner, that he remembered this place. The sound of their chatter carried across the courtyard, attracting other women, who emerged from doorways in aprons and floral frocks. Those above us rested their arms on the wooden balcony and noisily joined in the conversation. Soon there were half a dozen women shouting to him from every corner of the courtyard. He asked if this used to be a hotel that belonged to a *Volksdeutscher* named Trenkler. '*Tak! Tak!*' The doors opening off the galleries, they said, were once the hotel rooms. And Trenkler's bakery used to be here too? '*Tak! Tak!*' Izzy told them he remembered Trenkler's and the well-to-do customers who went in for coffee and pastries. '*Tak! Tak!*' 'You see! Exactly what I told you.' The hotel was still open when Izzy went back to Konin in 1945. The women waved goodbye as we left.

Not far from the big square, close to the river, we found the Jewish gymnasium building, still rather imposing, standing firmly on the foundations that once had been the subject of so much scandal. It was closed but clearly still in use.

Back in the square, we found ourselves outside Miriam Grossman's former home. Before leaving Omaha, I had made a promise that if I visited Konin I would stand outside her house – if it was still there – and think of her. I opened the Memorial Book to consult the old photograph on which I had marked her windows. I looked up. They were still there; and those of her good neighbour, Wodzinski, the Polish lawyer who so delighted in the sound of Jewish hymns on Sabbath afternoons.

62

IT FELT UNREAL, dreamlike, to be walking through streets I had walked through so many times before in my mind. I had the old town map in my hand but I had little need of it. I knew which street would lead where, what vista would greet me round each corner, which turning would take me towards the river or the Tepper Marik or the park. Seeing the landmarks in the main street – the Town Hall, the Catholic church, the medieval milestone – I felt a jolt of recognition, like a reincarnated soul returning from a previous life.

I stood in Third of May Street, and opened the Memorial Book at the pre-First World War photograph of the Town Hall in what was then 'Long Street, Konin, Russian Poland'. Long Street became Third of May Street, which became Hermann Göring Strasse, which was now Red Army Street. (After the fall of the Communist regime it went back to Third of May Street.) A few details had changed since the photograph was taken. A memorial to the Red Army stood in front of the Town Hall. Some trees had disappeared. But in most respects the view I was looking at – the white building with its pretty hexagonal clocktower – was the one my grandparents saw a hundred years ago when they walked along ulica Dluga (Long Street) and glanced up to check the time. The streets running along either side of the Town Hall, the houses, rooftops, iron balconies in the old picture, were still recognizable today, despite the post-Tsarist incursion of a satellite dish.

The place still had the feel of a provincial country town, small enough to be explored by foot, with views over meadows, fields and river. The construction of the new town had been the saving of the old, removing the incentive to expand. The new highway bypassed the town, keeping heavy traffic away. Shabby in parts, cheapened wherever new building replaced the old, stagnant in its atmosphere because it no longer had an indigenous economic life of its own, the old town retained a measure of dignity. Standing in the main street near the Town Hall with the sun shining and the locals coming and going, I could understand why those one-time locals now dispersed in distant lands had thought Konin a pleasing place.

The shops were on a village scale, yet for the most part without village charm. Dull and dingy, symptoms of decline rather than historical continuity, their tiny windows were more than adequate to accommodate the paucity of goods. Three pairs of braces, some buttons and a few drab hats comprised the total contents of a window near the Town Hall. Might this be the very shop where Rivka Lewin tempted officers' wives with her millinery *à la mode*?

I consulted the scattering of dots on my map, each representing a Jewish home or shop or *cheder* or place of worship. The small scale of the map made its reliability dubious. In some cases the position of the dots depended on shaky memories. But walking down the main street, I could tell – with help from Izzy – that here is where Fordoynski sold ropes, Strykowski iron goods, Bonzdrow herrings, Krauser cloth, Walkowicz gramophones, Rachwalski dishes; where Zucker made wire fencing, Ancer kept his horses, Kleczewski had his tinsmith's yard, Monczka his timber yard, where Ejzen put up his advocate's brass plate, and where Artur Lipschitz worked at his tailor's bench, remembering – or trying to forget – his university days as a student of philosophy.

Nowhere did I feel the sense of loss more acutely than in the Tepper Marik, now Plac Zamkowy, Castle Square, where the first Jewish settlement in Konin began. I shall go on calling it by its old name: it was part of my childhood, and I have not met a single Koniner who can hear those two words without an aching recollection of time past.

They would not have recognized the Tepper Marik I was looking at. One entire side of the old square had been demolished, so that what used to be a separate street – Piasceczna – had become the new south side of the enlarged square, twice its former size. The human scale was gone. Dozens of homes, sharing the fate of their occupants, had been wiped out. Nazi vandalism, years of neglect, uncertainty about ownership, leaking roofs – all led to decay, degeneration and demolition.

The three remaining sides of the original square were a melancholy sight: a blackened, boarded-up house, a prefab hut, gaps where demolished buildings had not been replaced. A new building jarringly at odds with its surroundings was going up on the site of Gluba's house, once the most imposing building in the square. The whole place had a disjointed, bedraggled look, as though what remained of the old Tepper Marik was simply waiting for another demolition gang to come along and finish the job.

An unkempt public garden occupied the centre of the square. Bus-shelters made of bilious yellow plastic stood on the perimeter of the garden, where old people sat waiting. The few tiny shops were nondescript to the point of invisibility. The most abject of them displayed two empty coffee packets and a dusty jamjar containing two cob nuts. Only a liquor store showed any signs of life.

Rabbi Lipschitz's house was still there, dark and heavy with a wrought-iron balcony. Here I began my Konin *mezuzah* hunt, which yielded not a single trophy, not even a trace of the nail holes where the *mezuzahs* were once fixed to the doorposts. I went into the empty entrance hall of the Rabbi's house and stood at the foot of the shadowy staircase leading to his apartment. The flats were occupied but it was deathly still. I followed the Rabbi's daily route from his front door, down a few steps, along one side of the square, past the empty building site – where once upon a time a small boy looked through his basement window and watched the Rabbi's feet go by – and across the road, past the *bes-medresh* to the *shul*: a minute's stroll.

Every trace of Jewish life had been expunged, and only in the mind could that life be resurrected, perhaps more easily at a distance from this dismal place, which only seemed to deny its past. This was not the market square so many Koniners had described to me, crowded with people buying and selling and haggling, the fishmonger Bim-Bom scooping a wriggling carp from his barrel, shopkeepers leaning in doorways, porters and wheelbarrows, Aryeh-Leib going by with his milk churn, country women with eggs and home-made cheeses, *buba* Mindl selling vegetables fresh from Glinka, Zalman Ryczke's gramophone horn booming from his tailor's workshop, Jews arguing over Judaism, Zionism, socialism, others hurrying to prayer, Simcha Sarna on his way to the Chevre Shas, the Lame Ryczke limping back to his *cheder*, peasants and pedlars, pots and pans, noise and chatter, and everywhere the lively, singsong cadences of Yiddish . . . Only memory can keep that world alive. To quote the Yiddish poet Abraham Sutzkever, mourning for his lost *shtetl*:

Can the whole measure of five hundred years
Grow less because of our bit of now?
Who says you have vanished? No, you live!
Else how could I walk through you, in the way I do?[1]

A drunk lurched towards us in the Tepper Marik, one of several we encountered in Konin, the sort who once made sober, hard-working Jews feel superior. My instinct was to back away from the *piyak*, but Izzy got talking to him and mentioned that I was a Ryczke. 'Ryczke!' Breathing fiery fumes in my face, he said he remembered Aron Ryczke, pumped my hand vigorously, and wished me good luck. Were there any Jews living in Konin today? No, he said, none left. He described an incident he witnessed as a young boy in 1941 or perhaps '42. The Germans had taken a bunch of Jews to the top of the *bes-medresh* – he pointed at the building as he told the story – and there they shot them off the roof with a machine-gun. 'They made a show out of it,' he slurred. He shook hands and lurched off.

I walked towards the Krum Gesl, the short cut between the Tepper Marik and Third of May Street. Here, as I discovered from Lola Birnbaum in New York, is where my Sarna grandfather once had his home and crockery business. In this little street Lola sold her *galanteria*, and the Jewish cloth merchants had their stores – Slodki, Iwanowicz, Zandowski, Kowalski . . . The street's Polish name – ulica Kramowa – was unchanged but one entire side of it was in the process of being flattened. Even as I approached, a bulldozer was demolishing the last remains of Lola's shop.

63

WE MOVED across the open ground like detectives searching for the body, poking at bushes, probing under clumps of trees, scanning the ground for clues. We were searching not for a body but for graves, on the site of Konin's Jewish cemetery, the 'new' cemetery founded nearly two centuries ago. Rabbis and revolutionaries, octogenarians and stillborn children, victims of cholera and typhus . . . generations of Jews were buried here, their deaths mourned but accepted as part of the divine plan, for this was before Auschwitz.

Some Christians were buried here too: the town's Polish intelligentsia, shot in 1939. Jewish forced-labour gangs from surrounding villages who had not yet been deported were brought in to destroy the cemetery itself. A photograph in the Memorial Book shows the scene after the devastation, the broken lumps of granite and marble piled up like heaps of rubble. Most of it disappeared in time, taken away – so it is said – to be used as building materials. When historian Jozef Lewandowski visited his home town in 1947 and went looking for the graves of his family, he found lying on the ground 'fragments of the shattered tombstones and human bones, crushed even more'.[1] Several Koniners who had been back assured me I would find no vestige of the cemetery, that the postwar Polish authorities had finally cleared the site when they built a new sports stadium nearby. Nevertheless, I hoped to find some trace, if only a stump of stone sticking out of the ground or a fragment of inscription pressed into the earth.

It was a quiet spot close to the park and river. A man watched us suspiciously for a while, asked what we were doing, and then wandered off. There was indeed no sign of a cemetery to be seen, not one shattered gravestone, not a single scrap saved from the heaps of debris. No sign to mark its site, no plaque to tell the people of Konin that this was once the holy burial ground of the Jews.

Towards the end of our search, pulling back some shrubbery, I discovered three shallow depressions in the ground, rectangular in shape, side by side in a row: unmistakably graves. And we found one slender strip of stone hidden in the grass, the foot of a memorial snapped off at its base. When the mourners consecrated that memorial, they recited the traditional words from the prayer book: 'As for man, his days are as grass; as the flower of the field, so he flourisheth. For the wind passeth over it, and it is gone; and the place thereof shall know it no more.'

Close to the site of the cemetery, in front of a screen of trees, stands a stone cenotaph on top of which the Polish eagle spreads its bronze wings. It is the town's memorial to the victims of Nazism. The inscription reads: 'TO THE FAITHFUL SONS OF THE HOMELAND, MURDERED BY THE NAZI FASCISTS IN THE YEARS 1939–1945. Association of Combatants for Liberty and Democracy. Society of the District and Town of Konin.' It may well be that the Association of Combatants for Liberty and Democracy counted the murdered Jewish men, women, children and babies of Konin among the 'faithful sons of the homeland'. I nevertheless wish that somewhere in the town the citizens of Konin had erected a memorial to the Jews who lived among them for five hundred years and were exterminated.

There *is* one Jewish memorial in Konin, though it is extremely hard to find. It is in the large Catholic cemetery that spreads across a steep hillside above the road to Kolo: a peaceful place, close to an old Franciscan church and monastery. Mature chestnut trees shade the well-tended graves, the simple marble crosses and extravagant family tombs. Candles flicker amid bunches of newly laid flowers. There are many reminders of war: monuments to soldiers who fell in battle, and civilians who were 'innocent victims of the Nazi terror'.

An old man told us where the Jews were buried. He pointed to a path leading to the upper boundary of the cemetery where, among the crosses and holy statues, we found a solitary Star of David, engraved on a simple tombstone. This is where Jewish prisoners from the labour camp – the 'House of Bondage' – near Konin's railway station at Czarkow were interred. By the time of their deaths the Jewish cemetery was already in ruins.

Rabbi Aaronson recorded in his diary:

> We buried the dead of the Konin camp as best we could according to Jewish rites and traditions, but they would not permit us to bury them in the Jewish cemetery, only in the Christian graveyard. In every grave I tried to place a bottle in which there was a note giving the name of the dead, date of death etc. On 17 July 1942, some twenty men were taken from us for work in the Polish cemetery. Some Jews had been buried in special graves among those of the Poles, and the mayor of Konin ordered these bodies to be exhumed and reburied in a communal grave at the south-west corner.
>
> There a pit was dug, about twenty metres long and two metres wide. Into this pit were placed all the dead and the killed who had previously been buried separately on a hill opposite. The work was hard as well as saddeningly painful, the more so as it was carried out under the supervision of an armed guard who obliged the Jews to labour to the end of their strength. With his watch in

> hand, he allowed five minutes for the removal of each corpse to the new place. He would not allow a single minute to be spent on taking a look at the bodies of the martyrs. This was the method of removal: the bodies were lifted by garden forks poked into the eyeholes or the skull or body. Then lime was thrown onto each body before it was thrust into the pit. Those who carried out this work included relatives of the dead. They were forbidden to take the bottles containing details of each of the dead. I did manage to throw a few of these bottles into the pit without the guard noticing, but most of these bottles remained where I had first put them – though the dead, to whom they refer, do not lie there.[2]

The memorial marking the mass grave where we stood bore the inscription: 'TO THE JEWS ABOMINABLY MURDERED BY THE NAZI OPPRESSORS IN THE CAMP IN CZARKOW IN THE YEARS 1941–43. Compatriots. Konin XI 1945.' Thick clusters of marigolds not yet in bloom filled the long rectangular space. The grave was well cared for, and so it was a pity that the ground next to it was used as a dumping-place for rotting leaves, broken glass and litter.

Postscript At the end of 1994, after I had finished writing this book, I learned about the work of Dr Lucja Nowak, the director of a local history museum near Konin. She has sought out the few Jewish gravestones to have survived the war, and made it her business to preserve their inscriptions. Not Jewish herself, she has learned Hebrew in order to read them.

64

IT WAS IMPOSSIBLE to miss the house where the Ryczkes lived. It stood in the middle of the road, astride the promontory where the road to Kalisz takes a fork near the Protestant church. It had a continental flamboyance that not even years of neglect and a layer of grime could suppress. The architect had gone too far with his ornate stone dressing and cone-roofed, fairy-tale turrets. For the Jewish tenants who once lived in it, I doubt that it ever was the stuff of fairy tales.

I looked up at the balcony below one of the turrets. It belonged to the apartment where my father's eldest brother, Itsik Hirsh, lived. The Germans murdered him and his wife. Below him, on the ground floor, lived the Leben family. The Germans murdered most of them. On the far left-hand side of the ground floor lived my father's sister, Bayla, and her family. The Germans murdered her and her two young sons. My grandfather lived at the back of the house up some steps leading from the courtyard. The Germans murdered his wife, his stepdaughter and my father's two stepbrothers who lived with him. What would my father's fate have been had he not crept out of this house one day in 1912, leaving a note to say he was on his way to London? I thought of him as he was then, and the eighty-nine-year-old lying in a hospital bed twenty-four hours after his leg had been amputated, shortly before he died, uncomplaining, humming Beethoven. Tears pricked at the back of my eyes.

The entrance to the house was open. I considered knocking at doors and asking if I could look around, but my nerve failed me. I remembered Fella Leben's return to this house in 1945, the moment when she reached out to open the door of her former home – and turned away. I peered through the window of what was once Bayla's grocery store, and entered a time-warp. Two men, one bent over an ancient sewing-machine, the other stitching with needle and thread, sat engrossed in their work. The scene was a perfect example of dozens of such tailoring workshops that gave Jews a precarious livelihood in prewar Konin. One of the men, aware of being watched, looked up at me suspiciously, came to the door and asked gruffly what we wanted. Izzy explained my family connection with the shop and asked if I could look inside. Of course, said the tailor, instantly affable. He did not know the shop had been Bayla Prost's grocery store all those years ago, long before he was born. I looked around the tiny interior, where Felunia's mother struggled to make ends meet during the years following her husband's suicide.

The tailor said: 'All I know is that the man who lived here before the war hanged himself from a hook on the door.' He might have been referring to an event of last year rather than over half a century ago. 'There was a doorway over there.' He pointed at a wall where a doorway had been blocked up. 'The room through there was where they lived. I'm not sure if he hanged himself from that door or the door of the shop here.' The tailor had learned about the suicide from the previous owner of the shop.

A few doors away stood the house where Sarah, the partisan, grew up. Across the road the Leszczynski flour mill, now State-owned, was still working within its white-flecked walls. And not far from that stood another former Jewish enterprise, the Spielfogel distillery with its tall brick chimney, where the Ryczkes and Lebens used to collect free hot water. This, too, had become part of a State monopoly.

Crossing the road we bumped into Feliks, our taxi-driver, emerging from a barber's shop looking like a shorn sheep, and a minute later we were inside the shop chatting to the barber and his assistant. The antiquated chairs, with round head-rests that moved up and down on iron ratchets, might have been there since the Twenties. The barber was a nimble little man with wily blue eyes and grey stubble; he was born in 1909 and had lived here all his life. He could not recall the Ryczke family but the name Prost drew an immediate reaction. He tugged at his Adam's apple, jerked his head back and produced a terrible, strangulated 'Aaaarchhhh!' The suicide happened in 1934 but he remembered it clearly. 'He hanged himself from a door and there was a big commotion. Everyone was running across to have a look.'

My map had a cluster of dots in this part of the town, most of them collected from a Koniner I had met in Haifa, Yitzhak Lipinski. One of them marked his own home. I pointed at it and said: 'Lipinski?' The barber threw up his arms: 'Lipinski!' Of course he knew Lipinski. 'He lived here in this very house.'

The barber nodded in agreement as I read out the names of other Jewish families who lived nearby: Weingarten the tailor; Zeidlitz – 'a good footballer'; Kowalski – 'he owned the mill next door'; Leszczynski – 'he owned the other mill'; Feinstein, Zelkowicz, Ozerowicz . . . 'The Jews were clever,' he said, 'clever and yet foolish. They should have gone away from here while they could.' I bridled at the word clever. As for the Jews getting away while they could – easy to say with the benefit of hindsight. The news that Lipinski was alive drew one comment from the barber: 'Ask him to send me a ticket so I can go there and visit him.' I read the sub-text: all Jews are rich.

Izzy pluckily raised a thorny subject, the complaint I had heard so often from Jewish Koniners, that their gentile neighbours failed to help them in their hour of need. 'The talk abroad is that the Poles murdered the Jews,' the barber rejoined, 'but the truth is that a lot of Poles helped Jews.' I could tell Izzy was not convinced, either then or on other occasions during our visit when locals dismissed the charge. It was impossible to help Jews, they said, when there were so many informers and when the penalty was death for the offender and his family.

It was not for me to ask Poles to examine their consciences. My inability to converse with them directly meant I could not pick up clues and nuances. Mike Jacobs had tried to discuss the war years with his former neighbours and got nowhere. In any case what would I achieve? 'We got on all right with the Jews,' the barber said to Izzy. 'We did not hate each other,' commented another local. How could I look into their hearts and know what they really felt?

65

BEFORE LEAVING London, I had called my honorary religious consultant, Uncle Leibish, to put a question to him: if, by good luck, I were to be allowed to enter the *shul* in Konin, what suitable holy words might I offer up by way of thanksgiving? He did not hesitate: 'How goodly are thy tents, O Jacob, thy dwelling places, O Israel.'

Luck – or rather the God of Israel – was on our side. The main door of the synagogue was open and we simply walked in. The building was not open to the public and I braced myself for problems. Izzy, never interested in problems until he has to face them, strode straight in. A door off the entrance vestibule led into the synagogue. American pop music, pulsating from a loudspeaker resting on the *bimah*, greeted us as we entered. Three young women sorting books gave us a welcoming smile. Yes, they said, we were free to look round. They were preparing for the opening of the new pubic library later in the year. Rows of pine bookshelves occupied the space where the congregation once sat.

The synagogue interior was a blend of grace and grandeur,

magnificent without being overpowering. No one, not even the architect in Tel Aviv (I had brought his drawing with me), had prepared me for the visual impact of the four pillars in the centre of the hall. Grouped close together, one on each corner of the *bimah*, they soared to the lofty ceiling where they supported four slender arches forming a canopy, decorated at each corner with a Star of David.

From the centre of the canopy hung a sixteen-branched brass chandelier. The pillars, lightly marbled, were ringed top and bottom with rich, vaguely oriental designs painted in terracotta, ruby, blue and turquoise, an artist's idea of temple style in ancient Israel. The fleurs-de-lis added a pleasing anachronistic touch. The freshness of every brush stroke testified to the recent work of a restorer. The entire place, every inch of its surface and fittings, looked new: not a mark, scratch, dent, or sign of human use anywhere. Reflections flashed off the brass orbs and delicate branches of the beautiful chandeliers. The wood strip floor gleamed. The wall-lamps in the shape of menorahs were the only lapse in taste, more suited to the lobby of the Tel Aviv Hilton.

For practical reasons, the floor had been raised to remove the original different levels. The steps on the architect's drawing, the traditional steps going down when you entered and those leading up to the *bimah*, were gone. The deep-set Moorish windows – positioned precisely where the architect had recalled them – had lost their stained glass. Varnished tongue-and-groove lined the high arched ceiling, agreeable enough to look at if one did not know that the ceiling was once an azure sky with golden stars. The side gallery for women worshippers was gone, but the main balcony remained, embellished with new and graceful iron railings. Izzy looked up and focused on the spot where his mother used to sit. It was the only time I saw him, momentarily, close to tears. He stepped onto the *bimah* and stood exactly where he did when he last sang here as a twelve-year-old choirboy, forty-nine years ago.

At that time, balustrading surrounded the *bimah*, creating an intimate enclosure, a small stage raised in the middle of the congregation. Koniners remember the table covered with a velvet, gold-embroidered cloth, and the pointer with a tiny silver hand waiting to be guided along the lines of holy text. They remember the seat where an honoured congregant cradled the Torah scroll on his lap before it was read, while another honoured male, often a boy, removed its velvet cover, its silver breastplate and the silver finials with their tinkling bells. The balustrading was gone. The *bimah* was just an empty square of shiny flooring. The former choirboy reminisced while the pop music blared.

The Holy Ark, once the building's most splendid feature, no longer graced the east wall. No one could tell me when the Nazis destroyed it. They probably smashed it up while the Torah scrolls were burning in the square outside. The place where the Ark had once stood, rising almost to the ceiling, was now an area of blank wall. A pair of modern cupboard doors covered the niche where the Torahs had been kept. No steps leading up to the Ark. No eternal lamp burning in front of the Ark: it was extinguished for ever in September 1939.

The east wall had not lost all its glory. Decorating the deep embrasures of the windows on either side of the Ark was a floral design that looked like faded tapestry. From below the cornice of the ceiling hung draped swags, fringes and tassels – all *trompe-l'oeil.* On either side of the empty space where the Ark stood were *trompe-l'oeil* columns with capitals that made up in exuberance for what they lacked in classical purity; and between the columns were panels incorporating the Star of David. From the tops of the columns rose an arch of spuriously three-dimensional moulding, designed to frame the Ark. On the east wall we found the sole surviving fragment of Hebrew lettering, a few partly obliterated – the signature of the original artist: M. Milchman, Warsaw.

One longed for some lingering aura of holiness. Religious devotion has a mysterious way of soaking into the walls of places of worship, but I did not feel its presence. There was no one to pray here any more, no rich Jews seated near the east wall, no poor Jews standing at the back, no bearded Jews rocking to and fro. To their credit, Poles had gone to costly and painstaking lengths to preserve this landmark of Konin Jewry, and yet – perhaps the unavoidable price of restoration on this scale – something had been lost as well as saved. The patina of age, the dark-timbered pews worn smooth by generations of worshippers, the cupboards crammed with prayer books had gone, like those who once prayed here. The building had been preserved, and that is cause for thanks, but it was no longer an expression of *hemshekh*, continuity. You cannot have *hemshekh* without Jews.

A few days later we met Roman Sobczak, the friendly director of the library. He ushered us into his office, gave us tea and offered help. The synagogue, he told us, had been saved in the nick of time. By 1970 it had deteriorated to the point where demolition seemed inevitable. A local citizen and museum director had campaigned to save the building, and eventually the necessary public funds were granted. The restoration work, carried out by the Ministry of Culture, had taken three years. The chandeliers and lamps – made by an artist/craftsman in Poznan – cost two and a half million zlotys; restoration of the murals another three and a half million.

I asked the director if the library had any books or booklets on the Jews of Konin. One of his staff flipped through a card index. They had books on the history of the Jews in Poland, on the Warsaw ghetto and a few other Jewish subjects, but alas, nothing on the local Jews. We were having this conversation in the former *bes-medresh* building, where once there were vast cupboards filled with religious books. Had any of them survived? '*Nic.*' None.[1]

A pair of flimsy metal gates opened onto a yard behind the *bes-medresh* building. The communal hearse was once kept here in a wooden shed. Now there was only a boiler house, a pile of logs, and a heap of coal spilling onto concrete paving-stones. I had a bizarre reason for looking at this bleak space. It began with a phone call I received one evening from Mark Natel, the former Konin cobbler, who knew I was about to set off for Poland. After wishing me a safe journey, he informed me – and this was really the point of his call – that buried treasure lay hidden in Konin: Jewish treasure. He had never mentioned it in the course of our talks, but now that I was going to Konin, the time had come to tell all.

During a visit to Konin in the Sixties he had met a Konin-born Jew then living in Lodz who had sworn that treasure was buried 'under where the hearse used to stand'. It was communal treasure, more particularly synagogue silver: Torah breastplates, beakers, candlesticks . . . maybe Holy Scrolls and precious books. Was the man still living in Lodz? No, he had subsequently emigrated to Israel and there, under the strain of great personal troubles, he had lost his mind and died.

When was the treasure buried? The answer again was guess-work. Probably soon after the Germans entered the town. It was surprising, was it not, that no one else had breathed a word to me about this? Nothing would shake the old man's conviction that the treasure was still there. He himself had tried to do something about it during his visit to Konin, but totalitarian surveillance, much tighter in those days, had made it impossible: 'Maybe you will be luckier,' he said. He pleaded with me to find the treasure and ensure that it found an honoured resting-place in Israel.

He gave me the name of an old Communist friend in Konin who could help me. I pointed out that the Pole, if he was still alive – which was unlikely – might be too old and infirm to help. In that case, my insistent Koniner countered, I should inform the local authorities and get permission from them to dig.

I stared at the paving-stones, wishing my eyes could penetrate the concrete and reveal, like a seismic scanner, the ghostly outline of a silver menorah. I went back to the yard several times over the next few days, hoping for an inspired idea. It never came. The Pole who might have helped me was long dead. I had no wish to become entangled with Polish officialdom, the passing from one office to another, the questioning, the bureaucratic formalities that might consume my entire stay and achieve nothing.

Another doubt nagged. Might not the man from Lodz have already been suffering from incipient dementia when he told my Koniner about the treasure? Would the police be likely to excavate the back of the public library on the basis of such evidence? Even if they were, I would be gone by the time the digging began. If treasure were found, what would happen to it? The thought of organizing my own clandestine nocturnal excavation was too risible, and in the end, rightly or wrongly, I decided against going to the authorities. Better to wait until these words appear in print.

Shall we ever know if there is treasure buried where the hearse once stood?

Postscript Among the Konin papers and photographs miraculously recovered from the back yard in Israel in 1992 was an old exercise book containing minutes of a Konin society meeting held in Tel Aviv on 12 November 1958. The Hebrew was in Haskel Ryczke's handwriting and included the following: 'As it is known that the committee of the *kehillah* has hidden the sacred objects and books of the community, and it is known roughly where they are hidden, it was decided to try with the help of Yad Vashem to explore the possibility of transferring these hidden objects to Israel.' I could find no other reference to the subject.

I sent a copy of the minutes to Yad Vashem in Jerusalem and asked them to consult their records. Five months later I received a reply from a senior official: 'I can now inform you that there is no documentation about it at Yad Vashem. Personally I believe that the matter of the buried objects is based solely on unsubstantiated rumours. In any case, it seems to me that even if the rumours are true, the likelihood of discovering the buried religious objects is nil.'[2]

66

STRANGE ARE THE ways of Orthodox Judaism, and none stranger than the criteria by which it decides who is and who is not a Jew, as in the case of Teresa. Her father was a Catholic. Her parents were married in Konin's Catholic church. She herself is a practising Catholic, married to a Catholic, and they have three children whom they have brought up as Catholics. Yet the most fundamentalist Rabbi would accept her as Jewish because of her matrilineal descent. According to Jewish law, therefore, my statement that Konin is *Judenrein* is not strictly true, for Teresa still lives in the old town.

Her mother, born Nadzia Lyfczak, came from a respectable Konin Jewish family. There was no parental lamentation when she married a Catholic because there was no family left to lament. Nadzia married in 1945 when there were just a handful of Jews in the town, recently liberated from the camps. Izzy was among them. One day, walking through the town, he saw Nadzia, young and beautiful in her white wedding-gown, on her way to the church to be married.

Soon after that, he left Konin for good. Nadzia subsequently gave birth to a daughter, Teresa, who was baptized, confirmed and eventually married in the same church as her mother. Within two days of our arrival, an old couple chatting to Izzy in the street happened to mention that a Jewess lived round the corner. They meant Teresa.

Kilinskiego Street, a quiet residential street not far from the synagogue, had lost its Jewish landmarks – the Chevre Tillim and a small *cheder* – but in most respects it was much as it had been when Jewish families lived there. Teresa's was the only commercial enterprise in the street: a laundry-pressing service run from a small annexe built onto the side of a tall house with the initials AR and the date 1910 carved in stone above the front door. The pleasantly humid smell of clean laundry greeted us when we entered. Two women were feeding towels and sheets into a pressing-machine. The elder of the two gave us that initial cautious look we had come to know. It was Teresa, nearing forty, plump and pretty, with the fair complexion of a young girl, and grey-blue panda eyes of amazing beauty. The caution fell away when we explained who we were. Eager to talk to us, she urged us to come back later when the shop would be closed.

That evening we met her husband Jozef, a miner, short and powerfully built, with braces stretched over muscular shoulders. He greeted us with a hand-crushing welcome and great joviality. When he laughed, the whole room seemed to shake. By Polish standards, their home was luxurious, the rooms high-ceilinged and solid, decorated in 'modern' style with reproduction landscapes, a veneered shelf unit with ornaments, a telephone, an enormous television set and a rubber plant trying to push its way through the ceiling. They also had an indoor flush lavatory. Modern sanitation and water piping came to Konin after the Second World War (though as late as 1962 one visitor to the town had seen 'women carrying pails of water hanging from halters round their necks. The water came from hand pumps in the square.').[1]

Teresa told us that the house had been built in 1910 by her Jewish great-great-grandfather, Avrom Ratajewski. She sat us down at the dining-table and brought out a family album. Her mother died quite young, she said, in 1956. Her father was also dead. Her eyes opened wide with delight when Izzy told her he had seen her mother on her wedding day. She showed us her parents' wedding-day portrait and

Izzy looked at it for a long time. The bride's face, the graceful long gown, were exactly as he remembered them.

Teresa left the room to fetch something she said would interest us. She came back carrying a long rectangle of white marble, broken in two. She fitted the pieces together and held them up for us to read the Hebrew inscription: *CHEVRE TEHILLIM*. What did it say? she asked. We told her it was the name of a *chevre*, a religious society that used to pray in this very street. The marble slab was probably a sign fixed by the entrance. Teresa's father, now dead, had found it during the war. The Germans had just gone round smashing up all the Jewish places of worship. He saw the slab of marble lying broken in the street, brought it home and hid it in the loft throughout the war. He had no idea then that he would one day marry a Jew. Teresa said she would never part with it.

I was in the home of a Polish Catholic family, a portrait of the Pope looked down on us from the wall, yet in one important respect this family's history differed from that of their neighbours: the Shoah was part of their story. Nadzia's parents and brother died in Treblinka. Teresa said her mother never wanted to talk about it. Nor did she ever say much about how she managed to escape the same fate. So far as Teresa knew, her mother, who did not look conspicuously Jewish, obtained false papers and was later sent to Germany like many other Polish gentiles to provide agricultural labour. Returning home after the war, she learned the fate of her parents and brother. Teresa's father travelled to Treblinka after the war on his wife's behalf to bring back some ashes from the crematoria, but for some reason his mission was unsuccessful.

I opened the Memorial Book and ran down the columns of names on the black-edged pages until I came to Lyfczak. Three people were listed. I read out their names. They were Teresa's grandparents and uncle. She stared intently at the names as though effort alone would enable her to decipher the Hebrew characters. She longed to make out the name Lyfczak, but the letters were totally alien to her. Of Hebrew, Yiddish, Judaism, she knew nothing.

She herself had not encountered anti-Semitism, she said, but her sister, a social worker who lived in another town, had faced difficulties for a while in 1965 when the question of her Jewish mother was officially investigated. Teresa, born and brought up a Catholic, mixing exclusively with gentiles in a totally gentile world, felt no religious or racial inner tug-of-war. She was a Christian and felt a Christian, but from the way she turned the pages of the Memorial Book, lingering over the pictures of bearded Konin Jews, it was clear that she wanted to know more about these strange people from whom she was partly descended, and the world they once inhabited here on her own doorstep – no, within these very walls built by Avrom Ratajewski.

Jozef felt it was time to have a drink. He poured out generous measures of Polish vodka and we clinked glasses: '*Na zdrowie!*' To health. Teresa brought in platters of bread and garlic sausage, slices of cold meat, and glasses of tea. What chance of total strangers walking into an English home unannounced and receiving hospitality like this? I raised my second glass of vodka in Teresa's direction with the traditional Jewish toast, '*L'chaim!*' – to life! She looked at me blankly. Jozef kept filling the glasses. I downed a third vodka, and a fourth. Izzy launched into Konin reminiscences, some of which drew deep-chested bellows of laughter from Jozef. Teresa plied us with more food. I declined a fifth vodka. After the meal a towel was passed round so we could wipe our sticky fingers. Our hosts urged us to come back another night for a proper meal.

Streams of Polish punctuated by Jozef's laughter floated over me as one reminiscence triggered off another. Izzy's prewar Konin world had vanished by the time Teresa was born. Her mother, she said, had only one Jewish soul-mate in the town after the war, the widow Madzia Leszczynska. She too had returned to Konin and stayed on. Teresa remembered the old lady coming to visit her mother on Friday nights, invariably greeting her with '*Gut shabbes!*' Teresa's intonation of the traditional Sabbath greeting, the only two Yiddish words she knew, was uncannily authentic.

For those two women, Madzia and Nadzia, the Friday night meetings were a last tenuous link with the world of their murdered parents. One had become a Catholic. Both were meeting in a Catholic home where there would be no Sabbath candles on the table, no *challah*, or glass of wine for the benediction. But each had memories of Friday nights in prewar Konin, the hush that descended on the Jewish quarter of the town, the spirit of rest that enveloped every Jewish home as night fell.

Jews had exchanged '*Gut shabbes*' greetings in Konin for five centuries. Though the words came naturally to Teresa's lips, they held no meaning for her, revived no Sabbath memories, had no ancient resonance. After her, there would be no one left even to mimic the words. *Di goldene keyt* – the golden chain – was broken.

67

I WANTED TO SEE the countryside that Leopold Infeld recalled during his émigré years – 'the Polish fields and meadows . . . the air smelling of flowers and hay . . . vistas and sounds which can never be found elsewhere . . .'[1] My Sarna grandfather, rare among religious urban Jews of his generation, responded in a similar way to the Polish countryside. He in turn influenced my mother, whose love of trees and flowers stayed with her until she died at nearly ninety. She, in turn, infected me. Is it far-fetched, therefore, to believe that my own harmony with the countryside, with flat meadows, orchards and rivers, owes something to Konin?

We set off in Feliks's Lada. It was a fine day with puffy white clouds sailing across a light blue sky. Soon we were bowling along country roads, scattering geese and chickens in our path. We plunged from brilliant light into shadowy forest, where a ribbon of silvery river glittered in the distance among the trees. Then out into the light again, past haystacks and blazing sunflowers. Villagers stared at us with that unashamed curiosity of country folk. Out of their sight, we snatched apples hanging temptingly over the roadside and sank our teeth into their sharp-tasting flesh. We overtook a classic peasant figure on a horse-drawn haycart, his gentle pace rebuking our modern haste. The countryside itself had a pre-industrial feel to it, not postcard-pretty but a bit rough and unkempt, a place for tillers rather than tourists. We passed roadside shrines awash with religious kitsch, plastic flowers, painted figures of the Virgin and Child, icons displayed behind little panes of glass and, hanging above it all, the figure of Jesus, the crown of thorns, the blood trickling down the ribcage, the nails driven through the palms . . . the martyred Jew.

An extract from my cousin Felunia's memories recorded on tape, and so nearly lost:

> After a few months [July 1940] it was announced that Konin must be *Judenrein*. Wagons and horses were supplied. Everyone had to put their little bits and pieces on the wagons. A few old people were permitted to sit on the wagons. The rest of us had to walk. It was terrible to walk in the street – the *goyim* were looking out of the windows at us. The SS lashed out with whips and shouted. Dogs barked. People wept. It was terrible. Along the way, the Germans treated us very harshly. When their eye caught someone, they just beat him to death.
>
> We walked a long time. In every village some families were ordered to stay. We came to a village named Krolikow [about 15 km from Konin]. Mother [Bayla] remembered that she had once attended the wedding of one of her customer's daughters and that the wedding took place here in this village. [The context makes it clear that she is referring to gentile customers.] When customers had a wedding, there was not one she failed to attend. If any of her gentile customers had to go to hospital and leave their children somewhere, they would deposit them with mother. She made friends with everyone.
>
> When we arrived at this village and learned that this is where we had to stay and that every gentile family had to take in a Jewish family, Mother said to one of the local women: 'Do you know so-and-so?' The woman said: 'Yes,' so Mother said: 'Do me a favour, go and tell her Prost is here with her family and would like to stay with her.'
>
> And so it was. The woman went to Mother's customer, who came immediately, began to kiss her, and cry, and said: 'You come to us, be with us,' and we stayed there. If I think back over the whole of the war – I was fourteen when it began and twenty when it ended – during all these years the best time was in Krolikow. It was almost idyllic . . .
>
> This woman took care of us. Mother began to help her in the kitchen. My brothers were taken out every day to work by the Germans, but relatively speaking it was not too bad . . . There was no lack of food because she shared everything with us. She used to cook a big bowl of potatoes in the morning; and she made curds

> from sour milk – it was for the pigs but it tasted like butter . . .
>
> As a child I enjoyed the forest all around. We used to go to collect wild berries and mushrooms, and to me it felt like a carefree vacation . . .
>
> Mother was very brave. She once went to another village, to six old customers of hers, and they sent her back with sacks of flour, meat, fat, eggs and everything . . . This was our period in the village and this also came to an end.

It ended in March 1941 with orders barked through loudhailers in village streets, another packing of a few possessions, another wagon trail, this time back to Konin and the railway station.

I wanted to find Bayla Prost's customer who helped 'redeem the name of mankind', to quote the phrase used by Yad Vashem for the 'Righteous Gentiles' who risked their lives to save Jews. I have no evidence that this country woman risked her life, but I do know that she took a persecuted mother and three children into her home without a moment's hesitation, a spontaneous gesture of love by a Christian towards a Jew in a society where such gestures were not the norm. Why did she do it? I suppose her reply would have been the same as that of the peasants of Le Chambon-sur-Lignon when asked why they helped the Jews. 'Why not?' they replied. Thanks to Bayla's gentile friend, a fourteen-year-old girl experienced a period of happiness before entering the charnel house.

Krolikow turned out to be a scattered community without a focal point. We looked across a panoramic vista of countryside with forest in the distance, perhaps the forest where Felunia picked berries and mushrooms. Izzy and Feliks pointed out realistically that it could take a week or more to knock at every door in the area. I did not even have a name. She might not be alive. Reluctantly, I abandoned the search for the good woman of Krolikow.

Passing a windmill with rotting timbers and broken sails, we arrived in Rychwal. Felunia had told me, posthumously, that this was where our grandfather died in 1941.

> Some of the food mother brought back was given to grandfather [Dovid Ryczke], grandmother and aunt. Occasionally I used to go to feed him. He had to be fed. He was very old and sick. He was

> paralysed, even his mouth, and one day Uncle Abramek [Dovid's son] came and gave Grandpa food and he choked and died. All the other old people nearby envied him for the reason that at this time, with such a war going on, he had died in his bed and was given a proper burial . . . He was buried in the winter of 1941 in Rychwal. There was a Jewish cemetery there . . . That is where he is buried – if the cemetery still exists.

Izzy asked a woman in Rychwal for the whereabouts of the cemetery. Gone, she said. It used to be on the road to Konin, but there was nothing there now.

A widow named Hannah was the sole Jewish inhabitant left in the little town of Kleczew, near Konin. Maybe the place was less torpid when the Jews lived here in considerable numbers. Mike Jacobs of Dallas had found Hannah on his last visit to the area and given me her address. We waited a long time before she appeared at the door, barefooted, a short, rotund woman with dark eyes and olive skin. She patted her dyed black hair into place while Izzy told her who we were.

Hannah led us into her room, sombre with dark furniture and a brown tiled stove. Seeing her unmade bed, I realized we had disturbed her afternoon nap. Above the bed were two religious pictures, one of Jesus bathed in a heavenly beam of light, the other of the Holy Virgin.

Hannah put on her shoes and glasses and smoothed her dress. I gave her a colour snapshot that Mike Jacobs's wife, Ginger, had asked me to give her. It was a photograph she had taken of Hannah standing next to her daughter's grave in Kleczew. Hannah looked at it silently for a while, then gave each of us an emotional kiss.

Hannah was born into a Yiddish-speaking family in Kleczew in 1910. She had forgotten all her Yiddish, she said, and could speak only Polish. In December 1939 she married a local gentile, and soon after that a helpful German gave her false papers. She hid for a time in a cellar in Kleczew. One day, through a keyhole, she saw the Germans rounding up the Jews for deportation. Later, one of her husband's relatives informed on her, but she managed to avoid arrest and left Kleczew.

She and her husband returned after the war. Parcels from her relatives in America helped them get by. The dress she was wearing today was made from material sent by an uncle in New York. She could have joined him in America but for one thing that prevented her ever leaving Kleczew: 'How could I leave my daughter's grave behind?' She showed us a portrait of the young woman who had been her only child. From the clues offered, I guessed that she had died of cancer. Five weeks after her death, Hannah's husband hanged himself. Since then she had lived here on her own, coping with heart trouble but managing to look after herself. She was in touch with Teresa in Konin, whose mother, Nadzia, had been a friend.

In 1948, with the help of two non-Jews, one of them a stonemason, Hannah erected a few simple tombstones in the nearby forest at Kazimierz in memory of the Jews buried there in mass graves. It took more than thirty years before the local authorities got round to erecting an official memorial.

In 1954 she experienced 'a period of hatred' when a group of local youngsters in their early twenties repeatedly scrawled 'Dirty Jew' on her windows. They were caught and given heavy jail sentences, and since then she had been left in peace. The religious pictures above her bed were a present from a friend. Her daughter had been baptized and brought up in the Catholic faith. She seemed unwilling to discuss this or to describe her own feelings about being Jewish: 'I am nearer death than life, so this is not the time for talking about such things and worrying about such things.' I could pursue the subject no further.

We had tea in the dim, cool room, its thick walls protecting us from the sweltering heat outside. Later, Hannah took us on a brief tour to show us all that was left of Jewish Kleczew: the Rabbi's house, the site of the synagogue (now a cinema), and a cement shack that was once the *mikve*. A drunk reaching out with one hand for a non-existent wall was the only sign of human life as we made our way back to the car, where Feliks was fast asleep, hunched over the wheel. Hannah, reluctant to let us go, took a deep breath and released a drawn-out Jewish sigh: '*Oy vey!*' she said, speaking Yiddish for the first time. '*Dos lebn iz shver*' – Life is hard.

We returned to Konin via my father's birthplace, Golina. It turned out to be a one-street village, as it had been a hundred years ago, with this difference: now it happened to be on the main Poznan–Warsaw highway. Juggernauts thundered through the once peaceful *shtetl.*

Postscript Hannah Zakrzewska (neé Sokaszewska) died a year later in Kleczew and was buried near her daughter in the Catholic cemetery.

68

EVEN KONINERS with bitter, festering memories of their Polish past cannot hear the word Glinka without a glow of nostalgia. It restores their childhood, a spring day, the scent of blossom and the annual Lag Ba'Omer picnic on Moishe Kaplan's estate. It brings back the songs they sang as they left their stuffy classrooms behind and made their way to Glinka along a country lane.

I wanted to walk in their path, along the same country lane. The idea set Feliks laughing. Country lane! No more. Glinka was a suburb of the new town, a mere ten minutes' drive from the hotel. He took us there in his taxi. First to the church at Morzyslaw, a stone's throw from Glinka. Kaplan's workers used to pray here. The old family retainer, Swendrowski, hid the squire's son in the churchyard when he was escaping from the Germans. I strolled among the old graves, wishing that Heniek – now Henry – was with me, to point out the tomb where Swendrowski brought him food and drink at night.

When I walked back to the road, Feliks and Izzy were chatting to an old lady opposite the church. Old ladies seemed to have sharper memories than old men. This old lady was a sprightly little granny figure with an adorable grin. Dressed as if for a Polish tourist poster, she wore a patterned apron over a patterned frock and a patterned kerchief round her head. She stood in front of a picture-book cottage with a picture-book garden filled with marigolds, mallow, daisies, hollyhock, phlox, nicotiana, all in flower. Her maiden name was

Swendrowski. The man who helped young Heniek escape was her father. Why should I have been astonished? We were destined to meet.

Mariana, who was eighty-five, remembered Heniek and his parents and eleven siblings. Her father had worked for the squire, the *dziedzic*, all his life until the war broke out. Her brother also worked on the estate. Everyone around here above a certain age remembered the Kaplans. A woman standing nearby, overhearing our conversation, dashed off and reappeared a few minutes later with Mariana's sister, Zofia, a youthful seventy-eight. She hurried towards us, impatient to meet the foreigners who had appeared out of the blue bringing news of the Kaplans. Her father, she said, had been like a second father to the Kaplan children. And the dziedzic had been a good man, a good employer. The sisters knew that he and his wife and most of the children had perished. After the war they received a parcel from Lucien, Heniek's brother in France, and then there was silence.

I told them I had spoken to Heniek the week before. Heniek! He is alive? Where does he live? Is he married? Has he got children? Grandchildren! The sisters seized on every scrap of information about the surviving members of the Kaplan clan. There were surges of excitement as I mentioned the names of people who had long vanished from their lives. They repeated each name with a gasp of recognition. Jacob! Lucien! Madzia! . . .

I told them I would be seeing Heniek soon; would they like to send him a message? I held out my recorder, first for Mariana, who found it difficult to put her feelings into words. Zofia looked fixedly at the small black box, addressing it as though Heniek himself were locked inside it like a magic genie, and poured out her emotions. Her voice quavered and broke and the tears streamed down her face. It was a moment that defeated every attempt to hold my own tears back. Two daughters of a faithful retainer weeping for the old master and his family; a scene out of old Russia rather than a People's Socialist Republic. They were still standing on the soil where they were born and where they belonged, while Heniek, who had once loved this soil and been ready to fight for it, had been driven out.

Promising the sisters that we would come and see them again before we left, we drove to Glinka, a couple of minutes away. We pulled into a new road and parked near what looked like two modern apartment buildings, one of which, said Feliks, was an old people's home, the other a hospital for alcoholics. A few patients were sitting outside enjoying the last sun of the day. We walked towards open land and found ourselves at the top of a grassy hillside high above the Warta.

We could find no trace of the Kaplan house, but it must have been close to where we were standing. It was on this land that Swendrowski taught the Kaplan boys to hunt and shoot, here that they learned to row and fish. And it was here that the *dziedzic* and his family led a life that their fellow Jews in Konin could only dream about, a life they glimpsed once a year, when they sprawled under the trees and drank the squire's milk fresh from the dairy.

A few days later we returned to Morzyslaw with some small gifts for Mariana and Zofia. We were seated on a wooden bench, chatting to the two sisters, when an old man walked by, a spade sloped against one shoulder like a rifle. He wore a peaked cap, had a bushy moustache and was perfect casting for a Chekhov servant. Mariana called him over and introduced us to her brother, Franciszek. Aged eighty-two, he had clear memories of the days when he worked for the Kaplans. Once again there was that spontaneous response to an old remembered name. 'Send my warm greetings to Heniek,' he said.

We sat outside the cottage and talked, inevitably, about the past. Nostalgia reigned, and I half expected to hear the sound of cherry trees being felled. But they had been chopped down long ago.

69

When I first tried to unlock the contents of the Memorial Book, the bulk of it written in three languages I did not understand, the handful of pages in Polish seemed unimportant compared with the nearly eight hundred pages in Yiddish and Hebrew. One of the Polish pages looked like a poem. The other seven were taken up with a text under the heading Protokol. It had no introduction in

Yiddish or Hebrew, nor any illustrations that might have given me a clue as to its subject-matter. Judging by the few words I could make out, the pages appeared to be concerned neither with the Protocols of the Elders of Zion nor with the subject of diplomatic niceties. Polish names were scattered about the text, as well as dates, mostly in the 1940s. The Polish word for Jews cropped up a few times, and the name of Konin. Yet the pages exuded a dry, official flavour, and I put them to the back of my mind.

Attending a friend's Passover Seder in London in the spring of 1987, I found myself seated next to a well-educated elderly woman of Polish birth. Our after-dinner chat turned to the subject of my book. I mentioned the Polish material in the Memorial Book that was still a mystery to me. The kind woman asked to see the material, and a few weeks later sent me her translation, neatly handwritten on exercise-book paper. What I thought was a poem turned out to be the school song of the Jewish gymnasium in Konin. In her accompanying letter my translator made no reference to the enclosed contents of the Protokol text. This is what I read:

PROTOKOL[1]

On 27 October 1945, Piotr Duleba, representative chairman of the Local Court in Konin, arranged a meeting at the mass graves in the State Forest in Kazimierz Biskupi in the district of Konin in Section 1 called 'Convenience' in order to show the place to the witness, veterinary surgeon citizen [F.Z.],[2] and examine him on the spot. Present were: Chairman of the village Council of Kazimierz Biskupi, Stanislaw Radecki, and citizen Aleksander Ciborski, representative of the village Dairy of Kazimierz Biskupi, as they knew the terrain well. After arriving at the mass graves, the condition of the area was ascertained, as it had been recorded in the report of the examination by the Chairman of the Local Court of Konin on 3 October 1945, whereupon Citizen [Z.], having recognized the place, and having been warned of the consequences of giving false evidence, in accordance with Article 107 of the Penal Code, made the following deposition:

I am [F.Z.] of Konin, born on 25 December 1910, veterinary surgeon, with no criminal record, a Pole and a Catholic.

In the middle of November 1941, at 4 o'clock in the morning, Gestapo men came to my prison cell and told me to get ready for a trip. They chained my hands and took me to a private car where I found two of my fellow prisoners, my comrades in misfortune. They were sitting in the back of the car with their hands and legs chained together. They were: Walenti Orchowsky from Golina and Kazimierz Tylzanowski from the village of Rzgow. I sat down by them and the Gestapo men chained my legs. They got into the car and drove away in the direction of the railway station, then turning off onto the road to Golina. Then it turned again by the flour mill and went towards Kazimierz Biskupi. It was light now, and as I was sitting facing the front I could watch the road. Past Kazimierz Biskupi, when we entered the forest the car turned left, onto a forest path. I recognize this path now: it is marked on the sketch as number 1. The car went past another path cutting across the one we were travelling on, came to another crossing and turned right. These paths are marked on the sketch as Number 2 and 3. Then the car turned again on the second crossing and went back and stopped between the first and the second crossing, a few metres from the second one.

I recognize the place well. Then they unchained us and we were taken out of the car and stood with our backs to a forest clearing, now the place of the mass graves, marked on the sketch as I and II. We stood like that for half an hour. Then we were taken to another clearing – which I now recognize well – marked on the sketch as 'A'. It was not so overgrown then as it is today. As far as the path marked as No. 1 on the sketch, across the clearing were two pits. The first one, nearer to the path, was about 8 metres long and 6 metres wide and 2 metres deep. Almost parallel to it, at the other end of the clearing across all its width there was the second pit of the same depth, 6 metres wide and 15 metres long. Between these two pits was open space. (The witness, accompanied by the judge and all those present, points out the places, the subject of his evidence as well as the location of the two graves marked on the sketch as I and II.) All around the clearing, except the edge where the paths cross, groups of Jews were standing or sitting – the place is marked on the sketch as 'B'. I cannot say how many there were, as they were standing among trees.

The largest group stood on the spot marked on the sketch as X. (Here the witness shows the place.) In the crowd were women, men, children, mothers with children in their arms. Whether they were all Polish Jews I cannot say. I was told later that they came from Zagorow. Among them I recognized a tailor and a shopkeeper from Konin, but I don't know their names. The paths, the clearings, the whole forest swarmed with Germans. Beside the three of us brought from Konin there were about 30 other Poles assembled there, I don't know where they came from. On the bottom of the larger pit I saw a layer of quicklime, I don't know how thick the layer was. There was no lime in the smaller pit. The Gestapo men warned us that the forest was surrounded and closely watched and if we attempted to escape we would be shot in the head. Then they ordered the assembled Jews to strip – first those who were standing near the large pit. Then they ordered the naked people to go down into both pits and jump into the larger pit. I could not describe the wailing and crying. Some Jews were jumping without an order – even most of them – some were resisting and they were being beaten about and pushed down. Some mothers jumped in holding their children, some were throwing their children in, others were flinging their children aside. Still others threw the children in first and then jumped in. Some were crawling at the feet of the Gestapo men kissing their boots, their rifle-butts and the like. We were told to go among the standing Jews and collect clothing and shoes. I saw Gestapo men come up to where we were heaping watches, rings, jewellery, and stuff their pockets with them. Seeing that, some of us, and I among them, stopped putting anything precious in heaps, but threw watches, rings, further into the forest.

At one moment the Gestapo men ordered the Jews not to undress any more, as the pit was full. Those of the Jews who hurried and stripped too soon were thrown by the Gestapo men onto the heads of those already crammed in the pit. And all the while we had to collect and sort out clothing, footwear, bundles, food, eiderdowns and the like. This lasted until noon and then a lorry came from the road and stopped on the path by the clearing. I noticed four vat-like containers. Then the Germans set up a small motor – it was probably a pump – connected it with hoses to one of the vats and two of them brought the hoses from the motor up to the pit. They started the motor and the two Gestapo men began to pour some liquid, like water, on the Jews. But I am not sure what that liquid was. While pumping, they were connecting hoses to the other containers, one by one. Apparently, because of the slaking of the lime, people in the pit were boiling alive. The cries were so terrible that we who were sitting by the piles of clothing began to tear pieces off the stuff to stop our ears. The crying of those boiling in the pit was joined by the wailing and lamentation of the Jews waiting for their perdition. All this lasted perhaps two hours, perhaps longer. When darkness fell we were taken along a forest path leading to the road at the edge of the forest and to a corner marked on the sketch as '4' (here the witness shows the spot to the judge and all those present) and here we halted.

We were given coffee to drink and a quarter of a kilo of bread each. Along the edge of the forest stood six or seven lorries covered with tarpaulins. We were herded into the vehicles in such a way that we were lying one next to another with our faces down so that we could not move. We were told to sleep like that. I could still hear the cries until I fell asleep, which happened rather quickly because I was so tired. Next morning the Gestapo men ordered us to cover the large pit with soil. The pit looked as if it had been dusted with a layer of earth. The human mass inside it seemed to have collapsed and dropped to the bottom. The bodies were so tightly packed that they looked as if they were standing, only the heads lolled in all directions. We did not fill the pit very thoroughly and the hands of some of the corpses were still sticking out, because lorries began to arrive, and we were stopped. We were told to throw into them all the sorted-out stuff: clothing separately, footwear separately, and so with other articles. In the afternoon a dark grey vehicle, looking like an ambulance, arrived in the clearing a number of times. When the back door was opened, human bodies fell out, men, women and children. They, too, were Jews. This grey car drove past me three times at hourly intervals. Whether it continued to come when I was taken away, I don't know. The bodies falling out of the cars were joined together, as if linked by a convulsive embrace in distorted postures, with faces bitten away. I saw one man's teeth sunk in another's jaw. Some had their noses bitten off, some their fingers. Many were holding their hands in a convulsive grip – they must have been members of the same family. These corpses we were told to separate by force. When this could not be done, we were ordered to hack them, cut off hands, legs and other parts. Then we had to put them in the smaller pit, heads to feet, packed very tightly. The severed limbs were to be put between the trunks. While I was there three layers of bodies were packed like that, and one car was not yet unloaded. Then we were taken away as on the previous night to sleep in lorries. We were given a meal of potato soup and bread.

The following morning my two companions and I were taken for an interrogation to the edge of the clearing. Some distance away, in a place marked on the sketch as III, we were made to stand along an already dug ditch, three or four metres apart. Opposite each of us stood an armed Gestapo man. I was standing with my back to the ditch. The Gestapo man told me to confess to some supposed offences, such as reading illegal press, helping other Poles and the like. When I turned to explain that these accusations were untrue he told me to turn around and face the ditch. He warned me a few times that if I did not confess he would shoot me, but if I did I would be allowed to go home and get a good position. When the warnings had no effect he fired. My nerve failed and I fell into the pit.

A thought crossed my mind, I remember it well, that I was killed. But then I was aware of everything happening around me. The Gestapo man yelled 'Out!' I got up quickly and scrambled out of the grave. I was not wounded. Whether the man missed or just wanted to frighten me I don't know. When I got out of the grave he beat me over my face with a riding-whip and took me back to prison in Konin chained together with my two comrades the same way we had been brought here.

After a few weeks we were removed from Konin to a camp in Inowroclawiu and from there to Mauthausen and Gusen. In Gusen I remained until I was freed on 5 May 1945. My two comrades had not survived the camps.

The corpses brought in the grey car were, apparently, victims of gassing. One could smell the gas coming from inside the vehicle and the clothes of the dead. I also remember that during the extermination of Jews in the forest, one of the Gestapo men snatched a small child from its mother's hands and smashed its head before her very eyes on the edge of his car. When the mother cried out, he lashed out with the body of the child so that the head hit her on her mouth and the brain stuck to it. Then he took something from his car – lime or plaster of Paris – and stopped her mouth. They treated in the same way other women who cried. I saw how one

Gestapo man caught a pretty young Jewish girl, tore off her dress, tied her hands behind her back and tied her by her hands and a leg to a tree, then with a Finnish knife he cut slices of her right breast, then he cut her belly and with his hands rummaged in her inside. She died on the tree. I did not know any of the Gestapo men.

Here ends the report of the report of the *in situ* examination (Signed) Chairman of the District Court (illegible) – [F.Z.] – Radecki – Ciborski Reported – (illegible). Confirming the result of the examination signed by Head of Chancery Irene Skonieczna.[3]

70

LEAVING THE tarmac road behind, we joined a track that cuts its way straight as a ruler through the thick forest. The day was wrapped in a hot, humid blanket. Sunlight filtered down through the upper foliage onto shadowy undergrowth. Nothing stirred. The village of Kazimierz Biskupi was not far off, yet a sense of isolation overcame us in the engulfing forest. Soon it became clear that we were lost. Feliks had not been here before, and Izzy could hardly be expected to remember the route he last followed in 1945, one of a small group of Konin survivors who came by horse and cart to visit the mass grave, say Kaddish and erect a homemade wooden plaque. Two of his relatives were murdered in the massacres that took place here. Other Koniners were among the victims – the parents of Sarah, the partisan, and, so I have been told, one of my father's brothers, Itsik Hirsh.

The forest went on and on, giving that awesome sense of unseen land stretching endlessly away. Jewish peddlers used to trudge by foot through lonely places like Kazimierz. Wagoners from Konin rumbled along here at night in fear of robbers. Veterinary surgeon F.Z. might have come along this very track as a prisoner of the Gestapo one November day in 1941, not knowing what he was about to witness.

We bumped along the rough track, splashing through rain-filled potholes. There were no signposts or people. We turned off at an intersection onto another track, and at the next intersection we turned again. Soon we had completely lost our bearings.

I was beginning to despair of finding the memorial when a man on a moped appeared in the distance, riding towards us, a leather pouch slung over one shoulder. He was not a country postman as I first thought, but a miner on his way home at the end of his shift. He was about forty and had fair hair, an open face and a beer belly. We were going in the wrong direction, he said. We turned and he led us onto another track. After a few minutes he pointed off to the right into the trees. At the far end of a grassy clearing stood a massive slab of concrete, the result, I would guess, of earnest deliberations by a People's Committee. Were it not for the inscription, one might have taken it for an army bunker. A short pathway of cement paving-stones led up to the memorial.

The Polish inscription read: IN TRIBUTE TO THE VICTIMS OF NAZI BARBARITY. COMMUNITY OF THE DISTRICT OF KONIN 9 MAY 1980. Laid on the scrubby ground to one side of the path were seven paving-stones, the same material as the path, placed so as to form the shape of a cross. How did it come here? Had some visitor removed paving-stones from the end of the path in order to create it? That a few Christians were buried here was possible. That the remains of some eight thousand Jews lay here was certain.[1] Stones almost buried in the grass marked the outline of a mass grave.

The miner stood at a distance, watching us. Izzy went silent. My own thoughts should have been with the dead. Instead, they turned to the vet. Did he observe the scene from the tree over there? Or on the spot where I now stood? The young miner joined us and began chatting to Izzy and Feliks. I had the Memorial Book in my hand. Having carried it so many thousands of miles, how could I not bring it here? These pages, it seemed to me, were a more fitting memorial than the block of concrete.

I knew that Feliks was aware in only a generalized way of what the Germans had done in this forest. I gave him the book, opened at *Protokol*. He leaned against his car while he read it. I watched him. After a few minutes he began pressing his hand to his forehead. When he finished, he repeated over and over again: '*Tragedia, tragedia, tragedia . . .*'

There were other mass graves not far away, the miner informed us. He offered to help us find them. We followed him as he trampled through the undergrowth. The sharp crack of snapping twigs sounded like pistol shots. Izzy asked: 'Have you noticed something about this place?' I had. No birds sang. Birds probably never sang here, even before it became an evil place. Yet their absence lent the forest a brooding silence; a silence broken only by the buzz of insects and, just once, by the sound of a distant train.

About a hundred yards from the concrete monument, the miner led us into a clearing. Here was another mass grave, smaller than the first, surrounded by wooden posts. Wild plants with large bright green leaves engulfed the area of the grave. A simple headstone, stained a mossy green, rose out of the lush foliage. The inscription read: THE GRAVE OF THE INNOCENT JEWISH VICTIMS FROM THE KONIN DISTRICT MURDERED BY THE NAZI OPPRESSORS 1941–1944. This simple piece of local stone, which Hannah in Kleczew helped to erect, blended perfectly with the forest greenery.

We would never have found it without the miner's help. He led us still deeper into the forest and brought us to yet another burial site, with an identical gravestone. The weeds and rough grass had been cleared to create a tidy patch of rich brown earth. A posy of plastic flowers lay at the foot of the stone. The miner told us that boy scouts came here from time to time to tend the graves. We stood there for a moment, paying silent tribute.

The miner was born in 1947, but his parents had spoken to him about what they had seen and heard. They had also told his three children about the war years in Kazimierz. 'My mother,' he said, 'told me that once a German truck full of Jewish children overturned in the village. They must have been driving too fast. A lot of the kids just fell from under the tarpaulin onto the road. The Germans slung them all back. They were unconscious, gassed . . . Only beasts could have done such things, not men.'

Izzy asked him the question he had put to other Poles, and got the same answer. Yes, there *were* Poles who had helped the Jews, he insisted, but we had to remember that people were frightened; they knew that helping Jews would lead to their own families being shot: 'As far as I am concerned, there's no difference between Jew and Christian. I know the word Jew, but for me it is only a word. To me, people are people.' He added: 'We must never allow such things to happen again.' On that note we shook hands. He slung his satchel over his shoulder and departed on his moped.

I had dreaded coming here. I remembered the first time I read those neatly written sheets of paper. When I reached one of the bestial details so sickening that I did not want to believe it, I fled into my back garden, where the roar of a low-flying jet drowned the roaring inside my head. Yet now, standing on the spot where it happened, I felt no emotions stir. Amid this serenity, the horror was impossible to grasp. When Izzy last came here, there were still personal reminders of the victims to be seen – a button off a child's dress, a pair of shattered spectacles, a piece of broken comb, some bits of teeth. These might have opened the floodgates of feeling for me.

Nothing about my visit to Kazimierz could heighten what the Polish vet had already told me. But when we were bumping along on our way back to the road, Izzy recalled something the miner had told him. For four or five years after the war, local folk gathering mushrooms near the mass graves would occasionally come across a gold ring lying on the ground, hidden in the grass or leaves. I remembered reading that F.Z. and his fellow prisoners had thrown rings and watches into the forest to deny the executioners their booty. The Germans would have spotted the watches quite easily, but some of the rings must have vanished into the undergrowth and remained there undetected until the mushroom-gatherers came along. Sometimes, the miner recounted, a mushroom would push its way through the ground at the exact spot where a ring lay hidden. Some lucky villager would come along and find the gold circle glittering on the velvety soft cushion of a mushroom like a magic ring in a fairy tale.

71

ON OUR FIRST evening in Konin, Izzy had asked Feliks and his wife to join us for dinner. They chose the venue, an inn run by a cooperative a few miles outside the town that displayed the sign of the Konin white horse. It was situated in a forest clearing close to the road, and maybe it was this that turned my thoughts to the forest at Kazimierz. As always, it was not only the Jews or their killers who filled my thoughts but the Polish witness who lived to tell the tale – the Konin 'veterinary surgeon with no criminal record, a Pole and a Catholic', born on Christmas Day 1910. The murdered ones lived on in me because of him. I heard their last cries because of him. Now that I was so close to Kazimierz, my curiosity about him sharpened. I wondered what became of him after he returned to the forest and gave his testimony, standing on the very spot where, four years previously, he had stuffed rags into his ears to silence the screams. Might he still be alive and living in the area?

We ate our way through the meatball soup and greasy roast chicken. Then came a lull in the chatter. I became aware of my self-absorption, as did the kindly Feliks, who smiled at me encouragingly across the table. I handed him a piece of paper on which I had written the vet's name. He shook his head blankly. I showed it to his wife, who said something to Izzy. 'She knows him,' he said. 'She says he used to be a vet.' One moment I was half asleep, the next as though doused by cold water. 'Is he still alive?' I asked. Primo Levi has commented on the disparity between time as measured by a chronometer, and subjective time. One objective minute spent waiting at a red traffic light, he observed, equals eight subjective minutes. I waited several years while Izzy interpreted my question and listened to her reply: 'So far as she knows, he's still alive.' 'Does she know where he lives?' The answer: 'Somewhere in Konin.' My excitement needed no interpreter. The couple conferred briefly. Izzy said: 'They are going to try to find him for you.'

Less than twenty-four hours later I was standing outside the vet's door in the old town. His house lay back from the road behind a thickly screened front garden with a door in the garden wall. We rang the bell and waited. Through a hedge we caught a glimpse of the house, a mellow, single-storey building set in a rambling, slightly overgrown garden of bushes, hollyhocks and old apple trees. Dappled light fell on a white wooden table and rickety chair planted in the tall grass, waiting for an Impressionist painter.

We rang the bell again. We had been warned that the vet was rather deaf. Perhaps his wife was out and he could not hear the bell. A more worrying thought: perhaps they were both away and would not be back before we departed from Konin. The door was locked and we could not get closer to the house. We rang a third time, then gave up.

That night Izzy dined in Feliks's home in one of the concrete tower blocks in new Konin. Feliks's wife, who used to live in the old town, telephoned the vet and spoke to his wife. It transpired that the vet had been at home when we called and had not heard the bell. Izzy spoke to the vet's wife and explained why I wanted to meet him. They arranged for us to call at the house two days later, after our visit to the forest.

Mrs Z. was waiting for us by the garden door when we arrived, a smiling well-groomed woman probably in her early sixties, wearing a smart, silk dress. She led us through the garden. In a small room overlooking the front garden, Mr Z.[1] stood up to greet us, a tall gentlemanly figure with a moustache and a lock of grey hair that fell across his high forehead. His jacket, dating from earlier years, hung loosely over his frail, bony frame. To me he looked utterly English, a touch Edwardian, maybe a retired, fondly remembered schoolmaster. As we shook hands he bowed his head slightly the way Poles do.

Izzy and the vet's wife perched on the edge of a bed that occupied much of the space in the room, while the vet and I sat on chairs. I threw out some mundane opening remark, which Izzy interpreted. The vet cupped a hand to his ear. Izzy repeated the remark. The vet leaned towards him, straining to hear. His wife repeated the words, loudly, carefully articulating each syllable. The vet stared at her lips, his face taut with concentration. She shouted the words. His hearing-aid began to emit a high-pitched whistle. He cupped his hands over both ears, making an even greater effort to hear.

His wife got out some books dealing with Nazi war crimes. She said they contained evidence that her husband had given after the war. The vet pointed at a number of references to his name and made some comments. His voice was steady, his eyes bright, his brain sentient. He possessed all his faculties, save one. When he needed to call on it, he relapsed into a state of helplessness. I made several attempts to get through to him, but in vain.

At one point the vet produced a set of well-thumbed black-and-white photographs. I recognized their subject: the shooting of the first two hostages in Konin, the Pole Kurowski and the Jew Slodki.

One of the pictures, the firing squad taking aim at the two men, was in the Memorial Book. But the vet had other pictures of the execution that I had not seen before: the hostages being led over to the wall, a priest in a long cassock walking behind them, and a picture of them after the bullets had hit home – two dark, crumpled heaps lying on the ground, a helmeted German bending over them, the priest kneeling beside them in prayer.

I asked if the vet knew who had taken the photographs. Izzy put the question to him with no success. His wife tried, raising her voice to a shout. She started to write out my questions on a piece of paper, an idea that had crossed my mind already – Beethoven's visitors got by well enough with a slate and a piece of chalk. Halfway through writing out the sentence, she lost patience and made another futile attempt to get through to him, shouting straight into his ear. The hearing aid began whistling again. She gave up with a gesture of exasperation and frustration. It was plain how badly she was suffering on his behalf.

I encouraged her to persist with pen and paper. She wrote another couple of words before hopelessness engulfed her again. She said something to Izzy, and the two of them embarked on an extended conversation in Polish. I toyed with the idea of writing my questions in German, but each time I was halfway to formulating a grammatical sentence, Izzy would suddenly interpret one of Mrs Z.'s remarks, and I would be diverted from my task.

I decided to try to find out more about the vet by putting questions to his wife, who seemed more than ready to speak for him, but Izzy kept a hold on her attention. I heard him mention the name Szwiatowicz and knew he was talking about his grandfather. Mrs Z. shouted 'Szwiatowicz' into her husband's ear: 'SZWIATOWICZ! SZWIATOWICZ!' Miraculously, he heard. With a grin that transformed his face, he made the gesture of a droshky driver cracking his whip. 'You see,' said Izzy elated, 'he remembers my grandfather.'

Mrs Z. and I realized we could just about make ourselves understood in German, but there was a problem: whenever she stumbled in German and groped for the right word, she would address Izzy in Polish and then forget to revert to German. I would try to tempt her back, but with no success. It was easier for her to speak Polish. I glanced across at the vet, slumped in his chair. We looked into each other's eyes, both of us frantic to communicate, both in our different ways deaf.

Mrs Z., according to Izzy, was aggrieved on her husband's behalf. She was angry that no one had shown any interest in her husband, who had been in the Polish resistance and gone through so much pain. He had not even been given a decent hearing-aid. The one he was wearing kept breaking down, and getting it repaired meant an exhausting trip to Poznan. They had spent the whole day there only yesterday, and we could see for ourselves what a waste of time it had been. She was resentful at the way the world had neglected him. What compensation had he received? She said I was the first Jew who had come back to see him. I bridled at the implied criticism of the Konin survivors. Their lives too, I pointed out, had not been exactly a bed of roses. They had lost their health, families, homes, everything. Did she expect them to return to Konin from all over the world to help her husband because he, like them, had suffered at the hands of the Germans? I did not know if my message got through. My German was probably unintelligible and perhaps I had misconstrued her remark. She was becoming over-excited, angry at the world's indifference to her husband's plight.

I tried to explain why I was interested in the history of the Jews of Konin, why I wanted to speak to her husband, who had seen for himself how some of the Jews had died. Izzy did his best to help when my German broke down, but again her reply in Polish would draw a comment from him and the two of them would get carried away. 'What is she saying, Izzy? What is she saying?' It was hopeless.

The vet's wife calmed down. She said we had to understand that our meeting was a difficult experience for her and her husband. He had taken special pills to enable him to cope with the stress. She had been in a labour camp during the war, and her own health was poor. His deafness was a terrible ordeal for them both. She began to cry silently. I looked across at the vet. He was bowed over, clutching his head tightly with both hands, staring down into his lap. I felt uncomfortable. Ought I to have come? Was I entitled to intrude into their lives?

The atmosphere revived the moment two attractive young women appeared from another room – their daughters, said Mrs Z. One was an engineer, the other an actress. They did not live in Konin and were visiting their parents for the day. Their spirited personalities brightened the room. Two young grandchildren scampered after them. The sisters brought in silver and china tea things and Mrs Z. served generous portions of cake. While we chatted, the vet sipped his tea, silent and withdrawn.

I awakened his attention by showing him the Memorial Book. He turned over the *Protokol* pages and looked at the illustrations of old Konin, recognizing each landmark with undisguised delight. He said he would love to have a copy of this book even though he could not read it. He flipped over the pages of Yiddish text until he came to the black-edged pages. I pointed out the name Ryczke printed in Hebrew letters. He said he remembered Aron Ryczke. Izzy rolled up his sleeve and showed the vet his Auschwitz number. The vet said he had been given a number too in Mauthausen, but his was on a tag round his wrist. He said he had seen people destined for the crematorium.

The sisters went in and out, preoccupied with the children playing in the next room. Mrs Z. told us she had three daughters, all gifted in their different ways. She brought in a plaster figure about fifteen inches high, which her other daughter had sculpted. It was the thin and elongated body of a man, head tilted back to an almost horizontal position, skeletal arms stretched up to the sky. Two strands of barbed wire, real barbed wire, embedded across the front of the torso gave the figure a grim power. A miniature Jesus stood at the base of the sculpture. One of the vet's experiences in Mauthausen had inspired the piece. One day, his wife related, when he was in the throes of despair, he decided to end it all by throwing himself against the electrified fence as others had done. He was about to run at the fence when his mother's voice came to him, holding him back.

While Mrs Z. told us the story, the vet looked on, knowing what she was telling us, adding nothing to it. I wished he were more loquacious. For much of our visit it was as though he had lost his power of speech as well as his sense of hearing. Perhaps he had got too used to his wife doing the talking. Mrs Z. asked us, almost pleadingly, if we could find him a better hearing-aid in London, and we promised to try.

The visit was drawing to an end on a relaxed and cordial note. The daughters came in to say goodbye. Then, as we were about to leave the room, they did something that took us both by surprise.

Reflecting on it afterwards, I realized they were giving us a parting present. Standing side by side in an open doorway, they began to sing a sweet and delicate melody, a song I had never heard before, perhaps a folk song. The engineer sang the words while her sister hummed. The two voices blended in unison, parted in melancholy harmony, came together again, separated, rising and falling with the graceful ease of birds floating on a current of air.

Their listeners had unwittingly arranged themselves as if for a painting, composed to lead the eye from one face to the next: the children gazing up, entranced; Izzy, absorbed yet instantly aware of being observed; Mrs Z., on the edge of tears, lost in maternal pride, and the vet, bent forward, head turned away, hand cupped to ear, trying to trap the sound waves carrying his daughters' music. I listened more closely to their words and realized that the language they were singing was Hebrew.

It was Modern Hebrew. That much I could tell without understanding the words. Their pronunciation was so authentic I might have been listening to an Israeli folk duo. I closed my eyes and tried to convince myself that I was not hallucinating, that I was indeed in a house in old Konin, long after all the Jews had departed, listening to two young Polish women singing a Jewish melody. I wished the sound were loud enough to carry to the nearby synagogue, where not a word of Hebrew, ancient or modern, had been heard for forty-eight years. I wished it were audible to Konin's Jewish dead. And to the vet.

The afternoon was drawing to a close and we had to be on our way. In the flurry of leaving, I failed to find out more about the song. Izzy vaguely remembered the sisters saying they had learned it at an academy in Poznan. (Later I discovered that the song was a modern romantic ballad from Israel.) I followed Mrs Z. out into the garden, and we stood talking for a moment near the table under the trees. She was a stalwart woman but she found her husband's handicap painful to observe day after day. She said in German: 'Oh, it is so sad, the way he sits here in the garden. He has no one to talk to.' Her eyes filled again. He used to address schools and talk about his experiences, but those days were over, she said. All he did now was sit and write. She knew we had visited the forest at Kazimierz. She could not let him go there again. The memories were too painful. As it was, he jumped and cried out in his sleep.

We had not talked about Kazimierz. The vet had said everything that was to be said many years ago. But his deafness had robbed me of an opportunity to converse with him about other things, had deprived me of insights into the past he might have given me. Yet I felt I had gained through being in his presence.

When we said goodbye and I put my arm on his shoulder, I felt the fleshless bones pressing through his jacket. He bowed and said something in Polish, which his wife translated: 'He says you have great luck that he, the last, the only one who still lives of those who saw those terrible things, is still here. And he says you are the first to come and see him.'

72

THE LAST DAY. A drizzle fell from a dirty sheet of sky as I crossed the meadows, turned off onto the old Slupca road and approached the river. It was all so familiar to me now, part of a daily routine. I stopped on the bridge and looked down at the choppy water, pewter grey. I had grown fond of the Warta in every light, but I was beginning to miss the other river in my life.

I had not yet visited the park. As a boy I had heard my mother talk of its lawns where the rich folk played croquet, the lake with a miniature bridge, the bandstand where the Russian cavalry musicians in their splendid uniforms played on Sunday afternoons, the tables under the trees . . . People went there to stroll, chat and, when they were old, just sit and admire the flower-beds. They liked nature this way: orderly and tamed.

From the Tepper Marik I walked up Mickiewicz Street, past the synagogue, towards the park facing the far end of the street. The entrance was solidly municipal: heavy iron gates, a green noticeboard with a map, a raised circle of blazing red flowers. Through the trees I could hear the rhythmic metallic squeal of swings and the sound of children's voices. The rain had eased off, leaving the bench seats with a glossy coat.

The park, much larger than I had expected, was partly floral and manicured, partly wooded with soaring trees. I came upon an open-air arena, a lake with swans and ducks, and an enclosure for deer. Near it stood a signpost with a single word that struck me with the force of a blow. There, in bold lettering, was my maternal family name: SARNA. What could it be doing here? Of course. It was the Polish word for deer. In the park that my mother loved so much, her name lives on.

It began to pour. Back in the Tepper Marik, I sat under a yellow bus-shelter and waited as the rain drummed on the plastic roof. Buses came and went. Bedraggled figures hurried down the street, past the house where the Rabbi once lived.

Early next morning, before going to the station to catch the Warsaw train, I stood alone on the edge of the new town, looking down over the meadows towards old Konin. The rain had washed everything clean, leaving the sky a piercing blue. Distance lost its meaning in the crystal light. It seemed as if the eye could pick out every blade of grass a mile away. The traffic coming and going over the iron bridge was powerless to pollute this flawless day.

From the beginning I had known I would have to come here. Now the journey was done. Curiosity was satisfied, an ache assuaged. To say I felt regret at leaving this place would be false and sentimental. I felt no emotion. Maybe it was spent. Or maybe the town was releasing me from its grip, for I knew now that it was not the place that held meaning for me but the people who once lived here. Their Konin would stay with me always, a persistent echo.

APPENDIX A: A Konin Chronology

1264 Boleslaw the Pious signs the Statute of Kalisz, giving Jews significant religious and economic freedoms in his domain of Wielkopolska (Great Poland).

1293 The first document to mention the granting of town status to Konin under the Magdeburg Law is dated 1293, but Konin almost certainly achieved that status before then, probably in 1284 or 1292, when the Prince of Wielkopolska, later King of Poland, Przemysl II, stayed in Konin.

1331 Crusaders destroy the wooden town.

1336 King Kazimierz the Great visits Konin.

1397 First recorded reference to a Jew in Konin.

During the second half of the century the town is rebuilt under Kazimierz the Great. By the end of the century Konin, a royal city, has become the capital of the district within the Province of Kalisz. A brick castle guards the river crossing, providing defence against attacks by the Teutonic Knights.

1425 King Wladyslaw Jagiello stays in Konin and grants the town important concessions, including the right to hold a second annual fair, which is of special benefit to Jewish traders.

In the later 15th century the town has approximately 150 Jewish inhabitants, engaged in moneylending, commerce and crafts. Local court books record the names and activities of some Konin Jews. At the end of the century a great fire destroys a major part of the town.

1628 Cholera decimates the population.

1656 The Swedish army burns down most of Konin. Pogroms follow the liberation of the town.

1662 Cholera again cuts a swathe through the population, reducing it to 200.

1707 Swedish forces attack Konin and destroy the castle. A slow improvement in Konin's fortunes continues through the rest of the century.

1765 Census of the Jews: approximately 168 Jewish inhabitants.

1763–6 Building of a synagogue marks the establishment of an autonomous Jewish community – a *kahal*, or *kehillah*.
1793 Second Partition of Poland brings Konin under Prussian rule. A wooden bridge is built over the Warta.
1794 Local support for the failed national insurrection led by Tadeusz Kosciuszko.
1795 Third Partition. Poland disappears from the map of Europe. Konin remains under Prussian rule.
1796 Fire devastates the town, destroying the medieval town hall.
1806–8 A new Jewish cemetery is founded.
1807–15 Konin becomes part of the semi-autonomous Grand Duchy of Warsaw, created by Napoleon.
1810 Jewish community appoints its first Rabbi, Tsvi Hirsh Amsterdam.
1815 Following Napoleon's defeat and the Congress of Vienna, Poland again leaves the map of Europe. Russia's vastly enlarged territory encompasses Konin, part of the new Congress Kingdom. Its administrative status is that of a district (*powiat*) within the provincial government (*gubernia* of Kalisz.
1829 The synagogue is rebuilt and enriched with new decorations.
1830 November Rising does not affect the town physically, but in 1831 its citizens participate in opposing the Russians.
1863 Jews participate in January Rising. Many skirmishes in the area.
1864 From this year on, the Congress Kingdom effectively ceases to exist; its territory, including Konin, is fully incorporated into the Russian empire.
1870 *Beth Hamidrash* (*bes-medresh*) is built next to the synagogue.
1872 Sir Moses Montefiore stops in Konin en route to St Petersburg.

Second half of the 19th century: Jews play a prominent role in Konin's commercial and industrial expansion.

1883 The Jewish inhabitants represent 52% of the town's population.
1905 Konin Bundists join in revolutionary demonstrations against the Tsarist regime. Founding of the Jewish lending library.
1914 August: battle between Prussian and Russian forces is fought close to the town; clashes in the streets. During the German occupation Konin has its first and last Jewish mayor.
1918 Poland gains its independence. Konin becomes a district (*powiat*) within the province (*wojewodztwo*) of Lodz. A coeducational Jewish gymnasium opens.
1919 Under the Treaty of Versailles, Poland's frontier with Germany is

shifted westward; Konin now lies 180 km from the nearest checkpoint.

1918–39 Economic situation deteriorates badly in the years of hyperinflation following the First World War and makes some recovery during the last years of the Twenties. Anti-Semitic boycott hits Jewish shops and traders.

1923 Completion of railway link with Poznan and Warsaw puts Konin on the main Berlin–Warsaw–Moscow line.

1928–29 Jewish synagogue closes.

1938 Changes in local government boundaries: Konin comes within the province of Poznan, which has a more overtly anti-Semitic tradition than Lodz.

1939 Konin's total population of about 12,000 includes approximately 2,700 Jews.

1939–45 Second World War. German forces enter Konin on 14 September 1939. Konin is annexed to the Third Reich as part of the newly constituted Wartheland. During the war years many Polish intellectuals in Konin are executed; other Polish citizens are removed eastwards to the territory of the General Government or transported as slave labour to Germany.

1939 22 September: public execution of a Pole and a Jew in the town square. Night of 30 November/1 December: first deportations of Jews to ghettos in the General Government; most went to Ostrowiec Swietokrzyski, some to Jozefow and other small towns.

1941 Last deportations mark the end of the Jewish community in Konin. During the Nazi occupation the synagogue interior, Jewish cemetery and parts of the Jewish quarter are destroyed. Many thousands of Jews from the Konin region die in massacres in the nearby Kazimierz forest.

1942 Massacre of Jews in Jozefow. Jews in the Ostrowiec ghetto are transported to Treblinka; those who remain are transferred to a local forced-labour camp. The Germans establish a forced-labour camp close to Konin's railway station.

1943 Revolt of Jewish prisoners in Konin labour camp.

1944 Labour camp in Ostrowiec is liquidated and inmates transported to Auschwitz.

1945 20 January: first Russian troops enter the town. 23 January: a Red Army communiqué declares Konin liberated. February: new district council under Communist control (PPR – Polish Workers' Party).

Postwar years Konin is designated as a new industrial centre, with open-cast coal-mining, power stations, an aluminium plant and other large-scale projects. A new town for workers goes up on the north bank of the Warta, near the railway station.

1975 The town becomes capital of the province of Konin.

1989 End of Communist regime in Poland. Konin's population has grown from 12,145 in 1950 to 80,290.

APPENDIX B: KONIN POPULATION STATISTICS TO 1939

(Source: *Pinkas Hakehillot, Encyclopaedia of Jewish Communities, Poland,* vol. 1, *The Communities of Lodz and its Region* [Yad Vashem, Jerusalem, 1976], p. 235.)

Year	Total Pop.	Jews	Jews as % of Pop.*
15th c.	–	180 (approx.)†	-
1764/65	-	168	-
1808	2,015	369	1831
1827	3,568	862	24.15
1857	5,147	2,006	38.97
1883	6,533	3,400 (approx.)	52.00‡
1897	7,823	2,502	31.72
1921	10,045	2,902	28.88
1.9.39	13,000 (approx.)	3,000 (approx.)	23.00 (approx.)

*Percentages calculated by author.

†'Approximately 150' according to the *Encyclopaedia Judaica*, vol. 10, p. 1179.

‡'The percentage for 1883 comes from Eugeniusz Biderman and Barbara Rewekant, in their paper, 'Dynamika Rozwoju Oraz Przemiany Struktury Ludnosci Miasta Konina W Drugiej Polowie XIX I W XX Wieku', in *Rocznik Koninski* No. 8 (Konin, 1980), p. 43.

Konin's Jewish population in 1939

The encylopaedia *Pinkas Hakehillot* and the *Encyclopaedia Judaica* both give the Jewish population in 1939 as 'approximately 3,000'. The former states the total population as 'approximately 13,000'. The Polish compilers of a table drawn from data in the National Archive state the total population in 1939 as 12,100, but they do not give figures concerning the Jewish population in that year. They do, however, provide some information for 1938, that shows the Jewish residents as 21.9% of the population (Biderman and Rewekant, cited above). Assuming that the total population and the percentage of Jews in 1939 were the same as in 1938, this would give us a Jewish population of 2,650. Taking other evidence into account, I have rounded this figure up to 2,700. It should also be borne in mind that the number of Jews in Konin fluctuated in the course of 1939, particularly during the period leading up to the German occupation of Konin in September of that year.

Glossary

aliyah: immigration to the land of Israel.

beth hamidrash (Heb.), *bes-medresh* (Yid.): combined place of study and synagogue, also used as a meeting-place.

buba: granny.

Bund: Jewish workers' party, banned in Tsarist times.

Cabbala: Jewish mystical philosophy.

challa: plaited white bread eaten on the Sabbath.

chalutz (pl. *chalutzim*): Zionist pioneer.

Chanukah: Festival of Lights.

chazan: cantor.

cheder: Elementary religious school.

chevre: association, congregation.

Chevre Kadishe: burial society.

chomets: leavened dough or bread, forbidden during Passover.

chuppeh: wedding canopy.

Eretz Yisrael: the land of Israel.

feldsher: old-time barber-surgeon, bone-setter, general 'paramedic'.

frum: religiously observant.

galanteria: fancy goods, haberdashery.

Gemoreh: part of the Talmud.

goy: Gentile.

Haskalah: the Jewish Enlightenment.

heym (as in *der heym*): the Old Country (literally, home).

Judenrein: cleansed of Jews.

Kaddish: Mourner's prayer for the dead.

kehillah: organized Jewish community.

kitl: white linen robe worn by men on some religious occasions.

Kol Nidre: the solemn prayer on the eve of Yom Kippur that ushers in the Day of Atonement.

Lag Ba'Omer: a mid-spring harvest festival.

landsmanshaft: association of immigrants from the same town or region in Eastern Europe.

landsman (pl. *landslayt*): compatriot from the same town or region.
maskil (pl. maskilim): follower of the Haskalah.
melamed (pl. *melamdim*): cheder teacher.
mezuzah: scroll inscribed with holy words, encased in a narrow container attached to the doorpost.
mikve: Ritual bath.
minyan: quorum of ten males over the age of 13, required for public worship.
mitzve: virtuous deed.
nadn: dowry.
Pesach: Passover.
Purim: Festival of Esther.
rebbetsn: wife of a rabbi.
Rosh Hashanah: Jewish New Year.
Seder: festive meal on the first two nights of Passover.
shammes: beadle.
Shavuoth: Festival of Weeks (Pentecost).
sheytl: wig worn by religiously observant married women.
shoychet: ritual slaughterer.
shtetl (pl. *shtetlekh*): small market town in Eastern Europe with a Jewish community.
shtibl: Chasidic house of prayer (literally: small room).
shtrayml: fur-edged hat worn by Chasidim on the Sabbath and Holy Days (also sometimes worn by rabbis in Eastern Europe).
shul: synagogue.
Simchat Torah: Festival of Rejoicing in the Law.
Sukkot: Feast of Tabernacles.
sukkah: booth erected for Sukkot.
tefillin: phylacteries.
treyf: non-kosher food.
tsimmes: vegetable (or fruit) stew.
Volksdeutscher: an 'ethnic German' loyal to the *Führer*.
yeshiva: rabbinic seminary for Talmudic study.
yeshiva bokher: *yeshiva* student.
yiches: family pedigree, status.
yidishkeyt: traditional Jewishness.
Yizkor: remembrance; the name of a memorial prayer.
Yom Kippur: Day of Atonement.
yortsayt: anniversary of a death, when Kaddish is recited.

NOTES AND SOURCES

All unsourced notes in the text come from interviews with former citizens of Konin, and their relations, conducted between 1987 and 1994.

Abbreviations

EJ *Encyclopaedia Judaica* (Jerusalem, 1971).
KMB *Konin Memorial Book*. Hebrew title, *Kehilat Konin be-Frihata u-ve-Hurbana* (*The Community of Konin: Its Flowering and Destruction*), ed. M. Gelbart (Association of Konin Jews in Israel, Tel Aviv, 1968).
PH *Pinkas Hakehillot, Encyclopaedia of Jewish Communities, Poland*, vol. I, *The Communities of Lodz and Its Region* (published in Hebrew, Yad Vashem, Jerusalem, 1976).
YVA Yad Vashem Archives, Jerusalem.

Introduction

1 Michael Ignatieff, *The Russian Album* (London, 1987), p. 2.
2 Rabbi Israel Ben Eliezer (*c.*1700–60), known to his followers as the Ba'al Shem Tov (Master of the Good Name).

1

1 I have drawn this from the legend given in KMB, p. 19. The KMB almost certainly took it from Zygmunt Pecherski's book, *Konin, Slupca, Kolo* (Warsaw, 1958), pp. 21–2. Simon Dubnow, in his great work, *History of the Jews in Russia and Poland* (translated from the Russian by I. Friedlaender: Jewish Publication Society of America, Philadelphia, 1946, vol. I, p. 40), provides another Prince Leszek legend: 'At the end of the ninth century a Jewish delegation from Germany waited upon the Polish Prince Leshek [*sic*], to plead for the admission of Jews into Poland. Leshek subjected the delegates to a protracted cross-examination concerning the principles of the Jewish religion and Jewish morality, and finally complied with their request. Thereupon large numbers of German Jews began to arrive in Poland, and, in 1905, they obtained special written privileges,

which, according to the same legend, were subsequently lost. These obscure tales, though lacking all foundation in fact, and undoubtedly invented in much later times, contain a grain of historic truth, in that they indicate the existence of Jewish settlements in pagan Poland and point to their German origin.'

2 The assassin, who was executed, was not a Koniner by birth. He painted the murals in Konin between 1904 and 1910.

3 She was not a Koniner by birth. Born in 1849, she came to Konin with her parents when she was fifteen, and lived there all her life. She died in 1939. Today, the street where she lived and a school in Konin are named after her.

4 In the 19th century it was moved to its present location in the churchyard of Konin's Catholic church of St Bartholomew.

5 Schwarmans, *Itinéraire de Napoléon* (Paris, 1911), 16 Dec. 1806: Napoleon left Posen at 3 am and travelled to Klodowa via Wreschin (present-day Wrzesnia). Konin lies on the highway between Wrzesnia and Klodowa. David G. Chandler, author of the definitive work, *Campaigns of Napoleon* (London, 1986), generously helped me in my attempts to establish a Napoleonic connection with Konin.

3

1 Ephraim Solomon ben Aaron of Luntschitz (Lenczyca), author of *Keli Yakar* (Precious Vessel), annotations on the Pentateuch, and other works; b. 1550; Head of *yeshiva* at Lemberg; Rabbi of Prague 1604–18; d. Prague 1619.

2 Known as the five Levi brothers, and famous in Poland in their day, they were: Asher Laemmle, Rabbi in Golina; Nahum, Rabbi in Szadek; Yaakov Yehuda Leib, Rabbi in Slesin; Yisrael, Rabbi in Posen (Poznan); Shlomo Zalman, Rabbi in Zloczew. The first three went to Jerusalem, where they were active in establishing the Orthodox neighbourhood of Meah Shearim. Their grandfather, Shlomo Zalman, was an eminent scholar in Posen. My maternal grandparents (they were first cousins) stemmed from this line.

3 Also spelled Abravenel and Abarbanel.

4 Leo Rosten, *The Joys of Yiddish* (London, 1970), p. 28.

5

1 The Yiddish writer I.L. Peretz wrote a short story, 'Bontshe Shvayg',

about a man, meek and poor, who suffered his misfortunes in silence. Perhaps this famous story inspired Sarah-Gitl's nickname.

2 Mordechai Moskowicz, KMB, p. 392.

6

1 Although it would be more correct to transliterate the Yiddish as 'Tepper Mark' rather than 'Marik', the latter conveys more accurately the way Konin Jews pronounce the word, with a rolling 'r'. The official Polish name for the square was Rynek Garncarski, which also means Pot Market.

2 Following Polish independence it was named Plac Wolnosci, Freedom Square, but continued to be known by local Jews and gentiles alike as 'the big square'.

3 Chanoch Neuman, KMB, p. 349.

4 In an exhibition, *Twilight of the Tsars*, at the London Hayward Gallery in 1991, I came across an item from the State Lenin Library, a paper wrapper 'for Renomé's *Bim-Bom* sweets'. Perhaps the fish-seller once had a weakness for them?

8

1 Karol Hahn came to London after the war with his brother. He died in London in September 1993.

9

1 Sometimes a touch of honey was dabbed on the cover of a prayer book and the boy was asked to lick it off.

2 The Yiddish word *rebbe* is used as a courtesy title and is synonymous with the Hebrew *melamed*; it is also used, in a different sense, to denote the head of a Chasidic sect. *Rebbe* is not to be confused with rabbi, though both derive from the Hebrew for teacher. A rabbi – *rov* in Yiddish – was one who had been to yeshiva and received ordination.

3 EJ, vol. 6, p. 429.

4 I have been unable to trace the actor's name. Another of *Rebbe* Meyer's pupils was Mendel Sachs, born in Konin in 1897. He studied philosophy at Warsaw University and emigrated in 1923 to Argentina, where he became well known as a Yiddish author writing under the pseudonym Emza.

5 Yeshia S. Zandberg, 'Melamdim and Cheder Boys, Memories from my Cheder Years' (my translation), KMB, pp. 208–11. Zandberg,

born in Kalisz in 1891, left Poland in 1919 and settled in Belgium, where he earned his living as a photo-journalist. He wrote lyric poetry (which he set to his own music) and other works in Yiddish, and also set French and Flemish poetry to music. Zandberg survived the Second World War, protected by the King of Belgium and died in Brussels in 1972.

6 Zandberg, KMB, p. 205.

8 KMB, p. 207.

9 Shmarya Levin, *Childhood in Exile*, trans. Maurice Samuel (London, 1939), p. 45.

10 Letter to the author from Rywka Diament, 5 Dec. 1991. She is the widow of the Yiddish author Zanvel Diament (*sic*). Her father, the *melamed*, who was born in Kolo, died in Konin in 1928.

11 KMB, p. 235.

12 Some were known by the towns they originated from: the Lodzer *melamed*, the Dobra *melamed*, the Kwaler *melamed*, and so on.

13 Zandberg, KMB, pp. 197, 198.

14 Zandberg, KMB, p. 201.

15 KMB, pp. 225, 226, author's translation.

16 The method was known as *ivrit b'ivrit* (Hebrew in Hebrew). The reformed *cheder*, the so-called *cheder mesukn*, existed in other enlightened Jewish communities of Poland towards the end of the 19th century. Zandberg (KMB, p. 199) mentions the *cheder mesukn* in Konin, and my grandfather's part in its foundation.

17 Asher Sarna, in conversation with the author. Asher and his brother Abie became Lichtenstein's pupils after the *rebbe* settled in England shortly after the First World War. Their elder brother, Jacob, studied under him for a while in Konin. (KMB offers a few more details about him on p. 219

18 He was almost certainly influenced by the Jewish educational reform movement in Poland, and used the *ivrit-b'ivrit* method of instruction.

19 One was called Yesoydas Hatorah, and was sponsored by the Orthodox Zionist party, Agudah Israel. Chasidic families favoured it and played a leading part in its administration. Some of the teachers of secular subjects were Christians, as there were no qualified Jews available to fill these posts. Its headmaster, Zalman Yankelewicz (not a Koniner), emigrated to Palestine in 1935, became influential in the Agudah Yisrael movement there, and was a deputy in the Knesset. He died in Israel in the 1950s (KMB, pp. 239–40). The other school,

which was part of the Yavne network of schools in Poland, came under the aegis of the Mizrachi party. As Zionists, they approved of the use of Hebrew as a modern language, for conversation as well as instruction. The Agudah Yisrael believed that Hebrew should be used only as a sacred language, and favoured Yiddish as the language of everyday use as well as the language of instruction. Both these schools transcended the traditional one-room, one-teacher *cheder*.

20 Freda Eisenstadt-Zandberg, 'Rivke the Melamedke', KMB, pp. 239, 240, author's translation.

21 Sarah Schenirer (1883–1935).

22 In 1929 the Agudah Yisrael took over the sponsorship of the Bes Yaakov schools.

23 Moishe Hirsh, writing about his grandfather, Menahel Ozerowicz, known as the Qvaler *melamed*, KMB, p. 222.

10

1 Called in Polish *Uciecha*, meaning pleasure, delight, joy.

2 The members of the governing body, known as *dozors*, were unpaid servants of the community, democratically elected by the Jewish adult population in accordance with, and under the supervision of, the Polish authorities. Police were in attendance during the counting of the ballots. Religious and political groupings of every hue were represented.

3 The rightwing National Democracy Party (*Narodowa Demokracja*), known by its acronym, *Endecja*.

12

1 My father learned English at evening classes and came to speak it perfectly without a trace of a foreign accent. His teacher, an Englishman who had difficulties with foreign words, urged him to change the name Ryczke. Unable to think of a new name, my father turned to his teacher for advice. He said: 'The first syllable of your name is pronounced like *rich*. I live near a town called Richmond, why not call yourself that?' He did, and it was not until I myself had lived in Richmond nearly twenty years that my father told me this story.

2 Fifty Years of Konin Jewry' by Leo Monczka, a typescript in German deposited in the archives of Yad Vashem, Jerusalem (YVA Ref. 0-3/3441, p. 65). Extracts in Yiddish appear in KMB, pp. 243–50

and 469–75. It is likely that Monczka wrote the original in German and subsequently had extracts translated into Yiddish.

3 Herman Krol served with the Polish army throughout the Second World War, ending up in Italy. In 1994, aged over eighty, he was still working as a bespoke tailor in London's Whitechapel, travelling to his workshop every day from his home in North London.

4 Testimony by Jacob Krafchik (YVA Ref. 0-3/4118, pp. 1–65). Krafchik came to Britain after surviving several concentration camps. He became a tailor in Preston, where he died. His testimony, quoted here in English, was almost certainly written by him in his adopted language.

5 Antoni Studzinski, 'Koninski Wrzesien 1939 Roku', in *Ziemia Koninska, vol. III, Materialy Na Sympozjum KTR* (Koninskie Towarzystwo Regionalne, Konin, 1972), p. 89. The Konin anti-aircraft duck theory appears in this symposium published in Konin. Alas, I have not been able to verify it with any of the pilots. There is some conflict of evidence on the subject of Konin's first air raid: Krafchik states (his testimony, p. 1): '1 Sept. 1939 . . . Konin had its first air raid at 2.30 pm. Ten people were killed and the railway station completely destroyed.' Monczka reports in 'Fifty Years of Konin Jewry', p. 65: 'On 1 Sept. German pilots pass over the town. They greet us with bombs thrown onto the station.' I have followed the Polish version in Studzinski, 'Koninski Wrzesien'.

6 Krafchik p. 2.

7 Studzinski, p. 93.

8 Ibid. The author mistakenly cites 2 Sept. as the date Britain and France entered the war. Many of the details in this and the following paragraphs come from Studzinski, pp. 91–8.

9 Monczka, p. 66. The next paragraph and the accompanying quote also draw on Monczka, pp. 66–8.

10 Krafchik, p. 4.

11 The wooden bridge was blown up on the night of 9/10 Sept. according to Studzinski, p. 99, and Monczka, p. 68.

13

1 KMB, p. 478.

2 See also Avrom Kempinski, KMB, p. 478.

3 Antoni Studzinski, 'Koninski Wrzesien 1939 Roku', in *Ziemia Koninska*, vol. III (Konin, 1972), p. 90.

4 Ibid.

5 Ibid., p. 100.

6 Jozef Lewandowski, *Cztery dni w Atlantydzie* (four Days in Atlantis) (Uppsala, 1991), p. 33. The young man's name was Gucio. Leo Monczka (YVA Ref. 0-3/3551, p. 73) describes the beating-up of a local ethnic German whose daughter was accused of being anti-German before the war.

7 Avrom Kempinski, KMB, p. 481.

8 Avrom Kempinski, KMB, p. 483. Kempinski escaped from Poland and entered Palestine as an illegal immigrant in 1940 via Lithuania, Moscow and Japan. After the war he was a leading light of the Association of Konin Jews in Israel, and served on the Memorial Book committee. He died in Israel (*c.* 1958) at the age of 48.

9 My maternal grandmother's brother, known to the family in London as '*der fetter Shmuel Leizer*' – Uncle Shmuel Leizer. The unintelligible word 'derfettershmueleizer' was one of the Konin-associated words imprinted on my memory at an early age.

10 Monczka, YVA, p. 68, text in German. Extracts from this testimony, given in Yiddish, are included in KMB, pp. 469–75.

11 Monczka, YVA, p. 69.

12 According to Studzinski, p. 103, the Germans claimed the killing of a soldier as a pretext for the execution.

13 Monczka, YVA, p. 69.

14 Studzinski, p. 103.

15 Mikhail Moskowicz, KMB, p. 428. Drumming is also mentioned by Avrom Kempinski, KMB, p. 479.

16 Monczka makes no comment on how the doomed men were chosen, and one is left with the impression that the Germans picked the names at random. Local Polish reports cast no light on this matter. According to Avrom Kempinski (who was in Konin at the time but not one of the hostages), the captives drew lots and two Poles were the losers. The Polish hostages then insisted that one of the two men to be shot should be a Jew. Another draw took place, and this time Slodki's name came up (KMB, p. 479). No evidence exists to confirm this.

17 From Avrom Kempinski's account, KMB, p. 479.

18 Monczka, YVA, p. 69.

19 The building was known as Dom Zamelki. In 1938 the Polish gymnasium moved from this building to new premises in Mickiewicz Street.

20 Moskowicz, KMB, p. 428.
21 Jacob Krafchik, YVA Ref. 0-3/4118, p. 5.
22 Studzinski, p. 104. Moskowicz, KMB, p. 428.

14

1 Leo Monczka, YVA Ref. 0-3/3441, p. 70. Also KMB, p. 472.
2 Meyer Winter, like Monczka a prominent member of the Jewish community, was active in many of its affairs, including the running of the Jewish library and Jewish bank.
3 Monczka, YVA, pp. 70–1. Also KMB, p. 472.
4 Monczka, YVA, p. 71. Also KMB, p. 472.
5 I have not been able to establish the exact date of the desecration of the synagogue. It occurred between 23 Sept. (Yom Kippur) and mid-November. According to one Polish source, *Jews in Konin*, a leaflet published by the Konin Public Library (1990), p. 3, the desecration took place 'a few days' after the public execution of the two hostages on 22 Sept., but other evidence suggests it might have been later, probably in early November. Most sources state that the burning of the scrolls occurred in the Tepper Marik, but one account, by Y.L. Hampel (KMB, p. 494), sites it in the synagogue courtyard. There may have been more than one bonfire. The Public Library leaflet states that during the burning of the scrolls the Rabbi was 'painfully beaten'. Other accounts, including the KMB, do not describe physical violence inflicted on the Rabbi.
6 Avrom Kempinski, KMB, p. 481.
7 Jacob Krafchik, YVA Ref. 0-3/4118, p. 5.
8 Ibid.
9 The deadline is given in the Yiddish text (KMB, p. 473) as four days. Ten thousand zlotys was an enormous sum, even for a prosperous merchant like Leo Monczka. The lowest grade of tailor at that time earned no more than about 10 zlotys a week.
10 Monczka, YVA, p. 72. Also KMB, p. 473.
11 Monczka, YVA, p. 72. The Memorial Book's editor was too genteel to include this detail.
12 Monczka, YVA, p. 73. Also KMB, p. 474.
13 Monczka, YVA, p. 74. Not included in KMB – see p. 474.

15

1 From a Berlin anti-Communist magazine, *Contra-Komintern*, 2 Nov.

1939, quoted in Martin Gilbert, *The Holocaust: The Jewish Tragedy* (London, 1986), p. 97.

2 István Deák comments in the *New York Review of Books*, 22 Oct. 1992, p. 43: 'Lukas [Richard C. Lukas] writes in the introduction to *Out of the Inferno: Poles Remember the Holocaust* that, during the war, the Nazis wiped out 45 percent of Poland's physicians and dentists, 40 percent of the professors, 57 percent of the lawyers, 30 percent of the technicians, almost 20 percent of the clergy, and most of the leading journalists. If we add to this the thousands of Polish professionals deported or killed on the order of Stalin, then we can get some idea of the catastrophe of Polish elites.' *Out of the Inferno*, ed. Richard C. Lukas (University Press of Kentucky, 19).

3 The figure of 56 is taken from information that the Polish National Archives office in Konin (Archiwum Panstwowe w Poznaniu, Oddzial w Koninie) supplied to the author, in a letter dated 18 Dec. 1992. Jacob Krafchik (YVA Ref. 0-3/4118, p. 6) also puts the figure at 56. Antoni Studzinski, in 'Koninski Wrzesien 1939 Roku', *Ziemia Koninska*, vol. III, *Materialy Na Sympozjum KTR* (Konin, 1972, p. 132, quotes the number of those executed as 200. Y.L. Hampel, writing in KMB, pp. 494, 495, gives a total of 40.

4 Studzinski, p. 132, testimony of Wladyslaw Dziobczynski.

5 KMB, p. 494.

6 Jozef Lewandowski, *Cztery dni w Atlantydzie* (Uppsala, 1991), p. 20.

7 Gilbert, *Holocaust*, pp. 88, 89, 97, 99.

8 One Polish account, Studzinski, p. 121, gives the date of the deportation as 9 November, but my own researches reveal that it took place during the night of 30 Nov./1 Dec.

9 Krafchik, YVA, p. 7.

10 Studzinski, p. 133.

11 Ostrowiec Swietokrzyski (usually referred to simply as Ostrowiec) lies about 50 km east of the city of Kielce. Jozefow-Bilgorajski, not far from Lublin, is about 40 km north-east of Ostrowiec. Some Konin Jews were deported to Opatow-Kielecki, about 15 km south of Ostrowiec. These were in the territory of the General Government, an administrative region created by the Germans in October 1939. It covered a large area of central Poland including Warsaw, Krakow and Lvov. Hans Frank was its governor.

12 Studzinski, p. 135. This is probably the place to mention an inaccuracy in a book written by the American son of a Koniner, Herb

Brin, *Ich bin ein Jude: Travels Through Europe on the Edge of Savagery* (New York, 1982), p. 130. The inaccuracy appears to have sprung from information given him when he visited Konin in 1962: 'Jews were lined up in the town square [of Konin], 10,000 of them, and massacred. None escaped. My family among the victims.'

16

1 EJ, vol. 10, p. 1179: Konin.

2 The Rabbi was Moses b. Israel Isserlis. EJ, vol. 13, p. 711.

3 The first Jews to arrive there in the late 12th century were minters. EJ, vol. 16, p. 1346.

4 When Boleslaw conquered the town in 1266, the Jews of Konin acquired the rights granted under the Kalisz statute. Kazimierz the Great's statute of 1334 further extended the rights of the Jews.

5 Eliezer Feldman, 'Tsvey Alte Yidishe Kehilas in Lodzer Kant', in *Lodzer Visnshaftlekhe Shriftn*, vol. I (Lodz, 1938), p. 25.

6 Maurycy Horn, 'Najstarszy Rejestr Osiedli Zydowskich w Polsce Z 1507 R.', *Biuletyn Zydowskiego Instytutu Historycznego* 3:91 (1974), p. 14. The year 1418, as the date when the Konin settlement was established, is also quoted by two encyclopedias, one German, *Encyclopaedia Judaica* (Berlin, 1928–34), the other Russian, *Yevreiskaya Entsiklopediya* (St Petersburg, 1908–13), vol. IX, p. 698.

7 Feldman, p. 26. Kanaan sometimes arranged loans in partnership with other Konin Jews such as one named Yordan: ibid., p. 27.

8 Feldman, p. 30.

9 Around 1436. Feldman, p. 30.

10 The king also visited Konin in 1403 and 1433: *Kronika Wielkopolski* 2:15 (1978), p. 23.

11 He probably died in this or the following year.

12 One of these debtors, a nobleman Pantek, acknowledged that he had received a certain sum of money from the 'perfidious Martha, a Jewess, daughter of the Jew Canahan of Conin'. Feldman, p. 32.

13 See also EJ, vol. 10, p. 1179. PH, p. 235, states: 'about 180 Jews . . . resided in 12 wooden houses.' The primary sources of the information regarding the number of Jews in Konin in the 15th century are not cited either in EJ or PH, but it probably comes from the work of W.I. Schipper, who in the early 20th century calculated the populations of Jewish communities, based on tax records and other sources; see his *Studja nad stosunkami gospodarczymi Zydow w Polsce*

podczas sredniowiecza (Studies on the Economic Situation of Jews in Medieval Poland), (Lvov, 1911). The present-day Public Library in Konin has published a leaflet, *Jews in Konin* (1992). While stating on p. 1 that the Jews 'could have come to Konin in the 14th century,' it maintains that 'no remaining documents confirm the existence of a Jewish community in the town during the 14th–16th centuries.' This does not accord with the other references to Jews in Konin mentioned here.

14 PH, p. 235; EJ, vol. 10, p. 1179.

15 KMB, p. 33. The concession cost Fishl 2,500 zlotys plus two stones of saffron and ten stones of pepper, which points to Jewish trading in these commodities. The concession brought considerable riches to Fishl, while the king and his two sons ended up disastrously in debt. The debt was settled by leasing Fishl the right to collect tax from Jews throughout Poland (KMB, pp. 32, 33).

16 Feldman, pp. 29, 30, KMB, p. 33.

17 Feldman, p. 30. Disappointingly, the Konin community is not mentioned throughout the existence of the Council of the Four Lands (in Hebrew *Vaad Arba Aratzot*), covering nearly two hundred years. The most likely explanation is that Konin was included in the representation of the Kalisz community. To add to the difficulty in untangling information about the early history of the Jews in Konin, I have it from the National Archive office in Konin (letter to the author, 25 July 1994) that: 'Professor Andrzej Wedzki has recently pointed out that in 1569, King Zygmunt August awarded his courtier Stanislaw Olszowski 50 zlotys which he was to take from the taxes paid by the Jewish population in various Wielkopolska towns which are listed by name, such as Kalisz, Gniezno, Kolo, Wrzesnia, Pyzdry. Konin is not listed which, according to him, can be considered indirect proof that, at that time, there was no Jewish population in Konin.'

18 Father Jan Wolski provided this information to someone who visited Konin on my behalf in July 1989. The record of the ecclesiastical visits to Konin is in the archives of the Gniezno Archbishopric. Further items of information about the Jews of Konin in the 17th century have been provided by the National Archive (letter to the author, 25 July 1994): 'The deeds of the Government Committee for Home Affairs in Warsaw in 1834 mention an ancient privilege, issued by King Zygmunt III on 7 January 1615, on the strength of which only Polish residents were permitted to settle in Konin. The

full wording of this document is not known and it has probably not survived. What we do know, however, is the text reporting a visitation to the Konin parish on 11 Oct. 1712 by F. Kraszkowski, who mentions in this report that by decree of the General Consistory in Gniezno, issued in November 1694, all Jews who had recently moved to Konin were to be expelled from the town. Evidently, this decree was never carried out, but it does give an indication that the second half of the seventeenth century saw a certain influx of Jewish people, which, however, does not rule out the possibility that there had already previously been individual Jewish residents.'

19 Piotr Maluskiewicz, *Konin i Okolice* (Poznan, 1979), p. 31.

20 Piotr Rybczynski, *Informator O Nazwach Ulic. Placow i Dzielnic Miasta Konina Do 1945 Roku* (Konin, 1989). In 1930 the name of the street was changed to ulica Targowa.

21 KMB, p. 35.

22 KMB, p. 35; Maluskiewicz, p. 31.

23 Maluskiewicz, p. 31.

24 *Kronika Wielkopolski*, p. 24.

25 Andrzej Czeslaw Nowak, *Konin, Turek, Dobra* (Poznan, 1987), p. 12.

26 KMB, p. 36. PH also quotes the figure of 168, but this may be an estimate. The Konin Public Library leaflet, *Jews in Konin*, (p. 1), quotes only the poll-tax total of 133. According to Table 1, KMB, p. 36, the figure of 133 is broken down as follows. Males: married 28, widowers 1, unmarried sons 36, journeymen and those employed 7. Total males 72. Females: married 28, widows 5, unmarried daughters 28. Total females 61.

72 Nowak, p. 12: 'At about that time [of the second partition of 1793 it had about 800 inhabitants.'

28 KMB, p. 37.

29 *Jews in Konin*, p. 1.

17

1 The second largest racial minority in the town, Protestants of German origin, formed 10% of the total population in 1883. There was a small Russian community, members of the civic and military authority, who were Russian Orthodox.

2 Ludwik Reymond.

3 Piotr Rybczynski, *Konin: 700 Lat* (Konin, 1993), p. 14.

4 KMB, p. 189. There seems to be some disagreement over when

the *bes-medresh* was built. Elsewhere in the KMB (p. 234) it is said to have been completed in 1890. A Polish reference work by Przemyslaw Burchard, *Pamiatki i Zabytki Kultury Zydowskiej w Polsce* (Remains and Monuments of Jewish Culture in Poland) (Warsaw, 1990), p. 106, states 1870 as the date of erection, as does an article in the London Yiddish newspaper, *Di Tsayt*, reprinted in KMB, p. 169. A notice-board sign on display in present-day Konin gives the date as 'at the turn of the nineteenth and twentieth centuries'. The Polish architect Anna Magorska has written a postgraduate diploma thesis in two volumes (Warsaw Polytechnic, 1980) on the architectural history of the synagogue in Konin. She suggests that the *bes-medresh* was built in 1844. I am still inclined to favour 1870.

5 *Jews in Konin* (Konin Public Library leaflet, 1992).

6 PH, p. 236.

7 I am grateful to Philip Lewin for supplying me with a copy of his father's unpublished memoir, 'My Home and Family'.

8 KMB, pp. 12–14. Maurice Lewin's contribution to the KMB occupies twelve of the fourteen pages of the book that are printd in English.

9 This information comes from notes recorded by Nick Lewin from a conversation with his great-aunt, Yetta Reingand, née Lewin (Maurice's sister), in Israel in 1982.

19 Monczka, YVA Ref. 0-3/3441, p. 40.

11 There is an account of Leszczynski's murder in KMB, p. 104. I have not been able to discover, either from Joe Fox or from the account of the murder in KMB, what happened to the miller who hired the hit-man.

12 Menahem Mendel Beilis (1871–1934) was charged with 'Jewish ritual murder' in Kiev in 1911, when a Christian boy was found murdered. Beilis was charged with the crime and imprisoned for two years before he was put on trial. He was acquitted. Bernard Malamud used this *cause célèbre* as the basis of his novel, *The Fixer* (1966).

13 He had two stepbrothers, Mordechai and Shimshon, who had already emigrated to London.

18

1 Leo Monczka, (KMB, p. 253; YVA Ref. 0-3/3441, p. 48.

2 Monczka, YVA Ref. 0-3/3441, p. 48.

3 The letter is dated Konin, 27 Feb. 1920, and was sent to my

grandfather's address in the East End of London. It bears the signatures of the *Dyrektor* (headmaster), Glogowski (initial illegible), and four members of the school board. My grandfather's business stamp giving the date of receipt reads, rather grandiosely: *S. Sarna, Shipping and Forwarding, Import and Export, 70 Sidney Street, London E.1.* The letter was found among the papers of my late uncle, Jacob Sarna, and I am indebted to his son, Nahum, for giving it to me.

4 Information from author's conversation with Natan Ahykam (né Strykowski).

5 Leo Monczka. My version of this passage conflates the Yiddish and the German accounts (KMB, p. 247; YVA Ref. 0-3/3441, pp. 50–51.

6 The process of closing down probably started in 1928. The Konin Public Library's leaflet, *Jews in Konin* (1992), cites 1926 as the year the school closed. This cannot be correct as the KMB contains a copy of a *Matura* certificate issued by the school dated '1927/28'.

7 Frances Taylor, née Franya Bulka.

19

1 The headmasters were, in chronological order, Alexander Rusak, Glogowski, Feuer (first names not known), Leopold Infeld, Jan Lipschitz.

2 Leopold Infeld, *Quest: The Evolution of a Scientist* (London, 1941).

3 Infeld, pp. 33, 46.

4 Infeld, p. 213.

5 Infeld, pp. 99, 184.

6 Infeld, p. 99.

7 Infeld, p. 300.

8 Ibid.

9 Infeld, pp. 300–1.

10 Infeld, p. 300.

11 Infeld, Ibid.

12 Infeld, pp. 99–100.

13 Infeld, pp. 102, 100.

14 Infeld, p. 195.

15 Infeld, p. 210.

16 Infeld, p. 208.

17 Infeld, p. 214.

18 Infeld, pp. 211–12.

19 Infeld, p. 291.

20 Infeld, p. 214.
21 Infeld, p. 305.
22 Alfred Schild, from his Foreword to Leopold Infeld, *Why I Left Canada, Reflections on Science and Politics*, translated by Helen Infeld, (Montreal and London, 1978), p. x.
23 Leopold Infeld, *American Scholar*, vol. 16 (1946–47). Quoted in *Einstein: The Life and Times* by Ronald W. Clark (New York, 1971), p. 247.
24 Jozef Lewandowski, in conversation with the author. Born in Konin in 1923, he was professor of history at Uppsala University, Sweden. He is now retired.
25 Infeld, *Quest*, p. 264.
26 Infeld, *Quest*, p. 215.
27 Wincenty Urbaniak, 'Z Dzialalnosci Rewolucyjnej w Latach 1920–1934', in *Rewolucjonisci ziemi koninskiej 1918–1948* ('Revolutionaries in the Konin Region' 1918–1948) (Warsaw, 1988), p. 80.
28 He was one of the original signatories to the Einstein-Russell manifesto of 1955 which led to the Pugwash Movement on Science and Public Affairs.
29 Leopold Infeld, 'Konin', *Szkice Przeszlosci* (Warsaw, 1964), later published in English as *Sketches from the Past*, translated by Helen Infeld and included in *Why I Left Canada*.
30 KMB, pp. 260–7.
31 Infeld, *Why I Left Canada*, p. 131.
32 Ibid.
33 They wrote an important joint paper subsequently published by the Royal Society. The result of their work became known as the Born-Infeld Theory: Alfred Schild writes of this theory: 'It was an attempt to explain the existence of elementary charged particles in terms of well-behaved solutions of nonlinear equations for the electromagnetic field' (from the Foreword to Infeld, *Why I Left Canada*, p. XI).
34 Infeld left in 1924; but the school did not close until 1928/29.
35 Infeld, *Why I Left Canada*, p. 134. Infeld describes the same encounter, using slightly different words, in *Quest*, p. 303, where he quotes Monczka as saying that the school 'was liquidated two years after you left'.
36 Infeld, *Why I Left Canada*, p. 135.
37 Ibid.

38 Infed, *Why I Left Canada*, p. 126. After writing this chapter on Leopold Infeld, I met a woman from Konin in Israel who recalled meeting someone in Tel Aviv a few years earlier whom she believed to be the first Mrs Infeld. She was then married to a respected music teacher in Israel, but that was all my informant could remember. Another Koniner, a former pupil of the gymnasium, told me independently that he believed Infeld's first wife had made *aliyah*. I subsequently scrutinized a list in the KMB (p. 258) that I had previously overlooked, which gives the name of the gymnasium teaching staff and their subjects. Among them is 'Infeld Masha – natural science'. This, I presume, was the name of his first wife, who must have been teaching at the school while he was headmaster.

20

1 Ezekiel xxiii, 13–16.

2 Frances Taylor (née Bulka), in conversation with the author. She was born in Konin before the First World War.

3 Maurice Lewin, 'My Home and Family' (unpublished MS), p. 4. His son, Philip Lewin, provided me with a copy of the manuscript, written during the Sixties.

4 One daughter died at the age of seven. The eldest son, Naftali, divided his time between a grocery store and religion. It was his son, Anszel Lewin, who so impressed Leopold Infeld, headmaster of the Jewish gymnasium: 'What happened to Lewin, the best in mathematics? . . . Murdered, murdered, murdered.'

5 KMB, p. 311.

6 Yetta Reingand (née Lewin), in conversation with her great-nephew, Nick Lewin, in Israel in 1982. He took notes of this conversation, which I have consulted. She died in Israel in 1986.

7 Ibid.

8 KMB, p. 313.

9 Her son became a writer, adopting the pen-name Yves Jamiaque. He served for a period as president of the Société des Auteurs.

10 Ralph A. Lewin, 'One Summer in Paris', *The Massachusetts Review*, vol. 3. No. 3, Spring 1962, p. 572. Ralph Lewin, born in London, is the son of Mark Lewin's elder brother, Maurice.

11 While Mark was making fur dogs in one part of Paris, Chaim Soutine was painting in conditions of extreme poverty in another. Born of poor parents in a Lithuanian *shtetl* in 1895, he received beatings

from his religious father for sacrilegiously spending his time drawing. When he was 16 he asked a religious Jew to pose for him. The man's family retaliated with physical violence, from which Soutine nearly died. He came to Paris in 1913. Marc Chagall, born in a *shtetl* in 1887, two years after Mark, was also painting in Paris during the years Mark lived there.

12 According to her son, Maurice, 'She was shot by the Germans in a wood near Lublin' – 'My Home and Family', p. 3. Her daughter, Yetta, calculated in conversation with Nick Lewin in Israel in 1982 that between forty-five and forty-seven members of her family died in the Shoah.

21

1 Irving Hower, *World of Our Fathers* (New York, 1976), p. 1.

23

1 The name of the B'nai Tsvi Amsterdam does not figure in the extensive lists contained in YIVO's reference works on New York Jewish organizations, and therefore I have not been able to establish a date for its demise. YIVO's head librarian, Zachary M. Baker, suggests an explanation for the omission from the lists: 'it is quite possible that B'nai Tsvi Amsterdam was a congregation founded on a *landsmanshaft* basis, as was often the case during the early years of mass immigration' (letter to Prof. Jonathan D. Sarna, 8 Nov. 1991). This is supported by the fact that KMB (p. 717) refers to the 'Chevre B'nai Tsvi Amsterdam'. (*Chevre denotes a congregation as well as a society.) At some point in the Sixties a Koniner by the name of Sherman Marks, since deceased, served as secretary of both the B'nai Tsvi Amsterdam and the Konin Society (KMB, p.* 721). KMB devotes only a few lines (p. 717) to the B'nai Tsvi Amsterdam, giving its date of foundation (27 Oct. 1879) and stating that it 'exists to this day'. Those words were almost certainly written some time – perhaps a few years – before KMB was published after long preparation in 1968.

2 This is the name of the Society as it appears on the 1923 charter. The Society's letterhead in 1964 had an expanded version: LADIES' AND MEN'S SOCIETY OF KONIN, INC. AND SURROUNDING TOWNS, followed by the names of those towns: SLUPCE, GOLIN, ZAGUROW, SHLESHIN, KLETCHEW, RACHVAL, SOMPOLNO, PAZER, RYSISZYCE, TULICHKOW. (In some

cases these are English translations of the Yiddish names and not the Polish spelling.) The first president of the Society (in 1923) was Isaac Bulka, followed by Philip Charof. In 1932 a Mrs Singerman was president (KMB, p. 719).

3 Son of Kopl-Dovid Charof, a frequent visitor to my grandfather's house in Sidney Street.

4 KMB, p. 719.

5 Among the 'veterans' from prewar days who helped re-establish the Society and played an active part in its affairs were: Sarah Apel, Sarah Bram, Murray Blum, Philip Charof, Sherman Marks, Dr Morris (brother of Leo Monczka), his wife, Rose, and Max Schwarz.

6 KMB, p. 721.

7 Irving Howe, *World of our Fathers* (New York, 1976), p. 189: 'Ideologues and intellectuals in the Yiddish world were always uneasy with these societies, sometimes mocking them as uncultured or deficient in the higher idealism . . . The men who dreamed of a rich Yiddish culture saw the *landsmanshaft* as a bulwark of parochial narrowness.'

8 Still in existence at the time of writing.

9 The last president was David Irwin (né Iwanowicz).

24

1 Franya Beatus, born in Konin of a Chasidic family, was a heroine of the Warsaw ghetto. Rose Kempinski, who lit the candle in her memory, was her friend in the Ostrowiec ghetto. In 1942 the Jewish resistance organization smuggled Franya to Warsaw, where she led a dangerous existence on the 'Aryan' side. She acted as a courier for the men and women who were to lead the Ghetto Uprising, which began on 19 April 1943. During the last days of the revolt, Franya maintained telephone communications with the outside world and helped to evacuate fighters through the sewers. On 12 May, after the resistance had been crushed, she committed suicide. She was seventeen years old. See Yitzhak Zukerman ('Antek'), *A Surplus of Memory: Chronicle of the Warsaw Ghetto Uprising*, trans. and ed. Barbara Harshav (Berkeley, 1993), pp. 345–6.

25

1 His surname was spelled Mycz in Poland, also pronounced 'mish'. Mycz means mouse in Polish. Some of Motek's relatives who came

to America earlier in the century changed their surname to Maus or Mawes.

27

1 Jozef Lewandowski, *Cztery dni w Atlantydzie* (Uppsala, 1991), p. 17.
2 Zygmunt Bauman, 'Adolf Rudnicki, the Jew and the Polish Writer', *Jewish Quarterly* No. 144, Winter 1991/92.
3 Lewandowski, p. 21.
4 Antony Polonsky (ed)., *My Brother's Keeper? Recent Polish Debates on the Holocaust* (London, 1990), p. 2.
5 *Zegota*, cryptonym for *Rada Pomocy Zydom* (Relief Council for Jews).
6 Francesca Bram (née Grochowska), KMB, pp. 526–7.

29

1 Lee Langley, *From the Broken Tree* (New York, 1978), p. 55. In the course of her researches for this novel, Lee Langley – my wife – talked to my mother about Konin more than I ever did!
2 Leopold Infeld, *Why I Left Canada* (Montreal and London, 1978), p. 133.

30

1 Mikhail Moskowicz, KMB, p. 430.
2 Ludwig Zepsuj, nicknamed Dokonch. KMB, p. 126.
3 The official name of the archives is Bund Archives of the Jewish Labor Movement in the Name of Franz Kurski. The archives are a symbol of Jewish survival. The first collection, mostly underground revolutionary literature, was established in 1899 in Switzerland, at a safe remove from the Tsarist secret police. Facing Bolshevik opposition after the Revolution, the Bund moved the archives to Berlin. In 1933 Nazi Storm Troopers confiscated the by now huge collection. It was nominally sold to the French government, whose ambassador in Berlin ordered it to be crated and dispatched to Paris. When the Germans entered Paris in 1940, the archives were again threatened with destruction. A hiding-place was found, and there they remained until the Germans began to evacuate Paris, at which time they discovered them and took them away in trucks together with other loot. The collection vanished without trace. Months later it was found strewn over an open field outside Paris. After the war, the archives were moved yet again, this time to New York. (See *A Great Collection.*

The Archives of the Jewish Labor Movement [New York, 1967].) Since I visited the Bund archives, in 1987, they have moved again, to be absorbed into YIVO (New York), where Leo Greenbaum is now in day-to-day charge of them.

4 J.S. Hertz (ed.), *Doires Bundistn* (Generations of Bundists) (New York, 1968).

32

1 Both died in the Shoah.
2 Mikhail Moskowicz, KMB, pp. 414–15.
3 Mrs Danziger. Her son, Beniek, appears in chapter 42.
4 *Oxford Companion to Medicine*, vol. I (Oxford, 1986), p. 270.
5 François Joseph Victor Broussais (1772–1838).
6 Charles Singer and E. Ashworth Underwood, *A Short History of Medicine* (Oxford, 1962), p. 282.
7 Lee Langley, *From the Broken Tree* (New York, 1978), p. 55.
8 Rachel Sarna Araten in her biography of her father, *Jacob Sarna: Here and There* (Jerusalem, 1991), p. 35.

34

1 Tsvi Ozerowicz, KMB, p. 57.
2 From records of ecclesiastical visits to Konin by the Gniezno Bishop, Albert Baranowski, 1595–1609. Archives of Gniezno Archbishopric. Father Jan Wolski of Konin unearthed this information in recent years while doing research on Konin churches. According to Father Wolski, the mention of fish suggests that the Jews had a lease on the local lakes.
3 The National Archive office in Konin states that the cemetery at Czarkow 'was probably started in the eighteenth century'. Letter to author, 18 Dec. 1993.
4 Ozerowicz, KMB, p. 57.
5 Ibid. This was the calligraphy used by the great French-born commentator on Bible and Talmud, Solomon Ben Isaac (1040–1105), known as Rashi.
6 Almost certainly Konin's first Rabbi, Tsvi Hirsh Amsterdam.
7 Ozerowicz, KMB, p. 58.
8 A custom continued today at the graves of great rabbis, such as those buried in Safed in Israel.
9 Ozerowicz, KMB, p. 59.

10 Descendants of Aaron the High Priest, *Kohanion* (Cohens) may neither see nor be observed while making a blessing.

11 The land was almost certainly wanted not for housing but for excavating silica-rich soil for the production of cement.

12 It is difficult to establish the year with any certainty. The recording of this event, like so many others, is beset with conflicting versions. KMB (pp. 56–63) says that the local government decree was issued in 1927 and that the bones were transferred the following year. Elsewhere, on p. 88, it states that the decree was issued in 1928 but gives no dates for the transfer of the human remains. PH, p. 237, also states 1928 as the year of transfer. However, KMB (p. 354) includes an extract from a Kalisz Jewish newspaper dated 1937, which says that the bones were transferred from the old cemetery 'only six years ago', which means 1931. To complicate the matter further, at least two Koniners have assured me they took part in moving the bones when they were young boys in about 1935. The only explanation I can think of is that human remains were discovered when development work took place on the site some years after the original transfer.

36

1 EJ, vol. 10, p. 1179 states: 'A magnificent synagogue was erected in Konin (1763–6), later (1829) decorated by the Jewish artist Zanvel Barash of Kepno.' I consulted two Polish experts on synagogue architecture in Poland, Maria and Kazimierz Piechotka. They wrote to me (letter dated 12 Dec. 1988): 'The information contained in *Encyclopaedia Judaica* about a synagogue erected in 1763–6 probably relates to the [earlier] wooden one.'

2 Maria and Kazimierz Piechotka have provided me with this information, drawn from the postgraduate diploma thesis by Anna Magorska (Warsaw Polytechnic, 1980) on the architectural history of the Konin synagogue building. The Piechotkas write that, according to Magorska: 'On 21 July 1818 the Konin Jews applied for an indefinite lease of the synagogue's grounds with a view to building a new one. Three months earlier, on 21 April, the town authorities received building plans . . . Those plans were not approved, and on 25 May 1825 revised plans were submitted in Warsaw. They were finally approved on 7 June 1825 . . . The synagogue was erected between 1825 and 1844.' The building underwent various reconstructions in later years.

The Moorish styling dates from reconstruction work based on plans drawn up in 1878.

3 Jacob Sarna, KMB, p. 190.

4 Chevre Tillim (Psalms), Chevre Tanach (Bible), Chevre Mishmorim (Guardians), Chevre Shoymer Shabbes (Keepers of the Sabbath), Chevre Chayotim (Tailors).

37

1 The dynasty was founded by Isaac Meir Alter in Ger (Yiddish) or Gur (Hebrew) or Gora Kalwaria (Polish), a small town near Warsaw.

2 *Di Tsayt* (London, 20 July 1915. See KMB, p. 169.

3 The Sephardic rite (*nusekh*) observed in Konin was a combination of the Polish Ashkenazi rite and the Sephardic rite of Palestine as arranged by the great mystic Isaac Luria, though there are variations among different Chasidic groups.

4 Hershl Perlmuter, in his book *Mein Stertzev*, quoted in Chester G. Cohen's *Shtetl Finder* (Maryland, 1989), p. 98.

38

1 In full: Tsvi Hirsh Ben Simcha: Deer, Deer, son of Rejoicing.

2 He was the son of Gaon Nachman Amsterdam, Rabbi and Chief of the Beth Din in Breslau, and a pupil of Rabbi Jonathan Eybeschutz, head of the Altona *yeshiva* among others. KMB, pp. 69, 91.

3 KMB, pp. 69–70. Bill Gladstone, a Canadian genealogist who has traced several paternal lines to Konin, notes that the Rabbi's name does not appear in the Jewish civil registration records of births, marriages, deaths kept in Konin in the 19th century, whereas the name of Rabbi Nachman appears in most marriage records until 1848. Although he has no positive proof, all his 'genealogical instincts' tell him that Rabbi Nachman and Rabbi Tsvi Amsterdam are one and the same person. 'It was not the custom for sons to be named after their fathers [Tsvi Hirsh Amsterdam's father was Nachman Amsterdam]. However, in the early and middle part of the last century, Jews often took on surnames based on a patronymic. Thus, someone called Hirsh ben Nachman [Hirsh son of Nachman] would have called himself Hirsh Nachman. Jewish surnames, which were only required after 1808 in many parts of Europe, were in a state of flux throughout much of the last and present centuries. Many Jews did

not appreciate the civil requirement that they call themselves after the Christian fashion. Perhaps Rabbi Amsterdam insisted on being known by his Hebrew name Hirsh ben Nachman, and shortened it to comply with civil regulations.' Letter to the author, 12 Jan. 1993.

4 KMB, p. 75.

5 His treatise, *Divrei Torah* (Words of the Torah), was published in Warsaw in 1881.

6 Menahem Mendel of Kotsk (1787–1859).

7 A member of my family recalls a story, possibly apocryphal, about a Rabbi whose only spoken language was Yiddish. At a lost how to claim knowledge of Russian without lying, he took advantage of classic Yiddish interrogatory circumlocution. Asked by a government official whether he knew Russian, he replied: 'Do I know Russian? I know Russian like I know Polish.'

8 KMB, p. 86.

9 This story told to the author by Mark Natel.

39

1 Ultra-Orthodox circles today also have a Yiddish term for the ceremony – *dos wort*, the word.

2 Known in Hebrew as Meyer Ba'al Na-nes.

3 The Technion (Technion-Israel Institute of Technology), founded in 1924, has an international reputation for scientific education and research.

4 Martin Gilbert, *The Holocaust* (London, 1986), pp. 793–794.

5 Isaac Ronch, *The Awakening of Motek* (New York, 1941), p. 41.

40

1 The poem, 'Yizkor', is by the Yiddish poet, Chaim Leib Fuks, who was married to a Konin woman, Chana (née Greenbaum). It is reprinted in KMB, (pp. 467–8) from his collection of poems and songs, *Sho Fun Lid* (Hour of Song) (Paris, 1951).

2 Tsvi Ancer, who at one time was in a camp with Leon Danziger, wrote: 'Fate also led Danziger to the gas chambers, and none of us had any pity on him' (KMB, p. 556).

3 Tsvi Ancer bears out Lefkowitz: '. . . our townsman Danziger achieved a high rank as senior prisoner. He was as savage as a German . . . When I saw how murderously they beat children, I begged Danziger to stop, for which he gave me a good beating

too. Danziger did everything he could to see that none of us should remain alive' (KMB, p. 556).

41

1 KMB, p. 657. I have been able to assemble the names of only some of the Konin Jews who returned after the war: Julius Ancer, Gedalia Behr, Niusia and Ewa Brzostowska, Chaim Czerwonka, Beniek Danziger, Fernbach (first name not known), Izzy and Karol Hahn, Henry Kaye (né Kawalek), Simon Kempinski, Jacob Kotowski (from a nearby town), Hanka Kowalska (née Zucker) and two children, Fella Leben, Louis Lefkowitz, Madzia Leszczynska and daughter, Nadia Lyfczak, Leo Monczka, Lola Moskowicz, Motek Mysch, two Obarszarnek brothers, Felunia Prost (née Ryczke), Janine Ryczke (née Meisels) and two children, Marcus and Lotka Yudkewicz (née Blum), Tola Zeidlitz and mother, and Motek Zelmanowicz.

2 Natasha Burchardt, book review in *British Journal of Psychiatry*, No. 6, July 1993.

3 Letter to author, May 1993.

4 Letter to author, 27 April 1993.

5 Completed in 1934, the bridge crossed a man-made canal designed to prevent flooding of the river near the town.

6 The English version given here is translated by Martha Price from the original German that Leo Monczka deposited in the archives of Yad Vashem (YVA Ref. 0-3/3441, pp. 78–82). A shortened Yiddish version appears in KMB, pp. 658–63. Where ambiguities arise in the German text, I have turned to the Yiddish for clarification. The German version of his return is headed 'February 1946'. This surely must be an error. Julius Ancer met him in Konin in February 1945, and others remember meeting him there in that year. Unfortunately, the Yiddish version in the Memorial Book fails to give any dates. Monczka says in the extract quoted here that his stay in Konin was 'short', yet he was still there when Motek Mysch went back for one night at some unspecified date the following year. This leads me to believe that he may have paid two separate visits to Konin, in 1945 and 1946.

7 Letter to author, 27 April 1993.

8 Chaim Czerwonka, a bachelor, was a glazier and carpenter before the war. His flat was in the biggest house in the Tepper Marik, owned by a Jew named Gluba. Czerwonka left Konin after the war

and emigrated to Toronto, where he died some years ago.

9 The American Jewish Joint Distribution Committee, founded 1914 to provide overseas relief and rehabilitation. In the aftermath of the Second World War it concentrated on helping victims of the Shoah in Europe.

10 He died in Montreal in 1991.

11 KMB, pp. 583, 584.

12 Letter to author, May 1993. The eight guests were: Eva Brzostowska (the bride's sister), Alex Kaliski, Hanka Kawa (née Lewin), Jacob Kotowski, Hanka Kowalska and her daughter Stella, Leo Monczka, Janina Ryczke.

13 The bridegroom was a Koniner by the name of Fernbach (first name not known). The bride was from Ostrowiec; her name is also unknown.

14 Robert S. Wistrich, *The Longest Hatred* (London, 1991), p. xv.

15 Letter to the author, 27 April 1993.

16 Ibid.

42

1 This is an error. The Polonia was a cinema. The 'nightclub' next door, was the Olympia.

2 Jozef Lewandowski, *Cztery dni w Atlantydzie* (Uppsala, 1991), pp. 35–7.

3 Tsvi Ozerowicz, leading light of the Konin society in Israel. My evidence is an envelope addressed to Ozerowicz that has survived. Postmarked 8 March 1958, it has Gdanski's name and Konin address on the back.

4 Letter to the author, 23 Sept. 1993.

43

1 Jozef Lewandowski, *Cztery dni w Atlantydzie (Uppsala,* 1991), p. 31.

2 Teresa Franco, née Zylberberg.

3 I first learned about the musical potty from an article about Maria Leszczynska and others by Hanna Krall, 'Ulica Bornsztajna', in the Warsaw journal Gazeta *Wyborcza*, 20 July 1991, p. 11.

4 I have taken these facts about the policeman from an article, 'Habsburzanka, by Katarzyna Meloch, in the journal *Wiez* (April 1993), pp. 31–46.

44

1 The Hebrew Immigrant Aid Society was founded in New York 1880 to provide aid for Jews immigrating to the United States.
2 Leopold Infeld, *Why I Left Canada: Reflections on Science and Politics*, trans. Helen Infeld (Montreal and London, 1978), p. 133.

45

1 *Bikher Velt*, a Bund-oriented journal (February 1922), pp. 474, 475. Bund archives Ref. M2–398.
2 These 1921 census figures are taken from EJ, vol. 10, p. 1179.
3 Only two Jewish libraries exceeded Konin in their total number of books: Bialystok (14,000) and Mir (6,065). Warsaw, with several more libraries, could claim the greatest total.
4 I know of only one other copy, which is in Israel. The widow of Maurice Lewin, who helped found the library in Konin, presented his copy of the catalogue to the Jewish National and University Library, Jerusalem, in 1978.
5 Lee Langley, *From the Broken Tree* (New York, 1978), pp. 81–2. Chapter 16 contains a fictionalized account of the forming of the library.
6 Maurice Lewin, KMB, pp. 6–8. Another contributor to KMB (p. 129) states that the library was established in 1902, as does EJ, vol. 10, p. 1179. But PH, p. 236, gives 1901. A photograph in KMB (p. 299) shows an event celebrating the 30th anniversary of the library, with the dates 1905–1935 displayed.
7 *Di Tsayt* (London), 20 July 1915.
8 Paul Johnson, *A History of the Jews* (London, 1987), p. 190.
9 Yehoshua Bram, YVA Ref. 0-3/3045, p. 2.
10 The charitable organization ran the lending library until 1938, when the local authority decided to establish a town library, named after the local writer, Zofia Urbanowska. Between the wars the Konin police club also maintained a modest private lending library and reading-room.
11 Jacob Krafchik, in his Yad Vashem testimony (YVA Ref. 0-3/4118), gives the larger number; I get the smaller number from J.S. Hertz, ed., *Doires Bundistn* (Generations of Bundists) (New York, 1968), vol. 3, p. 407. According to PH, p. 237, the library contained '8,190 books in Yiddish, Hebrew, Polish and German in 1936'.

46

1 Martin Gilbert provides a tragic sequel to Mike's story in his authoritative work, *The Holocaust* (London, 1986), pp. 809–10: 'When the American troops reached Mauthausen, they found nearly ten thousand bodies in a huge communal grave. Of the 110,000 survivors, 28,000 were Jews . . . Confronted by so many starving skeletons, well-meaning American soldiers brought chocolate, jam and other rich foods which the camp survivors ate, but which many could not digest, and died . . . These emaciated men and women here, as in other camps, were no longer used to such food, nor could their digestive systems cope with it. It was too rich, too fatty, too filling, and it killed, in the first hectic day of liberation, as surely as the bullets and the rifle butts of the day before.'

2 George Steiner, PEN lecture, London, 6 Oct. 1993.

47

1 Sarah Trybuch, KMB, pp. 628–41, my translation from the Yiddish.

2 In 1991, to mark the occasion of Sarah's eightieth birthday, her grandson, Sandy Bondorowsky, produced a translation (from the Polish) of his grandmother's account of her wartime experiences. If Sarah's and Eli's son did not already know his true relationship to his half-sister, he must have learned it then. Sarah's account was edited by Miriam Trybuch-Bondorowsky, and translated by Dr Romanowska of the University of Florida.

48

1 Sanniki (Sanik in Yiddish), in the Gostynin district west of Warsaw. Many of the other prisoners came from this area.

2 Zvi Szner, 'The Records Kept by the Rabbi of Sanik', in *Extermination and Resistance. Historical Records and Source Material*, vol. 1, p. 114. This valuable source, published in Israel by the Ghetto Fighters' House (Beit Lohamei Haghetaot, 1958), has provided me with much information in this chapter.

3 Szner, p. 115.

4 Ibid.

5 The prisoner was Feivish Kamlazh. See Szner, p. 107.

6 Szner, p. 116.

7 Eva Feldenkreis, the Director of Archives of the Ghetto Fighters' House in Beit Lohamei Haghetaot, having thoroughly investigated

all the evidence in her care, believes that the revolt occurred on 13 August. She has shown me the evidence, and it is convincing.

8 This last name is given mistakenly in the Yiddish text as Krapf. The correct name is Dr Hans Knopf. There is also some discrepancy between these eight names and those given by Zvi Szner. On p. 108 he names seven prisoners who lost their lives by suicide (I have added forenames in brackets): '[Feivish] Kamlazh, [Philip] Zielonka, [Abraham] Seif, Getzel Kleinot the gardener, Kamlazh's father-in-law Abraham Neudorf, Dr Hans Knopf of Berlin, and Zalman Nusenowicz . . .' Szner interviewed the survivors, including Rabbi Aaronson, and the Ghetto Fighters' House judges his list to be the more accurate.

9 Shmulek Ben Zion Mottel, KMB, pp. 623–4. He died in Israel in December 1980.

10 Abraham Seif and Feivish Kamlazh wrote parting letters, Seif's in the form of a Last Will and Testament. These were among the papers hidden in the bottles, now in the archives of the Ghetto Fighters' House. They are published in KMB (pp. 608–27) along with extracts from Rabbi Aaronson's diary.

52

1 KMB, pp. 535–40.

2 In Konin and in Israel she was called Fella. My father called her Felunia, and that is the name I have always known her by. In her Polish passport she was Freydl. She married David Fishkin in Israel.

3 My father, his brothers Itsik Hirsh, Haskel, Leib and Shimen, and his sister, Bayla, were Dovid Ryczke's children by his first wife, Ferka. Following her death, he married Gitl, who had one daughter, Marysha, by a previous marriage.

4 Garlic can relieve high blood-pressure.

5 He got a job as a porter, carrying flour sacks in Leszczynski's mill, across the road from where he lived.

6 Organization for Rehabilitation through Training – a Jewish international organization still active today.

7 Pre-decimal coinage: one shilling, eleven pence and three farthings.

8 A year or two before the war, my grandparents and their two sons moved to the big square (Plac Wolnosci), probably in order to be closer to the Jewish quarter and the synagogue. At the same

time – and this might have prompted their move – their eldest son, Itsik Hirsh, left Konin to work as a manager in a flour mill in nearby Golina.

9 The actual figure was closer to 50 per cent.

10 KMB, pp. 530–1. Among those who died in destitution was the wife of the *feldsher*, Jacob Strykowski. In these pages there is also mention of a Christian, Dr Leszek, who selflessly saved Jewish lives during the epidemic.

11 She found another relative in Ostrowiec, Mendel Ryczke, son of the *cheder melamed*, Benyumin Ryczke. Mendel survived the war but most of his family perished. He finally settled in Israel. Relations were strained between Felunia and Mendel, and there was little contact between them. He died in Israel some years ago.

12 Francesca Bram-Grochowska, KMB, p. 532.

13 KMB, p. 534. According to KMB, the Germans shot the Rabbi's wife at the same time, and their two adopted daughters.

14 Christopher R. Browning, *Ordinary Men: Reserve Police Battalion 101 and the Final Solution in Poland* (New York, 1992).

15 This is the date as stated both in Browning and in the KMB account (p. 533). The 13th of July 1942 was a Monday, yet Felunia says that the day she was picking berries was a Sunday and mentions villagers coming from church. They might well have been coming from church, on a day other than Sunday. She herself admits at one point in her recording to being vague about dates, and demonstrates this by even getting the time of the year wrong. In one sentence, not quoted here, she describes the events as happening in the spring, yet berries do not ripen in this part of Poland until midsummer. It occurred to me at first that she might be referring not to the massacre of 13 July, but to executions that had taken place earlier, in May. But the rest of her evidence all points to the events of 13 July. The Germans, the villagers told her, have 'killed all the Jews'. Furthermore, she quotes the forest warden as saying to her: 'I've been to the town and heard there is not one Jew there.' Had the executions been those which occurred in May, the warden and Felunia's Christian neighbours would undoubtedly have told her that there were still many Jews left in the place.

16 Browning, *Ordinary Men*, p. 61. The following extracts are taken from pp. 64–4.

17 Contrasting with the kindly behaviour of Bayla's neighbour, the

German testimonies that Browning investigated contained many accusations of Polish complicity in their crimes. He writes: 'The German portrayals of Polish complicity are not false. Tragically, the kind of behaviour they attributed to Poles is confirmed in other accounts and occurred all too often. The Holocaust, after all, is a story with far too few heroes and all too many perpetrators and victims. What is wrong with the German portrayals is a multifaceted distortion in perspective. The policemen were all but silent about Polish help to Jews and German punishment for such help.' *Ordinary Men*, pp. 157–8.

53

1 Isaac Bahevis Singer, 'A Friend of Kafka', in *Penguin Book of Jewish Short Stories*, ed. Emanuel Litvinoff (London, 1979), p. 121.

2 Eyal Sivan, a leftwing film-maker, whose provocative documentary, *Yizkor, Slaves to Memory* (1990), drew angry criticism in Israel.

54

1 Gershon Sirota (1874–1943) used to sing annually for Tsar Nicholas II. In 1903 he became the first cantor to make recordings. Moshe Kusevitsky, sometimes spelled Koussevitsky (1899–1966), succeeded Sirota as cantor of the main synagogue in Warsaw. His recordings and concert tours won him international renown as perhaps the greatest cantor of his time.

2 Hayyim Schauss, *The Jewish Festivals: From Their Beginnings to Our Own Day*, trans. Samuel Jaffe (London, 1986), p. 165.

3 A collection of ten labour camps about 50 kilometres west of Munich.

4 Underground Zionist military organization that disbanded when the State of Israel was declared in 1948. One of its functions was as a naval force assisting illegal Jewish immigration.

55

1 Jacob Sarna's wife, Millie, was a Horonchik from Poland.

58

1 M. Gelbart.

2 Brother of Sarah, the partisan I met in Florida.

3 Unrelated to the *feldsher* Strykowski.

4 After some years the original memorial stone deteriorated. Money was collected for a more ambitious memorial – the one I visited – on the same site.

62

1 A stanza from the poem '*Yidishe Gas' ('Jewish Street'), by Abraham Sutzkever (b.* 1913), today's foremost Yiddish poet. The free translation by Joseph Leftwich was published in *The Golden Peacock*, ed. J. Leftwich, pp. 450–1 (New York and London, 1961). The Jewish quarter of a town was traditionally known as 'Jewish Street'.

63

1 Jozef Lewandowski, *Cztery dni w Atlantydzie (Uppsala,* 1991), p. 32.
2 KMB, p. 618.

65

1 The director's successor, Lech Hejman, who is now in charge of Konin's public library, has done his utmost to respect and commemorate the synagogue's past. On 6 October 1988, a concert marked the official opening of the new library and the restoration of the building. There was a recital of Jewish and Yiddish songs, and an exhibition of *parokhot* – embroidered hangings for the Holy Ark. An information board provides visitors with a brief history of the synagogue building. In 1993 the public library acquired two Polish books bearing the stamp of the former Jewish library. Mr Hejman informs me that there are young people in Konin today who want to know more about the town's Jewish history.
2 Letter to author dated 27 Dec. 1993.

66

1 Herb Brin, *Ich bin ein Jude: Travels Through Europe on the Edge of Savagery* (New York, 1982), p. 131.

67

1 Leopold Infeld, *Quest: The Evolution of a Scientist* (London, 1941), p. 215.

69

1 KMB, pp. 18–24. The word *Protokol* is used here, as it can be

in English, to denote a formal record or agreement of an official nature, signed by the interested parties.

2 I have omitted his name, and these are not his true initials, for reasons that will become apparent later.

3 Translated by Maria Nicoll.

70

1 The figure of 8,000 Jewish victims is stated in Przemyslaw Burchard, *Pamiatki i Zabytki Kultury Zydoweskiej w Polsce* (Remains and Monuments of Jewish Culture in Poland) (Warsaw, 1990), p. 105. Another work suggests a larger total. According to *Wojewodztwo Koninskie. Monografia* (The Province of Konin, a Monograph) (Lodz, 1986), p. 110: 'In October 1941 in Kazimierz woods about 3,000 persons were shot. These were the Jews from the ghettos of the Konin district. In the first half of November 1941, near the gamekeeper's cottage, called 'Wygoda', near Kazimierz Biskupi, 8,000 Jews were exterminated.'

71

1 Although his name has appeared in official documents such as *Protokol* (see chapter 69 above), and has been published in at least two Polish books, he wrote to me after we met to request that to protect his family's privacy I should not reveal his name. One of the books he showed me was a Polish translation of Lord Russell of Liverpool's *The Scourge of the Swastika: A Short History of Nazi War Crimes* (London, 1954). On pp. 125–6 of that book the author gives a short excerpt from the vet's eyewitness account of the atrocity without identifying him by name. A footnote appended to the excerpt reads: 'The rest of this witness's description is too dreadful to print.'

ACKNOWLEDGMENTS

I wish to thank the following former Jewish citizens of Konin and its environs for giving me the benefit of their memories and, in many instances, for welcoming me into their homes in Britain, the USA, Canada and Israel. A more remarkable and courageous group of people it would be hard to find: Natan Ahykam, Leibush Aron, Julius and Niusia Ancer, Zalman Bayrach, Gedalia Ber, David Berendt, Lola Birnbaum, Shimon Bram, Rivka Brum, Tola Cymbler, Ginny Damashek, Rywka Diament, Shlomo Ehrlich, Joe Fox, Teresa Franco, Miriam Grossman, Sam and Eva Gruen, Gloria Gutwill, Izzy Hahn, Regina Rachel Haruvi, David Irwin, Mike Jacobs, Alexander Kaliski, Henry Kaplan, Henry Kaye, Simon Kempinski, Sam Klapstein, Leib Kleczewski, Herman Krol, Jozef Lasman, Mendel Leben, Louis Lefkowitz, Maria Leszczynska, Yitzhak Lipinski, Mikhail Moskowicz, Fella Nitzky, Alexander Piekarczyk, Sidney Prost, Abraham Rundbaken, Mira Ryb, Lola Sherer, Yitzhak and Hanna Sukari, Helen Trencher, Sarah Trybuch and Yehuda Wallis. Three of the above, Natan Ahykam, Shimon Bram and Mira Ryb, committee members of the association that published the Konin Memorial Book, kindly gave me permission to quote from it.

Sadly, the following have died since I had the privilege of interviewing them: Bertha Atzmon, Shimon Beatus, Natan Biezunski, Sarah Bram, Jacob Bulka, Miriam Cherniak, Rose Dolan, Yetta Ehrlich, Annie Glassman, Guta Katzenstein, Hanna Kowalska, Morton Mysch, Hirsh Majer Natel, Jacob Perelman, Avrom Soika, Avram Sukari, Lola Szafran and Frances Taylor. They bore my relentless questioning with noble patience.

I am indebted to the following relatives of Koniners for the insights and information they provided: Miriam Trybuch Bondorowsky, Lily Beyrack Cohen, Irene Fresko, Bill Gladstone, Claude Hampel, Ginger Jacobs, Philip Lewin, Professor Ralph Lewin, Rose Morris, Bella Natel, Hyman Offenbach, Merke Ronch, Eli Trybuch, and the late Ignac Grossman, remembered with special affection.

Thanks and acknowledgments are due to: Adam Bielecki, Librarian of the Jewish Historical Institute in Warsaw; Eva Feldenkreis, Director of Archives of the Ghetto Fighters' House, Israel; Dr Benjamin Nadel, former Director of the Bund Archives of the Jewish Labor Movement, New York; Suzie Sato of the Arizona Historical Foundation; the administrators of the Yad Vashem archives, Jerusalem; and members of the library staff at YIVO, New York. Professor David Chandler responded with kindness to my research enquiries. I am indebted to Professor Jozef Lewandowski, born in Konin, who not only contributed to my store of knowledge and gave me permission to quote from one of his books, but became a friend in the course of our long correspondence.

Several individuals in present-day Konin went out of their way to supply me with information that was hard, if not impossible, to obtain elsewhere. I therefore wish to express my appreciation to: Lech Hejman, Director of the Konin Public Library; Alicja Sadowska, Manager of the Konin branch of the Polish National Archive, and her historian colleague, Piotr Rybczynski. The warm welcome I received from Teresa and Jozef Blaszczynski during my visit to Konin will not be forgotten. My most memorable encounter in that town was with someone who, for reasons of his own, does not want his name mentioned. His testimony plays a significant part in this book, and I shall always be thankful for having had the opportunity of meeting him.

A lack of funds prevented me from using professional translators as much as I would have wished, so it was my good fortune to have two friends, Martha Price and Alexandra Gore, who gave freely of their time to translate long and difficult passages of Polish and German. I must thank Danuta Lyon and Maria Nicoll, too, for their help with Polish translations. When I had almost completed the book, the Society of Authors was good enough to award me a grant that paid for some of my translation expenses. I could not have written this book without having acquired the ability to read and translate Yiddish, in which so much of my source material was written. For this I must thank two gifted teachers: Yitzhak Niborski of the Sorbonne, who taught me during a crash course at Oxford, and Barry Davis, whose weekly Yiddish class at the Spiro Institute, London, brought delight as well as illumination.

I gathered facts and hospitality from a number of my relations, among them: Eva and Lewis Graham, Doris Leverson, Miriam Popoff, Chanoch Richka, Benny Ryczke, Abraham Sarna, Hettie Sarna and Gertrude Sarner. I should single out certain members of my family who went far beyond the line of familial duty in dealing with my tiring and, no doubt, tiresome stream of requests for information as well as assistance with Yiddish and Hebrew: Leibish Glassman, David and Varda Richke, Freda Ryczke, Rachel

Araten Sarna, Asher Sarna, Professor Nahum M. Sarna and his son, Professor Jonathan D. Sarna. It was to my advantage that the last two read the manuscript, as did my children Sarah and Simon, whose comments were of special help. I thank them, my son Jonathan, and the many friends who gave me much-needed encouragement.

There are others I must thank for not backing away when I foisted the bulky manuscript on them: Professor Antony Polonsky, Gerry Lewis and Harvey Mitchell. The last named was particularly generous with his attentiveness to nuance and detail. Any opinions expressed in the book and the responsibility for the facts given are entirely my own. Long before any publisher showed interest in this book, two strangers, David and Iris Freeman, heard of my quest for Konin, and spontaneously expressed their belief in what I was trying to do. I am grateful to them for being so generously supportive at a crucial time.

My literary agent, Toby Eady, took on an unknown and unproven author because of his faith in the subject of my book. I thank him for this and for encouraging others to have faith in it, especially my British publisher, Dan Franklin of Jonathan Cape, and my American publisher with the remarkably similar name, Dan Frank, of Pantheon Books. Both suggested cuts and changes with discernment and sensitivity, and I was lucky to have their advice as well as enthusiasm. I was also blessed with two superb copy editors: Steve Cox in London, and Ed Cohen in New York.

I have left to last the one person without whom etc. During the seven years I spent researching and writing this book, my wife, Lee Langley, supported me not only with her love but with the earnings from her creative writing as a novelist and scriptwriter. She was a tower of strength at times when I was a tower of weakness, in danger of toppling over whenever self-confidence grew shaky. Living with an obsessive was not easy, and she endured it with tender and selfless devotion. I inflicted every chapter on her as it was written, and there can scarcely be a page of this book that has not benefited from her constructive criticism.